"The first book on service user involvement in education and research that highlights its methodological and theoretical issues. It's impressive in its scope with the presentation of case-studies from all over the globe. With its reflections on what works in practice, it is a significant contribution to the contemporary debate of co-working with service users in human services education and research."

Dr Kristel Driessens, *Head Centre of Expertise 'Strengths Based Social Work', Karel de Grote Hogeschool, Antwerp, Belguim*

"This book that locates service user involvement in a historical and political context. The theoretical discussions in the book are followed by case presentations from different nations where efforts to implement user involvement in education and/ or research are discussed. To say that service user involvement is a very important thing, and that it is necessary, is not the same as saying that it makes a difference –this book begins to provide the evidence of the impact it can make."

Ole Petter Askheim, *Professor, Inland Norway University of Applied Sciences*

"As a 'user', lecturer, author and social debater, it feels 'obvious' that social colleges work actively with experiential knowledge in education, but as a 'user-representative', I know that it is unfortunately far from 'obvious'. The challenge is to take notice of the very useful experience for people to learn from me as a human being, a not scientific experiment. The knowledge of how to make the most of user competence in a proven and dignified way is available and this book provides an excellent basis for taking the form of such an ambition."

Malin Widerlöv, *User Lecturer*

"Service User involvement has been central to the process of updating the Global Standards for Social Work Education and Training. The IFSW/IASSW global consultation has revealed that, despite some progress in Service User involvement in research and education, there is a dearth of relevant literature. This seminal collection of essays helps bridge such gap. The editors of this handbook have managed to collect, document and analyse unique examples of Service User involvement in education and research. Crucially, the book also provides a powerful contextualisation of the barriers service users have faced in academic and research contexts. The authors make a passionate case for the necessity of genuine and meaningful co-production of knowledge. This is an essential handbook for all academics, students, service users and activists interested in co-production and the creation of inclusive and empowering academic environments."

Vasilios Ioakimidis, *Professor of Social Work- Head of Allied Health, Oral Health and Social Work, University of Essex. IFSW Global Commissioner- Interim Education Commission*

THE ROUTLEDGE HANDBOOK OF SERVICE USER INVOLVEMENT IN HUMAN SERVICES RESEARCH AND EDUCATION

Worldwide, there has been a growth in service user involvement in education and research in recent years. This handbook is the first book which identifies what is happening in different regions of the world to provide different countries and client groups with the opportunity to learn from each other.

The book is divided into five sections: Section One examines service user involvement in context exploring theoretical issues which underpin service user involvement. In Section Two we focus on the state of service user involvement in human services education and research across the globe including examples of innovative practice, but also identifying examples of where it is not happening and why. Section Three offers more detailed examination of such involvement in a wide range of professional education learning settings. Section Four focuses on the involvement of service users in research involving a wide range of service user groups and situations. Lastly, Section Five explores future challenges for education and research to ensure involvement remains meaningful.

The book includes forty-eight chapters, including seventeen case-studies, from all regions of the world, this is the first book to both highlight the subject's methodological and theoretical issues and give practical examples in education and research for those wishing to engage in this field.

It will be of interest to all service users, scholars and students of social work, nursing, occupational therapy, and other human service subjects.

Hugh McLaughlin is Professor of Social Work at Manchester Metropolitan University, UK. Prior to entering academia, he worked in local authority children's services. Hugh has a longstanding interest in participatory children's involvement that dates to his time in practice; it was further developed in academia, where his key interests are the meaningful involvement of service users in social work education and research, critical professional practice, and social service departments' ability to become learning organisations.

Peter Beresford is Professor of Citizen Participation at the University of Essex; Co-Chair of Shaping Our Lives, the national disabled people's and service users' organisation, think tank, and network; and Emeritus Professor of Social Policy at Brunel University London. He was awarded an honorary doctorate by Edge Hill University in July 2017. He is a long-term user of mental health services and has a longstanding background of involvement in issues of participation as writer, researcher, activist, and teacher.

Colin Cameron is a senior lecturer at Northumbria University, Newcastle upon Tyne, UK. He teaches sociology and philosophy on Guidance & Counselling and Health & Social Care degrees, and supervises postgraduate students in Social Work and Disability Studies. He has been involved in the Disabled People's Movement since 1992 and has published widely on Disability Arts and the affirmation model. He is a member of the Executive Editorial Board of the international journal *Disability & Society* and Chair of Shaping Our Lives' research committee.

Helen Casey is a lecturer with the Open University and has worked in social work education for fifteen years. As a social worker, Helen worked mostly with learning disabled adults, seeking to develop the innovative support people wanted in the community. Helen is currently studying a PhD part time at Durham University, exploring the effectiveness of service user and carer involvement in social work education. Helen introduced 'Mend the Gap' into social work in the North East of England and is an international co-ordinator with PowerUs.

Joe Duffy is Senior Lecturer in Social Work at Queen's University, Belfast, Northern Ireland. Joe is committed to transformative and pedagogic research by actively involving service users/ social work clients in helping social work students to understand difficult topics such as the impact of political conflict and lived experiences of trauma. He spent 2018–19 as a Fulbright Scholar in the US, introducing these initiatives to the social work curriculum, and has recently co-edited *International Perspectives on Social Work and Political Conflict* (Routledge, 2019) with J. Campbell and C. Tosone.

THE ROUTLEDGE HANDBOOK OF SERVICE USER INVOLVEMENT IN HUMAN SERVICES RESEARCH AND EDUCATION

Edited by Hugh McLaughlin, Peter Beresford, Colin Cameron, Helen Casey and Joe Duffy

Routledge
Taylor & Francis Group

LONDON AND NEW YORK

First published 2021
by Routledge
2 Park Square, Milton Park, Abingdon, Oxon OX14 4RN

and by Routledge
605 Third Avenue, New York, NY 10017

First issued in paperback 2022

Routledge is an imprint of the Taylor & Francis Group, an informa business

Publisher's Note
The publisher has gone to great lengths to ensure the quality of this reprint but points out that some imperfections in the original copies may be apparent.

British Library Cataloguing-in-Publication Data
A catalogue record for this book is available from the British Library

Library of Congress Cataloging-in-Publication Data
A catalog record for this book has been requested

ISBN: 978-0-367-52356-5 (pbk)
ISBN: 978-1-138-36014-3 (hbk)
ISBN: 978-0-429-43330-6 (ebk)

DOI: 10.4324/9780429433306

Typeset in Bembo
by Apex CoVantage, LLC

CONTENTS

Contents

Contents

Contents

FIGURES

TABLES

ABOUT THE CONTRIBUTORS

Nada Abdulla is a parent from Yemen.

Nafees Alam teaches social work at Boise State University. He specialises in macro practice. Dr Alam's research agenda focuses on quantitative analysis in the arena of service user involvement, diversity, and empowerment.

Larry Amadi-Emina relocated to the UK from Nigeria fifteen years ago. Larry is married to Lucinda Amadi-Emina, and they have four children.

Elizabeth Anderson is Professor of Interprofessional Education and lead for patient safety at Leicester Medical School. Elizabeth continues to advocate for patient involvement in the design and delivery of professional healthcare education, leading a 'Patient and Carer Group'.

Bini Araia is Regional Projects Manager of Investing in People and Culture (IPC), a North East-based charity that aims for the social inclusion of refugees and migrant communities (www.i-p-c.org). He also runs The Other Perspective CIC, a social enterprise that creates employment opportunities for new and emerging communities to utilise the skills they possess.

Raes Begum Baig is an assistant professor in the Department of Social Work at the Chinese University of Hong Kong. Her main research areas focus on gender, migration, and minority studies.

Katherine Baker graduated as a physiotherapist in 1999 and worked clinically with older adults and people living with neurological conditions. She is now Senior Lecturer in Physiotherapy at Northumbria University and has benefitted from engaging with service users in all aspects of her work.

Jim Bell, Unity Member. My life changed irreversibly in 1988 when I was involved in a fatal road accident. Although I was cleared of any blame, I felt responsible and became severely depressed. I have struggled with mental ill health ever since. I am passionate about working with students to help them to become the best social workers they can be.

Peter Beresford is Professor of Citizen Participation at the University of Essex; Co-Chair of Shaping Our Lives, the national disabled people's and service users' organisation, think tank, and network; and Emeritus Professor of Social Policy at Brunel University London. He was awarded an honorary doctorate by Edge Hill University in July 2017. He is a long-term user of mental health services and has a longstanding background of involvement in issues of participation as writer, researcher, activist, and teacher.

Kathy Boxall is Professor of Social Work and Disability Studies at Edith Cowan University, Western Australia. Kathy is from the UK and came to Australia in 2014. She was originally a social worker with people with intellectual disabilities and their families. Kathy also has experience as a mental health service user, and it is this experience – albeit some time ago – that provides ongoing motivation for her work.

Louca-Mai Brady is currently Senior Research Fellow at the UCL Institute of Ophthalmology, where she supports young people's involvement in eye and vision research, alongside work as a freelance researcher, consultant, and trainer.

Gary Broderick, Director SAOL (Women's Recovery and Education Project). Gary leads his service in reaching out to universities and other disciplines, designing curriculum, lecturing, attending conferences, and influencing policy makers.

Wendy Bryant is a retired occupational therapist and honorary professor at the University of Essex. Her research and teaching were based on collaborative work with an occupational focus, involving mental health service users, students, and staff. Her situation now has provided fresh insights into social and occupational perspectives on health and well-being.

Gillian Buck is Senior Lecturer in Social Work at the University of Chester. Her research interests include peer-led services, criminal justice, youth justice, and the voluntary sector. Before working in research and teaching, Gill worked as a social worker in a youth offending team.

Beverley Burke is a senior lecturer at Liverpool John Moores University, UK. She has worked as a youth and community worker and as a social worker. Beverley has published widely in the areas of anti-oppressive practice, values, and ethics. Beverley is co-editor of the Practice Section of the international peer-reviewed journal *Ethics and Social Welfare*.

Jim Campbell is Professor of Social Work in University College Dublin. Jim has published extensively on the subjects of mental health social work, and social work and political conflict. His co-edited book, *International Perspectives on Social Work and Political Conflict* (Routledge, 2019), with J. Duffy and C. Tosone, explores the role of social work and political conflict in a range of international contexts.

Colin Cameron is a senior lecturer at Northumbria University, Newcastle upon Tyne, UK. He teaches sociology and philosophy on Guidance & Counselling and Health & Social Care degrees, and supervises postgraduate students in Social Work and Disability Studies. He has been involved in the Disabled People's Movement since 1992 and has published widely on Disability Arts and the affirmation model. He is a member of the Executive Editorial Board of the international journal *Disability & Society* and Chair of Shaping Our Lives' research committee.

Maggie Cameron previously worked for Lothian Centre for Inclusive Living (LCIL) and was then seconded to Self–Directed Support Scotland, supporting the development of emerging disabled people's self–directed support organisations. She is a Deaf person who now works as a freelance Disability Equality Trainer in the North East of England.

Susan Carton trained as a nurse for people with intellectual disabilities and has been working at St Angela's College in Sligo since 2003. She worked on the first Disability Studies degree at St Angela's and is currently the Course Co-ordinator for the PG/Dip/MSc in Disability Studies.

Helen Casey is a lecturer with the Open University and has worked in social work education for fifteen years. As a social worker, Helen worked mostly with learning disabled adults, seeking to develop the innovative support people wanted in the community. Helen is currently studying a PhD part time at Durham University, exploring the effectiveness of service user and carer involvement in social work education. Helen introduced 'Mend the Gap' into social work in the North East of England and is an international co-ordinator with PowerUs.

Kar-Choi (K.C.) Chan is a full-time lecturer in the Department of Social Work, the Chinese University of Hong Kong (CUHK). His expertise and research interest include psychogeriatric care, dementia screening, health equity, and culturally competent practice.

Emilio José Gómez-Ciriano is an accredited professor in the Faculty of Social Work, Universidad de Castilla-La Mancha, Spain. His main research interests are migration policies and integration of migrants and refugees, and economic, social, and cultural human rights.

Holly Dale is currently a President's Doctoral Scholar at the University of Manchester; investigating the inter-relationships between serious mental illness, stigma, substance misuse, and suicidal thoughts and acts. Holly is currently using both her lived experience and professional knowledge to inform her work with the Survivor Researcher Network.

Ibrahim Dialllo is a parent from Papua New Guinea.

Jordan Dodds became involved with Investing in Children via the Young Adults Support Café (Y-ASC) and has helped out on projects relating to hate crime. He was brought into projects by his partner, Jack Etheridge, who has been instrumental in both Y-ASC and the Young Peoples Summit on Hate Crime. Jordan is a journalist in training at the University of Sunderland and has lived with Asperger Syndrome, a form of autism, for 11 years.

Elinor Dowson is a family carer whose life changed when a close relative was diagnosed with a mental illness. She is a member of the carers and users group in social work at the University of Dundee, a meaningful and rewarding experience.

Paul Doyle I went to two special schools. When I was at school, particularly a boarding school, I was not listened at all; I found this really frustrating and did not want anyone to go through this again. This is why I based my chapter upon supporting young disabled people in speaking up for themselves.

Joe Duffy is Senior Lecturer in Social Work at Queen's University, Belfast, Northern Ireland. Joe is committed to transformative and pedagogic research by actively involving service users/

social work clients in helping social work students to understand difficult topics such as the impact of political conflict and lived experiences of trauma. He spent 2018–19 as a Fulbright Scholar in the US, introducing these initiatives to the social work curriculum, and has recently co-edited *International Perspectives on Social Work and Political Conflict* (Routledge, 2019) with J. Campbell and C. Tosone.

Claire Ferrier is a qualified social worker working in adult care in Scotland with Perth and Kinross Council. Claire recently graduated with an MSc from the University of Dundee and was awarded the Jo Campling Memorial essay prize from the *Journal of Ethics and Social Welfare* for a paper on 'risk' in social work.

Ali Finlayson was born in Lima, Peru. Ali is a Scot who has lived in North East England for over forty years. Diagnosed with Parkinson's Disease in 2005, Ali started writing poetry in 2010, inspired by his family, and writes now about nature, Scotland, and living with Parkinson's.

Jenny Ford is a qualified speech and language therapist, and while Programme Leader at De Montford University she set up an interprofessional Service User Advisory Group. Jenny was also a board member of the UK Centre for the Advancement of Interprofessional Education (CAIPE) and helped pioneer board positions for service users and carers.

Rhiannon Foster is a mental health survivor researcher and PhD student at St George's, University of London. Her research interests include the value of experiential knowledge in mental health research and practice, and she is critically exploring professionalisation of peer support for her PhD.

Martin Fraser, Unity Member. My name is Martin and I have been a member of Unity for many years. I have experience of using mental health services and first became ill in 1984. I began to contribute to service user involvement in 1998 in the Falkirk area and am currently a care inspection volunteer.

Sascha van Gijzel is a lecturer at the Institute for Social Work and Researcher at the Research Centre for Social Innovation of Utrecht University of Applied Sciences, Netherlands. She specialises in the experiential knowledge of persons with a learning disability, and is working on developing inclusive education.

Steve Gillard is Professor of Social and Community Mental Health at St George's, University of London. His research focuses on the increasing role played by people with lived experience of mental distress in producing mental health services.

Merryn Gott I am a social scientist researcher whose work in the fields of palliative care and end-of-life care adopts a social justice perspective. I direct the Te Ārai Palliative Care and End of Life Research Group based at the School of Nursing, University of Auckland, Aotearoa, New Zealand.

Jill Grant is a person with lived experience of mental illness. She is Associate Professor of Social Work at the University of Windsor, Canada; her primary areas of research and teaching interests include relationships between service users and service providers and undergraduate social work education.

Shirley Hallam was born in Sunderland and is an example of lifelong learning. She has spent many years as a teacher, trainer, and senior manager developing and improving the lives of children and minority ethnic families.

Colin Hambrook is Founder/Editor of www.disabilityarts.online – a unique journal for discussion of disability arts and culture. Launched in 2004, Disability Arts Online is dedicated to critiquing the artistic practice of disabled artists/writers and performers and enabling debates around the curation and development of disability arts practice. He is currently working on *Fools' Gold*, a performance piece and research project reflecting on the history of psychiatry and the representation of mental illness in arts and culture. Colin has provided the picture for the book cover.

Paula Harriott is Head of Prisoner Involvement at the Prison Reform Trust and a former prisoner. Her work has a sharp focus on power, bias and system change, and creating space for those with lived experience of the criminal justice system both to be heard and to move into positions of leadership in the sector.

Ray Hegarty, CE Supervisor SAOL, provides video/photography expertise, supporting women in representing ideas through visual communication as part of their recovery. He provides both knowledge and support to the work of the collaboration.

Cecilia Heule is a university teacher and a PhD candidate at the School of Social Work at Lund University. She is one of the innovators of the Mobilization Course, which involves social work students and service users and was the start of PowerUs, which now has partners in nineteen countries with Cecilia as one of its coordinators.

Patricia Higgins I'm 65 years of age and I was diagnosed with autism two years ago. I'm also physically disabled. I have five children and I'm married. I am a poet, artist, and a member of Spectrum, a drama group for people with autism.

Sara Hitchin, Senior Lecturer in Social Work. I qualified in 1989 and worked in statutory social work services before moving to the University of Stirling. I am currently the MSc Social Work Programme Director and have been privileged to work with Unity members over the last ten years.

SeKwang Hwang, Senior Lecturer at Northumbria University, has a professional background in social work with disabled people in South Korea. His research and teaching focus on all aspects of disabled people's lives and their families in the international context.

Gillian Janes is a nurse academic with almost forty years' experience in clinical, management, education, and research practice. For over fourteen years she has partnered with patients, carers, and members of the public in developing and delivering higher education programmes.

Stephen Jeffreys After previous lives as a political activist, railway clerk, welfare lawyer, and parent, Stephen endured a long period of mental distress and social isolation. He currently does freelance work as an independent survivor/lived experience mental health researcher and serves in coordinating roles at Suresearch and the Survivor Researcher Network.

Ellis Jongerius, Caron Landzaat, Idman Nur-Voskens are trainers with lived experience. Together with a coach of LFB, they train people with intellectual disabilities and their support workers to become experts by experience and coaches. They work as co-lecturers and co-researchers at the Institute for Social Work of Utrecht and the Research Centre for Social Innovation at University of Applied Sciences, Netherlands.

Rebecca Jury is a lecturer in Social Work at Edith Cowan University, Western Australia. Rebecca worked in child welfare, mental health, and domestic violence services before moving to higher education. Rebecca is passionate about the centrality of lived experience knowledges for social work practice and education.

Peter Kearns In the mid-1990s, Peter established THE WORKHOUSE, a disability consultancy company that supports disability research/development. He also lectures part-time at St. Angela's College (NUIG) and Sligo IT and identified a need for an emancipatory–advocacy way of thinking and practice for and with disabled people.

Arianna Kennedy Having been challenged by mental illness since the age of 13, Arianna spends a lot of her time maintaining her mental health. She achieves this by swimming, walking, and spending time with supportive friends and family. At home in Vancouver, Arianna also spends time advocating for those with similar struggles.

Jeroen Knevel is a lecturer and PhD student at the Institute for Social Work at Utrecht University of Applied Sciences, Netherlands. He specialises in human rights, social inclusion, and persons with a learning disability.

Marcus Knutagård is a researcher and senior lecturer at the School of Social Work, Lund University. Knutagård's research interests concern social innovation from a welfare perspective, with a particular focus on service user influence in practice research, particularly in relation to housing/homelessness.

Janina Komaroff lives in Montreal, Quebec. She has a strong interest in mental health issues and is currently working in the pharmaceutical industry.

Arne Kristiansen is an associate professor at the School of Social Work, Lund University. He is one of the initiators of the Mobilization Course at the School of Social Work at Lund University. He is a part of the network PowerUs.

Annie Lambert is a professor–researcher at Sherbrooke's University Social Work School (Québec Canada). Her current work is focused on the decision-making process and risk management, but also on experiential knowledge of experts by experience in social intervention and social work training.

Susan Levy is Senior Lecturer in Social Work, University of Dundee, Scotland, UK. Her research interests are in user-involvement, disability, and the integration of the arts into health and social care. Her work has an international dimension, with a focus on Sub-Saharan Africa and indigenous social work.

Sarah Lonbay is Senior Lecturer in Advocacy and Engagement at Northumbria University, Newcastle upon Tyne. She is Programme Leader for BA Guidance and Counselling, and Academic Lead for the involvement of Educators by Experience in the social work programmes.

Hilda Loughran, Associate Professor, UCD, has a special interest in issues related to drug and alcohol policy, treatment, and research in social work. This collaboration has addressed education and research initiatives in social workers' role in responding to drug use issues.

Jacqui Lovell-Norton works with individuals, groups, and communities using approaches to effect social change that reflect the needs and aspirations of people at the bottom of the social hierarchy. She does so in her capacity as a White European cisgender lesbian, self-confessed granarchist, protest poet and doctor of critical community psychology. http://jacquiluvslife. blogspot.com/

Yvonne Lynch is Assistant Professor in Speech and Language Therapy in Trinity College, Dublin. Her research and clinical interests include augmentative and alternative communication (AAC), telehealth, and service delivery in speech and language therapy.

Karen Machin is a member of the Survivor Researcher Network. Following experiences of distress, including a caring role, she slowly returned to work through volunteering and then self-employment, which has included filmmaking, service evaluation, and training delivery.

Anna Makoni is a parent from Zimbabwe.

Kathleen Mason is a research assistant at the School of Nursing, University of Auckland for Pae Herenga. As a recent health science graduate, Kathleen has developed a keen interest in Kaupapa Māori research methods and how the stories of research participants are cared for and analysed.

Joanna Matthews is a freelance consultant and researcher working with various disabled people's organisations. She is trustee of Unlimited Oxfordshire, a user-led organisation supporting disabled people, and sits on Shaping Our Lives' National User Group.

Linda McCulloch, Unity Member. My name is Linda; I am a wife and mother. I have had problems with my mental health since my teens but was not diagnosed with bi-polar syndrome until I was in my forties. I have been a Unity member for several years now and have met so many lovely people with different experiences of using services.

Brendan McKeever has extensive experience of working in the field of housing, education, health, and social care. He has written extensively on issues relating to disabled children and their families and has published several books on these subjects. Brendan has a particular focus on and interest in user involvement.

Hugh McLaughlin is Professor of Social Work at Manchester Metropolitan University. Prior to entering academia, he worked in local authority children's services. Hugh has a longstanding interest in participatory children's involvement that dates to his time in practice; it was further developed in academia, where his key interests are the meaningful involvement of service users in social work education and research, critical professional practice, and social service departments' ability to become learning organisations.

Becki Meakin is General Manager of Shaping Our Lives. For more than twenty years, she has worked in the voluntary and community sector. She is a disabled person with expertise in the inclusive involvement of people from marginalised and underrepresented communities.

Stuart Meredith uses a communication aid for daily interactions. In the past, he was employed by a communication aid supplier to be part of assessments and offer training and mentoring. Currently, he is a board member for a national specialised AAC service. Stuart was involved as a co-researcher on the I-ASC project.

Damian Milton is a part-time lecturer at the Tizard Centre, University of Kent, and for the National Autistic Society, and chairs the Participatory Autism Research Collective. Damian's primary focus is on increasing the meaningful participation of autistic people and people with learning disabilities in the research process.

Tess Moeke-Maxwell is a founding member of the Te Ārai Palliative Care and End of Life Research Group, School of Nursing, University of Auckland. The methodological lens she brings to her work is Kaupapa Māori and Māori-centred, highlighting the importance of indigenous ways of knowing and doing death care.

Joanne Molloy-Graham I am married to Peter Joseph Graham and proud mother of Matthew and Bethany. My experiences of my own health issues have meant getting involved with, and fighting for, disability rights. I returned to education in 2017 as a Guidance and Counselling student at Northumbria University, where I am currently working on my dissertation, looking at disabled students' experience of higher education.

Yvonne Mondiwa is a parent from Zimbabwe.

Paul Morin is Director of Sherbrooke's University School of Social Work and Director of L'Institut universitaire de première ligne de santé et de santé et de services sociaux 'du CIUSSS de l'Estrie-CHUS (Québec, Canada). He has worked more than twenty years in mental health advocacy.

Lynda Morrison, Unity Member. My name is Lynda. I experienced abuse from the age of 8, and because of this, I have suffered with depression and self-harm throughout my life. I trained as a psychiatric nurse and have worked in many hospitals. I am a member of Unity and get a lot out of working with students and a great deal of support from other members.

Liz Moulam is the parent of a young woman with cerebral palsy who uses a communication aid for daily interactions. From 2015 to 2019, Liz was a public involvement co-researcher on the Identifying Appropriate Symbol Communication Aids for Children who are non-speaking project: Clinical Decision Making (I-ASC).

Janice Murray is Professor of Communication Disability and AAC at Manchester Metropolitan University, UK. She is currently Communication Disability Research Lead, former Chair of Communication Matters, and founding member of an All-Party Parliamentary Group for Assistive Technology.

Sidsel Natland is an associate professor in the Faculty of Social Sciences, Oslo Metropolitan University, Norway. She teaches and researches within social work, with a special interest in practice research and co-production of knowledge, in particular the involvement of service users and social work practitioners in research.

Andrea Newman currently works as a senior lecturer at Liverpool John Moores University, UK. Andrea's research interests have focused on research and evaluation with minority communities, and is interested in participatory action research approaches.

Joanne Newman is from Busselton, Western Australia. She works part-time as a lived experience educator at Edith Cowan University's Bunbury campus, where she co-teaches mental health to third-year social work students.

Sophie Nobert-Bordeleau is a student at the School of Social Work, University of Sherbrooke, Canada, and has been involved in many user involvement projects over the past two years.

Leila Nunes holds a BA in Psychology and Psychologist Training from Universidade Federal do Rio de Janeiro (1970), a master's degree in Special Education from Peabody College, USA (1977), and a PhD in Special Education from Vanderbilt University, USA (1985). She teaches in the Graduate Program of Universidade do Estado do Rio de Janeiro (UERJ). She teaches on and researches human development, language and communication, social interaction, alternative communication, and experimental research methodology.

Opeyemi Odejimi is a researcher at the Birmingham and Solihull Mental Health NHS Foundation Trust. She has worked as a visiting lecturer and an online tutor at the University of Wolverhampton and Dundee respectively.

Annie Patenaude is a service user. She is involved in all the projects of services users at the School of Social Work at the University of Sherbrooke, Canada.

Émilie Pothier-Tessier is a student at the School of Social Work at the University of Sherbrooke, Canada, and has been involved in many user involvement projects over the past two years.

Charden Pouo graduated with an MA from Marien Ngouabi University in Congo Brazzaville 2007 and is currently a BA student at Northumbria University, UK. Charden is the founding president of Couleurs Congolaises Association, an NGO that promotes human rights.

Konstantina (Dina) **Poursanidou** has been a university-based social science researcher since 2000. She started using mental health services in 1991. She is a member of the Asylum radical mental health magazine editorial group as well as a member of the Survivor Researcher Network (SRN) Working Group.

Jordan Risbridger is currently studying for his MSc in Social Work at the University of Dundee, Scotland, UK. Jordan is pursuing a career in social work after years of volunteering in and around the Tayside area of Scotland.

Claire Russell has thirty years of receiving secondary mental health care and ten years of delivering social work training. She was involved in facilitating servicer user feedback in the evaluation of a national fast track social work qualifying programme.

Kemi Ryan is co-founder and manager of Reformed Development CIC, specialising in young people's behaviour and the aftermath of crime.

Natasha Ryan is co-founder of Reformed Development CIC. She has lived experience of the criminal justice system with areas of focus in the aftermath of crime, underrepresentation of race, youth and community engagement, criminal justice aftercare, and educational awareness.

Joanne Sansome holds a Master's in Social Research Methods. She is a researcher and activist with a physical disability from Northern Ireland. Joanne has significantly shaped the concept, research, and delivery of service user and carer involvement within social work education.

SAOL Women's Group are, as part of their work, directly involved in educating professionals on drug issues. They want to enhance social workers' knowledge, understanding, and skill in responding appropriately to issues that arise for women in drug use and recovery.

Carolina Rizzotto Schirmer is an adjunct professor at Rio de Janeiro State University. She is a member of the Alternative Language and Communication Research Group and is experienced in speech therapy and education.

Laura Serrant is Head of Nursing and Professor of Community and Public Health Nursing at Manchester Metropolitan University, UK. She has specialist expertise in enabling wider diversity in patients and public engagement with research and was awarded an OBE in the Queen's Birthday Honours list 2018 for services to health policy.

Felicity Shenton was originally a qualified social worker in London and is former Strategic Director of Investing in Children, a children's human rights organisation in the North East of England. She has maintained a strong commitment to service user involvement and rights-based practice.

Emma Smith has had an integrated role as a service user representative, for Interprofessional Education with the Health and Medical Schools at the two Leicester Universities. She suffered significant injuries and is now a service user board representative for CAIPE.

Roger Smith is a former probation officer and youth justice practitioner. Since becoming an academic, he has worked at the University of Leicester, De Montfort University, and Durham University. He has extensive experience as a social work educator and has worked on a number of collaborative projects with service users in both teaching and research.

Elaine Spencer is a social worker.

Marie-Josée St-Jean is a service user. She is involved in all the projects of services users at the School of Social Work at the University of Sherbrooke, Canada.

John Stephens previously worked as a chartered physiotherapist before becoming a senior lecturer–practitioner with Northumbria University. He is involved in interdependence projects with other healthcare professionals, people with experience, and students.

Angela Sweeney identifies as a trauma survivor and survivor researcher. She has a particular interest in survivor-controlled research, trauma-informed approaches, survivors' perspectives on and experiences of psychiatric services and treatments, and alternatives to mainstream biomedical psychiatry, including trauma and social models of causation.

Luwam Tekeste is from Eritrea and plans to train as a social worker.

Philippa Tomczak is Senior Research Fellow at the School of Sociology and Social Policy, University of Nottingham, UK. She co-ordinates CRIMVOL: the international criminal justice voluntary sector research network.

Dan Vale is Director and Co-Founder of Ginger Giraffe, a cooperative-owned and democratically run by service users, students, carers, and professionals to provide spaces in health, social care, and communities to challenge power dynamics and develop radical coproduction.

Petra Videmšek is an assistant professor at the Faculty of Social Work, University of Ljubljana. Her main research interests include social inclusion in the field of mental health and handicap and the involvement of service users in research and education.

Jijian Voronka is an assistant professor in the School of Social Work at the University of Windsor, Canada, where she teaches primarily for their Disability Studies Program. Her research explores confluences of power in mental health community, research, and institutional spaces.

Nick Watson is Chair of Disability Studies at the University of Glasgow and a member of the research staff at the Strathclyde Centre for Disability Research. He has published extensively in the area of Disability Studies and is an active campaigner for access to mainstream education for disabled people.

Sheila Weatheritt was born into a family of six children, including her sister Ann, who has learning disability. She has cared for Ann for thirty-two years, is a kinship carer, and is a point of support for other family members. Sheila also shares her experiences with students at Northumbria University, Newcastle upon Tyne.

Helen Whittle is a speech and language therapist who has worked in the field of augmentative and alternative communication (AAC). Recently she has been a lecturer at Manchester Metropolitan University, UK, where she has been involved in the I-ASC project, exploring the decisions around children's alternative communication systems.

Jean Pierre Wilken is Professor of Social Work at the Research Centre for Social Innovation of Utrecht University of Applied Sciences, Netherlands. He is head of the research group Participation, Care, and Support, which is focused on social inclusion of persons with a disability.

Deb Wise Harris is a writer and editor in the mental health field. She has worked as a peer researcher and as Research Coordinator at the Centre for Research on Inner City Health (CRICH) at St. Michael's Hospital. Deb has a Master of Education with a focus on mental health from the University of Toronto (OISE).

Maryam Zonouzi is the chair of the first user-led placement cooperative Ginger Giraffe. Maryam is a social work and social care academic with a particular interest in co-production, knowledge democracy. participatory research, and disruption. Maryam is a disabled woman and lives in London.

ACKNOWLEDGEMENTS

We have many people to thank for making this book possible. First and foremost our contributors for their time and effort on this project. We are so pleased that such a diverse range of people, service users, practitioners, educators, and others from so many parts of the world made their ideas and experience available from many fields of professional activity to advance the practice and theory of involvement in professional education, practice, policy, and services. We also want to thank the team at Routledge, our publishers, for their support for this project from the start and for their capable help bringing it to fruition. Among them we want to thank Catherine Jones from Routledge for her continued support and encouragement throughout. All of us as editors also owe debts to particular friends and colleagues, who have helped us identify possible issues and contributors valuable to include in the book. While we can't list all and would want to offer general thanks, we hope that some won't mind us singling them out for thanks.

We would like to acknowledge the work of many others, in the United Kingdom and elsewhere who have pioneered the developments we discuss in this book. There have been key organisations which were at the forefront, particularly user-led and disabled people's organisations, but also others which have advanced both the understanding and practice of user and carer involvement. These include the National Institute for Social Work, General Social Care Council, Central Council for Education and Training in Social Work, Social Care Institute for Excellence, Health and Care Professions Council, Northern Ireland Social Care Council, PowerUs, and the Social Work Education Partnership.

We also owe a massive debt to those people who have pioneered user involvement and helped us all get to where we are. The list is a long one and we can only mention some, but we would like to acknowledge our particular thanks to the following: Enid Levin, Fran Branfield, Dame Denise Platt, Nasa Begum, Ann Nutt, and Patricia Chamber.

Finally, we would like to acknowledge the kindness of Colin Hambrook for permission to use his painting 'The Sky's Falling Down Again' as the art for the book's front cover.

FOREWORD

"Service User involvement has been central to the process of updating the Global Standards for Social Work Education and Training. The IFSW/IASSW global consultation has revealed that, despite some progress in Service User involvement in research and education, there is a dearth of relevant literature. This seminal collection of essays helps bridge such gap. The editors of this handbook have managed to collect, document and analyse unique examples of Service User involvement in education and research. Crucially, the book also provides a powerful contextualisation of the barriers service users have faced in academic and research contexts. The authors make a passionate case for the necessity of genuine and meaningful co-production of knowledge. This is an essential handbook for all academics, students, service users and activists interested in co-production and the creation of inclusive and empowering academic environments."

Vasilios Ioakimidis, Professor of Social Work- Head of Allied Health, Oral Health and Social Work, University of Essex. IFSW Global Commissioner- Interim Education Commission

The front cover.

The Sky's Falling Down Again (oil on canvas; 2013) is one of a series of psychological landscapes depicting a sense of being 'othered' by Psychiatry. Since the days of the witch trials, society has perpetuated systems for victimising those seen as mad or bad, legitimised by the mental health system. Psychiatric drugs disable the majority of those forced to take them, reaping multi-billion-dollar profits for Big Pharma.

Colin Hambrook is the founder/editor of www.disabilityarts.online He has exhibited his artwork widely and is the author of two illustrated poetry collections. He is currently working on *Fools' Gold*, a performance piece and research project reflecting on the history of Psychiatry and the representation of mental illness in arts and culture.

In remembrance

Very sadly, one of the authors we originally asked to contribute to this collection could not do so. In order to acknowledge her major contribution to participatory inquiry and action involving people with Asperger's Syndrome, we include a link to her ground-breaking doctoral thesis in the hope that this work lives on:

by Roger Smith

www.dora.dmu.ac.uk/handle/2086/11040

INTRODUCTION
TO THE BOOK

Peter Beresford and Hugh McLaughlin

Quietly, almost unnoticed, a fundamental change has been taking place in human and helping services in recent decades. Such policies and provision were once based essentially on an unequal model of professional and policy dominance, with end users on the receiving end of others' prescriptions rather than equal partners in the process; however, this has been challenged and has begun to change. Instead of continuing as a kind of self-perpetuating mechanism, with one generation of professionals training the following generations – drawing on their own ideas of what was needed and assumptions about their 'expertise' and 'expert' knowledge – there has been pressure for something different.

This is the movement for public and particularly service user involvement in human service education and research: that is to say, the knowledge base of the services and practitioners we may all need to turn to at particular times in our lives for help and support. The impetus for this development can be traced back at least 50 years, with the first pioneering efforts emerging at grassroots, but it has really taken off during the course of the twenty-first century. It is now a truly international, not to say global movement, albeit one that had its first flowerings in the Northern hemisphere – often indebted, though, to radical and emancipatory thinking and developments in the Southern hemisphere. Its progress has been complex rather than uninterrupted, and there are still many obstacles in its way, particularly facing those areas and groups that continue to be marginalised and discriminated against in our world.

But this is also a movement that we can see has truly come of age; for that reason, it seems especially important to produce this book – and, we believe, it is particularly timely to do so.

Knowledge of and learning for human services are never abstract and isolated issues. They serve a very practical purpose as part of a process to make people's lives better and restore their well-being. Here, thinking, reflection, doing and action must be inseparable. We are talking about a *praxis* that combines the two. The praxis here, where we are talking about user involvement in education and research for human services, has to be a participatory, emancipatory and inclusive one. Thus, this book encompasses both practice and theory and seeks to make their connections. It explores key underpinning concepts like involvement, difference, experience and identity and critiques them in action; it also checks out opportunities and barriers facing this new paradigm for learning and knowing. We have tried to provide both exemplars from existing experience and challenges for the future.

We have sought to paint the pictures here with a broad brush. As editors, we all have experience of trying to do such involvement as well as trying to think it through, make sense of and theorise about it. We include people who identify as service users, as well as those who are professional educators and researchers – indeed, people with experience as both. We have also worked hard to include as diverse a range of contributors and as far-reaching focus as possible, although we have to be honest that our reach has sometimes exceeded our grasp. This reflects the broader barriers such a transformative development faces globally, which we hope our book will help break down.

User involvement in the human services is at its heart concerned with challenging traditional exclusionary roles, breaking down traditional barriers and assumptions and, at its best, enabling real co-production at both a personal and a policy level. For this reason, we have selected contributors to ensure that many have lived experience of the policies and services with which we are concerned. Many of the pioneers of this movement are represented within these covers, alongside others whose lives have been changed and their opportunities enhanced by becoming involved because of the prefiguring work of others. We have also sought to address the key issue of diversity with equality along lines of gender, ethnicity, sexuality, disability, age and so on in all contributions, as well as specifically also taking account of the particular marginalisation faced by indigenous peoples and people in the Global South. As such, our contributions include theoretical chapters, practice-based chapters, international chapters and chapters focused on examples of service user involvement in education and research. These chapters have been written by people who identify as service users; carers; service users with academics; academics; service users who are also academics; and academics who have been service users. A feature of this book is the inclusion of a number of 'Talking Heads', where service users reflect on their experience of professionals, services, educators and researchers. These provide a counterpoint to the traditional book, valuing the experiential knowledge of service users alongside that of traditional 'scientific knowledge' and practice wisdom.

We accept that we all may become service users at some stage in our lifecycle, if we have not already done so, and thus have a vested interest in how human service professionals are educated and how effective the services are that they may deliver for us and our families and friends.

We start from the premise that service users have a right to be involved in the development and control of policies and services they experience; part of this includes the education of those human services professionals who seek to serve and be involved in research which seeks to evaluate and develop new methods of intervention. It is our belief that policies, education and research for human services will be better targeted and more effective when they include those on the receiving end.

The following section summaries indicate the nature of the different sections; however, it should be noted that examples of education and research and different national experiences of service user involvement can be found in the different sections. Just because a section is primarily about education does not mean that examples of research will not be present and vice versa.

We are proud to say we have examples from a diverse group of human services, including social work, nursing, physiotherapy, speech and language, health, special education, prisons and palliative care, including statutory and charity/NGO providers. There are also chapters by carers and chapters covering the experience of children, adults and elders. We have not described the contents from all our chapters below, but provided a brief identification of some of these to wet your appetite to explore the book further.

Section 1: Service user involvement in context: theoretical issues

This section of the book identifies a range of theoretical issues confronting service user involvement in education and research; it begins with Duffy and Beresford setting the tone in identifying critical issues concerning the development of service user involvement. Shaping Our Lives is a national organisation and network of user-led groups, service users and disabled people who recently developed a guide to promote meaningful involvement of disabled people; this is featured here. This is then followed by McLaughlin, who reflects on the social constructions of service users within an increasingly hostile neo-liberal context, and Gillard et al., who unpick the nature of experiential knowledge and its under-representation and acceptance in traditional knowledge domains. Burke and Newman provide a much needed analysis on the ethical issues involving service users. Cameron et al. examine the ways in which power distorts relationships between professionals and disabled service users. McKeever similarly draws on his own experience as a carer for his son, who had a life-threatening condition, and the housing campaign he undertook to obtain appropriate housing for his son and others in a similar situation. The section concludes with two 'Talking Heads' chapters; one focuses on asylum seekers' perspectives and the other on training for the non-disabled.

Section 2: The state of service user involvement in human services involvement in education and research across the globe

The aim of this section is to identify examples of service user involvement from across the globe; this was the most ambitious and most difficult section. In some countries, the ideas behind the book did not resonate with local authors; meaningful service user was in its infancy; authors felt they did not have much to say; or people were unable to meet our deadlines.

However, we have contributions from 18 different countries throughout the book, with 11 represented in this section. It is with great pleasure that we have been able to include a range of examples, from Newham et al. re: Australian mental health activism to Lambert et al.'s discussion of mental health from the Canadian experience. The chapters concerning Congo Brazzaville (Pouo), Spain (Gomez) and the USA (Alam) all identify to differing degrees how service user involvement has not had the same traction within their country, elaborating on why this is the case and what this means for education, policy and practice. Baig et al. discuss challenging racism in Hong Kong, while Hwang discusses the experience of disabled user organisations in South Korea; Videmšek considers the development of service user involvement in Slovenia. Sansome reflects on her experience as a disabled person in Northern Ireland researching participation of people with disabilities. Casey et al. argue for a radical rethink of involvement by championing co-production in the UK; this is followed by some of Amadi-Emina's personal experiences of his journey from Nigeria to the UK.

Section 3: Service user involvement in human services education

Section 3 looks at experiences of service user involvement in professional education, beginning with the involvement of disabled activists in developing /teaching disability studies. Bell et al. describe how they developed, delivered and evaluated a professional skills practice workshop. Loughran et al. also highlight the importance of service users being involved in teaching professionals about substance use. Serrant et al. describe how service user involvement has developed with nurse education and its important contribution to educating the nurses of the future. Anderson et al. develop the importance of going beyond single professional groups in their chapter on interprofessional education, while Buck et al. remind us that education takes place not only in schools and universities but also within the criminal justice system. Nunes and Schirmer describe attempts to involve students in special educational teacher training in Brazil.

Bryant adopts a radical stance in her chapter on occupational therapists (OTs) equalising opportunities, while issues of human rights are also prevalent in 'Investing in Children' by Dodds and Shenton. Lonbay et al. remind us that we should not forget about the lived experience of older people if we wish to prepare our human service professionals to work with all age ranges and conditions.

Duffy reminds us that professional practice is not neutral and identifies the challenges of would-be professionals learning to practice in societies where conflict is present; he further considers how the important role of those affected by conflicts can support the development of professionals navigating such difficult and challenging terrain.

Moeke-Maxwell et al. provide a window into the Māori perspective of end-of-life care and remind us of the need for cultural humility and its importance in working with service users. Stephens et al. describe how they co-produced curricular material (primarily with service users, but also students) within pre-registration physiotherapy programmes. Levy et al. also provide further evidence on the longitudinal impact on service user and carer involvement in a social work qualifying course.

Section 4: Service user involvement in research in the human services

As previously recorded, the last chapter could just as easily have been included in this section. Wilken et al. begin this section by discussing research on their university's commitment to inclusive learning in social work education, including gap mending and tandem cooperation, with evidence on the outcomes and experiences. Lovell-Norton continues the section with the challenging chapter 'How can we survive and thrive as survivor researchers?' Nick Watson carries on this challenging theme by questioning how co-production is experienced in research. Moulam et al. use their experience of augmented communication to reflect on both the rhetoric and reality of patient and public involvement in research. Voronka et al. use a case study to explore the challenges and opportunities in developing a peer qualitative research group within a larger mental health and homeless project. Brady takes a different approach to look at similar issues within young people's involvement in health research.

Natland reminds us that not all (if any) research projects ever proceed smoothly and helpfully identifies the struggles of meaningful service user involvement within a Norwegian project. Russell and Smith use the developmental evaluation of a major UK research study on a new model of social work pre-qualifying education – 'Think Ahead' – as an exemplar to reflect on the role of the researcher and the role of the service users, highlighting learning from the process. The final chapters of this section include two Talking Heads. Doyle shares his experience as a researcher with multiple impairments researching young disabled people preparing for life beyond segregated schooling, followed by a curation of experiences compiled by Casey et al. on the impact of gap mending for all stakeholders: service users, students and lecturers.

Section 5: Future challenges and opportunities

The final two chapters provide some reflections by the editors: Colin Cameron, Helen Casey and Joe Duffy in relation to impact of service user involvement in education and Peter Beresford and Hugh McLaughlin in relation to research. Whilst this book unashamedly promotes meaningful service user involvement in education and research, it is not done uncritically and seeks to provide some evidence and conditions under which it can make a difference and positive impact upon people's lives.

Conclusions

We believe this book adds to our understanding on the current state of meaningful involvement by those on the receiving end of human services and how this can contribute to improved policy making, service delivery and professional practice. The book also reminds us how easy it is to turn involvement into tokenism and the challenges we face in developing and sustaining participation across diverse groups and in diverse human services.

Finally, the book can be dipped into or read section by section, but we believe you will find articles that are moving, challenging and inspirational and that will help all those in the human services education and research to make a difference. Enjoy the book.

SECTION 1

Service user involvement in context

Theoretical issues

1

CRITICAL ISSUES IN THE DEVELOPMENT OF SERVICE USER INVOLVEMENT

Joe Duffy and Peter Beresford

Introduction

Service user involvement continues to grow as an integral part of policy and practice in regard to many aspects of health and social care, professional education and research. This is particularly evident in the UK from where we as authors write, but more importantly, it has become an international development, and there are important examples of service user involvement in many other countries, to which this chapter will also refer. While much progress has been made with regard to service user involvement, it is also important to critically reflect on those key issues which have the force to encourage yet impede its development. Understanding the history of 'involvement'; its key ideological and policy influences; debates on knowledge and theory; and issues around tokenism, power, social exclusion and othering are aspects of the undergirding conceptual building blocks which are necessary to interrogate in the process of understanding why service user involvement is necessary in the overall architecture of human services policy and practice. This chapter will focus on these key issues and debates, leaving the reader with a critical understanding of service user involvement with regard to its history, development and the nature of the challenges and opportunities that lie ahead.

Service user involvement – historical and policy perspectives

We can expect that so long as there have been human services, there have been pressures to make them more participatory from both practitioners and people on the receiving end as service users: to enable more equal two-way relationships, rather than the kind of bureaucratic and punitive regimes traditionally associated with poor law and regulatory regimes. However, it is really not until well into the second half of the twentieth century that we begin to see structured, formal and systemic arrangements come into existence that were expressly intended to encourage more involvement from service users and other citizens (Beresford, 2005). This marked a significant departure from the predominantly paternalistic and non-participatory ways in which, for example, post-war welfare states were established and operated.

There were two early and important contexts for this participatory development in the 1960s and 1970s. The first found expression in the US as the 'War on Poverty' and in the UK as the community development programme. Both were focused on communities and disadvantaged groups, particularly Black and minority ethnic people, women and young people, and they sought to 'involve' people in challenging their deprivation by consciousness and skill-raising approaches. The second initiative was the implementation of provisions for participation, pioneered in the UK in land use and land development planning. The aim was for local people and communities to have a real say and stake in how their neighbourhoods and localities were shaped through involvement in schemes for public consultation and complaint in planning (Beresford, 2019a). These historic initiatives offer some early warnings about the possibilities and also limitations of adding such involvement to existing political and policy arrangements. We know that in the US and UK, the continuing existence of structural barriers relating to continuing (and in some cases worsening) economic and social inequality limited the capacity of programmes for positive discrimination either to engage or to uplift people effectively (Atkinson, 1983; Sheffield and Rector, 2014). Formal provisions for participation in planning have been notorious for their failure to engage large numbers of people and to address diversity effectively (Beresford, 2019a).

These problems are a reminder of the importance both of contextualising efforts to involve people and connecting them to broader political structures and ideological pressures and issues at work which may impact upon them. One approach has been to develop models of participation although these tend to be limited in their usefulness. Such uni-dimensional approaches to participation, while in some cases recognising power differences, often still struggle to address its essentially *political* nature. While they can have a helpful part to play in improving understanding, they also tend to be reductionist, over-simplifying and ill-suited to dealing with the real-life complexities and ambiguities of such involvement (Tritter and McCallum, 2006).

A more helpful alternative is to put such participation in the context of the development of modern democracy more generally. Here, four key stages in the development of public participation in health and social care and other policies and services can be identified. These historical phases are associated with:

1   Moves towards universal suffrage in representative democracy and the achievement of social rights, like the right to decent housing, education and health [first half of twentieth century, creation of welfare states in Europe];
2   Provisions for participatory democracy and community development;
3   Specific provisions for participation in health and social care [emerging internationally from the last quarter of the twentieth century];
4   State *reaction* and service user-led *renewal* as conflicts and competing agendas develop [emerging particularly in the second decade of the twenty-first century and problematizing more clearly international inequalities and Northern and Southern hemisphere differences].

(Beresford, 2019b)

We can see from this that the 1960s to 1970s examples we discussed earlier fall into the second phase. Significantly, we now seem to be in the grip of the fourth phase, where broader political shifts to neoliberalism internationally can be seen to have a reactionary effect against such participatory initiatives, while increasingly popular user- and community-led approaches continue to press – more overtly often – in the opposite direction. The contentiousness that this generates helps explain the particular interest in discussions like those contained in this book, as well as highlighting the importance and urgency of developing them at this time.

Although the dominance of neoliberal ideology has imposed limits on the development of user involvement and citizen participation, as well as on the rights and say of people as service users, it would be a mistake to assume that it has ended progress. Indeed, what we can see is an increasing focus and indeed, in some ways, a strengthening and redirection of activity. Thus, while experiencing much suffering in recent years, service users and their organisations have extended both their critiques and their action in relation to health and social care and other policies and services. Some key areas of activity include:

- Widening involvement and campaigning, challenging exclusions
- Involvement in professional and occupational training
- Involvement in research and knowledge production
- The development of 'Mad Studies'.

All of these areas of activity are explored in this Handbook.

Service user involvement – knowledge and theoretical perspectives

At the very core of involving service users is an essential recognition that this involvement in itself brings with it a particular type of *knowledge*. It is, therefore, arguable that a fundamental questioning and shift has occurred in what is regarded as knowledge in the domain of human services work (see Beresford, 2000; Beresford and Boxall, 2012; Levy et al., 2018). Inevitably, this has been seen as challenge to other types of knowledge regarded as more traditional and 'expert' and, implicit within this, a recognition that there are 'other knowledges' which also can make an equally important contribution. Rose, for example, argues that there can be no such thing as universal knowledge but instead differing knowledges from different standpoints should be recognised (2009). Linked to this, McLaughlin (2009), adopts the term *service user standpoint theory* to argue that service users occupy a particular *standpoint[s]*, and their experience of being social work service recipients facilitates their development of key insights, perspectives and understandings about these issues based on lived experience. Locating service user experiential knowledge within standpoint theory, defined as "theory based upon identity and, in particular, an individual's membership of a particular social group, whether this is women, disabled people or service users" (p. 12), McLaughlin (2009) builds on the works of Harding (1987, 1991), Collins (1986) and Swigonski (1994). The basis of standpoint theory is that "less powerful members of society experience a different reality as a consequence of their oppression" (Swigonski, 1994, p. 390). Developing this argument further in regard to service user involvement in research in particular, Swigonski asserts that "less partial and distorted understandings of nature and social relations will result from research that begins from the standpoint of particular marginalised groups of human beings" (p. 390). Beresford (2013a) adopts a similar view in his argument that service users having an important contribution to make from their experience of being on the receiving end of social policies.

Service users and carers have thus had a well-established formal position in key aspects of professional social work education in the United Kingdom since its reform in 2002. In this role, their experiential-based knowledge has helped social work students in their understanding of social work values (Duffy and Hayes, 2012; Gutman et al., 2012), linking social work theory to practice (Brown and Young, 2008), developing skills in preparation for practice learning (Duffy et al., 2012) and understanding difficult, threshold concepts in the curriculum (Meyer and Land, 2005), such as the impact of political conflict (Duffy, 2012). Service user-based knowledge has therefore had an important, recognised role at the heart of preparing social workers for human services work.

As mentioned already, acceptance of service user, experience-based knowledge can pose epistemological questions and debates when compared to other types of knowledge considered to be more objective, expert and scientific (Eraut, 1996; Fook, 1999). While Ramon (2003), for example, argues that service users bring valuable first-hand knowledge in terms of policy, practice and research, concerns about "ordinary people taking on powerful roles" express the types of fundamental challenge that face the gravitas of this knowledge (Rimmer, 1997, p. 33). Similar questions have been expressed by others, such as Prior (2003), who raises questions about lay knowledge being too subjective and lacking in wider applicability. The latter point, however, links back to Rose's argument about the need to accept knowledges from differing standpoints, and to Harding (1987) and Swigonski's (1994) contentions that there are different 'ways of knowing'. It also challenges old assumptions that there is such a thing as 'objective knowledge' in the social sciences (Beresford, 2003).

Trevithick's (2008, 2012) pioneering work on the key components of the social work knowledge base is also important in her positioning of service user knowledge within a *factual* domain of knowledge in social work. Similar to the points already mentioned about service users being directly impacted by social welfare policies, Trevithick argues it is important "to recognise and to acknowledge this pool of knowledge and to use this information creatively" (2012, p. 1226). Fundamental questions of power and power imbalances are inextricably interwoven with these processes, which will be discussed later in this chapter. The social work literature, for example, frequently negatively constructs service users in an 'othering' discourse as being in some way deviant and on the outside (Banks, 2006). Acceptance of service user knowledge is thus a fundamental challenge to such "anti-oppressive literature or theory" (Wilson and Beresford, 2000, cited in Beresford and Boxall, 2012, p. 161), which arguably has had a tendency to problematically portray perceptions of service users. Linked to this point, and important in this notion of comparing different sources of knowledge, there is an argument that all knowledge claims should be exposed to critical questioning, thereby promoting anti-oppressive practice (Dalrymple and Burke, 1995; Clifford and Burke, 2005).

Service user knowledge arguably also can align itself to well-established existing theoretical constructs, particularly the work of some critical social theorists. For example, pivotal to Recognition Theory (Honneth, 1996), according to Rossiter, is the argument that an individual's identity is a social construct "socially acquired and thus identity is a matter of justice because the acquisition of self-confidence, self-respect and self-esteem is the foundation of autonomy and agency" (2014, p. 93). Honneth therefore situates identity development as linked with the role of others, which will ultimately help with the promotion and advancement of social justice. "It makes you realise how much you have to share" (Duffy et al., 2012, p. 12) is arguably an extension of Honneth's thinking in practice. Here, a service user expresses confidence in the knowledge that lived personal experience is brought to bear in assisting social work students in their knowledge development. Such a comment also accords with Cotterell and Morris' (2012) observation about the lack of confidence that marginalised individuals can sometimes attach to the value of their lived experiential knowledge (Duffy, 2015). Facilitating opportunities for involvement, espousing Recognition Theory, thus can not only connect firmly to established social work values but also facilitate an emancipatory and social justice-based dialogue. Paulo Freire's seminal *Pedagogy of the Oppressed* (1972) quite makes the point: "only a critical consciousness of the knowledge in one's possession can in turn lead to action and transformation" (cited in Cotterell and Morris, 2012, p. 60).

Service user involvement – power perspectives

Traditionally, helping services have often been rooted in an unequal distribution of power, with service users placed at a disadvantage. To make matters even more complex, they often intervene in the lives of people who are already disempowered or going through disempowering experiences in their life. While the focus of such 'helping' services has tended to be on the individual changing themselves, service users, their organisations and movements have also been concerned with changing those services themselves as well as the wider worlds in which they themselves live. If there is one generalisation that seems to hold irrespective of when and where research is undertaken, it is that service users get involved to change their and other people's lives for the better. To do this, they need to be able to have power, know that they have it and be able to make use of it.

The political sociologist Steven Lukes developed the idea of three dimensions of power. The third dimension refers to the social construction of practices, ideologies and institutions that secure people's consent to or at least acceptance of domination (Lukes, 2004). Community and developmental educationalist John Gaventa drew on this to support approaches to social change rooted in the perspectives of marginalised communities. Instead of looking for the sources and solutions of social problems in the theories and ideas of social science and social policy experts, he validated the narratives of the oppressed populations involved. In Gaventa's theory, such methodological subjectivity makes it possible for the framing of a social problem and its solution to arise from within the group. This both has an empowering effect on the group and provides a basis for it to take collective action to challenge dominant discourses and develop alternatives (Gaventa, 1982).

When it comes to people's involvement, power issues operate at both a macro and micro level, and service user involvement is impacted by both. Thus, at a macro level, there are the insidious impacts of neoliberal ideology and its associated managerialism. Their values, based on individualisation and regressive redistribution of wealth and opportunities, collide with those that underpin and are core to the emancipatory involvement sought by service users. The devaluing of service users' 'lived experience' and 'experiential knowledge', compared to traditional knowledge deemed more 'scientific', 'objective' and reliable, can be seen as another manifestation of such macro power. This both deters service users from feeling valued and getting involved and places significant barriers in its way. At a micro level, we can see how power imbalances are expressed through tokenistic approaches to involvement, which fail to address diversity with equality: the box ticking culture, creation of consultation fatigue, lack of sensitivity to practical considerations of physical, communication and cultural access.

At the same time, we now have many international examples of how such exclusionary and negative ideological and organisational pressures can be challenged and overcome. This book brings together many such examples. One such is PowerUs, which is showcased in this book, where an equalising of power relationships between educators, students and service users, building trust and shared understanding, can result in really productive and innovative outcomes in education, which have lasting effects for more equal and effective practice (Askheim et al., 2017). Also reported later in this book is pedagogic research undertaken in Northern Ireland with victims and survivors of political conflict, which has clearly evidenced the positive impact on students' knowledge skills and values by being directly introduced to these important personal lived experiences in the classroom (Duffy, 2012; Coulter et al., 2013; Campbell et al., 2013). These types of innovations in social work education would have been unthinkable during the 'Troubles' (the term used to describe over 30 years of violent political conflict) but were positively aided by the wider peaceful societal milieu heralded by the Northern Ireland Peace Agreement in 1998. Working in close partnership with citizen educators who have lived through and been adversely affected by violent political conflict has yielded important learning outcomes for social work students. Central to the success of this initiative, however, has been the value and respect given to experiential knowledge and the important contribution that this can provide. Without this, these significant achievements would have been impossible. Other international contexts are also evidencing ways in which students are learning from service user knowledge. The literature provides examples from the US, Middle East and Europe of ways in which service users and academic staff work together in helping students to understand the impact of living with mental ill-health (Gutman et al., 2012), and there are notable innovative examples also of students and service users studying alongside each other (Kjellberg and French, 2011).

Service user involvement – challenges and opportunities

We are now arriving to the final part of our chapter, where we can think positively yet realistically going forward about the key challenges that lie ahead and how these can be turned to opportunities. We will of course be reflecting back on the key messages from the three preceding sections, but we will also signpost readers in an important way as to what can be achieved when service user involvement is approached through the critical lens that our chapter is advocating.

While there is much more still to be done, there seem to be some key lessons from all the experience we already have from the development of user involvement in professional learning and education. We know there are challenges, but there are also real opportunities.

The first thing to work for is clarity. This is not necessarily easy or straightforward, given that user involvement is a relatively new idea and a common language can obscure very different assumptions, understandings and intentions. So, we must try in all we do to be clear. What kind of involvement is on offer? Is it just to hear what people have to say: perhaps their concerns or complaints or misgiving? Or is the plan really to try and listen to these and do something about them? That really is the key point, because we know that people really want to be involved to make a difference, for their views both to be heard and acted upon. Not many of us are content with just hearing the sound of our own voice! We want it to have an impact, bring about change, make things better.

And that brings us on to another key issue: how we can be involved. It has to be in ways that work for us: which feel familiar, comfortable and are appropriate, rather unfamiliar, inaccessible and perhaps even intimidating, such that we are reluctant to express our true opinions. We must feel safe. We must have encouragement to feel as confident and assertive as possible. We need to be offered a sympathetic setting and good conditions for our involvement, without hidden and unmet personal or financial costs. Involvement must be accessible regardless of our particular access requirements, communication needs and so on (Beresford and Croft, 1993).

Which leads to an even broader issue – ensuring that as wide a range of people can get involved as possible. We know from existing participatory arrangements that many groups face barriers of one sort or another, which means that they can readily get left out. We have to work to challenge those barriers and exclusions (Beresford, 2013b).

Conclusion

Participation, user involvement in one sense, is not rocket science. It doesn't demand vast amounts of specialist knowledge or special qualifications. Some might say it is mainly a matter of taking trouble and common-sense. That might in one sense be true, except many service users might conclude that there is a very common lack of common-sense around if that is the case, because they have so many experiences of poor and unpleasant involvement. Perhaps this really means two things. First, we have to be committed to involving people as positively and inclusively as possible. Second, as with any serious activity or new venture, we have to check out what other people have already done and learnt and what we ourselves have learnt from that, instead of rushing in where angels might fear to tread! We have to take trouble; we have to be serious. And, of course, we will have to allocate a sensible budget – as with any activity – to ensure that things work out well. And, finally, we need to keep people posted about what has happened and what has been learned. That is the key next step. And it is almost, but not quite, the last step. Because that, as we have already heard, is to make sure that what people say is acted upon! Involvement and action should be seen as inseparable. Involvement is not some kind of academic exercise. It is about real change for the better in real people's lives, in the real world. And working for such change in professional learning and practice, based on service users' experiential knowledge and lived experience, is clearly at the heart of this.

References

Askheim, O.P., Beresford, P. and Heule, C. (2017) Mend the gap – strategies for user involvement in social work education. *Social Work Education* 36(2), 17 February: 128–140.

Atkinson, A.B. (1983) *The Economics of Inequality*. Oxford: Clarendon Press/Oxford University Press.

Banks, S. (2006) *Ethics and Values in Social Work*, 3rd edn. Basingstoke: Palgrave Macmillan.

Beresford, P. (2000) 'Service users' knowledges and social work theory: Conflict or collaboration? *British Journal of Social Work* 30(4): 489–503.

Beresford, P. (2003) *It's Our Lives: A Short Theory of Knowledge, Distance and Experience*. London: Citizen Press in association with Shaping Our Lives.

Beresford, P. (2005) "Service user": Regressive or liberatory terminology?' *Disability & Society* 20(4): 469–477.

Beresford, P. (2013a) From 'other' to involved: User involvement in research: An emerging paradigm. *Nordic Social Work Research* 3(2): 139–148.

Beresford, P. (2013b) *Beyond the Usual Suspects: Towards Inclusive User Involvement, Research Report*. London: Shaping Our Lives.

Beresford, P. (2019a) Rethinking 1980s Social Policy: The struggle from powerlessness to participation. *Back To The Future: 1979–1989*. National Library of Scotland. Available online at: https://digital.nls.uk/1980s/society/social-policy/

Beresford, P. (2019b) Public participation in health and social care: Exploring the co-production of knowledge, policy and practice review article. *Frontiers in Sociology*, January, www.frontiersin.org/articles/10.3389/fsoc.2018.00041/full

Beresford, P. and Boxall, K. (2012) Service users, social work education and knowledge for social work practice. *Social Work Education* 31(2): 155–167.

Beresford, P. and Croft, S. (1993) *Citizen Involvement: A Practical Guide for Change*. Basingstoke: Macmillan.

Brown, K. and Young, N. (2008) Building capacity for service user and carer involvement in social education. *Social Work Education – The International Journal* 27(1): 84–96.

Campbell, J., Duffy, J., Traynor, C., Reilly, I. and Pinkerton, J. (2013) Social work education and political conflict: Preparing students to address the needs of victims and survivors of the Troubles in Northern Ireland. *European Journal of Social Work* 16(4): 506–520.

Clifford, D. and Burke, B. (2005) Developing anti-oppressive ethics in the new curriculum. *Social Work Education – The International Journal* 24(6): 677–692.

Collins, B.G. (1986) Defining feminist social work. *Social Work* 31(3): 214–219.

Cotterell, P. and Morris, C. (2012) The capacity, impact and challenge of service users' experiential knowledge. In M. Barnes and P. Cotterell (eds) *Critical Perspectives on User Involvement*. Bristol: The Policy Press, pp. 57–70.

Coulter, S., Campbell, J., Duffy, J. and Reilly, I. (2013) Enabling social work students to deal with the consequences of political conflict: Engaging with victim/survivor service users and a pedagogy of discomfort. *Social Work Education – The International Journal* 32(4): 439–452.

Dalrymple, J. and Burke, B. (1995) *Anti-oppressive Practice, Social Care and the Law*. Buckingham: Open University Press.

Duffy, J. (2012) Service user involvement in teaching about conflict – an exploration of the issues. *International Social Work (Special Edition on Social Work and Armed Conflict)* 55(5): 720–739.

Duffy, J. (2015) *Illuminating Pedagogy Through Experiential Knowledge*. Heslington/New York: Higher Education Academy.

Duffy, J., Das, C. and Davidson, G. (2012) Service user and carer involvement in role-plays to assess readiness for practice. *Social Work Education*. doi:10.10 80/02615479.2011.639066

Duffy, J. and Hayes, D. (2012) Social work students learn about social work values from service users and carers. *Ethics and Social Welfare*. doi:10.1080/17496535.2012.654497

Eraut, M. (1996) *Developing Professional Knowledge and Competence*. London: Routledge.

Fook, J. (1999) Reflexivity as method. *Annual Review of Health Social Sciences* 9: 11–20.

Freire, P. (1972) *Pedagogy of the Oppressed*. New York: Herder and Herder.

Gaventa, J. (1982) *Power and Powerlessness: Quiescence and Rebellion in an Appalachian Valley*. Chicago, IL: University of Illinois Press.

Gutman, C., Kraiem, Y., Criden, W. and Yalon-Chamovitz, S. (2012) Deconstructing hierarchies: A pedagogical model with service user co-teachers. *Social Work Education* 31(2): 202–214.

Harding, S. (1987) *Feminism and Methodology*. Buckingham: Open University Press.

Harding, S. (1991) *Whose Science? Whose Knowledge? Thinking from Women's Lives*. New York: Cornell University Press.

Honneth, A. (1996) *The Struggle for Recognition: The Moral Grammar of Social Conflicts*. Cambridge, England: Polity Press.

Kjellberg, G. and French, R. (2011) A new pedagogical approach for integrating social work students and service users. *Social Work Education* 30(8): 948–963.

Levy, S., Aiton, R., Doig, J., Dow, J.P.L., Brown, S., Hunter, L. and McNeil, R. (2018) Outcomes focused user involvement in social work education: Applying knowledge to practice. In H. McLaughlin, J. Duffy, B. McKeever and J. Sadd (eds) *Service User Involvement in Social Work Education*. London/New York. Routledge.

Lukes, S. (2004) *Power: A radical view*, 2nd edn. Basingstoke: Palgrave Macmillan.

McLaughlin, H. (2009) What's in a name: 'Client', 'patient', 'customer', 'consumer', 'expert by experience', 'service user' – what's next? *British Journal of Social Work* 39(6): 1101–1117.

Meyer, J.H.F. and Land, R. (2005) Threshold concepts and troublesome knowledge (2): Epistemological considerations and a conceptual framework for teaching and learning. *Higher Education* 49(3): 373–388.

Prior, L. (2003) Belief, knowledge and expertise: The emergence of the lay expert in medical sociology. *Sociology of Health & Illness* 25(1): 41–57.

Ramon, S. (2003) User research: Reflection and action. In S. Ramon (ed) *Users Researching Health and Social Care: An Empowering Agenda?* Birmingham: Venture Press.

Rimmer, A. (1997) Power and dignity: Women, poverty and credit unions. *Gender Development* 5(3): 26–34.

Rose, D. (2009) Survivor-produced knowledge. In A. Sweeney, P. Beresford, A. Faulkner, M. Nettle and D. Rose (eds) *This Is Survivor Research*. Ross-on-Wye: PCCS Books Ltd, pp. 38–44.

Rossiter, A. (2014) Axel Honneth's theory of recognition and its potential for aligning social work with social justice. *Critical and Radical Social Work* 2(1), March: 93–108.

Sheffield, R. and Rector, R. (2014) The war on poverty after 50 years. *The Heritage Foundation*. Available online at: www.heritage.org/poverty-and-inequality/report/the-war-poverty-after-50-years

Swigonski, M.E. (1994) The logic of feminist standpoint theory for social work research. *Social Work* 39(4): 387–393.

Trevithick, P. (2008) Revisiting the knowledge base of social work: A framework for practice. *British Journal of Social Work* 38: 1212–1237.

Trevithick, P. (2012) *Social Work Skills and Knowledge: A Practice Handbook*, 3rd edn. Maidenhead: Open University Press.

Tritter, J.Q. and McCallum, A. (2006) The snakes and ladders of user involvement: Moving beyond Arnstein. *Health Policy* (76): 156–168.

Wilson, A. and Beresford, P. (2000) 'Anti-oppressive practice': Emancipation or appropriation? *The British Journal of Social Work* 30(5), October: 553–573.

2

IMPROVING UNDERSTANDING OF SERVICE USER INVOLVEMENT AND IDENTITY

A guide for service providers and practitioners organising involvement activities with disabled people

Becki Meakin and Joanna Matthews

Introduction by Colin Cameron

In 2017, user-led research was carried out by Shaping Our Lives (SOL), a UK-based network of disabled people's organisations, to improve understanding of service users' perspectives on their experiences of involvement activities with health, social care and local government services. The research was developed as a response to a comment made by one of SOL's disabled Board members, Patricia Chambers, that such experiences had left her feeling confused. On the one hand, Patricia said, when she was involved with services in a consultation role, as an 'expert by experience', she felt listened to and taken seriously, as if her views mattered. Outside those contexts, though, back in her day-to-day role as a service user, she felt patronised, unequally treated and as if what she had to say was considered unimportant. A lot has been written by professionals about how well they are doing at listening to and acting upon the views of those who use their services, but there are questions to be asked about how deep this commitment is.

In April and May 2017, 22 disabled women and men from across England were interviewed by a team of five disabled researchers. Everyone who was interviewed had experience of being both a service user and a service user representative. Some had many years working with services in a representative capacity (for more than 20 years); others were newer to the role. Interviewees had been representatives in a wide range of public sector organisations.

A great deal is known about the advantages of service user involvement for services or professionals. In this study, SOL wanted to find out about:

- the impact of being a service user representative for the people who put themselves forward to take on the role
- how service providers can make sure they manage service user involvement well
- how being a service user representative can be a positive experience for those who give up their time to do it

The findings revealed a range of conflicts for disabled people when they use services and are also a service user representative. Most representatives got involved because they wanted to share their experiences of being a disabled person and make services better for others. Although there were some positive experiences, more people had had negative experiences of involvement. There were practical access issues, a breadth of communication problems and poor attitudes from professional staff. As well as producing a report of research findings, SOL produced two practical guides summarising these: *A Guide for Service Providers and Practitioners Organising Involvement Activities for Disabled People* and *A Guide for Disabled People Who Are Interested in Being a Service User Representative.* The first of these guides is reproduced here. The others can be found at:

> www.shapingourlives.org.uk/resources/our-resources/all-publications/improving-under standing-of-service-user-involvement-and-identity

Improving Understanding of Service User Involvement and Identity was funded by the National Lottery through the Big Lottery Fund:

> Shaping Our Lives
> Improving Understanding of Service User Involvement and Identity
> A Guide for Service Providers and Practitioners Organising Involvement Activities with Disabled People
> November 2017

Introduction

Shaping Our Lives is a national organisation and network of user-led groups, service users and Disabled people. It is a user-led organisation committed to inclusive involvement. It specialises in the research and practice of involving diverse communities in policy, planning and delivery of services.

Listening to and respecting service users' voices and perspectives is increasingly known to be an essential part, and often a statutory requirement, of developing quality services.

Shaping Our Lives has undertaken a piece of research to gather the experiences of Disabled people who have taken part as service user representatives in the policy, planning and delivery of health, social care and local government services.

From these experiences, we have produced this guide for professionals. The guide provides essential information for professionals who want to hear the views of Disabled people and to use this knowledge to make services efficient and effective for the people who use them. You should aim to co-produce services with your users. The advice and tips for successfully involving Disabled people detailed in this report reflect the principles of the social model of disability, and the adoption of working methods that reflect that the barriers that Disabled people experience are from society and not because of the impairments and health conditions they have.

It may be your role to manage involvement activities in your organisation. You may have been asked to run an involvement activity with little training or experience. If you are reading this guide, you are probably thinking ahead to what the task might involve and how to get the best out of it. When you have finished reading the guide, you will have picked up some top tips about how to improve the experience for service user representatives.

If you don't understand the following terms or their use in this guide, there is an explanation of them towards the end of this document:

- Disability Equality Training
- Involvement activity
- Organisation
- Professional(s)
- Service user
- Service user representative (Representative)
- The medical model of disability
- The social model of disability

Section 1

What makes a good and bad involvement experience?

Getting service user involvement right can be difficult. However, from the research findings there are some clear actions that are commonly mentioned that can make the difference between a rewarding experience and one that leaves both professionals and service users feeling demoralised. Service user representatives say the following things contribute to a positive involvement experience:

- Feeling part of a team.
- If the activity has a clear purpose and role for service user representatives.
- That lived experience and service user knowledge is valued.
- When service user contributions are acknowledged and make a difference.

The following things were commonly mentioned as leading to poor involvement experiences:

- No meaningful outcome from the involvement.
- Inflexible, too long or tokenistic processes.
- Not listening to and acting upon service user views.
- Power imbalances between professionals and the service user representatives.

Top tip!

Build on this research. Ask people who are currently involved in your engagement and involvement activities what makes it a good experience and what makes it a bad one.

Tackle the bad experiences in your actions for change (see Section 6).

Do more of the good things!

Section 2

Essential elements for effective involvement

There are seven essential elements for effective involvement activities from the perspective of a service user representative, as follows:

1 Equality

When involving service user representatives in involvement activities, it is important to value their lived experience and consider them as experts. Power imbalances can be avoided by involving service users at each stage of the process, including deciding what the purpose of the activity is, agreeing objectives and outcomes, setting a time frame and evaluating the outcomes.

Things that can lead to power imbalances are: not listening to service users, using professional jargon, not meeting the access needs of everyone, not providing accessible papers in advance, not sharing all the relevant information, not involving service users in setting the agenda, putting all the service user agenda items at the end (and leaving the meeting when these agenda items are eventually discussed).

2 Mutual respect

Involvement activities should be an opportunity for professionals and service users to listen to each other and gain mutually beneficial knowledge and understanding. There is considerable evidence that when service users become involved in designing policy and services, there are improvements in efficiency and often cost savings for services.

However, many service user representatives feel that their knowledge is not respected:

> *It is diminishing to realise how the service providers see service users. It is frustrating in the meetings to sense how little credence most of them actually give to service user viewpoints. If our view chimes with theirs they are positive and pleased with how things are going; if the service user perspectives challenge their views then they tend to offer platitudes and try to swiftly move the discussion on.*

3 Ownership

If service user representatives are involved equally and shown mutual respect, they can become fully involved, play an active role and contribute to the outcomes. If left on the side-lines, people will not be able to develop a sense of ownership and contribute to the success of the activity.

4 Structure

There needs to be a clear plan for the involvement activity developed in consultation with the service user group which is represented in the process. This plan should describe the purpose of the activity, state the expectations of people involved and provide the functional details such as frequency, length and duration of involvement activities. It is particularly helpful to develop role descriptions for service user representatives when the involvement activity is an ongoing process.

5 Commitment

Service user representatives often comment that involvement activities are most effective when there is a commitment from professionals, including senior managers, from all the relevant departments. This commitment is interpreted in many ways, including the following:

- Providing appropriate funding for the activities – so all access requirements can be met, expenses are funded and service user representatives are rewarded, either financially or in other ways, such as opportunities for personal development or accreditation.

- An understanding of inclusive involvement of people with a range of impairments and health conditions – all professionals need to have disability equality training, have knowledge about inclusive involvement and understand the principles of the social model of disability.
- Provide appropriate support for service user representatives – it may be necessary to provide some training or mentoring for people to be able to complete the required tasks.
- Realistic timescales – by allowing sufficient time for a service user involvement activity, it can change the outcome from a tokenistic experience to a meaningful and productive one.

6 Feedback

Many service user representatives say that they do not receive feedback on the outcome of the involvement activities they take part in. This makes people feel worthless and uninclined to take part in future activities.

7 Personal development

Personal development is a key motivator for service user representatives and includes training, acquiring new skills, gaining knowledge, opportunity for paid or voluntary work, increased confidence, opportunity to network/make new friends, increased self-worth and finding out about services and organisations in the area.

> *I think the best one for me used to be the Partnership Board because they had a mentoring system and I was getting some training that helped me be a representative.*

Top tip!

Provide the opportunity for service user representatives to talk to you about what you are trying to achieve, how you are planning to do it and what will be involved for the representatives.

This gives the service user a chance to decide if the involvement activity is appropriate for them and how it might feel to be part of the whole process.

Section 3

Managing relationships and conflict

Service user representatives say that sometimes professionals behave differently towards them when they meet using services compared to when they meet in an involvement activity. It is important to consider that someone taking part in involvement activities may also need to use services, and this may cause awkwardness. However, in both situations service users and professionals should be in a collaborative relationship, and this is the basis for meaningful involvement activity.

Top tip!

Provide a single point of contact for service user representatives. This person can ensure that any concerns are addressed appropriately.

Make sure you provide contact details for phone, text and email.

Section 4

Ensuring the process is inclusive and accessible

Service user representatives say the most important thing to ensure an involvement activity is successful is to make it accessible.

> *It's about developing inclusive practice. It's about making them aware that service user representatives are integral to the meeting and they shouldn't treat us as an add-on. If they were able to do that they would be able to make much more valuable use of the service users and develop much better services as a result of that.*

These are systems to put in place to make activities accessible:

- An overview of the activity, what it aims to achieve and what the outcomes will be.
- Terms of reference for service user representatives taking part.
- Role descriptions for longer involvement activities.
- Clear guidance to the amount of time service user representatives will need to commit and for how long.
- Payment policy for reimbursing expenses with details of how to claim and how long it takes for a claim to be processed.
- Involvement payment policy with details of how to claim and how long it takes for a claim to be processed.
- Including a skills audit to check participants have the appropriate skills for the involvement project.
- Completing an access audit before any activity starts.
- Confirmation of practical arrangements, such as times and places for meetings (although this should be part of the process to agree these details with the service user representatives).

The following things may help service user representatives meet their potential:

- An induction for the service(s) the involvement activity refers to.
- Training on the range of impairments and health conditions that people taking part may have and how this impacts on their participation.
- Professional training that is relevant and can be extended to service user representatives.
- A mentor from the service and/or a buddy with experience of involvement activities.

There is often an assumption that any Disabled person can be an effective service user representative, and generally this is true if they have the appropriate skills and knowledge. However, service providers organising involvement activities should do a skills audit or similar to establish any training and support needed for service users to take part successfully.

Section 5

Benefits and advantages for service users

It is useful to consider why service users become representatives. It will help you provide motivational opportunities – and encourage more people to sign up to be representatives.

People become service user representatives because:

- It is a pathway to paid and voluntary roles.
- They wish to make a positive difference to services, to affect change.
- It leads to involvements with other voluntary organisations or to other involvement activities that can expand knowledge and skills.
- It provides new activities and opportunities through increased confidence. For example, people said they had gained enough confidence to write articles, challenge decisions, attend regional/national conferences, do radio interviews – 'opening up a whole new world'.
- It is an opportunity to network and join user-led groups or voluntary sector organisations.
- It often also leads to invitations to aspirational events, other consultations and involvement events.
- Finally, some people find that being a service user representative benefits their health and wellbeing, helping them to get well and to manage their impairments and health conditions.

How it helped me

For me it was a start to getting back out into the world and a step on the journey to being well again.

Top tip!

Ask for feedback from participants about why they got involved. If you can, offer some or all of those opportunities as incentives on your next wave of recruitment for service user representatives.

Section 6

Good practice recommendations for improving service user involvement

Training

- Provide training in inclusive communication jointly for everyone (staff and service user representatives) who will be taking part in involvement activities.
- Offer opportunities for service user representatives to take part in relevant training and up-skilling activities.
- Find ways of accrediting participation in training.
- Establish accreditation of all service user involvement, for example, a Certificate or Record of Participation will attach merit to the time and effort Disabled people give to the role.

Access

- Ensure meetings are fully accessible – involve service user representatives in identifying what the access requirements are.
- Identify a person who is the central point of contact for matters leading up to and following meetings.
- Ground rules – at the start of meetings, use ground rules to help establish strategies for ensuring everyone can have their say. These should be used to clearly signal that all contributions will be treated respectfully.
- Everyone should be required to listen carefully and be polite.

Equal participation

- Involve service user representatives in setting the agenda for the meeting.
- Avoid having service user input as the final item on the agenda to ensure service user feedback gets the time and attention it requires.
- Make sure service user representatives have advanced receipt of all papers to be discussed in accessible formats well before the meeting.
- Ensure a welcome and inclusive event – have someone to meet and greet service user representatives.
- Follow through on suggestions and input made by service user representatives and have a strategy for feeding back on this.

Top tip!

If you have not had disability awareness and disability equality training, then get some. It will help you to understand simple practical, low-cost steps you can take to make activities accessible for everyone taking part.

Section 7

Actions for change

Here are some easy actions you can take to immediately set about improving involvement of service user representatives. These are small and doable action steps and habits that will create more respectful and inclusive service user participation and are key to making sure that people who take on the role of service user representation have positive experiences and outcomes from being involved. Don't be alarmed: these steps are often small (some will take ten minutes or less to complete!). Over time, they will improve involvement of service user representatives in ways that will make it more and more possible to drive through better quality, efficient, cost-effective services that Disabled people value.

Four essential steps to improving involvement of service user representatives

Step 1 – Profile the service users you currently work with and build better connections with them

Have you ever written up a list of exactly who the service user representatives are that give their time to development of the services you deliver? Building a list of the people you already involve can be a hugely clarifying activity. Understanding who you involve as service user representatives will help you identify essential access requirements for meetings and also help you identify the gaps in service user representation to address missing perspectives. To improve involvement of service user representatives, you could get in touch with those already taking part and ask for their ideas on how participation could be improved. Better connections, and building genuine relationships with service user representatives, are a great way to strengthen the impact service users can make to your service and also to ensure the role is positive for them.

Step 2 – Set some 30-day goals for improving involvement of service user representatives

Having identified what needs to change in your practices – hopefully by getting feedback from existing participants – set some goals for change. It might be to let service users know more about how they can get involved, a financial goal to reimburse travel costs quicker, improved access to meetings, a plan to make contact with existing representatives and ask them for feedback on how things are going, a new email update on service user recommendations – those are just a few ideas. We suggest 30-day goals because they are short enough to be manageable and will kick-start real change. In 30 days of focused action, you can achieve incredible progress for improving service user involvement based on the rich and varied ideas in the sister report to this guide.

Step 3 – Include a call for service user involvement in any communications you send to your service user community

This is something that will only take a few minutes to write and can be included in every correspondence sent out to service users. Get into the habit of always promoting the value of service user representation, and spell out the benefits for both providers and users who take on the role; this will have a massive impact on raising the value of the activity. Better communication will lead to greater involvement to support service development.

Step 4 – Follow up and ask for feedback

When service user representatives make suggestions, follow these through. We know not all suggestions can be fully realised but have in place mechanisms for reporting back on how and whether suggestions have been responded to. Following up with service user representatives, including asking for new suggestions when recommendations get stuck, can be game changing for your service and shows respect for service user representation.

Contact Shaping Our Lives for help from our Service User Involvement Advisory Service.

In conclusion

Service users welcome being able to contribute to service design, delivery and evaluation of the services you provide and the processes you use. Many service users want to do this to help others in the same position as them, to 'give something back'. Service users have valuable lived experience from which you and your organisation can benefit.

However, service users cannot automatically become useful representatives – they need induction, training and support, just like any paid member of staff would. They need to be valued and motivated and rewarded, too.

Good processes and systems for involving service user representatives will lead to better, more efficient and more effective services which are valued by their users. Bad processes and systems will not improve your services; they will put service user representatives off being involved, and in some cases can cause aggravation and distress to the service users who have been subjected to them.

There are simple, practical things you can do to provide inclusive and accessible involvement activities. Be realistic with your goals and make affordable and quick changes to your systems.

Top tip!

Think about all the good practices you have for valuing staff in your organisation. Think about how they can be applied to service user representatives, too.

Supporting information

This best practice guide for service user representatives is one of three documents in this series. The other documents are the report of the research findings and a best practice guide for professionals.

You can find these under the heading 'Improving Understanding of Service User Involvement and Identity' in the Resources section of our website – www.shapingourlives.org.uk/resources.

Other resources on our website that may also be of interest are:

- Guide to accessible meetings and events.
- Inclusive ground rules.
- Definition of a service user written by people who use services.
- A series of publications, including electronic resources in the 'Beyond the Usual Suspects – Towards Inclusive User Involvement'.

Or contact Shaping Our Lives about our inclusive involvement service:

Email: information@shapingourlives.org.uk
Telephone: 0845 241 0383

Glossary of terms

Disability Equality Training   Training developed within the Disabled People's Movement which outlines the distinctions between the medical and social models of disability and the implications for professional practice and service delivery of these different ways of understanding.

Involvement activity   An activity, series of activities or group set up by an organisation to engage and involve service users in designing, overseeing and/or evaluating one of the organisation's services or processes.

Organisation   A body providing a service. Can be a public body (like a local council or GP, a university), a charity (e.g. drug and alcohol services) or a private company (e.g. a residential home).

Professional(s)   This term is used interchangeably with service provider(s) and practitioner(s) in this document. It is taken to mean someone who is paid to work for an organisation in a particular role, like a social worker, nurse or commissioning officer. It is used as a noun and not as a descriptive term suggesting particular behaviours.

Service user   A person who uses a service provided by an organisation, often in a social care or health care setting. A service user is not always a Disabled person. However, in this document we have used 'service user' to mean a Disabled person who is a service user. Anyone can self-define as a service user.

Service user representative (Representative)   An individual service user who joins in with an activity to share their lived experiences and sometimes speak on behalf of other service users.

The medical model of disability   Disability is 'any restriction or lack of ability (resulting from an impairment) to perform an activity in the manner or within the range considered normal for a human being, for example the ability to climb the stairs or walk to the shops' (WHO, 1981). Technically, the answer is yes, but the quote marks didn't appear in the report by Shaping Our Lives.

The social model of disability Disability is 'the loss or limitation of opportunities to take part in the normal life of the community on an equal level with others due to physical and social barriers' (Disabled People's International, 1981). Technically, the answer is yes, but the quote marks didn't appear in the report by Shaping Our Lives.

Guidelines for making events accessible

Access is about providing people with equal opportunity to participate fully in whatever is being offered. Meeting people's access needs should be done in a positive and affirmative way, which should be reflected in the language we use when discussing access requirements. All disabled people are individual and will therefore have different needs at different times. People with the same impairment/condition may manage it very differently and also have different access needs. However, here are some guidelines that Shaping Our Lives National User Network suggests are good practice.

Before a meeting/event

As a matter of good practice, participants should be asked prior to a meeting/event if they have any access requirements.

It is absolutely essential that anything people ask for is available at the meeting/event. This means that events/meetings need to be planned well in advance as, for example, palantypists, lip speakers and BSL interpreters cannot be booked at short notice. Hearing loops in venues are notoriously unreliable, and venues must thus be made aware of the importance of them working and be reminded of this closer to the event, with testing carried out prior to the event.

An agenda should be sent out in advance of each meeting/event. The agenda should include a paragraph under each heading explaining what will be discussed/covered etc. in this item. This will allow people to think about it or discuss it with a support worker if necessary before the meeting. (Funding must be made available to support this.)

Getting to the meeting/event

Disabled people who drive, or who are being driven, need reserved, well-signposted car parking nearby. People who take enquiries about public transport to the event need to be able to advise on accessible travel arrangements.

Getting in

Entrances to venues should be level or ramped, and if there are steps as well, these need to have a handrail and preferably step edges clearly marked. Some people with walking difficulties prefer steps to a ramp. Revolving doors are not suitable for wheelchair users or for many other people with different impairments. The position of the entry door needs to be clear, with glass doors well identified. It is a good idea if someone can meet and greet people at the entry into the building.

The place

Venues should have natural lighting and be well ventilated without air conditioning, which can be noisy and thus be a barrier for many impairment groups.

A 'quiet room' should be available so that if any participants want to take 'time out' there is a space set aside for this. Make sure all participants know where it is.

Water should be available throughout the event and a supply of plastic drinking straws is useful.

Food should be clearly labelled and not mixed.

During the meeting/event

Housekeeping: At the start of meetings, it should be explained to people where the toilets (accessible and non) and the fire exits are. This should be done in an inclusive manner, avoiding pointing, for example 'over there', and should take into account different people's access needs. For example, if the meeting is taking place in an upstairs venue, how wheelchair users will evacuate in the case of fire, are the lifts operational in a fire and so on.

Agendas must be stuck to so people can follow where they are in the day's proceedings.

Timing is an access issue. At the beginning of meetings (even if they start late due to unreliable public transport), times of breaks, lunch and ending need to be agreed and stuck to.

During meetings, 'ground rules' should be agreed.

If it is intended to include people with learning difficulties in a truly inclusive way, then it is important that this is taken into account when the agenda is planned, as well in the practice that is adopted in running the meeting/event.

Before the meeting starts, it might be a good idea to discuss the need for break times. Some people need regular breaks for a variety of reasons. For example, a break every ten minutes in order for people with learning difficulties to take 'time out', talk with their support worker, talk to each other or whatever they wish, might be necessary. This can be positive and have benefits for the entire group and for some specific impairment groups, for example, hearing-impaired people who are lip reading or following a sign language interpreter, people with pain who need to move frequently or those with continence problems. The interpreter themselves may need a break.

It is important that the venue is checked in terms of access. Staff attitudes are a major factor in determining whether a venue is suitable or not. If possible, it is advisable to seek personal recommendation from user groups.

It is important to remember that a solution for one group of service users might become a barrier to another impairment group. It is good practice to have more than one option available.

Access is about providing people with equal opportunity to participate fully in whatever is being offered.

Acknowledgements

This report has been produced by Shaping Our Lives in honour and memory of our great friend Patricia Chambers.

Patricia, a prominent member of the black and minority ethnic mental health user/survivor movement, and a dear friend and colleague, passed away in May 2016. For over 25 years, Patricia worked tirelessly to address issues at the intersections of race/culture and madness, within services, within the wider user/survivor movement and within research and policy.

In 2009, Patricia took over as the Network Manager of Catch-a-Fiya, the only (and now defunct) national network for people from black communities. It is impossible to list all the places and platforms she contributed to/through: BUGS, the Afiya Trust, Shaping Our Lives, Black Women's Mental Health Project, the Forward Project, the DRE Ambassadors programme,

NIMHE's Making a Real Difference programme, the Count Me In census, Dancing to Our Own Tunes . . . and the many local/informal user groups where she acted as an advocate and friend to people who needed that.

We developed this project from an interest Patricia had in the conflicts for people who use services and who also work to improve them. The project has been funded by the National Lottery through the Big Lottery Fund. All of us at Shaping Our Lives hope it will go some way to keeping the very fond memories we have of Patricia alive as well as bringing about the kind of positive change she worked so hard and wisely to achieve.

The Research Team was led by Becki Meakin of Shaping Our Lives. The team comprised Dr Colin Cameron from Northumbria University, Professor Michele Moore, Ann Nutt and Charley Bell-Moore.

There are many other Disabled people who have given their time and expertise to the research findings and guides in this series. Shaping Our Lives is very grateful for their invaluable contributions.

Authors: Becki Meakin and Joanna Matthews.
Shaping Our Lives
www.shapingourlives.org.uk
Email: information@shapingourlives.org.uk
Telephone: 0845 241 0383
Facebook: @shapingourlives
Twitter: @Solnetwork1
YouTube: shapingourlives1

3

WHO ARE THE SERVICE USERS? LANGUAGE, NEO-LIBERALISM AND SOCIAL CONSTRUCTIONS

Hugh McLaughlin

Introduction

In 2009, I published an article: 'What's in a name: "Client", patient', 'customer', 'consumer' 'expert by experience', 'service user' – What's next?' McLaughlin (2009a). As part of this article, I suggested 'the nature of the language we use is imbued with meaning and power, is dynamic and changing and that I would not be surprised for us to have developed an alternative term within the next ten years' (McLaughlin, 2009a, p. 1115). Ten years have now passed; this chapter revisits the debate but also locates it within the current context of social work practice, arguing that our attention to language has never been more important than it is now – something that was sadly missing from the original article.

The current context

When the article was written it was 2008; Gordon Brown (Labour) was still Prime Minister, and we were still yet to fully to understand or experience the impact of the international financial crisis. This crisis was triggered by the greed of bankers, which led to the breakdown in the sub-prime mortgage market in the US and the collapse of Lehman Brothers on 15 September 2008. This collapse sparked an international banking crisis and, as Dorling (2018, p. 3) notes, most 'governments in power in affluent countries were voted out of office at the subsequent general election'. Brown, the Labour Prime Minister, was replaced by Cameron for the Conservatives in 2010, who had previously claimed at the Conservative Party Conference 2009 that 'we're all in this together, which is why we'll freeze public sector pay for all but the one million lowest paid public sector workers for one year to help protect jobs' (Cameron, 2009, n.p.).

In response to the financial crisis and the introduction of government-chosen policies on austerity (Jones, 2018), many governments chose to reduce 'public spending' and, in particular, the 'welfare bill'. Austerity, in this sense, is a situation in which people's living standards were reduced. From Cameron's statement, it could be considered everyone's living standards – those who were rich and those who were poor – would suffer equally because of the economic crisis. Surprisingly (Dorling, 2018), the bankers who had caused the financial crash escaped much blame, and many even took home larger salaries and bonuses than previously. As Dorling (2018) noted, both the UK and US, the two most unequal societies in the world, have become even more unequal since the crash, while increasing evidence has shown the social harm of inequality.

> If increasing austerity alongside high and rising economic inequality had been a medical trial, that trial would have had to be halted on ethical grounds.
>
> *(Dorling, 2018, p. 18)*

This has resulted in those who are social work's major service user groups – the vulnerable, the poor, the disabled, the elderly and those whose lives are symbolised by precarity – all being targets for budget reductions, as were those who provided the services in the first place. In 2018, Professor Phillip Alston, the United Nations Special Rapporteur on Extreme Poverty and Human Rights, claimed in a highly critical report on the UK that:

> British compassion for those who are suffering has been replaced by a punitive, mean spirited, and often callous approach apparently designed to instill discipline where it is least useful. To impose a rigid order on the lives of those least capable of coping with today's world, and elevating the goal of enforcing blind compliance over a genuine concern to improve the well-being of those at the lowest levels of British society.
>
> *(Alston, 2018, p. 3)*

Alongside the impact of government-chosen austerity, we have experienced an increased momentum and legitimacy of a neo-liberal orthodoxy worldwide whereby governments have been able to make public sector reductions by claiming that that they are a necessary requisite for getting out of the financial crisis. This has also been seen in an increasing emphasis upon individualism and a dismantling of the broader welfare safety net through benefit reductions and increasing eligibility criteria. This was particularly apparent in the government's desire to review payments for people with long-term conditions or disabilities and their commissioning of ATOS and Capita (private firms) to undertake the assessment for personal independence payments. Both of these companies' first responsibility is to their shareholders and thus needing to profit from their Department of Work and Pensions (DWP) contract by helping the DWP reduce the welfare bill. Far from being a success, the assessments by ATOS and Capita have been highly controversial, with an increase from 64% to 71% in successful appeals to social security tribunals between the last quarters of 2016 and 2017 (Disability Rights UK, 2018). Any other scheme with such a high degree of successful appeals would be seen as not fit for purpose, but only 5% of Atos and Capita reports were questioned by the DWP. Currently, there is no evidence that the DWP has made any commitment to change the medical assessment process.

Alongside this, there has been an 'othering' (Chauhan and Foster, 2014) of those in receipt of services as somehow different from the rest of us, as though they are non-beings because of these differences, thus making it possible for 'us' to treat the non-others as less human and reduce their rights to welfare. As Alston (2018, p. 18) noted:

> The costs of austerity have fallen disproportionately upon the poor, women, racial and ethnic minorities, children, single parents and people with disabilities. The changes to taxes and benefits since 2010 have been highly regressive, and the policies have taken the highest toll on those least able to bear it.

At the same time, we have also seen reduced local authority funding leading the National Audit Office (2018) in the UK to claim that there has been a 49% reduction in funding in real terms between 2010 and 2017; there is no sign that this direction of reducing budgets will be changed anytime soon. It would be no surprise if the current Brexit (non-)negotiations result in further cuts on welfare budgets and local authority spending in the UK.

Hayek (1944) identified the key tenets of neo-liberalism as, firstly, the supremacy of the market as the most effective means for the distribution of resources and liberty, and, secondly, the importance of liberty as the key political value. Liberty in this sense meant freedom from the state or other outside interference. Friedman (1962) famously argued that market mechanisms were so superior that they should be applied in most, if not all, areas of life. The mantra of individual choice and competition were deemed ways of improving education and health and social care. In England, we have seen schools removed from local education authority control with the introduction of academies and free schools; the growth of a private sector in health and the provision of adult residential care; and fostering services and residential children services by not just NGOs but also private, for-profit organisations whose primary responsibility is to their shareholders and for making profits. As Harris (2014, p. 8) has argued, 'neoliberalism's priority is the creation of conditions attractive to capitalist profitability in the global market'.

Alongside the growth in equality (Alston, 2018; Cummins, 2018), there has been a growing individualisation in attitudes, where the poor are believed to be poor because of personal failings and are therefore 'undeserving', thus permitting further reductions in services. This reduction in compassion (Alston, 2018) has provided fertile ground for increasing stigmatisation of those who are in receipt of social work and other welfare services. As Cummins (2019) argues, Goffman's (1963, p. 3) use of stigma is important here in signifying how stigma moves the stigmatised from 'a whole and usual person to a tainted, discounted one'. Wacquant (2012) also notes neo-liberalism is not merely an economic project but also a political one. This takes for granted that what is needed is a retrenchment of the welfare state and a reduction in the state's welfare net, to encourage its citizens to become economically active and avoid becoming a drain on the nation's resources. All of this personalising of individual ills neatly sidesteps the social and structural elements. In recent years, Bywaters (2018, 2015) has sought to show how poverty is linked to child protection, where, for example, a child living in one of the most deprived towns in England, Blackpool is eight times more likely to be in the care of the local authority than one in Richmond, one of the wealthiest areas.

Having provided a context against which patients, survivors, service users, clients, experts by experience or those with lived experience inhabit, it is time to consider how our language and labels impact upon our practice and open opportunities while also providing limitations on how human services construct these for those with whom they work. One other aspect the previous article ignored was the issue of interprofessional work, which is discussed next.

Interprofessional practice

McLaughlin (2013) noted that interprofessional practice has become so pervasive that it is rarely questioned and is often discussed as not only the best way of working but the only way. Lethard (2003, p. 5) eloquently described interprofessional working as a 'terminological quagmire' with terms like 'interprofessional collaboration', 'collaborative practice', 'multi-disciplinary working', 'multi-professional working', 'interprofessional practice', 'transdisciplinary practice' and 'interprofessional working'. Banks (2010) notes that interprofessional practice is symbolised by two or more professionals working closely together, sharing common goals, and where there may be an interchangeability of roles. In the context of social work, the most common interprofessional partners include teachers, who refer to those whom they teach as pupils or students; doctors, psychiatrists, health visitors, district nurses and other health care professions who work with patients; the police, who have both victims and perpetrators of crimes; and lawyers, who have both defendants and those being prosecuted. This is not an exhaustive list, but it illustrates that different occupational groups refer to those to whom they provide a service by different names that indicate different types of relationships. A change in one profession's claims is likely to have a knock-on effect on the others. The words used by the different professions represent differing social constructions of the same person, reflecting different political, social and cultural contexts, each embedded with meaning from their own professional grouping.

It also highlights that professions like social work, paediatricians, psychiatrists, nurses, teachers, lawyers or the police are laying to a claim for jurisdictional boundaries and for the legitimate control of a particular area of practice; these are not necessarily self-evident claims but can be political ones.

It is assumed that by bringing different skill sets and expertise to work on the teacher's pupil/ health visitor's patient/lawyer's client/ policewoman's victim and social worker's service user will inevitably lead to better outcomes for the child and their family. There is a sense at that, at its simplest, 'the whole is greater than the sum of the parts'. Alongside this is an assumption that interprofessional practice represents a pooling of 'resources' and expertise beyond any single agency's ability to mobilise and deliver. This also potentially results in greater surveillance of service recipients. As Haggerty and Ericson (2007) observed, we are all subject to surveillance, but we are not surveilled in the same way or for the same purpose. An interprofessional team of a social worker, health visitor, nursery nurse, teacher and community police officer may monitor a single parent's child rearing, which may not be viewed as necessarily supportive by the single parent or her children. It cannot be assumed that all surveillance will be experienced as either benign or helpful (Banks, 2010).

Labelling social work

The labels we use to define the social work relationship – or should we say the service user relationship – create different pictures and ideas about the nature of this relationship and its construction. From the very beginning, it is important to recognise that you cannot have social workers without people for social workers to work with, on and/or for. Similarly, you cannot have 'service users', 'patients', 'clients', 'experts by experience' or 'people with lived experience' without first having service providers to provide services. There is a symbiotic relationship between the two. To have one, you need the other.

Secondly, the relationship is not based on binaries. One may be a social worker or a service user, but one can also have been a service user and is now a social worker or vice versa. In a survey of children and family social workers in England, Johnson et al. (2019) found that one in seven (14%) of their total of 5,621 respondents mentioned that they had had personal experience of social services, which had been a factor in their motivation to become children and family social workers. Nine percent had had a positive personal experience and 5% a negative experience, with 1% indicating that they had experienced both. It is also possible to have been a social worker and then, following a mental health episode or physical injury, to become a service recipient. It is also quite possible to have moved between the two different positions on more than one occasion as the conditions causing the need for services has improved and then deteriorated again. It is also possible to need services for different reasons at different times. Lastly, it is also possible to be a social worker while in receipt of services. All these permutations are to remind us to never forget there is no essentialism about whether one is a service user or service provider; we can all move in and out at different times or even during the same time in our lives.

At this stage, it is important to consider the power of our labelling and the conceptualisations of those who are in receipt of human services.

> The words we use to describe those who use our services are, at one level, metaphors that indicate how we conceive them. At another level such labels operate discursively, constructing both the relationship and attendant identities of people participating in the relationships, inducing very practical and material outcomes.
>
> *(McDonald, 2006, p. 115)*

As McDonald argues, we should be both aware of the nuances of language and consider the messages we are delivering when we use it. The labels we use in in social work act as signifiers in identifying and constructing identities and relationships, highlighting different issues and espousing differing assumptions about power and the nature of the professional relationship. Baron and Mitchell (2018) importantly identified how young people were identified in a Scottish secure unit as being so behaviourally difficult they required a strict regime of control; however, when assessed for trauma, they were reconceived as in need of specialist support which, when delivered, resulted in better outcomes for the young people, staff and families.

To examine this further, this chapter will consider various social constructions of this relationship, symbolised by the terms 'client', 'customer', 'expert by experience' and 'people with lived experience'. Other terms are also used to signify this relationship, including 'patient', 'consumer' 'survivor', 'activist' or 'citizen', some of which will also be touched upon in the discussion.

Client

In the late 1970s, when I qualified as a social worker, 'client' was the most common term used and was reflected in significant texts of the period. Mayer and Timms' (1970) *The Client Speaks* was the first book to privilege the perspective of those on the receiving end of social work practice. In 1975, Bailey and Brake (1975) published their classical text, *Radical Social Work*, which similarly used the term clients. While this is a term that is still internationally recognised and used, its origins come from the early 'almoners' who worked as medical social workers in hospitals and who referred to those they worked with as 'patients' as well as 'clients'. The term 'client', while sounding quite neutral, is suggestive of a relationship much like that of the traditional 'doctor' and 'patient', whereby it can be argued that the good client was someone who was passive and acted on the professional's expert assessment. Power is located within the social worker, who is the one with the specialist knowledge and skills and is thus able to decide upon the best course of action to ameliorate the client's problems.

Within the British context, the election of Margaret Thatcher in 1979 was seen as a turning point at which the neo-liberal agenda could be seen to replace the welfare consensus. The introduction of the NHS and Community Care Act (1990) set to open the 'closed' market of adult social care to a mixed economy of welfare, redefining the role of social services from being a provider of social services to becoming a 'commissioner' or 'purchaser' of services. The commissioners and purchasers were expected to commission or purchase services less from the local authority and more from a mix of private and not-for-profit providers. At the same time, Thatcher was keen to reduce the power of professionals who were viewed as managing services too much for their own ends (McLaughlin, 2009b). Thatcher's solution was to introduce managerialism, which Adams (2002) notes put managers at the centre of organisations and imported practices from the private sector to ensure economy, efficiency and effectiveness of services.

As part of this organisational change, there was a push to relabel clients as 'customers' or 'consumers', following private sector norms. The social services recipient was recast as a 'customer' or 'consumer' who was able to choose between differing options from public or independent providers and to exit from a provider if they so wished (Harris, 1999). This empowering of human service recipients was more a case of smoke and mirrors. It was not really practical for someone facing a mental health assessment to suggest they wanted another GP or social worker from another local authority to do their assessment. The same could also be said for child protection investigations. While these changes could be argued as challenging the paternalism of the professionals, they could not be fully operationalised, although the seeds for increasing privatisation were clearly visible.

The defeat of the Tories at the 1997 election did not reverse this trajectory but rather gathered pace under Blair, the Labour leader's big idea captured by the term 'modernisation'. Modernisation (Cabinet Office, 1990; Department of Health, 1998) was viewed as the necessary process for updating public services to match the needs of modern-day consumers. It continued the attack on provider dominance while maintaining a focus on business solutions (Newman, 2000).

Denser Platt, when Chief Inspector for Social Services, summed up the government's approach in her annual report:

> The present government is committed to reforming the public services. Its vision is of public services where the services are designed around the needs of the people who use them, rooted in the values of the community. To deliver the agenda and to modernise the services we are asking the people who work in social services to work in new ways.
>
> *(Platt, 2002, paras 1.4–1.5)*

While this could be seen as potentially empowering for service users, Barnes and Mercer (2006) claimed that the move to greater use of scrutiny, inspection, audit and performance targets, far from increasing delegated authority, in fact reduced service user influence over service provision.

The service user

The acknowledgement of the importance of the service user mandate can be seen as an extension of the consumerist or customer tradition already discussed. As such, it can be viewed as a top-down approach (Ferguson, 2008). In opposition to this, it can also be traced to a more democratic tradition, or bottom-up, approach of promoting participation to ensure that services are fit for purpose.

> The origins ('bottom up', emerging out of collective movements rather than 'top down'), its aims (social change and social justice, rather than simply involvement in services), ideology (a social rather than an individual or bio-medical model of health and disability) and its methods (often involving collective action, rather than 'partnership' with its service providers.
>
> *(Ferguson, 2008, p. 70)*

The 'bottom-up' approach is therefore more radical than the 'top-down' approach and contains within it an inherent challenge to the status quo. In recent years, we have seen the development of user-led organisations, e.g. Shaping our Lives (www.shapingourlives.org.uk/), which is a national, independent, user-controlled organisation, with a network of 430+ user-led organisations, service users and disabled people advocating on behalf of service users, challenging service provider dominance and the status quo. Internationally, there is also PowerUs (http://powerus.eu/about-us/introduction/), an international organisation of social work academics and representatives from service user organisations seeking to develop 'methods of mutual learning in order to change social work practice to be more effective in supporting the empowerment of marginalized and discriminated groups in society' (PowerUs, n.d.).

In a research report by Shaping Our Lives (2017, p. 17), it is clear that there is still significant work to do, as a service user commented:

> It is diminishing to realise how the service providers see service users. It is frustrating in the meetings to sense how little credence most of them actually give to service user viewpoints. If our view chimes with theirs they are positive and pleased with how things are going; if the service user perspectives challenge their views then they tend to offer platitudes and try to swiftly move the discussion on.

As the use of the term service user has become more prevalent, it is important to note that this is not without its critics. In social work, professionals can refer to 'service users' as a way of defining a group of people, e.g. those with mental health needs, people with disabilities, families in need of support and or crisis, children looked after and so on. What is important here is that this labelling of human beings is viewed through the prism of their status as service users and neglects all the other statuses that they may have which may be viewed as more positive. Thus, a service user may also be a school governor, a manager, magistrate, researcher, volunteer or grandmother, but what is viewed as the most significant by service providers is their status as being in receipt of services – a more inferior status than that of manager, magistrate, researcher, volunteer or grandmother. There is a danger that the use of the term 'service user' can be a way for professionals to restrict service user identity, suggesting a hierarchical relationship between those who commission and deliver services and those who are in receipt of them.

The use of the service user also neglects those who are either unable to access services or do not access services to which they are entitled. For example, Memon et al. (2016) found that for members of the Black and Minority Ethnic Community (BME), issues like cultural identity and stigma, financial factors, waiting lists, communication, cultural naivety, insensitivity and discrimination all resulted in their being less likely to access mental health services.

Shaping Our Lives (n.d.) helpfully redefines service user in a more positive reframing, highlighting that it should be considered an 'active and positive term', in that it acknowledges we live in 'oppressive relationship with the state'. It is about 'entitlement to receive welfare services', resulting in some people considering service users as inferior as they have needed services for a long time, and being able to recognise that their shared experiences of using services gives members 'a strong voice to improve services'.

How we define those we work with, serve, help, care for, advocate on behalf of or wish to empower is not simple or straightforward. It is thus not surprising that other terms have also been used. I would now like to move on and discuss 'experts by experience and 'people with lived experience'.

Experts by experience

Banfield et al. (2006, p. 30) provide the rationale for experts by experience when they claim that:

> Service users can be the best people to tell professionals what they want and need from any particular service, because it is intended for them and their knowledge of it is based on direct experience.

It could also be added that it is they who experience both the intended and unintended consequences of service delivery.

Experts by experience is also the term favoured by the Social Care Institute for Excellence (2019) and the Care Quality Commission (n.d.), which manage an 'experts by experience' programme that involves the public in health and social care inspections:

> Experts by Experience are people who have personal experience of using or caring for someone who uses health, mental health and/or social care services that we regulate.
>
> *(CQC, n.d.)*

It is important to first consider what an expert is. The Cambridge Dictionary (n.d.) defines it as a 'person with a high level of knowledge or skill relating to a particular subject or activity'. This definition clearly opens the way for anyone to claim they are an expert; there is no requirement for any specific educational training or professionally regulated activity (Johnson, 1972). Traditionally, expertise is viewed as the successful completion of a prescribed higher education training programme, followed by time spent learning in practice and potential promotion.

While this is a common perception of an expert, it is by no means exclusive. As Scourfield (2010) has noted,

> the adoption of the term 'expert' in the context of 'experts by experience' can be understood as a self-conscious and deliberate attempt to confront the power of the professions and democratise 'experience' in the domain of health and social care. It is used to equalise power differentials and to suggest that expertise by experience is every bit as valid as professional expertise.
>
> *(Scourfield, 2010, p. 1892)*

Alongside this, we should note that in the UK, Statista (2019a) claims that 88% of households in the UK own a home computer, up from 13% in 1985. Statista (2019b) also claims that nearly 50% of all households worldwide have a computer at home, up from just over a quarter in 2006. This growth in access to computers at home has opened up the potential for most of us to use search engines like Google to self-diagnose our illnesses, compare evidence on services, contribute to service evaluations or link up with others who have similar concerns or wish to make changes to service delivery. Knowledge is no longer the sole preserve of the professional.

This claim to expertise is at one level a recognition that those on the receiving end of services have a right to be involved in the decisions that affect them. It also acknowledges that we cannot assume that professionals will always act in service users' best interests and that their privileged position should be open to question and challenge. It also provides opportunities for both positive and negative experiences to be identified. While answering some questions, it also creates others. How much experience does an expert by experience require in order to make this claim? Is it just one session with a professional, living with a disability for a month, a year, five years or a lifetime? The definition is also problematic in comparing and contrasting different experiences of 'experts by experience' who have the same needs but where one experiences the same service positively and one negatively. As McLaughlin (2009a) asks, which one is right? Or are both right? Also, what about someone who wanted the service someone else received, believing it to be better suited for them? Can we take it for granted that they are right (or wrong)? 'Experts by experience', while helpfully drawing attention to the power imbalance between professionals and those they work with, highlights that the importance of service user voices and credibility of their experiences is imprecise and fails to differentiate between individuals who use services.

In recent years, we have also seen the emergence of 'people with lived experience', where the expert part of the label is no longer claimed. This has been evident in improving service through co-production (Curtice and Greig (n.d.) and in the commissioning of mental health services (Rethink Mental Illness, n.d.). It is interesting that the commissioning report also uses 'experts by experience', noting that these terms can often be conflated. 'People with lived experience' again highlights the importance of people on the receiving end of service providers intentions, but it fails to help us decide as to which person's experiences should be listened to. The terminology also fails to help us distinguish between conflicting experiences where one may be viewed as positive while someone in a similar situation views the same service as negative. Both references, however, argue for the importance of co-production and the facilitation of conversations between service recipients and service providers.

Conclusions

This chapter has highlighted that the way we speak about those in receipt of social services or any other human service must be considered not only in terms of the meaning of the word but also in relation to the context in which it is used. It also challenges us to consider the underpinning ideological nature of wider society, and in this case the neo-liberal hegemony. Keywords such as 'patient', 'client', 'customer', 'expert by experience' and 'service user' are integral to social work's discourses. Looking beneath the surface of these key terms offers us the opportunity to 'cultivate new habits of disruptive thinking' (Fritsch et al., 2016, p. 116), interrogating discourses that are often insufficiently questioned within mainstream social work (Chihota, 2017). Beckett (2003, p. 627) rightly warns us against 'naivete about the extent to which changing the names of things (using anti-oppressive language for example) can change the world itself'.

It is important to accept that we currently have no single term that is acceptable to all. However, whatever term is used, it needs to acknowledge that people who are identified as clients, customers, experts by experience or service users are more than the services they receive. They are not merely passive receptacles of professional assessment, whether in social work service delivery, education or research, but are also active actors in their own story. In the previous article (McLaughlin, 2009a), I suggested that we would find a better word to identify the relationship in the future, and maybe we will. However, what is probably more important is to recognise how many of the same terms are currently used without question, having become re-constructed within our current experience of austerity and neo-liberalism. In the end, maybe the best way forward is for social workers, educators, researchers and others to ask those with whom they are working to identify how they would like to be labelled and to be open to a discussion about the negative and positive implications of any particular term. Importantly, the 'professional', 'educator' or 'social researcher' should also reflect on the implications of their role identity and how it also impacts upon the encounter and its implications for those with whom they work.

References

Adams, R. (2002) *Social policy for social work*, Basingstoke: Palgrave.

Alston, P. (2018) Statement on the visit to the United Kingdom, by Professor Phillip Alston, United Nations Special Rapporteur on extreme poverty and human rights, www.ohchr.org/Documents/Issues/Poverty/EOM_GB_16Nov2018.pdf

Bailey, R. and Brake, M. (1975) *Radical social work*, London: Edward Arnold.

Banks, S. (2010) Interprofessional ethics: A developing field? Notes from the ethics and social welfare conference, Sheffield, UK May, 2010, *Ethics and Social Welfare*, 4(3): 280–294.

Barnes, C. and Mercer, G. (2006) *Independent futures: Creating user-led services in a disabling society*, Bristol: Policy Press.

Baron, I. and Mitchell, D. (2018) Adolescents in secure accommodation Scotland: Exposure and impact of traumatic events, *Journal of Aggression, Maltreatment and Trauma*, 27(7): 777–794.

Beckett, C. (2003) The language of siege, *British Journal of Social Work*, 33(5): 625–639.

Branfield, F., Beresford, P., Taylor, J., Chambers, P., Staddon, P., Wise, G. and Willcome-Findlay, B. (2006) *Making user involvement work: Supporting service users networks and knowledge*, New York: Joseph Rowntree Fellowship.

Bywaters, P. (2015) 1 Jan 2015, Inequalities in child welfare and child protection services: Explaining the 'inverse intervention law, *British Journal of Social Work*, 45(1): 6–23, 18.

Bywaters, P., Scourfield, J., Jones, C., Sparks, T., Elliott, M., Hooper, J., Mccartan, C., Shapira, M., Bunting, L. and Daniel, B. (2018) Child welfare inequalities in the four nations of the UK, *Journal of Social Work*, https://doi.org/10.1177/1468017318793479 Accessed 09/11/2019.

Cabinet Office (1990) *Modernising government*, Cm 4310, London: Stationery Office.

Cambridge Dictionary (n.d.) Expert, https://dictionary.cambridge.org/dictionary/english/expert Accessed 21/08/2019.

Cameron, D. (2009) Full text of Davide Cameron's speech: The Tory Leader's address in full, *The Guardian*, 8th October, www.theguardian.com/politics/2009/oct/08/david-cameron-speech-in-full Accessed 08/05/2019.

Care Quality Commission (n.d.) *Experts by experience*, www.cqc.org.uk/about-us/jobs/experts-experience Accessed 21/08/2019.

Chauhan, A. and Foster, J. (2013) Representations of poverty in British newspapers: A case of "Othering" the threat?, *Journal of Community & Applied Social Psychology*, 24(5): 390–405.

Chihota, C. (2017) Critical language awareness: A beckoning frontier in social work education, *Aotearoa New Zealand Social Work*, 29(2): 56–66.

Cummins, I. (2018) *Poverty, inequality and social work*, Bristol: Policy Press.

Cummins, I. (2019) Social work and austerity, in A.L. Pelaez and E.J. Gómez-Ciriano (eds) *Austerity, social work and welfare polices: A global perspective*, Navarra: Thomson Reuters.

Curtice, L. and Greig, N. (n.d.) *How people with lived experience and people who work in services can have good conversations and build connections to co-produce wellbeing*, www.coproductionscotland.org.uk/files/8014/2788/6655/4._People_Powered_Health_and_Wellbeing.pdf Accessed 26/08/2019.

Department of Health (1998) *Modernising Social Services: Promoting Independence, improving protection and raising standards*, Cm 4169, London: Stationery Office.

Disability Rights UL (2018) *95% of Atos and Capita PIP medical assessments reports unquestioned by DWP*, www.disabilityrightsuk.org/news/2018/august/95-atos-and-capita-pip-medical-assessment-reports-unquestioned-dwp Accessed 27/08/2019.

Dorling, D. (2018) *Peak inequality: Britain's ticking time bomb*, Bristol: Policy Press.

Ferguson, I. (2008) *Reclaiming social work: Challenging neo-liberalism and promoting social justice*, London: Sage.

Friedman, M. (1962) *Capitalism and freedom*, Chicago: University of Chicago Press.

Fritsch, K., O'Connor, C. and Thompson, A.K. (2016b) Introduction, in K. Fritsch, C. O'Connor and A.K. Thompson (eds) *Keywords for radicals*, Chico, CA and Edinburgh, Scotland: AK Press.

Goffman, E. (1963) *Stigma: Notes on the management of spoiled identities*, New York: Simon and Schuster.

Haggerty, K.W. and Ericson, R.V. (2007) The new politics of surveillance and visibility, in K.W. Haggerty and R.V. Ericson (eds) *The new politics of surveillance and visibility*, London: University of Toronto Press.

Harris, J. (1999) State social work and social citizenship in Britain: From clientelism to consumerism, *British Journal of Social Work*, 29(6): 915–937.

Harris, J. (2014) (Against) neoliberal social work, *Critical and Radical Social Work*, 2(1): 7–22.

Hayek, F. (1944) *The road to serfdom*, Chicago: University of Chicago Press.

Johnson, C., Coburn, S., Sanders-Early, A., Winterbotham, M., McLaughlin, H., Pollock, S., Scholar, H. and McCaughan, S. (2019) *Longitudinal study of local authority child and family social workers (Wave 1): Research report*, Government Social Research, www.hpsc.mmu.ac.uk/departments/social-care-and-social-work/profile.php?id=12 Accessed 09/05/2019.

Johnson, T.J. (1972) *Professions and power*, Basingstoke: Palgrave Macmillan.

Jones, R. (2018) *In whose interest? The privatisation of child protection and social work*, Bristol: Policy Press.

Lethard, A. (2003) Introduction, in A. Lethard (ed) *Interprofessional collaboration: From policy to practice in health and social care*, Hove: Brunner-Routledge.

Mayer, J.E. and Timms, N. (1970) *The client speaks*, London: Routledge and Kegan Paul.

Memon, A., Taylor, K., Mohebati, L.M., et al. (2016) Perceived barriers to accessing mental health services among black and minority ethnic (BME) communities: A qualitative study in Southeast England, *BMJ Open*, 6: e012337. doi:10.1136/bmjopen-2016-012337 https://bmjopen.bmj.com/content/bmjopen/6/11/e012337.full.pdf Accessed 19/08/2019.

McDonald, C. (2006) *Challenging social work: The context of practice*, Basingstoke: Palgrave Macmillan.

McLaughlin, H. (2009a) *Service user research in health and social care*, London: Sage.

McLaughlin, H. (2009b) 'What's in a name: "Client", "patient", "customer", "consumer" "expert by experience", "service user" – What's next?' *British Journal of Social Work*, 39(6): 1101–1117.

McLaughlin, H. (2013) Motherhood, apple pie and interprofessional working, *Social Work Education: The International Journal*, 32(7): 956–963.

National Audit Office (2018) *Financial sustainability of local authorities 2018*, 8 March, pp. 10–11, www.nao.org.uk/report/financial-sustainability-of-local-authorities-2018/ Accessed 06/08/2019.

Newman, J. (2000) Beyond the new public management? Modernizing public services, in J. Clarke, S. Gerwitz and E. McLaughlin (eds) *New managerialism new welfare*, London: Open University in association with Sage.

Platt, D. (2002) *Modern social services: A commitment to reform*, London: Stationery Office.

PowerUs (n.d.) http://powerus.eu/about-us/introduction/ Accessed 18/08/2019.

Rethink Mental Illness (n.d.) *Progress through partnership: Involvement of people with lived experience of mental illness in CCG commissioning*, www.rethink.org/media/2591/progress-through-partnership.pdf Accessed 26/08/2019.

SCIE (2019) *How to work together to achieve better joined-up care*, www.scie.org.uk/integrated-care/better-care/guides/work-together Accessed 21/09/2019.

Scourfield, P. (2010) A critical reflection on involvement of 'experts by experience in inspections, *British Journal of Social Work*, 4(6): 1890–1907.

Shaping Our Lives (2017) *Improving the understanding of service user involvement and identity: A report of research findings*, www.shapingourlives.org.uk/wp-content/uploads/2017/11/Service-User-Identity-Research-Findings2.pdf Accessed 18/08/2019.

Shaping Our Lives (n.d.) www.shapingourlives.org.uk/about/about-sol/definitions Accessed 19/08/2019.

Statista (2019a) Percentage of households with home computers in the United Kingdom (UK) from 1985 to 2018, www.statista.com/statistics/289191/household-penetration-of-home-computers-in-the-uk/ Accessed 26/08/2019.

Statista (2019b) *Share of households with a computer at home worldwide from 2005–2018*, www.statista.com/statistics/748551/worldwide-households-with-computer/ Accessed 26/08/2019.

Wacquant, L. (2012) Three steps to a history of anthropology of actually existing neoliberalism, *Social Anthropology*, 20(1): 66–79.

4

EXPERIENTIAL KNOWLEDGE IN MENTAL HEALTH SERVICES, RESEARCH AND PROFESSIONAL EDUCATION

Steve Gillard, Rhiannon Foster and Angela Sweeney

Context – knowledge, power and mental health

We situate this chapter in an understanding that knowledge and power are inextricably linked. For Foucault, knowledge is defined as the particular common-sense view of the world that prevails in a culture at any one time. The power to act in certain ways, to claim resources or to control others depends upon the 'knowledges' currently prevailing in a society, allowing these actions to be represented in an acceptable light. As such, particular constructions of events, people and social phenomena will have a greater likelihood of being viewed as 'fact' or 'truth' than others, in any given time, location and culture. For example, versions of events provided by science and medicine can be given greater acceptance (viewed as fact) than those offered by religion or superstition. What we call knowledge, then, refers to the particular construction of a phenomenon that has received acceptance in our society at that time. Where scientists have not yet been able to explain fully a phenomenon (such as psychosis), these things are assumed to have an underlying rational explanation which science, in time, will uncover (Foucault, 1980; Lather, 1990).

Social constructionists have argued that power can be conceptualised as the extent of a person's access to valued resources, such as money, respected occupations or the impact they may have on others' lives through important decision making processes (for example, as politicians or doctors), with some groups of people in society having less power than others (Burr, 1995). For Foucault, the common-sense view of the world that prevails in a culture at any one time is inextricably linked with power because it can be associated with the potential for acting in one way rather than another, and for marginalising alternative ways of acting. What it is possible for one person to do to another, under what rights and obligations, is given by the version of events currently taken as 'knowledge'. This means that the power to act in certain ways, to claim resources, to control others or be controlled depends upon the 'knowledges' currently prevailing in a society (Foucault, 1982). Thus, to understand inequalities in society, we need to examine how particular ways of knowing serve to create and uphold particular forms of social life (Burr, 1995). This approach can be used to unravel the complex dynamics that may be at play in the formation and use of knowledge about mental health in research, education and practice.

What is experiential knowledge?

We locate the concept of experiential knowledge in phenomenological philosophy. Phenomenology suggests that we come to know our world through living in the world, a process that the 18th-century philosopher Husserl termed 'lived experience'. As such, our working knowledge of the world, social as well as material, is not something we passively receive in an essentialised or 'ready-made' form. Rather, we actively produce what we know through our actions and interactions with the world around us. Another 18th-century phenomenologist, Heidegger, suggested that the process of knowing is therefore shaped by our prior experiences and what we have already come to know about the world, or in other words, by who we are in terms of our previous social and material interactions. This experiential way of knowing is further described by the 20th-century philosopher Merleau-Ponty as embodied, physically and temporally, in our senses, perceptions and behaviours, in the things that we do and the people that we meet, as we go about our everyday lives.

Echoing this phenomenological view of the world, an extensive health professions literature contrasts formal, technical or codified knowledge about health and healthcare practice, acquired as objective knowledge through professional education and training (Mol, 2002), with an informal, 'tacit' knowledge subjectively acquired by healthcare professionals through hands-on experience and interaction with patients (Collins and Evans, 2007). Similarly, experiential knowledge about health and illness held by people on the receiving end of care is also increasingly recognised as an important discourse in healthcare delivery (Komporozos-Athanasiou et al., 2011). It is noted that this subjective or tacit knowing derives both from experiences of illness and experiences of using healthcare services (Mazandurani et al., 2013). Further, this subjective knowing about health and illness is experienced both bodily and temporally, in actual things that happen to the person at particular times (Mol and Law, 2004): feeling unwell, receiving treatment, feeling better and so on.

Medical anthropology has similarly noted how we produce our own 'local biologies', situated in our embodied experiences of health, illness and treatment (Lock, 2001). As such, subjective, experiential ways of knowing about the body and mind often work in tension with the more formal, objective knowledge of illness held by trained professionals (Barry et al., 2001). For example, Oborn and colleagues (2019) note that peer workers – people employed to use their experiences of mental distress and mental health services in support of others – bring tacit, experiential knowledge of living with mental distress and of receiving treatment to their work, contributing a distinctive and critical body of knowledge to mental health care.

Thus, our working understanding of experiential knowledge about mental health – as we consider it in this chapter – is of knowledge derived from living with mental distress and/or from being on the receiving end of psychiatric treatment and mental health care. Experiential knowledge articulates the way in which people make sense of things that happen in particular times and places. Experiential knowledge is therefore socially situated knowledge and is not separate from who people are in multiple other ways. As such, experiential knowledge is shaped by the way people's experiences are gendered, racialised or otherwise impacted by discourses of power, alongside their experiences of mental health and mental health care. This intersectionality between mental health and other sites of disadvantage and discrimination in people's lives arguably shapes the inequalities that characterise access, experiences and outcomes of mental health care for many people (Hatch and Dohrenwend, 2007). As such, we should be careful not to reduce experiential knowledge to a simple counter-psychiatry discourse. In the sections that follow, we consider the wider implications of experiential knowledge for mental health practice, research and professional training.

Experiential knowledge as emancipatory discourse

Our understanding of the role of experiential knowledge in mental health services, research and education owes much to the social constructionist understanding of the relationship between knowledge and power discussed above. For example, standpoint epistemology (Harding, 1991), with its roots in critical feminism, proposes that we come to know the world around us in socially situated ways – standpoints – that derive meaning in relation to gendered structures of power, and experiences of privilege and oppression. Likewise, in the field of race studies, Ladner (1973) has argued that a mainstream, or 'White', sociology has functioned to uphold the status quo in race relations in the US by, in effect, denying knowledge held by Black US citizens about the differing historical conditions that underpin US cultural experience. Science in different disciplines (psychology, psychiatry, genetics) has been argued to be highly politicised in nature, including racialised theories of intelligence (Rose et al., 1984) and gendered understandings of reproductive science (Tavris, 1993; Martin, 1991).

Thus, knowledge can be hegemonic and work to perpetuate inequity, exercising what Foucault termed 'sovereign' or repressive power; or knowledge can be emancipatory, resisting and challenging the assumptions that underpin and perpetuate hierarchy and privilege. As such, we suggest that experiential knowledge about mental health offers the potential to critique dominant or taken-for-granted understandings of mental health that are the common currency of psychiatric treatment, mental health research and professional education. Indeed, Foucault argues that the power implicit in any one discourse is only made apparent by the explicit resistance of counter-discourse. Thus, while experiential knowledge of mental health might be viewed as emancipatory discourse – as an expression of resistance to a dominant medical model of psychiatry – we also suggest that resistance to experiential knowledge (expressed by psychiatry or academia) is evidence of the power of survivor voices to bring about change.

Experiential knowledge – implications for mental health practice

Medical hegemony

> Hegemony is defined as the preponderant influence or authority over others, the social, cultural, ideological, or economic influence exerted by a dominant group. Medical hegemony is the dominance of the biomedical model, the active suppression of alternatives as well as the corporatization of personal, clinical medicine into pharmaceutical and hospital centred treatment.
>
> *(Weber, 2016)*

Weber views the doctor–patient interaction as an unequal social relationship based on power imbalance, where rules are dictated through exclusivity of information, status and money. In this way, the dominance of medical institutions such as psychiatry position themselves beyond criticism and reproach from non-doctors and create an elitism that does not serve the individual. Using the context of alternative medicine, Weber defines the hegemonic alliance as the dominant economic force, which is comprised of political society, medical universities, medical societies and the pharmaceutical industry. This hegemonic alliance has achieved dominance as the standard of knowledge production, which has subjugated other forms of medicine and knowledge. Biomedicine has taken a scientific approach to establishing efficacy with standardised and systematic scientific protocols that are methodologically incompatible with alternative medicine's underlying philosophy and nature of its practice; yet, it has still achieved dominance as the standard of knowledge production and, by extension, how the hegemonic alliance has achieved dominance over which knowledge is put into practice in healthcare.

A further extension of this hegemony is argued by Turner (2001), who problematises the concept of expert knowledge. He argues that expert knowledge can be seen as a threat to democracy and equality, whereby knowledge can be viewed as a possession to which some have access while others are excluded. Solutions to such a conceptualisation cannot be achieved by egalitarianisation through access to education when the difference in access to knowledge (expertise) is understood as a difference in viewpoint, in contrast to a quantity of knowledge. Turner (2001) argues that expert knowledge masquerades as neutral fact but is susceptible to ideology, whereby each claim or presentation of reality by an expert is a discursive structure that can often be an expression of patriarchy, racism or other injustices. He identifies a key feature of expert knowledge that makes it more powerful and persuasive as being that the 'real' character of this knowledge is hidden. It is easy to see the arguments here in the light of biomedical, traditional psychiatric knowledge and expertise claims.

Thus, in clinical practice in mental health, we see examples of discounting of experiential knowledge in favour of the wisdom of the clinical expert. Initiatives such as shared decision making have invited people using mental health services into the clinical encounter as partners, although systematic reviews have shown no impact of interventions to support shared decision making on either treatment or perceived decision making ability of service users (Stovell et al., 2016). It is possible that assumptions underlying shared decision making – that the professional brings expertise in understanding medical problems while the patient brings expertise related to values, goals and preferences (Drake et al., 2009) – work to mitigate the impact of experiential knowledge on treatment decisions that remain, primarily, the preserve of the treating clinician. Similarly, the introduction of advance directives and other forms of crisis plan are intended to provide a means by which an individual's knowledge about 'what works for them' is respected and actioned, especially when they might temporarily not be in a position to make decisions about their own care. However, such advanced planning has been shown to have little or no impact on either the care that is provided or the outcomes of care, often not being given dedicated time outside of routine clinical review and with service users reporting that their wishes are not subsequently followed (Thornicroft et al., 2013). Conversely, people routinely find their credibility questioned and their accounts of their mental health pathologised or dismissed as 'lack of insight'. This has been described as testimonial or epistemic injustice and variously attributed to the irrationality, bizarreness, incomprehensibility or moral susceptibility of the patient (Sanati and Kyratsous, 2015; Kyratsous and Sanati, 2016).

Experiential knowledge, culture and exclusion in mental health practice

If experiential knowledge is socially situated and intertwined with who people are in multiple other ways, this intersectionality is likely to be reproduced as different knowledges interact in mental health service spaces. Naidoo (1996) has observed how psychology has traditionally been both ethnocentric and Eurocentric (deriving from a White middle-class value system) in its orientation, training and practice, and has neglected the mental health concerns of other racial groups as well as the socio-political injustices they endure on a daily basis. Highlighting the ethnocentric nature of counselling research, Naidoo explores how knowledge is produced by Western, white researchers and therapists working almost exclusively within white client systems, and how key assumptions are made about important concepts such as individualism, competition, family structures, communication norms and emotion regulation, to name a few.

Naidoo argues that when these same therapeutic practices are applied to members of other cultural groups, they may in fact represent values that are antagonistic to that culture and as such may unwittingly become tools of cultural oppression (Naidoo, 1996, p. 13)

Similarly, Cruza-Guet (2008) illustrates how the Western bias in counselling practices has impacted on mental health treatment options in Ecuador. Among a vastly diverse population are several important cultural values that unite the population, including familism, social networks and the patriarchal structure of social relations. In addition to an enduring influence on Ecuadorian life is the resistance against historical domination or hegemony of outside cultural groups. Native people of Ecuador have a history of being invaded and colonised, and traces of such conquests remain significant and have discernible effects on many aspects of life, not least on the practice on mental health. Many of the attitudes and behaviours of the Ecuadorian population reflect a pervasive tension between what is foreign and what is perceived to be authentically Ecuadorian; such tensions can be magnified by the education and training pathways in mental health service provision and subsequent counselling practices being 'Western-centric' and how these conflict with the needs and worldview of the Ecuadorian population.

Experiential knowledge – implications for mental health education

The history of medical training and the lecture theatre suggest that the roles of patient, doctor and audience have always been characterised by performance, voyeurism and complex issues of morality, as much as by their educative purpose (Brockbank, 1968; Guerrini, 2006). It is perhaps in this context that the involvement of people with a psychiatric diagnosis in the teaching of psychiatry and other mental health disciplines might be considered, almost as anatomical specimens, objects, to be dissected and revealed, rather than as knowing subjects. While both healthcare students and people bringing their experiences of mental health and treatment to the lecture theatre report a range of potential benefits, including increased empathy in the clinical encounter (Happell et al., 2014), concerns remain about the status afforded to experiential knowledge in an educational context. People involved in mental health education from the experiential perspective have reported being concerned that lived experience is not valued in comparison to knowledge acquired through formal learning, and that staff and students are more interested voyeuristically in their lives than about the knowledge they offered (Meehan and Glover, 2007). Students and trainees are concerned that 'service users' involved in healthcare education may be too emotionally involved in the subject matter, have irrational expectations of training, be unable to deliver learning in a structured way, be unrepresentative of other patients, might have their own agendas and that this involvement might lead to shifts in power from psychiatrists to service users (Babu et al., 2008). As such, we see that subject or experiential knowledge – associated with emotions, irrationality and agendas – is both devalued and seen as challenging to existing power structures.

More recently, psychiatry and other professional teaching programmes have embraced the use of 'virtual patient' technologies, whereby students explore a range of clinical presentations through a digital interface, with both the content and algorithms underpinning the virtual exchange derived to a greater or lesser extent from consultation with people who have been on the receiving end of treatment. A recent review identified, alongside practical convenience, lack of variation in patient behaviours and absence of patient recall problems as benefits of the approach (Combs and Combs, 2019). While authors also identify lack of diversity as a current limitation to virtual patient technology, the prospect of both objectification and commodification of experiential knowledge is raised, with a proliferation of virtual patient software applications and mobile apps becoming commercially available (Culpepper and Thase, 2019).

It has been some time since a plea was made that knowledge based on the direct experience of people using mental health services should inform the theory-building that underpins education and training in the health and social care professions (Beresford, 2000). There is a well-established tradition of critical pedagogy in the health sciences that states that teaching is necessarily a political activity, operating within existing structures of power, and that teachers as such have a responsibility to expose the oppressive structures which confine and limit the health professional experience and to train professionals with a critical conscience (Harden, 1996). More recently, there have been calls for the full diversity of values that people bring to the clinical encounter – as clinicians, patients and family members, of different cultural heritage and so on – to inform training and practice within psychiatry, alongside and critiquing the knowledge claims made by evidence-based medicine (Fulford, 2011). We suggest that legitimacy challenges for experiential knowledge remain considerable in the field of mental health teaching, and that much more needs to be done to integrate experiential knowledge into the curricula of the medical school and the health and social care faculty.

Experiential knowledge – implications for research

We must no longer think of academia as out of bounds to us and our knowledge as survivors. Instead we should have the courage of our convictions that our lived experience has a real contribution to make to the development of human knowledge. We can see the survivors who are already advancing mad studies and disability studies within universities as an advance guard of a new kind of academic. This is an academic true to the founding principles of academia – to explore and share new knowledge, while equally committed to the aspirations of new social movements to advance people's human and civil rights and challenge disadvantage and disempowerment.

(Beresford, 2015)

While many health service research systems now advocate for the involvement of service users and members of the public in research, Russo (2012), among others, has warned that involvement alone does not ensure that mental health research is shaped by, or even integrates, the experiences and priorities of people the research might be about. Scientific conventions prioritise knowledge that demonstrates a tightly defined reliability and validity, enforced through peer review of research protocols and research papers, and predicating against minority or dissenting voices. The discourse this creates, most notably around biomedical psychiatry, is largely seen as objective, universal and incontestable. When survivors challenge these norms by engaging in research and education, biases can emerge that relate to survivors' historical exclusion from knowledge generation – who is seen as having legitimate claims to study whom. These biases can operate most vehemently against survivor research – arguably the most radical form of survivor involvement in knowledge generation – as they also rest in part on epistemological assumptions about survivors' ability to conduct impartial, methodologically robust research.

Experiential knowledge and survivor research

Epistemologically, survivor research occupies an interpretative paradigm in which our identity is foregrounded, and the relationship between our identity and experiences, on the one hand, and research activity, relationships and outputs, on the other, are considered as part of a reflexive, participatory approach to inquiry. This means that the standpoint from which survivor research is conducted is explicit and interrogated, rather than hidden or obscured. This is in stark contrast to the positivist paradigm within which much psychiatric (and indeed health) research operates, and where attempts to secure objectivity, neutrality and distance are prized (Beresford, 2003). Consequently, complexity, multiplicity and positionality can be lost to the seemingly trump card of objective, positivist science, resulting in suspicion and dismissal of experiential knowledge (e.g. Russo and Beresford, 2015; Sweeney, 2016). This serves to maintain the status quo in which survivors are objects, rather than legitimate producers, of knowledge.

In recent years, survivors and allies have made ethical, as well as methodological, arguments for our inclusion in knowledge generation. It has been shown how research working from a service user or survivor perspective, as members of multi-disciplinary mental health research teams, makes a distinctive contribution to both qualitative (Gillard et al., 2010; Sweeney et al., 2012) and quantitative (Goldsmith et al., 2019) enquiry. Yet while methodological arguments are vulnerable to dismissal, ethical arguments are far harder to counter, particularly in an open forum. Unusually, in relation to the field of medical sociology, Prior critiques the concept of experiential knowledge, writing:

> experience on its own is rarely sufficient to understand the technical complexities of disease causation, its consequences or its management. This is partly because experiential knowledge is invariably limited, and idiosyncratic. It generates knowledge about the one instance, the one case, the single 'candidate'. . . . Above all, lay people can be wrong.
>
> *(2003)*

The belief that experiential knowledge is partial, biased and often plain wrong fails to acknowledge the critical reflexivity inherent to survivor research. But, perhaps more importantly, this open challenge to experiential knowledge is highly unusual: the dismissal of survivor knowledge is typically more insidious and implicit, creating a hidden rejection among those who aren't convinced. This rejection can be brought to life through the anonymity of the peer review process.

Knowledge authentication and epistemic violence

Publication in peer-reviewed journals is a key way in which knowledge is authenticated in the current academic system. As survivor researchers foreground identity, contravening dominant (positivist) epistemological frameworks dictating who gets to study whom, peer reviewers can consider our work inherently biased, lacking in objectivity and methodologically weak. Survivors can be seen as incapable of preserving, representing and honouring the worlds of research participants, and instead as having an agenda to further. This complicates access to publication, with survivor researchers at times having to epistemologically defend research afresh each time publication is sought. This preserves the status quo regarding who has the right to study whom.

While this may seem somewhat innocuous – surely all researchers face bad reviews – we argue that it is about a more fundamental battle for who has the right to create dominant narratives about mental distress. This attempted invisible exclusion serves as a form of epistemic injustice that mirrors the silencing of survivors' voices within psychiatric service encounters (e.g. Russo and Beresford, 2015; Sweeney et al., 2019). Liegghio (2013) offers the following definition of epistemic violence:

> A concept originating from postcolonial studies, epistemic violence describes and explains the institutional processes and practices committed against persons or groups,

such as Aboriginal peoples, that deny their worldview, knowledge, and ways of knowing and, consequently, efface their ways of being . . . it is a form of silencing that renders certain persons and groups unable to speak and to be heard.

(pp. 123–4)

Liegghio continues:

Applied to the experiences of psychiatrized people, epistemic violence is the treatment of their knowledge and ways of knowing as something other than knowledge and other than legitimate.

(p. 124)

This, according to Liegghio's assertion, is about denying people as 'legitimate knowers', and can only be challenged by changing the structures and institutional practices and processes that deny survivor knowledge. It is important to state that we are not suggesting that any bad review is an act of epistemic violence – survivor research should be judged by the same standards as any other research (within the interpretative paradigm). Instead, what we are describing are reviews that challenge – often angrily – survivors' rights to produce knowledge.

Research, race and epistemic exclusion

The exclusion of survivors' voices from mainstream psychiatric research in some ways mirrors the positioning of people from racialised communities on the margins of survivor research and Mad Studies. Gorman writes:

With the emergence of Mad Studies, there is a danger that Mad identity – historically a product and cultural extension of the consumer/survivor movement – will be absorbed into white, middle class narratives of disability.

(2013, p. 269)

In reflecting on the ethics and politics of knowledge production, Macias observes:

This biopolitical condition of research cannot be avoided simply by identifying 'better' or 'more ethical' research approaches. Rather, it requires critical reflection that renders problematic the role and location of researchers in the contextual and politically relevant work of research.

(2016, p. 2)

The epistemic violence that occurs against survivor research is likely to be amplified for research into racialised or otherwise marginalised communities. Beresford and Rose (2009) note the paucity of user-controlled and survivor research focusing on and conducted by Black and Minority Ethnic (BaME) mental health service users and survivors in comparison to research controlled by their white counterparts. Kalathil (2013) argues that hierarchies of power, familiar from the organisational and professional structures of mental health services, are re-invented in user involvement spaces. Here, well-meaning professionals – involvement specialists – retain the role of expert and assume control of agendas. And these meeting spaces are often doubly disempowering for people from racialised groups as a result of failure to openly discuss race and the discrimination that characterises mental health services. King (2016) has noted the contemporary relevance of Fanon's (1967) exploration of the 'white mask' – assumed as a means of becoming culturally invisible in order to stay safe in racially hostile environments – to the experiences of men of Black African cultural heritage in their encounters with psychiatry. Clearly, this matters. Access to knowledge authentication not only creates a legitimate body of knowledge but also influences who has access to future knowledge production through impacts on our ability to secure research funding. Inequitable access to knowledge authentication therefore has a circularity to it, confirming who is a legitimate knower and who has the right to study whom both now and in the future.

Towards some conclusions: liberal, radical and critical perspectives on experiential knowledge

We have considered a range of ways in which experiential knowledge has played a role in mental health services, research and professional education. We have consistently encountered reservation, caution and hostility about what might be termed a liberal or consumerist approach to including experiential knowledge, wherein people are offered a voice – a seat at the table – but with no opportunity for what they know, experientially, to challenge what is habitually known, professionally or medically. While we do not wish to devalue either the commitment or the contributions that people make in this way, we have also seen how experiential knowledge can be systematically discounted; service user voices are considered unreliable, irrational or emotional, speaking to individual preferences or values rather than bringing reliable, technical expertise. Experiential knowledge is either formally discounted – for example, through research conventions that privilege knowledge that demonstrates good fit with dominant frameworks – or casually discounted by academically initiated professionals and trainees in clinical or educational encounters. A theme throughout this chapter has been the many ways in which experiential knowledge has been subject to epistemic discreditation.

Instead, we have seen the power to 'talk back' to dominant knowledge frameworks in mental health (Morrison, 2005) inherent in critical and radical approaches to experiential knowledge. We suggest that while the two approaches might be very different, there is value and space for both. Radical approaches to involvement in mental health research, such as survivor-controlled research and Mad Studies (e.g. Sweeney, 2016; Le Francois et al., 2013; Russo, 2012), propose an alternative knowledge base to that produced by dominant clinical academic research. Survivor researchers have consistently argued, for example, that the 'closeness' of the survivor researcher to the enquiry increases validity (Faulkner and Thomas, 2002; Beresford, 2003). Mirroring perhaps separatist spaces found in some peer- or user-led mental health services (e.g. Jenkinson, 2004), radical approaches directly refute constructions of mental health as psychiatric disorder, imposed on people's experiences of distress, and aim to give voice to the full diversity of survivor experiences and understandings of mental health (Gorman, 2013). As noted at the top of the chapter, the resistance we have seen to experiential knowledge – from across the arenas of treatment, teaching and research – and the discomfort and at times dismissive responses that experiential knowledge elicits, is in itself a measure of the potential power of experiential knowledge. We suggest that radical ways of producing and voicing knowledge about mental health are essential both to moving forward what it is possible to know about our mental health – shaped by the full diversity of identity and experience – and to remind all of us that taken-for-granted assumptions about psychiatry and psychiatric treatment are partial knowledges, embedded in structures of power, that can work, wittingly or otherwise, to silence survivor voices.

We noted above how critical approaches to understanding knowledge are grounded in standpoint epistemology (Harding, 1991). Harding, among others (e.g. Fox Keller, 1985), proposes that situated ways of knowing – standpoints – are relational; that the apparent dualities that characterise our social and political worlds (male: female, Black: White and so on) are not autonomous, ontologically or epistemologically, but derive meaning as they are experienced and understood in relation to each other (as social constructions). Similarly, insofar as experiential and medical understandings of mental health – for example – are co-produced through the clinical encounter (through diagnosis and treatment), experiential knowledge about mental health has the potential to offer a critique of psychiatric models of mental health (Rose, 2017). We note, of course, that far from all experiences of mental distress are shaped through the clinical encounter, hence the essential importance of radical thinking about mental health, as indicated above. But we also note that many people do find their experiences and the way they come to know their mental health constructed and reconstructed by the mental health system, hence the parallel importance of critical thinking. Critically, from an experiential perspective, clinical understandings of mental health – medical, psychological, sociological and so on – are not necessarily rejected out of hand (these disciplines will have utility for some people some of the time for a variety of reasons), but their partiality is foregrounded. Furthermore, the extent to which a knowledge framework is privileged and thereby works to discount other ways of knowing is examined and critiqued. The critical approach thereby envisages an engagement between experiential and psychiatric knowledge – or psychological knowledge, for example – as a means of challenging and changing the way that mental health services are routinely delivered, or the way in which clinical academic research is habitually done and so on (especially where taken for granted assumptions about mental health and its treatment are shown to be ineffective and/or oppressive).

Experiential knowledge, co-production and community participation

While we might note that the health sciences have arrived comparatively late to critical enquiry, survivor involvement in healthcare development through participatory methods such as co-production has been described as a new 'zeitgeist' (Palmer et al., 2018). Similarly, co-production in mental health research invites a re-distribution of decision making about how research is done, across teams contributing a range of experiential, clinical and academic knowledge, with critical reflection on the way in which research knowledge is habitually produced an essential part of the process (Gillard et al., 2012). It has been noted how community participatory approaches to research, creating safe spaces that enable people from different social worlds – academic and community actors – to interact, offer the potential to expand our thinking and move co-production from the dialogical to the transformative (Durose et al., 2011). Community participatory research has been characterised as a democratising approach, supporting the participation of underprivileged demographic groups and empowering community 'co-researchers' to make confident use of the knowledge they bring (Bergold and Thomas, 2012). Further, community participation has been offered as an approach to enhance the 'cultural competence' of health and social care research (Meleis, 1996) and challenge health inequalities by embedding 'the cultural context and beliefs of community researchers into the research study' (McQuiston et al., 2005). The potential of participatory research to move towards addressing the 'silent dynamics of race' and its powerful and unspoken role in reinforcing Eurocentric methodological frameworks has also been noted (Mosavel et al., 2005).

To conclude, we have described above how experiential knowledge represents a distinct knowledge base embodied in the way in which people make sense of their day-to-day experiences of mental distress and mental health services. We describe how experiential knowledge is highly differentiated from more formal ways of knowing – underpinning much clinical practice, training and research – that seek to codify (and so constrain) what can be known about mental health through academic and clinical processes that society has come to accept, uncritically, as 'good science'. Importantly, we note that the ways in which we know our mental health are shaped by the full diversity of our social and political lives, including the inequities that people experience in relation to race and racism, gender inequality and violence and so on. We acknowledge that understanding the intersectionalities between mental health and the full range of inequity that people experience in relation to their identity is incredibly complex and diverse, something that much of survivor and co-produced research has historically neglected. We also see the various ways, across mental health services, education and research, in which experiential knowledge is discredited and dismissed, and note that this epistemic injustice is emblematic and inextricably linked to the oppressive power that, for many people, characterises their engagement with mental health services. But we are not (always) disheartened by this; the power of experiential knowledge to invoke this resistance is indicative of the potential of experiential knowledge as emancipatory discourse. While there is much to be done, experiential knowledge represents a vital force for change, challenging and critiquing those reductive assumptions about mental health – reproduced through professional training and education – that perpetuate both ineffectiveness and injustice in mental health services. Research led by survivors and driven by communities, as well as research that creates safe, democratising spaces where community and survivor researchers are empowered to challenge and change the way clinical academic research is habitually done, has the capacity to transform mental health services so that they properly respond to the full diversity of people's experiences of mental distress.

References

Babu, K. S., Law-Win, R., Adlam, T. & Banks, V. (2008) Involving Service Users and Carers in Psychiatric Education: What Do Trainees Think? *Psychiatric Bulletin*, 32: 28–31.

Barry, C., Stevenson, F., Britten, N., Barber, N. & Bradley, C. (2001) Giving Voice to the Lifeworld. More Humane, More Effective Medical Care? A Qualitative Study of Doctor–Patient Communication in General Practice. *Social Science & Medicine*, 53(4): 487–505.

Beresford, P. (2000) Service Users' Knowledges and Social Work Theory: Conflict or Collaboration? *British Journal of Social Work*, 30: 489–503.

Beresford, P. (2003) *It's Our Lives: A Short Theory of Knowledge, Distance and Experience*. London: OSP for Citizens Press in Association with Shaping Our Lives.

Beresford, P. (2015) *Speaking as a Survivor Researcher*. Available from: www.madinamerica.com/2015/03/speaking-survivor-researcher/ Accessed April 2019.

Beresford, P. & Rose, D. (2009) Background. pp 11–21 in A. Sweeney, P. Beresford, A. Faulkner, M. Nettle & D. Rose (eds) *This Is Survivor Research*. Ross-on-Wye, England: PCCS Books.

Bergold, J. & Thomas, S. (2012) Participatory Research Methods: A Methodological Approach in Motion. *Historical Social Research*, 37(4): 191–222.

Brockbank, W. (1968) Old Anatomical Theatres and What Took Place Therein. *Medical History*, 12(4): 371–384. doi:10.1017/S0025727300013648

Burr, V. (1995) *An Introduction to Social Constructionism*. London: Routledge.

Collins, H. & Evans, R. (2007) *Rethinking Expertise*. Chicago: Chicago University Press.

Combs, C. D. & Combs, P. F. (2019) Emerging Roles of Virtual Patients in the Age of AI. *AMA Journal of Ethics*, 21(2): E153–E159.

Cruza-Guet, M. C., Spokane, A. R., Leon-Andrade, C. & Borja, R. (2008) Diversity, Hegemony, Poverty, and the Emergency of Counseling Psychology in Ecuador. Ch 30 in L. H. Gerstein, P. P. Heppner, S. Ægisdóttir, A. M. A. Leung & K. L. Norsworthy (eds) (2009) *International Handbook of Cross-Cultural Counseling: Cultural Assumptions and Practices*. Thousand Oaks, CA: Sage.

Culpepper, L. & Thase, M. (2019) Virtual Patient Challenges in Psychiatry: Evidence-Based Approaches to Adjusting Treatment based on Response. *Medscape*, Friday, May 24.

Drake, D., Cimpean, D. & Torrey, W. (2009) Shared Decision Making in Mental Health: Prospects for Personalized Medicine. *Dialogues in Clinical Neuroscience*, 11(4): 455–463.

Durose, C., Beebeejaun, Y., Rees, J., Richardson, J. & Richardson, L. (2011) *Towards Co-production in Research with Communities*. Scoping Study Report to AHRC Connected Communities Programme.

Fanon, F. (1967) *Black Skin, White Masks*. London: Pluto Press.

Faulkner, A. & Thomas, P. (2002) User-Led Research and Evidence-Based Medicine. *British Journal of Psychiatry*, 180: 1–3.

Foucault, M. (1980) *Power/Knowledge: Selected Interviews and Other Writings, 1972–1977*. Edited by C. Gordon, Translated by C. Gordon, L. Marshall, J. Mepham & K. Soper. New York: Pantheon Books.

Foucault, M. (1982) The Subject and Power. *Critical Inquiry*, 8(4): 777–795.

Fox Keller, E. (1985) *Reflections on Gender and Science*. New Haven, CT: Yale University Press.

Fulford, K. W. (2011) The Value of Evidence and Evidence of Values: Bringing Together Values-based and Evidence-based Practice in Policy and Service Development in Mental Health. *Journal of Evaluation in Clinical Practice*, 17(5): 976–987.

Gillard, S., Simons, L., Turner, K., Lucock, M. & Edwards, C. (2012) Patient and Public Involvement in the Coproduction of Knowledge: Reflection on the Analysis of Qualitative Data in a Mental Health Study. *Qualitative Health Research*, 22(8): 1126–1137.

Goldsmith, L. P., Morshead, R., McWilliam, C., Forbes, G., Ussher, M., Simpson, A., . . . & Gillard, S. (2019) Co-producing Randomized Controlled Trials: How Do We Work Together? *Frontiers in Sociology*, 4: 21.

Gorman, R. (2013) Mad Nation? Thinking Through Race, Class, and Mad Identity Politics. Chapter 19. pp 269–280 in B. Le Francois, R. Menzies & G. Reaume (Eds.) *Mad Matters: A Critical Reader in Canadian Mad Studies*. Toronto: Canadian Scholars Press.

Guerrini, A. (2006) Alexander Monro Primus and the Moral Theatre of Anatomy. *The Eighteenth Century*, 47(1): 1–18. doi:10.1353/ecy.2007.0018

Happell, L., McAllister, M., Lampshire, D., et al. (2014) Consumer Involvement in the Tertiary-level Education of Mental Health Professionals: A Systematic Review. *International Journal of Mental Health Nursing*, 23: 3–16. doi:10.1111/inm.12021

Harden, J. (1996) Enlightenment, Empowerment and Emancipation: The Case for Critical Pedagogy in Nurse Education. *Nurse Education Today*, 16(1): 32–37.

Harding, S. (1991) *Whose Science? Whose Knowledge? Thinking from Women's Lives*. New York: Cornell University Press.

Hatch, S. & Dohrenwend, B. (2007) Distribution of Traumatic and Other Stressful Life Events by Race/Ethnicity, Gender, SES and Age: A Review of the Research. *American Journal of Community Psychology*, 40(3–4): 313–332.

Jenkinson, P. (2004) The Wokingham & West Berkshire Mind Crisis House. *Mental Health Review Journal*, 9(1): 13–16.

Kalathil, J. (2013) 'Hard to Reach'? Racialised Groups and Mental Health Service User Involvement. pp 121–134 in P. Staddon (ed) *Mental Health Service Users in Research: Critical Sociological Perspectives*. Bristol, England: Policy Press.

King, C. (2016) Whiteness in Psychiatry: The Madness of European Misdiagnoses. pp 69–76 in J. Russo, A. Sweeney (eds) *Searching for a Rose Garden: Challenging Psychiatry, Fostering Mad Studies*. Ross-on-Wye, England: PCCS Books.

Komporozos-Athanasiou, A., Oborn, E., Barrett, M. & Chan, Y. (2011) Policy as a Struggle for Meaning: Disentangling Knowledge Translation across International Health Contexts. *Knowledge Management Research and Practice*, 9: 215–222.

Kyratsous, M. & Sanati, A. (2016) Epistemic Injustice and Responsibility in Borderline Personality Disorder. *Journal*. https://doi.org/10.1111/jep.12609

Ladner, J. (1973) *The Death of White Sociology: Essays on Race and Culture*. Baltimore: Black Classic Press.

Lather, P. (1990) Postmodernism and the Human Sciences. *The Humanistic Psychologist*, 18: 64–84.

Le Francois, B., Menzies, R. & Reaume, G. (eds) (2013) *Mad Matters: A Critical Reader in Canadian Mad Studies*. Toronto: Canadian Scholars Press.

Liegghio, M. (2013) A Denial of Being: Psychiatrization as Epistemic Violence. pp. 122–129 in B. A. LeFrançois, R. Menzies & G. Reaume (eds) *Mad Matters: A Critical Reader in Canadian Mad Studies*. Toronto, ON: Canadian Scholars' Press.

Lock, M. (2001) The Tempering of Medical Anthropology: Troubling Natural Categories. *Medical Anthropology Quarterly*, 15(4): 478–492.

Macias, T. (2016) Editorial: 'The Ethics and Politics of Knowledge Production', Critical Reflections on Social Work and Social Sciences Research. *Intersectionalities*, 5(1): 1–7.

Martin, E. (1991) The Egg and the Sperm: How Science Has Constructed a Romance Based on Stereo-typical Male-Female Roles. *Signs*, 16(3): 485–501.

Mazanderani, F., Locock, L. & Powell, J. (2013) Biographical Value: Towards a Conceptualisation of the Commodification of Illness Narratives in Contemporary Healthcare. *Sociology of Health & Illness*, 35(6): 891–905.

McQuiston, C., Parrado, E., Phillips Martinez, A. & Uribe, L. (2005) Community-Based Participatory Research with Latino Community Members. *Journal of Professional Nursing*, 21(4): 210–215.

Meehan, T. & Glover, H. (2007) Telling Our Story: Consumer Perceptions of Their Role in Mental Health Education. *Psychiatric Rehabilitation Journal*, 31: 152–154.

Meleis, A. I. (1996) Culturally Competent Scholarship: Substance and Rigor. *Advances in Nursing Science*, 19: 1–16.

Mol, A. (2002) *The Body Multiple*. Durham, NC: Duke University Press.

Mol, A. & Law, J. (2004) Embodied Action, Enacted Bodies. The Example of Hypoglycaemia. *Body and Society*, 10: 43–62.

Morrison, L. (2005) *Talking Back to Psychiatry: The Psychiatric Consumer/Survivor/Ex-Patient Movement*. New York: Routledge.

Mosavel, M., Simon, C., van Stadec, D. & Buchbinder, M. (2005) Community-based Participatory Research (CBPR) in South Africa: Engaging Multiple Constituents to Shape the Research Question. *Social Science & Medicine*, 61: 2577–2587.

Naidoo, A. V. (1996) Challenging the Hegemony of Eurocentric Psychology. *Journal of Community and Health Sciences*, 2(2): 9–16.

Oborn, E., Barrett, M., Gibson, S. & Gillard, S. (2019) Knowledge and Expertise in Care Practices: The Role of the Peer Worker in Mental Health Teams. *Sociology of Health & Illness*, 41(7): 1305–1322.

Palmer, V. J., Weavell, W., Callander, R., Piper, D., Richard, L., Maher, L., . . . & Iedema, R. (2019) The Participatory Zeitgeist: An Explanatory Theoretical Model of Change in an Era of Coproduction and Codesign in Healthcare Improvement. *Medical Humanities*, 45(3): 247–257.

Prior, L. (2003) Belief, Knowledge and Expertise: The Emergence of the Lay Expert in Medical Sociology. *Sociology of Health and Illness*, 25: 41–57. doi:10.1111/1467-9566.00339

Rose, D. (2017): Service User/Survivor-led Research in Mental Health: Epistemological Possibilities. *Disability & Society*. doi:10.1080/09687599.2017.1320270

Rose, S., Lewontin, R. & Kamin, L. (1984) *Not in Our Genes: Biology, Ideology and Human Nature*. NY, USA: Pantheon Books.

Russo, J. (2012) Survivor-Controlled Research: A New Foundation for Thinking about Psychiatry and Mental Health. *Forum: Qualitative Sozialforschung/Forum: Qualitative Social Research*, 13(1).

Russo, J. & Beresford, P. (2015) Between Exclusion and Colonisation: Seeking a Place for Mad People's Knowledge in Academia. *Disability & Society*, 30(1): 153–157. doi:10.1080/09687599.2014.957925

Sanati, A. & Kyratsous, M. (2015) Epistemic Injustice in Assessment of Delusions. https://doi.org/10.1111/jep.12347

Stovell, D., Morrison, A. P., Panayiotou, M. & Hutton, P. (2016) Shared Treatment Decision-making and Empowerment-related Outcomes in Psychosis: Systematic Review and Meta-analysis. *The British Journal of Psychiatry*, 209(1): 23–28.

Sweeney, A. (2016) Why Mad Studies Needs Survivor Research and Survivor Research Needs Mad Studies. *Intersectionalities*, 5(3).

Sweeney, A., Greenwood, K., Williams, S., Wykes, T. & Rose, D. (2012) Hearing the Voices of Service User Researchers in Collaborative Qualitative Data Analysis: The Case for Multiple Coding. *Health Expectations*, 16(4): e89–99.

Sweeney, A., Perôt, C., Callard, F., Adenden, V., Mantovani, N. & Goldsmith, L. (2019) Out of the Silence: Towards Grassroots and Trauma-Informed Support for People Who Have Experienced Sexual Violence and Abuse. *Epidemiology and Psychiatric Sciences*, 28(6): 598–602.

Tavris, C. (1993) The Mismeasure of Woman. *Feminism & Psychology*, 3(2): 149–168.

Thornicroft, G., Farrelly, S., Szmukler, G., Birchwood, M., Waheed, W., Flach, C., et al. (2013) Clinical Outcomes of Joint Crisis Plans to Reduce Compulsory Treatment for People with Psychosis: A Randomised Controlled Trial. *The Lancet*, 381(9878): 1634–1641.

Turner, S. (2001) What Is the Problem with Experts? *Social Studies of Science*, 31(1): 123–149.

Weber, D. (2016) Medical Hegemony. *International Journal of Complimentary & Alternative Medicine*, 3(2): 00065. doi:10.15406/ijcam.2016.03.00065

5

ETHICAL INVOLVEMENT OF SERVICE USERS

Beverley Burke and Andrea Newman

In this chapter, we critically reflect on and explore examples taken from our experiences of service user involvement in our various professional roles. By focussing on some of the concerns and dilemmas which have arisen during our practice when involving service users, we have developed a set of ethical practice principles which we believe would support and facilitate meaningful and ethical involvement of service users. As Black female social work educators, we bring to our discussion particular insights based on our multi-layered, intersectional identities, shaped by personal and professional experiences of power, oppression and inequality. Black feminist theorising and anti-oppressive values and principles inform our critical reflective analysis of our practices (Hill-Collins and Bilge, 2016; hooks, 2013; Hill-Collins, 2009; Clifford and Burke, 2009; Crenshaw, 1991).

Within the UK, there are a range of social, political and ethical arguments and drivers supportive of the involvement of service users in all aspects of social work, health and social care and social work education. Over the past three decades, service user involvement has become accepted practice and is compatible with the social work values of 'respect, independence, self-determination' (Croft and Beresford, 1990, cited in Robinson and Webber, 2013, p. 926) and anti-oppressive practice. The principle and practice of involvement is mandated by various major pieces of legislation (for example, Community Care Act 1990), policy and guidance frameworks (DOH, 2002; Webber and Robinson, 2012; Robinson and Webber, 2013). There is statutory recognition that service users must have a say in the development, implementation and evaluation of institutional processes which affect them (United Nations Convention on the Rights of the Child, article 12; Equality Act 2010). Since September 2014, service user involvement has been a prerequisite for the approval of social work programmes by the profession's regulator, the Health and Care Professions Council (HCPC). Practitioners are directed in section 1.2 of the HCPC standards to 'work in partnership with service users and carers, involving them, where appropriate, in decisions about the care, treatment or other services to be provided' (HCPC, 2018). However, we are aware that legal mandates for participation and involvement have been criticised for being partial, contradictory and ineffectual (Braye, p. 15, in Kemshall and Littlechild, 2000) and do not always lead to involvement that is meaningful. The legal framework has to be supported by practice underpinned by the values of respect, solidarity and mutuality (Moran and Lavalette, 2016) and committed to genuine and ethical involvement of service users.

Discourses regarding the level of service user involvement have shifted focus over the years, developing from an earlier emphasis on collaboration and consultation of service users to that of partnership and latterly co-production with service users. In fact, it should be noted that the Care Act 2014 is one of the first pieces of legislation specifically to include the concept of co-production (SCIE, 2015). Co-production embodies a more complex approach to understanding the fluid nature of power within relationships with service users and has the potential to facilitate a more equitable relationship where power is shared with all concerned (Braye, 2000). Earlier models of participation and involvement have focussed on the ladder metaphor beginning with the seminal work of Arnstein (1969) and adapted by Hart (1992) and others. These models centre on the progression up the ladder from passive participants with limited power, to more actively engaged participants, where there is an acknowledgement of the need for power sharing. It is important to recognise the various levels of participation in relation to the development of decision making processes to foster more meaningful involvement, while ensuring robust monitoring and reviewing systems are in place to support change (Shier, 2001). Whereas elements of the range of approaches to service user involvement are being used within the practice context today, McLaughlin (2006) suggests that levels of involvement below that of collaboration are more prone to misuse and abuse. It is therefore important to acknowledge that 'different levels of participation may be appropriate for different individuals and groups at different times and in different contexts' (Warren, 2009, p. 50). Incorporating a whole systems approach (SCIE, 2006) informed by an intersectional analysis recognises service users' experience of multiple oppressions and how this impacts their engagement and inclusion.

The current legislative context features the more potentially empowering concepts of partnership and co-production. This shift to a more liberal democratic perspective of service user involvement is suggestive of the desire by those in authority to involve service users in a more meaningful and ethical way. A critical understanding of concepts such as service user(s), partnership and co-production, participation and collaboration is necessary, as these often-used terms are intrinsically value laden and often presented as unproblematic.

Academic debates have highlighted the ethical and moral complexities of the concept of service user(s) (Braye, 2000). These range from concerns about reductionist implications that a person's most defining characteristic is that of passive recipient of services rather than an active, engaged individual with a variety of social identities (Beresford, 2005; Shaping our Lives National User Network, 2003).[1] Failure to take into account values, ideological perspectives and interests can lead to a myriad of positions and practice interventions in relation to the involvement of service users. It is important that the implications and impact of power, oppression and difference (Taylor, 2006) within relationships are addressed systematically if the end goal of transformative practice is to be achieved.

Negotiating and sharing power in our relationships with service users can be challenging for all concerned. This is particularly so within established mainstream structures, formal consultation mechanisms and traditional ideologies (Warren, 2009) within inter-professional arenas (Taylor, 2006), where notions of partnership can be hijacked by management priorities of cost effectiveness and efficiency. Fundamental to the ethical involvement of service users is an understanding of not only their individual and collective experiences of marginality, disadvantage and oppression, but also their narratives of resistance, struggle and challenge. Service users should be treated as equal participants who have agency and who adopt an active role in social and welfare processes and practices (Newman and Mcnamara, 2016).

We must not forget the strengths, agency, activism, new perspectives and insights service users bring to the relationship (Scheyett and Diehl, 2004). Ethical involvement should also take account of the whole range of service users, including those minority individuals and groups who are often on the periphery and viewed as marginal. It is important to engage such seldom-heard individuals, groups and communities so that those who are least represented in society are able to meaningfully participate in decision making processes which have or may have an impact on their lives (Fitzhenry, 2008; SCIE, 2015). Failure to do this can reinforce and deepen further inequality, oppression and exclusion (Cowden and Singh, 2007; Warren and Boxall, 2009; Tanner et al., 2017).

The experiences and narratives of both service users and practitioners provide the backdrop against which the processes of involvement become more visible, and new practices which encourage and facilitate ethical involvement are developed. We believe that to facilitate ethical involvement, the experiences and views of service users have to inform the actions taken in relation to their involvement. This, however, is not a straightforward process. It is important to acknowledge that practitioners, through their role and the institutional structures in which they are located, have power and influence with the potential to discriminate and oppress. Therefore, genuine dialogue between practitioners and service users regarding the quality of involvement can only begin if there is a good understanding of how unequal social relationships can and will impact on that involvement. An understanding of how the contested, socially constructed concepts of power and oppression operate within social situations will provide a legitimate foundation for practice regarding the ethical involvement of service users.

Practice which underpins ethical involvement is informed by our understanding of the writings of Black feminists in relation to dialogue, identity and intersectionality, anti-oppressive principles and values, as well as a critical understanding of ethical theory and related ethical concepts. Black feminist theory advocates the need to systematically analyse oppression by exploring personal and structural levels of power and powerlessness and highlighting the interconnections between various social divisions as they impact on individuals, groups and communities (Hill-Collins and Bilge, 2016; Lorde, 2007; Crenshaw, 1989). These ideas also inform the key principles of anti-oppressive practice, which seeks to maximise genuine partnership, working at both organisational and individual levels, and to minimise the dangers of tokenistic service user involvement (Wilson and Beresford, 2000; Barnes and Bowl, 2001). This knowledge supports practice which is relational, respectful, caring and sensitive to the needs, wishes and feelings of others (Barnes, 2012). It is important to foster a sense of both belonging and mattering to those who have traditionally been excluded from decision making processes (Rosenberg and McCullough, 1981; Schlossberg, 1989). This is particularly relevant in relation to those groups who are less likely to be represented in the traditional service user groups or forums, for example, those from BAME backgrounds, individuals who have communication challenges and other seldom-heard groups.

When working with service users, it is important to pay attention to the implications for how they experience their involvement and the impact this involvement has personally for them. This sense of 'mattering' signifies the need to appreciate, value and validate their contributions. An ability to understand these complexities and nuances around involvement will help professionals adopt appropriate support and skills to enable effective participation (Marchant and Kirby, 2004). Moral philosophy, ethical theories and anti-oppressive theorising deepen our thinking on, and understanding of, the diverse and multi-layered moral issues which surround the ethical involvement of service users. This is within a global context of diminishing resources, where needs are becoming increasingly more complex, and neoliberal social, political and economic policies dominate (Mattson, 2014). Genuine service user involvement is key to the development of policies and practices which begin to challenge the structural arrangements that maintain and sustain inequalities.

The ethical involvement of service users has not been without its difficulties, as it involves navigating and managing a range of 'morally contentious and ambiguous situations' (Clifford and Burke, 2009, p. 58). This is due to the competing interests, different perspectives and agendas of service users and those seeking to involve them (Goossen and Austin, 2017). Membership of different social divisions, values, beliefs and ethical positions may cloud understanding of the 'others' position within this relationship. The range of professional roles, status and responsibilities, and the values held by those professionals (Robinson and Webber, 2013), further complicate the relationships that exist between practitioners wishing to involve service users in a range of activities: for example, in social work admissions, teaching, curriculum design, research and practice. Factors including the growth of service user movements, the personal and professional commitment of practitioners, varied levels of commitment to service user involvement within organisations and the policy and legislative context have led to a much more nuanced debate regarding the nature and quality of the relationship between individual practitioners and service users at an individual level and the social work profession and service user movements at a more structural level. This is a debate to which we wish to contribute by sharing our experiences of involving service users in our roles as educators, practitioners and researchers.

Reflecting on practice examples

Like many social work educators working in the area of service user involvement, we have experienced the process of involvement as complex, challenging and rewarding, with at times unexpected outcomes. We found ourselves having to negotiate the competing tensions existing between organisational needs and goals, the needs of service users and our professional roles and responsibilities. We are aware of how service users may perceive our position as experienced academics. Our membership of various social divisions not only adds to the complexities of the nature of the relationships we have in our professional roles but also shapes the perspectives and understanding we may bring to our work. In the following section, we critically reflect on our experiences in the areas of social work education and admissions in an attempt to develop principles which would support ethical involvement of service users.

Involving service users in the development of the new social work degree at Liverpool John Moores University in early 2002 provided valuable insights developed over the years and has been used to guide our involvement practice with service users within a range of teaching and learning activities. The work was undertaken by a small group of consultant service users who later went on to become members of a small steering group; their remit was to review and evaluate an anti-oppressive ethics and values social work module. The group also contributed to the development of teaching materials. The experience of working with this group of service users was particularly instructive, and the following points made by this group of service users has helped to inform our teaching practice and provided a useful framework in which to develop our discussion of the work undertaken with young people in relation to their involvement in our work around social work admissions. We believe these interconnecting points are supportive of anti-oppressive values, concepts and principles, consistent with the humanitarian and social justice ideals of social work.

Box A   Ethical and practice insights from the service user steering group

Creating safe spaces to build meaningful relationships is a necessary starting point in order to begin the process of relationship building. Meaningful relationships take time to develop, to enable

---

any assumptions and prejudices to be worked through. This mitigates against a reductionist view of service users.

Communicating across differences is an important step to building honest, open and trusting relationships, which are informed by the multiple identities of all those involved. Opportunities for dialogue between service users and professionals are important in facilitating the often complex process of relationship building.

Reflecting on personal and social history and being aware of the impact of this on both personal and professional levels helps to develop relationships that are honest and authentic.

Awareness and acknowledgement of power differentials is essential in terms of service users being able to express their own opinions in relation to decision making. It is important that opportunities for dialogue are provided so that alternative views can be articulated and actively listened to.

Box B   Involvement in social work admissions

There has been a long history of involving service users and carers in our social work admissions process. We worked in partnership with a service user forum which provided support and training to service users and carers wishing to become involved with various aspects of social work education. While this was generally working well, it was very evident that young people's voices were missing from the whole of the admissions process. We wanted to actively engage and encourage involvement in a way that was meaningful, genuine and not tokenistic. We wanted their involvement in the decision making process to be full and not partial, on par with the experiences and involvement of adult service users and carers. This meant that they would contribute fully to all aspects of the assessment of candidates, which entailed a written task, group work assessment and an individual interview. They would be part of an admissions panel which included an academic member of staff, with whom they would be working throughout the assessment day. We wanted to achieve positive outcomes for the young people involved in relation to their personal, educational and future career development while ensuring they positively contributed to the rigorous selection process of future social workers. An evaluation of the young people's experience was jointly undertaken and co-produced by the voluntary organisation and the University, and from this we highlight some key areas of learning gained from the process of involvement.

Learning point

Establishing genuine partnerships and relationships with individuals and organisations.

The first step in this process was to establish a partnership with a voluntary organisation which supported young people. It was important to negotiate and agree on the nature of the partnership with the young people themselves. A relationship with the organisation had already been developed over time, so some trust had been built between the admissions tutor in the University and the Senior Social Work Practitioner in the organisation. It was important in achieving a partnership with the young people themselves to develop a dialogue. This was not a straightforward process, as the organisation had responsibilities in terms of their duty of care to the young people and the University and staff did not have a relationship with the young people. Time was needed in order to develop and maintain a positive working relationship with the young people in order to facilitate effective decision making, which required open and honest dialogue. This process took some time, as it was important to go at the pace of the young people; this involved honest conversations with them around the nature of their involvement, including understanding the task, support needed to carry out the task and clarity around intended outcomes for both organisations and the young people themselves. What was in it for the young people? This was a central question asked by both organisations, as we did not want their involvement to be experienced as a tokenistic, box-ticking exercise that left the young people feeling disempowered by the process (Tyler, 2006). All professionals involved wanted their experience to be a positive and rewarding one, and clear outcomes were agreed at the beginning of the process between the young people and the two organisations. As a result, the Senior Social Work Practitioner from the organisation supporting the young people asked a range of questions of the University staff involved in the initiative in order to ensure that the young people's contributions would be valued and validated within the relationship.

Is the relationship going to be safe and ethical?
Are expectations clear and achievable?
Is their interaction going to be a positive learning experience?
Is there opportunity to talk through any worries or issues that may arise?
Is this experience likely to reinforce any negative perceptions that the young people may already have about themselves?
Questions provided by Senior Social Work Practitioner

The above questions present important challenges which need to be met in order to develop and maintain a good relationship and ensure that the needs of the service user were central to the process. These questions could be used to cultivate and sustain any service user involvement.

Learning point: Preparation and support for involvement.

We realised we had to make changes to the processes we had already developed in order to meet the differing needs of the young people. The Senior Social Work Practitioner had already completed some preparatory work with the young people prior to us meeting them before the assessment day, when we undertook further preparation and training around the assessment day process. The young people visited the University before the assessment day to familiarise themselves with the University environment and all that it might represent to them, as well as meeting the staff member they would be working with on the assessment day. This was the start of building relationships with the young people and gave them the opportunity to ask questions and voice any concerns.

The young people valued being sufficiently prepared for their involvement. One of the young people reflecting on the preparation and support they had received recounted:

> I did feel prepared as was given a booklet beforehand and also we met with B and A, prior to the interview, to be more relaxed, knowing what to expect. You're not having to get to know the interviewer that you're working with; you feel like you already know and connect with them a bit better.

The aim of the preparation process was to introduce the young people to a staff member, clarify expectations, roles and responsibilities as well as to convey to the young people that they were to be equal partners and fully involved in the admissions decision making process. While we had discussed the level of involvement during the preparation sessions, it was evident from the young people's feedback that they were surprised at the extent of their involvement and that their contributions were taken seriously and valued. One young person reported:

> Before I got there, I expected my role to not be as significant, more as an observer, but as the day went on, I realised that my opinion was really valued so I felt really involved in the process, so that my contributions made a significant difference as to whether people get put forward or not.

Support for involvement is an ongoing process which required checking how the young people were experiencing the different aspects of the day and ensuring they had regular breaks and were not feeling overwhelmed, as well as being able to voice any concerns or worries they had, particularly those which might connect to their own personal biographies or experiences. Regular debriefing and feedback were provided throughout the day to check how the young people were responding to the emotional content of the candidate's answers. After the assessment day, focussed written feedback was provided to the young people through the Senior Practitioner, who helped them to debrief and identify learning gained and areas for further personal development.

Learning point: Personal and organisational impact of involvement.

Young people's participation in the assessment day has added new perspectives to our social work admissions processes and to the quality of decision making. In relation to consolidating more and longer-term outcomes for the young people, their involvement in the assessment day helped to foster confidence to think about other opportunities which they would not have previously contemplated. This could be considering further and higher education as an option or contemplating future career aspirations. This is voiced in one young woman's reflections:

> Now that I've met some people who go on degrees, I would consider going to College or Uni myself. They are mostly like me (except the older ones). I've never went in a Uni before and it's quite scary but it's ok when you get to know it, and the staff treat you like you're a grown up and listen to you. But not too much; they know you're still only a teenager, which is important.

This young woman has since being involved in the assessment day become a member of the local service user and carer forum, working with us independently now, and has also enrolled in a degree programme. An introduction to the local service user and carer forum would provide a range of opportunities for involvement on a broader level with different Higher Education Institutions (HEIs) and practice organisations. This furthermore resulted in changing the demographic makeup of the membership of the forum, ultimately contributing to the long-term outcome of increasing the number of young service users and carers in the social work admissions process.

Meaningful and ethical engagement is challenging, and therefore relying solely on formulaic practice guidance is not sufficient in meeting the realities of involving service users. The learning points above alongside the following questions can assist discussion, analysis and development of practice with service users. We have not provided an exhaustive list of questions; they can be added to, modified and further developed. However, they can provide a starting point for stimulating critical reflective and reflexive discussions within the areas of social work education, practice and research.

Questions

What strategies do you have in place to engage with a range of service users?
Do you have links with service user groups and involvement with local grassroots developments?

What power do you have individually, as part of a team, as part of an organisation to ensure that involvement practice with service users is ethical and meaningful?
What mandate from your organisation do you have to implement changes and make challenges in relation to issues that may arise through the involvement activity?
What commitments has the organisation made in relation to service user involvement?
Have these commitments been met?

How are values supportive of ethical involvement demonstrated in your practice?
How do you and the organisation translate values which underpin partnership working and co-production into practice so that new and powerful change perspectives on social inequality are not only developed but are acted on?

How are relationships with service users sustained and developed?
What support can service users expect in relation to their ongoing involvement?

Conclusion and future challenges

Service user involvement is an evolving, dynamic process characterised by uncertainty and ambiguity. Professional competence, ethical sensitivity and an understanding of the complex nature of power relationships is required in order to navigate the range of issues needing consideration when working within this area. The skills of interested and committed professionals cannot be assumed and may need to be further developed in relation to partnership and participation work. Joint training for professionals and service users is a good mechanism for knowledge transfer and skills development.

While a range of literature clearly highlights the benefits of involving service users, there is, we would argue, room for further development of practice in this area. By reflecting on our own experiences, we propose that involvement practice with service users should be informed by anti-oppressive ethical principles. These principles, by addressing issues of power, social diversity and inequality, underpin practice which is honest, authentic and ethical. Working collectively with service users requires a real change in political and ideological perspectives where the ideals of equality and social justice move from rhetoric to reality. Ideological and practice transformation are key challenges, particularly in relation to embedding service user involvement into complex bureaucratic organisational structures which lack a degree of flexibility. This often obstructs the development of a culture which can nurture, support and sustain creative and committed service user involvement. Without a supportive and service user-sensitive environment, organisations will continue to rely on the good will of interested individuals, leading to individualised, reactive, ad hoc and short-term initiatives.

The perennial problem of funding is a major issue and one which will continue to be so given the current global economic and political climate. Limited funding and competing priorities will have a deleterious impact on organisations' commitment to developing creative and sustained ways of involving service users. Finally, given our increasing globalised connections and inter-dependency, it is crucial to consider the range of needs presented by increasingly diverse service user communities. Engagement strategies informed by an intersectional analysis are essential if not only the voices of all are to be heard but also the differences within those voices.

Acknowledgements

We would like to thank the voluntary organisations, staff and young people who have over the years been involved in the social work admissions assessment days.

Note

1 Various terminology has been used over the years, reflecting the changing power relationships between those who receive or access services and those who provide services (Barnes, 2012). However, there is broad agreement that the term 'service user' is now a more acceptable part of the social work lexicon.

References

Arnstein, S. (1969) A ladder of citizen participation, *Journal of the American Institute of Planners*, 35(4), pp. 216–44.

Barnes, M. (2012) *Care in Everyday Life: An Ethics of Care in Practice*. Bristol: Policy Press.

Barnes, M. and Bowl, R. (2001) *Taking Over the Asylum: Empowerment and Mental Health*. Basingstoke: Palgrave Macmillan.

Beresford, P. (2005) 'Service user': Regressive or liberatory terminology? *Disability and Society*, 20(4), pp. 469–477.

Braye, S. (2000) Participation and involvement in social care: An overview, in H. Kemshall and R. Littlechild (eds.) *User Involvement and Participation in Social Care: Research Informing Practice*. London: Jessica Kingsley Publishers Ltd, pp. 9–28.

Clifford, D. and Burke, B. (2009) *Anti-oppressive Ethics and Values in Social Work*. Basingstoke: Palgrave Macmillan.

Cowden, S. and Singh, G. (2007) The 'User': Friend, foe or fetish? A critical exploration of user involvement in health and social care, *Critical Social Policy*, 27(1), pp. 5–23.

Crenshaw, K. (1989) Demarginalizing the intersection of race and sex: A black feminist critique of antidiscrimination doctrine, feminist theory and antiracist politics, *The University of Chicago Legal Forum. Feminism in the Law: Theory, Practice and Criticism*, pp. 139–167.

Crenshaw, K. (1991) Mapping the margins: Intersectionality, identity politics, and violence against women of color, *Stanford Law Review*, 43(6), pp. 1241–1299.

Croft, S. and Beresford, P. (1990) Learning the lessons of user involvement: Implications for training, *Social Work and Social Sciences Review*, 2(1), pp. 51–60.

Department of Health (2002) *Requirements for Social Work Training*. London: Department of Health.

Fitzhenry, S. (2008) *Service User and Career Involvement in Social Care and Social Work Programmes*. Scottish Social Services Learning Networks, unpublished report available online at http://data.learningnetworks.org.uk/workforce/218/serviceuserreport.pdf.

Goossen, C. and Austin, M. (2017) Service user involvement in UK social service agencies and social work education, *Journal of Social Work Education*, 53(1), pp. 37–51.

Hart, R. (1992) *Children's Participation: From Tokenism to Citizenship*, UNICEF Innocenti Essays No. 4. Florence: UNICEF.

Health and Care Professions Council (HCPC) (2018) *Standards of conduct, performance and ethics*. London: HCPC.

Hill Collins, P. (2009) *Black Feminist Thought*. Routledge Classics ed. Abingdon: Routledge.

Hill-Collins, P. and Bilge, S. (2016) *Intersectionality*. Cambridge: Polity Press.

hooks, b. (2013) *Writing Beyond Race: Living Theory and Practice*. Abingdon: Routledge.

Kemshall, H. and Littlechild, R. eds (2000) *User Involvement and Participation in Social Care: Research Informing Practice*. London: Jessica Kingsley Publishers Ltd.

Lorde, A. (2007) *Sister Outsider: Essays and Speeches*. Berkeley: Crossing Press.

Marchant, R. and Kirby, P. (2004) The participation of young children: Communication, consultation and involvement, in B. Neale (ed.) *Young Children's Citizenship: Ideas into Practice*. New York: Joseph Rowntree Foundation.

Mattson, T. (2014) Intersectionality as a useful tool: Anti-oppressive social work and critical reflection, *Journal of Women and Social Work*, 29(1), pp. 8–17.

McLaughlin, H. (2006) Involving young service users in as co-researchers: possibilities, benefits and costs, *British Journal of Social Work*, 36(8), pp. 1395–1410.

Moran, R. and Lavalette, M. (2016) Co-production: Workers, volunteers and people seeking asylum – 'popular social work' action in Britain, in C. Williams and M. J. Graham (eds.) *Social Work in a Diverse Society: Transformative Practice with Black and Minority Ethnic Individuals and Communities*. Bristol: Polity Press.

Newman, A. and McNamara, Y (2016) Teaching qualitative research and participatory practices in neo-liberal times, *Qualitative Social Work*, 15(3), pp. 428–443.

Robinson, K. and Webber, M. (2013) Models and effectiveness of service user and career involvement in social work education: A literature review, *British Journal of Social Work*, 43, pp. 925–944.

Rosenberg, M. and McCullough, B. C. (1981) Mattering: Inferred significance and mental health among adolescents. *Research in Community & Mental Health*, 2, pp. 163–182.

Scheyett, A. and Diehl, M.J. (2004) Walking our talk in social work education: Partnering with consumers of mental health services, *Social Work Education*, 23(4), pp. 435–450.

Schlossberg, N. (1989) A model for analyzing human adaptation to transition, *The Counseling Psychologist*, 9(2), pp. 2–18.

SCIE (2006) Guide 11 Involving children and young people in developing social care. https://www.scie.org.uk/publications/guides/guide11/index.asp accessed 29-5-2020

SCIE (2015) *Making It Co-Production in Social Care: What it Is and How to do it – At a Glance SCIE at a Glance 64*. Published October 2015, available online at www.scie.org.uk/publications/guides/guide51/at-a-glance/

Shaping Our Lives National User Network (2003) Shaping our lives, from outset to outcome, in *What People Think of the Social Welfare Services They Use*. London and New York: Joseph Rowntree Foundation.

Shier, H. (2001) Pathways to participation: Opening, opportunities and obligations, *Children and Society*, 15, pp. 107–117.

Tanner, D., Littlechild, R., Duffy, J. and Hayes, D. (2017) Making it real: Evaluating the impact of service user and career involvement in social work education real, *The British Journal of Social Work*, 47(2), pp. 467–486.

Taylor, I. (2006) What do we know about partnership with service users and careers in social work education and how robust is the evidence base? *Health and Social Care in the Community*, 14(5), pp. 418–425.

Tyler, G. (2006) Addressing barriers to participation: Service user involvement in social work training, *Social Work Education*, 25(4), pp. 385–392.

Warren, J. (2009) *Service User and Carer Participation in Social Work*. Exeter: Learning Matters Ltd.

Warren, L. and Boxall, K. (2009) Service users in and out of the academy: Collusion in exclusion? *Social Work Education*, 28(3), pp. 281–297.

Webber, M. and Robinson, K. (2012) The meaningful involvement of service users and Careers in advanced-level post-qualifying social work education: A qualitative study, *British Journal of Social Work*, 42, pp. 1256–1274.

Wilson, A. and Beresford, P. (2000) 'Anti-Oppressive Practice': Emancipation or appropriation? *British Journal of Social Work*, 30, pp. 553–573.

6

A MATTER OF POWER

Relationships between professionals and disabled service users

Colin Cameron with Joanne Molloy-Graham and Maggie Cameron

Introduction

In this chapter, I want to examine ways in which power distorts relationships between professionals and service users. I will specifically be discussing relationships between professionals and disabled service users. I will draw on observations made by disabled service user representatives interviewed by Shaping Our Lives (2017) and by Joanne Molloy-Graham and Maggie Cameron, two other disabled people with whom I have talked during the process of writing this chapter. My arguments will hopefully be applicable to the situations of other service user groups as well, though. My focus will mainly be on relations between professionals and disabled people in contexts of service user involvement in the evaluation, planning and co-production of health, education and social care services, though more incidental interactions will also be considered. While I shall be coming at this from a social model perspective – identifying disability as an oppressive social construction or social relationship rather than as an embodied individual condition or problem (UPIAS, 1976; Oliver and Barnes, 2012; Cameron, 2014a) – I shall also be using symbolic interactionist (SI) and structural symbolic interactionist (SSI) (Stryker, 2002, 2008) perspectives to inform my argument. As Forte (2004) points out, core concepts within symbolic interactionism include, for example, symbols (words, looks, gestures), interactions, attitudes, socialisation, role-taking, reference groups, roles and definitions of situations. Structural symbolic interactionism, Stryker (2008) states, places emphasis on the impact of social structures on social interactions.

Rather than reify the idea of power as a 'thing', as a personal attribute belonging to an individual or group, I shall characterise power as a property of social relations (Emerson, 1962). As Mast (2010, p. 26) puts it:

> Power does not exist in a vacuum, it is interpersonal by nature and unfolds in interpersonal behaviour among two or more social interaction partners. Power is affected by both interaction partners' behaviour and their mutual perception thereof.

In other words, in this context, even in situations where a formal commitment to equalising relationships has been made – where it has been stated that service users are recognised as 'experts by experience' and that their understanding and knowledge is regarded as valid – power is at work within assumptions being made about what is going on and in terms of meanings and interpretations made of experience. Central to this, in terms of this chapter, is the understanding of the meaning of disability. While service providers' views remain rooted in an individual model perspective (whether this is identified in medical model or biopsychosocial terms), it is my contention that service user consultation will remain of limited value, often proving an unsatisfactory experience for disabled participants.

I will structure my discussion in four parts. In the first, I will consider the nature of professionalism in health, education and social care. I will argue that power inequalities between service providers and service users persist not because service providers are 'lovers of power' or are unwilling to relinquish power, but because they are inherent in the professional role. Reflecting on ways in which service providers and service users interact, I shall secondly focus on generic processes in the reproduction of inequality (Schwalbe et al., 2000) – means through which inequality is reproduced within interactions, whether intentionally or unintentionally. Schwalbe et al. (2000, p. 422) identify these processes as including:

- Othering
- subordinate adaptation
- boundary maintenance
- emotion management

Thirdly, I shall illustrate ways in which these processes are experienced, both in contexts where service users have been actively involved as service user representatives and in everyday life situations. Finally, I shall conclude by suggesting that progress in terms of establishing genuinely respectful interactions, in which unequal power relations are minimised between service providers and service users, depends upon a shift in thinking about disability from an individual and personal tragedy model view to a social and affirmation model view. I shall outline what this means, why I think it is necessary and why – given the disappearance over the past few years of so many disabled people's organisations due to public funding cuts (Shaping Our Lives/National Survivor User Network, 2019) – this seems at times an aspiration with little chance of fulfilment.

I think it is important to state here that I am writing this as a disabled academic. I have experience as a professional who has worked in various roles in social care, in community development and in higher education, as well as many years' experience of being a disabled health services user. I have worked in and with services organised by local authorities and voluntary sector organisations *for* disabled people with physical impairments and with learning difficulties. These have largely been services organised by non-disabled professionals and have been based on such service philosophies as normalisation, social role valorisation (Wolfensberger, 1972, 2000) and, later on, 'empowerment'. In other words, they have involved plans and strategies about what to do about disability that have been constructed by non-disabled people. Within these, disability has largely been regarded as an unfortunate personal condition requiring professional help to be overcome, adjusted to or made the best of. I have also worked in and with voluntary sector organisations *of* disabled people, established and run by disabled people. The visions, aims and day-to-day practice within these have been based upon social model principles, regarding disability as being about physical, social and cultural barriers which prevent people with impairments from accessing and participating fully in mainstream community life. The ideas underpinning these organisations have been developed by disabled people and have involved addressing these barriers. I make no secret of my commitment, as a disabled person, to the social model. Like good disability research, developing disability theory involves 'the surrender of falsely-premised claims to objectivity through overt political commitment to the struggles of disabled people for self-emancipation' (Priestley, 1997, p. 91). If it appears that I am arguing that the main obstacle to successful partnership working lies with non-disabled professionals, there is a reason for this. As Schwalbe et al. (2000, p. 443) have pointed out,

> it remains true that far more research focuses on action by subordinates than on action by elites. While this has given us a detailed view of how subordinates adapt to inequality, it has left us with a relatively sketchy view of how elites act strategically to perpetuate it. To understand inequality we need to understand how it is maintained by those with the power to do so, not to continually focus on victims of the process.

I suggest that by taking a look at what is problematic about the way professionals relate to disabled people, a better understanding may be gained of how unequal power relations may be addressed in order to enhance the effectiveness of user involvement and service user representation within health, education and social care services.

Professionals in context

Young (2011) has asserted that oppression is experienced by many as part and parcel of everyday life. Oppression is something so routine and ordinary that it often passes unnoticed and uncommented upon by others while being felt intensely by those who have to deal with it. Young states that oppression does not necessarily have to involve ill intent or ill will upon anybody's part but makes itself felt in the details of everyday life, in the 'often unconscious assumptions and reactions of well-meaning people in ordinary interactions' (2011, p. 41). Sexism, racism and ageism work in this way, and it can also be found in disabling practices and encounters. Professionals know that for a person to be disabled means that they have something 'wrong' with them. This, after all, is stated in the definition of disability given in the 2010 UK Equality Act (GOV.UK, 2019), for example, in which a person is disabled if they 'have a physical or mental impairment that has a substantial and long-term *negative* effect on [their] ability to do normal daily activities' (my italics). Disability is clearly identified here in negative terms, as a flaw or a failing that is the result of an impairment or condition. It is identified in terms of aberration from a normal ideal. Within this definition, there is implied a need of something to be fixed or of a problem to be resolved. This task is assigned to professionals.

What makes the discussion of relations between health, education and social care professionals and disabled people complicated is that, behind the lexicon of 'care', 'special needs' and 'anti-oppressive practice' prevalent within professional discourse, there is a long history of coercion, containment and control. Both professionals' and clients' identities and role perceptions are formed within ideological contexts. Oppression is evident in the words, deeds, thoughts and gestures of everyday professional life, but so routine are these, so ubiquitous, that they are rarely considered problematic.

> The conscious actions of many individuals daily contribute to maintaining and reproducing oppression, but these people are usually simply doing their jobs or living their lives and do not understand themselves as agents of oppression.
>
> *(Young, 2011, p. 42)*

This is, perhaps, hard to accept. No professional wants to consider themselves as personally responsible for oppression or as being part of a system that perpetuates oppression. This would be considered an affront. Yet a brief examination of disabled people's history provides illumination.

People with impairments have been part of every human society since history first started being recorded (Barnes, 1997). While life for impaired people would never have been particularly easy, this was the experience of most other people, too (Wrightson, 2002). Prior to the Industrial Revolution of the 18th and 19th centuries, however – during which time economy was based on the principle of subsistence rather than profit and most labour was either agricultural or cottage-based – disabled people were part of an undifferentiated mass poor: 'clustered at the lower reaches of society, but not excluded from it' (Borsay, 2002, p. 103). Gleeson (1999) has remarked on evidence that people with physical impairments were regarded as part of the everyday pre-modern social order. Impairment was commonplace, regarded as inevitable rather than as something separate from ordinary life.

Industrialisation changed everything. The mass movement of the population to the rapidly expanding towns and cities meant that greater numbers than ever before lived in close proximity. Coupled with a shift to a factory-based system of production, this created a need for new forms of self-consciousness, discipline and a greater attention to individual bodily comportment and behaviour than had ever existed previously (Elias, 2001). Davis (2013) describes the way in which the word 'normal', in terms of its current usage as an expectation of physical and behavioural conformity, first started being used around 1840. The requirement which emerged for a standard-sized, standard-shaped worker of standard ability to work machines in the factories resulted in the simultaneous appearance of a population regarded as surplus to production requirements. Disabled people found themselves removed from ordinary life and incarcerated within new systems of asylums, long-stay hospitals and other isolated spaces where they came under the surveillance of the increasingly powerful medical profession (Barnes, 1997; Cameron, 2018). It is here that disability first became regarded as a medical issue (Oliver, 1990), where the bodies of impaired people began to be treated as markers of disorder and disruption, of unruly nature threatening to hold back and destroy the achievements of modern society (Davis, 2013). With the growth of Eugenics (Barnes and Mercer, 2010) and the rise of Victorian charities (Borsay, 2002), a discourse was established which viewed impairment as a mark of moral inferiority or a trial to be pitied and overcome. Impairment was no longer considered an unexceptional part of social life, but had become a metaphor harnessed in the business of establishing the boundaries of acceptability in the new social order (Cameron, 2014b).

Once disabled people's disorderly bodies had been removed from the social mainstream, there was considered no need to plan for their inclusion in the design of public architecture, workplaces, public transport systems, homes, schools, places of recreation, worship and so on. The social environment developed within industrialised society was built with a view that there was no need to take the needs of people with impairments into account, for it was presumed they had no role in society.

Throughout the 20th century, the supervision of disabled people's lives became an increasingly sophisticated business, resulting in the emergence of what Albrecht (1992) has described as a *disability and rehabilitation industry*. Oliver (1996, p. 37) has added:

> The medical profession, because of its power and dominance, has spawned a whole range of pseudo-professions in its own image; physiotherapy, occupational therapy, speech therapy, clinical psychology . . . each one geared to the same aim – the restoration of normality.

The 'scientific' knowledge and skill sets developed within these and related professions have given legitimacy to the power that professionals hold in relation to service users. In terms of Abbott and Meerabeau's (1998) trait model, the acquisition of theoretical knowledge as a qualification for the practice of highly skilled work is identified as the primary requirement for entry to the 'caring' professions. Each of these professions has carved out its own specialist area of 'interventions and intrusions into disabled people's lives' (Oliver, 1996, p. 37) and developed its own knowledge base and set of skills to practice this. The movement of training for professionals such as teachers, nurses and music therapists, for example, from colleges to universities has been about adding authority to these roles (Swain et al., 2003; Cameron, 2015a). In Abbott and Meerabeau's (1998, p. 13) words:

> The caring professions are powerful because they not only aim to change and control behaviour but also help structure the context of social and cultural life in a more general sense – through their power to command definitions of reality by which the lives of their clients are shaped.

Professionals' knowledge has been regarded as having objectivity and validity, while service users' knowledge has been looked upon as subjective and invalid. This understanding has been expressed by McKnight (2005, pp. 82–83), who states that, in defining need as personal deficiency, 'caring' professionals have communicated a number of propositions to service users:

> *You* are deficient.
> *You* are the problem.
> *I*, the professionalised servicer, am the answer.
> *You* are not the answer.
> *Your peers* are not the answer.
> *The political, social and economic environment* is not the answer.

The requirement for professionals to consult with service users has come about as a result of collective advocacy by service user movements rather than as a result of professional initiatives. The disabled people's movement, for example, has been raising concerns about professional assumptions for many years now. At the time of writing, it is 30 years since Richard Wood (1989, p. 201), then Chair of the British Council of Organisations of Disabled People, stated that

> the truth is that this view of disabled people as 'sick people' or people in need of 'care and protection' is the view most often held by governments and the professionals, and it is the view that dominates services, policies and strategies which other people have imposed on us.

Making the point that care seems to many disabled people 'a tool through which others are able to dominate and manage our lives' (1989, p. 201), Wood lays the blame for disabling professional practices firmly within individual model thinking:

> So strong is this medical model of disability that many disabled people have also come to believe that they must let others manage their lives since they are not competent to do so themselves. Thus, disabled people's lives are often dominated by professionals and services which de-skill us and turn us into passive recipients of care.
> *(Wood, 1989, p. 201)*

Wood's comments were made as part of the Disabled People's Movement's Campaign for Independent Living, established during the 1980s. Established in a social model understanding, this placed an emphasis on

> breaking down the barriers which prevent disabled people from living as equal citizens in the community. We believe that these social barriers are the true cause of disability

and that the solution to the independence of disabled people lies in using their direct experience to inform social policy which would be designed to remove these barriers.

(Wood, 1989, p. 202)

From a perspective 30 years further on, we can look back at the ways in which the Campaign for Independent Living was hijacked during the first years of the present century by the personalisation agenda (Garabedian, 2014); at the closure by the Department of Work and Pensions of the Independent Living Fund in 2015; and at the transference of responsibilities to fund independent living to cash-strapped local authorities which have had to deal with a decade of cuts to social care budgets as a result of austerity policies. While disabled people's vision of independent living had been about transforming 'the whole of disabled people's interactions with society; its organisations, facilities and structures' (Elder-Woodward, 2012), Beresford (2014, p. 25) identifies personalisation as part of a market-centred cost-cutting exercise involving the privatisation of services and reliance on unpaid caring: 'In some authorities, personal budgets have been used to mean little more than a re-branding of existing and traditional arrangements'. Far from receiving support to live independently, increasing numbers of disabled people are receiving what Inclusion London (Pring, 2019, n.p.) has termed an extremely basic *clean and feed* model of care:

> The most basic choices such as when to get up, go to bed or use the toilet, when and what to eat, and the choice to leave the house are no longer in the hands of disabled people but subject to local authority budget allocations which are becoming ever more restricted.

At the same time, disabled people identify professional practice within social care as persistently paternalistic: 'making unhelpful assumptions about what service users can and can't do' (Beresford, 2014, p. 23).

I stated in the introduction my intention to argue that change-preventing power inequalities between service providers and service users persist not because service providers are 'lovers of power' or are deliberately unwilling to relinquish power. Many professionals are very lovely people with the best interests of their 'clients' at heart. The problem lies in professionals' inability to see their own practices in terms of the wider picture. While, as McKnight recognises, most social human service professionals have a theoretical understanding of the structural causes of individual problems, their everyday practice isolates the individual service user from this structural context. Because the professional's 'tools and techniques are usually limited to individualised interaction, the interpretation of the need becomes individualised' (McKnight, 2005, p. 79).

What has been apparent to disabled people for decades – that the real causes of disability are to be found in the way that contemporary society is organised rather than within their own individual bodies – still seems to baffle professionals. In spite of professionals' professed commitments to listen to service users' voices, it is the unwillingness of professionals to take on board the implications of the social model for health, education and social care practice which perpetuates disrespect and oppressive power.

Power, social structure and role

In terms of Stryker's structural symbolic interactionism, society is:

> a never-ending process of routinisation of solutions to repetitive problems. Both persons (humans with minds and selves) and society are created through social process: each is constitutive of the other.

(Stryker, 2008, p. 16)

Who we are able to be as individual people depends on when, where and how we find ourselves thrown into the world. This is not to say that we are completely conditioned by the social organisation and structures we find around us, for we exercise considerable individual autonomy in how we respond to our situations (in turn shaping the ongoing emergence of these). It is, however, to say that we are all creatures of our own times and places and that 'behind cognitive organisation lies social organisation' (Stryker, 2008, p. 17).

As self and identity are produced by our life experiences, these are bounded and given meaning within social structures, understood as pre-existing patterned interactions and relationships, characterised by durability, resistance to change and the capacity to reproduce themselves (Stryker, 2008). Society is made up of 'organised systems of interactions and role relationships and . . . complex mosaics of differentiated groups, communities and institutions' (Stryker, 2008, p. 19), intersected by a variety of marked categories based on class, age, gender, ethnicity, religion, disability and so on. These large-scale structures operate through structures more immediate to individual experience, such as professional or human service settings, to impact on interpersonal social relationships: shaping roles, expectations and the contents of interactions. As Schwalbe et al. (2000, p. 420) state:

> the reproduction of inequality, even when it appears thoroughly institutionalised, ultimately depends on face-to-face interaction, which therefore must be studied as part of understanding the reproduction of inequality.

Experiences are not distributed randomly through society. Rather, the content of and the meanings derived from experiences are shaped by where people are located within structures of class, ethnicity, gender, age, religion, disability etc. (Stryker, 2008). Large-scale structures (like disability) channel people into smaller-scale social structures (like local human services), which in turn channel them into interpersonal relationships with people they encounter (like professionals). The interactions people experience within these will importantly impact upon their self-concepts, attitudes and behaviours (Stryker, 2008, p. 23). Society is in a constant process of change and new approaches to problems emerge as, individually and collectively, people adapt existing meanings and behaviours to deal with new contingencies. Processes of service user involvement, user representation, co-production and joint planning represent attempts to bring about change to the way human services are conceived, planned and delivered. These activities are, however, complicated by professional assumptions and role expectations involved.

Disabled people are not just disabled people. Service users are not just service users. Instead, they are people with multi-faceted personalities who may have many different roles. They may be professionals, too. They may be activists. They may be seasoned and experienced campaigners. They may be self-advocates or spouses or parents or lovers or students or artists. Perhaps something like this is what is meant by many professionals who self-righteously emphasise the importance of using the term 'people with disabilities', preferring to see people in terms of their individuality first (although this misses the point in that it often involves an assumption that overlooking impairment is a kindness and, besides, reflects an individual model perspective which regards disability as something people 'have'). In terms of identity salience, though, self-identification as a disabled person (or as a Disabled person) involves taking on a political identity, regarding oneself as among the disenfranchised who have decided to do something to change things (Cameron, 2014d). Participation in service user involvement activities, though, made a frustrating experience (Shaping Our Lives, 2017; Cameron et al., 2019a; Cameron et al., 2019b) when human service professionals cannot get beyond the idea that disability signifies something wrong with a person.

From a symbolic interactionist perspective, social order is a negotiated process and not something that 'just happens' (Sandstrom et al., 2010). Structural realities such as inequality are understood as embedded ultimately in terms of the countless ongoing everyday negotiations that occur in individual interactions and negotiations:

> A social system depends on individuals acting towards other individuals in particular ways. However, it is not simply the behaviours themselves that create the social structure, but rather their sedimentation into a system that individuals understand as normatively appropriate.
>
> *(Sandstrom et al., 2010, p. 164)*

I have already stated that I am not suggesting that professionals intend their words, thoughts and actions to be oppressive, but that unequal power relationships between professionals and disabled service users are often reproduced in interactions that professionals consider normal and unproblematic. Schwalbe et al. (2000, p. 422) have identified four processes (and numerous subprocesses) central to the reproduction of inequality which I contend can be related to common practices of professionals in relation to disabled service users.

Othering

In Fine's (1994) terms, Othering refers to the process whereby a dominant group defines into existence an inferior group. As discussed earlier in this chapter, during the industrialisation of society in the 18th and 19th century, people with impairments were physically removed from the social mainstream and placed within isolated settings. This was the first time 'the disabled' were identified as a group separate from society. It involved the establishment of abnormalcy in order that normalcy could recognise itself (Cameron, 2014d).

Oppressive Othering occurs, for example,

> when one group seeks advantage by defining another group as morally and/or intellectually inferior. . . . It is a process which entails the invention of categories and of ideas about what marks people as belonging to these categories.
>
> *(Schwalbe et al., 2000, p. 423)*

Eugenic terms such as *incurable degenerates*, *mental defectives*, *feeble-minded* and *idiots* (Quarmby, 2011), along with offensive medical terms such as *cripple, spastic* and *handicapped*, are echoed in professional judgements about service users' *challenging behaviours* or *inappropriate behaviours*, as well as in descriptions of people as *moderately*, *severely* and *profoundly* disabled. The latter may sound less harsh, but they have the same purpose of negatively marking out, of establishing difference as deficit. Descriptions such as *the most vulnerable* are used to justify professional interventions into disabled people's lives, for example in providing segregated 'special' education. Labelling disabled people as vulnerable identifies disability as *their* problem and directs focus away from physical and social barriers which close off opportunities to gain life experiences (Cameron, 2014e). Hasler (2004, p. 229) has explained that the word vulnerable first started to appear in social care jargon in the late 1990s, stating that this is 'a concept that owes nothing to disabled people and everything to professional concerns'. It is now, however, a word used widely and uncritically in professional practice.

Stereotyping is another form of Othering. Stereotypes are 'vivid but simple representations that reduce persons to a set of exaggerated, usually negative characteristics' (Barker, 2004, p. 263). The practice of stereotyping is found overtly in professional practices where a disabled person's impairment is regarded as their most important characteristic. It is also found more subtly in workplace participation in and endorsement of scripted cultural events such as BBC television's annual charity event *Children in Need* or the Paralympics. Events such as these are key locations for the public recycling of old disabling stereotypes such as *the poor pathetic victim* or *the tragic but brave, plucky struggler against adversity* (Cameron, 2014f). Such activities create and reinforce meanings that shape perceptions and interactions in ways that reproduce inequality. The message is transmitted again that to be disabled is to be a victim of personal tragedy. As 'people who care', the moral identity of professionals is re-established.

Subordinate adaptation

Schwalbe et al. (2000, p. 426) clarify what they mean by subordinate adaptation by describing this as 'trading power for patronage':

> One way to adapt to subordinate status is to accept it, while seeking to derive compensatory benefits from relationships with members of the dominant group.

The individual model of disability – the view that for a person to be disabled is to have something *wrong* with them, something they need professional help to deal with – is so pervasive and so dominant that it is little surprise that many disabled people accept this view of themselves (Oliver, 1996). When the discourses of dominant culture relentlessly present disability as involving personal tragedy, dependence and incapacity, then it is to be expected that many disabled people come to accept poverty, unemployment, restricted life chances and social exclusion as a consequence of their own characteristics as not-quite-good-enough human beings (Cameron, 2007). Given the unequal power relationships between professionals and disabled service users, approval from professionals in service user consultation contexts is likely to be something which can sometimes enhance self-worth. There is status to be gained for telling professionals what they want to hear. Discussing involvement as a service user representative, one participant in Shaping Our Lives' research (2017, p. 14) said they felt the experience was:

> Pointless as they have their regular service users who get listened to more than others.

The suggestion that professionals sometimes prefer to have passive and compliant service user representatives who can be relied upon to agree with them and will be unlikely to challenge the way things happen seems, perhaps, outrageous. It is, however, supported by the following statement taken from Shaping Our Lives' research report:

> My experience is that the professionals prefer to have victims. I experience an attempt to disempower me. They prefer to make decisions about me without me.
> *(Shaping Our Lives, 2017, p. 15)*

The following service user's statement underlines this point. As long as service users' voices assent to those of professionals, then things go well. When service users begin to express dissent, though, their views are dismissed as invalid and naïve. So long as the process of consultation can be shown to have occurred, then this seems to be what is regarded as important:

> It is diminishing to realise how the service providers see service users. It is frustrating in the meetings to sense how little credence most of them actually give to service user

viewpoints. If our view chimes with theirs they are positive and pleased with how things are going. If the service user perspectives challenge their views then they tend to offer platitudes and try to swiftly move the discussion on.

(Shaping Our Lives, 2017, p. 15)

It should really be unsurprising that many disabled people get involved as service user representatives out of a need to feel valued and important or that they should take pride in their involvement. To gain approval from people who seem important will have its rewards, especially if there seems little else to feel good about, but this does not necessarily signify greater respect or equality.

Boundary maintenance

Schwalbe et al. (2000, p. 435) state that:

> Preserving inequality requires maintaining boundaries between dominant and subordinate groups. These boundaries can be symbolic, interactional, spatial or all of these. By preserving these boundaries, dominant groups protect the material and cultural capital they have acquired and upon which they rely to preserve their dominance.

Structures which legitimise professionals' authority – e.g. codes of conduct, performance standards, registered monopolies over areas of work, membership of selecting, safeguarding and controlling professional bodies (Abbott and Meerabeau, 1998) – are used to establish institutional boundaries between professionals and service users. McKnight (2005, p. 83) notes that to be professional is 'to distance – to ensure that the relationship is defined in terms that allow the client to understand who is *really* being serviced'.

Patricia Chambers, a disabled member of Shaping Our Lives' Board of Directors, spoke of the role confusion she experienced as a result of the different ways she was addressed by professionals on the basis of whether she was being regarded as a service user representative or as 'just' a service user. It was Patricia's comments that led to the development of Shaping Our Lives' 2017 research project *Improving Understanding of Service User Involvement and Identity* (discussed more fully in Chapter 2). Patricia talked about the conflict she felt in being treated, on the one hand, with respect – as an 'expert by experience' – when involved as a service user representative, seen as someone who had a potential contribution perceived as of value to service provider organisations wishing to engage her; and, on the other, outside those situations, finding herself relegated to being 'just a service user' by the same professionals who had extracted expertise from her service user representation:

> In the meetings the say 'Hello, Patricia, how are you?' But when they next see me on a corridor they act like they don't know me.

(Cameron et al., 2019b)

It seems clear from Patricia's statements that the respect shown to her by professionals in situations of service user involvement was superficial. Once her service user's expertise had been gained, it was her experience that normal disabling, distancing relations resumed. It is little wonder that, as Shaping Our Lives (2017, p. 9) states, service users are often left feeling 'confused over status and concerned about having been used or exploited' (SOL, 2017).

In terms of the core argument of my chapter, I would argue that professionals' primary means of boundary maintenance is through regulating discourse. In Schwalbe et al.'s (2000, p. 435) terms, discourse is

> more than talk and writing; it is a way of talking and writing. To regulate discourse is to impose a set of formal or informal rules about what can be said, how it can be said, and who can say what to whom.

Discourse regulates the conversation that can be held on any matter, creating openings for the circulation and exchange of certain meanings and closing down possibilities for others. Within current health and social care provision, as I have already argued, disability remains predominantly talked about, thought about and acted upon as an individual problem, or in terms of individual model discourse as opposed to social model discourse. While many professionals acknowledge the existence of the social model of disability, it is far from clear that they understand it. In spite of the many campaigns organised by disabled people rooted in social model principles, and in spite of the volumes of academic writing that disabled people have produced about the social model, many professionals have seemed disinclined to comprehend it or take it on board. For this reason, it is important here to make clear what I am talking about.

The social model of disability needs to be regarded as the response of the disabled people's movement to the individual model, and so the individual model must here be explained first. The individual model of disability, also known as the medical model (Oliver, 1996), while having characterised professional thinking about disability for many decades previously, was most succinctly summarised in the World Health Organisation's 1980 International Classification of Impairments, Disabilities and Handicaps (ICIDH) (WHO, 1980, pp. 47, 143). An important distinction is made in ICIDH between the concepts of impairment and disability.

> Impairment: any loss or abnormality of psychological, physiological, or anatomical structure or function
> Disability: any restriction or lack (resulting from an impairment) of ability to perform an activity in the manner or within the range considered normal for a human being

It can clearly be seen that, within this framework, disability is regarded as the direct outcome of impairment and is measured in terms of deviance from normality. Disability is viewed here as an individual problem rather than a structural issue. WHO's later revision of ICIDH, the International Classification of Functioning, Disability and Health (ICF), redefined disability as:

> an umbrella term, covering impairments, activity limitations, and participation restrictions.
> *(WHO, 2019, n.p.)*

While purporting to be rooted in a biopsychosocial model of disability (WCPT.ORG, 2019), the ICF definition continues to conflate disability and impairment, treating these both as the same thing, and thus reproduces individual model thinking.

ICF overlooked Drake's (1999, p. 14) point that 'the medical and social models are two fundamentally opposed ways of understanding disability'. It allowed professionals to retain focus on addressing individual physicality and behaviour as the source of people's problems and to overlook the social contexts in which disabled people live – which they were largely powerless to do anything about anyway.

The social model, originally formulated in 1976 in the UK by the Union of the Physically Impaired Against Segregation (UPIAS), and developed in 1982 by Disabled People's International (DPI), redefined the terms impairment and disability.

> Impairment: lacking part of or all of a limb, or having a defective limb, organism or mechanism of the body
> Disability: the disadvantage or restriction of activity caused by a contemporary social organisation which takes little or no account of people who have physical impairments and thus excludes them from the mainstream of social activities
> *(UPIAS, 1976, p. 14)*

The DPI 1982 classification built on the UPIAS definitions by adding what it termed mental and sensory impairments so that, for example, people with learning difficulties, people with mental health issues, Deaf people and blind people were included as disabled people.

> Impairment: the functional limitation with the individual caused by physical, mental or sensory impairment
> Disability: the loss or limitation of opportunities to take part in the normal life of the community on an equal level with others due to physical and social barriers
> *(DPI, 1982, in Fougeyrollas and Beauregard, 2001, p. 177)*

Both these social model classifications identify impairment as signifying physical or functional lack or limitation. The added difficulty to life caused by impairment is implied within these definitions. Disability, however, is identified in terms of the way society excludes people with impairments from ordinary community life, whether intentionally – through the establishment of segregated environments and institutions, for example, which reinforce perceptions of Otherness – or unintentionally, through lack of thought, in the circulation of disabling stereotypes or the poor design of new public spaces that are still frequently inaccessible (Heaton, 2014). In terms of the social model, people with impairments do not 'have' disabilities, but they are disabled by society and its practices. Identifying as a disabled person involves a shift in thinking from medical model to social model terms. Being disabled becomes a political identity. It involves having to deal with choices and decisions made by other people, often professionals, which have a significant limiting impact on life opportunities.

The endless recurrence of individual model discourse within professional practice closes down opportunities to think differently about ways in which both impairment and disability may be experienced. Unending sequences of interactions where only individual model discourse can be heard establish demoralising contexts in which impairment can only be made sense of negatively. While individual model discourse remains the norm within professional interactions with service users, it involves both a regulation of emotion and a regulation of action (Schwalbe et al., p. 435).

Conditioning emotional subjectivity

A core principle of SI is that people act towards things on the basis of the meanings they learn to give to things (Chalari, 2017). The sense that disabled service users can make of their experiences as people with impairments in a disabling society depends largely on the meanings and narratives that circulate in the culture they are part of – or are excluded from (Cameron, 2007). As Schwalbe et al. (2000, p. 437) argue, emotional subjectivity can be conditioned in ways that reproduce inequality and may 'also entail conditioning one's self to accept as normal the feelings that are attendant to subordination'.

One disabled service user representative interviewed by Shaping Our Lives (SOL, 2017, p. 20) observed that:

> Many professionals mean well but can be tokenistic and patronising, especially in the health sector. It is a huge mind set for health to realise that disabled people want choice and control over their own lives although many disabled people who have not had the same experience as some disabled people simply accept this kind of treatment.

What the service user representative describes here is her view of the situation of other disabled service users who have – often because no other options have seemed available – taken on what French (1994) has described as 'the disabled role'. The disabled role is given legitimacy within everyday interactions, practices and contexts in which assumptions equating impairment with tragedy go unchallenged. It is characterised by a number of features. These include being required to aspire above all things to independence; to aspire to appear less disabled and more normal; moving towards acceptance of and adjustment to the tragedy associated with impairment; and taking responsibility for the feelings that non-disabled people have about impairment and disability. It is an oppressive role for a number of reasons.

While unequal relationships of care can create their own problems by developing mutual dependency, pressures placed by professionals on disabled people to carry out time-consuming physical tasks for themselves in order to demonstrate their independence can be regarded as equally oppressive. The thinking underlying such requirements is that 'this is how normal people go about things' and that normality is something disabled people should aspire to. Many disabled people believe that spending hours of indignity, pain and stress in order to complete tasks for themselves for the sake of appearances is a waste of time when they could get a personal assistant to do these things instead. This would free them up to do more interesting things with their lives. In terms of Independent Living philosophy, independence is about being in control of what happens rather than about being physically able to do things (Garabedian, 2014). The expectation that disabled people will aspire to normality leads to situations where disabled people cannot be open about their impairments or access requirements for fear of other people's responses. The requirement to accept and adjust to the 'loss' that 'disability' involves makes it very difficult to think about impairment other than as tragedy or to find anything of value in the experience. Finally, the expectation that disabled people will take responsibility for the feelings non-disabled people have about impairment and disability is wearing:

> People with epilepsy may, for example, be expected to explain constantly their condition and offer reassurance, deaf people may struggle to lip-read, and visually-impaired people may endure boredom rather than 'spoiling other people's fun'. . . . In contrast, non-disabled people are not expected to understand deafness, blindness, epilepsy or paralysis, or to alter their behaviour in any substantial way.
>
> *(French, 1994, p. 56)*

The disabled role, imposed through unequal power relations in countless daily interactions with professionals, often appears the only role available to disabled people and can be very hard to resist. As Jane Kroger (2000, p. 20) has noted, people 'are largely ascribed identities according to their manner of embedding within a discourse – in their own, or in the discourse of others'. The imagination is given little to build on with which to make positive sense of the experience of living with impairment. Disabled people often find themselves caught up in playing a part, and receiving social approval for playing a part, which does nothing to challenge the disabling social relations they experience.

Trying to break out of the disabled role and to assert oneself can be difficult and challenging, particularly when, as one service user representative said, there is a feeling that:

> They are working against me, not with me. They are making decisions in what they think is best for me but not really listening to me.
>
> *(SOL, 2017, p. 19)*

Another service user representative spoke of the emotional impact of having tried to challenge the professionals with whom he was meeting (SOL, 2017, p. 24):

> Just thinking about the impact that can have on you, not just the experience of being humiliated but the experience of trying to explain why that has an impact on you and that being disregarded as well, then that can undermine your confidence and then it becomes more and more difficult then to access services in the future.

The damaging impact upon service user representatives' confidence and self-esteem is not something that is lightly brushed off but can have a deeper demoralising effect. As another service user representative reflected:

> Those negative experiences become part of your private experience, very negative, very harmful.
>
> *(SOL, 2017, p. 24)*

If service providers intend consultation with service users to be meaningful and effective in bringing about real change, there is a requirement to recognise and address the unequal power relations inherent in the nature of their practice. This inequality does not stem from who they are as individual practitioners, but is rather the outcome of wider structural contexts to which perhaps they haven't really given much thought.

Apart from in a minority of cases, the unequal power relations discussed here are not attributable to individual professionals but to the disabling structures of society – to 'the system' or to the flux of a multitude of separate systems to do with disability, gender, race, ethnicity, age and religion. Within symbolic interactionism, structure is recognised as a metaphor for recurrent patterns of action involving large numbers of people (Schwalbe et al., 2000, p. 439), some of whom are human service professionals. There is no superimposing structure to be discovered out there, just the endless activity of other people in other settings doing similar things. What people do in any of these settings depends on the ideas, feelings, procedural rules, tools and habits available to enable their individual and joint action (Schwalbe et al., 2000, p. 440). In these terms, it has to be the responsibility of 'caring' professionals to examine the meanings they adhere to as well as their own values and beliefs about disability if they want to be part of the solution.

Disabling encounters with professionals

During the time I have been preparing and writing this chapter, I have talked about some of these issues with two other disabled people, Joanne Molloy-Graham and Maggie Cameron.

Joanne is currently a third-year undergraduate student at Northumbria University and Maggie is a freelance Disability Equality Trainer. Both were able to recollect numerous encounters with non-disabled professionals in which they had felt discriminated against by medicalising, individual model judgements and comments, and some of these are included here. These were comparatively small incidents happening in the flow of everyday life. Presumably it would never have occurred to the professionals involved that their words and actions were oppressive. These incidents will have been considered unimportant and have been long forgotten by them. Yet, in contexts in which disability 'is lived in the midst of the meanings given to it' (Titchkosky and Michalko, 2014, p. 101), these encounters have remained with Joanne and Maggie as examples of ongoing unwelcome professional invalidation.

Joanne Molloy-Graham

I remember arriving at college once to be told by one of my tutors that the lift was out of order and that this meant I could not gain access to the class room. When I asked if the room could be changed, I was told that it could not, and I should either go home or stay in the library. I felt it was assumed that I was the inconvenience. Angry, fed up and tired of having the rug pulled from underneath me, I went home. I was angry and upset and it raised some past issues from other occasions. I remember also attending a lecture at college in my wheelchair and being asked by a lecturer if I should be there. I felt it was assumed that somehow because I was in my chair, I was not capable of the work. It left me feeling annoyed, judged and embarrassed. I felt very self-conscious and stressed.

When I applied for a student representative role, I was asked to attend a chat in which the member of staff suggested that I withdraw my application given my illness. I felt the assumption was being made that I was not good enough or capable of managing myself. I was so angry. It made me fight harder, but my self-esteem and confidence were affected. I am scared to be myself sometimes. Also, she asked me why I was applying to be a disabled representative when I don't look disabled. I felt that the assumption was being made that I was somehow lying and I had to justify myself. I felt judged and it impacted upon my sense of self.

In one of my lectures I was having a seizure. I was asked by the lecturer why I was pulling faces and told to stop doing it or leave. I felt it was assumed that I was somehow trying to be disruptive. I felt embarrassed, stressed and anxious. I didn't go back for two weeks.

I get fed up at the amount of times staff tell me I am an inspiration and that I am so brave. Like I am not a burden or a trouble maker or a complainer but some form of hero that should be a poster for what people with illness or disability can achieve. The truth though is I am not brave or a hero. But just a mother, a wife, a student and a woman who loves her family, who wants to enjoy life. I am from my family's long line of stubborn pig-headed women, not a burden or a hero. Most of these issues need more staff training and awareness. It is lack of understanding. It is those who lack understanding in power that prevent the world from seeing me for who I really am.

Maggie Cameron

I remember being asked by one of my social work tutors at university if I wanted to go for a coffee while the other members of my group watched a DVD that wasn't subtitled. When I questioned this, she offered to let me take the DVD home for the week. Of course, it still wouldn't have been subtitled at home either. She seemed to have this idea that with constant repetition I would somehow be able to hear it. Stuff like this leaves you feeling exasperated and frustrated because you constantly have to validate yourself over trivial incidents. It's not so much the single incident itself so much as that you have to deal with stuff like this over and over again, every day.

Once when I was working in Edinburgh I had gone with a colleague to check out new premises for the disabled people's organisation Self Directed Support Scotland – to check the place in terms of access and room sizes. I had already explained to the receptionist that I was deaf, but when I asked her to repeat her directions to the meeting room she turned to my colleague and told her instead. You just say to yourself 'What the . . .?' It's always disbelief that someone you're talking to responds in such a dismissive way. You always think well, what happened there? Have I missed something?

I had explained to the minister of our parish church, who was also a speech therapist, why I had a positive regard towards my deafness. He responded by saying simply 'No, I can't accept that'. I was struck by his disbelief, at the fact that he could simply negate my opinion of myself. I don't know how he had the arrogance to just say what he did. I was gobsmacked and couldn't think of how to respond.

I was refused a telephone call to a professional at social services. The person on the receiving end of the call just kept putting the phone down while the person from Type/Talk tried to explain. You just feel a sense of annoyance and resignation. It happens again and again. It's the ignorance among professionals who haven't got the wit to understand. Surely access and communication with disabled people should be a key part of their training?

Thomas (1999, p. 47) has argued that as well as social barriers, recognised by social modellists as externally imposed restrictions of activity,

> there are also social barriers which erect 'restrictions' within ourselves, and thus place limits on our psycho-emotional well-being: for example, feeling 'hurt' by the reactions and behaviours of those around us, being made to feel worthless, of lesser value, unattractive, hopeless, stressed or insecure.
>
> *(Thomas, 1999, p. 47)*

Both Joanne's and Maggie's accounts of disabling encounters with professionals vindicate Thomas's assertion here. Professionals' complacent imposition of individual model values and judgements in the ongoing interactions of everyday life have a cumulative wearing effect. 'I am scared to be myself sometimes,' says Joanne. 'You constantly have to validate yourself over trivial incidents . . .' 'It happens again and again,' says Maggie. The problem is to do with the nature of the individual model as dominant discourse in that, on the basis of disabled people's statements considered in this chapter, it prevents professionals from seeing, relating and interacting with respect towards disabled people. The identification of disability with personal deficit allows professionals to presume an asymmetrical relationship between themselves and disabled people. In Sandstrom et al.'s terms:

> A relationship is asymmetrical when one of its participants establishes control or dominance, disproportionately imposing his or her will on the other participants and setting

conditions, making decisions, and engaging in actions that determine the form and course of the relationship.

(2010, p. 158)

Joanne and Maggie describe feelings of anger, tiredness, upset, self-consciousness, stress, exasperation, annoyance and frustration at professionals' presumed rights to impose their own understandings on what is going on in their encounters with disabled people. Yet this is not all they express. The passage by Sandstrom et al. continues. In spite of power inequalities that exist within interactions:

> We include the term 'disproportionately' in our definition because we recognise that subordinates, or less powerful people, are not without power or resources; indeed, they often have ways to initiate action and evade the control of superordinates, or more powerful people.
>
> *(2010, p. 58)*

In spite of their experiences of inequality, neither Joanne nor Maggie are victims. Both identify a requirement for professionals to receive training on disability equality issues. They identify the deficit in the interactions they have talked about as being in terms of professionals' understanding. The stress and frustration they feel is not the outcome of their experiences of impairment but of having to deal with professional condescension. Joanne rejects the roles professionals try to place her in, either as inconvenience or as hero. She identifies herself as 'just a mother, a wife, a student, and a woman who loves her family'. Maggie observes that professionals 'haven't got the wit to understand'. Like the voices of the disabled people who took part in SOL's research discussed earlier, these are the voices of disabled people who can see what is going on and have developed their own subversive discourse.

Conclusion

The affirmation model is the theoretical development within Disability Studies of the Disability Arts Movement's concept of *Disability Pride* (Swain and French, 2000; Cameron, 2015b). Expressive of transgression, resistance and self-confirmation, the affirmation model summarises in abstract terms the assertion of non-compliance captured in a line penned by the blues singer and disabled artist Johnny Crescendo:

> I'm in love with my body. It's the only one I've got.
>
> *(Holdsworth, 1989, p. 16)*

There is a self-respectful defiance in Crescendo's words and a refusal of expectations that, as a disabled person, he will only be able to relate negatively to his own embodied experience. His point is that impairment is an important part of his everyday experience but not something he intends to waste his time lamenting. This is expressed in the affirmation model in the following definitions (Cameron, 2015b, p. 118):

> Impairment: physical, sensory, emotional and cognitive difference, divergent from culturally valued norms of embodiment, to be expected and respected on its own terms in a diverse society.

Disability: a personal and social role which simultaneously invalidates the subject position of people with impairments and validates the subject position of those considered normal.

The disabled people's words in this chapter – the participants in SOL's research on service user identity, Joanne's and Maggie's, Johnny Crescendo's – articulate a demand to be recognised and valued for who they are as disabled people. While impairment can sometimes be messy, tiring and painful, it is not the end of the world. It is something to be lived with, not to be ashamed of. The real difficulty in life is disability which, as UPIAS (1976, p. 14) stated, is 'something imposed on top of our impairments by the way we are unnecessarily isolated and excluded from full participation in society'. Impairment is not the cause of incessant regret, but a common part of human experience which has much to teach about the ambiguity and temporality of human existence. Pointing out what should be obvious to most people, Hamilton (2014, p. 1) reminds us that:

Everyone knows that life contains many adversities: we all experience loss, failure, disappointment, waste and pain in various different forms and ways.

In other words, impairment is simply a variant among the difficulties life throws at all people. Jennie, a disabled woman with various impairments who I interviewed during my PhD research (Cameron, 2010), made this point when she remarked:

There are all kinds of terrible situations in life that I wouldn't be . . . I mean, for instance, the average person in Scotland now reads six books a year . . . it's hard for me to imagine being in that situation . . . and not being terribly unhappy with myself . . . obviously people are just different like that.

To Jennie, the idea of being someone who only reads six books a year would seem an unthinkable shame, something she would not enjoy. She accepts the fact that some people – the average person in Scotland, she says – may spend most of their time without their nose in a book, but that would not be a life she would choose. She enjoys being who she is, but feels sorry for those with less cerebral lives.

Roshni, a blind woman quoted in Cameron (2014g, p. 5), said:

I've yet to meet the person who's jumping up and down, celebrating that they've got dodgy eyesight . . . but, having said that, it's certainly not a cause for me to cry and weep and wring my hands and give up on the world . . . there are lots of things I'm not happy about. . . . I'm not happy about the fact that I've got dry rot in the next room and the ceiling needs replacing. . . . I think my visual impairment is on the same scale as that . . . life happens.

Disabled people's knowledge seems to elude most 'caring' professionals. Disabled people know that it is possible to live with impairment and to feel all right about being yourself, or that it would be if it weren't for physical barriers everywhere and for the fact that most people – including professionals – seem unable or unwilling to move beyond or to stop imposing individual model thinking. I have recently discovered two books by the South Korean Buddhist monk Haemin Sunim. The first is entitled *The Things You Can See Only When You Slow Down* and the second *Love for Imperfect Things*. Both are international bestsellers, with millions of copies sold. The wisdom suggested by the titles, though, could be related by any disabled person for nothing.

I conclude by quoting Mast (2010, p. 28) again:

> Power emerges in social interactions and affects social interactions in turn. The expression of power of the interaction partners and their perception of each other's power are interwoven in actual social interactions and determine how each individual feels, thinks, perceives, and acts.

For so long as professionals' understanding of disability remains rooted in individual model terms, their relationships with disabled service users will remain asymmetrically structured. Thinking of, speaking of, regarding and acting towards disability as abnormal deficit closes down possibilities for valuing impairment as a characteristic of human difference to be expected and respected on its own terms. Professionals need to learn to listen to what disabled service users have to say.

References

Abbott, P. and Meerabeau, L. (1998) 'Professions, Professionalism and the Caring Professions'. In Abbott, P. and Meerabeau, L. (Eds.) *The Sociology of the Caring Professions*. London: Routledge, pp. 1–19.

Albrecht, G. (1992) *The Disability Business: Rehabilitation in America*. London: Sage.

Barker, C. (2004) *Cultural Studies: Theory and Practice*. London: Sage.

Barnes, C. (1997) 'A Legacy of Oppression: A History of Disability in Western Culture'. In Barton, L. and Oliver, M. (Eds.) *Disability Studies: Past, Present and Future*. Leeds: The Disability Press.

Barnes, C. and Mercer, G. (2010) *Exploring Disability*. 2nd ed. Cambridge: Polity Press.

Beresford, P. (2014) 'Personalisation: From Solution to Problem?' In P. Beresford (Ed.) *Personalisation*. Bristol: Policy Press, pp. 1–26.

Borsay, A. (2002) 'History, Power and Identity'. In Barnes, C. Oliver, M. and Barton, L. (Eds.) *Disability Studies Today*. Cambridge: Polity Press.

Cameron, C. (2007) 'Whose problem? Disability narratives and available identities'. *Community Development Journal*, Vol. 42, No. 4 October, pp. 501–511.

Cameron, C. (2010) *Does Anybody Like Being Disabled? A Critical Exploration of Impairment, Identity, Media and Everyday Life in a Disabling Society*. PhD thesis. Queen Margaret University. http://etheses.qmu.ac.uk/258/1/258.pdf

Cameron, C. (2014a) 'The Social Model'. In Cameron, C. (Ed.) *Disability Studies: A Student's Guide*. London: Sage, pp. 137–140.

Cameron, C. (2014b) 'The Historical Construction of Disability'. In Cameron, C. (Ed.) *Disability Studies: A Student's Guide*. London: Sage, pp. 65–68.

Cameron, C. (2014c) 'Identity'. In Cameron, C. (Ed.) *Disability Studies: A Student's Guide*. London: Sage, pp. 72–74.

Cameron, C. (2014d) 'Normalcy'. In Cameron, C. (Ed.) *Disability Studies: A Student's Guide*. London: Sage, pp. 107–109.

Cameron, C. (2014e) 'Vulnerability'. In Cameron, C. (Ed.) *Disability Studies: A Student's Guide*. London: Sage, pp. 153–156.

Cameron, C. (2014f) 'Stereotypes'. In Cameron, C. (Ed.) *Disability Studies: A Student's Guide*. London: Sage, pp. 144–147.

Cameron, C. (2014g) 'The Affirmation Model'. In Cameron, C. (Ed.) *Disability Studies: A Student's Guide*. London: Sage, pp. 4–7.

Cameron, C. (2015a) 'Does Disability Studies Have Anything to Say to Music Therapy? And Would Music Therapy Listen if it Did?' *Voices: A World Forum on Music Therapy*, Vol. 16, No. 3.

Cameron, C. (2015b) 'Turning Experience into Theory: The Affirmation Model as a Tool for Critical Praxis'. *Social Work and Social Sciences Review*, Vol. 17, No. 3, pp. 108–121

Cameron, C. (2018) 'Social Policy and Disability'. In Beresford, P. and Carr, S. (Eds.) *Social Policy First Hand: An International Introduction to Participatory Social Welfare*. Bristol: Policy Press.

Cameron, C., Moore, M. and Nutt, A. (2019a) 'User Involvement and Identity: Disabled People Bringing Ourselves out of the Half-Shadows'. *Social Work and Social Sciences Review*, Vol. 19, No. 4

Cameron, C., Moore, M., Nutt, A. and Chambers, C. (2019b) 'Improving Understanding of Service-User Involvement and Identity: Collaborative Research Traversing Disability, Activism and the Academy', *Disability & Society*, DOI: 0.1080/09687599.2019.1632693

Chalari, A. (2017) *The Sociology of the Individual: Relating Self and Society*. London: Sage

Davis, L. (2013) 'Disability, Normality and Power'. In Davis, L. (Ed.) *The Disability Studies Reader*. 4th ed. London: Routledge, pp. 1–16.

Drake, R. (1999) *Understanding Disability Policies*. London: Macmillan.

Elder-Woodward, J. (2012) *Independent Living: The Frontier of Communication Welfare*. Lancaster: ESRC Seminar Series, Lancaster University.

Elias, N. (2001) *The Society of the Individual*. London: Continuum.

Emerson, R.M. (1962) 'Power Dependence Relations'. *American Sociological Review*, Vol. 27, No. 1, pp. 31–41.

Fine, M. (1994) 'Working the Hyphens: Reinventing Self and Other in Qualitative Research'. In Denzin, N. and Lincoln, Y. (Eds.) *Handbook of Qualitative Research*. London: Sage, pp. 70–82.

Forte, J.A. (2004) 'Symbolic Interactionism and Social Work: A Forgotten Legacy, Part 1'. *Families in Society*, Vol. 85, No. 3, pp. 391–400.

Fougeyrollas, P. and Beauregard, L. (2001) 'An Interactive Person Environment Social Creation'. In Albrecht, G.L., Seelman, K.D. and Bury, M. (Eds.) *Handbook of Disability Studies*. London: Sage, pp. 171–194.

French, S. (1994) 'The Disabled Role'. In French, S. (Ed.) *On Equal Terms: Working with Disabled People*. London: Butterworth-Heinemann.

Garabedian, F. (2014) 'Independent Living'. In Cameron, C. (Ed.) *Disability Studies: A Student's Guide*. London: Sage, pp. 81–84.

Gleeson, B. (1999) *Geographies of Disability*. London: Routledge.

GOV.UK (2019) *Definition of Disability under the Equality Act 2010* [Online] www.gov.uk/definition-of-disability-under-equality-act-2010 Accessed 05.07.19.

Hamilton, C. (2014) *How to Deal with Adversity*. London: Macmillan.

Hasler, F. (2004) 'Disability, Care and Controlling Services'. In Swain, J., French, S., Barnes, C. and Thomas, C. (Eds.) *Disabling Barriers: Enabling Environments*. London: Sage, pp. 226–232.

Heaton, T. (2014) 'Access'. In Cameron, C. (Ed.) *Disability Studies: A Student's Guide*. London: Sage, pp. 1–4.

Holdsworth, A. (1989) *Johnny Crescendo Revealed*. London: Self-Published.

Kroger, J. (2000) *Identity Development: Adolescence Through Adulthood*. London: Sage.

Mast, M.S. (2010) 'Interpersonal Behaviour and Social Perception in a Power Hierarchy: The Interpersonal Power and Behaviour Model'. *European Review of Social Psychology*, Vol. 21, No. 1, pp. 1–33.

McKnight, J. (2005) 'Professionalised Service and Disabling Help'. In Illich, I., Zola, I. K., McKnight, J., Caplan, J. and Shaiken, H. (Eds.) *Disabling Professions*. London: Marion Boyars, pp. 69–91.

Oliver, M. (1990) *The Politics of Disablement*. Basingstoke: Macmillan.

Oliver, M. (1996) *Understanding Disability: From Theory to Practice*. Basingstoke: Macmillan.

Oliver, M. and Barnes, C. (2012) *The New Politics of Disablement*. Basingstoke: Macmillan.

Priestley, M. (1997) 'Whose Research: A Personal Audit'. In Barnes, C. and Mercer, G. (Eds.) *Doing Disability Research*. Leeds: The Disability Press, pp. 88–107.

Pring, J. (2019) 'Breakthrough Lords Report Gives Boost to Campaign for Free Care'. July 4, 2019 [Online] www.disabilitynewsservice.com/breakthrough-lords-report-gives-boost-to-campaign-for-free-care/?fbclid=IwAR1mya0-7KgaQ9KH-MCOJ0q1P19soCnJy1rmHiJtI3cnLmwKnMOfEQv IiUY Accessed 08.07.19.

Quarmby, K. (2011) *Scapegoat: Why We Are Failing Disabled People*. London: Portobello Books.

Sandstrom, K.L., Martin, D.D. and Fine, G.A. (2010) *Symbols, Selves and Social Reality: A Symbolic Interactionist Approach to Social Psychology and Sociology*. New York: Oxford University Press, p. 158.

Schwalbe, M., Godwin, S., Holden, D., Schrock, D., Thompson, S. and Wolkomir, M. (2000) 'Generic Processes in the Reproduction of Inequality: An Interactionist Analysis'. *Social Forces*, Vol. 79, No. 2, December, pp. 419–452.

Shaping Our Lives (2017) *Improving Understanding of Service User Involvement and Identity* [Online] www.shapingourlives.org.uk/resources/our-resources/all-publications/improving-understanding-of-service-user-involvement-and-identity Accessed 28.06.19.

Shaping Our Lives/National Survivor User Network (2019) *The Future of User-Led Organisations* [Online] https://shapingourlives.us10.listmanage.com/track/click?u=d3e11cfe1dce72cdbc9c40bb4&id=06f803 ca02&e=eb761b4ad2 Accessed 04.07.19.

Stryker, S. (2002) *Symbolic Interactionism: A Social Structural Version.* Caldwell, NJ: The Blackburn Press.

Stryker, S. (2008) 'From Mead to a Structural Symbolic Interactionism and Beyond'. *Annual Review of Sociology*, Vol. 34, pp. 14–31.

Swain, J. and French, S. (2000) 'Towards an Affirmation Model'. *Disability and Society*, Vol. 15, No. 4, pp. 569–582

Swain, J., French, S. and Cameron, C. (2003) *Controversial Issues in a Disabling Society.* Maidenhead: Open University Press.

Thomas, C. (1999) *Female Forms: Experiencing and Understanding Disability.* Buckingham: Open University Press.

Titchkosky, T. and Michalko, R. (2014) 'Narrative'. In Cameron, C. (Ed.) *Disability Studies: A Student's Guide.* London: Sage, pp. 101–104.

Union of the Physically Impaired Against Segregation (1976) *Fundamental Principles of Disability.* London: UPIAS.

WCPT.ORG (2019) *The ICF: An Overview* [Online] www.wcpt.org/sites/wcpt.org/files/files/GH-ICF_overview_FINAL_for_WHO.pdf Accessed 12.07.19.

Wolfensberger, W. (1972) *The Principle of Normalisation in Human Services.* Toronto: National Institute on Mental Retardation.

Wolfensberger, W. (2000) 'A Brief Overview of Social Role Valorization'. *Mental Retardation*, Vol. 38, No. 2, April, pp. 105–123.

Wood, R. (1989) *Care of Disabled People* [Online] www.psi.org.uk/publications/archivepdfs/Disability%20 and%20social/WOOD.pdf Accessed 07.07.19.

World Health Organisation (1980) *International Classification of Impairments, Disabilities, and Handicaps A Manual of Classification Relating to the Consequences of Disease.* Geneva: World Health Organisation.

World Health Organisation (2019) *Health Topics: Disabilities* [Online] www.who.int/topics/disabilities/en/ fAccessed 14.07.19.

Wrightson, K. (2002) *Earthly Necessities: Economic Lives in Early Modern Britain, 1470–1750.* London: Penguin.

Young, I. M. (2011) *Justice and the Politics of Difference.* Princeton, NJ: Princeton University Press.

7

THE HOUSING CAMPAIGN – USER INVOLVEMENT IN ACTION

Brendan McKeever

Introduction

We can get immersed in discussions and debates on concepts. Maybe we spend our time analysing and scrutinising details that seem, and may be, so very important. But the reality is that often those most impacted by concepts have little or no idea themselves what all the fuss is about. If the truth is told, does it really matter?

User Involvement has become a major focus in health and social care, particularly in relation to professionals who work in social work and Allied Health Professionals. In the past twenty to thirty years, it has gradually influenced health and social care policy and planning as well as the education of health and social care professionals. There have been many academic articles written on the subject in some of the most influential journals.

However, twenty years ago, when such involvement seemed to be in its infancy, developments occurred that would dramatically change the lives of some users. User Involvement was not a concept for them; it was a way of life. This cannot be emphasised enough: the living experience and reality of users often is what we term "User Involvement".

The focus of this chapter is seeing and understanding User Involvement, primarily through the user perspective, and appreciating that how services are delivered is quite different from how they are received. Elsewhere, there are many opportunities to study the wider implications of User Involvement; these opportunities can help in a fuller appraisal of the personal approach to such involvement featured in this chapter.

Often-contested terms, such as users, service users, carers, survivors, victims, experts by experience etc., have several interpretations. In this chapter, when the term user is articulated, it refers to those who use services (primarily health, social care and housing) on behalf of themselves and/or their disabled children (often referred to as carers or parent carers, though many parents do not see themselves in this role; they are simply parents). In many instances, the term user will not be used at all; as already highlighted, it is not an everyday term used in these situations by those most impacted by service delivery. However, by implication, this is what is meant.

Furthermore, in this context, this is not about occasional access to service, an intermittent visit to a health professional; rather, it is an intense, ongoing relationship or involvement with a range of professionals, often on a regular basis over a period of time. This explanation of involvement can be and often is contested when claims are made that we are all users at some time or other; this is true, but in this chapter, the intensity of that involvement is paramount in understanding the user perspective in the particular experience highlighted below.

This is not a story, a journey or a particular narrative. It is about real-life experiences lived out day to day and daily by families of disabled children as well as the professionals in the voluntary and statutory sector who work with them. It is about learning: learning through life and interactions and learning from others. But, most of all, it is about resilience, not giving up, despite what you are told. It is about change.

The context

Back in 1998, when I was approached to become involved in a housing campaign, I had no idea what I was letting myself in for. My main concern at that time were the daily concerns that we faced as a family in relation to our son, who had been diagnosed a number of years previously with a life-threatening condition.

Issues and campaigns, to be honest, were not my priority, because as a family we were focused on our lives, our situation, not what was going on outside. However, helping to set up and work with an advocacy group of parents of disabled children – the Family Information Group – the previous year, in 1997, had begun to influence my thinking about stretching beyond our own particular circumstances. Although, I would stress, this was in its infancy.

But even at this early stage, the wider User Involvement agenda was not even on the horizon. Indeed, if truth be told, very few of us as parents saw ourselves as users; our main interest was each of our own children.

When I was approached by a researcher in England involved in the housing campaign – Homes Fit for Children – I was very surprised. I had worked with her on the provision of accessible information once before, but no mention had been made of this campaign, which started in 1997 in England. What surprised me was their issue related to adapted accessible housing provision for disabled children, an issue that we had frustratingly addressed for our son in the recent past without ever knowing there was a related campaign.

I was invited to participate, as were some other parents – a strategic decision by the members of the steering group that would eventually change everything as the seeds of what, in hindsight, became User Involvement were planted.

Although the issue around accessible housing and disabled children seemed quite complex, the main problem was that there was a Means Test on parents associated with the grants process, called the Disabled Facilities Grant. This Means Test, which is associated also with a number of other benefits, was preventing many families from accessing the grant for their disabled child. During the campaign, it was discovered that the calculations involved in this process did not reflect actual costs of living to the family. There was no acknowledgement (proved through research) of the additional costs associated with disability, and many parents just could not afford to pay the calculated contribution.

Even more frustrating was that although the disabled adult was assessed in the adult process of this grant, when applying for the housing provision for the disabled child, it was the child's parents who were assessed, not the child themselves. The result of all this was that many families pulled out of the grants process or went into debt to pay for the work, both of which negatively impacted the disabled child and their family. Eventually, because of this detrimental impact on families of disabled children, the core thrust of the campaign began to focus on "abolishing the Means Test" rather than making slight changes to it.

It probably is very difficult to take on board for those with no direct experience, but often the isolation and marginalisation associated with having a disabled child makes you feel, as a parent, that you and your family are the only people experiencing specific issues – and so you have to "fight" for your child. In hindsight, then, it is no real surprise that I did not know about this campaign; nevertheless, I had, and we had as a family, experienced all the turmoil and bureaucracy that went with this grants procedure.

Yet, the individual "fight" experienced by so many parents of disabled children and others in these circumstances inspired, encouraged and sustained them to carry on, even when there seemed no hope. This was not a campaign or an issue; it was their lives, their child, their quality of life, and no one would deny them this. "Something Inside So Strong" is a popular Labi Siffre song; the title conveys exactly how parents felt. They would not give up.

Involvement

The seeds of the thrust of the campaign were now unknowingly being planted. I agreed to be involved, even though travelling to England for meetings would be alien to me. We knew that we had to engage with more families of disabled children to help them see that this particular housing policy was not just peculiar to them; it involved other families, too. The "fight" was not just for one individual family, but for all relevant families. More professionals who worked with families and understood the issues needed to be involved.

Of course, many know that the classic foundation of User Involvement is partnership working. At that time, we as parents might not have known this, even as we actively tried to work with many groups and agencies – partnership working. Ironically, our partnership working emerged out of necessity; we did not have all the skills and knowledge to develop and run a campaign – a campaign that increasingly relied on the expertise and knowledge of the families themselves alongside those other "experts" who knew how to do the right thing.

The involvement of occupational therapists and housing officials was very encouraging in the rolling out of the campaign. Although encouraging from the outside, their professional status prevented them becoming involved in what was to become a political campaign around this issue, they did use their expertise and research skills to identify the problems associated with the then-current provision. Their research was done in a very open and transparent way and was authorised from very senior positions within their organisations. Their input on this issue was critical to creating the eventual change necessary; without them, this would not have been possible. The willingness of the professional Occupational Therapy Body (COTSSIH) to support their professionals in collating information, although unable to support the campaign directly because of professional restrictions, was also critical.

The campaign

Critical too was the building up of evidence, through independent research, of the impact of the Disabled Facilities Grant not just from the occupational therapists and housing officials. Evidence-based practice has become very important in recent years; back then, it may have taken different forms, but in reality, it was the same. The presenting of these findings, particularly to key organisations, again had a significant impact towards creating change. The individual experiences of families of disabled children were essential elements in these findings, particularly as previously there was not much recognition of their situation.

Researchers in England carried out studies and published their findings, supported in this by the Joseph Rowntree Foundation. A growing number of voluntary and other organisations, notably Contact a Family and HoDiS (National Disabled Persons Housing Service Ltd), engaged with the researchers and helped make contacts. I carried out research into families in England who had a child with a specific disabling condition. Support for the campaign was growing, even among those who initially felt this was not a priority issue. Alongside that support was the added bonus of the expertise they brought with them. If we did not know how to do something, we gradually got to know someone who could: a very powerful approach.

However, despite the growing campaign and, I must add, continued government resistance to us, we still strove to be focused on the user – or, rather, on the parent/family of disabled child. We continually tried to protect families from increasing interest from the press, which was requesting a family to come forward for interview. In some instances, families themselves agreed to go forward when they were approached, but any requests directed to us were discussed in detail with the family first, to ensure they knew the potential impact of being interviewed. If they still wanted to proceed, we would support them. We did not want the press to convey the "poor, poor me syndrome", as often happens.

It may seem disheartening, but as the campaign grew, I became less and less confident that we would succeed. This was a private thought; in public, we continued to grow the campaign through publicity, information and awareness-raising sessions with many voluntary and statutory bodies in Northern Ireland, England and Wales. The public did not know the issue, so we had to bring the issue to them, sometimes through road shows.

Why was I not confident? Sometimes part of me persisted in being that parent of a disabled child who did not believe we could ever make things happen. That no one would listen to us or believe our experience – that things were as they were for a reason and could not change. I recall in later years, while on a visit to Huddersfield on the campaign, a parent of a disabled child came up to me in tears and said nothing ever changes for parents; this is how I felt.

We had our significant key people in place, organising and coordinating activities for years: solid, dependable trustworthy help in England, Wales and Northern Ireland (Scottish legislation was different). Our families were on board throughout the UK – not thousands, but more than enough, and the heart of what we were at. Professional occupational therapists, housing officials, researchers, some key statutory agencies and voluntary groups and organisations were all helping us or directly on board, and Joseph Rowntree Foundation supported our information work . . . yet there was a missing link.

The regulation associated with the Means Test and the Disabled Facilities Grant had to be changed so that the Means Test would be abolished. This was a government policy in Northern Ireland, England and Wales. Both the Children's Law Centre and the Law Centre in Northern Ireland had identified that regulations could be changed in Northern Ireland; this was a major breakthrough, as full legislation did not need to be changed.

But all our efforts would come to nothing unless we had politicians on board. Of course, we knew this and from time to time we did receive individual support from certain politicians. The daunting task was that initially the widening of support at a political level had to be driven by parents. Did they not have enough to contend with already with family support, without us pulling them into the campaign?

Let me go back to the "fight". This was not a campaign for families; this was not a political platform. This was about life and their experience. This is what families do daily: they try and create the best quality of life for their disabled child, their other children (if any) and for themselves. Many families, including our son, had already been through the Disabled Facilities Grants process before the campaign and had either sorted something out or not. But we still got involved. This was the voice, our voice, emanating from the many frustrations, bureaucracy and painful experiences of the past. If you like, this was real User Involvement, without the frills and debates; this is what it was like. This was about families reaching out to those genuine and supportive professionals in the statutory and voluntary fields, saying we are in this together as we mutually respect each other.

The stage was set.

Politics

It is not the easiest task to engage politicians when you are not used to it. It is not something that many families would feel comfortable with or indeed would see as having any relevance to them in their lives. There are also restrictions for some professionals when it comes to engaging with politicians, and indeed, offering political support can be prohibited. The voluntary sector usually has no problems engaging with politicians when they support an issue that is relevant to them.

Each of our steering group (as we now called the key drivers) was responsible for engaging politicians in their own areas; for me, that included Northern Ireland. In Northern Ireland, our politicians are primarily working on the ground and do not seem as aloof as some other politicians, so I began at the local council area in Derry. Preliminary work with individual councillors paid off, and our local council supported the campaign. This was greeted with disbelief by fellow campaigners in England and Wales, who had never experienced support at this level before in the campaign. I was very proud of Derry City Council, as this also opened up opportunities with other politicians at different levels.

Sometimes contact was made in person with other NI politicians, explaining what the campaign was about. Phone calls were made and information and letters were sent. Sometimes other families met directly with politicians. In all cases, politicians were encouraged to discuss the issue with party colleagues. Such activities were repeated in England and Wales, with families playing a key part in all this with politicians and media coverage.

The message was getting across as television, radio and newspapers began to explore the issue in depth. In the final stages, in addition to MPs, Welsh assembly members, MLAs, local councillors and all the MPs in Northern Ireland supported the campaign. What an incredible change from when parents felt that this was a private issue in which no one was interested.

It seemed that the world had turned upside down. Those of us who had been driving this campaign for years were genuinely surprised at how far we had come through the support of many people. Bringing families into the centre of the campaign had been our greatest achievement. Even if this was all we had achieved, it was more than enough. Their voices were heard over this issue in a way that we never could have imagined or foreseen. Could we go another mile? I just was not sure; we had done everything that we could, but circumstances overtook us in Northern Ireland.

First breakthrough

On 4 December 2003, I helped to organise a housing conference with the Joseph Rowntree Foundation in my home town of Derry, Northern Ireland. The theme of the conference was "Where do the children live?" The conference was primarily targeted at occupational therapists, housing officials, a few parents of disabled children, civil servants and some staff from the Department of Social Development (under whose authority housing falls) and interested voluntary groups. Housing issues with regard to disabled children and their families were at the fore, and our campaign on the Means Test was not included as it did not seem to fit the agenda.

Within a few minutes of the conference starting, I stood dumbfounded on the stage after being invited up by the senior civil servant from the Department for Social Development to read a framed notice. Jokingly – I had never known him to joke before, in any of my encounters with him – he referred to me as "a pain in the backside" because of all the campaign letters I had sent and which he received. I naturally thought he was presenting me with "a pain in the backside" certificate. It was not.

My head spun and my eyes filled as I read the words on what I thought was a certificate but which in reality was a press release from the British Minister, John Spellar, responsible for the Department for Social Development. The Means Test in Northern Ireland would be abolished from February 2004. Just like that, with the applause ringing in my ears, our cameras recording the event and the senior civil servant emphasising the significance of this decision to the rest of the UK, I walked out of the room in total disbelief.

We had won. The voices of those most marginalised in our society had been listened to and acted upon. Northern Ireland had led the way in policy change. Usually it was the other way around, but common sense had prevailed.

Of course, everything exploded after that: press statements, interviews, requests for comments, acknowledgements. For days, I was not sure what was going on as England and Wales responded to this breaking news. We had no time to evaluate or review what had happened as expectations grew in England and Wales in response to our news in Northern Ireland. But I was glad my lead role was now over in Northern Ireland. I was exhausted; I had lived this issue for years. There was nothing more now I could do; I was glad I had played my part in Northern Ireland.

Back to basics

But life is not like that, of course; it never is. Months passed and frustration grew in England and Wales. One key politician, reportedly John Prescott, said it would never happen in England. Several of our key steering group members were called in to reviews of housing in England, thus absenting them from the campaign. I was asked to visit several parent and voluntary groups in England and Wales to help support the campaign.

The dramatic events on that Derry stage could never be repeated. Or could they? Remember, our group had filmed the housing conference; when I looked at the footage, I saw the moment of the announcement, a dramatic moment in life but also one captured on film. We got our local film company to edit this particular piece into a very short film clip, and then I took this with me to England and Wales.

When I showed the film, parents in particular could not believe it. For some of them, it was the first time that they had actually seen the power of parents and their influence in action. And, because I was there in person at the gatherings in England and Wales, as a parent, it had even more significance.

When studying User Involvement as a subject, we often disregard the emotions in such involvement, perhaps seeing it as diminishing objectivity and rational debate. Yet, emotion and feelings are an integral part of involvement and are essential in trying to make sense of the subject. Emotions and feelings have become a critical part of social work education and training as delivered in universities in Northern Ireland by users. It is how we handle such emotions and feelings that matter.

In England and Wales, I do not think I had ever experienced the raw emotions of parents in the manner I did in those visits. Their frustration over what had happened in Northern Ireland, coupled with the lack of response from government in England and Wales, was palpable. But instead of weakening the campaign, this emotion, these feelings, was the impetus to drive forward with the campaign, to keep working with others for change. To me, this is the reality of User Involvement, as the emotions and feelings of these parents emanated from their experience of caring for a disabled child and other family members. This experience and the emotions linked to it provided the stamina and resilience that these families needed. As I mentioned earlier, they just could not give up; it was their children that were important, not some big obscure policy.

No, the story did not continue; the journey did not move on. There was not another narrative working its way out. What happened was that the reality of the family's experience came to the fore, driven by the families and facilitated by their supporters. Lessons were learned from the Northern Ireland experience as well as from the experiences in England and Wales; there was no preciousness over geography here.

Even more voluntary groups became involved, and some of these had particular experience in lobbying and political activity. Their expertise facilitated the political activity needed in England and Wales to move the issue along. As all the different regions had been working in tandem up to this point, it was now only a matter of increasing the various activities, such as awareness raising (of the issue), political pressure, gathering support and utilising the skills on offer from the various supporters. If you did not know how to do something, you asked someone else who could. All this came together, first in Wales and then in England.

Victory Solidified

Just over a year after abolition in Northern Ireland, the Means Test in relation to parents of disabled children was abolished in Wales, on 30 September 2005; just a few months later, it was abolished in England, on 30 December 2005. Eight years of campaigning came to an end with victory for all those involved – but particularly for families of disabled children, who had never considered that one day their lives might be changed.

Lessons learned

As this campaign developed, people were literally learning as they went, as much of what went on was new and unfamiliar to them. However, it only has been in hindsight, with some distance from actual events, that I began to appreciate that more general lessons have been learned, lessons which could apply to almost anywhere in the world.

Disability knows no colour, no culture, no class, no belief system. Parents and families know this, and even in Northern Ireland, where religious differences have had and still do have negative impacts, they never surfaced during the campaign. The demographic breakdown and categories of children, young people, older people, ethnic minorities, male, female and sexual orientation were irrelevant and never had to be addressed, as participants and supporters came from many diverse backgrounds. Disability is a leveller; those who experienced this had no focus on any issues other than the impact of disability.

For the families of disabled children, dramatic learning occurred as many moved from a dependency culture over which they had little or no control to a position where they had a voice and that voice was listened to. Barriers had to be removed which over the years had seen these families treated as "special", different and often excluded from everyday activities. They learned to be assertive, to speak out, to appreciate that their lived experience was valued and valuable. They really had something to offer.

But, most of all, whether it was called User Involvement or not, they knew at the end of this campaign that they could make a difference to both their lives and the lives of others. User Involvement was shown to work, in their lives, in a way never thought possible. In the past, they had experienced determination, resilience, commitment and perseverance as they battled through accessing services, but this was different. The campaign had a real, beneficial outcome.

Representatives from statutory and voluntary organisations learned that real partnership working can make a difference, and many appreciated more fully the issues facing families of disabled children. Researchers were also encouraged that their meticulous work had contributed greatly to this change. Politicians, too, particularly in Northern Ireland (where party politics often alienate) learned that political engagement with people on the ground can make a real difference. A shared workload with different expertise can work in partnership and can create change for all involved. It was incredible.

Personal reflections

Homes Fit for Children impacted my life in a way I had never thought possible. I stood speechless on that stage in Derry when the announcement of the abolition of the Means Test was made public. Several years earlier, I had similarly sat in silence as the diagnosis of our son was given to us in a Belfast hospital. Times had changed since that day in Belfast and I had learned so much.

Most of the learning was through the direct experience of living with a disabled child and his family. Our family. It was not through reading, research, lectures or seminars but rather through life.

The formation of the Family Information Group was another step, as the group raised the "family view of disability" to whomever would listen, including university students in Northern Ireland. After the housing campaign settled, we now had a unique tool in the video of the announcement, a real concrete example of how User Involvement can work. There were many presentations to various voluntary and statutory groups after the housing campaign which were positively evaluated. The video constantly came out on top as the piece that had the most impact.

One presentation stands out for me personally. I was invited to the middle of County Donegal, just over the border in the Republic of Ireland. The venue was literally in the middle of nowhere. It was a Saturday and seldom did I work on a Saturday. The families of children who were being educated in the Irish language were having a working weekend away in Donegal. My theme was User Involvement and I showed the video as part of it. I could not have imagined the response as the participants unanimously applauded and welcomed the presentation; they got it from the start. Then it hit me: this group felt marginalised in their own particular way and understood fully what families of disabled children faced and what they had achieved. The message of this campaign certainly has a more universal message.

Evaluations were built into the presentations, and these were analysed afterwards. Most of the responses were very positive and any issues were addressed by me in response to any criticism. On other occasions, the facilitators of the events were asked to evaluate and then feed this through to me.

The outcome of this campaign became a central message in future presentations to a whole range of groups and organisations and has had a special place in my presentations to social work students in Northern Ireland.

Conclusion

This campaign is only part of the lives of families of disabled children. However, there were many barriers to overcome to get to this outcome. I have highlighted the barriers some families faced in relation to dependency and feeling downtrodden. However, there were wider barriers around perception, as many in the wider community believed that families of disabled children were well supported and provided for. The reality for many families is much different.

At a policy level in government, there were many who believed that no change in housing policy was possible, as the Means Test was associated with many other benefits and just could not be changed. Some people even believed that parents just wanted money to improve their homes.

Only when the reality of the family experience was introduced to the campaign did these barriers begin to disintegrate. The voices were heard.

But the campaign, and all we learned, was much more than the outcome. The underlying values of User Involvement evident in this campaign have more universal impact than simply a policy change. Trust in, openness and commitment to and respect and acknowledgement of human values were not just topics for discussion. They were thrashed out on the anvil of the campaign; they were real and evident throughout. Partnership and empowerment again were demonstrated daily as supporters struggled to get the message across that change was necessary.

In the midst of what could only be called a struggle, the dream of an accessible home and the quality of life it could offer drove all those who shared that dream to a level of commitment and perseverance that could never be imagined. User Involvement was the commitment to the disabled child and their family. Families just could not give up; it was their child, and no one else could fight for them. This was not a theoretical model.

In my work and life, I have seen User Involvement discussed, challenged and debated. But I have never seen such a concrete example of how it can work as I have seen through this campaign. I have seen it used as a tool in the education and awareness of a wide range of people, including students.

Earlier, I referred to the time of disempowerment in our lives when our son was diagnosed. Life then seemed so cruel, with no hope and no control. Years passed, and then, through the housing campaign, I realised I was empowered. There was hope, and life could be good because, as a parent, I was in control. Anyone who has an interest in User Involvement needs to hear these messages and hear them from users themselves. The challenge is: is anyone listening?

8

TALKING HEADS

Why asylum seeker parents are scared of social workers – mending the gaps between us

Nada Abdulla, Bini Araia, Helen Casey, Ibrahim Dialllo, Anna Makoni, Yvonne Mondiwa, Elaine Spencer, Luwam Tekeste

Introduction

'Mend the gap' is a model for the effective involvement of people who are at the receiving end of services, together with those who provide professional support. PowerUs is an international network of service users, students, academics, researchers and practitioners who use this model in education and practice (www.powerus.eu).

The aim of this approach is to promote an equal learning environment where people can share knowledge and experiences about their roles. Mend the gap courses have shown that when we identify 'gaps' between people, we open up a dialogue which challenges barriers and discrimination.

This chapter is about a mend the gap programme with single asylum seeker parents and social work students which was identified with the help of two local community organisations, Investing in People and Culture (IPC) and The Other Perspective CIC. These organisations exist to promote the social and economic inclusion and equal rights of marginalised communities, including refugees and asylum seekers in the North East region. It is the third gap-mending programme and took place in 2019, building on the work of the first programme in 2017 with adult refugees and asylum seeker groups and the second in 2018 with unaccompanied minors. The value of this approach to learning led to the establishment of 'mend the gap' as an educational model within the North East Social Work Alliance (NESWA) Teaching Partnership led by the Open University,

The programme was co-delivered by an Open University educator who is including the work and findings within a broader research project as a part time PhD student at Durham University.

Mend the gap programme

Fourteen parents took part in the programme, out of 60 single parents living in two hostels with children under 5 years old. Ten other participants included social work students, a qualified practitioner and an educator IPC (as introduced earlier) project manager. Key gaps were identified prior to the programme commencing by parents; it is a unique feature of the gap-mending approach for those in the most marginalised position to set the agenda instead of professionals. The gaps identified informed the themes for dialogue.

The main gaps identified were housing, finance, female genital mutilation, domestic violence, mental health, education and safeguarding – all contexts in which social workers have a role and influence yet lack a general cultural understanding. This was seen to be the main reasons why parents were not accessing the support they need.

This chapter was written over the eight-week period during which parents were participating in the gap-mending programme, to explore in more depth gaps around their strong negative feelings and reflect on how this could change through the programme. It has been written from the conversation which took place between four mothers, one father, a social work practitioner, a social work educator and an IPC project manager.

The starting point was agreement that everyone would least like to have a social worker coming to their home. The reasons for this were explored around the key theme of power. Parents described having a very clear perception in the community, shared widely among refugee asylum seeker parents, that even when struggling they would not want to see a social worker. They would rather struggle than put themselves in 'danger' of having their children removed.

Putting themselves forward to try to overcome these barriers with social workers and students, parents admitted that the first session where people came together was 'an eye opener' or, at least, 'not that bad'. People began to explore some of the mis-conceptions around the social work role. One woman had been contacted by a social worker to arrange a home visit; she decided that she would rather return to Syria than risk the social worker coming to her home, as she believed, to remove her son. This level of fear is very common. It is standard that a social worker will make contact with a Syrian family arriving in the UK to ensure they have the support they require, but this is not understood. The Syrian mother was terrified of losing her son from the moment she was contacted. Such mis-conceptions of the social work role come from the community, which believes that social workers hold the most power over them. If social workers were more immersed in the local community, building relations with BME organisations, they would be welcomed to come and meet with parents to explain their role. Social workers need to make time for this and be supported by their agencies.

Another example shared was of a parent who had left her children alone with the oldest child, aged 8, in charge of the youngest, age 2. When she returned from the local shop with her baby, she was met by a social worker and police officer in her home, who removed all three children. The distress that followed and the long delay with getting her children back could have been avoided had she understood that what was culturally acceptable in her home village in Africa was against the law in the UK. It is important that parents in the community are aware of safeguarding legislation to prevent problems.

Parents found that religious and cultural viewpoints are often dismissed during social work assessments, which results in them being viewed as bad parents. If social workers had better cultural understanding, assessments could be very different. Research conducted by Community Care supports this:

> Culturally competent practice can result in positive outcomes for service users, particularly in areas such as mental health, where cultural competence has been found to have had positive impact on service users from ethnic minority groups. This is due to workers being able to understand every aspect of the person's concerns, thereby enabling them propose interventions and care that are more likely to succeed.
>
> *(Thyer et al., 2010, in Community Care, 2018)*

Local authorities are seen by parents and organisations working to support the BME community to be institutionally racist due to a basic lack of awareness of cultural and religious importance. One mother described how upset she was that her social worker arranged her visits on 'her way home' on a Friday afternoon, presumably having the added bonus of an earlier finish. Fridays, 'Jumah', are the most important day of the week for Muslims to pray. Why is there not a standard sign in every social services office illuminating such facts to ensure that visits are not arranged on such days? Parents are unwilling to challenge anything the authorities do for fear that this will impact negatively on them. Parents feel powerless when it comes to appointments and making arrangements; a good practice message echoed across all professions is to ask the person receiving the service when would be good for them to meet. A starting point to empower parents would be to give options to meet, with information about the purpose of the meeting so that people do not feel terrified, like the Syrian mother, that they are coming to remove their children.

Involving men

Only one male parent joined the group; he explained how excluded men feel from conversations with social workers. He felt that the focus was always placed on the mother, as if men were in some way guilty of perpetrating something wrong. Where a family home is broken up i.e. where a child is removed, the father is asked to leave the home. Without any support, it is very easy for fathers to become depressed or destitute. This parent described one father's attempted suicide, stating that there is an unreported, growing number of asylum seeker fathers who have attempted to take their life and therefore a growing urgency to establish more support for men:

Men need to be involved in discussions affecting them and their families.

Female Genital Mutilation (FGM)

Another gap explored was about banning the practice of Female Genital Mutilation (FGM). Social workers need to be able to have these discussions with men as well as women. Since the law was introduced banning FGM in 2003, the first prosecution in the UK took place in 2019. FGM is a much-hidden, taboo subject which continues to be practiced in many cultures.

A recent report has highlighted how FGM is 'increasingly performed on UK babies' (BBC News, 2019). The findings highlighted how girls under the age of 3 not at nursery or school were hidden from authorities. The National FGM centre said there was 'anecdotal evidence from some communities that FGM laws can be circumnavigated by performing the procedure on girls at a very young age' (BBC news, 2019).

People in communities know that FGM is taking place; what they don't know is how to stop it.

The discussion points for mending gaps centred on how social workers raise the topic of FGM. It is important that practitioners have knowledge and cultural awareness of FGM and how girls and women can be protected. If someone is going away to a country where FGM is practiced, social workers can support them with having an emergency plan.

If it becomes suspected that a child may be taken abroad to undergo FGM, social workers and the police can intervene; it is not uncommon for people to be stopped at the airport. People know this, and therefore it becomes more hidden as people will be taken abroad without knowing why.

A scenario was discussed where someone wants to go abroad and arrives to discover a secret plan to take the child for FGM. What would you do? This opened up conversation about the importance of being prepared. Planning ahead should involve phone numbers for the foreign office or the local authority. It is important to have an escape route.

Accommodation

Housing was experienced as the biggest gap, creating lots of stress, cultural clashes and other problems which could lead to social work involvement.

There are approximately 600 asylum seekers in Middlesbrough (Asylum Seeker Statistics, 2018), three buildings of single mothers – approximately 30 women in each (two in Middlesbrough, one in Stockton) – with children under 11. Parents want their children to achieve more but would never seek help from social services.

Parents fear social workers and would not want their involvement at all.

As on parent stated:

If you don't have the language you cannot express your frustration. If you don't have status you have no choices.

This feeling of having no voice in processes was widely shared at the outset of joining mend the gap. Over the weeks, as people found their voices, they felt able to talk about their experiences; this helped to release their frustration. They also gained more information about their choices and their rights. The Immigration & Asylum Act 1999 (s95 & s4) entitles people to accommodation, whereby people could be dispersed anywhere. The provision clearly states this is on a 'no choice' basis. This message of 'no choice' is one parents heard over and over again. They said they had never heard any messages about their rights. G4S had a national contract with the government, and they subcontract to private landlords. Experiences were shared of unsatisfactory accommodation, families being forced to share, cultural clashes and tensions which were not at all addressed or supported by the landlord.

Parents reported that the landlord's employees enter the family's rooms at any time, unannounced, which feels intrusive and disrespectful. The feeling is that the landlords come to check up on them, catch them out and report them. The power the landlords had over them, to determine whether or not the family could stay in their accommodation, made them live in a permanent state of fear.

One mother explained that her son has to go to bed early as he is up for school the next morning, but she shares a flat with a mother with a toddler who stays up all night and sleeps during the day. They each have a bedroom – mother and child sharing – but the noise keeps her son awake so he is always tired for school.

Other parents described regular scenes where fights broke out due to insufficient space, especially the kitchen, which children witnessed. The police are called out regularly to deal with such disputes, but:

Nothing happens and nothing changes. No-one intervenes and helps.

Unsuitable accommodation arrangements put huge stress upon parents and children. We identified through the gap-mending programme that while it is a 'no choice' basis, this does not mean parents do not have any rights. Further, social workers are best placed to support parents with understanding and gaining their rights. Social workers are best placed to fight, to challenge, to mend these gaps by referring to housing policy which stipulates that 'people should receive fair treatment'. Clearly, when they do not this should be reported; as one parent summarised:

> Social workers need to find the right information and use their power to help those with no power.

The local provider housing policy is underpinned by the Home Office guidance on accommodation for asylum seekers (Gov.UK, 2019). This was a very timely conversation for our group, as the Home Office was about to review their guidance on accommodation as well as their guide to asylum seeker life in the UK. Hearing about our programme via the local migration support service, which was most supportive of mend the gap, we were contacted by the Home Office so that parents' experiences could inform their updated reports. Also, the decision had been taken to end the government's national contract with G4S, three years after they were exposed for making people highly vulnerable by painting the door of properties where asylum seekers are placed red (The Guardian, 2016).

The government's new contracts with a range of new providers provided an opportunity to end the local landlord contract and find a new local provider. Women's voices informed this process as conversations took place over who would take this on in the region. There is a saying in Eritrea:

> When the wolves are fighting the antelope escapes.

In this context, while landlords wrangled, parents got an even better deal as the Home Office was determined to ensure their situation improved. All parents have escaped the unsuitable, cramped housing conditions in which they had suffered so long and have been provided with single housing accommodation, one house – not room – per family.

This outcome demonstrates how the biggest gaps can be mended when people come together to share their lived experiences. Home Office guidance makes many positive efforts to ensure people access suitable accommodation, exercise their rights to fair treatment and have their complaints heard and resolved within reasonable time periods. Unfortunately, the reality for parents on our programme was very different to this. The Home Office listened to parents' experiences and new solutions were found. Mending gaps with policy makers is an essential way forward for improving outcomes for some of the most marginalised people in our society.

Messages for social work

> Whatever the perceived or actual challenges associated with cultural competence, social workers are required to acknowledge the importance of it in their engagement with service users and also recognise their professional commitment of 'respect for diversities' and promotion of social justice and human rights, themes which are embedded in the global definition of social work.
>
> *(Community Care, 2018)*

That is:

> Social work is a practice-based profession and an academic discipline that promotes social change and development, social cohesion, and the empowerment and liberation of people. Principles of social justice, human rights, collective responsibility and

respect for diversities are central to social work. Underpinned by theories of social work, social sciences, humanities and indigenous knowledge, social work engages people and structures to address life challenges and enhance wellbeing. The above definition may be amplified at national and/or regional levels.

(IFSW [International Federation of Social Workers], 2014)

One of the underpinning principles of this definition is that social workers advocate and uphold human rights, which are seen as the 'motivation and justification for social work'. This requires social workers to have an 'understanding of particular cultural values, beliefs and traditions' and 'via critical and reflective dialogue with members of the cultural group vis-à-vis broader human rights issues' (ibid.)

It is our view that the gap-mending approach is the way to achieve this global aim. People from the asylum seeker and refugee communities who have participated in mend the gap programmes have found out about their rights for the first time. Social work students and practitioners have developed their knowledge of human rights. Everyone has said they have a significantly improved cultural understanding, which has led to co-produced knowledge and learning. The poor image parents had of social workers at the beginning of the programme was changed in a matter of weeks. Parents stated that they no longer fear social workers now that they understand that the role of a social worker is to keep families together, be a support to them and fight for their rights.

Outcomes

This five-minute recorded evaluation demonstrates this:

https://vimeo.com/333943592/5bd335ecab

Unless students, lecturers and educators get out into the community to learn together with people, the barriers between people will remain.

One further outcome of the gap-mending programme has been the establishment of a drop-in, which is co-facilitated by a social worker and community project manager based at Investing in People and Culture. This ensures that parents from across the community can come to find out about how they can be better supported.

Conclusion

Final message from parents:

There is a lack of trust, an imbalance of power in communities. Social workers need to make links with community leaders and organisations. Parents, students, practitioners, educators and policy makers need to work together, sharing power and promoting rights in order to mend the gaps between us.

References

BBC news (2019) www.bbc.co.uk/news/uk-47076043 accessed 14/12/2019.
https://cityofsanctuary.org/2018/08/23/latest-asylum-statistics-to-june-2018/ accessed 14/12/2019.
www.gov.uk/government/publications/living-in-asylum-accommodation accessed 16/12/2019.

www.theguardian.com/business/2016/jan/26/g4s-jomast-bosses-admit-number-asylum-seeker-red-doors-too-high-select-committee accessed 14/12/2019.

www.ifsw.org/what-is-social-work/global-definition-of-social-work/ accessed 14/12/2019.

www.legislation.gov.uk/ukpga/1999/33/part/VI accessed 14/12/2019.

www.powerus.eu accessed 14/12/2019.

Thyer et al., 2010 in Community care, 2018: www.communitycare.co.uk/2018/10/24/tips-socialworkers-cultural-competence/ accessed 14/12/2019.

9

TALKING HEADS

Training for the non-disabled

Colin Cameron, Maggie Cameron and Colin Hambrook

Looking out of my office window, I see them. This year's first-year Nursing students doing their simulation exercises. It is their Practical 1 task. They have to 'find out' what it is like to lose one of the five senses. These are pretending to be blind. They are helping each other around the bit outside the library. I find this a bit depressing.

They have been told by their lecturers that this will help them understand better what it is like to be disabled. They have been told that disability is about what people cannot do as a result of impairment. They talk about disability as something 'wrong' with people. They talk about working with people 'who have disabilities'. Supposedly, spending half an hour blindfolded or using a wheelchair will teach them something about what it is like to 'have a disability'. It all involves a very medical model way of thinking.

In a few minutes, they will remove their blindfolds and feel a sense of relief that they can see again. They will make comments similar to those made by simulation exercise participants quoted by Valerie Brew-Parrish (2004):

> Trembling and shaking, I took my first steps blind. . . . I felt like I was in a small, dark room. . . . At the end of the day, I took off the blindfold. I was so grateful because so many people do not have the option of taking off the blindfold.

They will come away imagining that their experience has given them some insight into what life is like for people who have been blind since birth or who have long-term visual impairments. They will come away with the idea that blind people are primarily people in need of help. They will feel better able to share empathy, because now they have spent time similarly restricted.

It will be the same when the next lot of students get to ride in wheelchairs for half an hour. One minute they will be able to walk; the next minute, this ability will be 'snatched away'. They will spend half an hour navigating the inaccessible environment and then get out and reflect on the experience, thanking fortune that this is not really their fate. Their comments will again be similar to those collected by Brew-Parrish (2004):

> I briefly felt how it would feel to be wheelchair-bound for life. I couldn't keep the tears in my eyes.

The problem is that this isn't like disabled people's experiences. It doesn't give a real clue as to how disabled people relate to or feel about their impairments. Instead, it reinforces a personal tragedy view. It reflects non-disabled people's views of what it must be like to be disabled. Frankly, it is very unhelpful. As John Swain and Paul Lawrence (1994, p. 91) commented decades ago:

> Simulation exercises, by their very nature, focus on supposed difficulties, problems, inadequacies and inabilities of disabled people. They contribute to rather than challenge damaging stereotypes.

Critiquing simulation exercises that form a standard part of what is known as Disability Awareness Training (training about disability designed and usually delivered by non-disabled people, reflecting the assumptions of the non-disabled about disabled people), Swain and Lawrence (1994, p. 91) observe that these:

- provide false information about the situation of disabled people, who develop all kinds of strategies which cannot be simulated
- focus upon impairment rather than disability
- reinforce the view that disabled people, as a social group, are basically people in need of care and support
- have been rejected by disabled people

It is almost 50 years since disabled people first developed the social model, identifying disability as 'something imposed on top of our impairments by the way we are unnecessarily isolated and excluded from full participation in society' (UPIAS, 1976, p. 14). Within a social model view, disability is not something people *have*. Rather, people with impairments are *disabled* by society. Disability describes the unequal relationship experienced by people with impairments in a social world that has been organised without their inclusion in mind. Disability is created by inaccessible physical environments and within demeaning encounters where assumptions about inferiority and abnormality are made (Morris, 1991). People live with *impairment effects* (Thomas, 1999) and as individuals figure out countless ways of dealing with these in everyday life. What makes life difficult, however, is having to deal with misplaced reactions from those with whom we come into contact: condescension, tolerance rather than inclusion, sympathy predicated on the basis of our imagined suffering or wonderment at the 'inspirational' ways in which we simply get on with the ordinary tasks of daily living.

The personal accounts of disabled people refute the understanding of disability-that-can-only-be-experienced-as-loss perpetuated by simulation exercises. As Roshni, a blind woman from Glasgow, has remarked:

> I've yet to meet anybody who is a hundred per cent happy with who they are. . . . I don't necessarily think that because you're disabled you are extra unhappy with who you are . . . but equally I've yet to meet the person who's jumping up and down, celebrating that they've got dodgy eyesight . . . but, having said that, it's certainly not a cause for me to cry and weep and wring my hands and give up on the world . . . there are lots of things I'm not happy about. . . . I'm not happy about the fact that I've got dry rot in the next room and the ceiling needs replacing. . . . I think my visual impairment is on the same scale as that . . . life happens.
>
> *(Cameron, 2014:5)*

Or as Mary, a partially sighted woman from Portobello, has said:

> I don't think about my impairments in that sense. . . . I just think about myself as
> me . . . and feeling actually relatively quite okay . . . sometimes my impairment . . .
> my visual impairment . . . is inconvenient, but that's not because of my impairment
> but because signage is so small . . . stuff like that . . . those are the kind of things that
> make me angry . . . do they make me sob inconsolably into my pillow every night
> because I have a visual impairment? . . . no, absolutely not . . . do I choose to be any
> different in me? . . . well . . . only in the way we all wish we could be different about
> all sorts of things. . . . I wish I had nail extensions . . . all these kind of things . . . but
> do I fundamentally want to change myself . . . and wish my impairments away . . . no,
> I don't . . . to me, they're just part of me . . . they're an innate part of me.
>
> *(Cameron, 2010)*

Far from being a characteristic of life that can only be experienced negatively, many disabled
people have talked about the value to their lives that impairment has added. Reflecting on his
experiences of having lived with chronic depression, Brian, a psychiatric system survivor from
Brighton, has stated:

> I suppose I have an underlying kind of . . . erm . . . spiritual sense, that there is some
> reason . . . that . . . I don't know what it is, but it's . . . it's . . . there's something hap-
> pened that I'm being guided in some way that I'm living through experiences in order
> to . . . erm . . . learn something . . . and I think . . . it's about being honest about who
> you are.
>
> *(Cameron, 2010)*

Ben, an autistic man from Coventry, muses:

> Had things been different . . . I might have been a different person . . . but I wouldn't
> have been a better one.
>
> *(Cameron, 2010)*

Helen, a woman from Edinburgh labelled as having a personality disorder, asserts:

> It's hard to say I'd rather not have this illness because I don't know what I would be like
> without it . . . part of me thinks would I be a much more shallow, selfish, insensitive
> person . . . and I'd rather not be that person.
>
> *(Cameron, 2010)*

Jennie, a writer and journalist from Glasgow who has multiple physical impairments, contrasts
her situation favourably with that of the average Scots person. She is saying that she would
rather be who she is, as she is, than be someone else who perhaps did not have impairments but
did not share her enthusiasm for reading:

> It's just this whole pity thing . . . you know, you must be unhappy all the time . . .
> because of your terrible situation . . . well, you know . . . there are all kinds of ter-
> rible situations in life that I wouldn't be . . . I mean, for instance, the average person
> in Scotland now reads six books a year . . . it's hard for me to imagine being in that

situation (laughs) . . . and not being terribly unhappy with myself . . . obviously people are just different like that.

(Cameron, 2010)

The comments made here are illustrative of the claim made by John Swain and Sally French (2000) that, far from being necessarily tragic, living with impairment can be experienced as valuable, interesting and intrinsically satisfying. Swain and French's point does not deny there can be negative experiences resulting from impairment, but makes the point that this is not all that impairment is about. This is something simulation exercises can never, and will never, convey.

It is some 35 years since disabled people first developed Disability Equality Training (DET) (Gillespie-Sells and Campbell, 1991). In contrast with Disability Awareness Training, which seeks to 'improve attitudes' towards disabled people within a medical model framework, DET focuses on enabling participants

> to identify and address discriminatory forms of practice towards disabled people. Through training they will find ways to challenge the organisational behaviour which reinforces negative myths and values and which prevents disabled people from gaining equality and achieving full participation in society.
>
> *(Gillespie-Sells and Campbell, 1991)*

Rooted within the social model, and always delivered by disabled people, DET aims to 'challenge some of the common myths and false distinctions that relegate disabled people to the status of a discriminated-against minority' (Gillespie-Sells and Campbell, 1991). By creating different opportunities for critical reflection, DET involves a process through which participants are able to begin to understand the differences between individual (medical) and social model conceptions of disability. It equips participants 'with a working knowledge of disability which will enable them to recognise the discriminatory language and the visual images that help to perpetuate the inequality of disabled people' (Gillespie-Sells and Campbell, 1991). Practically oriented, DET sessions end with the formulation of 'an Action Plan of constructive changes which participants can make to their work situations and personal lives, and that will contribute to the gathering momentum for change in the social, economic, and political position of disabled people' (Gillespie-Sells and Campbell, 1991).

In my personal history, I have delivered more DET sessions for more organisations than I can recall. I am pleased to say that most people have got the point of it. It has changed some people's lives and transformed their work practices. Others have felt challenged and invigorated, but have returned to routines where institutionalised disablism is so much part of work culture that the social model will have been quickly forgotten. There have often been, as well, one or two within some groups who are resistant to change and who have dismissed DET as 'political correctness gone mad'.

Again, it is some 35 years since disabled people first developed DET. And yet, looking out of my office window, I see them again. This year's lot of first-year Nursing students doing their simulation exercises. Practical 1. No wonder I find this a bit depressing.

Maggie Cameron

I am a Deaf woman, a disabled professional. I devise and deliver Disability Equality Training (DET), basing the content upon the principles of DET as agreed by the Disabled Peoples' Movement. In short, I present the collective voice and view of disabled people, not the personal.

When training people, it is essential they understand that while you may have your own view on your own impairment/condition, you are not merely reflecting upon that. Rather, you are enabling them to work with disabled people across the board, irrespective of their specific impairment/condition. There are many purported DET options that may be seen to serve the purpose but actually only hinder understanding of inequality and prejudice by presenting information from a continued non-disabled perspective.

Due to this, training content in a DET session delivered from a disabled people's perspective usually covers: a discussion of the models of disability, language, cultural perception and barriers to equality as well examples from lived experience. It is typically concluded by developing a brief action for change plan. Of course, training may be tailored to meet specific requirements.

Often when commissioned to deliver DET, you have no idea of the participants' existing level of knowledge of disability issues, so determining and maintaining the appropriate pitch is an organic process. It can be difficult to know what to expect from the participants of a DET session. Much depends upon the brief, that is, what the commissioning organisation requires in terms of their aims and expected outcomes of the training. In many cases, the request merely states the need for staff to be trained in Disability Equality in order to meet legal requirements. It is then up to the trainer to determine upon which topics the emphasis should be laid and how best the expectations of the commissioning organisation and participants can be met.

I would like to focus here upon my experience of delivering DET sessions over the past few years. There are two in particular that I would like to discuss. These were different sessions for different organisations. One was for a Visitors Centre, training mainly frontline staff. That is to say, staff who are usually the first point of contact for visitors, disabled and non-disabled. The staff team was a varied group of a mixed age range who seemed keen to learn. My understanding of the brief was that the training would enable staff to develop a basic understanding of disability legislation and models of disability (specifically the social and medical models), and to become language confident.

The session at the Visitors Centre went well. The participants were engaged in the topics and contributed freely to the discussions. They seemed to enjoy the different activities, but it became increasingly clear that for some participants, at least, the training wasn't quite what they had anticipated. It was during the activity of effecting change through social model thinking that a comment was made to the effect that they had expected to learn what they could do to help disabled visitors, not explore their own attitudes towards disability. Further comments made it clear that, despite this, they thought the training useful.

I found it interesting that the participants, or at least some of them, had approached the training session with the idea of learning how to be more 'helpful'. The notion of helpfulness often seems prevalent in the minds of non-disabled people as a means of including disabled people. I would suggest, however, that more than a willingness to help is needed if we are to address both the overt and covert causes of discrimination and inequality that disabled people face.

On leaving the training session, I found to my dismay my car battery was dead. Some other drivers were extremely obliging and soon got the car going again. However, I remarked to a participant who was helping that apparently the car emitted a beep to alert drivers that their headlights were still on after the engine was switched off. But of course, I said,

> I can't hear it, it's a high-pitched beep, apparently, and I have no hearing at that level. It would be more useful if these alerts could come with a different register or a flashing light, for instance. I wouldn't then have to rely on other people to help me after the fact.

The participant appeared thoughtful and then remarked that she had never thought of that and commented that it must be frustrating for me having to rely upon other people in situations such as these. I think that at that moment, for her, the point of the training session came together.

To me, this reinforced the importance of DET which is underpinned by examples of lived experiences. It is our stories of everyday encounters with the barriers and prejudice which bring to life the need for change. It also helps people understand that in real terms the onus of change is not simply upon disabled people.

The other training session was to deliver to a group of health professionals, including health auxiliaries, who were responsible for transporting patients for hospital appointments and so on. This was a short session intended to give the participants an understanding of the models of disability, as mentioned above, as well as enabling them to become language confident and to explore disability etiquette and what was meant by reasonable adjustment in law. This group comprised significantly older participants than I had worked with before.

It was a difficult session from the outset. The participants were friendly and receptive to my comments and explanations about disability issues, but many would not, or perhaps could not, engage in the reflective thinking activities. It took considerable thought and adaptation on my part to keep the session moving forward. We were nearly through the programme and were just starting to explore the language confidence activity when I realised from comments made by participants that some of them had been expecting and wanting to be told what to think and say without engaging in any self-reflection.

It was the language activity which really highlighted this fact. The activity required participants, first individually and then as a group, to determine whether certain words from a prepared list could be considered offensive, inoffensive or neither. Usually participants really engage in this activity and seem to enjoy exchanging views and arguing their points to each other. On this occasion, the room remained remarkably silent and although one or two groups seemed engaged, the others remained quiet. When I went over to see what the problem was, a participant asked me what he should put. I again explained the purpose of the activity, finishing by suggesting that he didn't overthink the exercise, just put down what he thought. I added that we would discuss people's thoughts and reasons for their responses as a group, once everyone had had a chance to discuss it. His response was to say that he didn't know the correct terms and that was why he was attending the session, to find out what he should say. He seemed perplexed by the idea that discussion about language, terminology and its implications regarding people's perceptions of disabled people and resulting actions was warranted. He just wanted to be told what to say.

It would seem, then, that being told the perceived correct terminology was all that was needed for his expectations of the training to be met. This form of training could be considered to be little more than learning by rote, and I would suggest it is easy to forget an accepted term if you have not considered the reasoning and logic behind it. It is because reason and understanding are such key elements to effecting change in thinking that I believe that the best way to achieve it in a training situation is by offering participants the opportunity to explore, share, discuss and reflect upon their ideas and work practice.

Reflecting upon the delivery of DET over the years, I can recall the hostility I encountered from participants when I first started delivering training. Many participants disagreed vehemently with the view that qualified disabled people were best placed to deliver DET rather than non-disabled trainers. There were also assumptions that there was nothing new to learn as they already worked with disabled people and felt they knew what was best. This attitude was particularly noticeable from professionals who worked in the care industry. I recall one group of participants particularly, who worked for what was then known as the Department of Health and Social Security, remarking that they knew all about disability culture and didn't need to hear anything more. I was astonished by their comments. As far as I knew an exploration of Disability Art, which enables people to appreciate how disabled people think about their lived experiences and reflects a crucial part of disability culture, was only covered in sessions run by disabled trainers. It is to the detriment of DET, I feel, that this no longer the case. The fact that many sessions are now delivered by organisations run by non-disabled people, employing non-disabled trainers who frequently omit information regarding the social model of disability and have no lived experience of disability is, for me, a worrying trend.

Colin Hambrook

My life has been defined by Psychiatry and by the Disability Arts Movement that I grew into after getting involved with the London Disability Art Forum in the mid-1990s. I was a lad of 9 when a psychiatrist first came to my home to section my mother. He wanted his evidence and he took me into the bedroom my brother and I shared. He pulled up a chair, asked me to sit on my bed and proceeded to interrogate me about what my mother had been saying and to whom: 'I'm going to cure her', he promised, as if he could whistle a blessing from the stale air and turn back time and disassemble all of the confusion and pain and anguish and turn it into light. What he meant, of course, was that he was going to torture her to within an inch of her life for her 'religious mania' and keep enough of a breathing thread to be able to continue to torture her. To say I was frightened is an understatement. I was petrified by this arrogant, self-important man who demanded a betrayal from a child in order that he could wreak his revenge on a woman and her family, who he saw as easy pickings to vent his pathetic yearnings to exercise his power and privilege.

So, I told him some of the things my mother had been saying – her foolish rantings bedevilled by fear and confusion. She'd been shouting nonsense at our next-door neighbours, the Roses, and they had called the police, who in turn brought this man to our door. He took her away to Belmont Hospital – a gothic, Victorian asylum perched at the top of the hill beyond the edges of Sutton, Surrey – and he repeatedly plugged her brains into the electricity mains through a process euphemistically called Electro Convulsive Therapy.

When we went to visit her a few days later, her brains had been fried to the point that she could not remember her children. She didn't know who we were, and the mantle of guilt that descended took me down into hell itself. The earth opened on the gentle lawn outside the ward and I fell down through the earth to its molten centre. I literally felt something deep inside me crack open; I fell like Alice, except the world below that gripped me was dark, empty and barren. I was lost, alone, with nowhere to turn for any sense of the sense of what was happening to me, to our family or to any other of the souls trapped in the nonsensical tragic world of Psychiatry – where all these self-important, big ties pranced and strutted the Diagnostic and Sadistical Manual of Mental Disorders.

I became distracted and began to hear voices, telling me that I was a witch, that my mother was a witch and that we were to burn in hell. I sleep-walked through the days, doing the best I could to salvage some semblance of reality, emotionally bereft and empty.

My mother encouraged me to cry, to express the grief, and my younger sister held me. The family was torn to shreds, but we held together through a basic and primordial form of love that helped to transcend the fear: fear for our lives, a loss of identity and an ontological insecurity at the core of the consciousness we held together as a family.

On my 13th birthday, I incurred a brain injury that left me with short-term memory loss, violent mood swings and recurring hallucinations. 'Paint it all out', my mother advised, and it was art that saved my life. I developed a method of translating the voices and the dread into a series of watercolours that expressed what I was living through; it became a lifeline for putting an intangible inner turmoil into a concrete language. Being able to see what I was going through on paper, outside of myself, gave me an objectivity that, although it didn't stop the voices, did give me an external reference that allowed me to be able to not believe the auditory and visual hallucinations. With my mother's guidance, I found mantras that I could repeat in a way that gave me strength to put the hallucinations into abeyance and a determination that I wasn't going to allow myself to be further tortured by psychiatrists.

I had developed a language that I thought would be useful to others but was swiftly disillusioned when I left school to do an Art Foundation course. The tutors weren't interested or refused to take on board the value of my experience. I joined the Campaign Against Psychiatric Oppression, and we produced music and poetry gigs, pamphlets and a manifesto that challenged the authority of the psychiatric profession and the medicalisation of 'madness'. We saw mental distress as a result of our experience of being marginalised and oppressed, living in poor or difficult situations and being forced to do brain-damaging jobs in conditions that had no regard for health or safety.

It took me ten years to find Dartington College of Arts, which ran an art degree that understood the importance of art to the mechanics of society, where the social ramifications of art were valued and where I first began to learn about the practice of disabled artists like Frida Kahlo and Jo Spence. I was excited by the concept of art that was socially engaged, that challenged the medical model and its insistence on power remaining in the hands of an elite force of individuals living in an ivory tower, divorced from the experience of ordinary working-class people.

When in my twenties, I had made further attempts to advocate for my mother, who was living in a zombified state as a result of fortnightly injections of Largactyl. The idea of having the dosage slowly reduced to a point where she could find some quality of life seemed reasonable. It took me three years of writing letters and making phone calls to finally get to see her psychiatrist, Dr Norton. He saw my insistence as a confrontation. 'I have 600 patients under my care', he snorted. 'What makes you so important as to take up my time?' As if I were asking something unreasonable in putting my mother's request to him: as if he'd spent a second of his precious time considering how he was resigning her to a living hell. He said he had considered her request, but then used it as a way of punishing her further. He took her off the drug completely after enforced treatment over nearly two decades. In the backlash ensuing from the withdrawal of the neuroleptic drug, he then further increased the dosage. Largactyl inhibits the body's production of white blood cells, which made her immune system ineffective to the point she died of a coronary atheroma.

There was and is no outlet for challenging the abuses my family has suffered under the auspices of the psychiatric system. I was told repeatedly by 'professionals' I challenged that if the overdose of Largactyl hadn't killed her, she would have died as a result of the schizophrenia – as if schizophrenia were a proven fact; as if despite endless research programmes, the medical community had brought to the table a shred of evidence for a scientific basis for schizophrenia.

In response I dedicated my life to disability arts. I saw within disability arts individuals making work through visual art, performance and song – a resistance to the lies being perpetrated by the dominant medical perspective on our lives as disabled people. As an artist disabled by Psychiatry, I saw the work of other artists challenging the blatant abuse of the Hippocratic Oath, perpetrated particularly under the auspices of psychiatric intervention. If you research, there is a whole canon of literature relating the authors' stories of psychiatric abuse. Worldwide, there are passionate voices from individuals and groups challenging the vast hegemony that Psychiatry, the pharmaceutical industry and its zillion dollar power-base present.

Within the UK's Disability Arts Movement, you will find a rich source of artists and writers challenging the paradigm for misinformation and abuse that Psychiatry offers as a scientific understanding of madness and distress. Currently, the notion of 'stigma' is prevalent as a placebo to cover up the toxic core of the disabling effects of psychiatric practice. Artists like Dolly Sen, Bobby Baker, the vacuum cleaner, Vince Laws, John Hoggett, gobscure, Hamja Ahsan, Rachel Rowan Olive, Vici Wreford-Sinnott and the Mad Pride movement often use humour, with which we can arm ourselves in the struggle to assert our human right for respect and equality. Disability arts is the one place where protest continues to forge a community for mutual support and shared understanding in a world in which we find ourselves continually and irrevocably dismissed, marginalised and defeated.

Disability arts is the one place where we not only share our stories but also find a commonality of experience – within the social model of disability and its understanding of disability as representative of the barriers we face – in the struggle to challenge the powers that be and assert our demand that society learn to change for the better and desist from the medieval practices dressed up as Pharmacology that continue to oppress us.

Conclusion

It is clear from our statements that there are still important lessons that service providers and professionals need to learn. Disabled people have been saying these things for decades now, but we still find our perspectives and insights overlooked by those who think they know more about disability than we do. In closing, we would particularly emphasise that:

- Providers of education and training should avoid simulation exercises which reinforce medical model/personal tragedy model assumptions about disabled people.
- When organising training on disability, providers of education need to ensure that this is designed and delivered by disabled people and rooted in social model principles.
- Providers of education need to be critical of medicalising and pathologising labels that have been applied to disabled people, and should be reflective in terms of examining their own cultures and practices for institutionalised disablism.

References

Brew-Parrish, V. (2004) 'The Wrong Message – Still'. *Ragged Edge Online*. [Online] www.raggededgemag azine.com/focus/wrongmessage04.html Accessed 29.11.19.

Cameron, C. (2010) *Does Anybody Like Being Disabled? A Critical Exploration of Impairment, Identity, Media and Everyday Experience in a Disabling Society*. PhD thesis. Queen Margaret University, Edinburgh. [Online] https://eresearch.qmu.ac.uk/handle/20.500.12289/7340 Accessed 29.11.19.

Cameron, C. (2014) 'The Affirmation Model'. In Cameron, C. (Ed.) *Disability Studies: A Student's Guide*. London: Sage.

Gillespie-Sells, K. and Campbell, J. (1991) *Disability Equality Training Trainers Guide*. London: Central Council for Education and Training in Social Work [Online] https://disability-studies.leeds.ac.uk/wp-content/uploads/sites/40/library/Campbell-dis-equality-training.pdf Accessed 29.11.19.

Morris, J. (1991) *Pride Against Prejudice: Transforming Attitudes to Disability*. London: Women's Press.

Swain, J. and French, S. (2000) 'Towards an Affirmation Model'. *Disability and Society* 15(4) 569–582.

Swain, J. and Lawrence, P. (1994) 'Learning About Disability: Changing Attitudes or Challenging Understanding'. In French, S. (Ed.) *On Equal Terms: Working with Disabled People*. Oxford: Butterworth-Heinemann, pp. 87–103.

Thomas, C. (1999) *Female Forms: Experiencing and Understanding Disability*. Buckingham: Open University Press.

Union of the Physically Impaired Against Segregation (1976) *Fundamental Principles of Disability*. London: UPIAS.

SECTION 2

The state of service user involvement in human services involvement in education and research across the globe

10

A TSUNAMI OF LIVED EXPERIENCE

From regional Australia to global mental health activism

Joanne Newman, Rebecca Jury and Kathy Boxall

Introduction

This chapter is concerned with the involvement of mental health service users or survivors in social work education and research. In Australia, the terms 'lived experience', 'consumer' and 'activist' are more frequently used than 'service user'; however, recognising that we are writing for an international audience, we use all of these terms interchangeably. Our chapter discusses service user involvement in social work education and research on a small regional campus of Edith Cowan University in Bunbury, Western Australia. Bunbury is a two-hour drive south of Perth, the most isolated capital city in the world. It might be assumed, therefore, that this isolated context would place us at considerable disadvantage in relation to global developments in service user involvement in human services education and research. In this chapter, however, we argue that far from being disadvantaged by geographical location, Edith Cowan University's Social Work programme is powerfully connected to a global community of mental health activists and service users. We begin our chapter by discussing the regional university campus where we work and provide background information about our own connections to mental health and ways of understanding mental illness. We then go on to discuss user involvement in Australia and the first author's growing interest in mental health activism, which has been pivotal to our work together. The chapter then discusses our own work in the area of user involvement and some of the challenges we have encountered. Finally, we conclude by arguing for the establishment of place for the experiential knowledges of mental health service users within user involvement in higher education.

Working in a regional area

The three of us work on the Bachelor of Social Work course at Edith Cowan University's South West campus. Areas of Australia are categorised according to their remoteness and access to services and Bunbury, where the campus is situated, is regarded as 'Inner Regional' (ABS, 2018a), an area where geographic distance may result in restricted access to some services. It might be expected, therefore, that global higher education developments would be slow to impact on a small regional campus in Western Australia; however, the development of a globally connected internet, combined with the Australian government's (albeit limited) investment in a National Broadband Network, means that a view of regional Australian life as isolated from global flux can no longer be sustained. This applies as much to the work and interests of people outside the academy, including those who are service users, as it does to academic scholarship and research. We have not, therefore, limited discussion in this chapter to our local context in regional Australia, but have focussed instead on connection between the regional campus on which we work and a global community of mental health activists and service users. Much of that connection is due to the commitment of the first author, Joanne Newman, to challenging damaging stereotypes of mental health and illness through social media activism, including in her role as moderator for the *Drop the Disorder!* Facebook group, which has more than 8,600 members internationally.

All three authors also have a personal interest in mental health, as we explain below.

Joanne

I'm Joanne. I have voices. I have voices because of trauma. Trauma has been very present in my life – I experienced sexual abuse at ages 3 and 11, and sexual assault at 15. I also had learning difficulties at school, and when my family relocated from Geraldton to Perth (both in Western Australia), I was bullied every single day at my new primary school. Eventually, I was excluded from everyday activities. At high school, I experienced more of the same. Later, I met my now former partner, disclosed trauma and was believed. I then had years of re-traumatising therapy before meeting my current therapist, who inspired me to learn more about the Hearing Voices movement. The internet and social media have enabled me to connect with a worldwide community of mental health services users/survivors and make sense of my own experiences. Today, I have four voices. I think of them as a cheer squad who guide, support and protect me; they look out for me and give me some really great tips (especially when I'm writing poetry). I am awakening to life.

Rebecca

I am a social worker and an academic. My key area of focus for teaching and research is service user involvement in social work practice, policy, research and education. I have been interested in service user expertise and knowledges for many years. This interest stemmed from my observations of a family member's resistance to traditional medical approaches to 'treating' mental health issues and alternate, self-led approaches to maintaining wellbeing.

Kathy

I'm a survivor of the British psychiatric system. In my early twenties, my life was dominated by psychiatry and I was repeatedly told that I needed to accept that I was mentally ill (and would be for the rest of my life) and let go of any future plans or aspirations. Twenty years after my last contact with the psychiatric system, I was awarded a PhD for a thesis which explored service users' knowledges; and ten years later, I came to Australia to take up a post as Professor of Social Work and Disability Studies at Edith Cowan University in Bunbury, Western Australia.

Understandings of mental illness

There are multiple ways of understanding mental and emotional distress (Rogers and Pilgrim, 2014; Horwitz, 2013; Deacon, 2013). Biomedical approaches are based on a scientific understanding of the human body as a biological or physiological system which, if diseased, can be subjected to biomedical diagnosis and cure. The biomedical model is dominant in Western societies and has a strong foundation in physical medicine; applying this model to mental health involves understanding mental illness as located in the brain and administering pharmacological treatments (medications) to ameliorate brain-based disorders or disease (Whitaker and Cosgrove, 2015). A key difference between physical and mental health, however, is that there are no biomedical markers to support the diagnosis and treatment of mental illness – no blood tests or brain scans that can reliably diagnose mental illness or confirm its successful treatment or cure (Deacon, 2013; Whitaker and Cosgrove, 2015). Despite this, biomedical understandings of mental and emotional distress continue to dominate – something which the United Nations Human Rights Council has recently raised as a concern (UN, 2017, p. 4).

There are also a number of social approaches to understanding mental and emotional distress. Some of these accept mental illness as a given and explore social causes for its development in individuals. Others question the concept of mental illness itself by exploring ways in which our society produces so-called mental illness through social processes of identification, diagnosis and treatment (Rogers and Pilgrim, 2014; Horwitz, 2013). This latter social constructionist approach fits well with many mental health service users' own understandings of their experiences of mental health services. It is important to point out, however, that developing an understanding which runs counter to the dominant biomedical view of mental illness is not something that can easily be achieved or sustained as a lone mental health service user. It was coming together in activist groups, where recipients and survivors of mental health services shared their own experiences, that enabled the development of survivors' own understandings of mental and emotional distress (for example, Chamberlin, 1988; O'Hagan, 1993; Pembroke, 1994; Campbell, 2005). More recently, mental health consumers, service users, survivors and activists have come together via the internet and social media groups, where shared experiences and understandings can be validated from a distance.

User involvement in Australia

In Australia, *The Roadmap for National Mental Health Reform 2012–2022* (COAG, 2012) states that 'policy should be guided by, and respond to, people's lived experience' (COAG, 2012, p. 3). Brenda Happell and colleagues (2015) argue that this requirement for service user involvement should also extend to professional education. Nurse education in Australia has a growing track record of involving mental health service users, but there is less evidence of user involvement in social work education (Happell et al., 2014). One development of particular note is the Service User Academic Symposium, which has been held annually in Australia or New Zealand since 2011. The organisers make it clear that the symposium is open to 'anyone involved with, interested in, or aspiring to create co-produced and/or service user-led projects or programmes in mental health and addiction' (SUAS, 2018, n.p.). However, the greater involvement of mental health service users in nurse education in Australia, as opposed to social work education (Happell et al., 2015), appears to be mirrored in support for this symposium. While it is difficult to say why there is less evidence of user involvement in social work, one possible explanation may be the lack of a clear mandate for service user involvement in social work education in Australia.

The Australian Association of Social Workers (AASW) is responsible for accrediting social work programmes and publishes the Australian Social Work Education and Accreditation Standards (ASWEAS). The current edition of the ASWEAS (AASW, 2015) was published by the AASW in 2012 and revised in 2015; a series of guidelines (published in 2012) accompany this version of the ASWEAS. Guideline 1.1 outlines the essential core curriculum content which prepares social workers 'to identify and respond appropriately to clients with mental health problems' (AASW, 2012, p. 4). This emphasises respect for mental health service users and a commitment to 'mutuality, especially with clients and their family and friends' (AASW, 2012, p. 4), but does not require higher education providers to involve service users in social work education. It also has a strong focus on knowledge from within the dominant biomedical paradigm, rather than from people on the receiving end of mental health services. For example, Guideline 1.1 recommends that students are taught the following:

> A basic grasp of a psychiatric diagnostic framework, including differentiating between psychotic and non-psychotic conditions, and an introductory knowledge of how a client might present with behaviours characteristic of common mental health problems such as anxiety or depression, and also the less common, including bipolar disorder, schizophrenia, personality disorders, eating disorders, and post-traumatic stress disorder.
>
> *(AASW, 2012, p. 5)*

In August 2017, the AASW published a revised edition of the ASWEAS document. This advised that social work students should be supported to develop critical awareness of 'the issues inherent in using deficit models' and the 'medicalisation of personal and social problems' (AASW, 2017, p. 19). The inclusion of these critical approaches was a considerable improvement on the standards published in 2015, but the revised ASWEAS failed to provide any clear direction on service user involvement in Australian social work education. In February 2018, following representation from the Australian Council of Heads of Schools of Social Work, the AASW withdrew the 2017 ASWEAS, pending further amendment. The version of the standards currently in place, therefore, is the revised 2012 ASWEAS (AASW, 2015) which, as explained above, does not require higher education providers to involve service users in their social work courses.

Elsewhere, accreditation standards and regulating bodies play an important role in encouraging and supporting lived experience involvement in social work education. For example, in the United Kingdom, there has been a requirement for service user involvement in social work education since 2003 (DH, 2002), and the Health and Care Professions Council, which currently regulates social work education in the UK, has extended this requirement to all of the professional education courses it regulates (HCPC, 2014). The Global Standards for the Education and Training of the Social Work Profession (IASSW/IFSW, 2004) also advocate the involvement of service users in the planning and delivery of social work education; McNabb and Connolly (2017) argue for a strengthening of service user involvement in social work education in Australia and New Zealand, in line with these Global Standards. There is no guarantee that regulated involvement will be meaningful involvement, but accreditation standards and regulation do at least send a clear message to higher education providers regarding the contribution that people with lived experience can make to professional education. Without such regulation, 'lived experience involvement in Australian social work education seldom extends beyond guest lecturing', and there is little or no investment in capacity building for those service users who are involved (Dorozenko et al., 2016, p. 905).

Dorozenko et al. (2016) highlight a range of barriers to the involvement of people with lived experience in higher education, including pathologising epistemologies and competency-reducing understandings of mental health service users. They also discuss the Valuing Lived Experience Project (VLEP), which aims to address these barriers and to embed lived experience in social work education at Curtin University in Perth, Western Australia. With the exception of this work being undertaken at Curtin University, we are not aware of any other projects which support the capacity building and involvement of mental health service users in social work education in Australia. It is against this backdrop that we discuss the work we have been doing together at Edith Cowan University's South West Campus in Bunbury, Western Australia. We begin by discussing Joanne's perspective on user involvement.

Joanne's perspective

Joanne's participation is pivotal to the user involvement activities we describe in this chapter. The understandings Joanne has of her experiences of voice hearing form part of the knowledge that is taught to students studying the Social Work and Mental Health unit. As Joanne explains, she developed these understandings many years ago:

> I think I'd already found my own understanding way back even when I was first in hospital and I came to this thought, 'Well maybe this is all happening because at the age of 15 something happened.' When I tried to tell the psychiatrists they said, 'Oh perhaps you did something,' and I shut up because I felt I was being blamed. Way back then, I came to this understanding that maybe this is all happening to me because this happened when I was 15, and because I was bullied at school. I started to think about it then. So that's 30 something years ago.
>
> *(Newman et al., 2019)*

We are very aware of concerns about tokenism in service user involvement, where isolated service users may be invited to tell their individual story in contexts where support for biomedical approaches may leave little or no room for their own understandings (Beresford and Boxall, 2012; Costa, 2014; Byrne et al., 2016). But Joanne does not come to Edith Cowan University as an isolated service user; she is connected – via the internet – to a worldwide community of mental health service users and activists. This is particularly important in a regional area which does not have a vibrant mental health consumer movement. Joanne's understanding of her voices has been strengthened by learning from other mental health service users and survivors and their allies about the Hearing Voices approach and connections between trauma and voice hearing (Longden, 2010; Corstens et al., 2014; Longden et al., 2012). As Joanne explains below, much of this learning has occurred via social media and the internet.

Joanne: Before I got involved in the ECU social work course, I knew nothing about people coming to talk to social work students in universities – absolutely nothing! My therapist, Julie, had told me about the Hearing Voices movement which started in the 1980s (see Corstens et al., 2014). I'd done the Hearing Voices training but I only knew about the history behind the Hearing Voices stuff; I didn't know about activism, or the history behind activism.

I wanted to start a Hearing Voices group in Busselton with Lanie Pianta and I started reading. I read a whole load of books like *Models of Madness* (Read and Dillon, 2013), lots of articles and stuff about people like Eleanor Longdon, Jacqui Dillon and

Ron Coleman. I wanted to learn everything! I read Judith Herman's (2015) *Trauma and Recovery* and I really, really, really could relate to her ideas about survivor mission. I'd learnt about the Hearing Voices approach and it became a bit of mission, I guess, for me to tell everyone else about it, because for me it made sense in so many ways. I gave a talk to LAMP (an organisation of mental health service users and their parents and carers) in Busselton, and I got really good feedback from them and then Lanie emailed Rebecca and suggested I come and talk to the social work students at ECU, and I came along!

At first, I got a lot of resources from Lyn Mahboub at Curtin University and she supplied me with copies of papers, but everything else I've learnt has been from the internet and social media – it's amazing what you can learn from social media! I joined the Facebook page for *Intervoice – The International Hearing Voices Movement* and I started writing a few comments myself. I also contacted Rachel Waddingham (moderator for *Intervoice*) when people made comments that made me feel uncomfortable. Rachel was based in the UK, but she had a connection with Western Australia, and we started exchanging personal messages. When the *Drop the Disorder!* Facebook page was set up in 2016, Rachel put my name forward to be a moderator and I've been doing it ever since.

When I think about all the people I know from social media, they're not just Joe Blow from Bunbury, they're worldwide leaders! I'm friends with people like Darby Penney and Tina Minkowitz, who are really big in the US. And I see things that are put out by Jessica Eaton, who's almost finished her PhD in psychology in the UK. And Professor John Read, he's always publishing research he's done on *Drop the Disorder!* – it's amazing the information that's available. I get a first-hand look at articles that people have written, including Tina Minkowitz; she publishes quite a lot of stuff and puts it on Facebook, so I would say if it weren't for social media, I would be a long way behind. I wouldn't know half the stuff I know now – it's been like a tsunami, a tsunami of lived experience!

I can't get inroads into mental health services in Western Australia, because they're not interested in what I have to say, but worldwide I can! And I'm working at ECU as a Lived Experience Educator, teaching on a social work course. I always think it's amazing that this small campus has taken me on, because I don't know of anyone else who's been through services and doesn't have a degree who's teaching at a university. There are other people with lived experience of mental health services working in Australian universities – people like Lyn Mahboub at Curtin University, and people in the Eastern states like Ann Tullgren and Louise Byrne, but they all have qualifications or degrees.

We now go on to discuss Joanne's involvement in mental health teaching and research at Edith Cowan University's South West Campus.

Service user involvement at ECU

Rebecca has coordinated the Social Work and Mental Health unit on the Bachelor of Social Work course since 2011. From the outset, she invited people with lived experience to contribute to teaching the unit. Prior to working for ECU, Rebecca had been employed by the South West Aboriginal Medical Service (SWAMS), and drew on her networks from SWAMS to identify potential speakers. Aboriginal people's perspectives around mental health can be very different to dominant Western perspectives. For example, people may experience spirits and have stories of healing which, while totally accepted at SWAMS, may be discouraged by other mental health professionals. Rebecca felt it was important for social work students to hear these stories from Aboriginal people themselves. She also invited a range of other speakers with lived experience of mental and emotional distress to contribute to teaching, and in 2015, Joanne came to talk to the class. As soon as she heard her presentation, Rebecca wanted Joanne to co-teach the whole of the mental health unit, but there was no funding available to do this. Around the same time, however, funds were made available for short-term projects at ECU, and Rebecca applied for, and received, funding to develop a mental health learning resource.

Kathy had produced teaching materials with service users in the UK (for example, Boxall et al., 2004; Warren and Boxall, 2009; Boxall et al., 2009) and was mindful of the importance of payment for service users, respect for their perspectives and knowledges and negotiation of ownership of the resources produced (Branfield et al., 2006, 2007). After discussion between Joanne, Kathy and Rebecca, it was decided that the learning resource would take the form of a video film, which portrays Joanne's understanding of having, or hearing, voices. Using some of the funding received, Joanne was employed to work with Rebecca and Kathy to plan production of the learning resource and to decide which film company should be hired to professionally produce the resource under her direction. Joanne's therapist, Julie Dickinson, was also involved in planning part of the resource and had a key role in one of the scenes. (For discussion of how the resource was produced, please see Newman et al., 2019.) When the learning resource is viewed as a whole, Joanne's understanding of her voices and the place they have in her life is revealed through the different scenes of the film, each of which can be viewed separately and incorporated into face-to-face or online teaching. Joanne has ownership of the final resource and has chosen to make it freely available on YouTube for others to use (see www. youtube.com/watch?v=3Z88xtFc9j0&t=308s).

Once the learning resource was completed, we worked on a research project where we showed two scenes from the resource to a small group of first-year students who had not received any prior mental health teaching on the social work course. At the beginning of the research session, participants were asked to complete a preliminary self-answer questionnaire which asked about their understandings of mental illness. On analysis, all of these preliminary responses were found to be aligned with dominant biomedical approaches. After viewing part of the resource, participants were asked if anything during the research session had confirmed or changed their prior views about mental illness, and we found that their understandings of mental illness had changed. For example:

> It is new for me to consider the idea that people might want to keep their voices but after what Jo shares in the movie, it seems perfectly reasonable to me that a person (Jo, in this case) would be determined to see her voices as an effect of trauma, not as a symptom of mental illness.
>
> *(Student 05, Newman et al., 2019)*

Joanne and Rebecca now use the learning resource regularly in teaching with both on campus and online social work students.

As explained earlier, Rebecca was keen to involve Joanne in the whole of the Social Work and Mental Health unit, but there was insufficient funding available to do this. Nevertheless, they have continued to work together since 2015, with Joanne being paid to co-teach as much as possible. This was not ideal, but they felt it was important to go ahead and do whatever they could, and also include other mental health service users in teaching the unit.

Rebecca: Something that comes up for me time and time again in all of this is that service user involvement in social work education in Australia only seems to happen because of people's willingness to carry the risk and just take a chance. But some people kind of baulk at that because there might be barriers around paying people, which they're not willing to challenge – or they're feeling so constricted that they're just not willing to push the envelope. I don't think we've done anything special here at ECU, just looked for opportunities to do what we can. What you have to do is to make a place for user involvement – you have to prove that it's what needs to happen. This is going to be the first year [2019] that our line manager is going to fully fund two people [Rebecca and Joanne] to co-teach the Social Work and Mental Health unit. So, I think there are things that have to be done beforehand, you have to prove that someone belongs here first before they have a place, and that's not fair.

In addition to our user involvement in teaching and research, we have also presented at conferences and seminars and started to write about the work we have been doing together, linking it to the international development of Mad Studies (Newman et al., 2019). Mad Studies builds on the work of early survivor activists to explore alternatives to biomedical understandings of mental and emotional distress and aims to legitimise mental health service users' experiential knowledges within and beyond the academy (Ingram, 2016; LeFrancois et al., 2013, 2016; Beresford and Russo, 2016).

Challenges

We are aware that what we are doing is fundamentally challenging of dominant biomedical approaches to mental and emotional distress. It would be surprising, therefore, if we did not come across some resistance to our work. When teaching or presenting at conferences, we have found that many people are receptive to the approaches we present, but some students and audience members have challenged our understandings of mental and emotional distress, arguing in favour of dominant mainstream biomedical approaches. In 2017–18, 'one in five (20.1%) or 4.8 million Australians had a mental or behavioural condition' (ABS, 2018b). It is likely, therefore, that any classroom or conference room will include people who have themselves received mental health treatment. For some of these people, considering alternatives to biomedical concepts of diagnosis and treatment may be difficult.

Rebecca: We try and say to students that it doesn't matter what the diagnosis is, that's not what's important. But sometimes we have students in the class who have a mental health diagnosis themselves. What we say is if the diagnosis is useful to you, that's fine – we definitely don't say get rid of your diagnosis and chuck all your medication away!

Social work and mental health professionals who have many years' experience of working within the dominant biomedical model may also be reluctant to consider alternatives. This came up at a conference recently where we were talking about the learning resource film mentioned earlier in this chapter.

Kathy: We'd just shown two scenes from the film, when two members of the audience asked if we thought what we were doing was dangerous. I was a bit confused at first but then they started talking about risk, and the risk that viewing the film could lead mentally ill people to stop taking their medication which, they felt, could be dangerous.

The dominance of the biomedical approach is such that there will be few members of the public who will not be aware of medication treatment for people who hear voices.

Joanne: A question the students often ask me is, 'Are you taking medication, Jo?' When I say, 'No, I haven't done for years', that actually really surprises them.

Notions of the 'dangerousness' of mental health services users, especially those who stop taking medication, are also prevalent (Jorm et al., 2012). Large and Ryan (2012) argue that 'dangerousness' should be understood as component of 'sanism', a form of prejudice against mental health service users, which needs to be tackled in the same ways as sexism, ageism or racism. The vast majority of people with mental health diagnoses do not engage in violent behaviours and are more likely than members of the general population to be victims rather than perpetrators of homicide (Rodway et al., 2014). There are also serious adverse effects associated with long-term use of psychiatric medication, including irreversible physical impairments and premature death (Gøtzsche et al., 2015; Dorozenko and Martin, 2017; Roughead et al., 2017). In addition, there are concerns about systemic violence in Australia's mental health system (Ross, 2018), and the Australian Bureau of Statistics reported that the mortality rate (all causes) of people who accessed mental health-related treatments in 2011 was almost twice (1.9 times) that of the general population (ABS, 2017). Clearly, there is important work to be undertaken in countering sanism. Sapey and Bullimore (2013) argue that social work education has an important role to play in preparing future social work professionals for this challenge.

Conclusion

This chapter has discussed service user involvement in social work education and research at Edith Cowan University's South West campus and the pivotal role of Joanne Newman in connecting work on our campus to global mental health activism. As with many other universities, we have encountered institutional barriers to service user involvement, and a lack of clear direction on such involvement from the accrediting body for social work education in Australia. We have demonstrated, however, that it is possible to make headway through these barriers and to establish a place for service user involvement on our regional university campus. Our chapter has also highlighted the challenges inherent in user involvement initiatives which seek to counter dominant biomedical views of mental illness. A more urgent problem, therefore, is the establishment of place for the experiential knowledges and understandings of mental health service users within user involvement in higher education. Mad Studies and global mental health activism offer exciting possibilities for the development of these experiential knowledges, but without a clearly defined place for service users' knowledges, mental health user involvement in higher education risks being overshadowed by dominant biomedical approaches.

References

AASW (2012). *Australian Social Work Education and Accreditation Standards (ASWEAS) 2012 Guideline 1.1: Guidance on Essential Core Curriculum Content*, Canberra, Australian Association for Social Workers.

AASW (2015). *Australian Social Work Education and Accreditation Standards (ASWEAS) 2012 V1.4 (Revised January 2015)*, Canberra, Australian Association for Social Workers.

AASW (2017). *Australian Social Work Education and Accreditation Standards (ASWEAS) (May 2017)*, Canberra, Australian Association for Social Workers.

ABS (2017). *Mortality of People Using Mental Health Services and Prescription Medications, Analysis of 2011 Data*, Canberra, Australian Bureau of Statistics. www.abs.gov.au/ausstats/abs@.nsf/mf/4329.0.00.006

ABS (2018a). *The Australian Statistical Geography Standard (ASGS) Remoteness Structure*, Canberra, Australian Bureau of Statistics. www.abs.gov.au/websitedbs/D3310114.nsf/home/remoteness+structure

ABS (2018b). *National Health Survey: First Results, 2017–18*, Canberra, Australian Bureau of Statistics. www.abs.gov.au/ausstats/abs@.nsf/mf/4364.0.55.001

Beresford, P., & Boxall, K. (2012). Service users, social work education and knowledge for social work practice. *Social Work Education*, *31*(2), 155–167.

Beresford, P., & Russo, J. (2016). Supporting the sustainability of mad studies and preventing its co-option, *Disability & Society*, *31*(2), 270–274.

Boxall, K., Carson, I., & Docherty, D. (2004). Room at the academy? People with learning difficulties and higher education. *Disability & Society*, *19*(2), 99–112. https://doi.org/10.1080/0968759042000181749

Boxall, K., Speakup Self-advocacy and Eastwood Action Group (2009). Learning disability, in Higham, P. (Ed) *Understanding Post-qualifying Social Work*, London, Sage, pp. 103–121.

Branfield, F., Beresford, P., Andrews, E. J., Chambers, P., Staddon, P., Wise, G., & Williams-Findlay, B. (2006). *Making User Involvement Work*, York, Joseph Rowntree Foundation. https://shapingourlives.org.uk/wp-content/uploads/2015/03/Makinguserinvolvementwork_full.pdf

Branfield, F., Beresford, P., & Levin, E. (2007). *Common Aims: A Strategy to Support Service User Involvement in Social Work Education*, Social Care Institute for Excellence. https://shapingourlives.org.uk/wp-content/uploads/2015/03/Commonaims.pdf

Byrne, L., Happell, B., & Reid-Searl, K. (2016). Lived experience practitioners and the medical model: Worlds colliding? *Journal of Mental Health*, *25*(3), 217–223.

Campbell, P. (2005). From Little Acorns – the mental health service user movement, in Bell, A. & Lindley, P. (Eds) *Beyond the Water Towers: The Unfinished Revolution in Mental Health Services 1985–2005*, London, Sainsbury Centre for Mental Health. http://studymore.org.uk/pcacorns.pdf

Chamberlin, J. (1988). *On Our Own: Patient-controlled Alternatives to the Mental Health System*, London, Mind.

COAG (2012). *The Roadmap for National Mental Health Reform (2012–2022)*, Canberra, Council of Australian Governments.

Corstens, D., Longden, E., McCarthy-Jones, S., Waddingham, R., & Thomas, N. (2014). Emerging perspectives from the hearing voices movement: Implications for research and practice. *Schizophrenia Bulletin*, *40*(Suppl_4), S285-S294.

Costa, L. (2014). Mad studies – what it is and why you should care. *Mad Studies Network*, posted October 15. https://madstudies2014.wordpress.com/2014/10/15/mad-studies-what-it-is-and-why-you-should-care-2/

Deacon, B. J. (2013). The biomedical model of mental disorder: A critical analysis of its validity, utility, and effects on psychotherapy research. *Clinical Psychology Review*, *33*(7), 846–861.

DH (2002). *Requirements for Social Work Training*, London, Department of Health.

Dorozenko, K. P., & Martin, R. (2017). *A Critical Literature Review of the Direct, Adverse Effects of Neuroleptics*, National Mental Health Consumer & Carer Forum https://nmhccf.org.au/publication/critical-literature-review-direct-adverse-effects-neuroleptics

Dorozenko, K. P., Ridley, S., Martin, R., & Mahboub, L. (2016). A journey of embedding mental health lived experience in social work education. *Social Work Education*, *35*(8), 905–917. doi:10.1080/02615479.2016.1214255

Gøtzsche, P. C., Young, A. H., & Crace, J. (2015). Maudsley Debate: Does long term use of psychiatric drugs cause more harm than good? *The BMJ*, *350*, h2435.

Happell, B., Byrne, L., McAllister, M., Lampshire, D., Roper, C., Gaskin, C. J., Martin, G., Wynaden, D., McKenna, B., Lakeman, R., Platania-Phung, C., & Hamer, H. (2014). Consumer involvement in the tertiary-level education of mental health professionals: A systematic review. *International Journal of Mental Health Nursing*, *23*(1), 3–16. doi:10.1111/inm.12021

Happell, B., Wynaden, D., Tohotoa, J., Platania-Phung, C., Byrne, L., Martin, G., & Harris, S. (2015). Mental health lived experience academics in tertiary education: The views of nurse academics. *Nurse Education Today*, *35*(1), 113–117.

HCPC (2014). *Standards of Education and Training: Guidance for Education Providers*, London, Health and Care Professions Council. www.hcpc-uk.org/publications/standards/index.asp?id=195

Herman, J. L. (2015). *Trauma and Recovery: The Aftermath of Violence – from Domestic Abuse to Political Terror*, New York, Basic Books.

Horwitz, A. V. (2013). The sociological study of mental illness: A critique and synthesis of four perspectives, in *Handbook of the Sociology of Mental Health* (pp. 95–112), Dordrecht, Netherlands, Springer.

IASSW/IFSW (2004). *Global Standards for the Training and Education of the Social Work Profession*, International Association of Schools of Social Work and International Federation of Social Workers. http://cdn.ifsw.org/assets/ifsw_65044-3.pdf

Ingram, R. (2016). Doing Mad Studies: Making (non)sense together. *Intersectionalities. A Global Journal of Social Work Analysis, Research, Polity, and Practice* [Online], *5*(2). http://journals.library.mun.ca/ojs/index.php/IJ/article/view/1680/1327

Jorm, A. F., Reavley, N. J., & Ross, A. M. (2012). Belief in the dangerousness of people with mental disorders: A review. *Australian & New Zealand Journal of Psychiatry*, *46*(11), 1029–1045.

Large, M., & Ryan, C. J. (2012). Sanism, stigma and the belief in dangerousness. *Australian and New Zealand Journal of Psychiatry*, *46*, 1099–1103.

LeFrançois, B. A., Beresford, P., & Russo, J. (2016) Destination mad studies. *Intersectionalities. A Global Journal of Social Work Analysis, Research, Polity, and Practice* [Online], *5*(2). http://journals.library.mun.ca/ojs/index.php/IJ/article/view/1690/1342

LeFrançois, B. A., Menzies, R. J., & Reaume, G. (Eds) (2013) *Mad Matters: A Critical Reader in Canadian Mad Studies*, Toronto, Canadian Scholar's Press Inc.

Longden, E. (2010) Making sense of voices: A personal story of recovery. *Psychosis*, *2*(3), 255–259. doi: 10.1080/17522439.2010.512667

Longden, E., Madill, A., & Waterman, M. G. (2012). Dissociation, trauma, and the role of lived experience: Toward a new conceptualization of voice hearing. *Psychological Bulletin*, *138*(1), 28.

McNabb, D. J., & Connolly, M. (2017). The relevance of global standards to social work education in Australasia. *International Social Work*. https://doi.org/10.1177/0020872817710547

Newman, J., Boxall, K., Jury, R., & Dickinson, J. (2019) Professional education and Mad Studies: Learning and teaching about service users' understandings of mental and emotional distress. *Disability & Society*, 1–25. https://doi.org/10.1080/09687599.2019.1594697

O'Hagan, M. (1993). *Stopovers on My Way Home from Mars: A Journey into the Psychiatric Survivor Movement in the USA, Britain and the Netherlands*, London, Survivors Speak Out. www.maryohagan.com/resources/Text_Files/Stopovers%20on%20my%20Way%20Home%20from%20Mars.pdf

Pembroke, L. R. (1994) *Self Harm: Perspectives from Personal Experience*, London, Survivors Speak Out. http://chipmunkapublishing.co.uk/shop/index.php?main_page=product_info&products_id=230

Read, J., & Dillon, J. (Eds) (2013). *Models of Madness: Psychological, Social and Biological Approaches to Psychosis*, Abingdon: Routledge.

Rodway, C., Flynn, S., While, D., Rahman, M. S., Kapur, N., Appleby, L., & Shaw, J. (2014). Patients with mental illness as victims of homicide: A national consecutive case series. *Lancet Psychiatry*, *1*(2), 129–134. https://doi.org/10.1016/S2215-0366(14)70221-4

Rogers, A., & Pilgrim, D. (2014). *A Sociology of Mental Health and Illness*, Maidenhead, Open University Press.

Ross, D. (2018). A social work perspective on seclusion and restraint in Australia's public mental health system. *Journal of Progressive Human Services*, *29*(2), 130–148.

Roughead, L., Procter, N., Westaway, K., Sluggett, J., & Alderman, C. (2017) *Medication Safety in Mental Health*, Australian Commission on Safety and Quality in Health Care. www.safetyandquality.gov.au/wp-content/uploads/2017/06/Medication-Safety-in-Mental-Health-final-report-2017.pdf

Sapey, B., & Bullimore, P. (2013). Listening to voice hearers. *Journal of Social Work*, *13*(6), 616–632.

SUAS (2018). *8th Service User Academia Symposium – Nesting Our Knowledge*, University of Melbourne. https://healthsciences.unimelb.edu.au/departments/nursing/about-us/centre-for-psychiatric-nursing/engage/service-users-academic-symposium

UN (2017). *Report of the Special Rapporteur on the Right of Everyone to the Enjoyment of the Highest Attainable Standard of Physical and Mental Health*, United Nations Human Rights Council, Thirty-fifth session, 6–23 June, Agenda item 3. http://ap.ohchr.org/Documents/E/HRC/d_res_dec/A_HRC_35_L.31.docx

Warren, L., & Boxall, K. (2009). Service users in and out of the academy: Collusion in exclusion? *Social Work Education*, *28*(3), 281–297. https://doi.org/10.1080/02615470802659464

Whitaker, R., & Cosgrove, L. (2015). *Psychiatry Under the Influence: Institutional Corruption, Social Injury, and Prescriptions for Reform*, New York, Palgrave.

11

THE MEETING PLACE BETWEEN SERVICE USERS[1] AND STUDENTS

Mediums of learning at the School of Social Work of the University of Sherbrooke

Annie Lambert, Paul Morin, Sophie Nobert-Bordeleau,
Émilie Pothier-Tessier, Marie-Josée St-Jean, Annie Patenaude

Introduction

The field of social work is driven by values of respect, integrity, dignity and social justice. This daily calls for professionals to come alongside people in trying situations; they often live under difficult life circumstances, whether circumstantial or long term, that are shaped by different challenges. The vulnerability of these users requires the professionals who accompany them to develop important relational skills.

In a like manner, approaches that encourage the involvement of service users at the heart of the intervention process are currently important in the field of social work. Within a school of social work, these approaches guide and are reflected in necessary pedagogical choices in educating future social workers capable of overcoming relational obstacles and achieving the requirements of the professional practice.

In light of these considerations, the School of Social Work at the University of Sherbrooke (Quebec, Canada) has been working over the past few years to create an academic program structured by and for the involvement of service users[2] within its undergraduate and graduate programs. These innovations are supported by two motives that can be found in academic literature. Studies show that user involvement adds significantly to academic training because it creates better social workers (Cabiati and Raineri, 2016; Hitchin, 2016) and facilitates the empowerment of people (Beresford and Boxall, 2012; Hernandez et al., 2010). It's also a manner to adhere to the basic values of social work.

In Canada, patients' involvement is quite popular in the medical field (UBC, 2018), but much less for services users in social work education (Watters et al., 2016). It is hard to pinpoint the causes of such a discrepancy, but it is the actual reality. In social work education, a Canadian specificity is the implication of First Nations. A good example is the creation in 2016 at the University of Toronto of an MSW specialization: *Indigenous trauma and resiliency* (ITR). It was developed in partnership with the Ontario Federation of Indigenous Friendship Centres. Community Elders, as such, are very much involved in the program.

The goal of this chapter is to present findings concerning the involvement of users in the context of the academic training of future social workers. The findings presented are supported by several academic projects conducted from 2015 onward, as well as the data gatherings that accompanied them. The acquired understanding and benefits of such involvement for the service users and for students will be exposed as well as the associated challenges.

Service user involvement in the training of future social workers

Since 2012, the initial social work training[3] at the University of Sherbrooke has been built on a professionalization course. In other words, it promotes the development of professional competencies and the acquisition of resources through significant learning experiences that resemble the professional practice of social work (Bélisle, 2011). Several training activities in real and simulated environments are offered to students. These activities are anchored in the professional practice and are approved by professionals.

The integration of knowledge – scientific, professional and experiential – is the guiding principle of the program of initial training and is inserted in the continual and transversal process of developing the professional identity of the students. The links between theory and practice, as well as training grounded in the reality of social work practice, ensure a relevant curriculum for future social workers. The participation of several practicing professionals allows the combination of practical and scientific knowledge to be valued. This is in contrast to the traditionally scientific knowledge predominant in university curriculums.

However, an inconsistency was collectively highlighted in November 2015 during a pedagogical meeting that took place between several parties involved in the School of Social Work. The initial training encourages the links between theory and practice as well as interaction with different areas of practice. The training supports also values of social work and the concepts of co-construction, self-determination and user participation. However, users were not part of the academic program and the expression of their experiential knowledge was not encouraged. At that time, the priority of user involvement in the initial training in social work was voted upon. The work then began in order to develop projects that are structured by and around user involvement in the academic program.

This priority brought about in the spring of 2016 the *Community of Knowledge*, which is a meeting place joining different parties that represent scientific, professional, and experiential knowledge. It has the objective of merging different forms of knowledge. This committee is made of service users, caregivers, students, professionals, lecturers and professor-researchers. This mechanism was created to put in practice the School's priority of encouraging user involvement in the academic curriculum as well as to recognize the importance of merging different forms of knowledge.

The Swedish philosophy of gap mending was used as a foundation for the different projects that were put in place. In other words, this concept implies the reduction of the social distance between users and professionals. Gap mending is defined as

> a concept, which is used to create reflection and analysis of gaps that exist between actors in social work. The gaps we are focusing on are explicit or implicit distinctions between individuals, groups or organisations that are connected in Social Work. It can involve gaps, which are obvious and sometimes even open conflicts, but also cultural assumptions that can seem free from contradictions. Common to the gaps is that they contribute to injustice, subordination and exclusion in social work and society. The gaps inhibit, or sometimes even paralyze, activities in social work to contribute to

the positive development of their target groups. The power structures are important grounds for the emergence of the gaps, which are prevailing in society. Power relations between social workers and service users, or between welfare organisations and service user organisations enforce the gaps.

(Kristiansen and Heule, 2016, in Chappirini, E., 2016, p. 37)

Examples of user involvement[4] in the university curriculum

To remain coherent with the principles of knowledge merging and gap mending, a participative approach is used by the different actors to build upon previously attained knowledge as well as to create new knowledge. This approach allows for the building of bridges between traditional pedagogical experience and the expertise of users (Angelin, 2015; Mobiliseringkursen, 2016) while considering the service users as partners who invest through different levels of participation (McKeown et al., 2010). The service users devote themselves to more than simple testimonies, as is often the case within university programs. A testimony is often the first step towards disclosure. The road before being able to participate in other type of activities requires time and a thorough analysis of their lifecourse by the person before opening up to students. The three following activities illustrate different types of possible involvement.

The Barometer project: appreciating experiential knowledge

The initial training for future social workers includes an array of intervention learning workshops that are practical activities to train students for social work intervention. As such, students are enabled to develop intervening and analysing skills. They are also trained to reflect on their professional posture. Practicing social workers, named practitioner-trainers, head these activities in small groups of a dozen students, structured around clinical cases that are realistic and inspired by real situations. In several of these activities, services users are acting as comedians from their own experience, as the goal is to create realistic situations.

One of these intervention learning workshops was created to promote user involvement and enable a first meeting between users and students. Beginning in 2017,[5] during their first academic year, students experience a workshop where, as a triad, they autonomously lead an interview with a service user with the "Barometer" tool as support. The Barometer tool is online and interactive. It allows for an exploration of quality of life indicators. Within this exercise, the user is encouraged to share their own story by playing his/her own role; this way, the students are face to face with a person that has a lot to say about his/her life. This interview invites students to explore the person's reality and to seek their experiential knowledge so as to allow the users to evaluate their own quality of life. Services users participate in these discussions and make use of feedbacks to the students. The encounter between the service user and the student – and for both of them – can be stressful or querying.

To this point, this workshop has benefitted students in the 2017 (n=54) and 2018 (n=69) school years. It is comprised of three parts: a training given by a practitioner-trainer and service users on the online tool, a meeting between a user and students and feedback given by the different participants. The created learning context allows for students to develop relational skills and to be confronted by the exercise of co-construction.

The final project: widening roles

Since 2015, graduating students of the School of Social Work must take part in an activity at the end of the school year. The objective of this two-day activity is to promote the students' integration projects at the undergraduate and graduate levels. In April 2016, for the first time, a service user and a caregiver were present for this activity to testify of their experience. In 2017, the theme of user participation was central to this activity. An interactive panel then took place to bring together both users (4) and professionals (4) during an exchange with the cohort of graduating students (65).

More than simply an opportunity to discuss user involvement in the academic program, this school activity allows for users to become evaluators of the students' work. In fact, every student has the opportunity, through a poster and an oral presentation, to present the results of their work. An evaluation committee, including a professor, a practitioner and a user, evaluate the students in the perspective of merging knowledge. About a hundred students per year gain from this experience and from users' life experience with regard to the subjects presented. So, in this way, they can confront their views with the user's reality. As for the users, they can use their communication skills, and by the bias of their exchanges with the students, they can also realize that they really have expertise. The evaluator's status is also positive gain for the service users who grant good value to this role. They can share their experience with students and be positively critical about their works, with concretes examples and their points of view.

Summer school: *"The merging of knowledge for the renewal of practices": immersion in the encounter*

A five-day intensive summer program[6] called "The merging of knowledge for the renewal of practices" was developed and experienced for the first time in June 2018. This course, at the master's level, reunited a mixed group of 19 service users and 18 students. Students came to this activity to develop their abilities with the goal of a better social work practice. Users came to gain competencies in order to become user-trainers within the academic programs.

The experience of the encounter guides the activity for the participants. It is an opportunity for them not only to come to terms with certain challenges but also to begin breaking down barriers.

The academic environment provides participants with the space to realize the importance of relationship in social practice and encourages a human-to-human relationship. Inspired by an active learning approach, several learning methods are used – from theoretical to practical, traditional to creative and from within the university walls to inside the community. That being said, more than half of the educational activities are experienced outside of the university with the collaboration of several practice settings, such as non-profit community groups in the area. The participants sign up for lectures, small group activities, a theatre-forum, a world café and a community meal. Of course, these activities all serve the purpose of mending the gap, meaning reducing not only the social distance between students and services users but also diminishing the power relation between them. The encounter between persons, in the context of the summer school, acts as a consciousness raising facilitator: human relations are essential to the social work profession.

> The gap-mending concept can be characterized as a reflective tool that helps teachers and researchers to consider what, in their practices increases, maintains or mends gaps between policies, services and professionals – as well as service users. Gaps always exist in a context. Gaps can develop and be maintained because of prejudices based on social work's categorization of people, because of language barriers, because of institutional hierarchies and the roles we have created for people within them. They can

also exist because of lack of knowledge. Contextual knowledge is therefore essential in gap-mending reflections, as well as a good understanding of existing gaps.

(Askheim et al., 2017, p. 3)

Acquired knowledge and results for students and service users

Since the implementation of the orientation of involving users in the initial training of future social workers, over 250 students have experienced meeting a staff of 12 service users. To document these experiences, the following data gathering methods were used: the analysis of reflective cards (n=54) and essays (n=18); individual interviews with service users (n=12), students (n=22) and a professional (n=1); informal discussions with users (n=1); forums with users, students and professors (n=3); feedback from users and students (n=4) and with partnered organizations (n=6); and working seminars with French co-workers (n=1). So, the pedagogical activities have been used for the analyses and also personal interviews with the different stakeholders. Thematic syntheses were produced to identity the important elements for users and students.

The following statements are supported by these analyses so as to highlight what was learned and the impact of the experiences on users and students.

Learning to live the relationship: an essential learnt ability for the students

Encountering the other

The experience of human contact, the "face-to-face" between students and users, is a determining factor in every activity. As one student noted:

> The most important element to remember in this experience [the summer school] for me is that the intervention is first and foremost a human relationship. The connection with the other person is paramount in order to establish a therapeutic relationship.
>
> *(Caroline, student)*

The expression "real people" that was brought up by many students refers to the privileged access they have to a user's life experience. This allows them to better understand their reality. The confrontation with the emotional aspects of the relationship is determining and influential, as this service user expresses:

> Human contact. . . . I have seen the looks of certain students. Being confronted by a "real" person. Some were afraid. Sometimes some maybe had judgement in their eyes. But . . . I believe that the human-to-human exchange . . . it makes all the difference because walls fall. And then, we have a real heart-to-heart conversation. All the wall fall down. It's almost tangible.
>
> *(Marc, user)*

This privileged learning environment brings out students' know-how and postures that were acquired within their academic training. Time is in short supply in real-life situations, so it is really helpful for the students to acquire these relational skills. It also provides space for students to reflect on the importance of the relational aspect of the intervention. In other words, it helps them develop empathy, sensitivity towards others and authenticity. This contributes to students reflecting upon their roles and the intervention models learned in their courses as well as makes them aware of their effect on the relationship. The challenge of having a good professional distance and the just proximity are then pondered through the prism of the encounter experience.

Within these meeting contexts, students must put their resources in action in order to make a connection with the users. These resources, through their experiences, guide them:

> If my life experience can help you be more available to make contact with an individual without holding prejudice and without fear, you will be able to develop connections with them. The way you approach an individual represents the cornerstone.
>
> *(François, user)*

Through face-to-face contact, the expertise and the unique features of each individual represent relevant starting points in the merging of knowledge. Every person takes advantage of the richness and experience of the other. The crossroad of experiential, professional and scientific knowledge contributes, on one hand, to the creation of a collective *us*. On the other hand, it reduces the distance between users and professionals in a perspective of empowering the individuals (Morin and Lambert, 2017). Each individual learns to recognize the life experience and knowledge of the other:

> To see the different sides of the people with whom we are working. For me, that's valuable. I feel like when I start working I may forget. . . . It's important to remember that the service users are not only service users. They will not always be service users. It's possible that some they will be, but not everyone.
>
> *(Valérie, student)*

Learning to understand the other

The encounter and the diversity of the groups in the activities involving the users raise the issue of mutual comprehension and connecting the different realities and experiences. This issue can be both an advantage and a challenge. In fact, it allows participants to have access to a multitude of life experiences. This access comes with the obligation of deconstructing prejudices that are presented both ways: students and services users.

> We know everyone has prejudices. And . . . it allows me to confront my own prejudices. My little hidden preconceptions that I didn't even know really existed. But then, I recognized them because I could hear myself think. It really made me take a step back. . . . Yeah, to have even less preconceptions as before.
>
> *(Laura, student)*

However, in order to break down barriers, special attention must be given to the creation of a common language that facilitates the full participation of everyone involved. This language must allow each individual to understand the other's world (Scheyett and Diehl, 2004). The absence of a common language can have the effect of discouraging or halting participation in discussions and can bring about conflict. The observations that were made bring to light that discussions stemming from academic knowledge and those stemming from experiential knowledge are very different. The challenge resides in the recognition of the knowledge of each individual as well as the creation of favourable conditions for the merging of knowledge. A service user explains such thoughts well in his own words:

> For me, the only theory that can be taught is the one that teaches students how to approach people as well as the different intervention models that can be used. . . . Why use words that people won't understand? . . . It takes a common language to be able to be invested.
>
> *(François, user)*

Reflecting on one's professional identity

With the different activities involving service users, the students dive into an exercise of co-construction, an essential principle in their training. Meeting users brings out questions and thoughts about their role and their professional posture. "I finally understood my role of accompaniment!" underlined a student at the end of an activity. Confronted by their judgements and their timidity in the acknowledgement and use of the user's experiential knowledge, the students question their professional identity.

To encounter users is be confronted by the issues of power in the professional relationship between service users and social workers. The students are made aware of their position with regard to others. They are called to reconsider the logic of taking care and expert positions in the helping relationship:

> I had a hard time with the equal to equal approach, because I found that this approach is almost utopian. It made me wonder at what extend can someone be equal to equal when they are intervening. The activity confirm to me that it could be done.
>
> *(Annie, student)*

Regaining control over one's life: major benefits for service users

Reinforcing self-esteem

Being involved in the training activities with social work students has a major positive impact on the service users. It contributes to reinforcing their self-esteem and affirming their social role or function:

> It's validating to say that I'm involved at the University of Sherbrooke in one of their programs and to say that I already see little positive results in what I am doing.
>
> *(France, user)*

It also impacts their feeling of usefulness. Several service users who are involved in the training have not had much schooling and find it difficult to maintain a social role according to collective standards. As such, participating in academic activities, integrating a higher education environment and contributing to the development of future social workers represents a useful action that makes sense to them:

> It's the feeling of being useful, of changing things, of . . . of offering my experience. . . . I don't do nothing in life. I'm socially involved and that gives me validation.
>
> *(France, user)*

The reactions of the students towards the service users are also significant to the image that the users have of themselves. The thought process of one user – "the world listens to my point of view, the students really listen to me" (Emilie, user) – demonstrates well the impact that an encounter between a user and students can have on the self-validation and self-esteem of the users.

Giving meaning to one's story

Every service user recognizes the importance of going through a process of personal growth before getting involved with the academic program. This growth refers, primarily, to the fact that the person has attained a level of balance and the ability to take a step back to reflect on their own life. This prevents them from being shaken by their participation and having a negative experience. That being said, entry into the academic training and communication with the students contribute to the "recognition of their own story" (Gabrielle, caregiver) and allow them to reconstruct its meaning:

> For me, it's all my life experience, my experience with social workers, in mental health, I was also a young mom, and I had a lot of personal baggage that I wanted to bring to others and that I could transform into something positive. . . . I thought, at first, that they [the students] would look down on me . . . kind of like "you only have secondary 1, who do you think you are?" But no, instead, there was a beautiful openness, they are happy that we're there, it makes sense in their program.
>
> *(Maria, user)*

In such an environment, the service user's life experience is transformed into knowledge that is useful for students. This starts by the recognition and the appreciation of experiential knowledge as a source of learning. The trials and difficulties encountered by the users become a shared asset, generating a feeling of competence which serves as a starting point towards empowerment (Beresford and Boxall, 2012; Hernandez et al., 2010).

Taking advantage of the domino effect: impacts on individual realities

Not only does user involvement affect the users' self-esteem and contribute to the recognition of their life experience, it also echoes significantly in their individual lives. Maintaining a goal, overcoming obstacles, organizing their schedules and regaining motivation are elements that are brought up by users as part of the domino effect caused by their participation in the university training. Moreover, their participation the recognition from their social circles through the acquisition of a certain social status.

> I know that it's not a job, the user-trainers, but at least I have a role in society. It's big. My nephew, this young 16-year-old man, who sees his godmother being fulfilled, well for me, it's gratifying.
>
> *(Jane, user)*

The feeling of being someone and being recognized as such changes the attitudes of the users and can contribute to the improvement of their social integration. Whether by the increase of their personal confidence, a better openness towards others, a more positive attitude towards life or meaning given to their actions, the experience of their involvement in the educational training of social workers is motivating and encourages users to get involved in other ways in their personal and social life. The acquisitions of new knowledge and the development of diverse competences are linked to a better self-esteem and as such are a source of motivation and opportunities.

Challenges associated with user involvement in the university curriculum

Creating openings in the university program

The recognition of user involvement in educational institutions remains an important challenge for this type of learning model. On one hand, formal recognition is important for the service users – to be recognized for what they do, just as other parties in the program are. On the other hand, however, formal university structures do not allow easily for this form of recognition, including their status and monetary compensation. Within this context, in order to innovate and do differently, certain actions are required to inform, explain and sometimes demand a fair place for these service users.

Discussions with the users have led to the creation of a formal role by which users are recognized for their participation. They are given the title of user-trainers. This status allows for a better comprehension of the role given to them within the academic training, facilitates a better personal recognition and makes the administrative demands clearer.

In Great Britain and in France, there has been a formal recognition of service users' expertise in social work education, and on a broader geographical level – Europe – diverse networks and grant opportunities contribute greatly to the expansion of user involvement (Casagrande, 2019). However, status and monetary compensation can vary greatly between countries. In Canada, there is no formal recognition, so each social work school has its specific context, and it can be sometimes an uphill struggle to advance the cause.

The remuneration of service users remains a significant challenge. For the majority, the participants live or have lived in vulnerable social and financial situations. Their participation requires certain expenses (transportation, meals) that appear to be impossible to reimburse. Also, the invested time must be compensated for, as is the case for other participants. Whether by formal payment contracts or by alternative means (grocery cards, gift cards, etc.), financial recognition is imperative. In order to create breathing room within the institutional context, time-consuming steps must be taken to ensure the remuneration of user-trainers.

To overcome these challenges and guarantee a recognition and a remuneration that is worthy of the investment of the users, it is important to structure formal activities and ensure valuable collaborations with decision-making bodies. Without said recognition and remuneration, the participation of users may provoke a shift towards the commodification of those involved.

Creating a trajectory of accompaniment

Involving users in the training of future social workers implies the reconciliation of two worlds: the academic framework of the students and the experiences of the users. The former must distance themselves from their habitual learning contexts and the latter must allow themselves to uncover their own story. They must also each be accompanied in some way to properly accomplish the goals of the activities as well as to prepare and support them in every part of the process. Inevitably, their participation in the proposed activities can touch them emotionally, as is the testimony of a service user:

> The fact of opening up like that, it was like there was no longer . . . no longer any balance. There was really an imbalance between the student and me and even with the other people involved.
>
> *(France, user)*

And that enables a form of resistance in the students:

> The loss of meaning was challenging. What was the goal and what were we looking for? At the same time, it's an experience, and after, everyone continues to reflect . . . there are moments where the students disclosed part of their story too and that's okay but at the same time that may not be the goal of the exercise.
>
> *(Jessica, student)*

The learning models that include user involvement allow for learning that is not only academic. It is then important to guide the participants to ensure that they have a positive experience. Informing, preparing, accompanying and supporting become imperative to counteract the possible emotions that are added to the activity. Also, these essential actions require time, an important issue within the academic curriculum. Questions regarding structure (i.e. respecting the rhythm of each individual) and responsibility (i.e. who is responsible for the accompaniment?) remain important.

Added to these questions is also the line between accompaniment and intervention. Even though the service users are asked to have attained a certain level of personal balance and growth as well as to have taken a step back from their hardships, the emotional impact of their participation requires some form of care. This context can create tension between one's belief in self-determination and one's responsibility to protect and take care of the participant. It can be difficult for the leaders of the activities to set boundaries between their accompanying role and their responsibility of ensuring the achievement of their set goals.

In order to counteract these challenges, the decision of developing a training program for user-trainers was made. In conjunction with the decision-making bodies at the University of Sherbrooke, plans are underway to structure the accompaniment of the users through three activities (taking place during the fall, winter and summer trimesters 2019–2020). Users will be able to sign up for free and will receive university credits for their participation. The goal of these activities is to develop the necessary competencies for the exercise of the role of user-trainer. Therefore, structuring the training and the accompaniment of users as well as allowing them to develop competencies ensures the recognition of their role as key actors in the training of future social workers.

Conclusion

Finally, how does user involvement in social work training make the training better?

> I think that the biggest benefit is the real experience . . . in any case, my dream would be that social work students, when they finish their education, would see that there aren't many differences that separate people. There is birth status, bad experiences; there is only a hair's distance that separates their social position and the social position of those with whom they will be working. . . . Also, simply accepting that I'm not so far from becoming who I don't want to become is enough to create space for empathy.
>
> *(Alexandre, professional)*

In order to develop this empathy and sensitivity towards others – essential values in social work – and to decrease the distance that separates service users and social workers, user involvement in university trainings is not only possible but crucial. This pedagogical direction allows for coherence between academic language and the learning opportunities that are offered to students, just as Campbell describes as between "what we teach, how we teach, and what the students learn" (Campbell, 2002, p. 29).

User involvement in the universities is fraught with challenges, so changes are essential to meet them. Three keys seem to us fundamental:

Firstly, breaking academic knowledge out of its mould. Knowledge acquisitions must not be perceived unidirectionally between professors and students. Also, the aperture to the mixing of knowledge and the recognition of different types of knowledge are essential to the advance of students' formation. Administrative university structures must also be ease off so we can have a real user involvement in contexts that are not instrumental; these persons must have also an explicit status for their involvement.

Secondly, the aperture of the universities towards the community is fundamental; this way we can encourage user involvement in social work education. The links between organizations and community groups are really helpful in developing the credibility of program orientations that has user involvement as one of its goal. These links also favour work group ethics that are profitable for each stakeholder. Finally, these links allow potential service users to invest in the formations.

Thirdly, the formation and the support of service users are essential to the success of such a way of doing. The work must be done with the outlook of developing the competencies necessary to their involvement in a university program. As such, this favours users' empowerment and permits a higher level of pedagogical investment with the students. In brief, despite the challenges, the gains of such a pedagogical approach are real.

The academic training is thus enhanced. "I learned more during that activity [the summer school] than I think . . . my God, all of my other classes combined!" a student, Laura, explains. Through the encounter of another, it becomes possible to break down walls, reduce the distance between people and stand between the dichotomy of "them", the users, and "us", the social workers. This dichotomy, in contrast, contributes to the power differentials of relations. Within this pedagogical context, the training of future social workers of the University of Sherbrooke reiterates the essential values of social work: respect, dignity, integrity and social justice. That being said, service user involvement in the academic training is a pedagogical orientation that can make a difference and, we hope, can empower people to take action:

> Because I think it can make a difference in the lives of future social workers . . . it can even help them in their personal lives. And the future service users that the social workers will see will benefit from it, too.
>
> *(Emilie, user)*

Notes

1 The School of Social Work of the University of Sherbrooke promotes the participation of service users and their caregivers in its academic trainings. Because the field of caregiver involvement is currently ongoing, this publication will focus on the involvement of service users only.

2 The term service users refers to citizens who, by their life experiences, depend or have depended upon the care of social workers.

3 In Quebec, an initial training of three years at the university level allows students to practice social work and be admit to social worker associations.

4 As part of the department's orientations, different research and pedagogical innovation grants were acquired. Three discussion forums – gathering around 20 users, students and professors each time – were facilitated (2016, 2017, 2018) and participation in several conferences and conventions was made, including the conference for l'UNAFORIS (l'Union nationale des acteurs de formation et de recherche en intervention sociale) and the EASSW in June of 2017, where a delegation comprised of users, students and professors presented the work of the University of Sherbrooke on the subject. The School of Social Work is also a member of the international association called PowerUs and maintains tight relations with l'Institut universitaire de première ligne en santé et services sociaux (IUPLSSS) of the Centre universitaire de santé et service sociaux de l'Estrie that considers "act for and with the users" as a priority.

5 The Faculty of Arts and Human Sciences of the University of Sherbrooke has supported this project financially through the Pedagogical Innovation Funds program (2016–2017).

6 The Faculty of Arts and Human Sciences of the University of Sherbrooke has financially supported this project through their Pedagogical Innovation Funds program (2017–2018).

References

Askheim, O. P., Beresford, P. and Heule, C. (2017). Mend the gap – strategies for user involvement in social work education, *Social Work Education*, *36*(2), 128–140.

Angelin, A. (2015). Service user integration social work education: lessons learned from Nordic participatory action projects, *Journal of Evidence-informed Social Work*, *12*, 124–138.

Bélisle, M. (2011). *Perceptions de diplômés universitaires quant aux effets d'un programme professionnalisant et innovant sur leur professionnalisation en contexte de formation initiale*. Thèse de doctorat en éducation, Université de Sherbrooke, Québec.

Beresford, P. and Boxall, K. (2012). Service users, social work education and knowledge for social work practice, *Social Word Education*, *31*(2), 155–167.

Cabiati, E. and Raineri, M. L. (2016). Learning from service users' involvement: a research out changing stigmatizing attitudes in social work students, *Social Work Education*, *35*(8), 982–996.

Campbell, C. (2002). The search for congruency, *Canadian Social Work Review*, *19*(1), 25–42.

Casagrande, A. (2019). Associons nos savoirs: pour une démocratie des expériences, *Vie Sociale*, *25–26*, 61–70.

Chappirini, E. (2016). *The service user as a partner in social work projects and education*, Barbara Budrich Publishers, Opladen, Berlin & Toronto.

Hernandez, L., Robson, P. and Sampson, A. (2010). Towards integrated participation: involving seldom heard users of social services, *British Journal of Social Work*, *40*, 714–736.

Hitchin, S. (2016). Role-played interviews with service users in preparation for social work practice: exploring students' and service users' experience of co-produced workshops, *Social Work Education*, *28*(8), 970–981.

Kristiansen, A. and Heule, C. (2016). Sweden: power, experiences and mutual development. using the concept of gap-mending in social work education. In Chappirini, E. (ed.), *The service user as a partner in social work projects and education*, Barbara Budrich Publishers, Opladen, Berlin & Toronto, 37–53.

McKeown, M., Malihi-Shoja, L. and Downe, S. (2010). *Service user and carer involvement in education for health and social care*, Wiley-Blackwell, London.

Mobiliseringkursen. (2016). *It's our lives & andra texter*, Kompendium, Université de Lund.

Morin, P. and Lambert, A. (2017). L'apport du savoir expérientiel des personnes usagères au sein de la formation en travail social, *Revue Intervention*, *145*, 21–30.

Scheyett, A. et Diehl, M. J. (2004). Walking our talk in social work education: partnering with consumers of mental health services, *Social Work Education*, *23*(4), 435–450.

UBC Health. (2018). *Patient engagement in education in UBC Health programs*, The University of British Columbia, Canada, 17 p.

Watters, C. E., Cait, C-A. and Oba, F. (2016). Social work curriculum review case study. Service users tell us what make effective social workers, *Canadian Social Work Review*, *33*(1), 27–44.

12

TALKING HEADS

The non-existence of meaningful service user consultation in Congo Brazzaville

Charden Pouo

Introduction

In this chapter, I want to reflect on the non-existence of meaningful service user consultation in my home country, Congo Brazzaville. I will offer an explanation for and critique of this situation. I will then give an account of the activity of Couleurs Congolaises, a non-governmental organisation I established with some fellow university students in 2007, through which we tried to raise social consciousness and awareness among some of the most disenfranchised people in the country. We did this so that all Congolese citizens might have not only an understanding of their rights as human beings and as citizens, but also knowledge of how to act to assert those rights.

Critique

Congo Brazzaville became an independent country 60 years ago, having been liberated from the coloniser France on 15 August 1960. This liberation swept in a sense of national pride and unity and the promise of a new set of values for a brand-new Republic. Among these values was the notion of public service. The Congolese vision of public service is one of equality, in that services should be offered to all on an equal basis. Yet, I would suggest that only a small section of the population is even aware of the services to which they are entitled, never mind having a voice in the planning and delivery of these. The truth of the matter is that the gap has really increased significantly between the public services, as originally promised, and empty speeches on the delivery or the effectiveness of the same. Public services in Brazzaville have tended to speak on behalf of the service users in the name of what Rousseau (2012) called *l'interet general* or, in other words, the general will. In effect, this means that the state behaves as if it knows the needs of the service users better than they actually know themselves. And by doing so, service users are effectively denied a basic and fundamental opportunity or right to have a say in the making of services that directly affect them.

The need for social care is apparent, but nothing is being done to address the issue. In fact, there is no social care system in place as things stand. The health care system, almost non-existent, is an area of public service where service users are seen by professionals as merely passive objects with no real agency. They are regarded just as patients needing the help of professionals.

In short, and I know this may come as a surprise to some, but it is the reality: in Congo Brazzaville, service users are systematically excluded from the whole decision-making process.

The system is confusing. It bears flaws inherited from the time of colonisation. The idea of specialists of public service, of experts who know what is best, has only contributed to the remoteness of the user from the service initially designed to serve them. There is no communication structure whatsoever. Service users are generally confined in a position of isolation and submission. Subsequently, they don't understand or know where decisions affecting them come from. This leads to a real *disempowerment* of patients by professionals. Alienation and oppression of patients is a very concerning issue. Frantz Fanon (2001), writing about *The Wretched of the Earth*, can help us understand what at stake here because tyrannical rulers still oppress their people. Although we are in a post-colonial era, Fanon's work is still very much relevant. It is just that the colonisers wear white coats and make diagnoses now instead of wearing military uniforms and carrying guns. Patients with mental health issues, for example, are automatically seen as mad or crazy. They are literally ostracised by the very people supposed to help them heal. This sort of oppression and dehumanisation by professionals of health care, be it purposely or unconsciously, will only end when the service users, namely patients, are finally recognised as having a voice.

There is no system in place that allows the consumer to complain. Complaints departments or survey agencies don't exist in the Congolese public sector, let alone in the health care or education fields. Access to services is a real struggle on all fronts. Staff (working under horrible conditions) are generally not courteous or welcoming. It is often the case that patients at hospitals will be treated or defined by how much money they can pay.

From top to bottom, the system is rigged. Those running the services act as if they were superior to the very people they seek to serve. They treat service users with disdain, as if they were the roots cause of society's misery and therefore nothing good can come from them. Conversely, services users have no means to challenge staff. To put it simply, services users in Congo Brazzaville are disfranchised. There is no way they could ever give their view on how the service is being delivered to them. Just as much, they are unable to fight the exclusion. Users don't even know that they have the right to complain or report, and this is mainly because those structures don't actually exist.

Couleurs Congolaises

In the spring of 2003, I had just got my A levels and was ready to embark on a new journey. I was full of ambition and imagination. I originally wanted to be a musician, a rapper or just a famous artist, for I believed that was the only effective way to affect and bring about real changes in the lives of those I felt were not listened to. But my parents were against that idea, as they felt it wasn't representative of the family status or reputation. Having understood my motivation behind the ambition of becoming a famous artist, my family thought that the best course of action was for me to go university.

Now, it is common knowledge that where I come from no one sends their kids to university to learn music, or art for that matter. So, I had to choose either to study French literature and eventually end up as a teacher, or study law. My parents, especially my mum, convinced me that law school was my best shot. So, going to university (going to university unfortunately is still a luxury to this day) was a great thing and an eye opener for me.

Up until that time, I had always thought that only disabled people or people with learning difficulties, women and those who are still in Congo Brazzaville called *les pygmey* were the marginalised of our society. These were the people I had decided to commit my life to representing.

137

University then showed me a different perspective. I realised that we were all disfranchised and not listened to.

I met people that otherwise I would have never met. I met people whose parents had had to sell off everything they ever owned so that they could send their children to university. I also met people who were so rich that they had a sense of entitlement and always got things their own way. People with great talents and ambitions talked about leaving the country for new horizons as their opportunities for self-expression and success were so limited. I myself was tempted to go abroad. I started to question some of my beliefs about the kind of society we lived in. At university, I realised that in general the state didn't care about our ambitions, our aspirations.

So many things were happening, but we felt powerless and unable to have an impact. So, in summer of 2003 I, along with a couple of mates, decided to start publishing a journal in which students expressed their concerns. We would give copies away for free and post it on the walls of the university. We would publish it every two weeks – but because of lack of funds, and the university's unwillingness to help, we eventually had to stop. A great lesson was learned from that experience, however, in terms of how much people wanted to be heard but didn't know if they even have the right to be heard.

So naturally, in my second year, I wanted to do something about this. In the search for a good way to be useful, I joined several different organisations or associations. But one thing always bothered me: lack of representation for people that needed to have their voice heard, the way that privilege worked in these organisations so that the same old people always got the benefit while the unprivileged were always forgotten and ignored.

I found myself almost lost for about three months before I came across *Couleurs Tropicales*, a musical radio program run by Claudy Siar. Claudy Siar caught my attention not because of the music he played but rather because of his commitment to giving voice to young people across French-speaking countries in Africa. He was very aware of how much the young generation had to say but, more importantly, to learn. The format of the program was designed in a way that people all around the world would call him and express their feelings about a situation they were facing. Claudy would always have some hope to give them, encouraging us to vent our frustration but at the same time reminding us about the responsibilities we have to create the changes we want. Inspired by his work and words, I knew I had to do something.

In 2006, I had just come back from holiday with my granddad. I wasn't sure if I wanted to go back to university to complete my master's degree. I had just spent a great time with my grandparents in the village, where I was able to appreciate with a great sense of gratitude how blessed some of us have been. I had seen people living in conditions of desperate poverty and hardship. There was no access to education or health care, but there was also no expectation of these things. People had nothing, and made do with nothing, but had no sense that anything could or should be different. And there I had learnt that it is not that people are unwilling to change their conditions; rather, it was a case of many not even knowing that this was a possibility. I realised that people had grown into thinking that the way things were was the only way they ever could be. I realised that if people's lives were to change, then we needed a radical change in ways of looking at the situations they were in. I can remember my granddad sharing my frustration as to why I couldn't do something meaningful. But then he turned around and told me that if I wanted to be helpful to others, I might need to help myself first. I paused and gazed at him in bewilderment. He said: you need to change your mentality first, then you will be able to create the same level of enthusiasm and ambition in others.

As part of trying to follow my grandad's advice, I decided to create a platform where we would embark on a mission of creating what Benedict Anderson (2016) has called *a new consciousness*. So, with two of my friends, we founded the association Couleurs Congolaises. My frustration was born out of the fact that I knew so many people with great potential and who were incredibly smart but who couldn't pursue their education because of the way the system is set up. Some because they were dyslectics, some because they had physical impairments and some just because they stuttered when they spoke. These are issues that could have been addressed if indeed the policy makers had dared to talk to service users.

The aim of the group was simply to raise consciousness of personal and social rights – of basic human rights – among young people. My ambition came from the belief that if we could give a platform to voice their concern or just to put forward their ideas, there was always an opportunity for positive change. That aim gave us a very targeted audience in colleges and universities. We started by posting on university and college walls the things we thought students were entitled to while using those services. While this was very popular with the young people, the institutions didn't like it quite so well. We regularly found that our posters had been torn down and destroyed. We had to change strategies. We decided to offer free music concerts.

Inspired by Gramsci's *Prison Notebooks* (2005), we understood that in order to create and maintain a new society, we also needed to create and maintain a new consciousness. And the breath of consciousness is culture. A new public service culture was needed in Congo Brazzaville. So, we challenged people to think differently and be more proactive. We would invite young musicians that otherwise would have never performed in front a crowd to perform for us. We created opportunities for artists to showcase their work. We had, of course, to fund it ourselves. We would use those moments to effectively talk with people about their rights as women, as disabled people, as children, as students and so on. The concerts would most of the time turn into a debate, but always in a very constructive way. The first three events and workshops, we struggled to attract the big crowd. But then we were taken by surprise when at our next meeting we ran out of seats and room to accommodate everyone. The word had spread, and people now wanted to find out more about us.

As we became more successful we grew as an organisation, but we made sure that we were always representative of the communities we worked with. On our board of directors we had people with learning impairments, people with physical impairments, people who had had no opportunities for education, people as young as 16, people from the divided north and the south of the country. We started to apply for funding to various sources including, Le Centre Culturel Francais, but with no success until 2009, when the United States Embassy in Brazzaville took a gamble on us. We now had the funds, so we hired a bigger room, namely Memorial Pierre Savorgnon de Brazza. As we wanted to keep it real, we decided that we would do everything, including the speaking. By this I mean that we did not involve big-name academics or celebrities to draw the crowds; we kept it low-level and authentic. The themes were always about human rights and development. We emphasised the fact that human rights only make sense when they contribute to the development and emancipation of humans. We drew thousands of people. That alone put us on the government radar. We had gained momentum now.

Even the schools and colleges that initially said no were now calling us to come and address their students. We organised conferences across the country to help people realise that they have rights just as much as they have duties. We spoke to school children in a language they could understand. We held meetings for the most vulnerable people in our society: for poor people and for disabled people. These people were outright denied access to basic human rights. And at times we could see that they felt guilty and responsible for their conditions. Freire (2017) talks about this in his *Pedagogy of the Oppressed*. So worn down have they become, so few opportunities have they had, that they assume that because of who they are as people they literally have no entitlement to anything. In 2010, we launched a campaign of what Freire (2017) calls *conscientisation* across the whole country, though at the time I would not have used this word as I had not yet heard of Freire. We opened a youth centre within our headquarters. We hosted conferences on the rights of disabled people in the army. In 2011, we joined the YALI group, the Young African Leadership Initiative established by Barack Obama, and we went to the United States. After this, we put in place RJLC – the Rassemblement des Jeunes Leader in Congo, establishing a platform where we helped the focus remain on people who had been disfranchised for too long. In 2014, we became part of the Mandela Washington Fellowship. We organised courses educating people about HIV because of the dehumanising stigma around this.

These activities gave people a new perspective and an understanding that whatever their situation, wherever they had come from, whoever they were, as Congolese citizens they had the same rights as anybody else. They realised that as ordinary people they were entitled to be active in civil life and to speak out for themselves. We were just ordinary Congolese speaking about our rights, and that had a big impact. Suddenly people were able to see that this was a possibility for them, too.

The government took an interest in us by offering for us to campaign for them at election time. This was an offer that we naturally turned down. We started engaging with people as young as 10 years. We engaged with anyone who wanted to fight for social justice. We travelled all over Congo Brazzaville, addressing people in their own dialects, taking the same message that people need to know their rights before they can actively participate as citizens, working towards the betterment of their conditions and, by extension, of the whole society. The way we mobilised young people and encouraged them to be more active citizens and voice their concerns led to the government creating a new ministerial post in 2017. Since then, we have had a Minister for Youth, although we still have doubt as to what he is actually doing for young folks.

Conclusion

Now, I am sure I am going to get stick from some people, especially those in favour of the status quo, from those who profit from the way things are. They will attack me as being disloyal, for painting such a dark picture of Congo Brazzaville. They will argue that syndicates of consumers and various associations play the liaison between the public services and users. These syndicates and organisations are consulted and do engage, on behalf the service users, with the way services are structured and delivered. Therefore, they will argue, service users are effectively involved. They will certainly claim that the idea that it should be a direct dialogue with service users themselves is ludicrous. But these are like the organisations *for* disabled people rather than *of* disabled people in the UK. Their right to speak on behalf of service users needs be questioned when service users have no voice themselves. My guess is these people will try to accuse me of being anti-government.

But the truth is that all these syndicates, "people with competence", associations and so on, may well at a very specific point in time in the past have played the necessary role of representatives to fill a void. But the suggestion that they are still to this day fulfilling that same role is just not right. In one word, these spokespersons existed as a default position. But this does not mean that we should seek to maintain them if indeed they now impede new and better ways of user participation.

It is important to stress that I am not suggesting that we should get rid of them totally (even if I think they are useless in the sense that they are mostly focused on self-interest). I do not suggest that we exclude but rather that we add, share and participate:

- We should add because a proper representation of service users will help eliminate oppressive practice. For example, a patient is best placed to understand how their own life is experienced.

- We should share because this will allow for a redefinition of responsibilities from both decision makers and service users in the process. This willingness to share will put an end to the monopoly of representation and give way to a direct dialogue.
- We should allow participation because this will foster the creation of structures organised on the basis of more equal relationships between service providers and service users.

This, in my view, is the only serious way we will be able to improve the quality of public services that are provided. Only when service users are treated with respect within any public service, able to identify themselves without stigma being attached, when they are able to know when and who to speak to as the need arises – only then will I believe that things are any better.

The activities of Couleurs Congolaises were disrupted with the political unrest that followed the 2016 civil war in Congo Brazzaville. Our leadership has been dispersed and we have experienced "discouragement" to continue our activities. Nevertheless, there are signs that a new dawn is rising. In October 2018, a public meeting was held to re-launch the organisation. We are far from having achieved our goal, but we sure will continue the fight. And, as Gil Scott-Heron (1970) said, *the revolution will not be televised*.

Further Reading (and Listening)

Anderson, B. (2016) *Imagined Communities: Reflections on the Origin and Spread of Nationalism*. London: Verso.

Fanon, F. (2001) *The Wretched of the Earth*. London: Penguin.

Freire, P. (2017) *Pedagogy of the Oppressed*. London: Penguin.

Gramsci, A. (2005) *The Prison Notebooks*. London: Lawrence and Wishart.

Rousseau, J-J. (2012) *Of the Social Contract and Other Political Writings*. London: Penguin.

Scott-Heron, G. (1970) *"The Revolution Will Not Be Televised"*. *Small Talk at 125th & Lenox*. London: Ace Records.

13

SERVICE USER INVOLVEMENT AND GAP-MENDING PRACTICES IN SWEDEN

Cecilia Heule, Marcus Knutagård and Arne Kristiansen

Introduction

In the last 15 years, a practice of service user participation has been developed in the School of Social work at Lund University which has involved around 300 service users and over 50 service user organizations in the region. The urge to mend gaps between social workers and different service user groups was due to a perceived tendency to categorize "the other" based on prejudiced views and perceptions. We also noticed that people who became clients of social work practice seldom were mobilized into any kind of partnership within the social worker organizations, which we wanted to encourage. We will share some of our learning outcomes in this chapter, but first we will give you some idea about how service user organizations have developed and operate within the Swedish system.

History of service user involvement in Sweden

In the 19th century, a number of organizations were developed in Sweden to promote the interests of people with disabilities. These organizations were initiated by philanthropists and dedicated doctors. In the middle of the 20th century, people with lived experiences of disability or social and economic marginalization began to have an impact on the development of the service user movement. DHR (promoting people with disabilities) has existed since 1923 and has grown since the 1970s, inspired by the Independent Living movement, to become an important voice in protecting the interests of people with disabilities. PRO, an organization that protects the rights of the elderly, was founded in 1942 and has over 300,000 members. In 1945, Länkarna was formed as a peer support organization for people with alcohol problems. They conduct services in several Swedish municipalities. In 1956, Alcoholics Anonymous was established in Sweden, and since then it has grown to be an important movement with self-help groups throughout the country. In the 1960s, several service user organizations were formed in a collaboration between service users and professionals to improve policy and promote human rights for their members. RFHL was initiated in 1965 to promote the rights of drug users, while RSMH, which promotes rights for people with mental health problems, was founded in 1966. In the 1990s, a number of social enterprises developed in which formerly marginalized groups such as people with disabilities or persons with a background in drug use or criminality developed businesses together. Basta, 50 km south of Stockholm, was one of the first social enterprises in Sweden. Another example is Vägen Ut, which developed in Gothenburg (Meeuwisse and Sunesson, 1998; Larsson, 2006; Mathiesen, 2004).

An important part of Swedish history is the tradition of social movements and the significant role membership-based organizations have played in developing the democratic system and the Swedish welfare state at the beginning of the last century. Service-led and other voluntary organizations have been important parts of Swedish politics in their areas of expertise. One example is the disability movement, which played an essential role when rights-based legislation for people with disabilities was introduced in 1994 (the Swedish Act concerning Support and Service for Persons with Disabilities). The service-led organizations are also taking on growing responsibility for producing services financed by the state. There is increased recognition regarding the importance of service users' voices in the development of public services. Several national initiatives have been developed recently, planned by organizations such as the Swedish Association of Local Authorities and Regions (SKR) and dialogue groups consulting the government (Johansson et al., 2011). The National Board of Health and Welfare has since the 1990s tried to influence the social services to take greater account of service users' perspectives. It is clear that in recent years, some service user groups in Sweden have gained greater influence over the design of various care and support interventions. This applies, to some extent, to people in elderly care and people with physical or intellectual disabilities. However, the development of influence has not been positive for all service user groups. When it comes to people with substance abuse problems, people in poverty or people suffering from mental illness, there are many examples which indicate that their influence has diminished in recent decades. The development of service user influence in social work practice in Sweden is also hindered by insufficient resources for municipal social work. A large percentage of social workers have a very heavy work load, which makes it difficult to find time to develop cooperation with service users. In addition, the choice of intervention is governed by the municipalities' finances rather than by the needs of the service users (Kristiansen and Heule, 2016).

Service users and the education of social workers in Sweden

In Sweden, approximately 2,500 people are annually accepted as new university students in social work. Most social work programs in Sweden have courses that deal with the problems faced by service users. Often these courses are *about* different service user groups. They sometimes include lectures in which service users talk about their life experiences. There are problems with this type of strategy; namely, it rarely allows a critical analysis of the dominant perceptions of service users and social workers, which too often focus on the service user as a problem and the social worker as an expert on those problems. This entails a risk that such stereotypes are preserved (Heule and Kristiansen, 2018).

We believe it is fair to say that the School of Social Work at Lund University is an exception because of opportunities for service users to be a part of its curriculum as both students and teachers and supervisors. This practice has been developing since 2005, when the first so-called Mobilization course was given, which focuses on community planning and change and is given both to social work students in their last semester and to students who have been recruited from different service user organizations.

The first Mobilization course was developed within an EU-sponsored partnership funded by the EQUAL program. EQUAL was a program within the EU's structural funds that dealt with the inclusion of marginalized and discriminated groups in society. Through innovative projects carried out by organizations from different sectors of society that formed national and transnational partnerships, EQUAL aimed to influence structures and policies for the benefit of discriminated groups. It was together with the social enterprise Basta, which is run by former drug users, that the idea of a gap-mending course emerged. The School of Social work in Lund and Basta were formal partners in the development partnership, but other service user organizations were also invited to participate in the planning of the course, such as the Swedish clubhouse movement (Fountain House), the National Association of Roma people, members of the National Association for people with neuropsychiatric disabilities and others. The initiative of the course thus came from service user-led organizations in collaboration with teachers at the School of Social Work. The purpose of the cooperation was to include members from different service user organizations in the development of social education. The initiating teachers wanted to create a cross-boundary platform for change through the Mobilization course as well as conditions for future cross-boundary cooperation.

The design of the Mobilization course

Pedagogically, the Mobilization course is based on methods which assume that learning and development are social processes that require action, interaction and reflection and in which students have influence over the educational situation. A goal is to transcend the problem-based perspective, which dominates in social work (Kristiansen, 2005; Heule and Kristiansen, 2018). We believe that the strength-based perspective is significantly more constructive (Rapp and Goscha, 2012). The service users, as well as their organizations, are important forces for the development of social work. With the gap-mending concept, we want to give students from the service user organizations and social work program opportunities to study together on equal terms, while emphasizing that experience-based knowledge is an important complement to research and social workers' experience-based knowledges. There are several ways to develop gap-mending practices, and over the years we have made small adjustments in order to better frame the joint learning situation. We will first share with you how the course is presently conducted, and then share some of our learning outcomes.

The Mobilization course comprises six weeks of full-time studies and gives students 7.5 university credits (ECTS). The social work students take the course as part of an elective and advanced course in the seventh and final semester of the social work program. The students from service user organizations take the course as a six-week commission course in social work at the basic level. However, this difference is only a formal and administrative issue. In practice, it is a course with the same content and basically the same requirements for all students. The students who study at an advanced level have three additional weeks in which they deal with theoretical literature and reflect upon the common six-week course. Commission courses are an opportunity for Swedish universities and colleges to offer authorities and companies qualified education for their employees. Commission courses makes it possible to make exceptions from the admission requirements that apply to ordinary courses at universities and colleges. The fact that all students get university credits has been an important factor. Although the students who come from the service user organizations have different educational backgrounds, most of them belong to a group in the community that is normally excluded from university studies. On a personal level, it is therefore very valuable for many of the students from service user organizations to get this validation (Heule et al., 2017).

Since the first course, which took place in 2005, 25 Mobilization courses have been held. Students and teachers at the Mobilization course have interacted with more than 50 different service user organizations. Many of the commission students have experiences of mental illness. Another common background is long-term drug abuse, with the marginalization that often follows this lifestyle. People with physical disabilities or people who, because of their ethnic background, have difficulty entering the labor market have also participated, but not to the same extent. Several of those who attend the course have been in situations involving complex difficulties. A variety of problems have reinforced their experiences of marginalization and exclusion from society, such as experiences of homelessness, debt, family problems, addiction and mental or physical disabilities. In the first few years, we had to spend quite a lot of time recruiting students from service user organizations. Today, the course is well known among service users and social workers in our region. Students who have participated in the course tell their friends and colleagues about it. Facebook and other social media are also important resources for providing information about and promoting the Mobilization course.

The first day of the Mobilization course is devoted to information about the schedule, textbooks and various practical details. Through various exercises, the students briefly introduce themselves to each other. We discuss the ethical and social framework that will apply to the course. During the weeks following the course introduction, time is devoted to personal presentations, as well as to lectures and group work on power, discrimination, social mobilization, project development and social change.

After the first two weeks, the teachers and students spend two days at a guesthouse in the countryside about 50 kilometers from the university. The purpose is to jointly develop alternative project ideas to improve social work, but also to get time to deepen relations between the course participants by living collectively for a couple of days. During the days in the countryside, we use a model called Future Workshop (Jungk and Müllert, 1987), which is a democratic method that is well suited for groups facing new challenges and changes. At the end of the Future Workshop, students form project groups based on their own interests and on what they want to develop in social work practice. These groups develop their projects in the weeks that follows.

During the project development, the groups work independently, under supervision from the teachers. The project plans are presented by the students to an external panel of experts during the fifth week. The panel consists of a variety of persons who have considerable experience of working with and evaluating projects. We strive to have different experts represented in the panel and therefore usually invite a politician, a researcher, a social service representative and a representative from a service user organization. The day after the presentations of the project plans, we meet with the students to follow up and review the panel's views on the project plans. It is the teachers on the course that decide whether a project plan is approved. In our assessment, we rely not only on the content of the project plan but also the degree to which students have been involved and active in the project development. During the last week of the course, the students work on an individual assignment, which consists of a personal reflection of what they have learned from the joint co-production with the other students. These reflections are presented and discussed at a seminar. Thereafter, the Mobilization course ends with a joint course evaluation (Figure 13.1).

The paradox of categorization

The Mobilization course has taken on the challenge of creating a community between social work students and students from service user organizations. Social work students are educated to be part of a professional assembly, while those who come from different service user organizations are normally outside the professional demarcation. A concept that is often used in contexts characterized by categorical identification of people is the word *prejudice*. Social psychologist Gordon Allport describes how the evolution of the English word prejudice (from *Praejudicium* in

First week	Second week	Third week	Fourth week	Fifth week	Sixth week
Introduction Personal presentations Lectures Group work	Personal presentations Lectures Group work	Future work-shop Project deve-lopment	Project deve-lopment Supervision	Project deve-lopment Presentations of projects	Reflection Examination Course evalua-tion

Figure 13.1 Course outline. The Mobilization course at Lund University

Source: (Kristiansen and Heule, 2016)

Latin) in the American language has changed, from having meant "an assessment based on past decisions or experiences" to also include assessments taken on bad grounds, often with an emotional tone of approval or non-approval. He does this in his classic *The Nature of Prejudice*, which first was published 1954 and still counts as one of the most important works on the dynamics and emergence of prejudice. Just as we judge others, we place ourselves in different categories that are close to us, such as family, neighborhood, region or nation. Race, religion, politics and social traditions also play into our self-categorization. Allport calls this self-categorization a form of *ingroups*. The opposite of an ingroup is what Allport calls an *outgroup* (Allport, 1979)

In the Mobilization course, a former outgroup has been integrated into an ingroup at the School of Social Work, and a new overarching ingroup has been formed. The initial prejudices between the student groups are evident in the qualitative study conducted by Cecilia Heule (forthcoming), which shows how the social work students and the students from different service user organizations perceive each other at the beginning stage of the six-week course. They look at each other not as subjective individuals but rather as part of a binary category: social workers (to be) and (former) clients. Figure 13.2 summarizes the way they perceive the others initially.

These initial impressions show perceived differences between students from service user organizations and social work students. Gordon Allport's account of the concept of prejudice includes not only experience-based perception, but also emotionally approving or not liking. The reviews summarized in Figure 13.2 can be seen as a reduction of the other based on different value systems.

The first courses that were given were characterized by more unresolved conflicts, as the students from service user organizations came with a desire to educate the often-younger social work students about "reality". The social work students felt judged by the often-bad experiences that were communicated by the students from service user organizations and protested as they had not contributed yet to that practice. Because of this, a number of de-categorizing strategies were developed within the Mobilization course. Categorization, de-categorization and re-categorization have been discussed by Brewer and Miller (1984) in a study that focused on group differences when ingroups and outgroups met. They noted that contact between groups could lead to increased tensions, especially initially. Therefore, they recommended that the appearance of these differences should be suppressed by different de-categorizing processes. For example, they proposed a heterogeneity among the outgroup members to reduce the stereotypical similarities between them. They also encouraged more personal information during the contact to draw attention to differences within group boundaries. By reducing attention to membership in a category or group, they hoped to reduce tensions between ingroups and outgroups. Critics of the de-categorization theory have argued that, in particular for minorities, it may be unfavorable to weaken their group identities in the meeting with majority groups.

Social work student's categorical identification of the commission students	Commission student's categorical identification of social work students
• Negative towards social workers • Emotional • Unacademic approach • Undiplomatic and judgemental • Defensive	• Young and inexperienced • Having "school book knowledge" rather than having experienced the "real life" • Anxious and performance-targeted • Judgemental

Figure 13.2 Students' initial identification of "the others"

The re-categorization model (also known as the "common in-group identity model") has also been discussed by Gaertner and Davidio (2000), who have argued that good results can be achieved if members from different groups accept joint membership of a sub-ordained group. Instead of dissolving categorical boundaries, they are thus reconstructing new boundaries that enclose both groups of origin in a more efficient community. There are several experimental studies that support claims about the model's effectiveness. One advantage of the model is considered to be that it seeks not an obliteration of original identities but rather an inclusion in a more inclusive and diverse community (Brown and Hewstone, 2005; Pettigrew and Tropp, 2011).

Figure 13.3 shows which aspects of the Mobilization course can be seen as categorizing, re-categorizing and de-categorizing (Heule, forthcoming).

The starting point is that participants have been recruited due to categorical inequality. Our research shows that the different student categories initially have prejudice towards the others based on organizational affiliation, or category. The re-categorization and de-categorization aspects of the Mobilization course have an impact on the boundary crossing that leads to increased trust, or community. They create the conditions for a changed attitude between the course participants. However, these conditions cannot be forced upon individual students, but require the active risk-taking and commitment of each participants. The gap-mending challenge has been to develop community and trust between groups that initially have a stereotype and not infrequently prejudiced perception of each other. One hypothesis has been that the boundaries between one or the other category may become less noticeable by participants distancing themselves from their categorical character. This has been possible by developing different strategies of de-categorization, such as the personal presentations that every student makes at the beginning of the course. The focus on experiential knowledge is not only about the experiences of the commission students, but also exists in order to develop common knowledge; each student's experiences are reflected upon in relation to the others. It has surprised many that the social work students carry so many experiences that can be compared to those who come from different service user organizations. After overcoming the categorical demarcation, students' views of the others have changed and they express a more nuanced picture of the others. The social work students perceive this as a risk in relation to previous positioning. The new role interpretation can be seen as common risk-taking that has been done through a number of chain reactions. A changed self-image has proved to be an important step in order to change the image of the other. This process is described in the following citation, expressed by a social work student:

> I felt like once I had done the presentation, I was one of the members of the group. Because the group began by being two separate groups, as the students from service user organizations and social work students were expected to be different. I often

Categorizing aspects	• Selection of people who belong to different sides of a boundary in relation to the School of Social work (in-group and out-group)
Re-categorizing aspects	• Equal conditions as students on the same course • Cooperation • Common objectives in the joint projects that they develop. • Theories and values that support this within the framework of the Mobilization course
De-categorizing aspects	• Stepping outside the comfort zone in personal presentations by showing a more complex narrative than the stereotype • Students' own gap-mending strategies in group work by being more personal with each other • Transcendental meetings backstage in smoke and coffee breaks or traveling to or from school

Figure 13.3 The elements of categorization, re-categorization and de-categorization within the Mobilization course

sat down with those from my own group and I felt that there were prejudices about that the social work students knew nothing about what it was like to be exposed to problems, and that the commission students knew nothing about how the system worked or how to help people. But after I made my presentation, it was like I suddenly belonged to both groups, at least that's how it felt for me. I felt that the students from the service user organizations accepted me in a completely different way than they had done before. One of them told me that they initially thought I was like any other social worker – young, naïve and not knowing anything about what it's like to be exposed to government practice or being on the social bottom. That I lived in a world of fine theories and hid behind an academic education. When I told my story, which they could recognize themselves in, the service users' picture of me had completely changed and they realized that maybe I might know what I was talking about, even though I was young and academically educated. That I also had been through things, but was lucky enough to get out of them. That I was also worthy of talking about social problems, because I myself was part of that world. I felt that it took longer for those who were not as open in their presentations to become part of the group.

By being vulnerable and outside her comfort zone, the above-cited student gained trust from the students from service user organizations. The citation also shows that this changed the binary categorizing mechanisms and opened up for earlier gaps to be mended.

An enabling platform

The Mobilization course is today an established part of the social work program at the School of Social Work, Lund University. More than 800 students have completed the Mobilization course. Of 260 students with their own experiences of social problems, a majority are active in different service user organizations. Many of them are also engaged as lecturers and supervisors at other courses at the School of Social Work in Lund. The Mobilization course has been developed into an action research-oriented platform for gap-mending-based networking, the development of alternative solutions to social problems and research on an emancipatory basis (Heule et al., 2017). It makes it possible to create enabling niches (Taylor, 1997; Ryke et al., 2004; Rapp and Goscha, 2012). In an enabling niche, it is possible to use the students' own strengths and resources. Many of the commission students have experienced entrapping niches that hinder their participation. At the core of an enabling niche is the building of trust.

Several of the project ideas developed during the Mobilization course have been realized in various contexts in society. Some new service user organizations have been developed based on ideas created during the Mobilization course. Many of our former students are active in development projects in various organizations and municipalities in Sweden. Teachers of the Mobilization course are often invited to participate in various contexts related to service user involvement and the development of alternative solutions to social problems. Over the years, we have participated in a large number of conferences and seminars on service user influence both in Sweden and abroad. The Mobilization course has been an important part of the development of the international network PowerUs and has been a source of inspiration for the development of gap-mending practices in several countries in Europe. The experience of and knowledge from the Mobilization course has generated other research projects. One example is a research project on Housing First. Housing First is a way of working with homelessness that is based on housing as a prerequisite. By providing independent housing for homeless people first, and connecting with relevant support that the tenant wants, the result is very high housing retention rates. The principles of Housing First move away from the idea of making people "housing" ready and the dysfunctional logics of staircase models, where homeless people are expected to prove, step by step, that they deserve housing. Housing becomes an end goal rather than a means. There have been many synergies between the research on Housing First and the enabling platform that the Mobilization course constitutes. Former students from the course have been engaged from the very start in promoting, planning and implementing the program. Another example is an action research project on the social housing program in the City of Helsingborg, which took place between 2014 and 2017 and was inspired by the gap-mending concept (Knutagård and Kristiansen, 2018). Cecilia Heule's forthcoming doctoral dissertation is based on the Mobilization course as an experimental platform for studying the mechanism of gap-mending. We are currently working on a three-year EU-funded research project that includes a follow-up study of those who have been students on the Mobilization course. Mending gaps in social work education, practice and research is not a straight road. There are many barriers to tackle, from small bureaucratic bumps to huge mountains of prejudice. However, mending gaps is possible, and by creating enabling niches, it is also possible to open up a new space for change.

References

Allport, Gordon (1979) *The nature of prejudice*. New York: Perseus Books Publishing.

Brewer, Marilynn & Miller, Norman (1984) "Beyond the contact hypothesis: Theoretical perspectives on desegregation". In Miller, Norman & Brewer, Marilynn (eds.), *Groups in contact: The psychology of desegregation*. Orlando: Academic Press.

Brown, Rubert & Hewstone, Miles (2005) "An integrative theory of intergroup contact". *Advances in Experimental Social Psychology*, vol. 37, pp. 255–343.

Gaertner, Samuel & Davidio, John (2000) *Reducing intergroup bias: The common ingroup identity model*. Philadelphia: Psychology Press.

Heule, Cecilia (forthcoming) *Att utveckla delaktighet inom Socionomutbildningen. En studie om iscensatt gemenskap*. Lund: Lund University, dissertation.

Heule, Cecilia, Knutagård, Marcus & Kristiansen, Arne (2017) "Mending the gaps in social work education and research: Two examples from a Swedish context". *The European Journal of Social Work*, vol. 20 (3), pp. 396–408.

Heule, Cecilia & Kristiansen, Arne (2018) "Gap-mending as an additional concept in analytical reflections about service user involvement". In Spatscheck, Christian, Ashencaen Crabtree, Sara & Parker, Jonathan (eds.), *Methods and methodologies of social work: Reflecting professional interventions*. London: Whiting & Birch.

Johansson, Håkan, Kassman, Anders & Scaramuzzino, Roberto (2011) *Staten och det civila samhällets organisationer i ett föränderligt välfärdssamhälle. Perspektiv på en överenskommelse*. Stockholm: Överenskommelsen.

Jungk, Robert & Mullert, Norbert (1987) *Future workshops: How to create desirable futures*. London: Institute for Social Inventions.

Knutagård, Marcus & Kristiansen, Arne (2018) *Nytt vin i gamla läglar: Skala upp Bostad först, boendeinflytande och om att identifiera och stötta "the missing hero"*. Lund: School of Social Work, Lund University.

Kristiansen, Arne (2005) *Flickor i tvångsvård. Utvärdering av tolvstegsinriktad §12-vård*. Stockholm: Statens institutionsstyrelse.

Kristiansen, Arne & Heule, Cecilia (2016) "Power, experiences and mutual development: Using the concept of gap-mending in social work education". In Chiapparini, Emanuela (ed.), *Teaching social work by involving service users: Concepts and evaluations of courses with gap mending approaches in Europe*. Opladen, Berlin & Toronto: Budrich.

Larsson, Stig (2006) "Det sociala arbetets intresseorganisationer". In Meeuwisse, Anna, Sunesson, Sune & Swärd, Hans (eds.), *Socialt arbete. En grundbok*. Stockholm: Natur och Kultur.

Mathiesen, Thomas (2004) "Om KRUM:s nedgång och fall". In Adamson, Monica, Grip, Lars, Modig, Cecilia & Nestius, Hans (eds.), *När botten stack upp: om de utslagnas kamp för frihet och människovärde*. Hedemora: Gidlund.

Meeuwisse, Anna & Sunesson, Sune (1998) "Frivilliga organisationer, Socialt arbete och Expertis". *Socialvetenskaplig Tidskrift*, vol. 5 (2–3), pp. 172–193.

Pettigrew, Thomas F. & Tropp, Linda R. (2011) *When groups meet: The dynamics of intergroup contact*. New York: Psychology Press.

Rapp, Charles A. & Goscha, Richard J. (2012) *The strengths model: A recovery-oriented approach to mental health services*. New York: Oxford University Press.

Ryke, Elma, Strydom, Herman & Botha, Karel (2004) The social niche: Conceptualising the human environment. *International Journal of the Humanities*, vol. 2 (3), pp. 1935–1944.

Taylor, James B. (1997) "Niches and practice: Extending the ecological perspective". In Saleebey, Dennis (ed.), *The strengths perspective in social work practice*. New York: Longman.

14

CHALLENGING RACISM IN HONG KONG

An e-learning approach to social work education

Raes Begum Baig, Kar-Choi Chan and Jim Campbell

Introduction

This chapter uses the case study of Hong Kong to explore innovative ways to enhance students' and other stakeholders' knowledge and skills in working with ethnic minority service users. The chapter begins with important background information about the needs of ethnic minority populations in Hong Kong. This is set in an historical analysis which highlights periods of colonialism that exacerbated systems of discrimination and racism. As a result, social work provision in Hong Kong is shaped by a particular mix of social welfare organizations often delivered by voluntary sector organizations, with relatively little direct provision by the state. These organizations have made piecemeal responses to issues of racism and discrimination which particularly affect migrant populations seeking employment and new lives in Hong Kong. However, the Race Discrimination Ordinance (RDO), finally enacted in 2008, ensured that dedicated social services for ethnic minorities were established. The second half of the chapter then focuses on issues of social work education, drawing upon international and national literature to set the scene for an explanation regarding the planning and delivery of e-learning videos to enable social work students to challenge aspects of discrimination and racism in Hong Kong. The project used a stakeholder approach to design the videos, in which ethnic minority actors were used to create 'real world' scenarios that highlight professional, legal and policy approaches to racial equality. The videos were constructed around four themes (education, employment, use of social media and housing) and evaluated by students and other stakeholders, with positive outcomes. Some respondents felt that the videos helpfully aided in raising consciousness of stereotypes about ethnic minority communities, although others felt that they tended to overemphasize the need to abide by laws. It was felt that one effect of the videos was to encourage a re-evaluation of anti-racist social work approaches and services in Hong Kong, which were thought to be inadequate. The chapter concludes with an appeal for more innovative approaches to social work education, policy and practice in order that the needs of ethnic minority service users are met in Hong Kong.

Meeting the needs of ethnic minority populations in Hong Kong

The change of sovereignty from the British to Chinese government in 1997 marked an important turning point on race relations in Hong Kong. Non-Chinese ethnic minorities, mainly from South Asian countries such as India, Pakistan and Nepal, came to Hong Kong as early as the 1840s to work for the British colonial government and were granted the right of abode. Concerned that the right of abode granted by the British colonial government would cease after 1997 due to an uncertain political situation, many South Asians migrated to Hong Kong right before 1997. Together with the increase in the number of foreign domestic workers, the non-ethnic Chinese population increased from 251,200 in 1991 to 343,950 in 2001 and consisted of 8% of the whole population in 2018 (HKSAR Census and Statistics Department, 2017). The increased number of ethnic minorities and the desegregation of a minority population through public housing allocation have changed the nature of Hong Kong society. There is growing evidence of racial discrimination where minorities reported that they were not able to access public and social services due to issues of communication and language barriers (Baig, 2012). With mounting concerns about racial equality, the Race Discrimination Ordinance (RDO) was finally enacted in 2008 and dedicated social services for ethnic minorities have been opened by the government and other NGOs.

By the start of the new century, a number of social services organizations began to address the increasing challenges faced by ethnic minorities. For example, there were new attempts to provide Cantonese language courses, parenting skills training and recreational activities. In order to have better coordination among service providers, the Hong Kong Council of Social Service (HKCSS) formed a network to facilitate communication and skills sharing (Baig, 2012). In addition, there have been calls for greater legal protection against racial discrimination. Cross-sectoral collaboration platforms were established, including human rights organizations and social service agencies providing dedicated assistance for ethnic minority groups. These platforms were used for information sharing and the coordination of anti-racial discrimination campaigns which called for the government to legislate against racial discrimination (Baig, 2012). A consultation exercise enabled these groups to raise their concerns on racial equality and lobby the government on the contents of the legislation. It is important to point out role differentiations among these groups and organizations; while human rights groups tended to provide legal information on international standards on racial discrimination, social service organizations played a key role on information dissemination and mobilization. Significantly, user participation has been a feature in anti-racial discrimination movements and alliances have been built with social workers so that processes of communication and dissemination and mobilization could take place. As a result, forms of advocacy and action took place, for example through on-street protests and the lobbying of meetings with government officials and legislators. Eventually, the RDO was passed in the Legislative Council in 2008.

The development of social services for ethnic minorities

Although policies and services for ethnic minorities have existed in Hong Kong since the late 1990s, since the enactment of RDO the government is now subjected to statutory duties to ensure equal access to social services and welfare of ethnic minorities. As stated in the Administrative Guidelines on Promotion of Racial Equality:

> In addition to compliance with the legal requirements, the Government has also been taking measures to promote racial equality with a view to ensuring that persons of different races have equal access to, and benefit from, resources and opportunities available in the society. This is achieved through public education and promotional activities, and strengthening support services to ethnic minorities.
>
> *(HKSAR Government, 2010, p. 1)*

As stipulated in the RDO, racial discrimination, harassment and vilification in the provision of employment, education, provision of goods, facilities, services and premises are unlawful. The RDO also extended the provision of the Equal Opportunities Commission (EOC) to eliminate discrimination, harassment and vilification and promote equality and harmony between people of different races; and to settle cases through reconciliation or bring the cases to court. To facilitate social integration and access to community resources, the government funds the establishment and operation of support service centres and sub-centres for ethnic minorities in districts which have high concentrations of ethnic minority population and are operated by social service organizations. These provide various tailor-made services dedicated to the needs of ethnic minorities, including learning classes, after-school tutorial classes, developmental programmes for ethnic minority youths, counselling and referral services and integration programmes. Social workers are employed in these centres and sub-centres to manage and provide professional social work interventions. In addition, various funding schemes were also established by the government, the EOC and the private funding bodies to sponsor a number of programmes. This resulted in the development of radio programmes, job training courses and language courses for these communities (GovHK, 2017). Finally, an interpretation service is provided for ethnic minorities' communities to enable them to access general government services.

It is important to consider how well social workers understand and intervene in the context of these changes; in particular, there are rising concerns about how well they are prepared to be culturally competent and able to deliver anti-racist practice. Such concerns have been raised by ethnic minority groups, given the core role that social workers play in such organizations and services. According to the Hong Kong Social Workers Registration Board's (SWRB) Code of Practice, social workers should uphold cultural awareness in which 'social workers should recognise the ethnic and cultural diversity of the communities being served' and 'should be acquainted with and sensitive to the cultures of clients and appreciate the differences among them in respect of their ethnicity, national origin, nationality, religion and custom' (Social Workers Registration Board, 2013, p. 3). In another document published by SWRB, 'Principles, Criteria, and Standards for Recognizing Qualifications in Social Work for Registration of Registered Social Workers', social work students are required to learn about diversity under the required subject area of 'human behaviour and social environment', and knowledge of and practices on diversity are also disseminated throughout the curriculum (Social Workers Registration Board, 2014). However, most of the 19 institutions offering social work programmes do not have a dedicated course on understanding ethnic and cultural diversities. The Department of Social Work of the Chinese University of Hong Kong offers the course 'Intercultural Intelligence: Meeting the Challenges of a Culturally Diverse Society', yet it is not compulsory all for social work students.

Multiculturalism and anti-racism in social work and social work education

The importance of anti-racist practice in social work is highlighted in the Global Standards for Social Work Education and Training (Global Standards) published by the International Association of Schools of Social Work (IASSW) and the International Federation of Social Workers (IFSW) in 2004 (IFSW, 2004). The document emphasizes social work's mission to uphold 'cultural and ethnic diversity and gender inclusiveness' (IASSW and IFSW, 2004, p. 7). This implies that social work educators should equip social work students with the necessary skills, knowledge and values to deal with the many issues faced by ethnic minority communities. As stated in the Global Standards document, students need to 'develop self-awareness regarding their personal and cultural values, beliefs, traditions and biases and how these might influence the ability to develop relationships with people, and to work with diverse population groups' and to promote 'sensitivity to, and increasing knowledge about, cultural and ethnic diversity, and gender analysis' (IASSW and IFSW, 2004, p. 8). These approaches resonate with existing notions of cultural competence in social work education and practice.

A growing literature on how ethnic minority students experience social work education highlight a range of problematic issues that need to be addressed to confront discrimination and racism. In a recent study, Hollinrake et al. (2019) argue that white academics need to be more aware of issues of power and privilege when working with Black and Ethnic Minority Students. Hillen and Levy (2015) recommend a strengths-based approach and the celebration of diversity in the classroom. A key role for social work educators is to find ways to challenge the discrimination and prejudice that often occur during teaching (Daniel, 2011). Fletcher et al. (2015) conclude their study by arguing for concrete, transparent changes to social work education at institutional levels. Social work students, educators and practitioners need to be aware of their own cultural values, beliefs and prejudices in order to understand the identities of others, and should develop skills to perform interventions that cater for cultural and ethnic differences (Nadan and Ben-Ari, 2013; Sousa and Almeida, 2016). However, criticisms have been made about only using models of cultural competence which fail to address the complexities of racism and race relations (Abrams and Gibson, 2007; Schoorman and Bogotch, 2010; Constance-Huggins, 2012; Tisman and Clarendon, 2018). Schoorman and Bogotch (2010) conducted a study of teachers' conceptualizations of multicultural education (MCE) in the US and found that they could identify diversity and cultural differences, but that issues of social justice were largely absent. Constance-Huggins (2012) suggests that such findings overemphasized group differences rather than the reasons that create such differences. In focusing on 'content integration, prejudice reduction, and equity pedagogy' (p. 3), the underlying problems of racial inequality were largely ignored. By placing emphasis on individual attitudes and beliefs, educators were missing the opportunity to focus on structural causes of racial differences and inequality. Given social work's core principles in promoting social justice, such limited approaches on cultural competence appear inadequate.

It has been argued that structural analyses on race and racial inequality are therefore required to enable the profession to confront racism (Dominelli, 1992; Keating, 2000; Constance-Huggins, 2012; Masocha, 2015). Early attempts to develop such ideas tended to focus on racial power differences between black and white (Dominelli, 1992) and that institutional racism tends to systemically disadvantage ethnic and cultural minorities (Abrams and Gibson, 2007). To address this, it was asserted that anti-racist social work practice should be used to eliminate racial oppression and discrimination at both institutional and individual levels. Initiated by black social workers, 'it has been black people, writing from a black perspective rooted in their experience of racism in Britain, that have begun to shift the eyes of white academics and social workers towards racism as a structural phenomenon' (Dominelli, 1992, p. 74). Later commentators highlight the need for social workers and educators, not just to acknowledge the individual and institutional experiences of racism and oppression that prevent equal access to social resources, but also to take action to fight against injustice (Nadan and Ben-Ari, 2013). For example, anti-racist social work practice aims to turn white social workers into anti-racist allies by challenging racial supremacy and the intrinsic advantage of whiteness (Abrams and Gibson, 2007; Williams and Parrott, 2012). More recently, it has been asserted that a blended approach may be appropriate where an holistic multicultural social work approach merges both cultural competence and anti-racist models to address individual, interpersonal and institutional attributions on racism and racial equality (Akintayo et al., 2018).

The e-learning project on anti-racial discrimination and racial equality

As a result of these concerns about perceived deficits in the education and training of social work students in this area, the first two authors of this chapter developed new e-learning approaches in the Department of Social Work and Social Policy in the Chinese University of Hong Kong. E-learning is designed to use electronic technologies to access educational curriculum outside traditional classroom by supplementing traditional forms of face-to-face teaching. These include novel forms of media, information and communication technologies; these could be real time or achieved and presented when needed (Phelan, 2015). Sometimes blended learning would be used, with a combination of e-learning technologies and traditional classroom learning. One major concern that has been expressed is the contrasts between conventional classroom learning and e-learning in their relative effectiveness in transmitting knowledge and practice skills. However, comparisons of learning outcomes between social work students receiving e-learning and traditional classroom learning found similar grade results (Kleinpeter and Potts, 2000; Glezakos and Lee, 2001). Forms of e-learning can affect learning effectiveness, especially for curricula involving sociocultural perspectives and value reconstructions. Students showed higher satisfaction when e-learning platforms helped them to voice their opinions and allowed them to explore the curriculum being taught (Oterholm, 2009). These platforms can widen the content and scope of information in a way not often available in traditional teaching contexts (Campbell et al., 2018). This is relevant to the issues of race and disadvantage discussed in this chapter, where students need space to understand situations of disadvantage and cultural difference and in doing so can challenge existing values and beliefs through cognitive process when interacting with others (Longoria and Diaz, 2014). This echoes the findings on the effectiveness of blended learning, where students are provided with additional information through e-learning and given in-depth theoretical knowledge support in class (Banks and Faul, 2007; US Department of Education, 2010).

The key factor that leads to effective e-learning is the importance of having clear objectives and theoretical foundations (Liebowtiz and Frank, 2011; Okech et al., 2014). Emotional arousal and value transformation could be made possible if the e-learning content is focused and has strong motivational objectives. Deepak and Biggs (2011) used the concept of transformative learning through e-learning to facilitate social work students' learning on racism and develop their commitments on anti-racism ideology and practice in social work. Based on constructivist theory in adult learning, transformative learning is used to change a person's perceptions with a shift in consciousness, challenge a person's preconceptions on experiences and knowledge and construct new meanings to these prerequisite positions. In their study, Deepak and Biggs challenge social work students' racial prejudice by focusing on the social contexts of students' lives. The study drew on Tatum's (1997) argument that white privilege is an invisible advantage and people could be passively racist without being intentionally committed to racism. They described how a lesson plan with YouTube videos showcasing the racial differences in the state's response to Hurricane Katrina helped interrupt students' prejudices and enabled them to create alliances with people of colour to take collective actions against racism.

This approach was used in the Hong Kong project as follows. An e-learning approach was used to allow students to:

1   Form a comprehensive UNDERSTANDING towards the situations of racial discrimination in Hong Kong;

2   Understand the conceptual and legal framework on determining racial discrimination and the violation of equal opportunities;
3   Be able to access possible situations of racial discrimination and actions to be taken on anti-racial discrimination.

In addition to facilitating this e-learning approach to anti-racist practice, it was also important to trial the effectiveness of e-learning as an experiential learning method in this important area of social work education. The e-learning materials developed in this project could be used as standalone online curriculum or as blended learning to be incorporated in classes and seminars to be used for interactive discussions.

The development of the e-learning videos

The project received funding from a Chinese University of Hong Kong Micro-Module Courseware Development Grant to development e-learning materials for the course 'Intercultural Intelligence: Meeting the Challenges of a Culturally Diverse Society' under the Department of Social Work. This course provides university students with fundamental and systematic knowledge on issues related to ethnic and cultural diversity. It includes lectures on contemporary theories and conceptual perspectives about cultural sensitivity and cultural intelligence, and also highlights major discourses and challenges in the areas of access, equity, social inclusiveness, cultural assimilation and integration. These are crucial issues which have substantial impact on ethnic minorities as well as wider social cohesion. It was important, as part of a social work programme, that there was a balance between interventions at the micro level and interpersonal relationships building to the macro level which engages with a legal and policy advocacy agenda on racial equality. A particular aspect of the project was a tripartite collaboration which included two academics from the Department of Social Work focusing on teaching and research on racial equality and minority rights, a former executive director of SKH Lady MacLehose Centre, an NGO which has a dedicated service unit for ethnic minorities, and two colleagues from the EOC, a statutory quasi-human rights body overseeing the implementation of anti-discrimination legislations in Hong Kong. It is argued that the breadth of this multidisciplinary partnership would contribute the necessary diverse knowledge and expertise to enable the construction of suitable e-learning materials. A significant innovation was the production of e-learning videos involving a process of user participation.

After reviewing real cases on racial discrimination received by the EOC, and analysing the literature on racism and racial equality, the team developed four e-learning components: education, employment, use of social media and housing. Ethnic minority actors and actresses, some of whom worked in the social service sector, and had experienced racism and discrimination, were recruited. During the course of video shooting, they were given the space to inform how the individual components could be constructed to capture the key issues faced by both minority and majority populations. Four videos lasting around five minutes were produced. In terms of structure, the first part featured a situation of racial discrimination; in the second, a colleague from EOC explains how the situation violated the Race Discrimination Ordinance (RDO). Details of the four videos, with scenarios, are now described:

Video 1: The scenario features a Pakistani Muslim girl wearing a hijab; when returning to school, she is asked to meet the discipline teacher. The teacher asks her to take off the hijab, which is not deemed to be part of the school uniform. The girl challenges the teacher by asking why other students could wear necklaces with a Christian cross, but that she cannot wear the hijab which is also a kind of religious symbol. The teacher argues, on the basis of rules and regulations, and insists that she remove the hijab. Based on this scenario, the EOC representative explains to the school that they have to respect minorities' religious practice as this may contribute to indirect discrimination.

Video 2: This scenario features an ethnic Indian civil engineer who is attending a job interview in an architectural firm. The interviewer asks him whether he could speak Cantonese and write Chinese; the Indian replies he could barely speak and cannot read these languages. The interviewer immediately offers him a job, but as a lower rank because of this issue of language. Yet, at the same time, a Caucasian colleague, who works as a professional in the firm, arrives speaking in English with the interviewer. Based on this scenario, the EOC representative explains that the interviewer has potentially committed direct discrimination based on the RDO by not offering the same opportunity for people with different ethnic backgrounds.

Video 3: This scenario features a Pakistani girl complaining to the representative of a social media firm about a news article posted on social media. It described how she was admitted to a medical school in a local university, and as a result racist comments were made about problems in having ethnic minorities as doctors. She complains to the social media representative, who explains that these posts cannot be taken down because they count as freedom of expression. Based on this scenario, the EOC representative explains to the social media firm that they may have committed an offence based on the RDO as such racist comments contribute to a hostile online environment.

Video 4: A documentary. An Indonesian woman shares her experiences on renting a flat in Hong Kong. Although working for the EOC, she has been stereotyped as a migrant domestic worker by the real estate agents many times. She explains how estate agents have been reluctant in showing her apartments and often ask for proof of salary before showing her any apartments, which her local friends never experienced. As a result, she felt discriminated against on grounds of both race and gender.

Evaluation

Students who had taken the course 'Intercultural Intelligence: Meeting the Challenges of a Culturally Diverse Society' were invited to participate in the preview and online survey. They were given a set of questions on the four e-learning videos respectively and about their experiences in using the e-learning approach. The evaluation tool used a 5-point Likert scale from 'none' to 'very much' to rate these two domains of learning. Additional questions regarding overall satisfaction and how the learning stimulated them were also asked using a 4-point Likert scale. A total of 16 students completed the online survey. Overall, 13 of 16 respondents rated the videos to be satisfactory or highly satisfactory, and that they allowed them to gain better awareness about the subject matter. In addition, 14 of 16 said that they were either satisfied or highly satisfied with the value of these micro-modules in raising their critical thinking.

The stakeholders' review session sought to test how such approaches could develop knowledge and practical skills on how to advance cultural sensitivity and deal with the racism that is often experienced on an everyday basis by ethnic minority populations in Hong Kong. About 20 participants attended the session, including primary and secondary school teachers, ethnic-Chinese and Pakistani social workers employed by services for youths and ethnic minorities, social work educators and colleagues from the EOC. Opinions on the contents of the videos and the use of e-learning on anti-racism education have provided several major reflective learning points for the project and the development of educational curriculum on racial equality and anti-racism. Several participants from the education and social work sectors felt that the contents of the video overemphasized the need to be law-abiding, which they felt was rather restrictive. Such a minimalist approach in educating for racial equality and anti-racism may only touch upon behavioural changes rather than inducing fundamental cognitive and value changes. One Pakistani social worker commented that the cases shown in the videos reflected the perceptions of the general public towards ethnic minorities. For example, in the hijab case, the teacher may not simply see wearing hijab from a school regulation perspective; it may involve the teacher's preconceptions about women who wear the hijab. She used her own experiences to explain that people are usually hesitant to talk to her when she herself wears hijab as they think she could not talk to men, but could do if she was not wearing hijab. The point being made here is that such forms of discrimination may have to do with people's misconceptions and stereotyping towards Muslim women than more overt forms of racism or sectarianism.

Participants also commented that the scenarios vividly demonstrated power differentials between ethnic minorities and the majority population. It would appear, as with the Muslim girl, there was a need to confront the ethnic-Chinese teacher, especially when the mainstream professionals are still dominated by the ethnic-Chinese majorities. It has been argued that in these contexts, anti-racist social work, for example when initiated by black social workers, needs to challenge the power relationships that underpin hierarchy and to focus on identity politics (Weedon, 1987). However, participants were worried, as black social workers historically pioneered that discourse on anti-racist social work, that it is important to re-visit and re-evaluate anti-racist social work in the context of Hong Kong where there are only few ethnic minority social workers in Hong Kong. Ethnic-Chinese social workers therefore need to understand the essence of anti-racist social work and push for fundamental racial hierarchical power changes within the social work sector.

It has been argued that in different countries, opportunities for policy advocacy and community organization social work interventions are becoming less possible (Rush and Keenan, 2014). In Hong Kong, dedicated social services for ethnic minority communities tend to focus on issues of integration through promoting cultural diversity and equal access and inclusion to social services, education and employment. Participants commented that however valuable such approaches may be, they may be unable to address the multidimensional oppressions experienced by ethnic minorities. The social workers and social work educator highlighted how such oppression could be understood by the concept of intersectional identities. For example, in the hijab case, the public may perceive hijab-wearing as a form of gendered oppression towards women. For the employment case, the social work educator suggested that such a situation often occurred with his ethnic minority students. It raised the dilemma of asking ethnic minority students and others to speak up when facing blatant discrimination yet having to consider that in doing so it may affect employment and other opportunities. In the social media example, participants considered how this touched upon the idea of conflicting rights, for example freedom of expression versus racial discrimination, which the social work education curriculum seldom covers. Participants thus suggested that social work education should not only cover different approaches on cultural competence and anti-racism but also incorporate the teaching on human rights and the intersectional identities' oppressions.

Coverage and usage of the e-learning videos

Participants collectively agreed that the e-learning videos should not be solely used in social work education. In order to expand the areas of discussion, the key learning point of the videos should not just focus on the violation of RDO but also address the controversial issues situated in each case demonstration. For example, on the hijab-wearing case, discussion points could include legal perspectives (the compliance of RDO), gender and religious perspectives (the connotation of hijab-wearing) and social perspectives (integration of minority students in mainstream education environment and the interaction with teachers and peers). Finally, participants provided technical suggestions on how to better use the videos in order to expand discussions on minority issues and user groups. The part on the EOC issues could be separated from the story body of the cases, and questions could be placed after the case stories to facilitate discussions. The educational facilitator could then include the EOC material at any appropriate moment, according to flow of discussion. A toolkit on how to use the e-learning videos with guiding questions on different discussion areas should also be developed to cater for the educational needs of different target groups, including school students, university students, employers, social workers and the general public.

Conclusion

This chapter has discussed key aspects of this project, which involved service users at different stages of production, and describes how the content and usage of the videos were made more relevant for different stakeholders to achieve a greater understanding of racial diversity and equality in the context of Hong Kong. It was initially targeted for social work students and those who were interested in social work interventions on racial equality, but, it is argued, such approaches have relevance for a range of sectors as a way of knowledge-building on racial equality and anti-racial discrimination. User participation in the process was crucial in order to identify impediments to change in this area, as confirmed in stakeholder feedback. There was a need to include different dimensions of diversity and equality issues in the curriculum and to recognize important intersections of identities. It was argued that social work education should critically analyse theories that seek to explain these phenomena in addressing dimensions of cultural and racial knowledge, for example through the concepts of cultural competence and anti-racism. A problematic issue in this respect is the way that multidimensional, multicultural social work educational approaches in Hong Kong tend to focus on behavioural aspects of racial discrimination instead of broader structural explanations for racism. The chapter highlighted challenges in using e-learning formats, particularly in standardizing the level and quality of information used in the videos, but also positive outcomes in terms of raising consciousness about important issues of racism and discrimination. It is hoped that these and other approaches to social work education will be made compulsory in the social work curriculum in Hong Kong and other countries. In raising students' interest in and knowledge of issues of racial diversity and equality, services to disadvantaged services users can then in turn be enhanced.

References

Abrams, L.S. and Gibson, P. (2007). Reframing multicultural education: Teaching white privilege in the social work curriculum. *Journal of Social Work Education*, 43(1), 147–160.

Akintayo, T., Hämäläinen, J. and Rissanen, S. (2018). Global standards and the realities of multiculturalism in social work curricula. *International Social Work*, 61(3), 395–409.

Baig, R.B. (2012). From colony to special administrative region: Ethnic minorities' participation in the making of legislation against racial discrimination in Hong Kong. *Social Transformations in Chinese Societies*, 8(2), 173–200.

Banks, A. and Faul, A. (2007). Reduction of face-to-face contact hours in foundation research courses: Impact on students' knowledge gained and course satisfaction. *Social Work Education*, 26, 780–793.

Campbell, J., Davis, M., Phelan, A. and Hanley, D. (2018). Dealing with the learning needs of child welfare social and health care workers: An interdisciplinary approach to blended learning with part time students. *Social Work Education*, 37(6), 746–760.

Constance-Huggins, M. (2012). Critical race theory in social work education: A framework for addressing racial disparities. *Critical Social Work*, 13(2), 1–16.

Daniel, C.T. (2011). The path to social work: Contextual determinants of career choice among racial/ethnic minority students. *Social Work Education*, 30(8), 895–910.

Deepak, A.C. and Biggs, M.J.G. (2011). Intimate technology: A tool for teaching anti-racism in social work education. *Journal of Ethnic & Cultural Diversity in Social Work*, 20(1), 39–56.

Dominelli, L. (1992). An uncaring profession? An examination of racism in social work. In: P. Braham, A. Rattansi and R. Skellington (Eds) *Racism and Antiracism*, pp. 164–178. London: Sage Publications.

Fletcher, J., Bernard, C., Fairtlough, A. and Ahmet, A. (2015). Beyond equal access to equal outcomes: The role of the institutional culture in promoting full participation, positive inter-group interaction and timely progression for minority social work students. *British Journal of Social Work*, 45(1), 120–137.

Glezakos, A. and Lee, C.D. (2001). Distance and on campus MSW students: How they perform and what they tell us. *Professional Development: The International Journal of Continuing Social Work Education*, 4(2), 54–61.

GovHK. (2017). *Embracing Social Inclusion* [online]. Available at: www.gov.hk/en/residents/housing/securityassistance/socialsecurity/SocialInclusion.htm [Accessed 20 Nov. 2017].

Hillen, P. and Levy, S. (2015). Framing the experiences of BME social work students within a narrative of educating for a culturally diverse workforce. *Social Work Education*, 34(7), 785–798.

HKSAR Census and Statistics Department. (2017). *2016 Population by-Census Thematic Report – Ethnic Minorities*. Hong Kong: The Department.

HKSAR Government. (2010). *Administrative Guidelines on Promotion of Racial Equality* [online]. Available at: www.cmab.gov.hk/doc/en/documents/policy_responsibilities/the_rights_of_the_individuals/agpre/adm_guidelines.pdf [Accessed 20 Nov. 2017].

Hollinrake, S., Hunt, G., Dix, H. and Wagner, A. (2019). Do we practice (or teach) what we preach? Developing a more inclusive learning environment to better prepare social work students for practice through improving the exploration of their different ethnicities within teaching, learning and assessment opportunities. *Social Work Education*, 38(5), 582–603.

International Association of Schools of Social Work (IASSW) and International Federation of Social Workers (IFSW). (2004). *Global Standards for Social Work Education and Training* (Final Document). Adelaide, SA, Australia. Available at: www.iassw-aiets.org/global-standards-for-social-work-educationand-training/

Keating, F. (2000). Anti-racist perspectives: What are the gains for social work? *Social Work Education*, 19(1), 77–87.

Kleinpeter, C.H. and Potts, M.K. (2000). Distance education: Teaching practice methods using interactive television. *Professional Development: The International Journal of Continuing Social Work Education*, 4(2), 54–61.

Liebowitz, J. and Frank, M. (2011). *Knowledge Management and e-Learning*. Boca Raton, FL: Taylor & Francis.

Longoria, D.A. and Díaz, H.L. (2014). Best practices in professional distance education: A hybrid social work distance education program in south Texas. *HETS Online Journal*, 4. Available at: www.hets.org/journal/articles/72-best-practices-inprofessional-distance-education-a-hybrid-socialwork-distance-education-program-in-south-texas

Masocha, S. (2015). Reframing black social work students' experiences of teaching and learning. *Social Work Education*, 34(6), 636–649.

Nadan, Y. and Ben-Ari, A. (2013). What can we learn from rethinking 'multiculturalism' in social work education? *Social Work Education*, 32(8), 1089–1102.

Okech, D., Barner, J., Segoshi, M. and Carney, M. (2014). MSW student experiences in online vs. face-to-face teaching formats? *Social Work Education*, 33(1), 121–134.

Oterholm, I. (2009). Online critical reflection in social work education. *European Journal of Social Work*, 12, 363–375.

Phelan, J.E. (2015). The use of e-learning in social work education. *Social Work*, 60(3), 257–264.

Rush, M. and Keenan, M. (2014). The social politics of social work: Anti-oppressive social work dilemmas in twenty-first-century welfare regimes. *British Journal of Social Work*, 44, 1436–1453.

Schoorman, D. and Bogotch, I. (2010). Moving beyond 'diversity' to 'social justice': The challenge to re-conceptualize multicultural education. *Intercultural Education*, 21(1), 79–85.

Social Workers Registration Board. (2013). *Code of Practice for Registered Social Workers*.

Social Workers Registration Board. (2014). *Principles, Criteria and Standards for Recognizing Qualifications in Social Work for Registration of Registered Social Workers.*

Sousa, P. and Almeida, J.L. (2016). Culturally sensitive social work: Promoting cultural competence. *European Journal of Social Work*, 19(3–4), 537–555.

Tatum, B. (1997). *'Why Are All the Black Kids Sitting Together in the Cafeteria?' And Other Conversations About Race.* New York: Basic Books.

Tisman, A. and Clarendon, D. (2018). Racism and social work: A model syllabus for graduate-level teaching. *Journal of Teaching in Social Work*, 38(2), 111–136.

U.S. Department of Education. (2010). *Evaluation of Evidence-Based Practices in Online Learning: A Meta-Analysis and Review of Online Learning Studies.* Available at: www.educause.edu/library/resources/evaluation-evidence-based-practices-online-learningmeta-analysis-and-review-online-learning-studies

Weedon, C. (1987). *Feminist Practice and Poststructuralist Theory.* Oxford: Basil Blackwell.

Williams, C. and Parrott, L. (2012). Anti-racism and predominantly 'white areas': Local and national referents in the search for race equality in social work education. *British Journal of Social Work*, 44, 290–309.

15

LESSONS LEARNED

The meaning making power of involvement

Joanne Sansome

Introduction

This chapter will primarily reflect on the experiential lessons learnt to date via the author's lived experiences of service user involvement as a person with a physical disability, within education and research throughout the region of Northern Ireland (NI). The reflections will focus on her research data analysis regarding the participation (involvement) of Persons with Disabilities. The author will utilise the method of reflexivity and the theories of Pierre Bourdieu (1987, 1992) and Michel Foucault (1975–2002) to discuss what is happening concerning service user involvement in NI. The chapter will conclude with a look at the possible challenges and opportunities of engaging with the field of service user involvement within human services now and in the future.

The author has enjoyed many opportunities via her lived experience of service user involvement within education, assisting, for example, with modules in the social work degree such as "Introduction to Social Work" and "Law and Preparation for Practice" at Queens University Belfast and Belfast Metropolitan College in Northern Ireland. Contributing to educating the potential social workers of the future in this way has also led to opportunities to assist in the delivery of a seminar within a special education module in the undergraduate teaching degree. Service user involvement has also allowed the author to contribute to research as a service user researcher in studies such as " 'Making It Real': Evaluating the Impact of Service User and Carer Involvement in Social Work Education" (Tanner et al., 2017) and *Personal and Public Involvement (PPI) and Its Impact. Monitoring, Measuring and Evaluating the Impact of PPI in Health and Social Care in Northern Ireland* (Duffy et al., 2017). The previously mentioned studies allowed her to transition from being researched as a person living with disabilities to achieving the skill set needed to undertake and complete a master's in social research methods to become a social researcher. During the master's program, the author completed a research study regarding the participation of Persons with Disabilities (PWD) in public life living in Northern Ireland (NI), underpinned with the international lens offered by Article 29 of the United Nations Convention on the Rights of Persons with Disabilities (UNCRPD), the *right to participate in political and public life*.

The research study comprised two surveys, one offline and one online, followed by two small, semi-structured focus groups with six participants of PWDs and Providers (public and voluntary sector service provider representation) with disclosed and undisclosed disabilities.

Relevant ethical approval was granted by Queen's University, Belfast. During the analysis of the study's data, it was essential to consider the analytical (investigative, questioning and reasoning) elements in the process of what Fairclough (2003) terms "meaning-making" – hence, the production (the producers, authors, speakers and writers), the reception (the interpreters, readers and listeners) and the interpretation of the text. Furthermore, the objective was to validate or give meaning to the analysis process, alluded to within the theories of "meaning" such as Semantic and Foundational. The term Semantic refers to a specification of words and sentences via symbolic systems, whereas Foundational attempts to explain how individuals and groups give words, sentences and language symbolic meaning.

To clarify meaning, it is vital to identify the intention of the author. It is important, for further clarification, to mention how participants wished to be identified – for example, as a PWD or a Provider – as this can impact upon the reader's interpretation of the meanings. *Meanings*, as Fairclough (2003) articulates, get communicated via what he terms the "Interplay" between the authors and the interpreter, in other words, from considering the impact of variables such as institutional position, interests, values, intentions and desires of producers. This analysis will, therefore, consider the relationship between the variables mentioned above within the audio-transcribed texts from the focus groups. The relationships, in terms of the group dynamics, were considered based on institutional positions, knowledge, purpose and values of the participants and the researcher.

Enablers and barriers – Providers and Persons with Disabilities (PWD)

During the research analysis for both focus groups, several themes emerged that could be broadly categorised as either enablers or barriers. The most common theme from the Providers' perspective was "supporting PWD", in terms of capacity building and exploring the barriers, as well as the enabling of giving financial assistance to foster, for example, the emphases on co-design/co-production involvement. In contrast, the most common theme from the PWD focus group was attitudinal/environmental barriers.

Through the lens of reflexivity, it was evident that the Provider focus group participants were using the group environment as an opportunity to conceptualise and debate their thoughts collectively. On the other hand, PWD used it as a platform to share their experiences of participation and involvement to create awareness, focusing on equality issues.

During the focus group, a PWD talked about disabled people using language such as "they" and "their", which demonstrates that even though she has self-disclosed health conditions ("I know myself with arthritis that it is very difficult for me sometimes to walk. I can't move sometimes at all . . . but people don't know, they think maybe you are drunk because you sway"), which affect her mobility and how the public perceives her, she still talks about disability in a non-disabled manner. This example demonstrates not only the hierarchical structure within society among PWD that Haslam et al. (1995) supports and Linville (1998) alludes to, but is also reminiscent of Bourdieu's conceptualisation that symbolic violence can come from how we experience and view the world via both our subconscious and unconscious. This discussion within the focus group demonstrated that the respondent sees political and public life as committee participation, with the main barrier being lack of equality. Therefore, people are not understanding or getting the relevance to the experiences of PWD to particular committees.

> Significant expectations from agencies in government that participation is a significant aspect of support and co-designing services. [Without] . . . much thought into how

you develop someone from a service user background to fulfil those roles, [there-fore] . . . missing significant gaps around supporting people with disabilities.

The above response suggests that government expectations of participation are based on the notion of service users supporting the co-designing of services, a message reflected in the Government's Disability Action Plan (2012–2016). It also highlighted that there is a lack of thought around developing capacity to fulfil that role and, as one respondent noted, to "make a real difference". This comment prompted discussions around the lack of understanding regarding what needs to be done or put in place for the participation of PWD to happen. The discussion led to further dialogues around barriers:

> There is no scheme there, there is no mechanism for us to help . . . 'cause we don't know what to do.

The facilitation of participation (involvement) going beyond the existing structures in terms of disability groups and committees was reflected as a barrier to participation by some participants within the Provider focus group. As the following respondent observed, there was "a huge effort in relation to how it would be facilitated", as there was deemed to be "no schemes or mechanisms to help".

The financial solutions from another participant within the Provider focus group, responding to the barriers given within the group, interestingly almost took on the role of a service user when reflecting and communicating his concepts to the group. The debating was fascinating to watch, as the points raised resonated with the researcher's knowledge and experiences regarding the reality of participating as a PWD.

On the other hand, it was quite worrying, as a person with a disability, that another respondent within the same group had not realised the negative impact of the welfare system towards paid participation. Seemingly, the former participant did not understand the point made regarding financially supporting existing user networks in stating "there is no more money". It would seem that another participant was trying to communicate that disabled people often sit on boards and so forth without financial gain because they cannot accept a paid role due to the welfare system and the payment could be paid to their networks to secure them financially.

> It is interesting that you mention the impact that benefits, you know, maybe if you are getting paid to attend which I think is legitimate because if you are part of a committee and everyone else is getting paid, so should you. If that had an impact negatively on your ongoing lifestyle that is not appropriate, and that is not something that has probably not been realised.

Although the above comment was responding to the barriers as mentioned earlier and solutions articulated by a fellow group participant, this participant chose to respond as though she was talking to a person with a disclosed disability, which could be reflective of the other participant's service user approach. The respondent continued to discuss the topic of financial payment in terms of "strategy" with "no money attached" while reinforcing the expectation held by the government for "the community to deliver". The latter thinking, however, could be reflective of government's inability to respond to alternative ways of utilising the existing structures, mechanisms and money differently to bridge the gap between legislative-derived policies and reality.

A Provider within the focus group, interestingly, seemed to be wanting the researcher's definition of *public life*, in saying "it has never been clearly defined", but after some thought gave an example clarifying that participating in public life can have a dualistic definition that encompasses everyday general public life and professional/political public life. The definition dialogue highlighted that the meaning of participation (involvement) is unclear; the conversation also highlighted that documents such as "Disability Action Plans" are written to interpret and attribute actions stemming from legislation. Legislation, however, can seem removed from the societal assumptions, beliefs and norms that define public/political life and, therefore, do not necessarily fit the societal view of disability. The previous interpretation would align with the difficulty around the meaning and outcomes of participation to attitudinal barriers and not necessarily to the defining of words. The latter is reflected in Foucault's theorising of power and resistance concerning social structures and institutions (Mills, 2003, p. 30). Notably, those aspects of Foucault's work take issue with the assumptions of governance and the role of marginalised individuals and groups resisting the oppression of regimes.

For another participant in the PWD focus group, involvement in public life meant dealing with public ignorance and laws that are on paper but not evident in reality:

> It could be carried out in law, but it isn't ever. It could be carried out, but it's not, and that makes me very angry. All very well putting it on paper but not putting it in action.

This participant felt that lived experiences of discrimination and unfair treatment due to inequality and attitudes would

> never go away [because] . . . I'm not up there – I'm down here [even though] all I ask is to be in the public.

The extract above powerfully suggests that equality and attitude are still significant obstacles (barriers) towards ever being accepted at any level of public participation or involvement. The previous participant's personal reflection of lived experiences is reminiscent of Tyler's (2013) suggestion that PWDs are a "core part" of the "underclass" emerging from the State formation, de-emphasising traditional liberal principles (neoliberal), which has created a populist politics that fosters the resentment of difference.

For a female participant within the PWD group, political participation meant being politically involved, from voting to talking to friends/groups, giving an opinion or sharing information to assist other people within society such as politicians, in making an informed choice or at least creating awareness:

> Politically, involvement can be a matter of anything, it can be voting for a start, I mean you have a right to vote, and if you don't vote then you do not have a voice then; you can't complain. Well if you have the right to vote . . ., then you can participate.

Capacity building

The concept of building capacity could work in reality, if people could "just ask" everyone involved what you need support with to enable achievement. Just asking would start the communication and learning needed to get PWD involved and participating politically within government offices at a local level. Asking would also begin the process of PWD gaining the political profiling needed to challenge all aspects of society. Political profiling or capacity building through personal development could be achieved, as was alluded to within the focus groups, via the existing structures of supported employment/employment opportunities as opposed to the few one-day internships (shadowing experiences) that have to get pursued. The intern-ships mentioned latterly are opportunities that are often attached to "gatekeeping" charitable organisations; this could further exclude PWD within small DPOs or, in Bourdieusian terms, increase the power and dominance (Capital) that the gatekeeping organisations have in the dis-ability sector (Field).

After discussing developing capacity-building opportunities for PWD from within political parties, the respondent below continued to reflect on experience of working within the politi-cal environment and said:

> I think there may be disabled politicians all over the place, but I am not aware of them, and they certainly wouldn't be the first thing I would think about except for Blunkett, who I am always using as an example of someone who is a Braille user, or was when he was a Member of Parliament . . . fantastic opportunity for all people, from all walks of life to see good role models.

Touching on the concept of role models during the discussion prompted the researcher to reflect on Shakespeare's (2015) article "Why Disabled Achievers Should be Remembered", which draws on the notion that disabled people, like this participant, need to see other disabled people as role models in society. Thoughts of the article caused the researcher to think about hidden disabilities and how to measure this if people do not wish to self-disclose and make this part of their public identity.

Awareness-raising and lobbying

> Being a member of the public who understands how to engage politically . . . means that they know how to go to politicians to get what they want, . . . how to com-plain – literally – I am an advocate of people learning this wherever they are, they have to learn to engage with the statutory bodies in this way – politically – that they understand how to activate publicly – lobbying – is terribly important . . . in Northern Ireland . . . I see it as a positive . . . because it engages us if we get a let-ter of complaint all public sectors will respond [as] you have to act on it . . . that is what I would call being active in public life. It is about understanding how to use the system.

As the participant above comments, the focus group discussed the idea that awareness-raising and lobbying can be achieved as an individual or as part of a collective voice through a letter of complaint. This point caused the researcher to reflect on her experience of lobbying and utilis-ing the education department within Stormont (the local government of Northern Ireland) to avail of short courses on lobbying, regarding getting to know the NI Assembly and methods of effective lobbying. On reflection, perhaps, one solution to raising awareness of effective lobby-ing could be for Stormont to make those short courses available through their website, which groups within the sector could then utilise. This concept could create an online toolkit of the training mentioned above, encompassing templates for documents such as a letter of complaint. The courses could also then be accessible to individuals and groups alike and encompass a vari-ety of environments within the sector to suit as many individual support circumstances as pos-sible. This online platform could also begin to achieve the government agency expectations of service user involvement and participation in the supporting and co-designing of services. One of the female participants within the Provider focus group also openly expressed the view that participation means getting involved and really in there, but that the reality is "government . . . do pick and choose . . . your views . . . you are an 'outlier'". The choice of language used during this phase of the dialogue, the word "outlier", is significant given the topic of conversation, as this is a term that is used in statistical analysis to describe statistical data which lies outside of the majority statistical response, and thus outside of the societal norms. The latter is reminiscent of Foucault's marginalisation theory (Gutting, 2005), which conceptualises social norms as derivatives of the dominant societal views, meaning that the dominant create the norms and values of society, further dominating the marginalised of society.

Participation/Involvement

The second question of the focus groups focused on getting specific examples of the types of participation/involvement activities that people get involved in or opportunities they chose. By way of additional prompt points, it was also essential to have some discussion around: the nature of opportunities, levels of involvement and any suggestions for improvements. These prompts ensured the research was not just focusing on one aspect or variable but was reflecting the "holistic" picture of the reality.

> I have been involved in developing government strategies for years . . . there was very little attention paid to minority groups of any type – disability, older people, although it was there under Section 75. It was as much a tick box exercise as anything else. We've moved on, and we are now part of a team and a new disability strategy, and we are trying to work out how we do this.

The statement above is a forthright admission of the tokenistic approach to participation in the past under Section 75 legislation of the Northern Ireland Act 1998, and indeed the fact that government is only beginning to think differently, more than ten years on from the UNCRPD (UN General Assembly, Optional Protocol to the CRPD, 13 December 2006). If nothing else, this response shows that the focus group provided a safe environment for the participants to reflect on their practice and question, debate and begin to conceptualise their thoughts towards future developments. The constant references to lack of "knowing what to do", "lack of understanding" omissions and so on caused the researcher to reflectively question if the Providers within the focus group really did not know what to do, or if they were trying to use the situation to hear the researcher's views and opinion as a PWD. It was hard to understand that the respondents in the group with the responsibility for overseeing the creation and implementation of government strategies relating to minority groups did not have a strategic plan to implement, for example, the co-design strategy. When the participants were prompted to think about what public participation meant to them, it was not that they could not define it but rather that they could not define it in a way that the stereotypical view of disability "fitted" the "constructed structures" and associated "societal norms". Constructed structures and societal norms could be attributed to as the reason why the Providers are stumbling over the co-design strategy, as they are seemingly trying to make PWD fit into their existing operations instead of, as one Provider stated, "tweaking operations".

Co-Design

The Provider group discussed and debated "co-design". This discussion questioned the ethos of the co-design strategy's intention of improving the participation of PWD. In many ways, this strategy arguably attempts to conceptualise the idealism that "everybody, in every part of society, should be involved with changing the system for all of us", as one participant observed, but possibly instead has created a barrier. It has given organisations the "cop-out" argument of "but you are picking on one person, and it could be different on the other end of the disabilities spectrum, so how do you know you've got it right". This respondent indicated that the concept of disabled service users (PWD) developing the co-design system should be a requirement. The respondent articulated that such a requirement would create a process from which to work. However, as Cameron (2013) argues, deficit models of disability have resulted in the aim of social (welfare) policies only having the "desirable aim" of integrating disabled people into "the social mainstream" of society and its processes. The "desirable aim" attitude is a result of historic societal developments that cannot change through paternalistic policy development (Oliver and Barnes, 2012). Additionally, Drake (1999) argues that there is no recognition that society is at fault or needs to change. Within society instead, there is a notion that PWD need to build their capacity or create ideas to fit the existing social norms. The dialogue within the focus group discussions reflected that this is a held notion.

The perfect experience of participation and involvement

One of the participants with a disability in the focus group seemingly felt that meaningful political participation would never get achieved without gaining public level acceptance. He felt the experiences of discrimination and not being treated fairly were major obstacles (barriers) towards meaningful participation, which will "never go away . . . it stems from people's attitudes". This participant reported not having very positive experiences of participation throughout life right from school days. However, that enabled reflection on the fact that a good or perfect experience of participation would be the opportunity to learn, to get a good education with the right support and help to do it. This participant powerfully added this: it "is like winning the lottery or the pools". Another participant reflected on personal life experiences of places that do not get suitably designed for the majority of service users:

> Hospital, it's not designed [for] . . . the main people who use it – it's designed for able bodied people, it is not designed for people, who not only have a disability, but, my mum had dementia as well.

The dialogue above highlights issues about building the design in terms of thinking of the purpose and end-user requirements and issues at the design stage, which could be a future development suggestion for future participation. It also highlights that sometimes people with relatively hidden disabilities are also carers of other PWDs. This response also reflected that the respondent did not view dementia as a disability but rather a health condition. The classification issue is reminiscent of the hierarchy of disability while further highlighting that there can be confusion relating to what constitutes or differentiates a health condition from a disability among society and even among PWDs.

How can opportunities for participation and involvement be improved?

On this question, the focus group discussions reflected the existing literature, suggesting that good or appropriate participation is also about a person's skill set and that involvement is not just about the fact that the person has a disability, as participation is not solely a matter of rights or formal opportunities but also practical capacities to act on such premises (Bellanca et al., 2011; Mitra, 2006; Trani et al., 2011; Saleeby, 2007). Perhaps this conceptualised thinking could be further developed. If participation focused on the skillset needed, maybe the tokenism often associated with participation would be reduced. Secondly, the cost of participation was discussed, voicing that often it does not take any extra money but "a tweak in operation" and "people understanding what to do". Thirdly, this participant summarised participation as being about raising awareness, reducing barriers and continually lobbying and reflected further to mention the importance of proper training.

Study results – reflections

This research study, therefore, suggests: opportunities for the participation of Persons with Disabilities within Northern Ireland society are, according to some participants, seen as "always awareness raising" and as "the only way to reduce barriers". This notion of participation resounded with this study's PWD conceptualisation of what participation means to and for them, a finding that is further supported by Sherlaw and Hudebine (2015, p. 14) regarding their discussion involving Disabled People's Organisations (DPOs). The discussion also noted the role of DPOs in raising awareness and influencing policies, a role made possible through initiatives such as the previously mentioned REAL Disability Network in NI and the Regionaux de L'inclusion in France. Both initiatives aim to involve all PWD irrespective of their perceived impairment to address and set common goals, create awareness and influence policy decisions, using the legislative framework of the UNCRPD.

The results of this study also show that while the participation of PWD is a legislative requirement within public and political life, in many instances (as highlighted within the analysis) this is not defined clearly within organisations, meaning that participation differs from organisation to organisation due to the seemingly open and individual way this is interpreted. This open and individual interpretation of participation could suggest, like the work of Williams (1996), that linguistics and societal norms are significant factors contributing to the attitudinal barriers PWD experience around participation. This further supports and advances the findings of Scotch (2009, p. 17) that "disabled people", due to being perceived by society "as a dependent, marginal, and often [a] morally questionable minority who required special care . . . were best kept out of public life through a combination of charity and social exclusion". This research demonstrates that, due to the present gap between the policy/legislative rhetoric and the reality, as discussed in the Provider focus group, this is still evident within society. Notably, there is a lack in the understanding regarding how to adjust operations or "cultural constructs and social opportunities" already existing (Scotch, 2009, p. 17). This notion regarding a lack of understanding towards implementing change challenges the argument made by Coleman and Lebbon (1999, p. 17) when they suggest that the challenge to organisations is not in understanding but changing culturally to reflect the emerging reality "of equal rights legislation and a vocal and demanding disability lobby". However, the results could also be interpreted as a fear of linguistics. The Providers clearly articulated definitions of words and concepts but stumbled when trying to ascertain where the participation of PWD would fit; this difficulty could be attributed to the dominant creating structures reflective of stereotypical "norms", as Gutting (2005) suggests. If participation is looked at in the broad sense of social inclusion, from the perspective of PWD, as in the study by Abbot and McConkey (2006), there are similarities between both the latter study's PWD focus groups and this study's PWD focus group. Within both studies, the PWD focus groups perceived participation as being treated in a similar way to everyone else, in ordinary, everyday environments. The following quotes further underscore these points:

> For the participants in this study, social inclusion meant meeting other people in ordinary settings and being treated similarly.
>
> *(Abbot and McConkey, 2006, p. 281)*

> All I ask for is to be in the public and not treated like I have 2 heads . . . that makes me very angry. . . . We are part of the public . . . but people don't accept that.
>
> *(this study's PWD focus group, July 2016)*

In comparing the above quotes, the inference is that participation for PWD in Northern Ireland is about gaining public acceptance. Therefore, whether participation is prefixed by e.g. Public Life or termed as Social Inclusion or Service User involvement, and so on, is possibly irrelevant, although this would require further research. Arguably, however, the research findings articulating with language like "being treated similarly", could lead to further confusion and misunderstanding among non-disabled persons. Should a person, for example, vacate the folding seat on a bus, to make space for a person using a wheelchair, or let them sit in the aisle? If the bus is full, would they stand to let another non-disabled person have their seat? What is the difference? Arguably, the main issue here is disability and, with this in mind, the following question can be posed: Are researchers and disabled people fostering difference and creating an air of expectation or entitlement?

Limitations of the results

When considering the limitations of the results, the failings of the research design and the peculiarities of the sample, it was essential to reflect on the time and financial constraints of the master's program and the dissertation timeframe, as both of these constraints could have a significant impact on the aforementioned results. The limitations of time and money created possible failings in terms of the research design, for example not having the time to conduct more focus groups or follow up interviews to clarify transcript dialogue. More time and access to resources may have also eradicated the peculiarities of the sample size and could have also enabled the focus groups to be held over a few dates so that participants could select a date and time to suit their schedules as well as having the funds to reimburse expenses such as travel. The factors described above impacted on the small sample, as did health issues.

Financial constraints

Financial constraints are an essential factor of which the researcher was aware and considered, particularly, concerning the PWD focus group. Financial expense in terms of, for example, accessible transport and so forth is a barrier to participation. Additionally, there is a need to make a barrier-free environment (as much as possible) by providing, for example, a sign language interpreter or personal care assistance if participants identify within their "expression of interest" that they require any such support or adjustments to participate fully.

Sample size and research design

The limitations, failings and peculiarities of the sample and research design was most notably the small sample size of six participants. The sample size, therefore, limited the generalisability of the findings, making it unrealistic to compare and contrast with larger mainland UK studies of the disability sector such as the Attitudes Towards Disability Study, Disabled for Life (Grewal et al., 2002), commissioned by the Department for Work and Pensions (DPG). In the latter study, the majority of the 2,064 respondents, of whom 47% had a disability, thought that the position of people with disabilities had improved in the prior two decades but substantial attitudinal and structural barriers remained. The study showed a continuum of attitudes towards disability from inclusive attitudes, characterised by a positive view of the lives of people with disabilities and a broad definition of disability to exclusionary attitudes that focused on differences negatively. In 2003 a continuum qualitative study, Diversity in Disability (Molloy et al., 2003), also commissioned by the DPG and involving 103 PWD participants, believed that substantial progress had increased societal opportunities for PWD. SCOPES Research regarding current attitudes towards disabled people (PWD) concluded disabled people are more likely to experience the attitudes of others as a significant barrier to life/opportunities outside the home (Aiden and McCarthy, 2014). The findings reflect and hence support the highlighting of attitudinal barriers towards participation within the PWD focus group of this study. Due to the limitation of sample size, it was therefore hard to validate the findings with other UK studies of this type. The researcher was still, however, able to make future recommendations for further studies, utilising the focus group data and the literature review to support the limited responses.

Emerging support and possibilities

The data emerging from the focus groups support the concept and influence of symbolic power. Symbolic power is the constitutive power of the state via legislation and is misrecognised or internalised, illuminating a lack of awareness or understanding of how to implement the strategies. In the research reported in this chapter, symbolic power as the power of the State, via the law, was alluded to as "being on paper but not action", which highlighted the power discrepancies between the rhetoric of State power and cultural (capital) power of societal norms. The concept of power could be further explored through the theoretical concepts of Bourdieu's notion that knowledge of constitutional State power and cultural power shapes and produces legislative law. Bourdieu's concept articulates that laws are the highest form of capital (power), an articulation supported by the power/knowledge lens of Foucault's theorising. Hence, the argument can be made that the UK signing and ratification of the UNCRPD is a significant move from PWD being "objects" of charity, to "subjects" with rights and the capacity to claim them. (UN.org, 2016) The latter argument may also signify that a rights-based paradigm (epistemic shift) gives power to the marginalised (docile bodies), for example, people with disabilities.

This research explored the linguistics of the sector, such as "disability", in relation to the UK and the UN. Within the focus group discussions, the current structures that facilitate or impede the participation of PWD were debated, illuminating the perspectives and key issues of disabled persons and providers. The respondents' perspectives were analysed to draw out the comparisons and contrasts of the emerging themes. This study found that for PWD, participation in public and political life pertained to Fraser's (2008) notion of participation as a means of citizenship and societal inclusion. The Provider participants of this study supported the work of Hastbacka et al. (2016) in terms of the apparent control from legislative requirements. The PWD group also alluded to the fact that they agreed with Hastbacka (2016) respecting that legislative "laws" aim to end social exclusion and discrimination by communicating that they are "laws that look good on paper, not actions" (PWD focus group, 2016).

The literature review for this research also illuminated the power of linguistics and issues surrounding the vast number of terms and models of disability. Before this work, the researcher was unaware of most models, despite being a PWD who is active within the field of disability.

The issue of linguistics caused the researcher concerns and reason for reflection, particularly in regard to, for example, which terms to use in an attempt not to offend any of her peers with disabilities. These issues resulted in the researcher thinking of words, their meaning and the corresponding political correctness to conclude that words are as much a barrier to participation, becoming fully inclusive of disability, as environmental barriers. The linguistic barriers of the written word, therefore, give way to so many contradictions for terms and conceptualised models of disability that it is not surprising that providers and academics alike could be worried about political correctness when talking to or engaging PWD.

Resulting from the analysis of this study, it could also be argued that the participation of PWDs in Northern Ireland reflects the state's symbolic power enacted in e.g. NI, UK and the UN via the specific previously mentioned laws and policy structures. Hence, these laws and structures, in Bourdieusian terms, are constituting the habitus of PWD to be more disposed to engage in, for example, citizenship (collective) participation as outliers of societal norms and, therefore, to be less disposed to participate via professional roles within public/political life. The previous reflection could be due to the attitudinal and environmental barriers discussed within the body of existing literature and the PWD focus group of the author's research.

Conclusion

This chapter primarily reflected on the experiential lessons learnt from the author's lived experiences of service user involvement within education and research throughout the region of Northern Ireland, with a focus on her research data analysis regarding the participation (involvement) of Persons with Disabilities. The author utilised the method of reflexivity and the theories of Pierre Bourdieu and Michel Foucault to discuss what is happening concerning service user involvement in NI, with a focus on participation in public life. The chapter reflected on what is happening regarding service user involvement within education and research in Northern Ireland to highlight the emerging themes pertaining to the enablers and barriers of involvement and participation such as capacity building and co-design, awareness raising and lobbying to explore what the perfect experience of participation and involvement is or could be. In addition, the chapter focused on suggested opportunities towards improving participation and involvement, while acknowledging that the author's reflections from her personal lived experiences and her analysis of a small study offer a snapshot with limitations regarding results, financial constraints, sample size and research design recognised.

It was also possible to highlight the potential challenges and opportunities of engaging with the field of service user involvement within human services now and in the future, to begin to explore the emerging support and possibilities as well as to think about what the key future challenges could be. Such future challenges, drawn from the findings of this study, are about raising awareness, simplifying interactions to reduce the fear of linguistics and implementing changes big and small to communicate and reinforce that participation and involvement matters. The latter would demonstrate that the lessons learnt via participation and involvement have the power to achieve the implementation needed to create meaningful societal changes. Demonstrating such implementation would show that participation and involvement opportunities no longer reflect meaningless "dust collecting reports" or "words without action".

References

Abbot, S. and McConkey, R. (2006). The barriers to social inclusion as perceived by people with intellectual disabilities. *Journal of Intellectual Disabilities*, 3, pp. 275–287. London: Sage Publications.
Aiden, H. S. and McCarthy, A. (2014). *Current attitudes towards disabled people*. London: Scope.

Bellanca, N., Biggeri, M. and Marchetta, F. (2011). An extension of the capability approach: Towards a theory of dis-capability. *European Journal of Disability Research*, 5(1), pp. 158–176.

Bourdieu, P. (1987). What makes a social class? On the theoretical and practical existence of groups. *Berkeley Journal of Sociology*, 32, pp. 1–17.

Bourdieu, P. (1992). *From rules to strategies*, Cambridge: Polity, pp. 59–75.

Cameron, C. (2013). *Disability studies: A student's guide*, London: Sage Publications.

Coleman, R. and Lebbon, C. (1999). *Inclusive design*, London: Research Centre, Royal College of Art.

Drake, R. F. (1999). *Understanding disability policies*, London: Palgrave Macmillan.

Duffy, J., Gillen, P., Agnew, C., Casson, K., Davidson, G., McGlone, A. and McKeever, B. (2017). *Personal and public involvement (PPI) and its impact: Monitoring, measuring and evaluating the impact of PPI in health and social care in Northern Ireland, Belfast*. Public Health Agency and Patient and Client Council, available at: www.knowledge.hscni.net/Topics/Index/823.

Fairclough, N. (2003). *Analysing discourse: Textual analysis for social research*, USA and Canada: Routledge, Taylor & Francis Group.

Foucault, M. (1977 [1975]). *Disciple and punish: The birth of the prison*, New York: Pantheon.

Foucault, M. (1979). *Discipline and punish*, New York: Vintage Books.

Foucault, M. (1989). *Archaeology of knowledge*, London: Routledge Publications.

Foucault, M. (1991). *Disciple and punish*, London: Penguin.

Foucault, M. (2002). *The order of things: An archaeology of the human sciences*, London: Routledge.

Fraser, N. (2008). *Scales of Justice,* Cambridge: Polity Press.

Grewal, I., Joy, S., Lewis, J., Swales, K. and Woodfield, K. (2002). *'Disabled for life?': attitudes towards, and experiences of, disability in Britain* (No. 173), Leeds: Corporate Document Services.

Gutting, G. (2005). *Foucault: A very short introduction*, Oxford University Press.

Haslam, S. A., Oakes, P. J., Turner, J. C. and McGarty, C. (1995). Social categorization and group homogeneity: Changes in the perceived applicability of stereotype content as a function of comparative context and trait favorableness. *British Journal of Social Psychology*, 34, pp. 139–160.

Hastbacka, E., Nygard, M. and Nyqvist, F. (2016). Barriers and facilitators to societal participation of people with disabilities: A scoping review of studies concerning European Countries. *European Journal of Disability Research*, 10, pp. 201–220.

Linville, P. W. (1998). The heterogeneity of homogeneity. In: J. M. Darley and J. Cooper (eds.), *Attribution and social interaction: The legacy of Edward E. Jones*, Washington, DC: American Psychological Association.

Mills, S. (2003). *Michel Foucault: Routledge Critical Thinkers*, London & New York: Routledge.

Mitra, S. (2006). The capability approach and disability. *Journal of Disability Policy Studies*, 16(4), pp. 236–247.

Molloy, D., Knight, T. and Woodfield, K. (2003). 'Diversity in disability: Exploring the interactions between disability, ethnicity, age, gender and sexuality.' London: Department for Work and Pensions.

Oliver, M. and Barnes, C. (2012). *The new politics of disablement*, Basingstoke: Palgrave Macmillan.

Scotch, R. K. (2009). Nothing about us without us: Disability Rights in America. *OAH Magazine of History*, 23(3), pp. 17–22.

Shakespeare, T. (2015). *Why disabled achievers should be remembered*, available at: http://m.bbc.co.uk/news/blogsouch30700874?ns_mchannel=social&ns_campaign=ouch_bbc&ns_source=facebook&ns_link name=news_central (accessed: 9 January 2015).

Sherlaw, W. and Hudebine, H. (2015). The United Nations convention on the rights of persons with disabilities. *Alter: European Journal of Disability Research*, 9, pp. 9–21.

Tanner, D., Littlechild, R., Duffy, J. and Hayes, D. (2017). "Making it real": Evaluating the impact of service user and carer involvement in social work education. *British Journal of Social Work*, 47(2), pp. 467–486.

Trani, J.-F., Bakhshi, P., Bellanca, N., Biggeri, M. and Marchetta, F. (2011). Disabilities through the capability approach lens: Implications for public policies. *Alter: European Journal of Disability Research*, 5(3), pp. 143–157.

Tyler, I. (2013). *Revolting subjects*, London: Zed Books.

UN General Assembly. (2006). *Optional protocol to the convention on the rights of persons with disabilities*, UN General Assembly, available at: www.un.org/disabilities/ (accessed: August 2016).

Welch Saleeby, P. (2007). Applications of a capability approach to disability and the international classification of functioning, disability and health (ICF) in social work practice. *Journal of Social Work in Disability & Rehabilitation*, 6(1–2), pp. 217–232.

Williams, G. (1996). Representing disability: Some questions of phenomenology and politics. In: C. Barnes and G. Mercer (eds.), *Exploring the divide: Illness and disability*, Leeds: Disability Press, pp. 194–212, Chapter 11.

16

BLANK PAGE

Involvement of expert by experience in social work education in Slovenia

Petra Videmšek

Introduction

Social work is the science of doing! Based on this assertion, not only social work practice but also education for future social workers should be oriented towards this assertion, and students need to recognise that theory and practice are interconnected. In the last decade, we have witnessed many attempts at involving experts by experience in education for social work (Duffy, 2006; Dorozenko et al., 2016; Urek, 2017; Gutman and Ramon, 2016; Cabiati and Raineri, 2016 etc.). However, in Slovenia, it is still not the practice that experts by experience will be key stakeholders in all aspects of the design and delivery of the study program. Although we are aware that by involving experts by experience in education, we are narrowing the gap between theory and practice, involving experts by experience in education is more optional and depends on the professor's personal choices. The involvement of experts by experience is recommended, but it is not mandated by the Faculty of Social Work at the University of Ljubljana. On the contrary, the UK experience is that of "an established future" (Duffy and Hayes, 2012, p. 368) and includes active involvement in design, management, delivery, monitoring and evaluation of social work programs (Duffy and Hayes, 2012).

The aim of this chapter is to present how students of social work can learn from first-hand experiences and recognise that experts by experience can be a valued contribution by not only changing existing social services (Ramon, 2003; McLaughlin, 2009; Beresford and Rose, 2009; Powell, 2009) but also making a contribution to the increase in gaining competences for future social workers.

The chapter is based on the assertion that involvement in the curriculum for future social workers by experts by experience mirrors the profession's values of respect, partnership, co-creation and partnership. Research suggests that a change in culture within universities and academia is needed; as Urbanc (2009) pointed out, inclusion in teaching requires the whole system be adapted in order to "prepare" the field for new participants (in our experience, experts by experience).

Involvement: an imperative or real change in education for social work

Increased emphasis on involving those who use social services in their design, delivery, evaluation, research and education has occurred in the last decade, following users' movements (Thompson,

2002; Videmšek, 2009, 2017). In many European countries, there is a widespread consensus that the involvement of experts by experience[1] in education has stipulated that service users and carers were to be key stakeholders in all aspects of the design and delivery of the study program. This represents best practice (Duffy et al., 2013) and is seen as essential in moving forward to achieve a more proactive partnership model of engaging and working with experts by experience and carers. Moreover, the Global Standards for Social Work Education and training contain several provisions related to the users' involvement, especially in social work practice – for instance, under the Paradigm of the Social Work Profession, paragraph 4.2.4, "respect the right and interest of service users and their participation in all aspects of providing programs and services" and under Standards with regard to the curricula in paragraph 3.3, "involvement of service users in planning and delivery of programs (Global Standards, 2014). The extensive literature review indicates that in the UK, involvement has become an important aspect of social work education (Cabiati and Raineri, 2016), as well as a mainstream educational activity (Yeung and Ng, 2010), and that the rest of Europe has followed this pattern as well (for instance: Denmark, Germany, Norway, Sweden [Agnew and Duffy, 2010], Bosnia and Herzegovina [Čekić Bašić, 2009], Macedonia [Bornarova, 2009], Serbia [Brkič and Jugović, 2009], Italy [Allegri, 2015; Cabiati and Raineri, 2016], Croatia [Džombić and Urbanc, 2009], and Slovenia [Zaviršek and Videmšek, 2009]). The history of Slovene education for social work, starting in 1955 (Zaviršek and Leskošek, 2006), shows that the involvement of experts by experience in education has been acknowledged, but integration into social work education has seldom extended beyond guest lecturing.

In Slovenia, the experts by experience have been involved in teaching since 1996 (Zaviršek and Videmšek, 2009, p. 215). The major shift towards the participation in teaching by experts by experience was facilitated by Tanja Lamovec (1995) and people around her who challenged the power/knowledge of different professionals as well as educators and became continuously involved in social work teaching (Zaviršek and Videmšek, 2009, p. 212). Another important person that still works on a non-permanent basis and runs his own selective module at the Faculty of Social Work is Marino Kačič, a person with visual impairment. Also influential has been Elena Pečarič, a wheelchair user with severe muscle dystrophy, who in 2006 became a teacher at the Faculty on a non-permanent basis. She still comes occasionally and gives lectures, whenever she is invited to do so. In the local context of Slovenia, the involvement of experts by experience in teaching would hardly be possible without professors who recognise the meaning of inclusion and value the contribution of experts by experience. One of these is Professor Darja Zaviršek, Department for Social Justice and Inclusion, who works in the areas of disabilities, gender and ethnicity; she invited all the aforementioned people to teach on her module. Another is Professor Vito Flaker, an innovator in many ways, especially in the field of deinstitutionalisation. He and his colleagues in the Department for Mental Health (Mojca Urek, Vera Grebenc, Jana Mali) also put a lot of effort into involving experts by experience in different fields (mental health, drug abuse, same sex, transgender etc.). Twenty years after the first involving experts by experience as teachers, we found many modalities of their involvement. They are involved in a wide range of teaching opportunities in the lecture room. One of them has his own selective subject; his selective module is always full. Some professors invited experts by experience as guest lecturers every year. Experts by experience are invited to give feedback in all practice learning in a student's placement; they are also invited to give feedback on the collaboration of students and experts by experience in developing individual care plans, preparing and delivering training programs (EX-IN project was one of these examples) and opportunities for contributing to module assessment.

Research shows that attempts at increasing involvement of experts by experience occurred almost always with the changing of study programs (from two-year study programs towards four years of study; other changes happened with regard to the Bologna system).[2] The research also shows that the involvement of experts by experience as guest lecturers is personally valued, avoids tokenistic attitudes and approaches and includes a re-shaping of the power structures within academia. Zaviršek and Videmšek (2009) pointed out that with regard to the history of involvement in teaching by experts by experience, one of the major obstacles is the view of professionals who see experts by experience as people who need care and are dependent rather than as competent people with valuable skills. If experts by experience are seen as being incapable of solving everyday difficulties, how can they be allowed to get involved in social work teaching and responsible communication with social work students? The paternalistic voices against involvement in teaching by experts by experience often repeated that an "unknown teaching situation might trigger trauma, stress, and can re-traumatise the person". Many experts by experience have the ability to confront new challenges and difficulties as well as the stress of being involved in an unusual and unknown environment of teaching (Zaviršek and Videmšek, 2009, p. 211).

The central idea of the involvement of experts by experience in education is the notion that experts by experience are partners and people from whom to learn, not only in social work practice but also in education. This assertion is based on the concept of partnership and the shift from "we know what is best for you" towards a more inclusive and co-creational social work education and practice. The discussion of the involvement of experts by experience in education offers opportunities for reflection and consideration of further attempts of involvement that will not be just seldom but rather a regular part of social work education. As pointed out by many authors (McLaughlin, 2009; Beresford and Boxall, 2015; Gutman and Ramon, 2016; Dorozenko et al., 2016), involvement of those with lived experiences can provide significant opportunities for capacity building and development of both service users and academics, and holds promise for service system improvements (Dorozenko, 2016).

Methodology

This chapter is based on the author's experiment "Evaluation of the Study Process, Students' Attitudes, When the Teachers Are Experts by Experience in Their Social Work Courses". The principles and values of participatory action research and co-production guided this evaluation, facilitating the empowerment of those involved and enabling new competences, knowledge and learning processes from first-hand experiences for students. In the evaluation, I involved students, more precisely third-year students, at the Faculty of Social Work, University of Ljubljana, who had chosen the elective "Users' Perspectives in Research" in the year 2016/17 and 2017/18 (sample: 28 students).

For research purposes, I invited as guest teachers people with different personal experiences (mental ill health, people with special needs, people with cerebral paralysis). All experts by experience were prepared and supported by the teacher (but did not have teacher training in advance), and they knew what they wanted to communicate in the classroom. Each of the lectures lasted three teaching hours, with one 15-minute break in between.

With the research, I wanted to see:

1 What difference does it make if teachers have their own experiences of using services?
2 How do students respond to their teaching?
3 Which competences do they learn and receive from first-hand experience?
4 The students' attitudes and their readiness to accept the idea that teachers may have first-hand service-using experiences.

For me, it is essential that students see and hear from people who can share their stories of recovery, mental ill health, users' research etc., to understand that what we are teaching in class at the university (the concepts, theoretical background) is not just text without practical background, that concepts are an integrated part of everyday practise, and to show that experts by experience can and do recover and have other identities as well. For a student's perspective, I had three research questions:

1   What will students learn from the first-hand experience?
2   Does the involvement of experts by experience increase emphasis on practice? Learning and equipping students with the knowledge, skills and tools for the job?
3   What are the main differences if the teachers are themselves experts by experience?

Data was collected through the application of four tools: reflection, evaluation forms, observation and concept mapping. For research purposes, I used a combination of qualitative methods. I used reflexive approaches (Ferguson, 2017), which I carried out with students after every session. The reflexive approach contained feelings of uncertainty and anxiety, how the students see the advantages of involvement of experts by experience and why they declare an expert's involvement in education a useful tool.

For the research purpose, at the second year of the research process I also added concept maps as a tool of learning. I often use concept maps (Videmšek and Fox, 2009) as teaching tools so students can see their progress in learning. The concept map task was to allow the students to respond by addressing concepts and theories they considered relevant for the perspective and involvement of the experts by experience in social work practice. Before we started the module, the students were asked to construct concept maps about the key features of the perspective of the experts by experience and how they conceptualised the knowledge production so far. At the end of the module, they created new concept maps. Pre- and post-construction of concept maps helped the students and myself to see the knowledge acquired and also the competences that students obtained with the lectures. Concept maps demonstrated their meaningful learning (Novak and Gowin, 1984) through the involvement of experts by experience.

The third tool was evaluation forms. The students were asked to fill in the questionnaire at the end of the elective module. As a fourth tool, I used participation observation and wrote all the actions and reactions of the students, which offered me a helpful technique for evaluating the outcomes relating to the attitudes and perceptions of students and for identifying the students' ability to integrate theory and practice (Fook et al., 2000).

Sample: A total of 28 students chose the elective "Users' Perspectives in Research" in the study. All 28 (100%) students completed the evaluation; 17(61%) students completed c-maps. I collected six reflexive approaches and did six participatory observations in the guest lectures.

The study was analysed thematically, following the thematic analysis approach developed by Braun and Clarke (2006). The themes were also systematically grouped together for each respondent from different research methods. This chapter will draw out some of the strengths and advantages of involving experts by experience in the education process with the aim that students recognise the importance and value of a partnership and an integrated approach from the start of their training, as pointed out by Levin (2004). The reflection shows, as stated by Jackie Powell (2009), that the real integration of theory and practice will not come about through a ponderous, rigid body of knowledge, but rather from the humility to learn from a practitioner's experiences (2009, p. 325).

The discussion of experimental involvement is first based on the reflexive approach and my own observations, which were part of the lectures that took place when experts by experience took on the role of a teacher. Participant observation was used as a means of participating in the activities of the people under study. In this study, observation was used to allow me to gather data through watching dialogue and listening to what people do and say. At the start of the session, I introduced the experts by experience and then sat down with the students. Only on one occasion, the first, did the students address a question to me, which I then put back to them to ask the expert by experience who was teaching.

I conclude this discussion with a view of what needs to be done so that the involvement of experts by experience will become a normal part of social work education in Slovenia and not an optional practice at the University.

Key findings

Question of trust as a core social work premise

I observed six sessions led by experts by experience. Straight after each session, I interviewed the students about their experience. As Howe (2009, p. 171) puts it, "reflective practice demands that you learn from experience. It requires you to be self-critical. It expects you to analyse what you *think*, *feel*, and *do*, and then learn from the analysis" (Howe, 2009). Schön's (1983) formulation of reflection in action and on action was intended to challenge the dominant perspective that professional practice is a technical–rational activity that merely involves the application of rules and expertise to solve problems. He argued that professionals use reflection to deal with the uncertainty that pervades their work, to shape their thinking and actions and to learn from experience. Reflection in our case was meant as a teaching tool. It was obvious that students needed to learn how to "behave" if the teachers are experts by experience. They needed to experience the experiential knowledge that experts by experience have to answer their questions and develop their learning.

Because of the issue of confidentiality, trust is vital to work with and learn from. When the experts by experience took the podium, we were able to see that there was some mistrust in the eyes of students, but there was also curiosity to see what would happen next. In the first lecture, where the lecturers were experts by experience in the field of mental health, this mistrust was evident through the questions the students asked and posed to me instead of to the experts by experience themselves. The students needed constant reminders to pose questions to the experts and not me. This can be interpreted as behaviour influenced by position in the social hierarchy. Students had some concerns and also confusion about to whom to pose the question. Beresford and Croft (2004) pointed out that not everyone values experiential knowledge as equal to other sources of knowledge, and this can lead to experts by experience feeling exploited rather than fully integrated into the education program.

Posing questions to me instead of the lecturer with experience also suggests stigma. Discussions about stigma are part of our curriculum in almost every subject in social work and are a particularly important topic in our social work education. Most of the experts by experience (if not all) that are in receipt of social work practice or education face some forms of stigmatisation. Thompson and Thompson (2008, p. 216) said that "being a client of social work is often enough to attract stigma." Education has, therefore, an important role to teach students how to address these issues and promote empowerment and collaborative social work practice. They need to learn how to support stigmatised people and avoid barriers to forming partnerships, as well as how to fight stigma and discrimination (Dominelli, 2002, 2008; Barnes, 2006; Banks, 2008; Thompson, 2006). Social work education has an important role to equip students with the knowledge and skills that support them in challenging and overcoming their stigmatising attitudes.

If we want students to overcome stigmatising attitudes, they need to develop critical understanding of how socio-structural inadequacies, discrimination, oppression and social, political and economic injustice impact on human functioning and development at all levels, including the global level (Cabiati and Raineri, 2016, p. 983).

Secondly, they need to have the chance to discover and reflect on their attitudes. Ferguson (2017) noted that reflective practice is a core concept in social work and probably the most well-known theoretical perspective across the entire applied professions of teaching, health and social care. Its origins lie in Schön's (1983) formulation of how professionals engage in "reflection *in* action" by thinking about their experience and what they are doing while they are doing it and afterwards using "reflection *on* action" to think about and link their practice to knowledge (Schön, 1983; Redmond, 2006; Mešl, 2008). At the second lecture, where the lecture was about cerebral paralyses, we saw some progress. We could even say that we saw a polarised reaction. Students wanted direct contact and a personal relationship with the experts by experience. They wanted to hear from their experiences, from them and not from the support worker who brought them to the Faculty. We can say that through this experience, students evidenced how they learnt to pose a question and to frame the different issues that they wanted to discuss.

Curiosity without questions is not possible

Another inherent feature was that students wanted to gain more shared experiences, but they didn't ask for this. From the questionnaires that were completed by the students after the session, we found out that students wished to know more about personal stories and more details about the experts, but they hesitated to ask. This motivated them to reflect and ask themselves why they didn't ask: respecting privacy and being afraid to be curious. The reflections showed that they were afraid to break the boundaries of respecting the users' privacy. Through the lectures, they learnt how to overcome the barriers they had. More students pointed out that they learnt how to ask questions. "I am not afraid to ask", "I realise that I have some stigmatised attitudes": this shows that students acknowledge the importance of interacting with experts by experience. They also developed communication skills and emphasised the value of listening. This was similar to the findings of Cabiati and Raineri (2016). Students realise that experts by experience have the right not to answer questions; that does not mean there is anything wrong with the question, however, just that they would prefer not to answer. The experts by experience also said to students: "ask us, don't think you know how to open the door for me, ask me if I want the door opened for me". Students learnt that active listening is a key to building a trusting relationship.

They discovered that involvement can be a tool for empowerment (Videmšek, 2014); feeling empowered and in control can contribute to unique professional knowledge. Learning from my experience is paramount to providing the conditions in which people can exchange knowledge. Students wanted to keep them at the centre of attention: "I wanted to hear what they had to say about the service, not what she told us. I recognise power imbalance". Another student pointed out that "I recognise that they really know what is the best for them and that we need to see them as equal partners in our relationship. It is probably hard but we need to work on that".

Changing stigmatising attitudes

Apart from gaining a "good learning experience", the involvement of different experts by experience brings multiple advantages to students. In the evaluation forms, students wrote that they learnt "how to establish trusting relationships with the experts by experience". Some of them also noticed that "I break the communication barrier and learn how to ask again if I don't understand what someone is saying to me. This allowed me to have more open and meaningful dialogue, allowed me to ask again without feeling bad". Students recognised that developing a trusting relationship with experts by experience is fundamental to successful engagement. Anghel and Ramon (2009, p. 187) point out that only when the experts by experience feel respected for what they can offer are they more able to share their perspective.

Another important aspect and learning outcome was the recognition of our own "prejudice and discrimination". Many students remarked that these experiences involving experts by experience as guest lecturers were invaluable, and they really appreciated not only the honesty and openness but also the direct suggestions and remarks on how to work and what not to do. "I discovered how much prejudice I have towards people with mental ill health"; "I learnt a lot about mental ill health"; "I found out that I had a lot of prejudice before the presentation about people with mental ill heath"; "I have learnt how to behave and change my attitude towards experts by experience". This finding is similar to Gutman and Ramon (2016). In Gutman and Ramon's (2016) research, students also pointed out that "users' involvement enabled them as, future social workers, to become more accomplished professionals by overcoming their prejudices and perceiving their clients' potential" (2016, p. 884). Students were encouraged to reflect on their assumptions and misconceptions.

Involvement with experts by experience has advantages for not only for students but also professors. New topics of what is important for experts by experience is definitely one of the models of good practice to be implemented in social work education when the lecturers are experts by experience. The invitations clearly illustrate which theory is relevant in the context of involvement of experts by experience and points out that power issues are at the core of social work values. Academics need to be able to give up the power and the position of "we know best" and revert to a balanced power-sharing relationship. On the other hand, it means that academics:

- Have enough courage to implement the social work concepts in education, do something new, be able to handle the potential emotional aspect of involvement.
- Enable students to learn from first-hand experience and be able to see experts by experience in this interaction with others.
- Open the space for reflection and, through reflection, enable students to gain new knowledge.

My reflection

I found that students show interest and listen very carefully to what people have to say. The research proves that involving experts by experience as teachers deepens understanding of the everyday experience of experts and challenges the dominant discussion of power and types of worthwhile knowledge. Sometimes I had the feeling (especially after the first presentation) that they asked many more questions; they were willing to listen to as much as they could. They showed an interest in the presented topic, and the questions were really good and could only be answered by the experts themselves. This was in contrast to certain findings (Zaviršek and Videmšek, 2009, p. 217) suggesting that "students were more silent during this class, they remained very formal and more careful". Today, students showed sensitivity for diversity and inclusiveness. Students have learnt that direct contact with experts by experience makes the connection between theory and practice. They produced rich and complex concept maps that show the understanding of the students' perception of experts by experience.

They have learnt how "to establish relationships" and how to get close to a person. These are all reasons for involving experts by experience in education; however, involvement still requires a lot of cultural and professional changes.

Benefits and challenges for the experts by experience in the process

The experts by experience reported many advantages of being a teacher. Many of these advantages relate to their everyday life routine and how they are commonly treated.

The experts by experience who participated in the process reported the following:

1   The most important shift took place with the change in their roles, as they take on the new role of being a teacher. "It is so nice to be on this side and to tell so many students about our needs, wishes, and life situations. I was not the one to receive the help but helped others to learn". "It was nice to see that students are interested and they pose questions". "From participating in education, the experts-by-experience achieve socially valued roles". "It is nice to be a teacher for future social workers and I like to go to the Faculty and present who I am again and tell them what I experience from the social worker".
2   For some experts by experience, being a teacher also meant they had the opportunity to share their experience and expertise: "valuing my experiences of mental health problems. I also see that this can bring so many changes, especially in further projects. I see that students take my experiences seriously and my story touches their feelings and also influences their prejudice". "I feel much more important being here!"
3   For others, participation meant a sense of appreciation: "I am treated with respect; student listened to me and posed so many questions. I wanted to stay longer in the class".
4   Inclusion in education also develops a sense of value from experts' expertise and a feeling of being important: "when our (mentor) told us that we are invited to the Faculty, I felt really happy. Everyone in the day centre knows when we are going to the Faculty. They wished me good luck and I received a great deal of support from others".
5   Some experts also mentioned that this experience enabled them to develop new skills. "I got a new skill and learned how to use a computer, and prepare the presentation". "I became more confident to talk in a bigger group". "I also see the progress. Last year I was much less confident that this year. Through practicing I have become a better talker and I think that this year I will have an even better presentation. I am proud".

Drawbacks of involvement

It is not enough only to invite experts by experience as teachers; they need to be supported to be teachers in the first place and to know what we expect from them, what is in the curriculum for the education program, why we want them to be involved and what they might get out of the experience.

Their roles need to be clear. Experts by experience need to have a more emancipatory role and play a central role in the construction and development of the program (curriculum) to develop closer links and collaboration between experts by experience, students and professors.

There is a risk that experts by experience will be seen as "case studies" instead of partners. There is also a risk that we will increase the distance between "us" and "them" (Beresford and Croft, 2004).

Results show that there are some prerequisites for the involvement of experts by experience in teaching:

Involvement should be planned and structured

1   We need to prepare experts by experience for their roles as teachers e.g. how much time they have and what we expect from them. At the Faculty of Social Work in Ljubljana, we have one good example for this. From 2005 to 2007, we were a partner in the European project EX–IN (Experience involvement, Flaker et al., 2007), which was coordinated by the author of the text. In this project, we established the teaching program together with experts by experience in the field of mental ill health. Experts by experience had different roles. Firstly, in collaboration they suggested and prepared the content of the module and then they taught. This can be one of the foundations for our future collaboration of the curriculum, which is the base step of inclusion. We need to assure collaboration in the preparation of the curriculum.

2   We need to assure enough time for their presentation. Sometimes people need more time, especially if the experts by experience have verbal problems, or they talk a lot and wish to say more.

3   Fees and expenses should be discussed. In one of our cases, we could not pay the expert for lectures because she was already employed at the faculty in another capacity. So we needed to find a way to cover her cost. The expertise of experts by experience should be fully recognised (see also Bornarova, 2009, p. 287).

4   There is a need for development of an anti-paternalistic, strength and resilience-oriented perspective from the academic staff towards experts by experience (see also Zaviršek and Videmšek, 2009).

5   We need to have the courage to let them take centre stage and be open to the diversity of knowledge.

6   We need to avoid tokenism and exploitation.

Conclusion

The involvement of experts by experience in teaching can take many forms, but not everyone values experts' knowledge as equal to other sources of knowledge (Beresford and Croft, 2004). The research highlighted that the new knowledge that comes from experts by experience is still devalued and connected to stigma. The students may integrate this knowledge into practice but not per se; first they need to build a trust relationship and overcome prejudice to see experts by experience as partners that can bring positive outcomes. More in-depth research is needed to sharpen and broaden understanding of the potential outcomes for all involved (not only for students but also for experts by experience). Involving experts by experience as teachers cannot be allowed to be one of the neoliberal concepts with the aim of reducing cost, but should rather be a way to empower experts by experience in the education sphere as well as in social work practice as such. It is about changing our future professional work in the University, being open to different kinds of knowledge and implementing our core concepts in social work. We are often too reluctant to involve "outsiders with experience" in teaching, and we feel insecure because we do not know what will happen. But to be honest, we are talking about power issues. Who controls what? Who can say what?

Many authors (Brown and Young, 2008; Morgan and Jones, 2009; Irvine et al., 2015) argue that the involvement of experts by experience in social work education is extremely valuable to all involved. Irvine et al. (2015) pointed out that many students realise how keeping experts' perspectives at the core of practice is paramount in order to actualise social work values. It is not enough for students to hear only from people who can share their stories of recovery from mental ill health or to hear their experiences with involvement in research; it is essential that students have the chance to reflect on their feelings and review and obtain feedback on them.

Research shows (Ramon, 2003; Gutman and Ramon, 2016; Dorozenkot et al., 2016) that a lack of training can be identified as a significant issue, and experts by experience can feel unsupported and unprepared for their roles.

Findings from this research shows that learning from lived experience promotes social work practice, which honours lived experience. Students identified what they had learnt from experts by experience and how their presentations had shaped existing knowledge and their ability to resist dominant biomedical cultures and disempowering practice, as also pointed out by Dorozenko et al. (2016, p. 908). They present a positive view of involvement of experts by experience and see it as an enriching element in their future social work practice as well as a positive element in education.

The role of experts by experience as teachers was a good opportunity to shape attitudes and future teaching structures in social work. As it is now, the involvement of experts by experience in teaching is relatively under-developed. Experts by experience are only guest lecturers. There is a total absence of policy guidance and resources in Slovenia to support and promote their participation in teaching. They do not play a part in the planning of the study curriculum or in, monitoring and evaluation of social work programs. It is important to acknowledge that there is a big opportunity for all involved for programs of social work to become more interesting, more alive, and for students to acquire more complex knowledge based on real-life experience. There are many hurdles to jump for full participation of experts by experience in education to come to fruition, but it is not an impossible task. The search for the optimum model of integration and involvement of experts by experience in education for social work is possible, but it needs to be debated and to be open to different strategies in order to avoid tokenism and exploitation.

Notes

1 An expert by experience is someone with experience of using social services now or in the past (read more about this in Van Haaster and Koster, 2005; McLaughlin, 2009). Expert by experience knowledge is in the literature also described as experimental or direct knowledge, as lived experience and as from experts by experience. The key point lies in the fact that people are experienced, and it is learned from personal experience. This is not to deny the existence or validity of professionals' knowledge or the fact that they are based on direct experience. It means first-hand experience and reflection.
2 In 1999, 29 European countries, including Slovenia, sang the Bologna declaration in Bologna as a main document of the Bologna process that started the reform in European Higher Education. It was agreed that until 2010, we would have a united Higher Education system in which students and graduates could move freely between countries, using prior qualifications in one country as acceptable entry requirements for further study in another. Slovenia started with the Bologna program in study year 2009/10.

Literature

Agnew, A. & Duffy, J. (2010). Innovative approaches to involving service users in palliative care. *Social Work Education*, 29:7, 744–759.

Allegri, E. (2015). *Service users and carer involvement in social work education: Lessons from an innovative Italian experience*. Paper presented at EASSW Biennial Conference "Social Work Education: Towards 2025", Milan.

Anghel, R. & Ramon, S. (2009). Service users and carers' involvement in social work education: Lessons from an English case study. *European Journal of Social Work*, 12, 185–199. doi:10.1080/13691450802567416

Banks, S. (2008). Critical commentary: Social work ethics. *British Journal of Social Work*, 38, 1238–1249. doi:10.1093/bjsw/bcn099

Barnes, M. (2006). *Caring and social justice*. Basingstoke: Palgrave Macmillan.

Beresford, P. (2000). Service user' knowledge and social work theory. *British Journal of Social Work*, 30, 489–503.

Beresford, P. & Croft, S. (2004). Service users and practitioner united: The key component for social work reform. *British Journal of Social Work*, 34:1, 53–68.

Beresford, P. & Croft, S. (2008). Democratising social work – A key element of innovation: From "client" as object, to service users as producer. *The Innovative Journal: The Public Sector Innovation Journal*, 13, 5–22. Retrieved from www.innovation.cc/scholary-style/Beresford_2_democrat_sw.pdf

Beresford, P. & Rose, D. (2009). Background. In A. Sweeney, P. Beresford, A. Faulkner, M. Nettle & D. Rose (Eds.), *This is survivor research* (pp. 11–22). Herefordshire: PCCS BOOKS Rose-on Wye.

Beresford, P. & Boxall, K. (2015). Where do service user's knowledge sit in relation to professional and academic understanding of knowledge? In. P. Staddon (Ed.), *Mental health service users in research* (pp. 69–87). Bristol: Policy Press.

Bornarova, S. (2009). User involvement in social work education: Macedonian perspective. *Ljetopis socialnog rada*, 16:2, 279–298.

Braun, V. & Clarke, V. (2006). Using thematic analysis in psychology. *Qualitative Research in Psychology*, 3, 77–101.

Brkič, M. & Jugoić, A. (2009). Experience of service user involvement in the education of social workers in Serbia. *Ljetopis socialnog rada*, 16:2, 469–481.

Brown, K. & Young, N. (2008). Building capacity for service user and carer involvement in social work education. *Social Work Education*, 27, 84–96.

Cabiati, E. & Raineri, M.L. (2016). Learning from service users' involvement: A research about changing stigmatizing attitudes in social work students. *Social Work Education*, 35:8, 982–996. doi:10.1080/026 15479.2016.1178225

Čekić Bašić, S. (2009). Service user involvement in social work practice, education and research in the federation of Bosnia and Hercegovina. *Ljetopis socialnog rada*, 16:2, 241–257.

Dominelli, L. (2002). *Anti-oppressive social work*. London: Palgrave: Macmillan.

Dominelli, L. (2008). *Anti-racist social work*. London: Palgrave Macmillan.

Dorozenko, K.P., Ridley, S., Martin, R. & Mahboub, L. (2016). A journal of embedding mental health lived experience in social work education. *Social Work Education*, 35:8, 905–917. doi:10.1080/02615 479.2016.1214255

Duffy, J. (2006). *Participating and learning. Citizenship involvement in social work education in the Northern Ireland context: A good practice guide*. London: Social Care Institute for Excellence (online). Retrieved, October 15, 2018, from www.scie.org.uk/publications/misc/citizeninvolvement.asp

Duffy, J., Das, C. & Davison, G. (2013). Service user and carer involvement in role plays to assess readiness for practice. *Social Work Education*, 32, 39–54. doi:10.1080/02615479.2011.639066

Duffy, J. & Hayes, D. (2012). Social work students learn about social work values from service users and carers. *Ethic and Social Welfare*, 6, 368–385. doi:1080/17496535.2012.654497

Džombić, A. & Urbanc, K. (2009). Involvement of persons with disability in the education of social work student. Zagreb: *Ljetopis socialnog rada*, 16:2, 375–394.

Ferguson, H. (2017). How social workers reflect in action and when and why they don't: The possibilities and limits to reflective practice in social work. *Social Work Education: The International Journal*, 34:4.

Flaker, V., Cigoj-Kuzma, N., Grebenc, V., Kodele, T., Kranjc, B., Pirnat, T., Smole, A., Urek, M., Videmšek, P., & Žnidarec Demšar, S. (2007). *Empowerment in theory and practice*. Ljubljana: Univerza v Ljubljani, Fakulteta za socialno delo.

Fook, J., Ryan, M. & Hawkins, L. (2000). *Professional expertise: Practice, theory and education for working in uncertainty*. London: Whiting & Birch.

Gutman, C. & Ramon, S. (2016). Lessons from a comparative study of user involvement. *Social Work Education*, 35:8, 1–14. doi:10.1080/02615479.2016.1221392

Howe, D. (2009). *A brief introduction to social work*. Basingstoke: Palgrave Macmillan. www.tandfonline.com/doi/full/10.1080/02615479.2017.1413083

Irvine, J., Molyneux, J. & Gillman, M. (2015). "Providing a link with the real world": Learning from the student experience of service user and carer involvement in social work education. *Social Work Education*, 34, 138–150. doi:10.1080/02615479.2014,957178

Lamovec, T. (1995). *Ko rešitev postane problem in zdravilo postane strup: nove oblike skrbi za osebe v duševni krizi.* [When solutions become the problem and the medicine becomes the poison: new forms of support for people in mental crisis]. Ljubljana: Lumi. Repinted 2006 by Faculty of Social Work.

Levin, E. (2004). *Involving service users and carers in social work education* (Report No. 4). London: Social Care Institute for Excellence. SCIE (online). Retrieved, October 20, 2018, from www.scie.uk/publications/guides/guide04/files/guide04.pdf

McLaughlin, H. (2006). Involving young service users as co-researchers: Possibilities, benefits and costs. *British Journal of Social Work*, 36:8, 1395–1410.

McLaughlin, H. (2009). What's in a name: Client, patient, customer, consumer, expert by experience, service user: What's next? *British Journal of Social Work*, 19:6, 1101–1117.

McLaughlin, H. (2010). Keeping service user involvement in research honest. *British Journal of Social Work*, 40, 1591–1608.

McLaughlin, H. (2015). Alternative futures for service user involvement in research. In P. Staddon (Ed.), *Mental health service users in research: Critical sociological perspectives* (pp. 153–169). Bristol: Policy Press.

Mešl, N. (2008). *Razvijanje in uporabna znanja v socialnem delu z družino*. Procesi soustvarjanja teoretskega znanja v praksi [*Development and practicability knowledge for social work with the families. Process of co-creation of theoretical knowledge into practice*]. Ljubljana: FSD.

Morgan, A. & Jones, D. (2009). Perception of service user and carer involvement in healthcare education and impact on students' knowledge and practice: A literature review. *Medical Teacher*, 31, 82–95.

Novak, J.D. & Gowin, D.B. (1984). *Learning how to learn*. New York: Cambridge University Press.

Powell, J. (2009). Developing social work research. In R. Adams, L. Dominelli & M. Payne (Eds.), *Practising social work in a complex world* (pp. 321–331). UK: Palgrave Macmillan.

Ramon, S. (Ed.) (2003). *Users researching health and social care: An empowering agenda*. Birmingham: Ventura Press.

Redmond, B. (2006). *Reflection in action*. Farnham: Ashgate.

Schön, D. (1983). *The reflective practitioner: Towards a new design for teching and learning in the porffesionals*. San Francisco, California: Jossey-Bass.

Thompson, N. (2002). Social movements, social justice and social work. *British Journal of Social Work*, 32, 711–722.

Thompson, N. (2006). *Anti-discriminatory practice*. Basingstoke: Palgrave Macmillan.

Thompson, S. & Thompson, N. (2008). *The critically reflective practitioner*. Basingstoke: Palgrave Macmillan.

Urbanc, K. (2009). Participation of service users in social work education – Teachers' perspective. *Ljetopis socijalnog rada*, 16:2, 327–354.

Urek, M. (2017). Unheard voices: Researching participation in social work. *European Journal of Social Work*. doi:10.1080/13691457.2016.1278525

Van Haaster, H., & Koster, Y. (Ed.), (2005). *What is an expert by experience?* http://www.ex-in.info/hinterground.php-expert_by_experience.pdf

Videmšek, P. (2009). From the margin to the centre: Service users as researchers in social work practice. In V. Leskošek (Ed.), *Theories and methods of social work: Exploring different perspectives* (pp. 179–194). Ljubljana: Fakulteta za socialno delo.

Videmšek, P. (2011). Vpliv družbenih gibanj na razvoj socialnega dela v Sloveniji [Role of user's movement in changing control of expert by experience]. *Socialno delo*, 52, 129–138. Ljubljana: Fakulteta za socialno delo.

Videmšek, P. (2014). From definition to action: Empowerment as a tool for change in social work practice. In A.L. Matthies & L. Uggerhøj (Eds.), *Participation, marginalization and welfare services: Concepts, politics and practices across European countries* (pp. 63–76). Farnham and Burlington: Ashgate.

Videmšek, P. (2017). Expert by experience research as grounding for social work education. *Social Work Education*, 36:2, 172–187.

Videmšek, P., & Fox, J. (2009). Concept mapping as a discovery and learning tool. In Ramon, S. and Zaviršek, D (Eds.), *Critical edge issues in comparative social work and social policy research*. Comparative research perspectives. (pp. 119–218). Ljubljana: University of Ljubljana.

Yeung, Y.W.E. & Ng, S.M. (2010). Engaging service users and carers in health and social care education: Challenges and opportunities in the Chinese community. *Social Work Education*, 1–18. doi:10.1080/02615479.2010.491542

Zaviršek, D. & Leskošek, V. (ur.) (2006). *Zgodovina socialnega dela v Sloveniji. Med družbenimi gibanji in političnimi sistemi*. Ljubljana: FSD.

Zaviršek, D. & Videmšek, P. (2009). Service users involvement in research and teaching: Is there place for it in Eastern European social work. *Ljetopis socialnog rada*, 16:2, 189–207.

17

EMERGENCE AND CLASHES IN DISABLED SERVICE USER ORGANISATIONS IN SOUTH KOREA

SeKwang Hwang

Introduction

Over the past three decades, there has been increasing internationally wide recognition regarding the importance of involving service users and their caregivers in the development of health and social care policy and planning processes, service delivery, monitoring, and research (Omeni et al., 2014). As Crawford et al. (2002) mentioned, service user involvement is becoming less discretionary but more compulsory (p. 163). In South Korea (hereinafter Korea), citizen participation was either absent or coerced until 1987 due to the deep-rooted tradition of a state-centred society under military governments. Since the early of 1990s, social support services for the elderly, disabled, and children have dramatically increased. For instance, the number of community centres in local authorities increased from 1,836 in 2006 to 8,052 in 2016 (MOHWp, 2017). Although there is a growing recognition of user involvement in health and social care, there is no agreed definition of "service users" and "service user participation or involvement" in Korea. Rather, several terms commonly refer to user involvement, including "citizen participation" and "consumer involvement", and to user organisations such as NGOs (*Mingandanche*), civil society organisations (*Simindanche*), civic movement organisations, (*Siminwoondongdanche*), and public interest corporations (*Gongickbubin*). Nevertheless, the social welfare service has been limited to socially marginalised groups in Korea. So, service user participation and voices are still largely restricted due to lack of information, low socio-economic class, limited social network, and lack of political action.

Service user involvement has its origins in the disabled people's movement (Beresford and Carr, 2012), especially the self-advocacy movement for people with learning disabilities. In Korea, the number of disabled service user organisations have increased since 2000 under the influence of the Disability Movement (Yu and Hwang, 2018), and social interest in the rights of disabled service users under the influence of disability *Dansajajuwei*[1] has increased. The importance of user participation is enshrined in Korean legislation for disabled people, notably the United Nations Convention on the Rights of People with Disabilities (UNCRPD). Nevertheless, service user involvement in social care and health is still at the nascent stage, and not enough studies have been done on service user involvement. Only limited areas such as theoretical understanding of service user participation (Kim and Kim, 2007) and user-oriented services (Kang et al., 2010) have been explored. In Korea, the term disabled people's organisations (DPOs) has been used without a clear distinction between organisations of the disabled and organisations for/with the disabled (see Oliver's typology, 1990). As a result, there are many clashes between DPOs who insist on referring to themselves as the truly "authentic and representative" organisation "of" or "for" disabled people (Ablenews, 2016). This chapter will look closely at this issue. This chapter also offers a conceptual analysis of the service user involvement in the context of Korean DPOs.

Contextualising service user movements in Korea

To begin with, it is important to briefly look at the development of service user involvement in Korea. Until 1987, user participation in social and political contexts was absent or coerced under military governments, but only selected organisations were mobilised in a range of pro-government activities to improve industrial and agriculture productivity (Kim, 2010). Those organisations were not run by user groups, and their activities did not represent genuine user involvement. In this period, military governments did not allow any opportunity for service user involvement in welfare policy. Welfare legislation and policy was used as a political instrument of the military regime to control citizens and weaken resistance of democracy and participation. As a result, welfare was largely left to the individual and their family members. In this period, there were few formal statutory support services for disabled people.

From the early 1980s, various civic organisations, such as women's groups and consumer advocacy groups, grew with the emergence of middle-class and university-educated groups as there was increasing awareness of the problems of the military regimes. In this period, non-disabled activist or family members of disabled people generally spoke for disabled people, but disabled people's rights to speak for themselves were generally neglected.

After the nationwide "Democracy Movement" in June 1987, the political system in Korea started to shift from an authoritarian state under military governments to a democratic state. After the 1990s, many user-led organisations were established and grew rapidly. During the Kim Dea Jung presidency (1998–2003), for instance, governmental agencies were encouraged and even pressured to delegate collaborative governance and devolve as much work as possible to market sectors and voluntary sectors, such as firms and user-led organisations. Collaborative governance was highlighted as an important policy goal of the Roh Mu Hyun government (2003–2008), which named itself as a "participatory government" (*Chamyeo Jeongbu*) with a focus on decentralisation, governmental innovation, and civic participation. In response to service users' increasing and diversifying needs, the Korean government has shifted its approach for social service to financing social services from direct funding support for service providers to the voucher system for service users since 2007 (Lee and Son, 2011). Service users are allowed to use social service vouchers to purchase services from any provider of their own choice. The number of individual voucher users increased from 636,093 in 2011 to 656,200 in 2014 (Kwon and Guo, 2019, p. 670). A boom of many newly established nationwide or local user-led organisations immediately followed to raise a voice for disadvantaged users to collectively express their views and priorities.

The past five consecutive governments in Korea, albeit with varying degrees of enthusiasm, have placed emphasis on so-called collaborative governance, defined as "a governing arrangement where one or more public agencies directly engage non-state stakeholders in a collective decision-making process that is formal, consensus-oriented, and deliberative and that aims to make or implement public policy or manage public programs or assets" (Kim, 2010, p. 166)

With the continuing influence of political changes, a substantial increase in social service infrastructures and social service policy implementations in an effort to meet the increased welfare demands have been witnessed. In the past, the top-down welfare service system and provider-centred paternalist approach was allowed no room for service user participation.

A decentralised social service system was introduced in 1995, and local authorities have focused on providing more social services (Kang et al., 2010). Moreover, user involvement in delivering social services was strongly demanded after several protests for introducing a social security system and ensuring stable security of the social welfare budget, but it was led by academics, lawyers, and a few civic organisations. Since 2000s, the importance of user involvement has slowly been acknowledged by the disabled people's movement.

Emerging disabled service user organisations

Before 1981, there were no appropriate support services for disabled people, and disabled people's rights were largely ignored and neglected. There were a few organisations for the disabled, such as Rehabilitation Korea (1954), Korean Association for Mental Retarded (1968), the Korea Polio Association (1966), the Korean Society for the Cerebral Palsied (1978), and Korea Disabled Welfare Organisation (1981), but those organisations were led by non-disabled activists, professionals, or parents of disabled children. The main work of the organisation involved creating petitions to help certain disabled people gain access to employment and education.

Influenced by the United Nations International Year of Disabled Persons in 1981, the Korean government enacted two major disability policies, for social welfare (the Act on Welfare of Persons with Disabilities in 1981) and education (the Act on Special Education for Disabled Persons in 1977). Many organisations for/with disabled people were established, such as the National Union of Students with Physical Disabilities (NUSPD) (1978). The main task of these organisations was to promote a mutual friendship, or to educate and to provide support to limited disabled people who were being discriminated against in education and employment. But these organisations did not work collectively to raise the voices of disabled people; rather, they were merely individual efforts.

Since 1987, the democratic movements in Korea changed to social movements that evolved in the context of the military and authoritarian regimes. During this period, two key organisations were formed. First, the Research Institute of the Differently Abled Person's Right in Korea (RIDRIK) was established by university-educated physically disabled people, academics, lawyers, and non-disabled activists in 1987 to lobby politicians and professionals to introduce disability rights-based policies and legislation. Second, disabled activists who were inspired by civil rights groups started to form their own organisations in reaction to social attitudes and barriers at the local and national levels. Disabled People's International Korea was formed with 20 disabled people, but this organisation was run by non-disabled professionals. NUSPD was transformed into a user-led organisation, "Ullimteo" (1986), which was a very small disabled user-led organisation, but this organisation introduced a new rights-based paradigm for thinking about disability against capitalism (Ullimteo, 1993). In 1987, key members of Ullimteo joined the National Organisation for People with Physical Disabilities (NOPPD) to take initiative for disabled people's movements, but the existing members of NOPPD struggled to collaborate with the newly arrived disabled young activists' radical and direct activism. As a result, Ullimteo was dissolved in 1992, and almost all disabled young activists from Ullimteo joined the Association for Young Disabled People's Activism (AYDPA). In 1987, AYDPA discovered that the total budget for the 1988 Seoul Paralympic Games was allocated more than four times that of the total welfare budget provided for disabled people (HamkkeGulum, 2003). In 1988, a new disabled user-led organisation called Korean Differently Abled Federation (KDAF) formed and collaborated with other organisations with/for disabled people to organise a mass public protest demanding the boycotting of the Paralympic Games and the enacting of legislation for welfare and employment for disabled people. This protest formed "Union for Enacting Two Acts", which was not a disabled people's organisation but a group of people, including well-known academics and non-disabled people of high social status, who were campaigning to achieve full human rights and equality for disabled people (Yu, 2017). From 1988, disabled organisations began to engage in mass radical, but non-violent, direct actions, such as demonstrations on streets, hunger strikes, and sit-in strikes at political party or government offices (HamkkeGulum, 1991). As a result, two key disability-related laws (i.e. the Welfare for People with Disabilities Act 1989 and the Disability Employment Act 1990) were enacted or amended during this period.

From the 1990s, human rights, self-determination, and autonomy were held as the core values for DPOs. The number of DPOs began to multiply but were divided into several nation-wide, user-led umbrella organisations (Yun, 2012). For instance, Korea Association of People with Physical Disabilities, Korea Association of the Deaf, and Korea Association on Mental Retardation in 1996 formed an umbrella organisation, entitled Korea Differently Abled Federation (KODAF); other organisations such as Korea Traffic Disabled Association, Industrial Injured Member Association, Korean Federations of Centre of Independent Living of People with Disabilities, and the Human Rights Forum for People with Disabilities in Korea formed another umbrella organisation, the Korean Federation for Organisations of the Disabled (KOFOD) in 2002. Other disabled activists that disagreed with the actions of the above two umbrella organisations also emerged. In 2007, the Solidarity Committee of the Disabled to Obtain Mobility Rights (SDOMOR) and other disabled people's organisations merged to become the Solidarity Against Disability Discrimination (SADD), advocating the use of radical and direct actions.

Since 2000, consumerism and the Independent Living Movement have been introduced to DPOs in Korea. Self-help organisations influenced by advocacy and self-advocacy movements in Western countries especially have emerged through various organisations such as Centre for Independent Living (CIL), the Community Rehabilitation Centre for the Disabled (CRCD) in local authorities, or the Korean Parents Society for the Disabled (KPSD). CIL focused on rehabilitation services for disabled people via vocational training, cultural activities, and education on disability rights, while CIL supports self-advocacy groups in collaboration with Japan's People First. KPSD started a programme for self-advocacy based on the People First Movement's values. The National Self-Advocacy Group Convention of People with Developmental Disabilities has been held annually since 2013; Korea's People First launched in 2016.

To summarise, disabled people's organisations influenced by activism, especially disability Dangsajajuwei, of disability people's movements, have increased significantly. As Table 17.1 shows, there are currently three umbrella disabled service user organisations in Korea. The demands of each organisation vary: citizenship issues, human rights, challenging societal attitudes and barriers, and welfare rights.

Clashes between Korean disabled people's organisations: disability Dangsajajuwei

While the Independent Living Movement was introduced through Japan's Human Care Association, the biggest change in disabled service user organisations started in the areas of health and social care from the late 1990s as a major ideological shift occurred in Korea in the name of "disability Dangsajajuwei". This was first introduced by Disabled Peoples' International (DPI) Korea in 1991 and became a key political ideology for disability activism; attempts have been

Table 17.1 Key umbrella disabled people's organisations in Korea

	Korea Differently Abled Federation	Korea Federation of Organisation of the Disabled	The Solidarity Against Disability Discrimination
Aims	Disability and human rights	Disability Dangsajajuwei and disability rights	Democratic movement
Key members	Disabled people's organisations and supporting organisations	Disabled people's organisations (physical impairments)	Disabled people's organisations and citizen-activist organisations
Main activities	Making policy and legislation proposals relating to disability	CILs	Radical public protests

made to use it to transform disabled people's organisations since 2002 (Yu and Hwang, 2018). However, there is no clear theoretical definition of Dangsajajuwei. Dangsajajuwei emphasises that disabled people must make their own decisions and have control over services and policy, and strongly resists creating/operating/managing content, systems, or facilities for disabled people by non-disabled activists or/and professionals (Yu and Hwang, 2018). Importantly, two main philosophies of Dangsajajuwei are "self-representation" and "rights of self-determination". So, the passive role of disabled service users in welfare support and policy has been strongly challenged by Dangsajajuwei. This argues that active users' involvement is imperative to make sure the needs and wishes of service users are heard.

ILM's philosophy, which emphasises consumer control and the idea that disabled people are the best experts on their own needs, was deeply integrated into Dangsajajuwei by the KOFOD (Lee et al., 2007) after key member organisations, such as DPI Korea, Korea Association of People with Physical Disabilities (KAPPD), and Korea Federation of Centers for Independence Living of People with Disabilities (KOIL), joined KOFOD from 2002 on.

However, there has been great debate among and criticism of disabled people's organisations. The main bone of contention is the role and function of non-disabled activists and families in operating and managing DPOs, because some DPOs include family members, mostly parents, or non-disabled professionals at governance and leadership level. For instance, KOFOD criticised that KODAF was an organisation "for" the disabled and thus incapable of being truly representative of disabled people's organisations because Rehabilitation International (RI) Korea, RID-RIK, and KPSD, which were key member organisations of KODAF, were managed with parents and non-disabled professionals. KODAF argues that KOFOD was a subject interest group only in order to use their own initiatives and power over DPOs. These controversial debates slowly died down after the Korea Blind Union (KBU) withdrew from KOFOD and joined KODAF in 2007 (Kim, 2012). Inhee Kwon, the representative of KBU, argued against KOFOD:

> *Dangsajajuwei* has achieved many key developments for the disabled. So, the current chauvinistic and exclusive character of *Dangsajajuwei* in KOFOD, which does not allow any input from non-disabled professionals and activists, needs to be changed to integrated character of *Dangsajajuwei* to accept contributions of non-disabled activists and professionals on disabled people's organisations.
>
> *(Ablenews, 2007)*

Finally, KOFOD's criticism was clouded because two big disabled people's organisations, KBU and the Korea Association of the Deaf, joined KODAF.

The second wave of clashing started from debates over the functions and actions of DPOs in 2007. KODAF and KOFOD'S work was mainly limited to seminars, conferences, education, public hearings, publications, establishing ties with other organisations, and so on. However, many disabled people's organisations opposed KODAF and KOFOD's indirect actions, especially in relation to mobility rights for disabled people. As a result, those disabled activists and their organisations which engage in mass radical and direct actions to obtain mobility rights for disabled people gathered to form a new umbrella organisation, called Solidarity Against Disability Discrimination (SADD). DPI Korea and KFCIL disagreed with SADD's direction and criticised SADD due to heavy involvement by non-disabled activists or professionals in their actions. Specifically, they argued that a disabled people's organisation should be "of" the disabled; if it includes non-disabled people to control and manage, it cannot be called a disabled people's organisation (Ko, 2007). However, SADD argues that conservative disabled people's organisations such as KODAF and KOFOD are further ahead in terms of becoming key partners of disability policy making and getting funds for running their organisations through Dangsajajuwei (Kim, 2017).

The third wave of clashing started within CILs. In 1993, DPI Korea introduced the independent living movement to Korea through the Japanese version of a book entitled *The Shock of the ADA*. ILM's philosophy, which emphasises consumer control and the idea that disabled people are the best experts on their own needs, was integrated into Dangsajajuwei in 2002 by the Korea Federation of Organisations of the Disabled (KOFOD) (Lee et al., 2007). In 2001, Jeongnip Center for Rehabilitation and Independence started to provide independent living services, including peer counselling and personal assistance services.

Ten Centres for Independent Living (CILs) were established in Korea in 2005 with government funding, and almost two hundred CILs were in existence in 2017 (Yu, 2017, p. 309). The Korean government revised the Welfare of Persons with Disabilities Act in 2008 to provide legal grounds for its support of CILs.

The independent living movement had become influential in the lives of disabled people, especially people with complex needs. After public demonstrations and direct actions on the street for 39 days by key members with complex needs under SADD in 2006, the Act on Activity Assistant Services for Persons with Disabilities was enacted and came into effect, which specifies introducing personal assistants for disabled people in 2007. Those disabled people contributed to establishing CILs. In 2003, 11 CILs formed Korea Council of Centres for Independent Living (KCCIL). Within KCCIL, however, there has been great debate on the orientation of ILM and the method by which it should be used to campaign for disabled people's rights. This has been between CILs who led public direct actions for mobility rights and CILs who focused more on support services based on disability Dangsajajuwei because of parents of disabled people involved in the later CILs. Parents have been working to receive services such as personal assistance for their disabled children. Parents and disabled people within those CILs have insisted that the priority for their CILs must be services for disabled people, not political direct actions to change policy. As a result, this clash caused CILs to split into two umbrella organisations in 2006: advocacy-oriented CILs (i.e. Korea Federation of Centres for Independent Living of Person with Disabilities (KOIL) and service-oriented CILs (KCCIL). KOIL has criticised KCCIL for failing to recognise disabled people's opinions. The basis of this viewpoint is that many non-disabled people and professionals function as the representatives of CILs (Yun, 2012).

As seen in the previous section, each DPO is rooted in different politics, strategies, and tactics, and each DPO is led by various leading groups, including the parents of disabled people, non-disabled activists, and professionals. They have seldom worked cooperatively at a national and local level, and occasionally have even been hostile to each other for taking initiative (Yun, 2012).

Current challenges and future directions of DPOs

As Beresford agues (2018), the emerging DPOs in Korea have brought significant changes for disabled people in terms of factors such as public and political understandings of disability, employment, housing, education, healthcare, income, social service, and the discrimination that disable people face for their rights. Nevertheless, it is evident that DPOs have faced several important challenges:

First, although the definition of DPOs is distinct from other disability sector organisations, the term "DPO" has not been clearly been discussed and defined in Korea. The type, structure, role, and governance of DPOs are varied; therefore, there are a variety of organisations that consider themselves DPOs. In particular, the term Dangsajajuwei has not been defined clearly within DPOs and the Korean Disability Movement. As a result, some groups that have been established primarily for the purpose of providing support services to members also claim themselves as a DPO. Yun (2005) classified three DPO characters under Dangsajajuwei: 1) single disability group organisations who have focused only on their own interests but do not fully integrate with Dangsajajuwei; 2) DPOs that collaborate with non-disabled activists to achieve solidarity for disability rights; and 3) DPOs that restrict non-disabled people's involvement.

The debates on Dangsajajuwei do not clearly define who the main party of DPO is that constitutes Dangsaja (a person/party), and it is very difficult and subjective to judge which DPOs should be included under Dangsajajuwei. For further development of DPOs, the identity and functions of DPOs urgently need to be debated and defined through Dangsajajuwei.

Second, excessively emphasising (i.e. Dangsaja) issues of disabled individuals under Dangsajajuwei led to neglect of the multiplicity and plurality of DPOs (Yu, 2004). Ironically, Dangsajajuwei creates exclusive and selective authoritarian groups among disabled people. Kim (2012) argues that Dangsajajuwei has been transformed into exclusive collective group activism that involves focusing advocacy on "only certain" disabled groups and becoming distant from the fight against oppression and inequality for all disabled people. Those DPOs exercise power over, and are being oppressive towards, other DPOs. Dae-Sung Kim, representative of DPI Korea, concurred (2003) that Dangsaja cannot be same as Dansajajuwei because all disabled individuals do not follow or agree with Dangsajajuwei. He argued that some disabled users, "namely Dangsaja", were involved in the decision-making process but tried to exclude other disabled users' participation without any careful consideration of the individuals' unique needs and circumstances. Some DPOs completely ignored the disabled service user's self-determination and participation. As a result, some disabled user groups are much more likely to be heard and listened to than others. DPOs must overcome the limitation of disability Dangsajajuwei around the wide range of issues of diversity and equality, such as gender, belief, disability, and age, to avoid exclusion of any disabled service users.

Third, there are approximately 347 local and regional DPOs, including single-disability and cross-disability organisations, in 2019. Nearly all DPOs act as representatives and stakeholders of a single disability group (e.g. Autism Society of Korea or the Association for People with Physical Disabilities). Each DPO must compete to obtain funding from the central and/or local government. The scarcity of available resources has also led to intense competition between the organisations. Under this environment, DPOs have hardly collaborated or allied with other user-led organisations in nationwide or local areas to provide a stronger voice for change. Occasionally they have even been hostile to each other over taking control of the initiative of welfare service and budgets from the central or local government, but have failed to create strong partnerships with each other (Yun, 2012). For instance, no DPOs have been appointed as national advisory board members who monitor the implementations of UNCRPD due to hegemonic disputes between DPOs. This was particularly evident during the preparation of the report to the UNCRPD monitoring body (Ablenews, 2010). As Campbell (2009) asserts, DPOs must recognise the importance of solidarity, sharing experiences and supporting each other to bring important changes and to make a difference.

Fourth, the rights of disabled people to participate in decision-making was legally guaranteed in Korea. But they are still excluded when it comes to being in positions to initiate, lead, and implement the policy or service decisions that affect their lives. The Parallel Report for the UN Committee on the Rights of Persons with Disabilities, written by Korean DPOs and a non-governmental organisation coalition (2014), stresses that there still are many limitations to improving disabled people's rights and their involvement in decision-making. Recently, the Korean government pledged to collect opinions of different types of relevant DPOs, to develop policies and services for disabled people. Collaborative work with DPOs was ensured mainly through information sharing, workshops, and regular consultations. For instance, the Policy Coordination Committee for Persons with Disabilities was established under the Act on Welfare of Persons with Disabilities. Half of those outside of commissioned committee members have not consisted of disabled people, having led to the participation of representatives of DPOs. Also, no official or regulatory route is in place to ensure the participation of DPOs. DPOs as the initiators of ideas for policy or service change are rarely enabled to be involved in the full procedure of policy and services that affects them. Most of the support services in social care and health areas have still largely been initiated, delivered, and managed by the provider, especially the state, and non-disabled professionals in Korea. DPOs must be involved in a range of different political activities to promote the participation of disabled people or to facilitate their participation.

Note

1 This term has a very similar meaning to the disability activism slogan "nothing about us without us", which emphasizes that no decision should be made affecting disabled people without their full and active involvement. Lee (2004) defines it as "a way of the disability right movement developed by disabled people to criticise and restrain unfair power relation of welfare service providing system and oppression toward disabled people in society, and to emphasise disabled people's rights, independence, self-help and decision making" (p. 12).

References

Ablenews. (2007). *Interview with a New Representative of Korea Blind Union.* http://m.ablenews.co.kr/News/NewsContent.aspx?CategoryCode=0033&NewsCode=13780 (Accessed: 10/5/2019). In Korean.

Ablenews. (2010). *We Insist to Withdraw the Response Report on UNCRPD.* www.ablenews.co.kr/News/NewsContent.aspx?CategoryCode¼0011andNewsCode¼0011201011109248836375 (Accessed: 18/7/2019). In Korean.

Ablenews. (2016). *A Staring Contest Between Disabled People's Organisations.* http://m.ablenews.co.kr/News/NewsContent.aspx?CategoryCode¼0044andNewsCode¼00442016110217057857433 (Accessed: 2/6/2019). In Korean.

Beresford, P. (2018). 30 years of service user involvement and advocacy. In: S. Jones (ed) *30 Years of Social Change.* London: Jessica Kingsley, pp. 136–142.

Beresford, P., & Carr, S. (eds) (2012). *Social Care, Service Users and User Involvement.* London: JKP.

Campbell, P. (2009). The Service user/survivor movement. In: J. Reynolds, R. Muston, T. Heller, J. Leach, M. McCormick, J. Wallcraft, & M. Walsh (eds) *Mental Health Still Matters.* Basingstoke: Palgrave, pp. 46–52.

Crawford, M., Rutler, D., Manley, C., Weaver, T., Bhui, K., Fulop, N., & Tyrer, P. (2002). Systematic review of involving patients in the planning and development of health care. *BMJ*, 325: 1263–1268.

HamkkeGulum. (1991). *For Establishing the Association for Young Disabled People's Activism.* www.cowalknews.co.kr/news/articleView.html?idxno¼1447 (Accessed: 21/2/2019). In Korean.

HamkkeGulum. (2003). Disabled people oppose to Paralympic. 12: 15–17. In Korean.

Kang, H. G., Kim, B. Y., Eom, T. Y., Kim, E. J., & Chung, S. J. (2010). *A Study on Developing a User-Centered Social Service System*. Seoul: KIHASA. In Korean.

Kim, D. H. (2003). The spirits of cooperation and participation of disabled Dangsajajuwei movement. *The Radical Review*, 18(Winter): 181–186. In Korean.

Kim, D. H. (2012). A critical understanding of Dansajajuwei. *The Radical Review*, 52(Summer): 172–190. In Korean.

Kim, D. H. (2017). A bird flies with two wings. In: *Korean Disability Studies Conference*, Seoul, pp. 62–65. In Korean.

Kim, S. (2010). Collaborative governance in South Korea: Citizen participation in policy making and welfare service provision. *Asian Perspective*, 34(3): 165–190.

Kim, Y. D., & Kim, M. O. (2007). Conceptual structure of user involvement and implications on Korean disability services. *Korean Journal of Social Welfare*, 59(2): 39–64. In Korean.

Ko, K. C. (2007). *Directions and Tasks of the Korean Federation of Centres for Independent Living of Persons with Disabilities*. http://cafe.daum.net/_c21_/bbs_search_read?grpid¼14oY2andfldid¼CKkZanddatanum ¼137andq¼%C7%D1%C0%DA%20%BF%ACand_referer¼V7kfJwkeLEGMZxGlgqZEmWdFocBZ ynzcC1k3ZoqmkKDcSGNo8cFK.A00 (Accessed: 8/6/2019). In Korean.

Kwon, S., & Guo, B. (2019). South Korean nonprofits under the voucher system: Impact of organizational culture and organizational structure. *International Social Work*, 62(2): 669–683.

Lee, I. S. (2004). *Disabled People's Dangsajajuwei and Disability Right Movements: Background and Ideology*. Seoul: Seoul DPI. In Korean.

Lee, I. S., Choi, J. A., & Lee, D. Y. (2007). An exploratory discussion on independent living model: Focusing on social exclusion perspective. *Korean Social Policy Review*, 14(1): 48–81. In Korean.

Lee, J., & Son, J. (2011). Market and industry in social service policy: Social service e-voucher program. *Trends and View*, 82: 45–84. In Korean.

Ministry of Health and Social Welfare. (2017). *2017 Statistics of Health and Social Welfare*. www.mohw.go.kr/ react/al/sal0301vw.jsp?PAR_MENU_ID=04&MENU_ID=0403&page=1&CONT_SEQ=343379 (Accessed: 29/4/2019). In Korean.

Omeni, E., Barnes, M., MacDonald, D., Crawford, M., & Rose, D. (2014). Service user involvement: Impact and participation. A survey of service user and staff perspective. *BMC Health Service Research*, 14: 491.

Ullimteo. (1993). *The Records of Disability Activism of Ullimteo (1986–1992)*. http://sadddan.tistory.com/cat egory/%EC%9E%A5%EC%95%A0%EC%9D%B8%EC%9A%B4%EB%8F%99%EC%9E%90%EB%A 3%8C/%EC%9A%B8%EB%A6%BC%ED%84%B0 (Accessed: 5/6/2019). In Korean.

Yu, D. C. (2004). The achievements and assignments of disability movement in Korea. *Social Welfare Policy*, 21: 5–33. In Korean.

Yu, D. C. (2017). History of Korean disabled people's movement. In: *Korean Society for Disability Studies Autumn Conference*, Seoul, South Korea, 19/5/2017, pp. 8–30. In Korean.

Yu, D. C., & Hwang, S. K. (2018). Achievements of and challenges facing the Korean disabled people's movement. *Disability & Society*, 33(8): 1259–1279.

Yun, S. H. (2005). Disability and politics. In: *Disability Academy Proceedings*, Daegu: DPI Daegu. pp. 72–76. In Korean.

Yun, S. H. (2012). Past and present of Korean disability movement – Focused on disability liberation and disability Dansajajuwei. International Seminar on Disability Studies 2012 – Debates on Disability and Disease in Korea and Japan. *Survival Studies Research Centre Report*, 20: 155–172. In Korean.

18

SERVICE USERS AND PARTICIPATION – THE SPANISH EXPERIENCE

Emilio José Gómez-Ciriano

An unframed framework

The return of democracy to Spain in 1978 paved the way for a real, structured implementation of social welfare. Prior to that time, some initiatives existed albeit insufficiently structured (Casado and Fantova, 2007). The new welfare state mirrored the Constitution and was inspired by its principles. Its development was characterized by three elements. Firstly was the recognition of the majority of the 'social rights' included in the text not as rights but rather as mere principles (Gómez-Ciriano, 2016). Secondly, a high degree of decentralization affected all areas of welfare and particularly social services due to the new political and administrative role played by the autonomous regions and local governments. Finally, there was a familistic-based care scheme that placed public intervention in a subsidiary position with respect to families (Rodriguez-Cabrero et al., 2011). These three elements influenced the degree and quality of participation of welfare recipients

Stigmatizing services for stigmatized poor

In Spain there exists a widely shared perception of the poor as idle, lazy people responsible for their own poverty. The main response to their condition has been punishment, forced work, forced enrolment in the army or confinement in closed premises until they became 'normalized'. This perception has been in existence for more than five hundred years in Spain (Vives, 1526; De Robles, 1545) and from time to time seems to be recast. Together with the homeless, migrants and Roma people, the poor are still portrayed as suspicious in the collective imagination, as reflected in periodic surveys by the Spanish Centre for Sociological Research on opinions and attitudes (CIS, 2017).

Along with poverty, there exists a perception – anchored in the past but still present – of services as stigmatizing. In the words of Spicker, a service is stigmatizing

> when it degrades the recipient or undermines his dignity, when it embarrasses or humiliates him and makes him feel guilty or ashamed, when it deters him or makes

him hesitate to seek help, when it deprives him of rights or treats him with contempt, when it marks him out from others or identifies him with someone who is socially rejected.

(Spicker, 1984, 31)

In Spain, historically orphan houses, hospitals, lunatic asylums or reformatories have had bad reputations, with tainted premises that inflicted stigma on its beneficiaries. These images have survived in the collective imaginary and, by a contagion effect, have been extended to premises and centres where social workers and carers now do their work. This explains why recipients of social services or charities live with a feeling of shame.

On user participation and citizenship

Participating means taking part, cooperating with others and creating consensus to achieve common aims. Participation is also a right of citizenry and, as such, must be exercised in a free, critical and responsible way in all aspects of life. As a fundamental right, it also requires governments to prioritize and normalize it. However, this is not the case in all areas or for all people, as participation is not granted in the same way or to the same extent. The Spanish Aliens Act is very explicit in distinguishing between Spanish nationals, EU nationals and relatives, non-EU nationals in regular situations and non-EU nationals in irregular situations. In addition, in the fields of social services, benefits and job allowance provisions are more and more influenced by conditionality, to such an extent that it can be said that the more conditionality is present, the less participation is possible.

The latest survey on citizenship feelings from the Centre for Sociological Research (CIS) depicted an emerging awareness regarding the importance of participation as a way of exercising citizenship. Around 84.5% of the interviewees supported the idea that everybody should be granted the right to an adequate standard of living, In addition, 62.9% of people interviewed were in favour more opportunities being granted for participation in public decisions of their concern. Finally, a significant 50.2% of respondents estimated that public officers did not really take their concerns and worries into account (Center for Sociological Research. CIS ISSP, 2014). From this survey, some elements deserve to be highlighted. Firstly, the right to an adequate standard of living is directly linked to article 25 of the Universal Declaration of Human Rights (1948) and article 11 of the International Covenant on Economic, Social and Cultural Rights (1966); thus, when people declared that they support an adequate standard of living for everybody, they were in fact supporting the implementation of this human right in everyday situations. Secondly, something has changed people's minds regarding their perception of social rights and their awareness of them; such consciousness was unthinkable just five years earlier, when the economic crisis had not yet impacted on people's lives and expectations. Finally, a significant number of respondents do not trust the government as the actor responsible for improving the living conditions of its citizens.

Participation has to do with the exercise of social rights, which are at the core of the concept of social citizenship (Marshall, 1950). However, to be effective, participation must be developed not only in a framework that enables it, but also in an environment that does not place obstacles in the way of its expression, promotes its creativity and in which service users are confident in terms of the importance of their inputs and able to feel a connection between what their counterparts say (in our case, social workers, lecturers and researchers) and their own contributions. This is known as a culture of participation. Participation paves the way for the exercise of rights;

its absence can be not only a consequence of poverty but also a defining feature and a cause of it. As the former UN Rapporteur on extreme poverty and human rights declares:

> Powerlessness manifests itself in many ways, but at its core, is an inability to participate in or influence decisions that profoundly affect one's life, while decisions are made by more powerful actors who neither understand the situation of people living in poverty, nor necessarily have their interests at heart.
>
> *(Sepulveda-Carmona, 2013, 4)*

Finally, participation means clarity in the procedures of access and in conditions for access in an understandable and sufficient way, the right to be actively heard on all decision-making processes the service user is involved in and the right to give or refuse consent at any moment. It also entails the possibility of going to court in cases of non-compliance or a wish to challenge the abuse of power by the state.

Participation gaining ground 'ma non troppo'

In social legislation

Without any exception, the right to participation of service users is formally acknowledged in all 17 social services laws actually in force in Spain. In some cases, the right is included as part of the bill of rights and duties for social workers and service users that appear in the laws. This is the case of Madrid (2003), Aragón (2009), Castilla-La Mancha (2010). Castilla y León (2010). Extremadura (2015). or Andalucía (2016). This recognition, however, does not mean that there exists a right to appeal in courts in the cases of non-compliance, as was previously said. Only in the case of the Canary Islands has this precaution has been made explicit in its recent law, Canarias (2019). This lack of enforceability is something the Committee of Economic, Social and Cultural Rights of the United Nations noted in its concluding observations to the VI periodic report issued by the Spanish government in May 2018.

> The Committee is nevertheless concerned that those rights (economic, social and cultural rights) continue to be viewed as nothing more than guiding principles and that as result they can be invoked only after having been incorporated into domestic law or in connection to other rights that enjoy greater protection such as the right to life.
>
> *(Committee on Economic, Social and Cultural Rights, 2018)*

The right to participation, although formally present in law, is not recognized in all its dimensions, as service users could experience times of crisis when benefits are cut and there are no other choices for exercising their rights than demonstrating in the streets.

In academia

The adaptation of the Spanish University System to the Bologna Process entailed an in-depth revision of curricula and study programmes in the different disciplines, and consequently in social work. The white book on the degree in social work (ANECA, 2004) and the report on criteria for the design of study plans in the degree of social work (Vazquez-Aguado et al., 2007), both approved by the Board of Directors of Schools of Social Work and the General Council of Social Work of Spain, reflect the willingness to involve service users not just as passive actors, but also in the planning, decision-making and evaluation processes. This can be seen in the following paragraphs of the report on criteria:

All faculties and schools of social work should elaborate a declaration of their mission on which the rights and interests of social services users would be respected and also their participation in all aspects of the development of the study programmes.

(translated from the original; point 1.4)

Services users should be involved in the design and development of study and training programmes.

(translated from the original; point 3.3)

A common work between Academia, agencies and services users to make decisions about formative actions and evaluation should exist.

(translated from the original; point 3.12)

Users should actively participate in the selection, admission and continuity and permanence of students.

(translated from the original; point 6.3)

In the formation of future social workers, educators, users and practitioners should intervene at all levels.

(translated from the original; appendix to the recommendation point 9)

However, an analysis of the different study programmes in social work schools and faculties reveals that the participation of service users is yet to be achieved, with some exceptions (Universidad de Alicante, Universidad del País Vasco). The absence is complete in postgraduate studies, where service users, as active participants, are neither present nor expected to be present, at least in the near future.

At the political level

According to the document 'Standards in Social Work Practice Meeting Human Rights', issued by the International Federation of Social Workers in Europe,

social workers must strive to work effectively with users to challenge the personal and structural inequalities that diminish civil, economic and cultural rights in Europe.

(IFSW – Europe, 2010)

In pursuance of this objective, which is also present in the global definition of social work (IFSW, 2014), collaboration between social workers and service users is crucial. Lecturers and researchers should not be left behind in this process (Ramon et al., 2019). This is something highlighted by the abovementioned report on criteria for the social work degree in Spain when it affirms that social work studies aim at training future professionals by providing them with a wide understanding of structures and social procedures to transform social and economic contexts (Vazquez-Aguado et al., 2007).

While social workers have played a central role in the development of the welfare state by assuming political and managerial roles at both national and regional levels, the fact of the matter is that political influence through professional practice is much less common. This is so even where, as is the Spanish case, the General Council of Social Work strongly supports it. The reasons for this passivity can be found as partly due to the fact that, as Martinez Roman clearly explains, practitioners at the frontline do not believe that their work should have to do with politics, but rather just being professional while doing their jobs. In addition, even when most of them question welfare policies and criticize politicians, they don't really trust the effectiveness of developing a more activist role, much less promoting service users' involvement in the promotion and defence of their own rights (Martínez-Román, 2012). The precariousness of the profession and uncertainty in the future are additional elements that constrain professionals from taking risks.

Academia should also play an important role in raising awareness on this topic among students by promoting a human rights perspective in the content of the different subjects, and particularly in those that link social policy and social work. However, there is still a long way to go. As Cubillos et al. observe:

> Introducing training in human rights is not only an indispensable tool for improving the compromise of students with human rights fundamentals but also their understanding of what human rights perspective means as a key method to face challenges that social problems entailed in a globalized world.
>
> *(Cubillos et al., 2017)*

Androff similarly expressed that human rights approaches are necessary to become effective social workers and agents of social change (Androff, 2016). Mercado, Valles and de la Paz (2017), in their comprehensive study of the content of human rights in different study programmes, also note that its presence is clearly insufficient.

Some examples of service users' participation

The context for service users' participation was clarified in the first part of this chapter. In this part, examples of users' involvement will be introduced. At this point, it is important to highlight that although these cases are still an exception, they represent the willingness of their promotors to challenge deeply rooted inertia by inspiring other ways of lecturing, doing research and influencing politics. However, in none of the cases has the degree of involvement reached the level of user control defined by Arnstein (1969) and Hanley et al. (2004).

The Orange Tide

'Is not the crisis. It is the system' (slogan from the Orange Tide movement)

'Orange Tide' is a movement led by the General Council of Social Work in Spain and replicated by the different regional and provincial councils as a response by the social work profession to retrenchment policies that have cut benefits, increased the vulnerability of service users and weakened the stability of the profession. This movement is particularly interesting because, for the first time, service users got involved in initiatives that portrayed them as citizens claiming their rights without any remnant of shame or reluctance. The orange T-shirt that they wore in their mobilization was no longer a symbol of shame and exclusion but rather a signal of pride, and one that was also worn by non-service users, social workers and students and academics – although in this last case, not to the same extent. By wearing the orange T-Shirt at work, social workers expressed their rejection of neoliberal policies. The T-shirts contained the slogan: 'Social services for all. No cuts, don't be silent'. Service users acted to defend their social rights to citizenship and to challenge a welfare model which was becoming more residual and conditional (Dwyer, 2018; Cummins, 2018, 2019).

Certainly, service users were not involved in the decision-making process of this movement, but their participation was not tokenistic, either. In fact, they joined the movement spontaneously at a moment in which their awareness as citizens had awakened and resistance to cuts was spreading in the different areas of welfare.

Follow up of the Orange Tide

The Orange Tide movement was the follow-up to a number of initiatives developed by the General Council of Social Work in which service users became more and more present. One example is the documentary series 'Social rights for dignity' (Consejo de Trabajo Social, 2015, 2019). This series was composed of two programmes. The first showed how service users and social workers participated in an open session at the European Parliament and denounced the violation of their social rights, while in the second it was explained how the day to day life of a person in need affected by the crisis changed her perception of social services and her relationship with social workers, who were portrayed as emphatic, receptive and committed to defending their rights.

At this point, it seems fair to recognize the crucial work made by the General Council of Social Work in making visible the important role service users can play in demanding their rights and in being supportive in this task.

The user tells us: an example of how service users and students can reflect on needs, benefits and rights

'The user tells us' is a pilot experience developed by third year undergraduate students at the Faculty of Social Work at Castilla-La Mancha University in the framework of the 6-ECTS credit subject 'Social services programmes and benefits'. Students who attend this module have necessarily passed two previous subjects that provided them with background on the structure of welfare in Spain and the importance of linking economic, social and cultural rights with benefits.

The main objective of this module is for students to acquire a working knowledge of the whole range of benefits provided by the social services system and to learn how to analyse them from a human rights perspective. Students are advised to not take for granted that benefits are just prescriptions which cannot be questioned by them as traditionally has been the case. Quite the contrary: they should have the capacity to critically analyse the way benefits are delivered, their accessibility and appropriateness to meet the user's needs and the possibilities of claiming in case of non-compliance. But they would do it by listening to service users' own words and context.

By developing this practice, students become aware on how there is a kind of 'fitting to be' adaptation process between the user and the benefit that takes time and effort. In this sense, it is essential to listen to how social services service users feel in relation to their benefits. How (if so) does this make them reflect on their rights? This is not always easy; in many cases, both service users and practitioners receive and deliver benefits as if they were market products and do not question either their content or their adaptability to the situation in need.

At the beginning of the assignment, students are told to focus on one of the benefits provided by the social services system and find a social services user who is neither a part of his/her family nor is connected with the placement to which the student has been ascribed. It may occur that, due to the limited number of benefits, some students choose the same benefit. This is not a problem. Quite the contrary: it enriches the experience.

Once the choice has been made, students are told to analyse the content of the benefit. What does it aim to do? What does it cover? What does it not cover? Is it aligned with any of the economic, social and cultural rights as defined by the International Covenant, and if so, which ones? For this purpose, students should analyse not only the article or articles of the covenant directly but also the general comments issued by the Committee on Economic, Social and Cultural Rights in which the full extent of the rights is explained.

The second part of the practice consists of the preparation of an in-depth interview with the service user to identify their views on the benefit's sufficiency. For this purpose, a questionnaire is drafted including the following elements: the identification of the need, the benefit, the sufficiency of the provision, the way the benefit is provided (accessibility, clarity, etc.) and finally, the conformity or not of the user with the benefit and the changes they would make if they were a policymaker. The draft would be approved by the board of teachers of the third course after being supervised by the lecturer. Service users would be anonymized in case if they don't wish to be identified, and the interview would be recorded only if the person interviewed gives their permission.

Once the interview has been completed, the student reflects on it and proposes a new edition of the benefit that takes into account the service user's perspective and the current state of conformity/non-conformity with the social right (or social rights) of the current benefit. The proposal has to be grounded, coherent, well supported by arguments and contextualized within the legal framework. When the proposal is finished, the student meets other students who have focussed on the same benefit to discuss their respective findings, insights and suggestions and to agree on a common, alternative new edition of the benefit to be publicly exposed in the big group and discussed with the rest of students.

This alternative edition, together with the other alternative editions of the different benefits made by students, when publicly presented and discussed in the fora will give a good overview of the current state of social rights in the provision of benefits; will empower the user's perspective; and will provide a holistic and critical perspective to students and practitioners.

Common design and development of activities between practitioners and lecturers with the participation of service users and students (University of Alicante)

'Vengan a ver lo que no quieren ver' ('Come and see what you don't dare to see') (song by Luis Pastor, Spanish musician)

The Faculty of Social Work at the University of Alicante has been a pioneer in developing initiatives of joint collaboration between HEIs and practitioners in their lectures, and more specifically in the subject 'initiation to the development of social skills in social work', which is taught in the first course.

The learning experience consists of a study visit guided by a service user (helped by this circle of support) to the centre for people with disabilities they attend. During the visit, students will be informed by the service user (who is an expert by experience) about the functioning of the centre, the professionals, the different activities developed and the other service users that receive attention there. Once the visit is over, students are told to complete an assignment by analysing the results of the visit and reading material previously provided by academics and social workers at the centre.

In a second phase, the service user who guided the visit, together with their support group, will visit the class and share their personal experience, their strengths and difficulties, as well as their plans and projects for the future. After the presentation, there is a time for discussion between students and the social services user (Martínez-Román et al., 2014; Martínez-Román, 2010).

As Martínez-Román and others explain, the collaboration between experts by experience practitioners and lecturers is very meaningful; people who receive care and their carers have a broad experience that enables them to participate in the management of the social services centres and in the theoretical and practical training of social workers. By being invited by the university to collaborate in the training of future social workers, service users feel respected and valued, and this is helpful for their self-esteem and social inclusion (Martínez-Román, 2010)

Some words about research

There are not remarkable examples in which users' participation in research goes beyond what Arnstein (1969) defined as 'tokenism' in its different degrees (placation, consultation and information) or Hanley et al. (2004) defined as consultation. In most cases, research on social services and care services has been pushed by public administrations as part of quality procedures (Sánchez-Pérez, 2016) or as part of more comprehensive research (FOESSA, 2014; FOESSA, 2019). At an academic level, research in social work has been mainly developed in postgraduate and doctoral studies and is still early in development.

Conclusion and road map

In this chapter, the main obstacles and opportunities for better involvement of service users in lecturing, researching and policymaking in Spain have been presented. Cultural and religious misconceptions, bureaucracy, resistance to change and academic inertia, together with a criminalization of the poor throughout history and a lack of culture of participation, mean that the involvement of service users remains a particularly difficult aim. However, there are some interesting glimpses for future hope.

There is an increasing awareness by service users of their rights, particularly their right to participation; this is noteworthy in the social services sector. Passivity and resignation have given way to assertiveness. This feeling, although still not generalized, is spreading due to events like the Orange Tide. A higher level of involvement of service users in social work studies has also been highly recommended by the General Council of Social Work and by the Board of Directors and Managers of Faculties of Social Work (Vazquez-Aguado, 2007).

Social work, as both a profession and academic discipline, aims at transforming oppressive structures and promoting human dignity. As Cubillos et al. (2017) showed in their research, there is an increasing correlation between social and economic compromise and the formative training acquired in social work studies. Also, there is more sensitivity towards human rights among social work students. However, Mercado et al. (2016) consider that the profession has a formative deficit in human rights that affects the way human needs are met, and this can affect not only the roles assumed in the relationship between service users and professionals but also the quality of their participation.

To avoid this, human rights perspectives should be introduced in all subjects of social work studies in a cross-cutting way. This, however, is not enough; the perspective of service users must be tangible in the way social work education is conceived and delivered. This requires the presence of 'experts by experience' in the design of lecture contents, in placements, in evaluation processes, etc. (Martínez-Roman et al., 2014; Vazquez-Aguado et al., 2007).

To conclude, it is important not to forget that social work and training and research priorities are in the midst of a neoliberal wave that affects lecturers, practitioners, service users and students. Di Rosa and others note that 'the liberalization of public assets, governance, the rhetoric on monetization, the managerial implementation, the erosion of universal rights and the contractual arrangements of social policy as aspects that undermine welfare' (Di Rosa et al., 2019). As they highlight:

> These ongoing changes have led to an erosion of the competencies embodied in public wellbeing and a transferral of these duties to the sphere of liberalization and privatization.
>
> *(Di Rosa et al., 2019)*

This phenomenon has also happened in Spain. The transferral of duties from the public to the private sphere means that service users are no longer covered by the contents of the law (in terms of rights of the service users), nor are the duties and obligations of professionals (who are not bound by the declarations included in law). In teaching, the appearance of new professional profiles, such as frontline social workers whose main aim is to deliver benefits and put conditionality into practice an effective way, portray service users as mere benefit recipients who are continuously under suspicion that at the same time weakens their possibility of participating. Finally, research is becoming more and more conditioned by the requirements and objectives of private donors and funders who, for the most part, are more interested in achieving results than in promoting human rights.

References

Agencia Nacional para la acreditación de la calidad de la evaluación (ANECA) (2004) *Libro Blanco del Título de Grado en Trabajo Social*. Madrid. Retrieved from www.aneca.es.

Androff, D. (2016) *Practicing rights: Human rights-based approaches to social work practice*. London: Routledge.

Arnstein, S.R. (1969) A ladder of citizen participation. *Journal of the American Planning Association*, 35:4, 216–224.

Cabiati, E. and Raineri, M.L. (2016) Learning from service users' involvement: A research about changing stigmatizing attitudes in social work students. *Social Work Education*, 35:8, 982–996.

Casado, D. and Fantova, F. (2007) *Perfeccionamiento de los servicios sociales*. Madrid: Fundación FOESSA.

Centro de Investigaciones Sociológicas (CIS) (2014) *Encuesta sobre sentimientos Ciudadanos*. Retrieved from www.cis.es.

Centro de Investigaciones Sociológicas (CIS) (2017) *Barómetro 3190 sobre opiniones y actitudes hacia la inmigración*. Retrieved from www.cis.es.

Committee on Economic, Social and Cultural Rights (2018) *Concluding observations on the 7th periodic report submitted by the Spanish government to the Committee on Economic, Social and Cultural Rights Geneva*. Retrieved October 12, 2018, from www.ohchr.org/.

Comunidad Autónoma de Castilla-La Mancha (2010) *Ley 14/2010 de 16 de diciembre de servicios sociales de Castilla-La Mancha*. BOE n°38, de 14 de febrero de 2011.

Comunidad Autónoma de Andalucía (2017) *Ley 9/2016 de 27 de diciembre de Servicios sociales de Andalucía*. BOE n°18, de 21 de enero de 2017.

Comunidad Autónoma de Aragón (2009) *Ley 5/2009, de 30 de junio, de Servicios Sociales de Aragón*. BOE n°201, de 20 de agosto de 2009.

Comunidad Autónoma de Canarias (2019) *Ley 16/2019 de servicios sociales de Canarias*. BOE n°141, de 13 de junio de 2019.

Comunidad Autónoma de Castilla y León (2010) *Ley 16/2010 de 20 de diciembre de servicios sociales de castilla y León.* BOE n°7, de 8 de enero de 2011.

Comunidad Autónoma de Extremadura (2015) *Ley 14/2015, de 9 de abril, de Servicios Sociales de Extremadura.* BOE n°108, de 6 de mayo de 2015.

Comunidad Autónoma de Madrid (2013) *Ley 11/2003 de 27 de marzo de Servicios Sociales de la Comunidad de Madrid.* BOE n°157, de 2 de julio de 2003.

Consejo General de Trabajo Social (2015) *Derechos sociales por la dignidad. Parte 1* (Social rights for dignity. Part 1). Retrieved from www.youtube.com/watch?v=a9poEy8RuQE.

Consejo General de Trabajo Social (2019) *Derechos sociales por la dignidad. Parte 2* (Social rights for dignity. Part 2). Retrieved from www.youtube.com/watch?v=qz2lQ1GAyrM.

Cubillos-Vega, C., Ferran-Aranaz, M., Mercado-García, E. and Pastor-Seller, E. (2017) Nociones y compromiso con los derechos humanos de los estudiantes de trabajo social en España. *Revista Mexicana de investigación Educativa, 22:175,* 1047–1075.

Cummins, I. (2018) *Poverty, inequality and social work.* Bristol: Polity Press.

Cummins, I. (2019) Social work and austerity. In López-Peláez, A. and Gómez-Ciriano, E.J. (cords.), *Austerity: Social work and welfare policies. A global perspective,* vol. 7. Navarra: Thomson Reuters Aranzadi, 111–136.

De Robles, J. (1545) *De la orden que en algunos pueblos de España se ha pues-to en la limosna para remedio de los verdaderos pobres.* Retrieved September 13, 2018, from www.cervantesvirtual.com/obra/de-la-orden-que-en-algu-nos-pueblos-de-espana-se-ha-puesto-en-la-limosna-para-remedio-de-los-verdaderos-pobres/.

Del Pino, E. and Rubio, M.J. (eds.) (2016) *Los Estados de Bienestar en la encrucijada: políticas sociales en perspectiva comparada.* Madrid: Tecnos.

Di Rosa, R.T., Mordeglia, S. and Argento, G. (2019) Social work and welfare state in Italy, challenges, critical issues and resiliencies. In López-Peláez, A. and Gómez-Ciriano, E.J. (cords.), *Austerity: Social work and welfare policies. A global perspective.* Navarra: Thomson Reuters Aranzadi, 111–136.

Dwyer, P. (2018) *Dealing with welfare conditionality: Implementation and effects.* Bristol: Policy Press.

Ferrera, M. (1996) The southern model of welfare state in Europe. *Journal of European Social Policy, 6:1,* 17–37.

FOESSA Fundación (2014) *VI informe sobre la situación social de España.* Retrieved from www.foessa.es.

FOESSA Fundación. *VII informe sobre la situacion social de España.* Retrieved July 2019, from www.foessa.es.

Gómez-Ciriano, E.J. (2016) *Human rights on trial.* Madrid: Fundacion FOESSA. Retrieved from www.foessa.es.

Hanley, B. et al. (2004) *Involving the public in NHS, Public health and social care research: Briefing notes for researchers.* Eastleigh: Involve.

International Federation of Social Work (IFSW) (2014) *Global definition of social work.* Retrieved from www.ifsw.org/global-definition-of-social-work/.

International Federation of Social Work – Europe (IFSW – Europe) (2010) *Standards in social work practice meeting human rights.* Retrieved from www.ifsw.org/regions/europe/.

Marshall, T.H. (1950) *Citizenship and social class and other essays.* Cambridge. Cambridge University Press.

Martínez-Román, M.A. (2010) La incorporación de los usuarios en la educación teótrica y práctica de los trabajadores sociales: ¿Convergencia con Europa? *Miscelánea Comillas, 68:132,* 223–239.

Martínez-Román, M.A. (2012) Trabajadores sociales influyendo en las políticas sociales. *Revista de Servicios Sociales y Política Social, 100,* 97–102.

Martínez-Roman, M.A., Domenech-López, Y. and Tortosa-Martinez, J. (2014) Aprender conociendo a las personas usuarias. *Azarbe, 3,* 93–98.

Mc Laughlin, H. (2012) *Understanding social work research.* London: Sage.

Mercado, E., Valles, M. and De la Paz, P. (2016) La formación en derechos humanos en los planes de estudio del grado en Trabajo social en España. In Carbonero, D., Raya, E., Caparrós, N. and Gimeno, C. (eds.), *Respuestas transdisciplinar esen una sociedad global.* Aportaciones desde el Trabajo Social. Logroño: Universidad de la Rioja, 1–23.

Ramon, S., Moshe, M., Allegri, A. and Rafaelic, A. (2019) Service users' involvement in social work education: Focus on social change projects. *Social Work Education, 38:1,* 89–102.

Rodriguez-Cabrero, G. et al. (2011) *Servicios sociales y cohesión social.* Madrid: Consejo Económico y Social.

Sánchez Pérez, M. (2016) Satisfacción de usuarios y profesionales en la evaluación de programas sociales. *Revista de Educación de Programas y políticas Públicas, 7,* 116–140.

Sepúlveda-Carmona, M. (2013) *Report of the special rapporteur on extreme poverty and human rights on the right to participation of people living in poverty*. A/HRC/23/36. Geneva: United Nations.

Spicker, P. (1984) *Stigma and social welfare*. London: Croom Hall.

United Nations (1948) *Universal declaration of human rights*. Retrieved from www.un.org/en/universal-declaration-human-rights/.

United Nations (1966) *International covenant on economic: Social and cultural rights*. Retrieved from www.ohchr.org/en/professionalinterest/pages/cescr.aspx.

Vazquez-Aguado, O. (coord.) (2007) *Criterios para el diseño de planes de estudios de Títulos de Grado en Trabajo Social*. Aprobados por la Conferencia de Directores/as de Centros y Departamentos de Trabajo Social, Barcelona, 14 septiembre 2007 y la Junta de Gobierno del Consejo General de Colegios de DTS y AA.SS.

Vives, J.L. (1526, 1991) *De subventione pauperum* (Tratado del socorro de pobres). Madrid: Ministerio de Asuntos Sociales.

19

SOCIAL WORK IN THE UK

A case for radical co-production replacing worn out structures

Helen Casey, Dan Vale and Maryam Zonouzi

The movement towards formalised involvement in UK health and social care

A key feature with the establishment of the new degree for social workers in 2003 was the formal commitment made to the involvement of service users and carers in all aspects of the curriculum, course management and delivery. This commitment was bold and welcomed, as it placed an appropriate spotlight on the importance of people being central to educational processes in the same spirit that policy commitments are made in practice (e.g. Community Care Act, 1991; Care Act, 2014; Children Act, 1989/2004; Mental Health Act, 2007). Such spirit can be found in other health and care professions; however, social work in the UK may be viewed as distinctive due to the funding commitment from the government to support and sustain involvement.

The social work profession has gone through considerable changes in recent years, which has affected review of the commitment to service user and carer involvement. The new regulation provider, "Social Work England", seems to be indicating a will to strengthen and develop sustained involvement, which presents a timely opportunity to review structures.

There has been a wide range of pro-active and creative developments across the varied routes into social work across the UK to achieve involvement. Equally, there continue to be many challenges, including a challenge to establishing an evidence base within research on the benefits of participation. Our own research has highlighted the limitations of an involvement model in higher education programmes, which generally require one lecturer to take on the role of arranging for people with different backgrounds and lived experiences to come into the classroom to share these with students. Often members of what quickly becomes a core reference group who regularly contribute to a social work programmes get involved in social work student interviews and course team meetings. Together, it is our contention that traditional classroom-based HEI models for involvement are outdated. Structures must change to co-produce learning between all participants.

While there is a broad-based consensus and appetite for co-production, it remains elusive and ill-defined. Put simply, the concept is currently defined as "an approach in which researchers, practitioners and the public work together, sharing power and responsibility from the start to the end of the project, including the generation of knowledge" (INVOLVE, 2018, p. 5).

The concept was first used in the late 1970s by Elinor Ostrom and colleagues at Indiana University. Ostrom and others recognised that public services "rely as much upon the unacknowledged knowledge, assets and efforts of service 'users' as the expertise of professional providers" (Co-production in London, 2017, p. 13).

A 2007 article by Tony Bovaird encapsulates the public policy meaning of co-production:

> Policy making is no longer seen as a purely top-down process but rather as a negotiation among many interacting policy systems. Similarly, services are no longer simply delivered by professional and managerial staff in public agencies but are co-produced by users and their communities.
>
> *(p. 846)*

In other words, policy makers don't just issue edicts from above because the government is more fragmented and services are now run by many different organisations, some of which are people in the community.

This is further emphasised in the Health & Social Care Act 2012, which places greater emphasis on individual patient influence and choice:

> Patients should be at the heart of everything we do. In Liberating the NHS we set out the Government's ambition to achieve healthcare outcomes that are among the best in the world by involving patients fully in their own care, with decisions made in partnership with clinicians, rather than by clinicians alone: "no decision about me, without me".
>
> *(Department of Health, 2012, p. 3)*

The most recent attempt to integrate co-production in policy was the Care Act 2014. The integration of co-production presented an opportunity for transforming services; however, it is a missed opportunity emphasising "influence" rather than transformation:

> Local authorities should, where possible, actively promote participation in providing interventions that are co-produced with individuals, families, friends, carers and the community. "Co-production" is when an individual influences the support and services received, or when groups of people get together to influence the way that services are designed, commissioned and delivered.
>
> *(Care Act, 2014, p. 44)*

As SCIE (Social Care Institute for Excellence) points out, "this definition is not as helpful as other definitions of co-production as it refers to how people can 'influence' services rather than work in 'equal partnership'". SCIE's analysis highlights the positive efforts made to include co-production at various points in the statutory guidance to achieve the overarching aims of the Act. SCIE also emphasises the positive focus the Act places on how people who use services, carers and the community should be involved in co-production, suggesting a range of activities for achieving this (SCIE, 2009, p. 6).

These legislative definitions present us with a reason for why co-production is advocated within public policy circles, but much like the statement of intent from INVOLVE, they do not reveal the theoretical differences behind the concept of co-production, which means there is an absence of a methodological framework for its practice.

The opportunity for a radical new agenda

In social work and social care, if professionals are expected to deliver services based on co-production principles, it is our contention that this should be taught within education so that students develop their learning within equal partnerships with people who use services.

Inroads to challenge the current university systems have started with the introduction of the first service-user owned service partner and co-production specialist, Ginger Giraffe – providing embedded social work placements and "ground up" participatory research opportunities.

Also, the introduction of "Mend the Gap" programmes has taken learning outside of traditional classroom contexts.

We will return to these innovative approaches; however, first we must fundamentally address the question of what co-production is and how we achieve it.

The challenge of conceptual promiscuity and elision

The Social Care Institute for Excellence recognises that

> there is no single formula for co-production and concedes that there are many different definitions and sub-categories. Broadly speaking in health and social care co-production has been divided into four sub-types; – co-design (usually of services), co-decision making (usually about treatment and resources), co-delivery (of services) and co-evaluation (of service quality and outcome).
>
> *(SCIE, 2015)*

Huge claims are then made about the power of co-production.

Needham and Carr (2009) distinguish between three levels of co-production, advocating that at its most effective, co-production can involve the transformation of services. The transformative level of co-production requires a relocation of power and control, through the development of new, user-led mechanisms of planning, delivery, management and governance. It involves new structures of delivery to entrench co-production, rather than simply ad hoc opportunities for collaboration. It can be "a form of citizenship in practice" (Needham and Carr in Askheim et al., 2016, p. 6).

INVOLVE, National Institute for Health Research (NIHR), SCIE and other organisations concerning themselves with giving guidance to professional researchers and service providers in health and social care tend to avoid precise definitions and conceptualisations, preferring to talk of overarching "principles" and "values". These tend to involve prescriptive "equality" (of importance), a focus on "assets" (valuing people's strengths), "diversity" (an implicit recognition that some service users' perspectives have been ignored), "accessibility" (an explicit recognition that many service users are excluded from service design) and "reciprocity" (which usually concerns quid pro quos, reward and remuneration).

The co-option of "vision", "mission" and "value" statements from business literature has helped to further conceptually confuse and elide these developments, to the extent that "co-production" is now often utilised to describe any collaborative or participative projects which focus on health and social care service design and delivery.

Much has been made subsequently of various "co-productive" methods, such as Experience-Based Co-Design (EBCD). Needham and Carr have pointed out that co-production is now a catch-all term with serious political cachet. It has been used to describe all manner of participative approaches, often without a critical understanding of conceptual underpinnings (Needham and Carr, 2009).

In practice terms, co-production is very widely touted as the answer to challenging traditional and oppressive top-down models of service design and delivery. In working with service users, co-production is often conceptualised as a collaboration within the therapeutic alliance between service user and professional practitioner. Used in this way, the key innovations are viewed as the primacy of the nature of collaborative negotiation and communication between staff and individual service users working together. By positioning it as an "alternative" to traditional gatekeeping, charity, "gift" or "top-down" models of care delivery, where resource eligibility, case completion and output deliverables are central, co-production is seen to magically deliver a relational and more evolved future for service delivery.

The language is often about power-sharing, mutual respect and acknowledgement of expertise, asset and knowledge on both sides. This is very powerful language, in that it has clearly persuaded many professionals that they are pioneers of co-production. But is it co-production in any meaningful sense? If any service approach which is more sensitive to the opinions, wishes and knowledge of service users and more participative in approach and transparency is defined as co-production, is there any benefit at all in the term? Or should it be rejected as an expedient trend with no long-term transformative conceptual power?

In recognition that this "elasticity" provides a conceptual challenge, there have been a number of attempts to leverage in conceptual thinking from a number of other disciplines.

Osborne and others have developed an integrated typology of co-production which draws on service management and public administration theories (Strokosch, 2013; Osborne and Strokosch, 2013). The idea of Service Dominant Logic posits that users of public services are always viewed as co-producers, whether or not their co-production is voluntary, conscious or active. This has been further developed by Hardyman and colleagues, who focus on the individual (in their case, the patient in healthcare interactions) as the locus of theory and as the co-creator of value, within an overarching system of "value-based" healthcare.

Combining management, marketing and service theories around the idea of "value" positions co-production and its related methods, practices and principles firmly within a business interaction conceptualisation. It draws on elements of design theory, which emphasise the importance of user experience and co-design iterations. Further elision and elasticity are then possible with the quasi-scientific trend towards patient-reported outcome measures and metrics of patient experience.

Even though some of these approaches explicitly recognise that differentials in power and expertise recognition and status and the brittle and unyielding nature of organisational cultures can present significant barriers to meaningful transformation (Gibson et al., 2012), there is no sense in which the structural conditions and dynamics that underpin these systems are being recognised or addressed.

The neoliberal individualist paradigm of co-production

The locus of all these ideologies is an individual beneficiary, an independent customer, a consumer, a patient or service participant who is defined as a co-creator of value. In this worldview, it is the customer of the service who determines and assesses the nature of the value that is co-created (Vargo and Lusch, 2008; McColl-Kennedy et al., 2012).

> Value is always uniquely and phenomenologically determined by the beneficiary.
> *(Vargo and Lusch, 2008, pp. 1–10)*

The result of this conceptual elision and elasticity is that a number of theoretical approaches have been introduced to the smorgasbord, all of which conceptually sit within methodological individualism. Methodological individualism is based on an atomistic ontological worldview in which human needs, motivations and capacities are conceptualised as arising from within the individual. This view dominates health and social care, situating interventions for health, psychological trauma and disabilities as individual problems. This view is also supported by neoliberalism and neoliberal conceptions of public service management and design theory, all of which are characterised by the primacy of individualism:

> Individualism causes its citizens and policy makers to locate the source of social ills within the individual and to develop solutions aimed at addressing these individual problems.
>
> *(Terling-Watt, 2000, p. 19)*

The calls for greater co-production go hand in hand with the shift of patient to consumer coupled with the promotion of a patient choice agenda. This redefines the focus of service provision and reframes providers as vendors. In this shift from service user to consumer, co-production becomes the way in which consumers feedback their views.

This presupposes that patients have the necessary information to choose, and that their choices change service provision or that their purchasing decisions change the demands of what is provided. Marinker argues that

> in contemporary Britain, citizenship is confused with consumerism and democracy with marketing. Choice and individualism are elevated to the status of moral imperatives. The consumer is characterised not only by the right to choice but also by entitlement to redress.
>
> *(1996, p. 13)*

Consumerism is currently presented as a mechanism for redressing the power inequality between professionals and service users. Longley suggests, however, that "the preference for consumerism and individual choice is more about customer relations than any enhanced rights which entail true partnership or power sharing" (1996, p. 147). Power sharing requires a robust methodological basis which is not offered by adherence to methodological individualism.

The reasons and motivations for governments and services to "co-produce" are often that of improving existing services and systems. For many service users, it is the whole paradigm which needs to be reframed. As one service user recently highlighted in a consultation exercise about how people had felt about the ways in which previous attempts at co-production had gone in the past for them:

> I recently attended a mental health conference and there were psychiatrists who were congratulating themselves for being anti-psychiatry and how they have worked in co-production with mental health patients to redesign a psychiatric ward. When they stopped and opened the floor for questions my friend stood up and said "I'm happy that you have got round to working with patients on making the ward a nicer place. . . . But I'm not interested in moving deckchairs on the Titanic is there anyone here that can tell me exactly what is the point of psychiatry?"

If we care to listen, we will find that service users have altogether different questions than the questions that professionals and services are prepared to look at. We argue that this is because many professionals and services do not realise the epistemological challenge they face in disrupting their own logic. Those operating within methodological individualism see co-production as a mechanism for achieving change within the existing paradigm. Consequently, those involved in co-production initiatives are either those who work in the sector or those who most use its services.

Unfortunately, this has the unintended consequence of reinforcing methodological individualism rather than overturning it:

> I have found that most co-production initiatives are limited to me commenting and scrutinising and developing something within the status quo, albeit that we are working together from the beginning until the end of the project.
>
> *(Ginger Giraffe service user, 2019)*

It is not clear how practitioners and researchers operating from within methodological individualism can be said to be co-producing at all. Researchers who work within methodological individualism assert that facts must be observed and recorded from a distance. Thus, people are treated as objects in positivist research and, most importantly, are considered incapable of investigating their own social reality.

Positivism views people as being biased and incapable of investigating their own social reality, so how can it be said that positivist researchers should incorporate the views of service users when their ontological orientation points them in the opposite direction? As Kuhn noted, the framework of a paradigm is a prerequisite to perception itself (1970, p. 113). We argue that there is an internal inconsistency in methodological individualists attempting to apply any of the principles outlined by INVOLVE, SCIE or the NIHR because the challenge they face is not a matter of principles but of ontology and epistemology. An issue which these agencies fail to address or resolve.

Two scientists may look at the same thing, but because of their different theoretical perspectives, different assumptions or different ideology-based methodologies, they may literally not see the same thing (Patton, 2002, p. 22). A set of principles cannot change this. Researchers are guided ontologically and episodically and not by a set of principles developed by well-meaning outside institutions. INVOLVE would be required to critique "clinical reason", questioning the conceptual foundations of the NIHR and much of medical research, which it cannot do without jeopardising its own position. By not making the case for an examination of the conceptual foundations for co-production, we are left to conclude that the kind of co-production that INVOLVE ultimately advocates is of the consensual type.

It is perhaps then of no surprise that consensual co-production is not delivering the kind of change that service users are calling for. We argue that while it remains tethered to methodological individualism, it will not be transformative. Perhaps this is why the King's Fund have found that "co-production, where it has been happening successfully, has generally been outside nationally funded services that are supposed to achieve this, and usually despite – rather than because of – administrative systems inside public services" (Boyle et al., 2006).

The conceptual problems that lie at the root of consensual co-production present social work with a unique opportunity to reframe the concept away from methodological individualism, replanting it into new and fertile soil from which it can grow. We would like to suggest radical co-production as an alternative to the existing hegemony of consensual co-production.

The case for radical or "dissensual" co-production

Unlike consensual co-production, which is predicated on objectivity and "fixing" the status quo, radical co-production is counter-hegemonic and operates to challenge existing systems and develop new theory and practice. It is rooted in Critical Theory, disrupting the existing conceptual framework offered by methodological individualism to ultimately bring about change in the way in which we think about and practice co-production.

By implicit acceptance of "what is", consensual co-production does not disrupt but rather adds to the perpetuation of this status quo. Furthermore, owing to professional and service interests, there is a reluctance to critique these basic theoretical assumptions; thus, the idea of co-production has been easily transformed into a set of reified ideologies which have become frozen to a set of conceptual foundations. Critical Theory, in some ways, acts as an "anti-freeze" to this because it is dedicated to finding alternatives to existing hegemony (Ngwenyama, 2003, cited in Zonouzi, 2016).

According to Habermas (1971), Critical Theory is aligned with what he describes as emancipatory knowledge. In other words, it is related to our concern for countering existing hegemonic thinking. Critical Theory is thus well suited as a foundation for the methodological approach to radical co-production because it is grounded in the understanding that people create the world in which they inhabit and, as such, can change it if they wish. In other words, just because methodological individualism holds the conceptual space currently does not mean that we cannot rupture this logic. In addition to Critical Theory, we suggest that radical co-production should be rooted in Social Constructivism, acknowledging that individually created realities are shaped and preceded by social relationships.

A commitment to Critical Theory and Social Constructivism as the theoretical grounding for radical co-production means that those coming together to practice it understand from the outset that the endeavour is about questioning the status quo, developing new theory and practice for the mutual benefit of those in the relationship of co-production.

We suggest that radical equality (Zonouzi, 2016) is an implicit principle within radical co-production. Radical equality presupposes that professionals and service users are equal from the outset and that the knowledge they possess is of equal value to the endeavour. In other words, radical co-production does not presume that service users are knowledge-poor and become empowered through co-production, as is assumed by consensual co-production. Instead, in radical co-production, equality is not the destination; it is the starting point. In this regard, it is not an approach which is concerned with changing individuals' minority positions to majority positions in the Materialist sense. Instead, it is about recognising the knowledge democracy (Cook et al., 2019) between professionals and social workers as a fifty–fifty mission for reciprocal change.

Case study 1 – Ginger Giraffe

Ginger Giraffe is a radical cooperative owned and run by a collective of mainly but not exclusively disabled service users, carers, practitioners and researchers in London. It has conducted Participatory Action Research looking to reimagine the personalisation agenda and the way in which disabled people are treated by health and social care services. Ginger Giraffe is the first service user-led organisation in the UK to validate placement learning opportunities for social work students. They have produced a conceptual map for co-production (Figure 19.1).

Ginger Giraffe's approach to putting radical co-production into action

Putting radical co-production into action requires a set of conditions and prerequisite conditions. Ginger Giraffe adapted the work of Bergold et al. (2012), which suggested four fundamental principles and eight distinguishing features:

The fundamental principles describe transparently:

- Democracy as a precondition for participatory research
- The need for a "safe space"

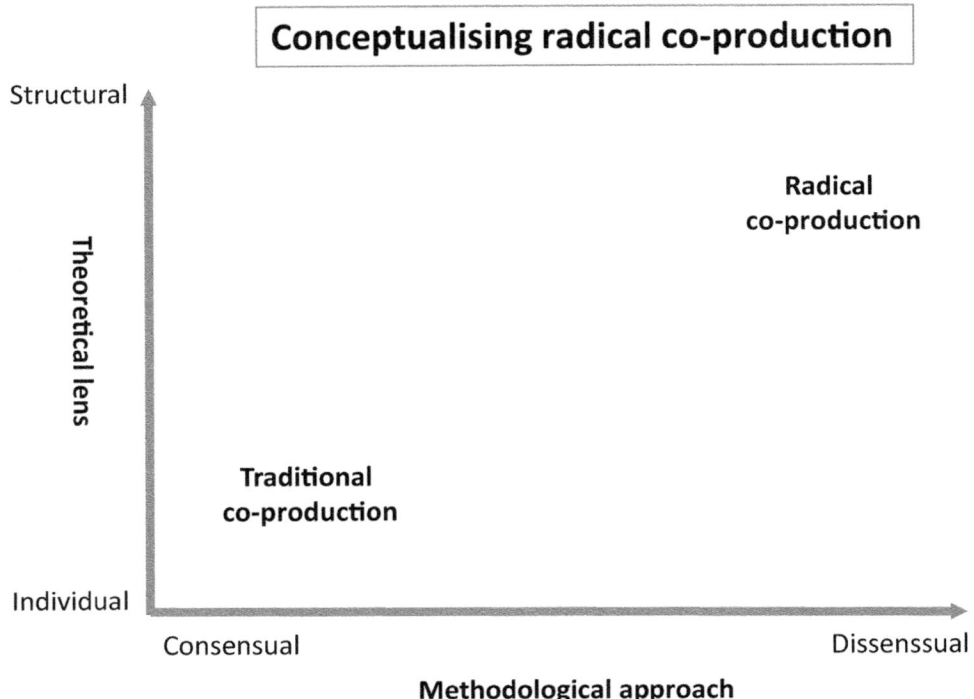

Conceptualising radical co-production

Figure 19.1 Co-production conceptual map

Source: Adapted from Ginger Giraffe 2019

- Defining the community inclusively
- Allowing for different degrees of participation

The distinguishing features are specific in how the following are dealt with:

- Material prerequisites
- Challenges and tasks facing all the research partners
- The importance of reflection
- Distinctive features of the production and analysis of the "data"
- Distinctive features of the representation of findings
- Academic requirements and funding conditions for participatory research
- Justification of participatory research projects
- Ethical aspects of participatory research

In addition, Ginger Giraffe, working iteratively on embedded placement PAR tasks, such as the reimagining of supervision as "intervision", developed a number of other key elements which need to be present in order for the radical turn to take place:

1   There needs to be an examination of theory between those involved
2   There needs to be theoretical turn breaking away from existing concepts, thus shifting the theoretical assumptions

3   There needs to be a move away from service redesign to designing services between people
4   Hearts and minds of all involved need to have fundamentally shifted so that new practices emerge
5   Each site is unique and thus the process can be replicated but not the outcome, as this will result in top down . . .

Many projects touted as co-production are merely exercises in involvement work between professionals and service users; there are few examples where one model of practice is moved to a transformed way of understanding and delivering in practice. The prerequisites identified above provide the basis for social workers and services to begin the process of radical co-production.

A critique of the current social work education environment

Lack of explicit focus in the regulation of education and training

The regulatory frameworks and standards produced by the regulating and validating bodies for social care in the UK mention and assess service user involvement and not co-production, so they are not actually useful in defining or helping HEIs to move beyond a consultation model and framework. What is more, the criteria for demonstrating involvement is essentially that of showing that service users were present and engaged with, regardless of the method, strategy or power differentials.

Lack of practical skills-based training on social work courses

The Social Work Professional Capabilities Framework does not have co-production as a central plank of professional practice. Courses often fail to cover the ethical and conceptual tensions explored in this chapter and certainly do not explore and hone students' skills in exercising the concepts in practice, whether that be in facilitating or challenging power structures. Much of the service user involvement aspects of the training are essentially left to the community organisations which host the community placement, many of which would certainly sit at the more consensual and traditional end of our axis (Figure 19.1).

Another key barrier for a more meaningful co-production is the fact that it requires not only new ways of relating to experts by experience but also learning new ways of working together. Developing such skills, abilities, methods and practices requires time, and social work academics, much like most social work practitioners, have very little of that resource. The public sector in general and higher education as part of it, in the UK and in many other Western countries, has become in recent decades more and more bureaucratised. This growing bureaucratisation involves complex and multiple procedures for measuring outputs, quality assurance, risk mitigation, auditing and much more. These mechanisms and procedures are multiplied on professional courses and even tripled in the case of social work as a highly scrutinised and criticised professional group. Currently, social work programmes must ensure their curriculum is aligned with the Professional Capabilities Framework (PCF) and Social Work England's Professional Standards as well as the Knowledge and Skills Statements (KSS) for children and families as well as that for adults.

One aim of these underpinning frameworks is to encourage and stimulate innovative ways of working; however, the result of this context could mean that social work programmes are constantly and endlessly busy with responding to a variety of internal (from inside their institution) or external bureaucratic demands that make new ways of working, learning and relating and any real change much more difficult.

Ethical misalignment in the culture of educational institutions

Contemporary universities and social work courses are themselves hierarchical and, in some ways, antithetical to the true spirit and ethics of co-production. In the UK and other Western countries, universities, and the education system more broadly, are well acknowledged, highly competitive and hierarchical paths to social mobility. The qualifications obtained in this long journey provide access to a range of professional and social opportunities and a variety of resources. Cynical critics of higher education will argue that it is just a "degree factory", but even without taking such a harsh view, it is clear that the degrees earned by students play a key role in their motivation, including if they are idealistic social work students who would like to "help people" or even "change the world". Such degrees help all students to distinguish themselves from others who don't have the same degrees, and ensure their greater access to jobs and opportunities. In *Distinction* (Bourdieu, 1984), Bourdieu described the French school system and attempted to explain how could it be that such a supposedly meritocratic system only reproduced class divisions. His book shows how students' habitus or "taste", which includes a range of aesthetic and cultural preferences in food, clothing, music and more, is shaped by their class belonging and positioning, and functions as a distinction that maintains the separation between class groups and reproduces the existing class structure. The education system, whether we acknowledge it or not, is an arena in which groups compete over power, access and opportunities. This is where the egalitarian idea of co-production is almost antithetical to the spirit of higher education and its hierarchical and competitive character, especially in contemporary neoliberal societies. It requires students – in the midst of their competitive journey, also aimed at distinguishing them from others with lesser qualifications – to disregard all hierarchies. They are asked to see experts by experience, who often have no formal degrees and qualifications, as their equals, at least for a short while. Without acknowledging these contradictions and the real meaning of co-production, it is not surprising it often happens only at surface level.

Social work academic members of staff are also exposed to both internal and external pressures. They are entangled in the hierarchical and competitive promotion trajectory offered by universities and supported by the neoliberal imperatives contemporary universities hold. Being promoted in contemporary higher education is closely tied with "income generation" through research grants, or with "cost cutting" and increasing efficiency. All these are rarely incentives to get involved in co-production, in either research or teaching, as in both cases it often requires gaining new skills and techniques and can be very time consuming, especially until one gains the appropriate skills and methods. Similar neoliberal imperatives around cost cutting and increasing efficiency also rule the lives of social work practitioners. Most social work organisations are just as hierarchical and competitive where higher salaries and better opportunities are often linked with higher degrees.

What potentially might make things more difficult for social work students is the fact that many of them come from relatively lower socio-economic backgrounds, often motivated by their own very difficult experiences. Overcoming such challenges required a lot of hard work and effort, and the way higher education acknowledges their achievements is by celebrating their qualifications, which serve to distinguish them.

Case study 2 – Mend the Gap

One approach that has developed in recent years has challenged the conventional ways in which service users/carers, students and professionals come together and learn together. Mend the Gap is an alternative educational model which promotes the benefits of substantive mutual learning outside of the classroom context.

"The gap-mending concept can be characterized as a reflective tool that helps teachers and researchers to consider what, in their practice increases, maintains or mends gaps between policies, services and professionals – as well as service users. Gaps always exist in a context.

Gaps can develop and be maintained because of prejudices based on social work's categorisation of people, because of language barriers, because of institutional hierarchies and the roles we have created for people within them. They can also exist because of lack of knowledge. Contextual knowledge is therefore essential in gap-mending reflections, as well as a good understanding of existing gaps" (Askheim et al., 2016, p. 5).

The gap-mending approach in social work education originates from Lund University, Sweden (since 2005), and was developed by PowerUs, the Social Work Learning Partnership (2012) (www.powerus.se), to promote new ways of learning that can come from sharing experiences, knowledge and skills within professional education. By creating a learning environment where people share their experiences and knowledge, traditional barriers that exist between people on the receiving end of professional support and those providing it can be removed.

There is a growing evidence base to demonstrate how the gap-mending approach provides an alternative model for social work education which meets the needs of communities, not just professionals (Chiapparini, 2016; Community Care, 2018; Beresford and Carr, 2018).

Elsewhere in this book there are chapters presenting examples and, most importantly, outcomes of gap-mending programmes. The gap-mending approach could further develop the aims of radical production through identifying and co-producing practical strategies for mending gaps that exist between people, policy and practice.

Implications for social work education and practice

The success of Ginger Giraffe to co-create placement and research opportunities provides a firm foundation for radical co-production to grow.

The successful establishment of Mend the Gap approaches in the north of England testify to how practitioners, managers and academics are seeking to find more effective ways of learning with and from those who are traditionally unheard and marginalised in educational processes.

Both of these approaches are rooted in collaborative methodology which promotes equal partnerships and mutual learning in order to transform support and services. They present new structures in the community to replace outdated structures dominated by academics.

Conclusion

We believe that having a clear consensus on the ideology embracing theory and principles of co-production would inform a methodological framework for co-produced learning within equal partnerships. Without this, weak attempts will continue to be made, diluting the potential benefits and confusing the aims of collaborative working. The roots of this confusion lay in the conflicting methodology of individualism which currently underpins co-production in health and social care contexts. We hope that an alternative radical model of co-production will provide new structures for learning, practice and effecting change which is very much needed in social work education and human services.

References

Askheim, O., Beresford, P. and Heule, C. (2016) Mend the gap – Strategies for user involvement in social work education. *Social Work Education*. doi:10.1080/02615479.2016.1248930.

Beresford, P. and Carr, S. (2018) *Social policy first hand: An international introduction to participatory social welfare*. Bristol: Policy Press.

Bergold, J. and Thomas, S. (2012) Participatory research methods: A methodological approach in motion [110 paragraphs]. *Forum: Qualitative Social Research*, 13(1): Article 30. http://nbn-resolving.de/urn: nbn:de:0114-fqs1201302.

Bourdieu, P. (1984) *Distinction: A social critique of the judgement of taste*. London, Routledge & Kegan Paul.

Bovaird, T. (2007) Beyond engagement and participation – User and community co-production of public services. *Public Administration Review*, 67(5): 846–860.

Boyle, D., Clarke, S. and Burns, S. (2006) *Hidden work: Co-production by people outside paid employment*. York, UK, Joseph Rowntree Foundation.

Care Act (2014) www.legislation.gov.uk/ukpga/2014/23/contents/enacted, accessed 11/12/2019.

Chiapparini, E. (2016) *The service user as a partner in social work projects and education: Concepts and evaluations of courses with a gap-mending approach in Europe*. Opladen, Berlin, Toronto: Barbara Budrich Publishers.

Community Care (2018) www.communitycare.co.uk/2018/04/13/learning-people-new-training-method-brings-together-service-users-social-workers/, accessed 11/12/2019.

Cook, T., Brandon, T., Zonouzi, M. and Thomson, L. (2019) Destabilising equilibriums: harnessing the power of disruption in participatory action research. *Educational Action Research*, 27(3): 379–395.

Co-production in London (2017) A Report by the co-production working group for The Way Ahead available at: https://thewayahead.london/sites/default/files/uploads/Co%20production%20Working %20Group%20-%20Final%20version%20April%202017.pdf

Department of Health (2012) *Liberating the NHS no decision about me without me*. 23 May, London, UK.

Gibson, A., Britten, N. and Lynch, J. (2012) Theoretical directions for an emancipatory concept of patient and public involvement. *Health (London)*, 16(5): 531–547.

Habermas, J. (1971) *Knowledge and human interests*. Boston, MA: Beacon.

Hajer, M.A. (1989) *City politics: hegemonic projects and discourse*. London: Avebury.

Involve and National Institute for Health Research (2018) Guidance for co-producing a research project.

Kuhn, T.S. (1970) *The structure of scientific revolutions*. University of Chicago Press.

Marinker, M. (ed) (1996) *Sense and sensibility in healthcare*. London, BMJ Publishing Group.

McColl-Kennedy, J.R., Vargo, S.L., Dagger, T.S., Sweeney, J.C. and van Kasteren, Y. (2012) Health care customer value cocreation practice styles. *Journal of Service Research*, 15(4): 70–389.

Needham, C. and Carr, S. (2009) *SCIE research briefing 31: Co-production. An emerging evidence base for adult social care transformation*. London, Social Care Institute for Excellence.

Osborne, S.P. and Strokosch, K. (2013) It takes Two to Tango? Understanding the Co-production of Public Services by Integrating the Services Management and Public Administration Perspectives. *British Journal of Management*, 24: S31–S47.

Patton, M.Q. (2002) *Qualitative research and evaluation methods*. Thousand Oaks, CA: Sage Publications.

SCIE (2015) www.scie.org.uk/publications/guides/guide51/what-is-coproduction/defining-coproduction.asp.

Strokosch, K. (2013) Co-production and innovation in public services: can co-production drive innovation? In *Handbook of innovation in public services*. Edward Elgar Publishing.

Terling-Watt, T., (2000) A communitarian critique of the child protective system. *Journal of Sociology & Social Welfare*, 27: 3–23.

Vargo, S.L. and Lusch, R.F. (2008) Service-dominant logic: continuing the evolution. *Journal of the Academy of marketing science*, 36(1): 1–10.

Zonouzi, M. (2016) Using a Participatory Action Approach to investigate the effects of a new social policy (Self-Directed Support): Reframing empowerment, independence and emancipation. PhD Thesis, Northumbria University

20

FACULTY PERCEPTIONS OF SERVICE USER INVOLVEMENT IN HUMAN SERVICES EDUCATION

Nafees Alam

Social work education in the United States

Social work curricula across the United States lacks service user involvement in the education of social workers, despite the trademark of the profession being service user-oriented. Social work education in the United States requires a four-year undergraduate degree, or a two-year graduate degree, in social work. Both undergraduate and graduate social work degrees require students to complete internship hours (a minimum of 450 hours at the undergraduate level and a minimum of 900 hours at the graduate level) working with individuals, families, groups, communities and/or organizations, with the goal of enabling and encouraging the application of social work-related knowledge, skills and values covered during classroom instruction (theory) within real-life settings (practice). For many students, the internship serves as the first encounter with service users of social service organizations, meaning they may have little to no understanding of service user experiences, or the skills needed to work collaboratively with service users, prior to this point in their academic careers.

Social workers are tasked with assessing service users of social service organizations for eligibility and need for services, thereafter working collaboratively with service users to meet these assessed need(s). Social workers in the United States are expected to adhere to the National Association of Social Workers (NASW) Code of Ethics, which emphasizes respect for service users, service user self-determination and preservation of the dignity and worth of every person (NASW, 2008). International professionals in the field of academia, as well as social workers and service users, have argued in favor of service users being included in the education of social work students to prepare and equip them with the knowledge, skills and values necessary to provide social work services to service users while on their internship and after graduation (Brown and Young, 2008; Levin, 2004). The consumer movement in particular has helped bring light to the importance of service user involvement, specifically within social work education.

The consumer movement

The consumer movement is an effort by service users of social services to gain control over their treatment and to eliminate associated stigma (Frese and Davis, 1997; Kaufman, 1999).

The consumer role is a social role based on experiential knowledge of the system with which they are affiliated (Kaufman, 1999). The consumer movement in the United States has recently begun shaping policy and practice (Bluebird, 2000) but not social work education. This movement emphasizes the recovery process, conceptualized as having three phases: a) reclaiming a positive sense of self in relation to the presenting issue(s), b) active pursuit of health and c) "moving on" and claiming meaningful roles outside of being a consumer of social services (Ridgeway, 1999). It would seem that service user involvement should be a logical component of social work education since activism and focus on recovery are in harmony with social work values, including partnership and self-determination (NASW, 2008).

Service user involvement in social work education around the world

Between 2003 and 2004, the involvement of service users receiving health and social work services became mandatory in social work education in the United Kingdom (UK). Service user involvement was viewed as important and necessary in order for the "new generation of social workers to gain a thorough grounding in clients' experiences and expectations from the very start of their training and careers" (Levin, 2004, P2). Universities and social service organizations varied in the extent to which service users were included, and some academics began to publish case studies and evaluations of service user involvement (Robinson and Webber, 2013).

Branfield (2009) explored service user perceptions of their own involvement in UK-based social work education, including barriers to, and components of, good practice. Service users reported that in order to employ and promote quality social workers, service users should take part in their education, which should include involvement in the selection of students into the program (admission), training and writing coursework (curriculum) and evaluating student progress (assessment). Service users reported potential barriers to their involvement, such as access to the university, inadequate training and negative attitudes from faculty and students toward their involvement. Alternatively, good practice was identified as accessibility to the university, identifying and providing training to service users and faculty and students being open and receptive to service user knowledge and experience (Branfield, 2009). Branfield (2009) and the service users concluded that best practice approaches to service user involvement remain relatively unknown.

Universities across Europe and the rest of the world have begun considering service user involvement in social work education. Robinson and Webber (2013) conducted a comprehensive review of literature on the models and effectiveness of service user involvement in social work education. The research reviewed was primarily conducted in the UK (where, as aforementioned, service user involvement is mandatory) and included only four studies – two from Croatia, one from Israel and one from the US. The US-based study was an evaluation of a small-scale project consisting of a one-day (six-hour) activity bringing social service users into a facilitated dialogue with social work students with the aim of changing student attitudes towards persons with mental illness (Scheyett and Kim, 2004). There is limited knowledge on the extent to which service users are included in social work education in the US and the potential benefits and drawbacks to involvement for students, service users and the overall social work profession.

Rationale for service user involvement in social work education

Self-determination, empowerment and partnership with service users are all central values to social work practice in the United States (NASW, 2008). Students, both undergraduate and graduate, are taught to establish collaborative relationships with service users during their coursework and internships. The very paradigm of social work is to act "with" and not "for" service users. Although service user input is incorporated in social work education in indirect ways (e.g. literature with first-person service user accounts and service user feedback on intervention literature), social work educators need to evaluate whether or not the aforementioned social work values are genuinely incorporated into the curriculum, or if the involvement is more tokenistic and superficial (Scheyett and Diehl, 2004). Schools of social work in the United States have emphasized incorporating content related to racial and ethnic minority groups taught by faculty members belonging to those groups (Bush et al., 1983; Ross-Sherriff, 1979) with service users occasionally being included as guest speakers or co-trainers in the classroom (Manthorpe, 2000). However, it cannot be assumed that the appropriate faculty will have the ability and availability to teach such coursework.

The New York State Office of Mental Health (NYSOMH) includes service users in the training of psychiatric hospital staff and found that service users reported feeling valued and empowered for having their opinions sought out, and service providers (including social workers) felt higher respect for service user rights, greater acceptance of service user self-advocacy and greater sense of importance of viewing each service user as an individual (Bassman, 2000). Scheyett and Diehl (2004) found that service users have a desire to participate in social work education through co-teaching, course content development and implementation, being included in curriculum committee and syllabus review processes as well as research and field practicum. Hence, the motivation is there for students and service users to welcome service user involvement in social work education.

Social work is defined as

> a practice-based profession and an academic discipline that promotes social change and development, social cohesion, and the empowerment and liberation of people. Principles of social justice, human rights, collective responsibility and respect for diversities are central to social work. . . . social work engages people and structures to address life challenges and enhance wellbeing.
>
> *(International Federation of Social Workers, 2014)*

As the definition highlights, social work aims to engage people to enhance wellbeing and values collective responsibility in achieving this aim. The empowerment of individuals, groups and communities in need requires their active involvement in the social work process of assessment, intervention and evaluation of services, yet service users' views and perspectives are often ignored during this process (Beresford, 2013; Munro et al., 2006).

Service users of social work services have formed advocacy groups to fight for involvement in the shaping of social services and have used the slogan "nothing about us without us" in their mission. Service users in the UK argue for involvement in all areas of social work services from the education of future social workers to the evaluation of services and consultation on policies (Beresford, 2013; Fox, 2011; Munro et al., 2006; Spiers et al., 2005).

Faculty perceptions of service user involvement in human services education

A 2018 study of 404 social work faculty across the United States shows that faculty favor a) service user empowerment and consumerism and b) service user involvement in social work organizations more than c) service user involvement in social work education. The study was an exploratory cross-sectional design employing non-probability, purposive sampling techniques, using a non-pre-existing quantitative questionnaire developed through a review of literature and theory. Data was collected through the electronic platform SurveyMonkey from March 1, 2018, to April 30, 2018. Findings suggest that social work faculty were split over service user involvement in social work education (mean composite score of 57.360%), while they were more in favor of service user involvement in social work organizations (mean composite score of 69.405%), and even more in favor of service user empowerment and consumerism (mean composite score of 76.322%). This was found to be both valid and reliable after several levels and methods of statistical analyses.

The majority of demographic bivariate analyses from this study show results that are not statistically significant. *Age, gender, race/ethnicity, geographic location, primary role in academia, years in academia, status of current social work practice, level of formal education* and *familiarity with the NASW Code of Ethics* were all originally hypothesized to show statistically significant correlations with attitudes on service user involvement in social work education. Such was not found to be the case, suggesting that *age, gender, race/ethnicity, geographic location, primary role in academia, years in academia, status of current social work practice, level of formal education* and *familiarity with the NASW Code of Ethics* have little to no bearing on attitudes on service user involvement in social work education.

Statistically significant demographic bivariate findings were two-fold: faculty experienced in teaching the client consumer movement were *more* likely to favor service user involvement in social work education ($p=0.001$). However, faculty experienced in teaching human behavior and the social environment were *less* likely to favor service user involvement in social work education ($p=0.005$).

Essentially, the only demographic characteristic of statistical significance predicting more positive attitudes toward service user involvement in social work education by faculty is experience teaching content pertaining to client consumer movement. The opposite holds true for faculty experience teaching human behavior and the social environment, as these faculty are predicted to have less positive attitudes toward service user involvement in social work education.

Composite bivariate analyses showing results that are statistically significant are both *attitudes on service user empowerment and consumerism* and *attitudes on service user involvement in social work organizations*, found to show statistically significant correlation with attitudes on service user involvement in social work education. Findings show that those who favor service user empowerment and consumerism are likely to favor some service user involvement in social work education ($p=0.030$). Findings also show that those who favor service user empowerment and consumerism are likely to favor more service user involvement in social work education ($p=0.000$).

Factor analysis was employed to conduct multivariate analyses between a) *attitudes on service user empowerment and consumers*, b) *attitudes on service user involvement in social work organization* and c) *attitudes on service user involvement in social work education*. The analysis shows three concepts, components or factors coming to the surface as underlying factors: Component 1 (C1) appears to pertain to *student development*, Component 2 (C2) appears to pertain to *professional development* and Component 3 (C3) appears to pertain to *service user compensation*. Linear regression creates a model that shows *student development* (C1) to be the most important of these factors.

Implications and contributions to social work

Implications gleaned from this study pertaining to social work practice suggest that practitioners should be aware of how they have been taught to view service users and the underlying policies that may make service users believe they are more involved in their own service plan than they really are. Implications gleaned from this study pertaining to social work education suggest that students and faculty should be more self-aware of how they view service user involvement. The CSWE (Council on Social Work Education) in the US may find it fruitful to reinforce the core social work values in encouraging (and when appropriate, requiring) service user involvement in social work education, just as the accrediting body does in the UK. Requiring social work faculty to teach at least some content pertaining to client consumer movement inside of all courses could get more social work faculty involved and on board with this type of initiative. This content is especially in need within human behavior and the social environment courses in order to counteract the aforementioned negative influence.

Considerations

There is a great deal of information to be gleaned from those with experiential knowledge on subject matter, beyond the limits of academic knowledge. The involvement of service users in social work academia could help bridge the gap between academic knowledge and experiential knowledge. More importantly, *meaningful* involvement of service users, defined as citizen power as opposed to tokenism or non-participation (Arnstein, 1969), is key in maintaining an environment where there is buy-in from all parties to advance social work theory and eventual practice.

However, cautiousness must be employed in aiming for meaningful involvement of service users, as there is a risk of re-traumatization through continual recollection. Service users should not be taken advantage of and coercion must be kept in check to ensure that service user involvement remains voluntary at all times. Not all service users may have an interest in advancing social work academia and that should be acknowledged by all.

References

Arnstein, S.R. (1969) A ladder of citizen participation. *Journal of the American Institute of Planners, 35*(4), 216–224.

Bassman, R. (2000) Consumers/survivors/ex- patients as change facilitators. In F. Frese (Ed.), *The role of organized psychology in treatment of the seriously mentally ill: New directions for mental health services* (pp. 93–102). San Francisco: Jossey-Bass.

Beresford, P. (2013) From "other" to involved: User involvement in research. An emerging paradigm. *Nordic Social Work Research, 3*(2), 139–148.

Beresford, P. (2013) From "other" to involved: User involvement in research. An emerging paradigm. *Nordic Social Work Research, 3*(2), 139–148.

Bluebird, G. (2000) A consumer's view of consumer providers. *National Association of Case Management Reports,* 2, 7–10.

Brown, K., & Young, N. (2008) Building capacity for service user and carer involvement in social work education. *Social Work Education: The International Journal, 27*(1), 84–96.

Bush, J., Norton, D., Sanders, C. & Solomon, B. (1983) An integrative approach for inclusion of content on blacks in social work education. In J. Chunn II, P. Dunston, & F. Ross-Sheriff (Eds.), *Mental health and people of color: Curriculum development and change.* Washington, DC: Howard University Press.

Fox, J. (2011) "The view from inside": Understanding service user involvement in health and social care education. *Disability & Society, 26*(2), 169–177.

Frese, F. J., & Davis, W.W. (1997) The consumer–survivor movement, recovery, and consumer professionals. *Professional Psychology: Research and Practice, 28*(3), 243.

International federation of social workers. (2014) *Global definition of social work.* Retrieved from https://www.ifsw.org/what-is-social-work/global-definition-of-social-work/ accessed 10.01.2020

Kaufman, C. (1999) An introduction to the mental health consumer movement. In A. Horwitz & T. Scheid (Eds.), *A handbook for the study of mental health: Social contexts, theories, and systems.* Cambridge: Cambridge University Press.

Levin, E. (2004) *Involving service users and carers in social work education.* SCIE Guide 4. London: Social Care Institute for Excellence.

Manthorpe, J. (2000) Developing carers' contributions to social work training. *Social Work Education,* *19*(1), 19–27.

Munro, K., Ross, M.K., & Reid, M. (2006) User involvement in mental health: Time to face up to the challenges of meaningful involvement? *International Journal of Mental Health Promotion, 8*(2), 37–44.

National Association of Social Workers (2008) *Code of ethics of the National Association of Social Workers.* Retrieved November 14, 2014, from www.naswdc.org/pubs/code/code.asp.

Ridgeway, P. (1999) *Deepening the mental health recovery paradigm, defining implications for practice: A report of the recovery paradigm project.* Lawrence, KA: University of Kansas School of Social Welfare.

Robinson, K., & Webber, M. (2013) Models and effectiveness of service user and carer involvement in social work education: A literature review. *British Journal of Social Work, 43,* 925–944.

Ross-Sheriff, F. (1979) *Implementation of minority content in social work education.* Paper presented at the Program Meeting, Council on Social Work Education, Boston, MA.

Scheyett, A., & Diehl, M.J. (2004) Walking our talk in social work education: Partnering with consumers of mental health services. *Social Work Education, 23*(4), 435–450.

Scheyett, A., & Kim, M. (2004) "Can we talk?": Using facilitated dialogue to positively change student attitudes towards persons with mental illness. *Journal of Teaching in Social Work, 24*(1–2), 39–54.

Spiers, S., Harney, K., & Chilvers, C. (2005) Service user involvement in forensic mental health: Can it work? *The Journal of Forensic Psychiatry & Psychology, 16*(2), 211–220.

21

TALKING HEADS

Nigeria to the UK

Larry Amadi-Emina

I trained as a social worker in Nigeria in 1994. It was a diploma route then, but I completed my degree in social work later in 2001. At that time, social work education was seen as a very lowly profession. Most people going to university wanted to study law or engineering. Social work was a fall-back option if people weren't successful. This reflected the way that social workers were seen in the community. They were seen as helpers without any authority. The police had the authority and so did the parents. That is a big difference to my experience now in a community in Teesside. In this country, BME families fear social workers more than the police. In my home country, the police were most feared. Lots has changed in Nigeria in the past ten years. Now most universities have social work courses, and human rights organisations have had a big impact. It is no longer acceptable for parents to abuse their children as they once did, when they were seen to have more rights over their children and the police were not very effective. Social workers can intervene and remove children to places of safety. Parents can be prosecuted, which used to be unheard of. Now social workers have more status.

My inspiration to become a social worker came from my family. In Nigeria, extended family provided support to people, not the Government. I saw how my grandmother supported vulnerable women and their children. She was always working to help people. My cousin studied social work in the UK, then studied an MA in India. He came home so enthusiastic about social work, saying it was the future way to help people. He saw how effective the Government was in the UK and felt that social work was the way to raise awareness and promote a campaign for more Government support in Nigeria. This is what happened in the early 1990s. The Government in Nigeria swept welfare under the carpet, whereas in the UK people's welfare was seen as a priority. I studied social work at this time of change.

Social work training and education in Nigeria includes service user involvement in different ways to here in the UK. People with experiences of services do not come into the classroom to talk with students about their lives. That would be something people would not want to do; they would feel too ashamed. It could stigmatise them, especially if they had a family connection with one of the students. Generally speaking, Nigerian people are very private; they do not want to share their problems in public. For example, people would never talk openly about having mental health problems like they do in the UK. The belief systems are so different. In Nigeria, if people have mental health difficulties, often they believe this is because they are possessed by evil spirits. In the UK, there is more understanding of different causes of mental health difficulties such as depression and anxiety. Generally speaking, people can talk about their experiences of having problems in the UK, whereas in Nigeria most subjects are taboo. People would worry about bringing shame upon themselves and their families if they admitted to their difficulties. The way people were involved in education in Nigeria was through giving feedback about social work students on placements. As a student, you have to sell yourself to the service user.

In Nigeria, the roles for social workers were mostly in hospitals, prisons, psychiatry services and school. Social workers were the main link between those institutions and the community. There is no National Health Service like in the UK. There is a National Health Insurance Scheme, to which some people are lucky enough to have contributions paid by their employers. For people not in employment, there is a lack of funding; support is usually from charities. My role involved helping people to be discharged from hospital by linking them up with charities for support in the community. My work with prisons involved lots of negotiating. It was very common for mass arrests to be made, which meant that lots of young people were locked up; legally this was meant to be for twenty-four hours, but this was always breached and they would be detained for days with no bail for release. They would then be moved to prison to await trail. This could be for two, three, four years. If they were found guilty, it was usually for a sentence of six months, when they had already spent a few years in prison. Social workers negotiated a lot for parole. They also were the main link with the family. Families rejected members who had committed a crime. It is probably the most shameful thing someone could bring upon their family. As a social worker, I would keep in contact with the family, let them know their son was being rehabilitated, speaking very positively about how he will be reformed on release. This was to help them to allow the person to return home and not reject them. I would take the person home, then help the person into education. It was a big part of my role.

Since coming to the UK in 2015, I have done lots of voluntary work supporting BME families in the community. I was very frustrated that, due to the limitations of my status, I could not work as a social worker. It is better for me to stay busy and involved with people, so I have always kept myself very busy. Since 2013, I have been a volunteer advisor supporting people with a range of legal and health claims.

I have always been shocked at how much people I have tried to help do not speak about. Full information is required, yet people feel so ashamed to talk about their problems. It is always at the very last minute that someone will actually tell you the information you need to know. For example, if someone has HIV, they just mention that at the very last minute when the form has been completed.

My experience of being involved with Mend the Gap was very new and different. It really changed how the BME community talked about things. By creating a trusting environment, I was so amazed at the way people talked about their problems in front of each other and with students and professionals. I had not experienced people speaking so confidentially. That never happens; people would always fear someone talking about them in the community. Mend the Gap was really important because it created the right space for people to talk about their problems, which helped them to find solutions. Also, it had a positive impact on policy makers, as recommendations from Mend the Gap have been taken up and accommodation for families has been much improved.

It is really important that social workers are involved with supporting families. Since my status was settled, I have been able to go back into social work. Unfortunately, my status for my family was settled just after my oldest son turned 18. This means that he did not automatically get the same status and now he has to fight for this in his own right. This is very unfair and stressful. It has been very hard for my children, who have not been able to do all the things they wanted to do because of their status. For example, they have not been able to go on school trips outside of England with their friends. Now my youngest child is very worried about her brother. There is a role for social workers to advocate for families by defending the best interests of the children whom they support. This is a big gap that needs to be mended.

SECTION 3

Service user involvement in human services education

22

DISABLED ACTIVISTS' INVOLVEMENT IN DEVELOPING AND DELIVERING DISABILITY STUDIES AT ST ANGELA'S COLLEGE, SLIGO, IRELAND

Peter Kearns and Susan Carton

A note on terminology

In this chapter, the term 'disabled people' will be used instead of 'people with disabilities'. The term *disabled people* is preferred because, within the social model of disability – on which Disability Studies is founded – people with impairments are considered to be disabled by prejudice, inaccessible environments and social barriers. They are not people 'with disabilities' but people with impairments who are disabled by society (Cameron, 2014).

Introduction

Colin Barnes wrote in 2008 that 'disability studies emerged from within the disabled people's movement. Its agenda and credibility has been closely linked to its ongoing relationship with disabled people and their organisations' (p. 15). The development of Disability Studies in St Angela's College has subscribed to this core belief since its inception in 2009. In this time, a range of Disability Studies courses (National Framework for Qualification (NFQ) levels 7, 8 and 9) have been developed and delivered in partnership with the Disability Equality and Specialist Support Agency (DESSA) and individual disabled academics who co-wrote, taught or acted as Extern Examiners for the courses. Positive feedback from disabled and non-disabled students, lecturers, stakeholders and Course Board members is attributable to this essential partnership.

The Irish context

While the causes of disablement, as outlined by disabled British academics (Barnes and Mercer, 2010; Oliver and Barnes, 2012; Davis, 2016; Slorach, 2016), have obvious resonances in Ireland due to the closely aligned development of societal structures between the two countries, there remain key challenges in Ireland to the dismantling of disabling barriers.

Alike as the two countries are, there is a gulf in culture and practice between Britain and the Republic of Ireland which affects engagement with the social model of disability in this country. There are several possible explanations for this. These may be attributable to the historical influence of the Church on the State here, the dominance of centre-right politics in this country and the difference in the relative size of the two economies.

The power and influence of the Roman Catholic Church on the State in Ireland has been well documented (Browne, 1986; O'Reilly, 1991; Ó hAdhmaill, 2013; Allen, 2017). A complex history of colonisation, revolution and civil war contributed to the formation of the national identity, in which being Roman Catholic was central (Allen, 2017; Ó hAdhmaill, 2013). The Church had a long-established responsibility for welfare and education in Ireland, given firstly by the British establishment and later by our own deeply conservative initial government. O'Reilly (1991) writes about the profound influence of the Church in Irish law right up to the latter quarter of the 20th century.

A second major difference in the socio-political landscape between Britain and Ireland is, as Browne (1986) suggests, the failure of a robust political Left to develop in Ireland in the first half of the 20th century. Having no large industrial working class in the country and the unprecedented alliance between the Fianna Fáil and the Church hierarchy set the scene for the development 'one of the most conservative societies in the world' (Allen, 2017). However, a strengthening of the Leftist political voice has been developing in Ireland in recent decades.

Finally, it has been argued that a small country with an open economy, being very susceptible to the varying external economic forces, has less autonomy in its governing decisions than larger economies. Ireland is dependent on its associations with the rest of the world and so far seems to have been swept along with rising capitalist and neoliberal ideologies.

The economic crash has dominated all the decisions of government since 2008. Draconian austerity measures imposed at the behest of the International Monetary Fund (IMF) have annihilated the provision of quality supports for marginalised people in Ireland and the dismantling of the barriers that impede disabled people's full participation in society has ground to a near halt since then. As the second decade of the 21st century draws to a close, however, there are green shoots of collective activism by disabled people in evidence.

Emergence of Irish disability activism and collectivism

According to disabled activist and broadcaster Donal Toolan, as with civil rights movements worldwide and closer to home in Northern Ireland, the 1960s and 1970 saw groups of disabled people become involved with an increased self-representation model, focused upon rights. Liam McGuire, a disabled activist and trade unionist, was involved with the politicisation of the Irish Wheelchair Association in the 1970s. Disillusioned with the slow pace of change in the 1980s, organisations of disabled people such as the Disability Awareness Movement (DAM) began advocating access to the same rights and opportunities as other citizens in 1980s Ireland. Co-author Peter Kearns was involved with DAM as a teenager and is certain that the focus of its activism was more on collectivism than impairment.

The ramp-up of collective activism was solidified with the 1990 launch of the Forum of People with Disability, the first 100% disabled activist organisation, which quickly lobbied the government and led to the publication in 1996 of the historic *Strategy for Equality* document. This detailed publication clearly established the need to move to a rights-based mode of addressing disability in terms of social, cultural and economic barriers. In all, it made 402 wide-ranging recommendations. The Forum of People with Disability published the first Irish Advocacy Strategy in 1998. This was followed by the State's progress report *Towards Equal Citizenship:*

Progress Report on the Implementation of the Recommendations of the Commission on the Status of People with Disabilities (2000), which made an attempt at measuring and explaining the progress – or lack of it – on the various recommendations. Co-author Peter Kearns worked as Development Officer for the Forum of People with Disability until the collective decided to wind up in 2006. Until autumn 2018, there had been a 12-year gap in having a replacement 100% disabled people's representative body. In 2018, a new social model-led collective was launched: the Independent Living Movement of Ireland (ILMI). Going to publication, this is one of the only Disabled People's Organisations (DPO) in the Republic of Ireland.

Interpreting 'service user involvement' with Irish universities and colleges

Yet, as the emerging Irish social model-led DPOs claim to speak with the voice of disabled activists in the Republic, the main players that Irish universities consult regarding the provision of supports and services to disabled people at the local level have traditionally been within the (mostly private-sector) disability service providers. These are made up of some very large voluntary and charitable organisations, which receive most of their multi-million-euro (€1.8 billion in 2018[1]) funding from the State. They have traditionally delivered specialised services to disabled people away from and separate to their local communities, although disabled consumers would usually have very little say in the content or aims of such '*special-needs*' resources. In the wake of the 1996 *A Strategy for Equality*, a State principle of mainstreaming of State services was developed and came into effect in June 2000.

Mainstreaming is supposed to deliver services for disabled people through the same organisations that deliver services for everybody else. It also challenges disability service providers to deliver quality services at a standard equivalent to their mainstream contemporaries. The mainstreaming ideal should have led us towards the disappearance or shrinking of facilities within the disability sector. In reality, the opposite has been the case, with the private-sector disability service providers continuing to be the main service 'carers' for disabled people.

The development of Disability Studies in St Angela's College

St Angela's College, in the northwest of Ireland, is a College of the National University of Ireland, Galway (NUIG). The College delivers higher education programmes at both undergraduate and postgraduate levels across the academic departments of Nursing, Health Sciences and Disability Studies, Home Economics and Education. One of the co-authors, Susan Carton, has a background in Intellectual Disability[2] Nursing and works in the Department of Nursing, Health Sciences and Disability Studies.

In 2009, the then Department of Nursing and Health Sciences decided to expand its remit and explore the possibility of engaging in the field of Disability Studies. It was decided that a level 8 course in Health and Disability Studies was feasible. The co-authors met at this point, to explore the development of the course.

At the time my co-author, Peter, was working with the Disability Equality and Specialist Support Agency (DESSA), lecturing in advocacy, facilitating Disability Equality Training and engaging in various Disability Arts activities. Direction from a disabled academic on the content of the Disability Studies stream of the course was essential. Peter oversaw the development of the vision, aim and objectives for the course in 2009, and these have remained established throughout the life of the programme. He was also involved in the writing of all the Disability Studies-related modules on the programme.

The BA (Health and Disability Studies) commenced in 2011. In 2014, Dr Colin Cameron (University of Northumbria) succeeded Dr Fazil (University of Birmingham) as External Examiner for the BA (Health and Disability Studies). He has been working with us since that time.

In 2014, St Angela's College and DESSA met to discuss the formulation of an online version of the course. At this point, we decided to concentrate on Disability Studies only and discussed the possibility of creating a UG Diploma and a PG Certificate/Diploma pathway. After several meetings between St Angela's and DESSA, it was decided to create the BA (Disability Equality Studies) course, a four-year, part-time level 8 course that would be delivered via blended learning.

The work of DESSA is guided by the principles of community development: collective action, empowerment, social justice, equality and anti-discrimination and participation. These principles were embedded in the curriculum as it developed and influenced the choice of modules that were included and the choice of lecturer to deliver the modules. This course commenced in September 2016.

After a departmental review in 2017, the decision was taken to develop the postgraduate pathway and continue to offer a level 7 undergraduate Certificate in Disability Studies. At the time of writing, the Post Graduate Certificate/Diploma/MSc in Disability Studies has commenced.

Disabled people's involvement in producing the course

As outlined above, my co-author was involved from the start of this process. Years later, I am still very grateful for his patience and persistence as I made my way over the 'threshold' of the social-model-of-disability concept (Morgan, 2012). The guidance from an academic who understood and advocated a social model stance has kept the development of the Disability Studies courses on the right track. All subsequent development depended on this solid foundation.

The Course Board Committee exists to facilitate the ongoing development, planning, delivery and assessment of an educational programme. It is usual for the developers of a course to seek relevant 'stakeholders' to be members of the Course Board Committee. Naturally, for a Disability Studies course, disabled people needed to be properly represented on this Board.

Carton and Kearns (2017) have described the disability sector in Ireland as consisting of 'two unequally sized categories: the large multi-funded disability service sector and the near non-existent disability representative sector' (p. 206). When planning the constitution of this Board, we looked for disabled representatives from both categories. The results were mixed in two ways. Firstly, finding disabled people who held positions in the larger service providers was not easy and, secondly, not all the disabled people we invited on to the Board had had the opportunity to explore the social model of disability. Members who contributed most critically to the development of the course were those who knew and understood this model.

Extern examiners are employed to assure and enhance the academic standards of courses, modules, programmes and awards. They also provide an important consultative and advisory function in supporting the development of modules and programmes as well as the enhancement of teaching learning and assessment practices (NUI, 2014). Externs are chosen for their expertise, in not only the subject area but also higher education in general. Having an extern in place who has the expertise in Disability Studies and lived experience of disablement has added immeasurably to the quality of the course. Dr Cameron's expertise has had an influence at many levels, from advice on the terminology used in the modules, to the relevance and application of different subjects, modes of assessment and the general quality of the course. But also, and more importantly, in the less formal conversations he has had with students and department staff. In these discussions, concepts were reinforced, ideas clarified and understanding was broadened.

It was in these spaces that the 'seismic shift' in thinking (Morgan, 2012) really took place, for those open to change.

Peter regularly provides Disability Equality Training in the college, which has also contributed to a more inclusive culture in the institution. This opportunity is available to all staff but is not mandatory, and it remains interesting to observe the individuals and groups who do not see the relevance of it in their professional lives.

Disabled students' involvement in the course

Over the years, we have sought to recruit disabled students onto the courses. The value that these students add falls into three broad categories. Their presence in the classes adds the dimension of the lived experience to the discussions, so that ideas and concepts are applied naturally and therefore meaning is made more easily among all students. Secondly, the insights offered at the evaluation of the modules and the course as a whole have positively influenced the quality of the content over the years. Finally, individual students' experiences of accessing the course content, and the College in general, has contributed hugely to our ability as a College to improve the service we offer.

St Angela's College and DESSA's partnership process of attracting more disabled people, and especially 'activists', into 3rd level learning entails defining creative access pathways into 3rd level education using mainstream community resources. As community support officer with DESSA, this co-author (Peter) would suggest that effective 3rd level pathways are about enabling a set of innate abilities and learned skills, plus facilitating capacity of disabled individuals within community-based collectives, to transcend accepted ideas and norms. I facilitated such by drawing on imagination and creative-arts group exercises to realise new ideas that bring additional value to human activity.

An important aspect to the St Angela's College and DESSA's partnership process is the collaborative nature of the access work between national and local government. St Angela's College is situated in County Sligo, and joint supports offered by DESSA and the College have helped Sligo County Council to adopt the social model in its 2019 *Disability Inclusion and Access Strategy*. Experiential and creativity-based learning and education pathways, such as those implemented by DESSA and St Angela's College, could be shown to be first steps towards 3rd level experiences for and with disabled people. This is particularly important for building capacity in already politicised activists. The disability equality-led experience saw DESSA, and myself as animator, design and deliver programmes that link the local community venue with university access courses such as that at St Angela's College.

The creative group-based experiential nature of the training with DESSA access 'Step-Forward' educational programmes include learning outcomes that enhance the capacity of the disabled people to:

1   understand what is meant by the term 'experiential' in a collective group setting, but always outside the disability service sector and with a local community centre;
2   provide an experiential environment, where information and issues can become active at the level of the disabled people participating in the advocacy and learning processes;
3   use group work exercises to devolve relevant information and further education knowledge to disabled people participating in the further education training process;
4   use appropriate group-based arts and creative exercises within a mainstream community development venue to help participants to explore solutions towards individual pathway visions to social model-identified attitudinal barriers within their own communities.

The DESSA and St Angela's College collaboration shows how a community development approach to confronting disabling learning barriers can complement a social model role in real and effective university entrance pathways for and with disabled people. DESSA recognises that the Irish mainstream community development sector is best to facilitate the capacity building of local disabled people towards effectively accessing 3rd level facilities. These strategic supports involve training, networking, advocacy and emancipatory mentoring which enable disabled people as activists to develop skills, experience and confidence to actively engage and participate within their chosen learning communities.

What difference did the involvement of disabled people make?

It is difficult to imagine what Disability Studies would look like in St Angela's without the collaboration of disabled academics. At a fundamental level, it would be unthinkable to run a course in any similar vein (studying oppression) without the involvement of the people experiencing the oppression, similar to running a women's studies course with no women involved. The difference made by having disabled people involved is evident in the quality of the courses. Committing to the social model of disability as the foundation of the Disability Studies education we offer has driven and directed the evolution of the content in the programme.

Committing to the social model of disability, in what continues to be a very 'medical-model world' in Ireland, is not without its difficulties. Pushing back against well-established and professionally reinforced beliefs about disability takes energy and resilience. In addition to the quality assurance of the content of our courses, referred to above, the involvement of disabled academics and activists has bolstered the dedication to delivering social model-based Disability Studies in St Angela's College.

Some comments taken from student evaluations bear this out:

> The further I get into the course, the further convinced I am of that, and not only am I benefiting from it as a disabled person but ultimately my fellow disabled people will too.
> Studying Disability Equality Studies has had a profound impact on my understanding of disability in Ireland today.
> My perception of disability has been transformed. I have come to understand that disability is caused by social injustice, social oppression, disabling environments and disabling structures.
> An ability to question critically the accepted status quo in today's society, is what has engaged me, and subsequently taught me the most.

In wider terms, I believe that working as we are, in close collaboration with disabled academics, is contributing to the generation of knowledge about disability and disablement in Ireland. Writing on the subject, holding and attending seminars and conferences and being members of national organisations affords us opportunities to share insights, debate the issues and contribute to social change.

The enabling role of Disability Arts in a disability equality-led academia

Through the collaboration of St Angela's and the disability equality-led community development processes of DESSA, 'power' is being transferred to disabled people as activists rather than them merely being disabled students contemplating their disabling status quo. The experts are the participants on the learning pathways, as these are the people who daily experience a disabling society.

An emancipatory 3rd level experience enables disabled activists to speak with academia, so they themselves become part of the struggle and the struggle becomes part of the academic effect. All that happens 'only happens because there is a struggle' (Freire, 1972). That is to say, the emancipatory learning process with access programmes and 3rd level pathways carries within itself an antagonism which makes the circumstances of a disabled person and activist move from what it is to what it should be in tandem with enhancing just academic knowledge.

By providing 3rd level environments with a community development process, information and issues can become active at the level of disabled activists participating in a learning processes which facilitates thinking as a form of action. The method supports the participants to discover any lived experience issues, and it provides a place for the university and activist to learn together. This emancipatory-informed 3rd level engagement can give the disabled activist the opportunity to express the learning to be identified from a lived experience of the medical model, together with the knowledge experience of the 3rd level institution embracing social model discourses. The decoding or deconstruction of medical model or oppressive narratives requires the university and disabled activist to move from the abstract to a social model transformation of mutually recognised disabling barriers. The nature of the learning and the knowledge experience is emancipatory for the disabled person as activist.

A primary objective of DESSA and St Angela's emancipatory learning processes is to enable thinking-as-an-action skills. There is also a need to identify space for *reflective* change and *transformation* within the 3rd level institution. DESSA and St Angela's emancipatory learning processes have shown that universities need to seriously engage with disability equality discourse and should not just be a supplier of educational premises, portraying existing medical-model knowledge and impairment-led narratives.

Barriers to developing and delivering Disability Studies courses

A significant barrier to developing and teaching Disability Studies in Ireland is the pervasiveness of a 'medical/individual model' of disability culture in both the academy and wider society. Deeply embedded beliefs and values about impairment and disability influence the responses that disabled people meet every day. Disability Studies has only recently begun to infiltrate the education of health professionals in Ireland and, therefore, the view that disability is a personal tragedy continues largely unchallenged here. A lack of awareness of the social model of disability exists, and the majority of people are in the position of 'not knowing what they don't know'. The role of being the 'expert' is highly valued among health professionals, and the idea of relinquishing the power associated with that status gives rise to resistance. This is further compounded by a dismissive narrative about the social model of disability, usually premised on a misconception of what it is, pervading the public discourse here in Ireland.

A *new* role for community development in 3rd level access by disabled people

The principles, or 'pillars', that underpin community development attraction to disabled activists, looking for new ways to enable other disabled people to access 3rd level learning 'power', include such terms as empowerment. The community development pillar of collective participation also must be a feature of effective learning in 3rd level institutions. Responses by activists to this author have recognised that support may need to be given to individuals to engage in decision making and that some individuals will need additional support to overcome barriers they face. They state that a social model-informed university engagement would be the ideal. Another pillar, self-determination, is about activists supporting the right of disabled people to make their own choices regarding 3rd level education and is about ensuring resources, skills and capabilities are used effectively (Jackson and O' Doherty, 2012) for and with disabled students at learning institutions. Empowerment processes can dis-empower if they are tokenistic (Adams, 2008).

Participation by disabled activists coming through the community development pathway into 3rd level Irish mainstream education refers to that part of the continuum of involvement where disabled people play a more active part, have greater choice, exercise more power and contribute significantly to decision making (Adams, 2008, p. 33). Third level participation is also about citizen engagement; key to this is that the disabled activist as citizen feels that their interactions are important, and that continuous engagement is regarded as significant (Adams, 2008).

DESSA and ILMI Role of disability equality and community development tutors

The aim of empowerment, in the context of community development impact on disabled people progressing into 3rd level, is to provide people with prospects to participate and gain control in decision making over matters that affect them and their community. It is about providing opportunities in education, learning development and capacity-building to engage. Ife (2016) says that empowerment is a means of providing individuals and communities with the opportunities, resources, knowledge and skills to increase their capacity to determine their own future progress. DESSA's connection with St Angela's Disability Studies set out to identify, promote and facilitate the early steps towards routes from community development programmes to St Angela's College's Access programme and on to degree-level education.

Learning from our experience and future challenges

DESSA and St Angela's Centre for Disability Studies, with the buy-in from the new DPOs e.g. the Independent Living Movement Ireland (ILMI, formerly Centre for Independent Living), are making sure that 3rd level empowerment is also linked to self-determination and autonomy. In the context of community development, self-determination and autonomy are about providing disabled people with supports to make their own decisions. Adams (2008) defines empowerment as a change process that develops those who are marginalised to achieve self-determination in decision making. This includes validating and normalising their views and social roles. Jackson and O' Doherty (2012) declare that the purpose of community development is to improve individuals' well-being by positive change. Key to community development is enabling disabled individuals to increase their well-being through self-determination, collaborative action and getting a better deal for people who are marginalised. DESSA and ILMI's future community development role could be to facilitate individuals to enter 3rd level learning by providing them with supports to take action to improve the quality of their life-long learning lifestyles and their communities at large (Jackson and O' Doherty, 2012). Cauchi and Murphy (2006, p. 3) state that one of the fundamental principles underpinning the empowerment of communities is self-determination. The inclusion of disabled people in the decision making in matters that most affect them is paramount in individuals' engagement with academic access pathways informed by the social model.

The experience of developing and delivering Disability Studies in St Angela's has been extraordinary. Learning has taken place on an individual, departmental and College-wide basis. The decision to develop Disability Studies in the department was based on recognition by the originators of the need for a change in how disability is perceived and responded to in Ireland. The involvement of disabled academics and activists in the process brought a depth and breadth to that learning which would have been otherwise absent. As attested to above in the student comments, what might have been limited to knowledge transference became transformative learning with the incorporation of the expertise and experience of disabled people in the process of developing and delivering the courses.

We hope to continue to attract students who are in a position to champion change. The growing strength of Disabled People's Organisations in Ireland is demonstrated in their demand to have disabled people 'at the table' in the development of education, policy and services. Disability Studies courses will only be acceptable in the future when disabled people have been key in their development and delivery.

In St Angela's College, we have introduced a Disability Studies module, 'Concepts and Paradigms of Disability', into the Bachelor of Nursing Science (Intellectual Disability) curriculum. We had developed the postgraduate pathway in Disability Studies which provides an opportunity for graduates to explore current perceptions and responses to disability and disablement in Ireland. In planning for this course, we drew together a Course Board with representatives from disability activism, disability education and Disability Arts. It is hoped that critical analysis from this group will facilitate the ongoing development, planning, delivery and assessment of an excellent educational programme.

Our future challenges include continuing to make the current culture and beliefs related to disability equality visible and promoting disability-led development in education and research.

Conclusion

Sometimes, education access supports for individual disabled students may unconsciously reflect a medical model approach, where the access and learning problems are perceived to lie with an individual rather than being shared by many disabled people outside mainstream 3rd level. The emancipatory learning pathway does not only meet and support disabled participants in an accessible college in order to induce information and knowledge on issues. Such information and knowledge findings will only become active in another arena. The 3rd level engagement process should be about coming to know through dialogue with disabled people both the reality of their situation and their perception of that situation (Freire, 1972).

McDonnell (2003, p. 35) writes persuasively about the two different structural levels at which educational systems work. He refers to the 'deep structure of theories, concepts, assumptions and beliefs, and a surface structure of day to day practices in the organisation and operation of schools'. He suggests that while the surface level is generally attended to, the deep structures have not been challenged or changed over the years. Disability Studies, which are founded on the social model of disability, provide access to those theories, concepts, assumptions and beliefs. The Community of Inquiry (CoI) model (Garrison and Arbaugh, 2007) is used on our courses in order to foster social constructivism as the foundation for teaching and learning. We are committed to the idea that knowledge is constructed through social interaction. In Disability Studies, that social interaction must involve disabled people (Sheldon, 2006; Barnes, 2008) as students and instructors, so that together we can construct and confirm the meaning of disability and disablement in 21st-century Ireland.

Notes

1 National Disability Authority: Fact Sheet October 2018.
2 Intellectual Disability is the term currently used in Ireland for people who may have impairments of intellectual and adaptive functioning and which has had an onset before the age of 18.

References

Adams, R. (2008) *Empowerment, Participation and Social Work.* Hampshire: Palgrave Macmillan.
Allen, K. (2017) Catholicism and the Irish State – Time to Separate. *The Irish Marxist Review* Vol. 6, No. 18. Available from www.irishmarxistreview.net/index.php/imr/article/view/238/229 [Accessed on 9/1/2019].
Barnes, C. (2008) *Disability and the Academy: A British Perspective.* Notes for an Oral Presentation, Le Handicap: Un Moteur Pour Les Sciences Sociales Journée d'étude organisée par le programme Handicap et sciences sociales de l'EHESS.
Barnes, C. and Mercer, G. (2010) *Exploring Disability.* Cambridge: Polity Press.
Browne, N. (1986) *Against the Tide.* Dublin: Gill and Macmillan.
Cameron, C. (Ed.) (2014) *Disability Studies: A Student's Guide.* London: Sage.
Carton, S. and Kearns, P. (2017) Ireland Disability Studies at St Angela's College – Tracing the Pathways Leading to the Current Understanding and Response to Disability. In: Głodkowska, J., Gasik, J. and Pągowska, M. (Eds.) *Studies on Disability: International Theoretical, Empirical and Didactic Experiences.* Warszawa: APS.
Cauchi, J. and Murphy, J. (2006) *Empowering Communities! Who Are We Kidding?* Paper presented at the Empowerment Conference with Noel Pearson, Melbourne May 16–17.
Commission on the Status of People with Disabilities. (2000) *Towards Equal Citizenship: Progress Report on the Implementation of the Recommendations of the Commission on the Status of People with Disabilities.* Dublin: Commission on the Status of People with Disabilities.
Davis, L.J. (2016) Disability, Normality and Power. In: Davis, L.J. (Ed.) *The Disability Studies Reader.* London: Routledge.
Freire, P. (1972) *Pedagogy of the Oppressed.* London: Penguin.
Garrison, D.R. and Arbaugh, J.B. (2007) Researching the Community of Inquiry Framework: Review, Issues, and Future Directions. *The Internet and Higher Education,* Vol. 10, No. 3, pp. 157–172.
Ife, J. (2016) *Community Development in an Uncertain World: Vision, Analysis and Practice.* Cambridge: Cambridge University Press.
Jackson, A. and O'Doherty, C. (2012) *Community Development in Ireland Theory, Policy and Practice.* Dublin: Gill Education.
McDonnell, P. (2003) Chapter 2: Education Policy. In: Quin, S. and Redmond, B. (Eds.) *Disability and Social Policy in Ireland.* Dublin: UCD Press.
Morgan, H. (2012) The Social Model of Disability as a Threshold Concept: Troublesome Knowledge and Liminal Spaces in Social Work Education. *Social Work Education,* Vol. 31, No. 2, pp. 215–226.
National University of Ireland (2014) *NUI Policy on Extern Examiners.* Dublin: National University of Ireland.
Ó hAdhmaill, F. (2013) The Catholic Church and Revolution in Ireland. *Socialist History,* Vol. 43, pp. 1–25.
Oliver, M. and Barnes, C. (2012) *The New Politics of Disablement.* Basingstoke: Palgrave Macmillan.
O'Reilly, E. (1991) *Masterminds of the Right.* Dublin: Attic Press.
Sheldon, A. (2006) *Disabling the Disabled People's Movement? The Influence of Disability Studies on the Struggle for Liberation.* Notes for an Oral Presentation, 3rd Disability Studies Association Conference, Lancaster, UK.
Slorach, R. (2016) *A Very Capitalist Condition: A History and Politics of Disability.* London: Bookmarks Publications.

23

SERVICE USER INVOLVEMENT IN PROFESSIONAL SKILL DEVELOPMENT

Planning and delivering a skills practice workshop

Jim Bell, Martin Fraser, Sara Hitchin, Linda McCulloch and Lynda Morrison

Who are we?

We are all members of Unity, which is a group of people who have experience of using services and teaching staff and student representatives on the BA (Hons) and MSc/Postgraduate Diploma Programmes in social work at the University of Stirling in Scotland. Unity was established in 2005 in recognition of the important contribution that people who use services have to make to social work education. Many of the group's founder members continue to be involved along with people who have joined more recently. The group contributes to teaching through a number of workshops with students and accompanies them on their journey from induction into the course right through to graduation. Unity members aspire to support students to become the best social workers they can be because people who use services deserve this.

In this chapter, we will share our experience of developing and delivering a skills practice workshop. We have decided to produce a step-by-step guide designed to help others to plan their own professional skills workshops. This is not to suggest that what has worked in our context will automatically work in other settings. In our experience, this type of workshop is more complex than others we have delivered. We would, therefore, encourage anyone thinking of following our guide to consider it within the context of your own setting. We value the concept of co-production, defined as *working in partnership through sharing power* (Social Care Institute for Excellence; SCIE, 2013). In our view, this is fundamental to effective workshop development, so we recommend that this should be your starting point.

Introduction

The use of skills rehearsal (role-play) in social work skills teaching might be seen as a *signature pedagogy* for the profession (Shulman, 2005, p. 52). It is a recognised method of teaching social work skills (Hargreaves and Hadlow, 1997; Skilton, 2011; Wilson and Kelly, 2010) and forms a central element of the Theory and Practice of Social Work module on the qualifying programme at the

University of Stirling. Role-play is also used in skills development teaching with medical (Nestel and Tierney, 2007) and nursing students (Babatsikou and Gerogianni, 2012).

Opportunities to develop core communication and engagement skills before embarking on placements are crucial if University staff are to be confident of students' readiness to work effectively with the people they meet (Scottish Executive, 2003; Moss et al., 2007, Skilton, 2011). Indeed, such readiness is assessed, on this module, through a video-recorded, role-played interview along with an accompanying written assignment.

Students learn about the foundation skills of communication and engagement with reference to Pam Trevithick's (2012) work. Through a series of skills workshops, they practice different elements of an assessment interview through role-play with each other, using fictitious scenarios. Although undoubtedly a valuable tool for skills practice, role-play between students has limitations. Some students struggle to get beyond the unreality of the scenarios into which they are asked to submerge themselves, in the roles of both service user and social worker.

In recognition of these limitations, the Unity skills practice workshop was designed to give student social workers the opportunity to practice their professional skills, in the form of initial interviews, with service users who are focused on student learning, in a safe classroom environment. The rationale was that this approach offers more in-depth learning and preparation for practice than student-to-student role-play alone. This is in line with Moss et al. (2007), who report that a higher degree of realism was achieved in skills labs when service users and carers were role-playing an agreed set of scenarios.

Student feedback has been universally positive and Unity members have also reported positive experiences of their involvement. We have, however, found this workshop more challenging to deliver than other teaching contributions. On this basis, we have decided to offer a step-by-step guide, drawing on our learning from the experience of delivering the workshops over the last four years (two workshops per year). We would suggest that a similar approach might also be used to focus on different types of skill development, such as nursing engagement with patients and doctor consultations. We have found that there are seven steps to effective development and delivery of the workshop. We would advise you not to miss any of these out:

Step 1: First establish your service user involvement group
Step 2: Decide on your learning objectives
Step 3: Hold planning meetings
Step 4: Design the workshop structure
Step 5: Meet immediately before the workshop
Step 6: Deliver your workshop
Step 7: Hold a debriefing meeting afterwards

Step 1: First establish your service user involvement group

Service user and carer involvement is integral to the development, re-approval and delivery of social work programmes at Scottish universities (Scottish Executive, 2003). The Unity service user and carers' group was established in 2005. In the early stages, the group convenor listened to group members and learned about their experiences of exploitative and disrespectful involvement with other groups where organisers assumed that they would be available with little notice; talked in jargon, making them feel excluded; did not offer them refreshments while drinking their own coffee etc. Together, staff and service user members worked to establish core principles underpinned by social work values. Regular meetings were scheduled for the full year, working around people's other commitments. A welcoming, inclusive environment was promoted where everyone's views were encouraged. Catering was provided in recognition of its symbolic messages of welcome and appreciation as well as the value of relaxed time together. Group membership increased and an underpinning philosophy emerged as it became clear that, for the group to work well, everyone involved should feel that they were getting something out of it; benefits should be reciprocal. Ager et al. (2005) report a similar process whereby group values were forged, and this is in line with guidance on service user and carer involvement set out by Levin (2004).

Unity was a well-established group with a solid foundation of trusting relationships by the time we decided to develop our skills practice workshop. While all service user involvement in professional education presents challenges, we would suggest that this type of engagement is significantly more demanding of service users than traditional forms of involvement, such as sharing personal stories. Unity members decided to draw on their own experiences, so participation in the workshop involved people stepping back from an *expert* role, where they share their views on what makes a good social worker, for example to return to a former situation where they needed help and experienced relative powerlessness. Unity members have reported challenges in terms of managing the emotional impact of this as well as rewards in terms of increased confidence and seeing how far they have come (Hitchin, 2016). Given that documented benefits to service users primarily relate to more traditional forms of engagement with students (Brown and Young, 2008; Moss et al., 2007; Scheyett and Kim, 2004), it is important to be mindful that taking part in skills practice with students is inherently different, and benefits to service user participants cannot be assumed.

The adoption of co-production principles – *reciprocity*, *equality*, *accessibility* and *diversity* (SCIE, 2013) – as well as experience of participation in other forms of service user involvement in social work education were important in creating the conditions whereby some members of the group felt ready for this new challenge.

Your group may not need to have been established for as long as Unity was before embarking on the development of a role-play workshop, but please do not rush this first step. We believe that for service users deciding to engage in skills practice with students, it is crucial that this takes place within a supportive environment and from a position of confidence. This can result in personal development and increased self-esteem (Hitchin, 2016), whereas participation without appropriate preparation could have the opposite effect.

Top tip from Sara: "Coffee, biscuits and laughter have proved to be essential ingredients in establishing Unity as an effective service user involvement group. Make sure that people feel welcomed and try to promote a relaxed meeting environment."

Top tip from Jim: "Discussing serious issues is made easier by doing this in in a fun, informal environment."

Step 2: Decide on your learning objectives

On the Theory and Practice of Social Work module, the main learning objective of skills practice is for students to develop their approach to professional communication and engagement in order to build competence and confidence before embarking on their first practice placement. The Unity workshop, therefore, shares this objective, aiming to provide a more realistic experience of interaction than student-to-student role-play alone.

The focus on foundation communication, engagement and assessment skills resulted in a need to set parameters around the types of scenarios that could be used within the role-play workshop. We agreed that each situation should lend itself to an initial meeting, rather than being part of an ongoing situation, and should not include overly complex information or that which might result in a child or adult protection response. This was intended to enable students to focus on using their inter-personal skills to engage with the individual, establish a rapport and begin to undertake an initial assessment rather than worrying about how they should respond to an urgent, high-risk situation. Hargreaves and Hadlow (1997) highlight the importance of setting clearly defined learning objectives for role-play in order to avoid distraction by the many interesting issues that are likely to arise.

Because of the large number of students, there are limited opportunities to work with Unity members. The structure of the interaction, therefore, attempts to maximise opportunities for students to meet people with a range of different experiences. The process of planning this is discussed in Step 4. A further learning objective, therefore, is for students to meet people experiencing a range of difficulties.

In addition, we aim for students to learn through observing how the other students in their triad approach the task; receiving feedback from service users and tutors; and giving feedback to each other. These powerful experiences also appear to help students to empathise with the people they meet and experience ways of translating feelings of compassion and respect into engagement with Unity members. A broader learning objective relates to the need to avoid the notion of *them* and *us*. Meeting Unity members in this way helps to reinforce the message that all of us will be service users at some point in our lives.

Here we have described a number of learning objectives in relation to the development of fundamental engagement and assessment skills; yours may be similar, or the workshop might be adapted to focus on different practice techniques, approaches or intervention stages. There are several key decisions to be taken at this point, and clarity about what you would like students to learn will help to shape your workshop structure.

Top tip from Linda: "I find that making the situation as real as possible can be challenging for students but gives them a more realistic experience. When I was ill I couldn't make eye contact with people and looked down all the time. I use this during the role-play."

Top tip from Jim: "Through experience of delivering the workshops, ideas about how to develop student-learning opportunities will emerge. I have had an idea to develop ours further by encouraging students to write up their interviews with us in order to practice professional writing skills."

Step 3: Hold planning meetings

Having established that your group would like to develop such a workshop, it is important that only people who feel ready to get involved should take part. Planning meetings enable people to find out more and decide whether or not it is for them.

Our annual planning meetings start with a discussion of the skills practice workshop aims and how it fits within the wider module and course teaching. Participants are given an explanation of why role-play is used and how it works. Hargreaves and Hadlow's (1997) guidance on the triad process offers a helpful explanation of the social worker, service user and observer roles.

The module tutor explains their commitment to skills rehearsal (role-play) as a way of supporting development of practice skills before students come into direct contact with service users. There is recognition that the more prepared students feel, the less likely it will be that the people they meet on placement will be exposed to underdeveloped skills and knowledge.

As previously stated, Unity members decided to use real-life experiences to develop the role-play scenarios. This may not work for all groups, and you might prefer to use fictional scenarios. Indeed, some writers have highlighted the potential emotional impact and risk of distress to service users through crossing the boundary between role-playing and acting out one's own issues (Duffy et al., 2013; Skilton, 2011). These concerns were discussed in the first planning meeting with members feeling that it should be their own decision. The main rationale for choosing to use real-life experiences was that it is easier to role-play our own experiences; we know what happened so do not have to imagine how something might feel or what happened next. As a consequence, members have reported that interactions feel more natural. This is not to dismiss the value of using scenarios that are not our own, however. In recent workshops, one Unity member has opted to draw on the experience of someone close to her in playing a role that she feels well able to relate to. This has also worked well.

Once service user group members have an understanding of how role-play works and have identified an aspect of their experience to focus on, we find it helpful to try it out. The tutor facilitating the workshop takes on the role of social worker in order for Unity members to practice going into role.

For one person, this was particularly useful as she undertook a practice role-play and realized that the situation she had chosen was still too painful for her to explore in this way. She considered withdrawing from the workshop at this point but was able to identify another, less painful issue to use (Hitchin, 2016). She decided to remain involved and has subsequently taken part in the workshops for four years. Another member tried out role-play and realised that they found it too difficult to stay in role, while a few others tried it out and decided it was just not for them.

In our experience, trying out role-play as part of the scenario development process is really important. It enables Unity members to make sure that they are comfortable revisiting aspects of their life that have been difficult for them. This seems particularly important as the students are learning fundamental interview skills and, as inexperienced practitioners, may not always handle the encounters with complete sensitivity.

Once members have settled on an aspect of their lives to focus on in the workshop, each person is supported to develop their scenario in the form of referral information. This is handed to a student just before they undertake skills practice with the Unity member so has to be brief and to the point, for example:

> You are meeting Michael for the first time and are visiting him at home. He has contacted the social work office, where you are on placement, with concerns about his housing support which is funded by social work.
>
> You are meeting Oliver for the first time and are visiting him at home. Oliver has a learning disability and lives with his father. He has been upset by young people in the area shouting names at him and throwing stones and would like some support in relation to this. (NB, Oliver is being supported to take part in the workshop today by Joe who will not be participating in the role play).
>
> *(Hitchin, 2016, p. 976)*

We have also spent time thinking about how to give feedback to students and what sorts of things to comment on. The "Feedback Sandwich" technique, where you comment on positive aspects of what the student did, discuss areas for improvement and then finish with more positive comments, is helpful in making sure that feedback is balanced.

We have found planning meetings useful in a number of ways; they have enabled the workshop to take shape and to evolve, taking everyone's ideas and experience into consideration. Those who have been involved previously are able to share their learning with people who are new to the workshop. Planning meetings have also helped Unity members to prepare for the emotional impact of engaging with students in this way and have enabled some people to opt out at a point when they are not experiencing the pressure of potentially letting anyone down.

Top tip from Jim: "Using real life experience is much easier than working with a scenario, as you don't have to think about your responses to questions; you have lived it so you don't have to imagine what it would have been like or to make any thing up."

Top tip from Linda: "For any service user thinking about what aspect of your experience to focus on in the role-play, make sure you feel comfortable with it. You need to ensure that it won't upset you too much. It can be emotionally draining and for me, it can bring back feelings of shame. I find that it can help to plan to do something nice afterwards."

Top tip from Linda: "Think about how to relate to the students in order to give feedback gently and honestly."

Step 4: Design the workshop structure

The structure of your workshop will be influenced by a range of factors; learning objectives are central to this. Practicalities such as room and staff availability as well as how much time you have for the workshop, the number of service users able to participate on the day and the number of students in the class all have to be considered.

We are typically working with 50–60 students with around six Unity members at a time. Although we generally know who is planning to attend, service user educators are variously living with mental health difficulties, caring responsibilities or have disabilities or illnesses. As a consequence of this, we cannot be absolutely confident about who will be there until the day. This requires some flexibility and an ability to adapt as we go. With this in mind, the following structure has worked well for us:

The Unity workshop generally takes place across two adjacent rooms or in one very large room.

A workstation is created for each Unity member. This consists of four chairs facing each other: one for the Unity member and three for the students who will be working in triads. These workstations are positioned around the room(s) to create as much space between them as possible.

Meanwhile, the whole class of students gathers in another large room with a tutor and are allocated to triads. When Unity members are ready to begin, a staff member gathers the same number of triads as Unity members and brings them to the workshop.

Before entering the room, students selected for the Unity workshop decide who, in each triad, will take on the role of social worker first. They are then given a printout of the referral information and are advised to undertake a ten-minute initial interview with the aim of building a rapport with the person and finding out about the issue of concern. They are encouraged to resist the temptation to offer advice and "fix" things but to use the time to develop as full an understanding as they can. Each triad is then directed to the person their referral relates to.

Students in the social worker role go straight into the role-play, while the other two students in each triad take on the role of observer.

Those who remain in the main teaching room undertake skills practice using fictitious scenarios. Working in triads, students take it in turns to undertake the roles of service user, social worker and observer. The student in the social worker role receives feedback from those in observer and service user roles as well as from tutors and participating practice educators on occasions.

Back in the Unity workshop: after the ten-minute role-play is complete, Unity members, observers and sometimes tutors and contributing practice educators give feedback to the students in the social worker role. We have found it important for service users to resume the role of student educator following role-play with students in order to experience benefits from their involvement. Giving feedback and general discussion with their triad allows them to do this. Sufficient time for this must be incorporated into the workshop (Hitchin, 2016).

Following around ten minutes of feedback and discussion, the tutor signals that it is time for triads to move on. Unity members remain in their place while students move to the next person, who gives their referral information printout to the student whose turn it is to take on the social worker role. The role-play followed by feedback pattern is repeated with a further rotation to a third service user.

Because of high numbers of students, it is only possible for each student to have one or, occasionally, two opportunities to practice skills with a Unity member. Working in triads like this enables them to meet three Unity members and observe two of their peers interviewing different people. By planning the order in which triads work with Unity members, we are able to influence their exposure to a range of difficulties that people experience and enhance learning from the workshop.

Once each of the students has had the opportunity to work with a Unity member and receive feedback on the skills demonstrated, students and Unity members take a break. The complete workshop process is then repeated with a new group of students with the first group returning to the main teaching room.

Over a two-and-a-half-hour period, we have found that it is possible to complete the workshop with two groups of students, typically meaning that 36 students have the opportunity to work with a Unity member. We therefore deliver the workshop again the following week to ensure that everyone in the class is able to participate. This, of course, means that service user educators are undertaking six role-plays a workshop, which can take its toll on people. This makes debriefing sessions and support during the workshop all the more important.

Top tip from Jim, Martin and Linda: "Noise levels from other groups around you can be distracting; be aware that this can have an impact on both service users and students; large teaching rooms can help with this."

Step 5: Meet immediately before the workshop

We have found that meeting and having lunch together before the workshop helps us to familiarise ourselves with the teaching room(s) and prepare for the session. At this point we can plan who takes up which position in the room and go over the workshop structure and expectations. People do sometimes forget the details, as they are involved in so many different workshops and events, so a reminder is helpful.

This time together also enables the group and/or tutor to be aware of and address any worries that a service user participant might have. Sometimes people are feeling more anxious than usual and it is helpful to know that there will be a tutor or Unity member they know well nearby in case they need support.

Having lunch together also provides a relaxed environment in which Unity members can be introduced to any practice educators who have volunteered to contribute.

Top tip from Martin: "The planning meetings on the day are important. It helps to remind me of the structure and timings. It is important to me that I know who I will be with, which room I will be in and where I will be positioned. This helps me to manage stress arising from my illness and gives me more confidence."

Top tip from Jim: "This preparation gets you in the zone and having lunch together whilst we talk helps us to relax."

Step 6: Deliver your workshop

In terms of resource commitment, at least one staff member who knows service user educators well should be present to facilitate the workshop. At the same time, at least one other tutor is needed to work with the remainder of the class as they undertake skills practice with each other. In addition, the availability of several practice educators who can observe role-plays and contribute to the feedback really enhances the student experience.

In addition to Unity members sometimes needing support, students may also need help. Some find the idea of the workshop stressful and will need additional encouragement to take part. It is also inevitable that some of the situations students encounter through role-play can trigger memories or remind them of current family concerns. As a result, there are times when students become upset, so tutors also need to be available to offer support if needed.

Keeping to time can be a challenge, as students as well as Unity members seem to really enjoy post role-play discussions. While allowing time for this is important, we also have to ensure that all students have the opportunity to work with service users, so keeping to the scheduled timescales is a necessity. This is something to be aware of in terms of both student and service user experience of the workshop. It may be that the logistics of your workshop enable you to incorporate more time.

At the end of the workshop, you might wish to ask students to evaluate their experiences; we do this at the end of the second day and invite students to complete a questionnaire. Students also use this session to express their appreciation to Unity members.

Top tip from Lynda: "It is important that we give balanced feedback; finding positives to comment on as well as areas for development. When the feedback is critical, this should be done sensitively."

Top tip from Linda: "Start by giving feedback on something the student did well, then something to work on and finish on a positive."

Top tip from Jim: "If the student messes up the role-play, try not to shatter their confidence and do be constructive in your feedback. I use an analogy about spray-painting cars; the ninth one is likely to be a lot better than the first!"

Top tip from Linda: "Sometimes students tell me that they are struggling to know how to respond, as they haven't had post-natal depression. I try to help them to develop empathy by encouraging them to imagine what it is like when they are feeling really down."

Top tip from Jim: "It can be helpful to point out to students that sometimes it is necessary to read between the lines of what people are actually saying."

Top tip from Linda: "When giving feedback it is important to be calm and reassuring."

Top tip from Martin: "I try to give students the message that they will get better going forward."

Step 7: Hold a debriefing meeting afterwards

Immediately after the workshop, service user group members and tutors spend time together to debrief. We have found that this enables both staff and Unity members to reflect on and learn from the experience and to ensure that individuals are feeling supported and have not been unsettled by taking part. At this stage, we also consider whether there are things we could do differently; for example, we adjusted the timing of the workshop delivery based on student feedback.

During refreshments, we explore any difficulties that may have arisen and recognise the potential for any of us to have an emotional reaction to the experience of taking part in the workshop. Some members anticipate this and have developed ways of managing it. One person always plans to do an enjoyable activity afterwards, for example, as she knows that spending so much time focusing on a difficult time in her life can leave her feeling low in mood.

We have found reading over student feedback questionnaires to be an uplifting and rewarding experience. Despite their nerves, students seem to get a great deal out of the workshop and their appreciation of Unity's contribution makes it all worthwhile:

> I really enjoyed it. I felt that the interview with the Unity member felt almost like I was in practice as it was their real problems which allowed me to feel empathy.
>
> *(student quote, 2015 in Hitchin, 2016, p. 977)*

Top tip from Lynda: "It is important to encourage students to give developmental feedback rather than just appreciation. We really value that students tell us they get a lot out of the workshops but we also want to hear about any changes we could make. For example, the first time we did the role-play workshop, it was earlier in the module and students fed back that they didn't feel confident enough to try things out with us. We took this on board and the workshops take place later in the module now. Students appear better prepared and more confident."

Top tip from Jim: "This meeting also allows Unity members to alert staff to any worries about particular students getting upset during role-play for example."

Conclusion

In this chapter, we have taken the reader through seven steps in planning and delivering a skills practice workshop. We hope to have shared our enthusiasm for and commitment to supporting student learning. We have found these seven steps particularly helpful in relation to this workshop but would suggest that a similar process is useful when developing any new service user involvement in human services education.

What we have described in this chapter is a process, which requires significant resources in terms of staff and service user time and commitment, as well as funding for catering and service user expenses. At a time when Scottish universities receive no direct funding for service user participation, ensuring the availability of catering and expenses is indeed a challenge and there is a risk that these are not seen as essential. We would argue that both are fundamental to effective service user involvement and are pleased that our institution recognises this.

Pressure on academics to deliver high quality teaching and tutoring and undertake research as well as administrative and governance roles means that staff are juggling many competing demands on their time. Without sufficient space to support service user and carer involvement, there is a risk of cutting corners, which could mean that the experience of those participating is compromised, co-production becomes notional rather than authentic or opportunities for service user participation are reduced. These are ongoing challenges, but we strongly believe that effective service user participation is worth fighting for. It significantly enhances student experience and influences their approach to practice. We have also found that it is beneficial to service user educators in terms of increased confidence and self-esteem (Hitchin, 2016).

In this particular workshop, a student receiving direct feedback on their practice from service users reinforces the message that service user views should be both sought and listened to. This is a practice principle we hope that students will take into their careers. This student testimony, given at the point of graduation, suggests some success:

> Feedback from service users will be at the heart of my practice in the years ahead when I will always remember the importance of core values such as respect, reliability and accountability when I begin to practice, in the future and forever.
>
> *(Wardrope, 2015)*

Reference List

Ager, W., Dow, J. & Gee, M. (2005) Grassroots Networks: A Model for Promoting the Influence of Service Users and Carers in Social Work Education, *Social Work Education*, 24:4, pp. 467–476. doi:10.1080/02615470500097033

Babatsikou, F. & Gerogianni, G. (2012) The Importance of Role-Play in Nursing Practice, *Health Science Journal*, 6:1, pp. 4–10. Available at: www.hsj.gr/medicine/the-importance-of-roleplay-in-nursing-practice.php?aid=5305

Brown, K. & Young, N. (2008) Building Capacity for Service User and Carer Involvement in Social Work Education, *Social Work Education*, 27:1, pp. 84–96. doi:10.1080/02615470701381491

Duffy, J., Das, C. & Davidson, G. (2013) Service User and Carer Involvement in Role-Plays to Assess Readiness for Practice, *Social Work Education*, 32:1, pp. 39–54. doi:10.1080/02615479.2011.639066

Hargreaves, R. & Hadlow, J. (1997) Role-Play in Social Work Education: Process and Framework for a Constructive and Focused Approach, *Social Work Education*, 16:3, pp. 61–73. Available at: http://explore.bl.uk/primo_library/libweb/action/display.do?tabs=detailsTab&gathStatTab=true&ct=display&fn=search&doc=ETOCRN613373549&indx=1&recIds=ETOCRN036409356

Hitchin, S. (2016) Role-Played Interviews with Service Users in Preparation for Social Work Practice: Exploring Students' and Service Users' Experience of Co-produced Workshops, *Social Work Education*, 35:8, pp. 970–981. doi:10.1080/02615479.2016.1221393

Levin, E. (2004) *Involving Service Users and Carers in Social Work Education*. SCIE, London [online]. Available at: www.scie.org.uk/publications/guides/guide04/files/guide04.pdf (Accessed: 3.2.16)

Moss, B. R., Dunkerly, M., Price, B., Sullivan, W., Reynolds, M. & Yates, B. (2007) Skills Laboratories and the New Social Work Degree: One Small Step Towards Best Practice? Service Users' and Carers' Perspectives, *Social Work Education*, 26:7, pp. 708–722. doi:10.1080/02615470601129925

Nestel, D. & Tierney, T. (2007) Role-Play for Medical Students Learning About Communication: Guidelines for Maximising Benefits, *BMC Medical Education*, 7:3, pp. 1–9. doi:10.1186/1472-6920-7-3

Scheyett, A. & Kim, M. (2004) "Can We Talk?": Using Facilitated Dialogue to Positively Change Student Attitudes Towards Persons with Mental Illness, *Journal of Teaching in Social Work*, 24:1–2, pp. 39–54. doi:10.1300/J067v24n01_03

Scottish Executive (2003) *Framework for Social Work Education in Scotland*. Scottish Executive, Edinburgh.

Shulman, L. S. (2005) Signature Pedagogies in the Professions, *Daedalus*, 134:3, pp. 52–59. doi:10.1162/0011526054622015

Skilton, C. J. (2011) Involving Experts by Experience in Assessing Students' Readiness to Practice: The Value of Experiential Learning in Student Reflection and Preparation for Practice, *Social Work Education*, 30:3, pp. 299–311. doi:10.1080/02615479.2010.482982

Social Care Institute for Excellence (2013) *Co-production in Social Care: What It Is and How to Do It* (Adults' Services: SCIE Guide 51). Social Care Institute for Excellence. Available at: www.ndti.org.uk/uploads/files/Coproduction_Guide51Fin.pdf (Accessed: 22.11.18)

Trevithick, P. (2012) *Social Work Skills: A Practice Handbook* (3rd ed.). Open University Press, Maidenhead.

Wardrope, E. (2015) *Student Testimonials*. University of Stirling. Available at: www.stir.ac.uk/testimonials/social-sciences/elaine-wardrope/ (Accessed: 30.12.18)

Wilson, G. & Kelly, B. (2010) Evaluating the Effectiveness of Social Work Education: Preparing Students for Practice Learning, *British Journal of Social Work*, 40, pp. 2431–2449. doi:10.1093/bjsw/bcq019

24

SERVICE USERS REACHING OUT TO HELP PROFESSIONALS

Shaping professional education on substance use and poverty issues

Hilda Loughran, Gary Broderick, SAOL Women's Group and Ray Hegarty

(SAOL IS THE TITLE OF THE SERVICE PROVIDER PARTNER)

Introduction

While engaging service users in the education and training of professionals is now an accepted and in some cases mandatory requirement (Health and care professions council), the nature of this engagement continues to generate debate (Goossen and Austin, 2017). Hatton cautions that service user engagement must be meaningful (2017, p. 155). The challenge, then, is to work creatively so that service user involvement can have real meaning and impact in the education of professionals. Ethically, the process should have added value for service users. Respectful and meaningful engagement with professional education should give voice to service users' experiences in a transformative way for students and service users alike.

Moving from traditional to transformative

As has been noted before (Hatton (2017, pp. 154–155), more traditional engagement of service users took the form of, for example, being expert speakers. In the area of substance use education, the inclusion of service users as guest speakers who had personal experiences of substance use, either as family members or as substance users in recovery, was fairly commonplace. Social work educators have made great progress in developing more appropriate and creative ways to work with service users in the substance use field, examples of which are discussed by Galvani and Allnock (2014). However, there are a number of challenges to be met in creating a form of engagement in which the voice of the service user can be heard while at the same time addressing curriculum requirements.

The importance of engaging service users in developing curriculum for social work students on addiction-related issues has been discussed in relation to women who were current service users (Loughran and Broderick, 2017). In this study, it emerged that there may be disparities between what educators and service users considered to be important. Loughran and Broderick (2017) found that the educators were focusing on signs and symptoms of substance use problems and were concerned that social workers be equipped to undertake assessments, make decisions about risks and identify suitable intervention. Service users were more focused on social workers' ability to understand their experiences of drug use and to make assessments which valued the service users' progress, resilience and attempts to make positive changes. They wanted social workers to acknowledge their successes in managing the substance use issues. Service users were also interested in helping social workers gain more in-depth insight into the lived experiences of drug-using women in a much broader social context.

On reviewing earlier experiences of engaging service users in social work education (Loughran and Broderick, 2017), a number of important factors were identified. The debate about defining who is a service user incorporates some concerns regarding, for example, failure to distinguish between current and former service users, and reliance on what might be termed as 'professional' services users. Educators working in partnership with service providers can provide support for current service users in their participation with professional education. This means that service users can be both protected and prepared for what, for some, is a stressful and challenging experience of interacting with professionals. This is particularly significant when the service users have ongoing relationships, not always positive, with these professionals in practice (for example, some service users who are still negotiating relationships with social workers managing access to their children). Being a current service user does inevitably pose a challenge for engagement with professionals in training, as the service user is trying to provide insight into their own experiences while at the same time acknowledging that not all experiences are the same as theirs. Another aspect of this is that current service users may be still involved in seeking resources and so may have some anxiety about speaking out with professionals. It was considered important that the engagement with professional education should address power differentials between service users and professionals. For this purpose, service users should clearly be recognised as providing expertise and sharing their knowledge with the professionals.

With this growing understanding of the value and challenges of current service users participating in professional education in meaningful ways, the next step was to consider if there were other, broader aspects of education that needed to be addressed and, even more importantly, if there were alternative forms of communication that might be more be more appropriate to enacting this engagement.

As there was an appreciation of the importance of the working partnership with service providers, it seemed appropriate to look at what was happening in the service in terms of direct work with service users that might translate into a more service user-friendly approach to education. The authors (academic, service providers and service users) looked at what activities had been effective in engaging service users not only in addressing their substance use issues but also in moving on to address broader issues such as self-esteem and skills to enable them to have their voices heard.

The initial iteration of the service user involvement did in fact focus more on the academic requirements (Loughran and Broderick, 2017); the evaluation and analysis of the whole process highlighted the need to redress the imbalance in focus and to redesign or add to the engagement so that it reflected more of what the service users valued. The research enriched debate among participants as to how service users' interests could be better represented and what format that should take.

Making a difference to service users

The process of broadening the remit of service users' contribution to the curriculum was further enhanced by a number of factors:

An unanticipated benefit to service users was the growing confidence in their engagement with third level institutes. The process served to legitimise the part of service users in contributing to social work education. The particular group of service users who participated in this earlier research gained additional levels of confidence in voicing their input into the process.

The confidence and legitimacy facilitated the service users and services providers in broadening their horizons. They developed independently of the social work educators and expanded to engage with other relevant professionals and social work educational institutes.

It became evident that such engagement served to address fundamental aspirations of the services mission. The service (SAOL) 'is a community project focused on improving the lives of women affected by addiction and poverty and is working towards transforming the way in which Ireland responds to substance use and poverty'.[1] It also highlighted that the initial focus on women and substance use had failed to deliver on providing insight and understanding in regard to the social context of poverty which is so often part of women's lived experiences. Yet the service itself, outside of the professional education forum, was engaged in very creative ways of working with service users towards developing a critical consciousness about power, politics and poverty.

Service users leading the way through visual arts

What resulted from these developments was recognition that, for service users, the individual deficit models of addiction are both unhelpful and misrepresentative of their experiences. Service users had been developing a critical consciousness through creative use of art, drama and literature and were in an ideal position not only to expand the input on substance use and poverty in professional curricula but also to provide support and model for professional educators the use of creative arts as a teaching and learning tool. Carlson et al. (2006) highlight the opportunities for photography to create an impetus for different levels of engagement and consider this art form as a way to enhance critical consciousness though emotional engagement. SAOL was already looking to arts to provide an accessible platform for service users to explore socio-economic, political and feminist issues. Hatton (2017, p. 160) promotes the employment of more imagination and creativity in 'releasing people's political imagination so they can envision an alternative experience'. The value of employing visual arts in education for social workers has been acknowledged (Walton, 2012). This is further developed by Bloomfield and Capous-Desyllas (2017), who comment that in relation to social work education, 'art has the power to transcend both language and culture, the images generated . . . served to uncover interconnections among diverse social identities, corresponding to their unique life experiences'. They (Bloomfield and Capous-Desyllas, 2017) present an argument for the place of one such visual method, Photovoice, as a pedagogical tool in social work education. This is supported by Ostaszewska (2018, p. 75), who views Photovoice as a valuable method for social work education as it has a role in 'shaping knowledge about social reality'. She adds that 'photographs can be an empowering tool. Through stories they show that they can inspire changes and bring the attention of the public and decision makers' (Ostaszewska, 2018, p. 75).

The value of using photographs to explore and express lived experiences was already an established approach in SAOL. This enabled the service users in partnership with Saol to use photography to, as Bloomfield and Capous-Desyllas (2017, p. 493) suggest, 'enhance experimental dimensions of learning that are more engaged and reflective compared to traditional teaching methods'. As a result, a decision was made to amalgamate the outcomes of a project that the service users had been working on, which they called Object Poverty, with designing input into professional education.

Visualising critical consciousness: Object Poverty

As was highlighted in Loughran and Broderick (2017), one significant feature of engagement in education was that service users' view of what they felt was important for professionals to be taught differed from the view of educators. As the service user group gained in confidence, they were able to articulate that they thought not only that professionals did not acknowledge their attempts at managing their difficulties but also that professionals had limited understanding of other factors that impinge on their lives. SAOL service users were developing awareness of socio-political and economic factors and were giving a voice to such social factors associated with problems of substance use. One of these factors that seemed to be particularly important was that people did not understand the part that poverty plays in making life challenging for service users.

It is very difficult to convey what poverty means to people, especially when trying to convey poverty to those who have not experienced it. Object Poverty was undertaken as a project through which SAOL Women's Group sought to express the experience of poverty through photographs. Object Poverty initially focused on developing service users' ability to articulate their experience of poverty. The impact of visually representing what poverty means is so powerful that its potential for transformative action in a political context was also recognised, and work on this aspect of the project continues. For the purpose of this chapter, we are focusing on the potential of Object Poverty to elicit emotional engagement and enhanced appreciation among students about what poverty means to service users.

The background to Object Poverty

In a drugs rehabilitation project like SAOL, talking about substance use is easy: when did you last take something? How was your use triggered? What is your plan for the next week? What are your care plan goals? It can be an easy conversation that keeps the addiction professional in control (share with them what they want to hear) and the real conversations for change can be relegated to 'some future date'. It's not that details of substance use aren't important; it's more that they are not as central as we might like to believe they are.

What is often more essential are questions like: how are you managing without your children? How violent has your partner been this week? How do you cook a meal without electricity? What is it like to live in a hostel/hotel bedroom/tent/parent's spare box room? When was the last time you ate? But these are the questions that are painful and personal and 'need to be avoided'; often, the isolation of addiction makes such questions feel like they are individual problems that are not shared or understood by others in a drugs rehabilitation project.

An opportunity came about for SAOL to create something that would draw attention to the issue of poverty. UN Day for the Eradication of Poverty is held each year on October 17, and a small grant was made available to create something to get people reflecting on poverty. Initially, when the topic of poverty was raised with the service users, they started talking about Africa and 'places that you see on the TV'. The group were challenged to look closer to home and talk about poverty in Dublin (their city). They talked a lot about homelessness and people stuck in hostel accommodation. Gradually, slowly, they talked about their own experiences: the click of the electricity metre as it ran out of money; the struggle of getting the right shoes/clothes for their children to wear to school; the fear of Christmas and the burden of going into debt so that Santa Claus would bring the right toys.

That year, many of the service users had experienced a major cut to their social welfare payments and had had to listen to endless debates about the need for austerity. They were angry that their payments were being cut so harshly, and this may have made it easier to discuss the topic. As a result of the workshops, they created a 'poverty washing line' as well as two short films highlighting both the experience of living in poverty in Dublin and an imagining of the debates being had by the ministers who chose to cut their social welfare payments.

Although following October 17, poverty was a topic that could be discussed more openly in SAOL (people openly asked for help when they were running low), poverty as a topic was generally left without much reflection for another year.

As UN Poverty Day emerged again, the same group created a series of art pieces reflecting on poverty and the senses: e.g. the smell of poverty (described by one woman as 'cabbage' as she suggested that 'every place dealing with poor people smells of cabbage') became a perfume brand, 'Pauvre'; the sight of poverty became a poster of rundown Georgian doors of Dublin mimicking a famous poster (the group went around the north inner city of Dublin taking these photographs, as anyone else might have been run out of the streets); the sound of poverty was an audio recording made by the group, the centre-piece of which was a mother trying to soothe her crying child as they waited for the Post Office to open so they could access their social welfare payment.

This set of art pieces got a lot of positive feedback, and they are displayed in the Project and shown to all visitors. Again, however, the conversation all but stopped after the event had finished.

Object Poverty was created in 2016, again to mark UN Day for the Eradication of Poverty. It is useful to highlight that during this time, the same group were involved in the work outlined in Loughran and Broderick (2017) with social work students.

Sitting before a group of social work students is a daunting experience for service users; add that they were master's students and the concern rises further. The fact that the service users going to the meeting were also active drug users who had experiences of social workers in their lives (both as children and as adults) and many had not completed secondary school meant that this was a huge challenge for them.

We worked closely with the group in preparation for the meeting. One phrase that took hold for the group was: Who is the student and who is the teacher? For a group of women who did not see themselves as having any wisdom to impart, this question became an important refrain for them. When they met the students and found them to be 'normal' human beings who didn't seem to know as much about addiction as they did, they began to acknowledge that they had insight to offer and could be seen as teachers, too.

This experience stayed with the group. Experiencing themselves as people who could guide social work students was a challenging discovery, and they were a significant part of the process that fed into the creation of Object Poverty (SAOL Project).

The group wanted to make something that people could see; with access to a professional photographer to help them make this work, they began to explore what poverty looked like. They decided to ask people what they thought, and the idea emerged that a questionnaire could be sent to people to ask them to say what things represented poverty for them.

More than 230 replies were garnered and from them a list of 16 'objects' which represented poverty for the service users were created. There was a list of objects, accompanied by a list of 'the absence of' objects; e.g. the absence of money, food, a home. The list was only restricted by the artistic eye and the visual appeal of 16 objects which decided matters.

The group worked with the photographer (Ray Hegarty) in taking the findings and turning them into a list of objects that could be photographed. Some items were easy to nominate as they were clearly named in the feedback: a sleeping bag (homelessness), the paper cup (street begging) and the cardboard (to sleep on when sleeping rough). Through discussions with the group, the lack of food was represented by the empty plate; poor clothing by the 'button'; and lack of money by the empty purse. For all of the objects, 'the image is the invitation to the story'.

The items chosen were also inspired by stories told by the group members of their own experiences of poverty (Figure 24.1). A 'toothbrush' was chosen to represent 'lack of dental care' or 'bad teeth'. The service user concerned told how she carried her toothbrush with her everywhere so that whenever she had access to running water, she could wash her teeth.

The 'boots' were given by a woman who used them to walk the streets while waiting for access to her hostel. After they were photographed, she refused to take them back, telling us that boots last only 12 weeks when you are homeless: 'by then they are worn out from the walking and the rain'.

Other items were used because of opportunity. A bar of 'soap', representing the grime and dirtiness of poverty, was given to us by a woman who had visited the site of an old Magdalen Laundry (former residential service for 'fallen women') and had permanently borrowed it as a remnant of the suffering women had experienced in that and other such places. In all, 16 items were photographed and collated as a poster under the title 'Object Poverty'.

However, the actual art piece that is Object Poverty is made up of the 16 full-colour images, each individually printed and framed on an old bread board that was sprayed gold. The boards could be connected together, hung individually or even made into cubes and were therefore adaptable depending on the exhibition space available.

On October 17, 2016, Object Poverty was displayed for the first time. It elicited many reactions, which were predominantly positive, with people telling their own stories inspired by the objects photographed. The 'negative reactions' tended to highlight the emotional disturbance caused by the images for some, and this was a very important reaction for the SAOL Women's Group to process. They suggested that more people should see the work. This included hosting a street exhibition of the work and inviting members of the public to tell us their reactions to the pictures. The owner of the building under renovation next to our Project agreed to hang the pictures on the walls, and the exhibition became a focal point of interest on the street for the rest of the month.

Service users working with educators and students

Service users' previous positive experiences of engagement with social work education encouraged them to take an opportunity to bring the Object Poverty exhibition to the School of Nursing in Dublin City University. What the women wanted to convey with Object Poverty was:

- A humanity and reality behind poverty
- An explanation about how poverty blocks full engagement
- An unspoken request to be heard as good people who happen to have been poor – the shame that shouldn't be there but is
- To talk about how hard it is to be poor (and homeless) and to be expected to respond to goals/tasks unrealistically quickly
- To name different experiences:

  - The cold of poverty
  - The hunger of poverty
  - The slowness of time when you are poor
  - The shame – and how helpful a pill is to hurry time along
  - The emptiness of poverty
  - The energy required to be poor – e.g. the boots are worn out

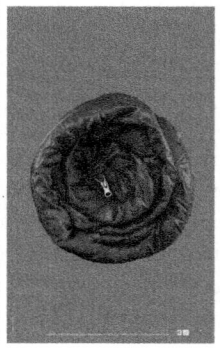	**Object Poverty 1: Sleeping bag** Borrowed from one of the homeless agencies, the sleeping bag came top of our poll on items that represent poverty in Ireland in 2016. We gave the bag back. There's probably a person in it tonight.		**Object Poverty 2: Boots** These boots belong to a homeless woman. She keeps her things as well as she can given that she doesn't know where she will be from one day to the next. She has been homeless for more than 20 years. Her name wasn't properly registered on the homeless list. She is likely to be homeless for some time to come.
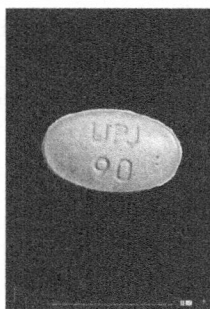	**Object Poverty 3: Addiction: Pill** Addiction was one of the recurring 'objects' named as representing poverty. We used a couple of images to help us see it more clearly. The first is a tablet or pill. Prescribed for every ill. Especially the gut wrenching fear of having nothing.		**Object Poverty 16: Empty shopping basket** When the everyday task of going to the shops becomes a daily stress, you know you are poor. When you cannot afford to buy 'in bulk' or to travel to the bigger (cheaper) supermarkets results in you paying more for daily provisions. The original phrase 'basket case' was used in First World War to describe soldiers who had lost all four limbs. Long term poverty is debilitating.

Figure 24.1 Examples of Object Poverty SAOL (2016)

All of this was risky – as the service users were not convinced that third level students would understand, and the fear was that they would merely write off their examples as stories being used as excuses.

The exhibition was launched with a workshop and discussion with nursing students, exploring the reality of poverty in people's lives. Going into a new setting to a different university and meeting a group that they had no history with was a big challenge. The service user group revised their concerns that they would find it difficult to talk to the third level students, believing them to be too intelligent and too far removed from their experiences. Building a partnership with educators and taking time to develop a relationship between educators and the service users had proved critical in the past and so, Dr Briege Casey, in her capacity as nursing educator, developed a relationship with the women before they went to meet the students.

The phrase 'Who is the student and who is the teacher?' became the mantra again. Having embraced the new identity as educators, the service users went to the workshops and exhibition launch believing that they did have something to offer. They were surprised when they arrived because their image of distant students was immediately challenged. The students shared stories of poverty with service users, telling of their own financial restraints and their struggles to keep warm, pay bills and eat regularly.

Object Poverty offered a structure for the discussion to take place. Each object framed experiences. But the meaning of objects expanded during discussions from the meaning originally given by the service users; the 'needle' moved from meaning 'addiction' to also meaning 'access to healthcare'; the button became 'mental health and hanging on by a thread' as much as poor clothing; and the coffee cup began to represent the cost of breakfast for a family for a week and access to warmth in a coffee shop as much as it was initially seen as representing a tool for begging. The women expressed different meanings of the objects as for nurses and themselves, for example 'We see that (the syringe) as a life-taker and you see it as a life-giver'.

The normality of the students and the surprise that they also had experiences of poverty impacted greatly on the service user group. They began to see the students as regular, ordinary people who shared some of their experiences. As a result, a transformation in 'self-image' seemed to be taking place for the group. They were re-constructing themselves as teachers and women with insight that professionals needed to have. They had seen how their work impacted social work students; now they were seeing how they could alert nursing students to the impact of poverty on their patients' lives and healing process. They were hungry for much more.

The SAOL women generously shared other art forms with students. They have written poetry and songs to express themselves and to help people connect with their experiences. Some examples of their work on experiences of poverty demonstrate the evocative nature of this art form. The experience of the women is that they feel this work is helping social workers and other professionals to more fully understand and appreciate the challenges they face, both as women and as service users. Employing art forms to capture their stories does appear to provide a more effective vehicle to express the resilience they demonstrate on a daily basis to survive and to thrive in the face of such adversity.

From a song that the women wrote:

> Born into poverty, it's a role with no say
> No escape, no relief, barely making each day
> The waiting the needing, the children need feeding
> The begging and crying, the constantly pleading

257

Poverty, misery in the world of today
No one should be starving in this day and age
(SAOL Sisters (2014) SAOL Project, Dublin)

From a poem written by two people from the group

Kids need to be clothed, fed and dressed and even though we do our best
It's never feels good enough, never enough to pass our test
No food, clothes or heating, just another beating
Life is so hard for us but still we don't make a fuss
(Byrne & Dawnay (2013) SAOL Project, Dublin)

Since then, sub-groups of the original group have presented to social care students; another group of social work students in a different university; student teachers; a group of government representatives (TDs) in Dáil Éireann (government); and internationally to social workers in Warsaw University and poverty activists in Paris and to MEPs in the European Parliament in Strasbourg.

Discussion

Object Poverty became a transformative experience for not just the service users but also the many students they encountered, political representatives and beyond the Irish experience to an international audience. The employment of visual arts in the form of photography demonstrated the ability to transcend culture and language constraints in the same way that at home in Ireland it transcended class and education. It should be acknowledged that a strong motivator in all of this work for the service users is that the groups that go to talk to students are seen as ambassadors for other women in similar situations who do not have the opportunity to be heard. This was particularly important when meeting social workers; the service users want to be seen as people and not as problems. They recognise that reaching out to professionals and helping them to understand their lived experiences have the potential to change the quality of the services they and others in their position will receive in the future. The use of Photovoice informed methods; the photo poster, in conjunction with poetry and song, appears to have contributed to helping students to understand and emotionally connect with the issues of poverty for the service users. It may well be that the connection generated though these art forms has the additional impact of transforming students' views of the women and, indeed, women's view of themselves. Through the 'performance' of the art forms, the service users build confidence in an alternative identity of themselves as creative and talented people. This in turn provides a deeper level of appreciation on the part of the students, who can see the service users beyond the service user identity.

The women put great importance on making a connection with the students, and, worryingly, they have commented that in relation to Object Poverty they felt that one group of social work students they encountered seemed unable to make an emotional connection to their experiences of poverty. Despite the limited evidence on this matter in the current project, it is nonetheless of concern. It is significant that the social work students in this situation did not manage to convey their empathic abilities. This is reflective of concerns raised by Forrester et al.'s (2008) research, which found that social workers were not employing their reflective skills and therefore pointing to concern about use or lack of use of empathy.

Conclusions

Certainly, the SAOL experience suggests that service user engagement in social work education contributes to more meaningful connection between social worker and service users. It can contribute to critical consciousness raising for service user and social worker (Carlson et al., 2006). It also has the potential to elicit appropriate reflective and emotional responses from social work students which are ultimately essential to the development of good working relationships. Perhaps, given the way in which art can transcend barriers, as discussed in Bloomfield and Capous-Desyllas (2017), developing engagement with creative and visual arts in social work curricula can provide a useful platform to assist students to engage in developing their emotional and reflective capacities in meaningful and positive ways. Photovoice, which is compatible with the participatory methods familiar to social work research, may be one tool which can facilitate these developments.

Note

1 https://www.SAOLproject.ie/

Bibliography

Bloomfield, N., & Capous-Desyllas, M. (2017) Photovoice as a pedagogical tool: Exploring personal and professional values with female Muslim social work students in intercultural classroom setting, *Journal of Teaching in Social Work*, 37, pp. 493–512.

Byrne, C., & Dawnay, M. (2013) Hard life, in SAOL Project, *Scéals and anthems of outstanding lives*, SAOL Project, Dublin, p. 62.

Carlson, E., Engebretson, J., & Chamberlain, R. (2006) Photovoice as a social process of critical consciousness, *Qualitative Health Research*, 16, pp. 836–852.

Forrester, D., Kershaw, S., Moss, H., & Hughes, L. (2008) Communication skills in child protection: How do social workers talk to parents? *Child & Family Social Work*, 13, pp. 41–51.

Galvani, S., & Allnock, D. (2014) The nature and extent of substance use education in qualifying social work programmes in England, *Social Work Education*, 33, pp. 573–589.

Goossen, C., & Austin, M. (2017) Service users involvement in UK social service agencies and social work education, *Journal of Social Work Education*, 53, pp. 37–51.

Hatton, K. (2017) A critical examination of the knowledge contribution service users and carer involvement brings to social work education, *Social Work Education*, 36, pp. 154–171.

Health and care professions council, HPCS (2020) https://www.hcpc-uk.org/education/resources/education-standards/service-user-and-carer-involvement/

Loughran, H., & Broderick, G. (2017) From service-user to social work examiner: Not a bridge too far, *Social Work Education*, 36, pp. 188–202.

Ostaszewska, A. (2018) Social work and participatory methods of empowering – Photovoice, *Tiltal*, 2, pp. 75–83. ISSN:1392-3137, ISSN:2351-6569 Online.

SAOL Project (2016) *Object Poverty*. https://saolproject.ie/UNDayfortheEradicationofPoverty2016.php

Walton, P. (2012) Beyond talk and text: An expressive visual arts method for social work education. *Social Work Education*, 31(6), pp. 724–741, DOI: 10.1080/02615479.2012.695934.

25

SERVICE USER INVOLVEMENT IN NURSE EDUCATION

Laura Serrant, Gillian Janes and Opeyemi Odejimi

Introduction/setting the context

Nursing programmes must prepare graduates who can effectively engage in the delivery of high-quality healthcare within a complex context. Across the world, there is variation in the models used to ensure the quality and effectiveness of preparing student nurses for their role as a fully qualified professional. In the UK, nursing education and training programmes leading to initial Registered General Nurse (RGN) qualification, whether this leads to adult, mental health, child or learning disability nursing, can only be undertaken at approved Higher Educational institutions (HEIs), with clinical practice training based in registered health and social care settings. Programmes leading to qualification as a nurse in the UK usually take a minimum of three years full-time study, although flexible entry routes are available at some HEIs, which take into account previous related learning and experience. On qualification, graduating students are eligible for entry the Nursing and Midwifery Council (NMC) register – the professional body responsible for ensuring the professional standards for nurses and midwives in the UK.

All NMC-approved programmes have an equal split between practice and theory hours for students undertaking training for first registration, which means that half of the programme is based in clinical practice with direct contact with patients and families. Clinical practice reflects the broad scope of places where nursing care is provided, meaning students work with service users and their families in the home, community, hospitals and independent and voluntary sector organisations.

During the nurse education programme, students are exposed to a range of situations and learning opportunities to develop their ability to understand, promote and facilitate safe and effective patient care. Their training involves learning about the profession, the evidence base (research) underpinning nursing practice and healthcare and their own professional role as a nurse, including working with other health professionals as part of a multidisciplinary team.

Successful completion of the programme, resulting in the newly qualified nurse being accepted onto the NMC register of licenced practitioners, reflects that the nurse is deemed 'fit to practise' (www.nmc.org.uk). Fitness to practise is a universal recognition of the standards required by national nursing associations and regulatory bodies worldwide, irrespective of the pattern or length of training across different countries. Being fit to practise is testament to a nurses' ability to provide effective, safe and appropriate care for service users and in addition reflects that the nurse themselves is of good health and character to do their job safely and effectively.

The *Professional Standards of Practice and Behaviour for Nurses, Midwives and Nursing Associates*, known as 'The Code of Conduct' (or The Code), sets out the professional standards that nurses (as well as midwives and nursing associates) must uphold in order to be registered to practise in the UK. During their training, students too are expected to conduct themselves in line with the professional standards outlined in The Code.

If an allegation is made that a nurse is not meeting the standards for skills, education and behaviour as expected in The Code, investigations take place which could ultimately lead to removal from the NMC register either for a set period of time or permanently. Similar sanctions exist in regulatory bodies across the world. This is called being 'struck off'.

The above gives a brief summary of the requirements for qualification as a nurse in the UK (adult, child, mental health or learning disability speciality) and outlines the equal emphasis placed on theory and practice-based learning in clinical settings. This chapter will not focus specifically on student nurses' engagement with service users in clinical practice, as this is core to completion of all vocational programmes – it will focus on exploring the opportunities, challenges and considerations in engaging service users in the 'taught' or HEI-based elements of undergraduate, pre-registration nurse training. The UK is used as an exemplar of the opportunities and challenges of engaging service users in first level training of student nurses – many of these approaches are used elsewhere in the world, but the UK is identified here as involving service users at all stages of the student journey from application to qualification as a nurse.

Service user involvement in education – clarification of terms and purpose

The term 'service user' has become more widely used in everyday language, with varying scope of who is included or identified by the term. Most commonly it is used interchangeably with the term 'patient and public engagement' (PPE) and often combined to include 'carers'. It is therefore important to clarify how the term is used and understood within nurse education and training as discussed here. Service user, as used in this chapter, refers to individual(s) who use health or social care services; carers are defined as 'individuals who provide care for others on an unpaid basis' (Fallon et al., 2012, p. 128). Both groups can be involved in the education of health and social care professionals. In this chapter, therefore, the term service users will be used to incorporate other terminology (such as patients, PPE etc.) which in essence relates to those with whom nurses engage as users of health and care services and should be read to include carers also.

Recent years have seen radical changes in the way healthcare services policy and service delivery are undertaken. The term 'patient' no longer denotes a passive recipient of healthcare but rather a key influencer with an active role in healthcare systems (Liabo et al., 2018). As concepts such as patient empowerment and shared decision-making become more of a reality in health and care provision (Sacristan et al., 2016), traditional top-down approaches to professional service planning and care delivery are rendered outdated. This invariably requires a re-distribution of power from professionals to service users to ensure both have a voice in determining mutual benefits, but it also means that professionals must find new ways to interface with service users and communities (Bovaird, 2007). Thus, more collaborative processes involving engagement and co-production with service users are adopted and deemed more appropriate as part of negotiations between a number of interacting policy systems.

Service user involvement in health and social care education has therefore become a key imperative internationally, largely in response to increased public and political expectation that user voices are prominent in the ongoing design and monitoring of care services. Internationally there is wide variation and a paucity of information concerning the systematic inclusion of service users in first level education programmes in nursing, particularly across the whole of the student journey towards professional registration in the range seen in the UK.

The roots of service user involvement are often linked to reactions to highly publicised failures in the healthcare system, such as those highlighted in the 'Mid Staffs enquiry' (Francis, 2013). This inquiry stressed the failure of hospital service staff and systems to listen to the issues and concerns of patients, leading to systematic failure to address their needs, resulting in poor care. This report led to a range of policy and professional recommendations, including the need for more patient-centred approaches to service development and delivery (National Institute for Health Research, 2019); and recommendations about nurse education, training and professional conduct (www.nmc.org; Department of Health and Social Care, 2019).

Subsequently, moves to include service users in health and social care education within HEIs increased, driven and supported by key policies such as the National Health Service (NHS) Constitution and government strategy for the NHS (2019) and national nursing strategies such as *The Compassion in Practice Strategy* (Cummings and Bennett, 2012), which stress the principle of shared decision-making. This policy reflects evidence that service users are best placed to evaluate their experiences and support the preparation of health and social care professionals (Bennett and Baikie, 2003; Debyser et al., 2011, DeMarco, 2010) and recognises the value of involvement in service planning, delivery and quality of care identified by Fremont et al. (2001).

Such contextual changes mean that as service users and wider communities play a much greater role in shaping healthcare policy and treatment decisions, this has been mirrored in the development of educational programmes designed to prepare graduates with this broader understanding and the skills to deliver effective care in this context. An important benefit of service user involvement in nursing education and learning is in helping develop student thinking about nursing in this broader sense. Individuals and groups not traditionally associated with healthcare delivery help promote awareness in students of a more holistic approach to care delivery that is integrated with other aspects of the individual's life. Furthermore, in addition to developing competence in clinical and treatment-specific skills, new practitioners must understand the wider role of nursing as a profession in society along with their own influence and contribution to this. Service user involvement in nurse education and learning can help to enable this by providing a broader public perspective on nursing and nurses.

Service user involvement in education has taken many forms, ranging from consultation on proposed nursing programme design at one end of the continuum, to partnering in the recruitment of students an development and delivery of nursing curricula as core members of the delivery teams at the other. HEIs in the UK, in general, engage with service users for all nursing programmes and students irrespective of whether they will ultimately work in adult, mental health, learning disability or children's nursing specialities.

The remainder of this chapter will outline the nature of service user involvement in nurse education at three stages of the education process:

- Student recruitment
- Programme development
- Programme delivery and quality assurance

SU involvement in recruitment of students

Service user involvement in student education is not unique to nursing. Medicine and social work initially led the way regarding user involvement in practitioner education Rhodes (2012).

Policy recommendations in the UK (DoH, 1994) and internationally (Happell et al., 2011) regarding mental health nursing programmes in particular have since meant that engagement with service users in nurse education is most established in this field. More recently, however, this imperative has extended to embrace the wider remit of all pre-registration nursing programmes.

Service user involvement in student recruitment is perhaps one of the most innovative changes in nurse education in recent years. Most HEIs involve service users in the selection processes for applicants to their programmes. The nature of the involvement varies across HEIs; however, this can include:

- Developing interview questions
- Co-interviewing shortlisted applicants alongside academic and/or practice staff
- Participating in open days for students considering nursing as a career
- Forming part of interview panels or advisory panels for final selection of students

The imperative for SU involvement in recruitment processes within HEIs arises from the call for 'values-based' approaches to recruitment and selection of health and social care professionals (Groothuizen et al., 2018). Values-based recruitment is defined as a process wherein individuals are selected or recruited to a programme based on their ability to demonstrate the values required for the role (Miller, 2015).

Values-based recruitment was a direct outcome from the Francis report (Francis, 2013), which recommended that applicants wishing to enter an undergraduate healthcare degree programme, or a post within a healthcare profession, should be recruited using a process that assesses their values (Francis, 2013). This was identified as an action required to prevent recurrence of the failures highlighted in the Francis report. As a consequence, individuals applying for places on nursing programmes, or their first nursing posts, are now exposed to different recruitment and interview processes designed to explore their personal values aligned to the Code of Conduct and NHS Constitution as well as their academic abilities or relevant care experiences (Groothuizen et al., 2018; Miller, 2015).

In the recruitment process, service users are equal partners in the recruitment team alongside academics and clinical partners. Their inclusion is based on an 'expert by experience' approach, which values their input as equal to that of the clinicians or academics involved. 'Experts by experience' is more commonly related to inclusive research approaches based on what Gillard et al. (2012) and others defines as co-production. These approaches espouse that including service users (experts by experience) as equal partners in decision-making enhances research findings (Batalden et al., 2016). Similarly, the value added by service users to recruitment of aspiring nursing students through their differential experiences of healthcare is seen as useful for identifying how service users can impact the future nursing workforce at the point of entry to nursing education.

Service users involved in education are inducted into the recruitment process by the HEI. There is no standard approach to this, but in general the service user will be briefed on the process as a whole and receive in-house training or briefing on their specific role in this. Values-based recruitment involves using case studies or exemplar stories to encourage students to explore their perceptions and views about some of the complexities of healthcare experiences from the perspective of the patient or clinician. At interview, the ability of service users to present the stories 'in real time', engaging the applicant in discussion with non-academics' observations, often facilitates a deeper discussion and exploration of views than previously achieved through direct questioning by academics in traditional interview settings.

SU involvement in programme development

In light of the healthcare policy changes outlined previously, service user involvement in the development or co-design of nursing programmes has become more commonplace. Indeed, it is now mandated (Nursing and Midwifery Council, 2010).

For most universities, service users have become an integral part of programme validation panels that oversee the approval to provide nursing education at undergraduate and postgraduate levels. The role of service users on validation panels commonly involves ensuring the programme team has taken account of the patient and public perspectives in all aspects of a planned programme. This works to ensure consideration of the service user/public perspectives is embedded as an integral part of the formal review/validation process. As service users have become more involved in programme design and development as partners within programme teams, they have increasingly contributed to the presentation of programmes to university and/or professional statutory and regulatory body validation panels, as illustrated in the example outlined in Box 1. This is a valuable means of making visible and giving legitimate voice to the service user contribution to programme development and has become routine practice. More recently, the new quality assurance standards for first level training, *Quality Assurance Framework for Nursing, Midwifery and Nursing Associate Education* (NMC, 2019), makes service user representation and inclusion in programmes a mandatory part of the approvals process – including the use of service user representation on the NMC's validation panels.

Box 1 Service user co-design of a suite of master's programmes (Teesside University)

In the development of a new Master of Arts and associated programmes, the development team and steering group included service users and carers as programme team partners through membership of the Critical Friends Stakeholder Support Forum (CFSSF) alongside academic staff and representatives of NHS employers/healthcare provider organisations. Via this group, service users/carers contributed to the programme design – including the programme content, assessment strategy and evaluation processes. Their specific contribution focused on providing guidance on what, where and how the practicalities of service user/carer input to all aspects of the programme development, delivery and evaluation could most effectively be achieved. This was based on mutual recognition of the specific expertise and roles of academic, service provider and service user/carer team members. As core programme team members and key partners, service users/carers were part of the group who presented and secured University validation for the programme. They also participated as full partners in formative and summative student assessment panels, specifically contributing the service user/carer perspective to the development of students' practice-based service improvement projects, and the summative assessment and feedback process for students, alongside academic and service delivery colleagues. As an example of their contribution to the whole programme design and delivery cycle, service user/carer members of the CFSSF also participated in the programme evaluation and ongoing management and development of the programme. This included the design of a formal evaluation study (Watson and Janes, 2019).

As the range of service user contributions built into the design of nursing programmes continues to develop, they are increasingly involved in student assessment. This is most commonly formative assessment but increasingly involves summative assessment, in which service users contribute to students' final grades. This is often undertaken in partnership with academic and healthcare service delivery staff, as described in the example outlined in Box 1.

The contributions outlined in the example in Box 1 required service users to adopt a much broader approach than is commonly required in many nursing programmes. To do this, their contribution drew but was not specifically focused on their own healthcare condition, setting or story. As opportunities for service user contributions to nursing programmes become more varied, it is important that service users are made aware of the range of contributions available to them and the requirements associated with each according to the specific programme, student group or activity. This helps ensure the best match between how and what they want to contribute to nurse education and learning and programme/student need but also has implications for the 'selection' of service users for specific programmes or learning activities. For example, some service users want to share their story and experience of healthcare directly with students, whereas others prefer to make a broader contribution. This should be a joint decision between the service user and education provider/programme team and includes consideration of service user preference, past experience and availability balanced with the student learning/programme requirements. Importantly, universities are increasingly putting into place the relevant organisational infrastructure, including a dedicated service user co-ordinator role to support this process, ensuring the best use of resources and maximising outcomes for service users, students and academic staff alike.

Resources development

Service user involvement in learning resource development has a relatively long history in nurse education and learning. Firstly, reusable learning resources developed by or with them is a well-established strategy. The second approach, of developing service users themselves as learning resources, is more recent and has developed as the scope of their involvement in education and learning has expanded and their contribution has become more integrated into organisations and curricula. For example, developing their knowledge of the learning environment, key processes and relevant policy and procedures and the curriculums to which they contribute, through extended induction, for example, is increasingly the norm, in a similar way as occurs for new academic staff. Specific examples include recruitment and assessment policy and processes, basic principles of adult learning and management of the learning environment, although these will vary according to which aspects of the learning process each service user is involved in.

Enabling direct service user input to specific learning sessions within a complex timetable and with relatively limited service user resources remains challenging for many reasons. These include service user availability and organisations' operational business constraints. Re-usable learning resources developed with or by service users can help mitigate these, however, while supporting high quality learning based on service user experience. There are a wide variety of possible reusable learning resource formats. One of the most commonly used is service user informed scenario writing. The flexibility of this type of resource means it can be used for multiple learning purposes, including: case study based, clinical decision making or problem-based learning activities. Increasingly, with better usability and accessibility of technology enabling non-IT specialists to produce high quality audio-visual outputs, the range of re-usable learning resources produced by different stakeholders in the collective healthcare education endeavour has increased. For example, one NHS Trust worked with a service user and her family to produce a short film of their experiences. This was then made freely available to support wider learning. A further example is outlined in Box 2.

Box 2   Service user involvement in re-usable learning resource production (University of Central Lancashire)

A service user worked with the academic team to create a video of his journey to an outpatient appointment at the local hospital. The film starred and was narrated by the patient himself. It illustrated, in real time, the significant challenges he faced and ingenious ways in which he overcame these to enable attendance for treatment. In cataloguing a real experience, supportive factors and encounters the patient experienced along the way were also captured. This resource was then used during learning sessions to stimulate learning and student-led service improvement projects to address aspects of this service user's experience, as well as to facilitate wider student learning regarding others facing similar healthcare journeys. The film was funded by the University, supported by competitive development funding as part of a nationally funded healthcare education development initiative.

As these two examples illustrate, although such resources feature specific healthcare experiences, they can be used very effectively to stimulate learning and student exploration of patients' experiences and therapeutic contacts within a wider context. This can stimulate a more holistic, person–centred approach by students, helping them to develop a different perspective on service user behaviour as a result.

In practical terms, re-usable resources like these also help increase the accessibility of patient experiences for students. Not only can they be used with large numbers of students over time, but students can also access them after specific learning sessions, through a virtual learning environment. This can enable reinforcement of the learning or further exploration of the topic and issues raised by the learning activities at a convenient time for the student. This promotes a deep approach to learning and is particularly relevant for nursing students juggling the practice-based and academic requirements of a vocational education programme within a complex and changeable healthcare environment.

Nursing Research Education

Traditionally, nursing education and learning has focused on service users primarily as research participants (Sacristan et al., 2016). This resulted in an emphasis on developing students' capability regarding the theory and practice of research, research skills development and ethical involvement of service users as research participants. As the context of healthcare research changes, however, so too do nurse education and learning in this area.

The UK government has recognised the value of public engagement for research and society but also that while the UK has a rich history of engaging the public with research, challenges remain (Stern Review, 2016). These particularly concern embedding public engagement activities in routine research practice and education as well as enhancing the scope and quality of public engagement activities. Over a decade ago, the National Co-ordinating Centre for Public Engagement (NCCPE) was established as part of the Beacons for Public Engagement programme to create a culture in Higher Education in which public engagement was formalised and embedded as a valued and recognised activity for staff and students.

The Concordat for Engaging the Public with Research, developed by UK research funding bodies in 2010, has been a key driver for public engagement in research and students' learning about research. The 2010 Concordat's emphasis on the importance of integrating public engagement in research within Higher Education-based teaching and learning was further reinforced by the Teaching Excellence Framework (TEF). This requires universities to spell out how they support 'engaged learning', with many choosing to do this by outlining the opportunities they provide for students to engage in learning with communities from beyond the classroom.

Although a systematic review (Domecq et al., 2014) found that the evidence on the best way to achieve this was lacking, examples of how service users are increasingly being involved as research partners and their contributions to nurse education and learning on this topic are emerging.

Some nursing programmes involve service users as partners in supporting student research and dissertation projects by providing a patient perspective on these. Box 3 provides one example of how the learning experience of a PhD student in nursing involved working in partnership with a service user to design, implement and disseminate research. It illustrates a number of challenges associated with involving service users in student-led research. For example, the un-funded nature of student-led studies makes it unlikely that service user participation can be formally remunerated. In addition, teaching staff may need to use their professional networks to enable students to access and engage service users with the relevant experience and skills. This is only one of many ways, however, in which service users can contribute as partners rather than participants in students' research education. Service user colleagues can also support student access to other service user groups and networks in much the same way as professional and academic staff use their professional networks to support access and enable student-led research.

Box 3   Involving a service user as a research team member in nurse researcher training (University of Wolverhampton)

A healthcare student undertaking a PhD exploring the recovery experiences of people under 60 years of age with an isolated traumatic fracture of the hip (Janes, 2016; Janes et al., 2018) engaged a patient with the characteristics of the target participant group as a 'critical friend' to the study throughout the research process. This was a voluntary arrangement as the student had no funding to support the study. This service user provided a patient perspective on all aspects of the study design and documents, including the participant information sheet and interview guide. She also provided feedback on the initial findings and study report, which enhanced the outputs/subsequent dissemination. In particular, her input led to some minor but important changes to wording and language in the study documents and outputs, but also clearly validated the study itself, the means by which it was conducted and the subsequent findings.

In addition, service user and carer members of an NHS Trust Patient and Public Experience and Involvement (PPEI) group with relevant experience also provided feedback on the initial findings in terms of to what extent these reflected/resonated with their own experiences. This further validated the findings from what was a relatively small qualitative study of 30 in-depth story-telling interviews and its contribution to addressing the gap identified in the nursing and wider evidence base on this topic. It also resulted in apparently unprecedented feedback from the PPIE group to the student, via the Trust PPEI co-ordinator, regarding the very positive involvement they had experienced during this study.

The final study report also included a section on the practicalities, benefits and challenges of involving service users in this aspect of nursing education. This illustrates the importance the student and academic supervisors placed on the central role of service users and their perspective within the study.

These examples illustrate how the aim of the UK Concordat (RCUK, 2010), to support public engagement in research through appropriate training support and opportunities for healthcare staff as researchers, is being enacted in Higher Education teaching and learning practice.

The discussions so far have illustrated how service user engagement is of increasing strategic importance for Higher Education, strengthening its accountability and building trust in its relevance and responsiveness. The evaluation and quality assurance of nurse education and learning intertwines with programme design and the university/professional, statutory and regulatory body approval processes governing nursing programmes, as identified earlier. As service user involvement in nurse education and learning develops, the need and scope for evaluation of its effectiveness increases. The outline in Box 4 provides a brief summary example of how this may be achieved.

Box 4   Service user engagement in education research

An innovative master's programme in which service users took on a much broader role than other similar programmes was evaluated from a multi-stakeholder perspective. This was important, as engaging service users as core members of the programme team responsible for the initial development, delivery and ongoing management of the programme was unusual. It was also the first time this had been attempted within the context of delivering very applied, advanced education in a range of healthcare settings within a fiscally challenged Higher Education and rapidly changing healthcare environment.

Service user team members were study participants in this evaluation study along with students, academic staff and healthcare delivery representative programme team members.

A specific aim of the study was to explore the service user experience of this new initiative and identify their perspectives on the challenges, opportunities and benefits this new form of involvement had had. The purpose was to inform future local education provision, preparation of subsequent service user programme team members and, through dissemination of the findings, nurse education and learning more widely by adding to the evidence base regarding service user involvement in healthcare education.

The single programme/suite of programmes focus and relatively small scale of the study outlined in Box 4 is typical of the growing but limited body of evidence regarding service user involvement in general nurse education identified in the systematic review by Scammel et al. (2015). It is also one of even fewer examples of research exploring the impacts or value added in service user involvement in post-registration/postgraduate education programmes.

SU involvement in programme delivery

Happell et al. (2011) argue there are many benefits, including that service user participation can usefully challenge the traditional power base apparent in much health professional education, which tend to privilege clinical perspective over individual experience. The regulatory body for nursing in the UK (Nursing and Midwifery Council, 2010) demands that education providers also demonstrate how service users contribute to programme design and delivery.

Service user involvement in programme delivery is a relatively recent development, perhaps spanning the last two decades. There are three main approaches:

User-engaged: involves consultation with service users on the delivery of learning rather than supporting their direct involvement in the delivery.

User-involved: is the commonest form, in which the service user contributes alongside a tutor, facilitating and supporting learning activities. Increasingly, the term co-design or co-delivery of learning is used to reflect a more equal partnership between education staff and service users. This principle can be applied to single or groups of learning sessions or activities.

User-led: the service user facilitates the learning/session themselves as a member of the education team. This is less common, and tensions exist for some staff around this approach for example in the mutual recognition of the skills, contributions and roles of all parties in learning.

Regardless of the categories identified above, service user involvement in programme delivery is commonly based on two forms of contribution: their experiences of specific healthcare conditions or contexts and/or their broader experiences of healthcare systems and processes.

Service user experiences specific to particular healthcare conditions or contexts

This remains the most common means of service user participation in nurse education and learning. Here the focus is on providing a service user perspective on their experiences of receiving care or advocating for someone else and/or answering questions about their own experience of healthcare and/or illness (Horgan et al., 2018). This is often then used to stimulate student learning. While this type of service user contribution can be very effective, there can also be challenges; for example, it could lead to service user perceptions of being 'wheeled in and out to tell a story', even if this was not the intention or the actual situation. Furthermore, a focus on a specific disease or service could potentially reinforce a siloed approach to care, the predominance of one person's experience or students' lacking a broader awareness of associated care needs. In addition, it is possible that service users may not be made aware that students continue to reflect on and learn from a specific learning activity over subsequent weeks or months of their learning experience – leading to potential related interrogation of their personal experiences over time. Avoiding such risks requires that service users are well briefed and prepared in advance, in much the same way as when participating in student recruitment. This requires an understanding of the learning activity as a whole and their contribution to it. The service user themselves also needs to be willing and able to balance student learning needs with their own need to share specific experiences, and/or skilled facilitation by academic staff during and after the learning event.

General experiences of healthcare systems and processes

This more recent development is becoming more widespread. One example relates to the programme outlined in Box 1. In this context, service users provide a service user perspective on quality and safety issues, systems and processes outside their own disease or healthcare experience. In this instance, the service users were interested in improving the quality and safety of healthcare more generally as required to meet the broader student learning needs and aims of the programme. This wider perspective did not suit all service users, with some preferring to focus on supporting learning within their own disease area/service setting, for example. This broader role, however, was attractive to service users who had previous experience of contributing to nursing programmes, for example by telling their story, but who could also draw on other experiences. These could include experiences of healthcare or different healthcare settings, as well as previously developed skills in leading teams and change in their personal/professional lives – although the latter was not a specific requirement.

Expanding the involvement in programme delivery and management can also provide greater opportunities for involving service users in shared dissemination of their own learning from the process of their involvement in nurse education and learning. Examples include joint presentations at academic conferences and co-authorship of publications. Watson and Janes (2019), for example, found that service users in their study relished taking on this broader role in nurse education and learning and envisioned development of this to further enhance student learning, service user empowerment and their own satisfaction.

Challenges of SU involvement in HEI

Service user involvement is generally perceived as beneficial to education and learning and in research is often presented uncritically, with little attention to its negative or challenging aspects. Most of the reported challenges associated with involvement are related to its resourcing and logistics (Speed et al., 2012). The challenges of involvement affect all stakeholders and are often related to preparation, resource allocation, recruitment of service users, diversity of service user/carers, skills development, role clarity, service users'/carers' welfare and power imbalances. Nevertheless, it appears that service users/carers and academic staff are those mostly impacted with these reported challenges, perhaps because both academic staff and the service users/carers view themselves as having a duty to develop competent healthcare professionals.

In some literature, academic staff resistance to involvement is documented and attributed to the power shift to service users and carers (Felton and Stickley, 2004; Lathlean et al., 2006). Odejimi (2018) also noted that staff resistance occurs due to disagreement between staff and SU/carers during delivery involvement, SUs venting opinions in a non-constructive manner based on their previous negative illness or caring experience, as well as SU straying off originally planned tasks. A PhD study (Box 5) to explore the impact of involvement on adult nursing and social work pre-registration degrees uncovered the reasons behind academic staff resistance. It appears that academic staff believe they are the ones who will bear more of the consequences should any error occur with student education (Odejimi, 2018).

Recently, it appears there is less resistance by academic staff which may be attributed to growing knowledge about involvement and strong recommendation for co-production. Possibly all stakeholders, particularly staff and SU, are realising there is no power shift and, rather, that all parties need to work collaboratively. More so, there is documented evidence that academic staff acknowledge the beneficial impact of involvement in students' education (Gutteridge and Dobbins, 2010, Chambers and Hickey, 2012). Besides, there are emerging studies indicating that academic staff now recognise involvement has been beneficial to their professional role as well as their skills, attitude and behaviour (Odejimi et al., 2019).

The challenge around service user diversity is a recognised, ongoing concern. It is believed that SUs who engage in education and research should be varied in terms of illness, age, gender, ethnicities, religion, sexual orientation, and disabilities. Many suggestions have been made to help improve this situation, including strategic recruitment of SUs, the use of alternative reusable learning materials and partnering with community groups (Chambers and Hickey, 2012; Odejimi, 2018). It should be noted that having diverse SUs engaging in education and research is best practice and should be strongly encouraged. Nevertheless, it should also be acknowledged that involvement is beneficial with or without SU diversity. Moreover, no policy has indicated that service users involved in education and research must be diverse; there is rather emphasis that SUs are represented, their voices heard and recognised.

Other practical challenges associated with the successful delivery of involvement in nursing education and research concern controversies around payment and recognition of service users. These are sensitive issues for all parties because institutions want SUs to feel valued and empowered. In particular, SU recognition involves major dissonance. For instance, giving SUs the same rights as other employees means they may have access to students' personal and academic records, commercially sensitive university information and staff records. At the same time, not having' staff permissions may make things like access to buildings, support prior to and after delivering a session and claiming expenses difficult. INVOLVE (2019) recommends averting this potential problem by having a clear co-designed payment and recognition policy to which the SU agrees prior to commencing involvement.

Box 5 A study to evaluate the perceived impact of service users' and carers' involvement in Higher Education institutions (University of Wolverhampton)

A PhD research study (Odejimi, 2018) was carried out to evaluate the perceived impact of service users' and carers' involvement from a multi-stakeholder perspective. In this study, the views of the three main stakeholders within Higher Education institutions (HEIs) were explored, that is, staff, students and service users/carers. The student and academic staff participants were from the adult nursing and social work degree.

Involvement was reported to occur in almost all educational activities, such as teaching, student recruitment, developing learning materials, module/curriculum development and student assessment. However, teaching and student recruitment were the most common educational activities with involvement.

It was generally indicated that service user and carer involvement is beneficial to all three main stakeholders. The study also reported challenges and recommendations to improve and sustain involvement of HEIs.

Concluding comments

This chapter has outlined the many ways in which SU involvement makes a positive and unique contribution to nursing education and research. This is evident in the manner the nursing degree has evolved in the last few decades. Hopefully, as a result of the interventions to include service users at all stages of the student experience, tomorrow's nurses will be more rounded professionals that deliver excellent care and services which take into consideration SU and their carers' perspectives. However, for involvement to be effective, co-production between all stakeholders is needed to facilitate equal partnership and beneficial outcomes for all stakeholders.

References

Batalden, M., Batalden, P., Margolis, P., Seid, M., Armstrong, G., Opipari-Arrigan, L., & Hartung, H. (2016). Coproduction of healthcare service. *BMJ Quality & Safety*, 25(7), 509–517.

Bennett, L., & Baikie, K. (2003). The client as educator: learning about mental illness through the eyes of the expert. *Nurse Education Today*, 23(2), 104–111.

Bovaird, T. (2007). Beyond engagement and participation: user and community coproduction of public services. *Public Administration Review*, September/October, 846–860.

Chambers, M., & Hickey, G. (2012). *Service user involvement in the design and delivery of education and training programmes leading to registration with the Health Professions Council*. London: Faculty of Health and Social care science, Kingston University and St. Georges University.

Cummings, J., & Bennett, V. (2012). *Compassion in practice: nursing, midwifery and care staff: Our vision and strategy*. London: NHS Commissioning Board.

Debyser, B., Grypdonck, M., Defloor, T., & Verhaeghe, S. (2011). Involvement of inpatient mental health clients in the practical training and assessment of mental health nursing students: can it benefit clients and students? *Nurse Education Today*, 31, 198–203.

DeMarco, R. (2010). Palliative care and African women living with HIV. *Journal of Nurse Education*, 49, 462–465.

Department of Health (1994). *Working in partnership: a collaborative approach to care. The report of the mental health nursing review*. London: HMSO.

Department of Health and Social Care (2019). *The NHS long term plan*. London: Crown. Available at: www.longtermplan.nhs.uk

Domecq, J.P., Prutsky, G., Elraiyah, T., Wang, Z., Nabhan, M., Shippee, N., Brito, J.P., Boehmer, K., Hasan, R., Firwana, B., Erwin, P., Eton, D., Sloan, J., Montori, V., Asi, N., Abu Dabrh, A.M., & Murad, M.H. (2014). Patient engagement in research: a systematic review. *BMC Health Services Research*, 14, 89. Available at: www.biomedcentral.com/1472-6963/14/89

Fallon, D., Warne, T., McAndrew, S., & McLaughlin, H. (2012). An adult education: learning and understanding what young service users and carers really, really want in terms of their mental well being. *Nurse Education Today*, 32, 128–132.

Felton, A., & Stickley, T. (2004). Pedagogy, power and service user involvement. *Journal of Psychiatric and Mental Health Nursing*, 11(1), 89–98.

Francis, R. (2013). *Report of the mid Staffordshire NHS foundation trust public inquiry*. London: The Stationery Office.

Fremont, A.M., Cleary, P.D., Hargraves, J.L., Rowe, R.M., Jacobson, N.B., & Ayanian, J.Z. (2001). Patient-centred processes of care and long-term outcomes of myocardial infarction. *Journal of General Internal Medicine*, 16, 800–808.

Gillard, S., Simons, L., Turner, K., Lucock, M., & Edwards, C. (2012). Patient and public involvement in the coproduction of knowledge. *Qualitative Health Research*, 22, 1126–1137. doi:10.1177/1049732312448541

Groothuizen, J.E., Callwood, A., & Gallagher, A. (2018). What is the value of values based recruitment for nurse education programmes? *Journal of Advanced Nursing*, 74(5), 1068–1077.

Gutteridge, R., & Dobbins, K. (2010). Service user and carer involvement in learning and teaching: a faculty of health staff perspective. *Nurse Education Today*, 30(2010), 509–514.

Happell, B., Moxham, L., & Platania-Phung, C. (2011). The impact of mental health nursing education on undergraduate nursing students' attitudes to consumer participation. *Issues in Mental Health Nursing*, 32, 108–113.

Horgan, A., Manning, F., Bocking, J., Happell, B., Lahti, M., Doody, R., & O'Donovan, M. (2018). 'To be treated as a human': using co-production to explore experts by experience involvement in mental health nursing education – The COMMUNE project. *International Journal of Mental Health Nursing*, 27(4), 1282–1291.

INVOLVE (2019). *Good practice for payment and recognition – Things to consider*. INVOLVE. Available at: www.invo.org.uk/good-practice-for-payment-and-recognition-things-to-consider/ [Accessed 13 May 2019].

Janes, G. (2016). Silent slips, trips and broken hips: the recover experiences of young adults following an isolated fracture of the proximal femur. PhD Thesis. University of Wolverhampton.

Janes, G., Serrant, L., & Sque, M. (2018). Fragility fracture in the under 60s: a qualitative study of recovery experiences and the implications for nursing. *Journal of Orthopaedic and Trauma Nursing*, 2(1).

Lathlean, J., Burgess, A., Coldham, T., Gibson, C., Herbert, L., Levett-Jones, T., Simons, L., & Tee, S. (2006). Experiences of service user and carer participation in health care education. *Nurse Education in Practice*, 6(6), 424–429.

Liabo, K., Boddy, K., Burchmore, H., Cockroft, E., & Britten, N. (2018). Clarifying the roles of patients in research. *BMJ*, 361, k1463. doi: 10.1136/bmj.k1463

Miller, S.L. (2015). Values-based recruitment in health care. *Nursing Standard*, 29(21), 37.

National Institute for Health Research (2019). *Patient and public involvement and engagement plan (2019–20)*. Twickenham: NIHR.

NHS England (2019). *The NHS long term plan*. London: Crown.

Nursing and Midwifery Council (2010). *Standards for pre-registration education*. London: Nursing and Midwifery Council.

Nursing and Midwifery Council (2019). *Quality assurance framework for nursing, midwifery and nursing associate education*. London: NMC, May.

Odejimi, O. (2018). An exploratory, descriptive mixed method study of active service users and carers involvement in adult nursing and social work students' pre-registration education. PhD Thesis. University of Wolverhampton.

Odejimi, O., Lang, L., Serrant, L., & Tadros, G. (2019). Perceived impact of service users and carers involvement in higher education on academic staff. *Nursing Education in Practice*. (in press).

Research Councils UK (2010). *Concordat for engaging the public with research*. Research Councils UK. Available at: www.ukri.org/files/legacy/scisoc/concordatforengagingthepublicwithresearch-pdf/ [Accessed June 2019].

Rhodes, C.A. (2012). User involvement in health and social care education: a concept analysis. *Nurse Education Today*, 32(2), 185–189.

Sacristan, J.A., Aguaron, A., Avendano-Sola, C., Garrido, P., Carrion, J., Gutierrez, A., Kroes, R., & Flores, A. (2016). Patient involvement in clinical research: why, when, and how. *Patient Preference and Adherence*, 10, 631–640.

Scammel, J., Heaslip, V., & Crowley, E. (2015). Service user involvement in pre-registration general nurse education: a systematic review. *Journal of Clinical Nursing*, 25, 53–69.

Speed, S., Griffiths, J., Horne, M., & Keeley, P. (2012). Pitfalls, perils and payments: service user, carers and teaching staff perceptions of the barriers to involvement in nursing education. *Nurse Education Today*, 32(7), 829–834.

Stern Review (2016). *Building on success and learning from experience: an independent review of the research excellence framework*. London: Crown.

Watson, P., & Janes, G. (2019). *The MA advancing quality, safety and governance in health and social care and constituent programmes: a multi-stakeholder perspective impact evaluation*. Middlesbrough: Teesside University.

26

THE POTENTIAL FOR INTERPROFESSIONAL EDUCATION

Elizabeth Anderson, Jenny Ford and Emma Smith

In this chapter, we will explore the central role of patients/service users and carers in interprofessional education (IPE). We base our chapter on experiences of delivering health and social care education in the UK. We recognise that social, economic and political context vary greatly between countries and therefore not all of our recommendations will be applicable elsewhere. Both IPE and service user involvement in health and social care education are innovative and push against traditional boundaries. These maybe more difficult to implement in countries where professions have more hierarchical paternalistic views. However, there is international impetus towards including patients in health and social care professional education.

The overarching purpose of IPE is for students from different professions to learn together in an interactive way, for the improvement of care and care delivery services. The UK Centre for the Advancement of IPE (CAIPE), which promotes effective IPE, places patients at the centre of their values and aims underlining the critical importance of their involvement.

We will share our experiences of working with patients and carers in the design and delivery of IPE, a central theme for the chapter. We will draw on over twenty years of our own experiences of delivering the "Leicester Model" of practice-based IPE. We will share the need for more rigorous understandings of what it means to place patients within faculty activity systems, considering patients not just as story tellers but also in leading teaching roles.

We will outline some of the barriers relating to faculty structure and consider the potential for patients to have active roles across healthcare faculty. We will also outline the stable place of patient experience at a time of greater complexity and uncertainly about future healthcare delivery structures. "Future proofing" may bring about robotics, new professional roles and patient interactions with artificial intelligence. However, this new era for interprofessional working must place still the patient experience at the centre.

Introduction

Interprofessional education (IPE) brings learners from different professions together to construct new learning collectively by sharing their uni-professional knowledge. The current internationally accepted definitions of IPE state that the sole purpose of the approach is to advance the quality of care that patients/service users[1] receive:

Occasions when two or more professions learn from and about each other to improve collaboration and the quality of care.

(UK Centre for the Advancement of IPE (CAIPE), revised, Barr, 2002, p, 6)

Interprofessional education occurs when students from two or more professions learn about, from and with each other to enable effective collaboration and improve health outcomes.

(World Health Organisation, 2010, p. 7)

IPE is an approach to professional education aimed at breaking down barriers between professions to improve collaboration and the quality of care. Regulators across the world now recognise and require this approach (Interprofessional Education Collaborative Expert Panel, 2011; The International Curriculum Renewal Forum, 2013; General Medical Council, 2011; Health and Care Professions Council, 2014; Nursing and Midwifery Council, 2010). Consequently, many pre-registration health and social care students in the UK and elsewhere now have interactive opportunities to learn inter-professionally. The UK Centre for the Advancement of IPE (CAIPE) remains a leader in this international movement and has helped to define and develop the principles and standards underpinning IPE (Barr et al., 2017). In 2010, the World Health Organisation (WHO) published aspirations for IPE and listed the main regional networks promoting IPE (WHO, 2010). There is an extensive body of work, such as the seminal 2005 text by Freeth and colleagues on the constituents of effective IPE (Freeth et al., 2005). Whether in the classroom or in practice, IPE enables students to consider together how the care each profession offers can align with others to provide optimal support for patients and carers.

In 2002, Barr introduced the term "collaborative competencies" to describe the knowledge, skills and attitudes needed for effective interprofessional practice. Today it is internationally accepted that IPE is designed to achieve collaborative competencies around the following themes: teamwork, roles and responsibilities of different practitioners, communication, reflection and, most importantly, the patient and ethics (Thistlethwaite and Moran, 2010). Specifically, six aspects of interprofessional practice place the patient firmly in the centre of any practitioner team. In this way, the views and perspectives of the patient, their carers and their families are heard, clarified and understood and ultimately translated into shared decision making (Box 1). The voices of patients/carers and family are therefore essential to ensure education is designed to achieve these outcomes.

Historically, patient involvement has sometimes focused paternalistically on the needs of the profession, whereas in an interprofessional setting the patient is placed at the centre, re-balancing the relationship in keeping with the principles of IPE (Spencer et al., 2011; Francis, 2013; Towle et al., 2016). Patients have been involved in uni-professional education for some time; however, the nature of this involvement has varied. Although some involvement has been long-standing in medicine, patients have often been perceived as illustrations of conditions with little or no power or status. Educational partnership with patients and carers has mainly evolved in the UK in social work and mental health nursing; aiming to bridge the gap between theory and practice and to make the felt experience of the patient a reality for the student. However, patient and carer involvement delivered uni-professionally tends to focus on profession-specific interactions and delivery of care. In an interprofessional learning environment, students can learn holistically from patients and carers as they have a unique ability to observe the whole interprofessional team along their patient journey.

Box 1   Learning outcomes for IPE relating to the patient

- The patient's central role in interprofessional care (patient-focused or centred care)
- Understanding of the service user's perspective (and family/carers)
- Working together and cooperatively in the best interests of the patient
- Patient safety issues
- Recognition of patient's needs/perspective
- The patient as partner within the team

In many countries, professional bodies require the involvement of patients in the education of health and social care professionals to enhance understandings of patient perspectives and to develop compassionate values in future practitioners (Australian Commission, 2012; Health Canada, 2007; Department of Health UK, 2010; National Health Service, 2014; General Medical Council, 2011; Nursing and Midwifery Council, 2010; Health and Care Professions Council, 2017). Following growth in understanding and propelled by regulation, universities delivering health and social care training have iteratively developed strategic approaches to build supportive communities, bringing together patients, carers and faculty members. A well-planned strategy involves patients and carers at all levels, from curriculum design through teaching and assessment to quality assurance. This is true in the UK and elsewhere, and there are global calls for such approaches (Towle et al., 2016). Partnership arrangements require faculty support and resources (Spencer et al., 2011).

Designing effective involvement for interprofessional education

Patients in the interprofessional environment in higher education – UK perspective

Developing IPE requires different professional schools to work together; this may involve relationships within and between universities. In this section, we will describe some of the enablers and barriers. The infrastructure must take account of the variations between the activity systems (AS) in the different professional schools. These systems must be aligned to create an AS for IPE (Anderson and Smith, 2010). In our experience, involvement of patients adds further complexity to the AS by integrating systems for supporting patients into the IPE system (Anderson et al., 2018). In Figure 26.1, the integration of patients into the IPE AS is outlined. The "subject" of the AS is the IPE involving patients and the "outcome" is the learning achieved through this educational process. The "community" comprises patients, students and faculty of each participating school from one or more HEI (Anderson et al., 2014). The "rules" which govern the AS consist of quality assurance processes, for example, cyclical gathering of evaluation data reported to partnership steering groups with faculty members and patients. All processes should be underpinned by ethical principles. The "tools" will include teaching design and delivery informed by patient participation and the processes for the employment of patients. Finally, the "division of labour" describes the contributions of educators, administrators and patients who participate in the education in various ways.

When patients are involved in IPE, they may have to navigate processes which vary between the different schools and potentially between different HEIs. This means educators and administrators

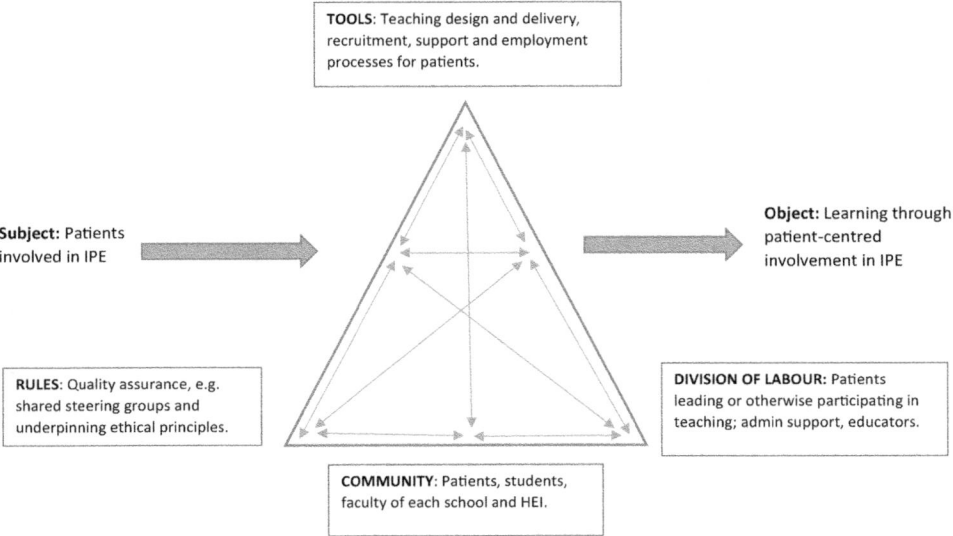

Figure 26.1 Integrated activity system for patient involvement in IPE

must provide information and support to enable possibly vulnerable people to feel confident in their place within the educational infrastructure. Variations in systems for payment, recruitment, quality assurance etc. can prevent people from participating and can lead to dissent and conflict. The IPE community must be mindful of this at an organisational, strategic and operational level.

Box 2   A patient's perspective of what it feels like to work in these HEI activity systems

Involvement depends upon effective communication. I work with two universities whose communication mechanisms are different. Patients often gravitate to work with different uni-professional students because of the value of their stories for different professions. For example, some people have more involvement in their lives with social work, others nursing and others medicine and hence teach with these students. Sometimes moving between these schools, say from medicine to social work, results in us comparing and contrasting our HEI experiences. It can feel very different in how HEIs receive and work with us.

HEIs often have designated administrators to liaise with us and inform us of what is happening, and if these change and there is inconsistency, then patients can fall through the communication gap. A personal touch for me and a sense of joining a family has been achieved by one HEI more than another – some of this is about consistency of staff, as it can be harder to form relationships when faculty change.

Many times HEIs forget that we are not in the normal communication loops of full-time and part-time academic staff. We need regular and constant contact to build working relationships. How we are welcomed and received influences how valued we feel and how enthusiastic we are

---

to work with the schools. Schools differ and vary, and in IPE we need clarity about who leads and coordinates our involvement.

On a positive note, both of the HEIs I work with involve us in preparation training events and ensure we are aware of how we can work (our role) with the faculty members.

How patients might become involved in IPE

Patient-centred IPE takes place in the current health and social care context, which is challenging. Table 26.1 outlines some current challenges facing future professionals internationally which have to be taken into account when designing professional education. The challenges relate to:

- Demographic population shift with a rise in the number of older people living longer and more people living with complex long-term conditions

Table 26.1 Examples of patient involvement in interprofessional education

Learning outcomes	*Patient involvement*
• The patient's central role in interprofessional care (patient-focused or centred care) • Understanding of the service user's perspective (and family/carers) • Working together cooperatively in the best interests of the patient • Patient safety issues • Recognition of patient's needs/perspective • Patient as partner within the team	***Involvement in faculty steering groups*** • Please see the Leicester Model below for details ***Involvement in providing case studies*** • Patients joining faculty writing groups to shape content (Kilminster and Fielden, 2009) ***Classroom small group conversations on the following*** • What matters to patients in their communications with members of the healthcare team (Anderson et al., 2011) • Shared experiences of positive and negative examples of care • Sharing their patient journeys • Understanding what listening means to patients (Anderson et al., 2011) • Carers' perspectives on the challenges they face in supporting people living with long-term conditions (Anderson et al., 2010) • Teaching students skills for how to communicate with people who have different needs ***Simulated activities*** • Patients can be simulators playing their own experiences or those of others and help to write scenarios (Kilminster and Fielden, 2009) ***Practice-based IPE*** • See the Leicester Model below ***Using technology for e-communication on patient shared decision making*** • Patients Know Best (the website – has been adapted for teaching www.patientsknowbest.com/). ***Involvement in assessment*** Work in open forums to design relevant assessment tools (Soklaridis et al., 2017; Dearnley et al., 2011)

Learning outcomes	*Patient involvement*

Examples of resources, including digital stories and films, which can be used in any classroom setting at HEIs or in practice so that patient voices can be heard for deeper understandings and reflection
- Patient Voices resources www.patientvoices.org.uk
- Open educational resources TIGER – has patient films taken from actual patient journeys (see Mr King; Mr Kirby; Mildred) http://tiger.library.dmu.ac.uk
- Care Opinion – patients sharing their stories and experiences of healthcare directly to the clinical team www.careopinion.org.uk/

- Changes in service delivery models towards, for example, integrated care and more community care
- Global shortages of professions such as medicine and nursing, leading to changing professional roles and boundaries
- Technological advances
- Patients viewed as equal partners in shared decision making and pivotal to improving the quality of care delivery

We began with sharing the overarching learning outcomes for IPE (Box 1); patient involvement is fundamental to their achievement. We now describe and share some examples of patient-centred IPE designed to deliver these learning outcomes and address these health and social care challenges.

Patient involvement in the Leicester Model of interprofessional education

This well-established teaching Model in the UK was set up as a partnership between university, practice, students and patients (Anderson et al., 2016). The original design came from focus groups involving students from two HEIs. Patients were then central to the iterative development of the Model, having been consulted at the outset before going on to become active steering group members. Patients designed variations on the original Model which have been delivered in different settings. Our approach to involving patients in refining and extending the Model used the principles of Participatory Action Research (PAR) (Lewin, 1946; Kuper et al., 2008). This meant listening to the experiences, meanings and realities of patients as well as other stakeholders to guide the educational design (Anderson et al., 2011).

The Model consists of four learning steps following the stages of the Kolb learning cycle (Kolb, 1984). Based in real-life practice settings, small interprofessional student groups meet patient(s) who have complex needs, sometimes with family, and receive input from several services. The IP groups analyse the patient experiences and their understandings of the patients' needs and how they are being addressed by those who care for them. The patient perspective forms the platform and is central to the learning. The IP student teams also meet the practitioners who support and deliver care to the patient. The student teams combine their IP perspectives with what they have heard from practitioners and the patient to develop a care plan. The outcomes are fed back to the practitioners and often bring new insights and enhance care. Students can spend more time with the patients than busy practitioners and often highlight concerns which had not been recognised by the practice team. These insights are achieved as students from different professions combine their expertise.

In some iterations, students report their learning to patients and receive feedback from them, for example, in the Listening Workshop. In this version of the Model, the IP student groups meet two patients who share their experiences of IP care and IP communication along their care pathways. The students are tasked with analysing the quality of care from the patient's perspective in order to reflect on how to improve their own practice when in an IP setting. In the Listening Workshop, as well as sharing their stories, patients have the opportunity to take on leading teaching roles ("Co-Tutor") and to support other patients who contribute ("Mentor"). These two roles, "Co-Tutor" and "Mentor", were designed through a PAR process as described above and have now been embedded in delivery of this workshop across two HEIs (Anderson et al., 2018).

Patients perceptions of involvement in the Listening Workshop

Being part of something from the very beginning was amazing. I first came and shadowed a Listening Workshop and straight away I felt I wanted to get involved. I wanted to see something positive come out of my experiences following my accident. Because my recovery was all about teamwork, I was so very excited that this was an IPE event to promote better team working and collaboration of care. I wanted to advance holistic person-centred care. This gave me a chance to share personally my story – tell it as it was and help students know and feel what had happened to me (emotions). Hearing me telling this story is so very different from reading about accident recovery in a book.

The workshop enables conversations with interprofessional groups of students and the combination of student professions might be different every time. So I have found that the way I tell my story changes according to which students are present. For example, midwifery students were not involved in my care but if they are present, I try and inspire them to think about what patients experience, the core skills they will utilise. Also, I feel sometimes my input varies according to the student personalities, their active listening skills and what they feel about their future professional roles, e.g. hierarchy.

Being involved over twelve years has increased my confidence and inspired me to take on a leading teaching role. I joined a training session a few years ago to learn more about what it means to teach, and ever since I have felt more involved as I became a "Co-Tutor". I have learnt from other patient Co-Tutors and they have inspired me. This workshop has developed a wonderful community of people and that has been important. I have been involved for so long that often academic tutors come along to teach with me and although I am the Co-Tutor, I may appear to know more about how to run the session than they do.

When I am telling my story (not as a Co-Tutor), I enjoy the feedback session. The student presentations at the end of the workshop have been wonderful as I often don't realise how much they have learnt from my story. But being part of this helps me see what they have gained from listening to me. I have seen students after the event in passing who remember me and tell me they have tried to implement what I told them.

As a patient, I give feedback to the students as the workshop ends. In this way, I can help the students to reflect on any communication errors they may have made when talking to me. This is often about how they present themselves and failure to actively listen to me. On the whole, they are often very commendable.

Co-working, in the design of the Leicester Model, which brings patients into HEIs, is based on agreed values and goals for partnership working. These cluster around the following themes: good communication; being open and honest; maintaining trust; consent; confidentiality; respect as colleagues; inclusiveness and accountability:

1   **Trust:** Working to make sure that patients involved in teaching are treated fairly and equally. Being mindful of the emotional vulnerability that patients and carers may encounter when sharing personal experiences.
2   **Consent:** A two-way consent process for all involvement which is aligned to the agreed values and assured through support for participants. Participants must be able to withdraw at any point in the process. Adherence to data protection regulation and consent where appropriate to access sensitive personal information, including clinical records.
3   **Confidentiality:** Patients who share their stories and who lead teaching need to be confident about the security of the information they share. Students are reminded of their professional responsibilities regarding the security of information and ethical principles concerning anonymous reporting.
4   **Respect and value as colleagues:** Patients and carers personally agree the terms for their involvement and are rewarded financially. Throughout their involvement their views are listened to and acted on. Suitable times and places are negotiated for their engagement. Support is provided at all stages and respect is shown by little things such as refreshments, courtesy and a welcoming atmosphere.
5   **Accessibility and inclusiveness:** All organisations involved in teaching comply with relevant policies and legislation, ensuring that no one is disadvantaged and all can access these opportunities.
6   **Accountability:** There are processes for ensuring safety and safeguarding and recording incidents or concerns identified by students, facilitators, clinicians or patients.

Reflections on patient involvement in IPE today

We have found remarkably little published work on patient involvement in IPE despite the central role of the patient in the accepted definitions of IPE (Barr, 2002; WHO, 2010). Truly participatory patient involvement in uni-professional education is uneven across different professions, with social work and mental health nursing taking the lead (Warne and McAndrew, 2005; Cairney et al., 2006). Medicine is progressing with many asking serious questions about what it means to have patients as equals in educational roles alongside practitioners and academics (Spencer et al., 2011). In a recent international meeting of health and social care education leaders, there were renewed calls for greater involvement in uni-professional education (Towle et al., 2016); however, little of this discussion focused on IPE.

As outlined earlier, health and social care in the twenty-first century faces many challenges across the globe. Common to all countries is the need to develop and retain an appropriately skilled workforce to meet population needs (WHO, 2016). We have identified three main challenges relating to IPE:

1   The push to re-balance the relationship between the patient and the clinical team so that patients become active partners in their care.
2   The redesign of the workforce and models of care delivery to meet the needs of the ageing population and those living with multiple co-morbidities.
3   Recognition of the central role of patients in ensuring that care is safe (Berwick, 2013; Loeffler et al., 2013).

Ladder of service user involvement in Interprofessional Education (adapted from Tew, Gell & Foster, 2004)	
LEVEL 5 *Partnership*	Patients as faculty members with a designated role to support IPE alongside academic staff. Partnership working is integral to the department values statement. Patients with secure contracts.
LEVEL 4 *Collaboration*	Patients as full departmental members involved in Level 3+ major aspects of faculty work for IPE. The department has a statement of values. Employment support given.
LEVEL 3 *Growing involvement*	Patients involved in TWO of the following for IPE: teaching design and delivery, assessment and evaluation. Payment at normal visiting lecturer rates. Training and support offered.
LEVEL 2 *Limited involvement*	Service users "tell their stories" to IPE student groups. No opportunity to shape the course. Payment offered.
LEVEL 1 *No involvement*	IPE curriculum planned, delivered and managed with no patient involvement.

Figure 26.2   The Ladder of Involvement in IPE

Source: Adapted from Tew et al., 2004

IPE with participatory patient involvement is the ideal approach. By bringing all students from different professions together to learn with and from patients, collective solutions can be developed and cascaded.

The Ladder of Citizen Participation offers a framework for evaluating the level at which the public are involved in any context (Arnstein, 1969). This has been adapted for use in health and social care, termed the Ladder of Involvement (Figure 26.2; Tew et al., 2004). At the lowest level, there is no involvement; at the intermediate levels, patients have specific roles but are not full faculty members. The top level places patients alongside faculty members as equal partners in all aspects of the design and delivery of IPE. We recommend its use to guide faculties in progressing patient-centred IPE (Figure 26.1).

Conclusion

IPE remains complex, challenging and fragile as it seeks to bring together professions which are managed, regulated and resourced uni-professionally. Future challenges include:

1   Establishing true partnerships between the interprofessional community of educators and the patients who work with them.
2   Developing strategic leadership to build and embed support and organisational processes to withstand the challenges of curriculum renewal.
3   Achieving successful transition from small pilots to delivery to whole cohorts of students.

There is emerging evidence that IPE involving patients can make a difference to patient outcomes (Anderson and Thorpe, 2014; Reeves et al., 2016). Our work in involving patients within IPE has led to a community of patients who are fully committed and inspired by IPE. Student evaluations continue to provide evidence of "light bulb moments" as a result of this learning, which bodes well for future practice. The quotes below demonstrate this emerging evidence regarding IPE involving patients and student evaluations:

> Gaining an insight into the service users' perspective – listening to their experiences and analysing this to identify how it can improve my individual practice.
>
> *(social work student)*

> The importance of communication within the multi-disciplinary team, as well as between the health care professionals and the service users became very apparent.
>
> *(midwifery student; Anderson et al., 2011, p. 49)*

> As a medical student, I found it was very very useful as I am now able to improve my communication and listening skills.
>
> *(student focus group, Anderson et al., 2018, p. 220)*

Note

1 Throughout this chapter we have mainly used the term "patient", mindful that there are several terms, such as "service user", which can be used for people who receive health and social care services.

References

Anderson, ES, Ford, J, Thorpe, LN (2011). Learning to listen: improving students communication with disabled people. *Medical Teacher*, 32, 1–9. http://dx.doi.org/10.3109/0142159X.2010.498491

Anderson, ES, Ford, J, Thorpe, LN (2018). Perspectives on patients on leading teaching roles a phenomenological study. *Journal of Interprofessional Care*. Accepted October 2018. doi:10.1080/13561820.2018.1531834

Anderson, ES, Hean, S, O'Halloran, C, Pitt, R, Hammick, M (2014). Faculty development and interprofessional education and practice. In Steinert, Y (Ed.), *Faculty development in the health professions: a focus on research and practice*. New York: Springer, Chapter 14, 287–310.

Anderson, ES, Kinnair, D, Ford, J (2016). Interprofessional education and practice guide no. 6: developing practice-based interprofessional learning using a short placement model. *Journal of Interprofessional Care*, 30(4), 433–440. www.tandfonline.com/doi/full/10.3109/13561820.2016.1160040

Anderson, ES, Smith, R (2010). Learning from lives together: lessons from a joint learning experience for medical and social work students. *Health and Social Care in the Community*, 18(3), 229–240. doi:10.1111/j.1365–2524.2010.00921.x

Anderson, ES, Thorpe, LN (2014). Students improve patient care and prepare for professional practice: an interprofessional community-based study. *Medical Teacher*, 36, 495–504. http://dx.doi.org/10.3109/0142159X.2014.890703

Arnstein, SR (1969). A ladder of citizen participation. *Journal of American Institute of Planners*, 35(4), 216–224.

Australian Commission (2012). *National safety and quality health service standards*. Sydney: Australian Commission on Safety and Quality Health Care. www.safetyandquality.gov.au/wp-content/uploads/2011/09/NSQHS-Standards-Sept-2012.pdf

Barr, H (2002). *Interprofessional education: today, yesterday and tomorrow*. London: Learning and Teaching Support Network: Centre for Health Sciences and Practice.

Barr, H, Ford, J, Gray, R, Helme, M, Hutchings, M, Low, H, Machin, A, and Reeves, S (2017). Interprofessional Education Guide. CAIPE. https://www.caipe.org/resources/caipe-publications [Accessed 28 April 2020].

Berwick, D (2013). *A promise to learn – a commitment to act: improving the safety of patients in England*. London, UK: The Stationery Office.

Cairney, J, Chettle, K, Clark, H, Davis, A, Gosling, J, Harvey, R, Jephcote, S, Labana, L, Lymberya, M, Pendred, B, Russell, L (2006). Editorial – involvement of service users in social work education. *Social Work Education*, 25(4), 315–318.

Dearnley, C, Coulby, C, Rhodes, C, Taylor, J, Coates, C (2011). Service users and carers: preparing to be involved in work-based practice assessment. *Innovations in Education and Teaching International*, 48(2), 213–222.

Francis, R (2013). *Report of the mid Staffordshire NHS foundation trust public inquiry*. London: The Stationery Office.

Freeth, D, Hammick, M, Reeves, S, Koppel, I, Barr, H (2005). *Effective interprofessional education: development, delivery and evaluation*. Oxford: Blackwell Publishing.

General Medical Education (2011). *Patient and public involvement in undergraduate medical education: advice supplementary to tomorrow's doctors (2009)*. London: GMC.

Health and Care Professions Council (2017). *Standards of education and training guidance*. London: HCPC. https://www.hcpc-uk.org/resources/guidance/standards-of-education-and-training-guidance/ [Accessed 28 April 2020].

Health Canada (2007). *Primary care healthcare transition fund. Collaborative care*. Ottawa: Health Canada. www.hc-sc.gc.ca/hcs-sss/alt_formats/hpb-dgps/pdf/prim/2006-synth-collabor-eng.pdf

The Interprofessional Curriculum Renewal Consortium, Australia (2013). *Curriculum renewal for interprofessional education in health*. Sydney: Centre for Research in Learning and Change, University of Technology, Sydney.

Interprofessional Education Collaborative Expert Panel (2011). *Core competencies for interprofessional collaborative practice: report of an expert panel*. Washington, DC: Interprofessional Education Collaborative.

Kilminster, S, Fielden, S (2009). Working with the patient voice: developing teaching resources for interprofessional education. *The Clinical Teacher*, 6, 265–268.

Kolb, DA (1984). *Experiential learning – Experience as a source of learning and development*. Upper Saddle River, NJ: Prentice Hall.

Kuper, A, Reeves, S, Levinson, W (2008). An introduction to reading and appraising qualitative research. *BMJ*, 333, 404–407.

Lewin, K (1946). Action research and minority problems. *Journal of Social Issues*, 2(4), 34–46.

Loeffler, E, Power, G, Bovaird, T, Hine-Hughes, F (Eds) (2013). *Co-production of health and wellbeing in Scotland*. Birmingham: Governance International.

National Health Service (2014). *Five year forward view*. NHS England. https://www.england.nhs.uk/wp-content/uploads/2014/10/5yfv-web.pdf [Accessed 28 April 2020].

Nursing and Midwifery Council (2010). *Standards for pre-registration nursing education*. London: NMC. www.nmc.org.uk/standards/additional-standards/standards-for-pre-registration-nursing-education/

Reeves, S, Fletcher, S, Barr, H, Birch, I, Boet, S, Davies, N et al. (2016). A BEME systematic review of the effects of interprofessional education: BEME 2016 guide no. 39. *Medical Teacher*, 38(7), 656–668.

Soklaridis, S, Romano, D, Fung, WLA, Martimianakis, MA, Sargeant, J, Chambers, J, Wiljer, D, Silver, I (2017). Where is the client/patient voice in interprofessional healthcare team assessments? Findings from a one-day forum. *Journal of Interprofessional Care*, 31(1), 122–124.

Spencer, J, Godolphin, W, Karpenko, N, Towle, A (2011). *Can patients be teachers? Involving patients and service users in healthcare professionals' education*. London: The Health Foundation.

Tew, J, Gell, C, Foster, F (2004). *A good practice guide. Learning from experience. Involving service users and carers in mental health education and training*. Nottingham: Mental Health in Higher Education. National Institute for Mental Health in England/Trent Workforce Development Confederation.

Thistlethwaite, J, Moran, M (2010). Learning outcomes for interprofessional education (IPE): literature review and synthesis. *Journal of Interprofessional Care*, 24(5), 503–513. doi:10.3109/13561820.2010.483366

Towle, A, Farrell, C, Gaines, ME, Godolphin, W, John, G, Kline, C, Lown, B, Morris, P, Symons, J, Thistlethwaite, J (2016). The patient's voice in health and social care professional education: the Vancouver statement. *International Journal of Health Governance*, 21(1), 18–25. https://doi.org/10.1108/IJHG-01-2016-0003

Warne, T, McAndrew, S (Eds) (2005). *Using patient experience in nurse education*. Basingstoke: Palgrave Macmillan.

World Health Organisation (2010). *Framework for action on Interprofessional education & collaborative practice*. Geneva: WHO. p. 7.

World Health Organisation (2016). *Global strategy on human resources for health: workforce 2030*. Geneva: WHO.

27

ALL OUR JUSTICE

People with convictions and 'participatory' criminal justice

Gillian Buck, Paula Harriott, Kemi Ryan, Natasha Ryan, Philippa Tomczak

Despite experiencing strong cultural messages that *they* are outsiders to be contained and corrected (Becker, 1963/2008), criminalised people play varied roles in the development and delivery of criminal justice services and advocacy around the world (Buck, forthcoming; Prison Reform Trust, 2017). These roles include peer listeners and mentors (e.g. Seppings, 2016), involvement in service design and commissioning (Revolving Doors, 2016), establishing innovative programmes (e.g. User Voice[1]) and creating service user 'voice' and policy lobbying formations (e.g. the Prisoner Policy Network,[2] Revolving Doors Lived Experience forums[3]). This work is often organised by voluntary organisations, from local to national scales. It has been driven by people with convictions themselves, and UK policy plans to i) blend volunteer and peer mentoring into criminal justice 'rehabilitation' services (Grayling, 2012; Gough, 2017), and ii) involve young people in the planning, delivery and evaluation of activities across youth justice (YJB participation strategy, 2016).

Notions of participation and engagement have become central to realising public services that are more democratic, sustainable and responsive to public values and human needs (Bovaird, 2007). Propelled by potent yet paradoxical forces of 'top-down' privatisation and user group movements as 'bottom-up' resistance, the prior monopoly of social care once held by state social work has been displaced by the empowered 'service user' (Carey, 2009). Nevertheless, criminalised people rarely feature in texts on service user involvement – despite overrepresenting, as a population, intersecting inequities (Prison Reform Trust, 2019 re England and Wales) and experiencing the inequities which flow from criminal justice contact (Turney and Wakefield, 2019 re the US). Criminalised people are overwhelmingly perceived, in discourse and practice, as *passive and problematic recipients of services*, designed by others who know best (Tomczak and Buck, 2019). This is especially true of criminalised children, who are punished for actions shaped by conditions they cannot affect (Phoenix, 2015, p. 135) and in turn become 'objects' of concern (Case et al., 2015), 'whose liberties and rights can be justifiably curtailed or dispensed with in the presumed public interest' (Weaver and Barry, 2014, p. 279). The clear limitation of participatory approaches in the context of criminalisation is that people are at best *merely consulted* and likely ignored, with little hope of being *meaningfully included* in decision-making processes (Haines and Case, 2015).

Involving people with convictions in criminal (and social) justice policy development and service delivery presents many avenues for analysis and theory-building, which we encourage others to develop. Our focus in this chapter is to explore how people with lived experiences of the criminal justice system are involved with, and too often excluded from, formal criminal justice knowledge production. We reflect on 'leaders' with lived experiences and how they produce, contribute to and constitute criminal justice knowledges. It is problematic that criminal justice services are not routinely associated with offering choice, control and involvement for their service users or wider stakeholders, as e.g. adult social work and care services have developed (Weaver, 2011, p. 1040). It is problematic that generalised services tend to label people with criminal justice experience as 'hard to reach' or 'seldom heard' (Beresford, 2012, p. 265), and that formal research and education settings often tangibly exclude people with convictions (Aresti et al., 2016). It is problematic that scholarly, policy and practice discourses often position criminalised people as subjects, and powerfully *other* them through terminology such as managing 'risk' (which often means managing human needs) and 'profiling' criminals (which often means laundering intersecting socioeconomic inequities into hyperindividualised interventions) (Goddard and Myers, 2018).

Following Beresford's (2016, p. 3) weaving of the personal and the political, this chapter adopts a reflective critical storytelling approach, drawing on 'experiential and academic knowledge; lived experience as well as research findings . . . in an attempt to reconnect [criminal justice] policy to the world in which it operates and to the reader'. This chapter is the product of five women's decades of knowledge of academic 'criminal justice' and 'service user' literature, criminalisation and 'support' work with criminalised people. We occupy a range of fluid identities, including a white female academic and former social worker (Gill); a white female criminal justice worker with lived experience of criminalisation, education and research (Paula); two black female criminal justice workers with lived experience of criminalisation and education (Kemi and Natasha); and a white female academic (Philippa). The 'data' we present was gathered through three prompts from Gill: *approach to involvement, enablers and barriers, and future challenges.* Loosely guided by these prompts, Paula (in writing) and Kemi and Natasha (in voice) reflected on their lived experiences of criminalisation; stigma; discrimination; and supporting others through the 'aftermath' of crime. Gill and Philippa used the prompts to analyse the existing literature. This contribution from five women is by no means representative of our field, and we encourage others to develop this area. There is further relevant literature and lived experience presented by e.g. Rod Earle, Andreas Aresti, Sacha Darke, Jason Warr, Stephen Wakeman and Matthew Kidd, but ethnic minority men and women are notably underrepresented in scholarship, raising questions for the disciplines and practices of criminology and social work.

This chapter illustrates the value of a range of perspectives. In Kemi and Natasha's words, the knowledges of people with convictions are not in 'place of anyone else's', but undeniably have much 'to tell us about the operation of punishment and the concept of justice' (Farrant, 2016, p. 23). The knowledges of people with convictions are vital for understanding and reconfiguring criminal and social justice; developing service user 'voice' and policy lobbying formations; adapting and revolutionising service delivery, design and commissioning; and balancing constructed 'criminal' narratives.

What is your approach and what difference has it made?

Paula

I am a senior manager at the Prison Reform Trust, leading prisoner involvement nationally. I have held several roles in the criminal justice user movement since 2010, having worked at User Voice and Revolving Doors Agency in senior roles. I am a woman with lived experience of imprisonment, having served an eight-year sentence for supplying Class A drugs (four years in prison and four years on licence). Reflecting on my life experiences and activating them for social purpose informs my approach to my work. But, why would traumatised prisoners want to help improve the very system that has traumatised them? Why do we get involved?

In prison, we generally engage in peer support and user involvement mechanisms such as Prison Councils because in such a confining and infantilising position it seems the only way to exert an identity, beyond offence and number. Peer work can aid in improving conditions in the short term; we are aware of this power. It's also about trying to negotiate an improvement, trying to influence for the better for others who are still to come, but in prison and the community, user involvement in service delivery is still focused on service delivery improvement. As such, user involvement can act to legitimise and assimilate critics into the existing system. However, along the way, the sharing of experiences, the support of peers and feelings of self-value and self-confidence emerge as beneficial and welcome side effects.

'User involvement' rarely addresses or educates prisoners about the wider structural issues which intersect with prison experiences. Therefore, in terms of shifting systems they do very little, but what they can do is offer a way in for people to activate lived experience and start to harness an energy/appetite for change.

Paula's concerns about assimilation echo Carey's (2009, p. 185) moral questioning of a 'government led culture that seeks to encourage service users and carers to integrate with, if not embrace, a political and economic system responsible for causing many of their problems'. He cites Humphries' (2008, p. 67) Foucauldian critique that participation can result in a disciplining of the self, 'empowering [people] to behave in ways that are confining and restricting, tantamount to "subjection"'. While we agree entirely with Paula's assessment, Gill and Philippa would like to add a note of hope for the future. We see the 'user movement' as a critical actor in any possibility of re-socialising an authoritarian penal welfare state that has resituated itself towards the market (Powell, 2009). We need to find forms of public input that can deconstruct our bloated penal system (Gottschalk, 2006), and we believe the participatory 'user movement' has a crucial role to play (Tomczak and Buck, 2019).

Kemi and Natasha

We created 'Reformed', a crime prevention community interest company, to address the lack of opportunity and encouragement available to many criminalised people. Our motivation was personal, as we were released from prison sentences to services which were offering unsafe and unsuitable housing options (i.e. offering young black women housing in a predominantly white, socially deprived area with known hate crime problems); low expectations and limited opportunities in relation to employment (the only opportunities were unpaid[4]); and very little practical or emotional support. Our approach is to educate community members positively in all aspects of the aftermath of crime, including the restrictions of a criminal record. We educate employers and professionals about the need to offer employment opportunities; we also give motivational talks and workshops in prisons, after which people can self-refer for mentoring. Despite the size and number of other criminal justice services and charities, we are inundated with self-referrals from people who want help to get into volunteering or paid work. People want to come to workers who have achieved the change, rather than people who don't understand. We believe in the potential of people to change. If workers do not have this belief and criminalised people do not believe in themselves, there will not be change.

Because we are embedded in our local community and active in community engagement and mentoring, people know us and what we are about. Our local area has a big problem with 'county lines'[5] criminal exploitation, yet formal services often struggle to gain the trust of affected families. Because we have our feet in those homes and have already earned people's trust and respect, Social Services now use us; they invite us to negotiate on their behalf as families will not engage. They call us for advice and to accompany them, as the families say they want Reformed. This has led to community resolution work with the police, who can see the relationships we have made.

Our success rate is heightened because service users can relate to us and we can relate to them; it opens up an honest exchange. We ask people why they come to us and *they say* it is because they have met patronising, judgemental staff who don't really want to help and don't believe in change. We can answer questions about how it really was to start over. It's not an easy journey, but we can help you with the challenges because we have been through it. We do not claim to be better or in place of anyone else; we need a range of perspectives, but we know the barriers created by a criminal record.

Barriers for criminalised people

Kemi and Natasha

A huge problem is our work not being *valued*. Often, we are invited to work with professional partners for free. Only when we have proved ourselves will we be paid. This is *discrimination*. When our work is funded, it is often on a case by case basis, rather than through arrangements which offer us stability and ensure we can pay our bills. There is a belief that if you've got a conviction your work should be charitable, but who can afford to work for free? Some services have tried to throw a lot of work our way and we have had to put boundaries in place to protect ourselves.

Another barrier to meaningful participation is the *exploitation* of people with criminal records for organisational ends. We have been brought in to 'educate' others and told what to say and no one is paid. When a person is trying to rebuild their life, they should be paid; there should be real opportunities and buy in to rehabilitation. *Rejection* is another huge problem; it restricts legitimate employment and can affect mental health. It makes us sad that the rejections we have faced for over a decade have not changed, but it fuels our passion.

Paula

Imprisonment creates objects of curiosity and revulsion. People objectified in this way become adept at negotiating relationships with people who act as voyeurs, extracting information about experiences and demanding stories of pain, reform and redemption which act to endorse a world view which justifies the pains of imprisonment. There is an immense distrust of the system, which is part of the barrier. Our life experiences divide us depending on where we sit in relation to power. Many prisoners reject involvement advances, sensing them as tokenistic and offering false hope, and those that do get involved are often merely seeking new identities that are acceptable within society.

These experiences echo Ross' (2015) continuum of prison voyeurism and Hayes' (2017) 'institutionalised humiliation': the failure of respect afforded to [in Hayes' case] homecare workers as a collective group; workers' own recognition of being unjustly treated; and the lived reality of economic and social detriment, all while delivering the neo-liberal ideal of 'DIY welfare' (Carey, 2009, p. 183). Criminalised people are at risk of *appropriation* and, because of their (never-ending) debt to society, are 'expected to labour (emotionally) intensively for little or no financial reward' (Buck, 2018, p. 197).

Enablers – and further barriers – for criminalised people

Kemi and Natasha

We are mentally strong because we have each other and put our energy into working for change; we haven't had to deal with the aftermath of crime alone. If we had, we wouldn't be having this conversation today. We would have been lost, maybe even developed addictions. Having no-one to relate to and being rejected damages people long term. It changes a human being and they want to block things out. This is why you sometimes hear people say they want to return to prison, at least there is some sense of belonging. This is why it's so important to be part of a team; we can relate to each other and when one is down, the other can lift.

We had an experience where some money went missing when we were working for a charity. We looked hard for the money. This made us look guilty and feel guilty, despite having done nothing wrong. People need to work in environments where they feel valued, yet you often meet with judgements and people who don't believe you can change.

Paula

I found a supportive organisation which embraced me and never asked me to disclose details of my conviction, which was unusual. My imposed script[6] was embarrassment, shame and a need to prove that I was not a risk to the public. When a member of my team told me of gossip about my conviction I froze with fear. I felt outed. My deepest shame – that I was emotionally not ready to discuss – was forced into the public space. I was frozen, locked in my office in a panic and whirl of emotions that kept me mute. A criminal conviction is a permanent stain on someone's character. This is how sentencing is experienced; the individual is guilty: judged, culpable and deserving of punishment. Society banishes '*offenders*' to prison, and prisoner stories of integration into society post-prison are few and far between. We prisoners know this; we know that few people in the workplace and in relationships with others are offered reprieve after a prison sentence.

Kemi, Natasha and Paula's reflections on workplace discrimination and rejection of people with convictions are not uncommon and illustrate how these messages can be internalised. Their experiential accounts are important. Grey and academic literature has raised similar points. A 2008 taskforce 'identified a culture and mentality of ingrained resistance to the concept of offenders, former offenders and their families as experts as perhaps the greatest barrier to their involvement in service design and review' (Martin et al., 2016, p. 37). Key concepts such as 'user-led or co-(words) mean little without first understanding the essential value lived expertise brings to our social purpose work' (Sandhu, 2017, p. 122). Artello (2014) has argued for a paradigm shift, for individual abilities to be acknowledged, to emphasise the 'strengths and assets' [of 'juvenile offenders' with severe mental illness], family members, front line workers and the wider community need to be *'indoctrinated' into a strength-based approach* (Artello, 2014, p. 385).

But perhaps 'strengths indoctrination' (by itself) is not a helpful approach. Perhaps experiential accounts, such as those presented here, enable us to see these 'offenders' as the (imperfect) people that they – *just like all of us* – are. Gill, Paula, Kemi, Natasha and Philippa are all imperfect people. By the luck of the draw,[7] three of us went to prison and two of us went to university (albeit with more 'speeding' convictions than desirable: but again, by the luck of the draw, Philippa[8] didn't hit anyone and end up in prison). By the luck of the draw,[9] Paula, Kemi and Natasha are labelled as a collection of 'deficits' and – by the 'progressives' – 'strengths' (e.g. Burnett and Maruna, 2006). But we are all just imperfect people.

As lead author, Gill had the power to shape the direction and language used to develop this piece, despite her participation involving much less personal or professional risk than co-authors. When Philippa is 'challenging', it is seen as a sign of her 'future research leadership', potentially warranting thousands of pounds in research funding. When a young, working-class black woman is 'challenging', then silencing of 'personal' or 'uppity' opinions often occurs (Buck, forthcoming 2019). Although *further* exposing for Paula, Kemi and Natasha, perhaps experiential accounts such as this can be useful in breaking down the delineations that position 'them' as a threat to 'our' order and solidarity (McMurray and Ward, 2014).

Indeed, personal storytelling is one of the most common ways that criminalised people are involved with knowledge production. It can be powerful, build relationships, influence individual and organisational practice; improve services; engender understanding, empathy and reflection; and benefit the teller by encouraging personal growth and resilience (Drumm, 2013; Peer Power, 2019[10]). But storytelling can create harms. Background checks (Blumstein and Nakamura, 2009) and media interest in crime increase the likelihood of shame provoking 'outings' like Paula powerfully described.

Peer Power's (forthcoming 2019) peer-produced *Code of Ethics for Storytelling* attempts to acknowledge lived experiences as a valid form of knowledge transfer and tool of engagement, while recognising the potential for exploitation or social and emotional harm if careful reflections on power and wellbeing are not central to plans. The *Code* encourages service user storytelling to include multiple stories, a consideration of the purpose of storytelling (e.g. to help other people; to challenge stigma; to raise awareness; for self-healing) and avoidance of storytelling that will (re)traumatise. *Code* is also clear that ethical service user involvement should avoid tokenistic stories which reinforce stereotypes and 'trauma porn', which invokes fascination or voyeuristic pleasure (Meek, 2011, p. 31). Paula has also written about the need to move beyond simplistic storytelling of individual experience, which can limit prisoners to their personal narrative of powerlessness in the face of the system (Harriott and Aresti, 2018). She notes the *indignity of speaking for others* (Foucault in Brich, 2008) and Maruna's (2017) call to frame desistance as a social movement for macro-social change, before advocating for *networks* which represent the lived experience of criminalised people, as a means of influencing grassroots confidence in self-determination, policy and service delivery. We reinforce the importance and potential of these considered activities.

Opportunities and enablers of participation

Kemi and Natasha

For us, a real enabler would be positive changes to the criminal records process. Do we need unspent convictions that limit people for the rest of their lives? People need to be provided with genuine opportunities to carry on with their lives; this includes buying in to rehabilitation and paying people for their contributions. The criminal record should be a protected characteristic in the workplace given the levels of discrimination it creates. There is also a need for diverse representation and to give voice to experiences of racism. We have noticed that there is a visible lack of black women (with and without criminal histories) in criminal justice roles. It is much harder for black people; people see black first and [criminal] record second. Akala (2018), provides an astute personal–political account of how (primarily male) blackness and criminalisation intersect.

Paula

Coming to terms with the conviction, a process commenced by speaking out about what I had experienced and examining it by sharing it with others, was healing, was cathartic, was freedom. It allowed me to integrate my experience into a strength, rather than hide it in the deepest recesses of my brain as an episode too frightening to acknowledge. Trying to move forward with that heavy load was going to be very slow progress.

The focus of my work recently has moved to *movement building* and development of lived experience leadership. User involvement remains a means to this end, identifying activists and leaders in marginalised communities and supporting allies from other sectors such as academia, who can work toward a collective agenda. The movement aims to nurture leaders and 'coproduce' as a group that *sets* rather than *responds to* the policy agenda. The network approach aims to build a critical mass of people who can challenge and create alternatives to the status quo. Development of lived experience leadership is a means to move beyond coproduction as guests of the system, to wresting higher degrees of control of the conversation.

Kemi, Natasha and Paula's reflections illustrate that speaking one's truth can be healing and may exert some educational/consciousness-raising influence but has limits in terms of systemic change. However, collective activism, driven by lived expertise, could begin to challenge barriers, including punitive criminalisation, systemic racism and a lack of social investment. Goddard et al. (2015, p. 77) argue that activism by community-based coalitions in the USA has triggered national conversations around police violence, racial disproportionality in incarceration and the racialised consequences of mass incarceration.

The current prominence of participatory approaches, as discussed in our introduction, signals growing recognition that the people and families who have experience of the criminal justice system are a vital source of knowledge (Clinks, 2018). At the functional level, user participation can 'enhance the credibility, meaning or legitimacy of interventions' (Weaver and McCulloch, 2012, p. 4) and increase levels of engagement and self-esteem (Creaney, 2014). At the macro-level, it can open up meaningful new opportunities (Little, 2015). In youth justice, it can provide a means to deliver individuals' right to express their views in matters affecting them and have due consideration given to their views (see YJB, 2016). The prisoner's voice is also essential for countering the de-humanisation, de-personalisation and stigmatisation of both prisoners and their families, exposing bad practice and helping to set standards of decency and acceptability within prison walls and during resettlement (Aresti et al., 2016, p. 13).

Some strands of collective reflection and learning could enable social changes and collective action, alongside individuals' personal and political goals. User expertise is often relegated to the bottom of the hierarchy of [mental health] 'evidence' (Rose, 2009, p. 176). Maruna (2015, p. 318) highlights a similar hierarchy in criminology, where the elevation of randomised controlled trials has often resulted in 'program fetishism'. Yet, British Convict Criminology (BCC) privileges the knowledges and standpoints of those with first-hand experience of prison (Aresti et al., 2016, p. 6). BCC aims to support prisoners and ex-prisoners as academics; develop research with/on prisoners and former prisoners; and influence policy change through academic work and connections to advocacy/campaign groups (BCC, 2019).

Learning Together sees 'students in universities and prisons learn degree-level material alongside one another in the prison environment' (Armstrong and Ludlow, 2016). It follows a long history of prisoners and 'outside' students learning alongside each other in the UK and USA.

Learning Together is not a user-led initiative but it based on the 'contact theory' of philosophy that 'meaningful interchange . . . between people who may hold prejudices against each other in situations that provide opportunities for people to cooperate, as equals, with common goals and the support of social and institutional authorities' can reduce overall prejudice' (Armstrong and Ludlow, 2016, p. 13). The UK pilot of Learning Together highlighted the power of education as a (potentially) socially transformative practice, when it involves collaboration through dialogically sharing knowledge and working together to achieve aims. The graduates of this initiative may also be vital contributors to and beneficiaries of any burgeoning user movement.

At a practice level, peer mentoring – which draws upon the knowledge of people with lived experiences of criminalisation, to support people in prison and the community – can provide a platform for previously submerged voices, position people in new ways and ask questions of established approaches, potentially opening up alternative solutions (Buck, forthcoming 2019). User Voice Prison Councils 'represent an important example of different actors co-producing alternative patterns of governance through innovations in democratic participation' (Weaver, 2019, p. 249). The effects of such 'bottom-up' practices 'include enhanced institutional legitimacy; improvements in prison officer-prisoner relations; and greater quality of life for prisoners' (Weaver, 2019, p. 249). While the effects of such co-production risk being 'more ameliorative than transformative', user councils can 'enable differently situated people to forge new norms of interactions and forms of democratic participation to achieve collective goals' (Weaver, 2019, p. 249).

But, while these initiatives represent opportunities for criminalised people to contribute their knowledge and potentially network and be nurtured as 'leaders', in most cases these opportunities lack pay or status relative to that of criminal justice or academic professionals. Moreover, it is unclear how well represented women and men from ethnic minorities are, particularly at the highest levels of these enterprises.

Three future challenges

In conclusion, we outline three future challenges for participatory criminal justice. First, it is important for service user involvement and coproduction to avoid tokenism, be sensitive to the needs of people sharing their shame/trauma-invoking life experiences and include substantial opportunities beyond volunteering or insecure contracts. It also requires honest reflections from service deliverers and policy makers on the power they hold and how much they are (not) prepared to share. This includes reflecting on how much our efforts may collude with *fixing* individuals at the expense of challenging and resisting structural inequities. Second, we do not know how to leverage the interest in coproduction to engage marginalised communities in a movement for change. Paula is a strong advocate for lived experience leadership development as a route to alternative approaches to knowledge production and practice, but we do not yet know if or how this will lead to systemic reform. As Kemi and Natasha note, *people cannot move forward and sustain employment if they have no house, poor mental health and no family support.* They require holistic, often long-term support, yet this is often not available or is beset with preconceived judgements. Third, local and collective user involvement cannot be representative. A single 'user voice' is not possible, and it is important that a range of perspectives are represented from activist/practitioner to managerial levels. Importantly, this includes black and minority ethnic men and women, who are overrepresented as recipients of punishment and underrepresented as leaders and influencers, with or without lived experience. As our own reflections indicate, people from different places, with different identities and histories, can often have differing priorities for changes required at personal and systemic levels.

Notes

1 www.uservoice.org/our-story/
2 www.prisonreformtrust.org.uk/PressPolicy/News/vw/1/ItemID/617?platform=hootsuite
3 www.revolving-doors.org.uk/blog/our-lived-experience-forums-celebrate-10-years-impact
4 See also Gough (2017) on volunteering with little hope of paid work.
5 The development of drug routes into the counties by drug running gangs in cities (Firmin and Pearce, 2016, p. 78). Gangs and organised crime networks exploit children to sell drugs. Often these children are made to travel across counties, and they use dedicated mobile phone 'lines' to supply drugs (Children's Society, 2019).
6 See Warr (2020) on narrative labour.
7 Luck meaning politically generated inequitable distribution of opportunities, and the activities which constituted 'criminality' at certain points in time (see Barton et al., 2010 for a discussion of 'deviance' as socially, structurally and historically contingent).
8 Critics may read such reflections as naval gazing (see Ellis, 2009), but for us they constitute an ethical imperative in researching criminalised people. If academics (with more than their fair share of power, resources and various forms of capital (financial notwithstanding)) 'invite' people who have been convicted, disadvantaged and marginalised to lay themselves bare, it is necessary (although insufficient) to acknowledge our own flaws, advantages and shared personhood.
9 Luck arguably meaning the gendered, classed and racialised playing field (Barton et al., 2010).
10 Peer Power is a social justice charity which aims to create platforms for the voices of those with lived experience of [youth justice and mental health], through storytelling and peer engagement www.peerpower.org.uk/about-us/.

References

Akala (2018). *Natives: Race and class in the ruins of Empire*. London: Two Roads.
Aresti, A., Darke, S., & Manlow, D. (2016). Bridging the gap: Giving public voice to prisoners and former prisoners through research activism. *Prison Service Journal*, 224, 3–13.
Armstrong, R., & Ludlow, A. (2016). Educational partnerships between universities and prisons: How learning together can be individually, socially and institutionally transformative. *Prison Service Journal*, 225, 9–17.
Artello, K. (2014). Shifting 'tough on crime' to keeping kids out of jail: Exploring organizational adaptability and sustainability at a mental health agency serving adjudicated children living with severe mental illness. *Criminal Justice Policy Review*, 25(3), 378–396.
Barton, A., Corteen, K., Davies, J., & Hobson, A. (2010). Reading the word and reading the world: The impact of a critical pedagogical approach to the teaching of criminology in higher education. *Journal of Criminal Justice Education*, 21(1), 24–41.
Becker, H.S. (1963). *Outsiders*. New York: Free Press. (Original work 2008).
Beresford, P. (2012). The personal is still political. In Beresford, P. & Carr, S. (Eds.), *Social care, service users and user involvement*. London: Research Highlights in Social Work, 265–271.
Beresford, P. (2016). *All our welfare: Towards participatory social policy*. Bristol: Policy Press.
Blumstein, A., & Nakamura, K. (2009). Redemption in the presence of widespread criminal background checks. *Criminology*, 47(2), 327–359.
Bovaird, T. (2007). Beyond engagement and participation: User and community coproduction of public services. *Public Administration Review*, 67(5), 846–860.
Brich, C. (2008). The Groupe d'information sur les prisons: The voice of prisoners? Or Foucault's? *Foucault Studies*, (5), 26–47.
British Convict Criminology (BCC). (2019). *Convict criminology*. Available at: http://convictcriminology.org/bcc.htm
Buck, G. (2018). The core conditions of peer mentoring. *Criminology & Criminal Justice*, 18(2), 190–206.
Buck, G. (forthcoming 2019). Politicisation or professionalisation? Exploring divergent aims within UK voluntary sector peer mentoring. *The Howard Journal of Crime and Justice*, 58(3), 349–365.
Burnett, R., & Maruna, S. (2006). The kindness of prisoners: Strengths-based resettlement in theory and in action. *Criminology & Criminal Justice*, 6(1), 83–106.
Carey, M. (2009). Critical commentary: Happy shopper? The problem with service user and carer participation. *British Journal of Social Work*, 39(1), 179–188.

Case, S., Creaney, S., Deakin, J., & Haines, K. (2015). Youth justice: Past, present and future. *British Journal of Community Justice, 13*(2).

Children's Society (2019). *What is county lines?* Available at: www.childrenssociety.org.uk/what-is-county-lines

Clinks (2018). *Service user involvement.* Available at: www.clinks.org/our-work/service-user-involvement

Creaney, S. (2014). The benefits of participation for young offenders. *Safer Communities, 13*(3), 126–132.

Drumm, M. (2013). *The role of personal storytelling in practice.* Insight 23. Available at: www.iriss.org.uk/resources/insights/role-personal-storytelling-practice

Ellis, C. (2009). Fighting back or moving on: An autoethnographic response to critics. *International Review of Qualitative Research, 2*(3), 371–378.

Farrant, F. (2016). *Crime, prisons and viscous culture: Adventures in criminalized identities.* London: Springer.

Firmin, C., & Pearce, J. (2016). Living in gang affected neighbourhoods. In Bernard, C. & Harris, P. (Eds.), *Safeguarding black children: Good practice in child protection.* London: Jessica Kingsley Publishers.

Goddard, T., & Myers, R.R. (2018). *Youth, community and the struggle for social justice.* Oxon: Routledge.

Goddard, T., Myers, R.R., & Robison, K. (2015). Potential partnerships: Progressive criminology, grassroots organizations and social justice. *International Journal for Crime, Justice and Social Democracy, 4*, 76–90.

Gottschalk, M. (2006). *The prison and the gallows: The politics of mass incarceration in America.* Cambridge: Cambridge University Press.

Gough, D. (2017). *Voluntary sector actors in community justice: A case study of St Giles trust and ex-offender peer mentoring* (Doctoral dissertation, University of Portsmouth).

Grayling, C. (2012). Justice Minister's 'Rehabilitation Revolution' speech, November 20, 2012. Available at: www.justice.gov.uk/news/speeches/chris-grayling/speech-to-the-centre-of-social-justice

Haines, K., & Case, S. (2015). *Positive youth justice: Children first, offenders second.* Bristol: Policy Press.

Harriot, P., & Aresti, A. (2018). Voicelessness: A call to action. *Journal of Prisoners on Prisons, 27*(2).

Hayes, L.J. (2017). *Stories of care: A labour of law: Gender and class at work.* London: Springer.

Humphries, B. (2008). *Social work research for social justice.* Basingstoke: Palgrave Macmillan.

Little, R. (2015). Participation and practice in youth justice. *Eurovista, 3*(3).

Martin, C., Frazer, L., Cumbo, E., Hayes, C., & O'Donoghue, K. (2016). Paved with good intentions: The way ahead for voluntary, community and social enterprise sector organisations. In Hucklesby, A. & Corcoran, M. (Eds.), *The voluntary sector and criminal justice.* London: Palgrave Macmillan.

Maruna, S. (2015). Qualitative research, theory development, and evidence-based corrections: Can success stories be 'evidence'. *Qualitative Research in Criminology, 1*, 311.

Maruna, S. (2017). Desistance as a social movement. *Irish Probation Journal, 14*, 5–20.

McMurray, R., & Ward, J. (2014). 'Why would you want to do that?': Defining emotional dirty work. *Human Relations, 67*(9), 1123–1143.

Meek, A. (2011). *Trauma and media: Theories, histories, and images.* Oxon: Routledge.

Peer Power (forthcoming 2019). *Storytelling code of ethics.* London, United Kingdom: Peer Power.

Phoenix, J. (2015). Against youth justice and youth governance, for youth penality. *British Journal of Criminology, 56*(1), 123–140.

Powell, F. (2009). Civil society, social policy and participatory democracy: Past, present and future. *Social Policy and Society, 8*(1), 49–58.

Prison Reform Trust (2017). *A different lens: Report on a pilot programme of active citizen forums in prison.* Available at: www.prisonreformtrust.org.uk/Portals/0/Documents/A%20Different%20Lens.pdf

Prison Reform Trust (2019). Bromley Briefings Prison Factfile Winter 2019. Accessed at: http://www.prisonreformtrust.org.uk/Portals/0/Documents/Bromley%20Briefings/Winter%202019%20Factfile%20web.pdf

Revolving Doors (2016). Commissioning Together. Available at: http://www.revolving-doors.org.uk/involvement/peer-research/commissioning-together

Rose, D. (2009). Is collaborative research possible? In Wallcraft, J., Schrank, B., & Amering, M. (Eds.), *Handbook of service user involvement in mental health research.* Chichester: Wiley-Blackwell, 169–179.

Ross, J.I. (2015). Varieties of prison voyeurism: An analytic/interpretive framework. *The Prison Journal, 95*(3), 397–417.

Sandhu, B. (2017). *The value of lived experience in social change: The need for leadership and organisational development in the social sector.* Clore Social Leadership Foundation. Available at: http://thelivedexperience.org/wp-content/uploads/2017/07/The-Lived-Experience-Baljeet-Sandhu-VLE-summary-web-ok-2.pdf

Seppings, C. (2016). *To study the rehabilitative role of ex-prisoners/offenders as peer mentors in reintegration models – in the UK, republic of Ireland, Sweden and USA.* The Winston Churchill Memorial Trust of Australia.

Tomczak, P., & Buck, G. (2019). The penal voluntary sector: A hybrid sociology. *The British Journal of Criminology, 59*(4), 898–918.

Turney, K., & Wakefield, S. (2019). Criminal justice contact and inequality. *RSF: The Russell Sage Foundation Journal of the Social Sciences, 5*(1), 1–23.

Warr, J. (2020). 'Always gotta be two mans': Lifers, risk, rehabilitation, and narrative labour. *Punishment & Society, 22*(1), 28–47.

Weaver, B. (2011). Co-producing community justice: The transformative potential of personalisation for penal sanctions. *British Journal of Social Work, 41*(6), 1038–1057.

Weaver, B. (2019). Co-production, governance and practice: The dynamics and effects of user voice prison councils. *Social Policy & Administration, 53*(2), 249–264.

Weaver, B., & Barry, M. (2014). Managing high risk offenders in the community: Compliance, cooperation and consent in a climate of concern. *European Journal of Probation, 6*(3), 278–295.

Weaver, B., & McCulloch, P. (2012). *Co-producing criminal justice*. Scottish Centre for Crime and Justice Research. Available at: www.sccjr.ac.uk/wp-content/uploads/2012/11/Co-producing_Criminal_Justice.pdf

Youth Justice Board (2016). *Participation strategy: Giving young people a voice in youth justice*. London: Youth Justice Board.

28

CONTINUOUS TEACHER TRAINING FOR PROVIDING SPECIALISED EDUCATIONAL SERVICES IN RIO DE JANEIRO, BRAZIL

Leila Regina d'Oliveira de Paula Nunes
and Carolina Rizzotto Schirmer

The process of school inclusion of children with special educational needs in Brazil (students with disabilities, autism spectrum disorders, and high functioning abilities) has resulted in the growing presence of these students in regular classrooms in recent decades. In order to support this process, the Ministry of Education (MEC) in 2008 instituted Specialized Educational Assistance (SEA), offered preferentially in Multifunctional Resource Rooms (MRR). The role of the SEA is to complement or supplement students' education by providing services, accessibility resources, and strategies that eliminate barriers to their full participation in society and the development of their learning.

In 2016, the city of Rio de Janeiro had 1,013 elementary schools and 514 Early Childhood Education Units, distributed across 11 Regional Education Coordination (REC). Of the 650,000 students placed in the public school system, 13,336 were of the special education target population. Of these, 8,758 were enrolled in 474 Multifunctional Resource Rooms (MRR), a number far below the care needed for this growing portion of the special student population.

Considering the complexity of the school routine and the need to attend to this special population, in January 2013 the Instituto Helena Antipoff,[1] through the Oficina Vivencial (Experiential Workshop (EW)),[2] invited researchers from the Universidade do Estado do Rio de Janeiro (State University of Rio de Janeiro) to enter into a partnership with the purpose of conducting research on continuing in-service teacher training, focusing on Assistive Technology (AT)[3] and Augmentative and Alternative Communication (AAC).[4] The main objective was to create a team of approximately 22 teachers who had already worked in these MRR and were interested in participating in this training program in order to expand the work of the Oficina Vivencial (OV) through the Multifunctional Reference Resource Rooms (MRRR). Thus, these rooms (MRRR) would serve as a reference for the development and dissemination of AT and AAC procedures, services and resources, accessible computing, and other pedagogical strategies to offer support to other teachers working in conventional MRR as well as to teachers in regular classrooms.

The extensive body of research on continuing in-service teacher training has criticized traditional models of training, considering them merely informative, disconnected from classroom reality, failing to address teacher and student needs, and contributing little to the modification of their conceptions and practices. A divorce between researchers, who plan educational practices, and teachers, who carry them out, disqualifies teachers' function. This seems to show that teachers' actions serve only to validate the scientific knowledge produced by researchers (Machado, 1999). Schön (2000) proposes that training be centered on the investigation of teaching work in the school context. This model became known as the reflexive practice model, and there is a consensus in the literature about the relevance of its incorporation in initial and continuing teacher education (Cochran-Smith and Zeichner, 2005).

Purpose and study steps

Based on the reflexive practice model, we devised this intervention research. The purposes of this study were to plan, implement, and evaluate the effects of offering continuous in-service training for MRR teachers. In so doing we used the problematization approach to the area of AT, with emphasis on AAC, with non-vocal students with disabilities and autism spectrum disorder.

Data was produced through various instruments, such as semi-structured interviews, observation records, questionnaires and checklists, content analysis of teacher verbalization in the research meetings, and postings in a WhatsApp[5] created by the group, among others.

Initially, using the responses to questionnaires, the MRR teacher's characterization was set up. We applied checklists and questionnaires before and after training to identify teacher conceptions and knowledge about AT and AAC resources, and we asked these teachers to describe their pedagogical skills. From this information, we planned the teacher training course using the problematization approach. This training program involved a set of activities, namely:

a) Offering lectures with experts about communication and interaction, alternative communication and language, MRR, specialized educational assistance (SEA), AAC systems, and various software. On these occasions, videos of non-vocal students using AAC resources were exhibited.

b) Presenting and discussing several case studies developed by the teachers themselves about some of their students with greater difficulties. Two teachers also participated in a study in which autoscopy[6] was employed as a critical element of training.

c) Demonstrating of the use of various AAC systems and technology resources.

d) Conducting 35 research meeting sessions discussing topics proposed by teachers, the Experiential Workshop staff, and researchers.

e) Creating a WhatsApp group, in which the participants discussed their difficulties, offered suggestions, and shared adapted or specially elaborated teaching materials and alternative communication resources.

f) Planning and implementing the so-called Open Rooms, consisting of lectures and workshops conducted by the MRR teachers who participated in this study.

g) Evaluating the training program.

h) Joint elaborating, including the participating teachers, the Experiential Workshop (EW) staff, and the research coordinators, of a book reporting all the research steps and findings.

Who are the participating teachers and the students they serve?

Of the participating teachers, 22% were 20 to 29 years old, 39% were 30 to 39, 28% were 40 to 49, and 11% were 50 to 59 years old (Table 28.1).

Table 28.1 Teachers' age

Teachers' age	Number of teachers (%)
20 to 29	4 (22%)
30 to 39	7 (39%)
40 to 49	5 (28%)
50 to 59	2 (11%)

Source: (Nunes et al., 2017)

Table 28.2 Teaching time in metropolitan schools

Teaching time in metropolitan schools (years)	Number of teachers (%)
0 to 5	4 (22%)
6 to 10	6 (33%)
11 to 15	6 (33%)
16 to 20	1 (6%)
21 to 25	1 (6%)

Source: (Nunes et al., 2017)

Table 28.3 Teaching time in special education

Teaching time in special education (years)	Number of teachers (%)
0 to 5	10 (56%)
6 to 10	4 (22%)
10 to 15	4 (22%)
More than 16	0 (0%)

Source: (Nunes et al., 2017)

For 67% of participants, teaching time varies from 6 to 15 years, with reasonable dedication to students with special needs (Tables 28.2 and 28.3). Also, 72% of teachers have been working in MRR for three years or less.

The majority (89%) had a college degree, and all of had attended specialization courses offered by the EW, as well as courses on basic AAC, before joining the research study. Many had attended scientific events in the area and customarily read about themes related to special student education. Data analysis concerning the students educated by these teachers confirm findings from a set of studies developed by 76 researchers from 21 universities located in 38 Brazilian cities, with the participation of 596 MRR teachers (Mendes; Cia; Tannús-Valadão, 2015). Our participants provided educational services to a total of 262 students between 2015 and 2016. The average number of students served per teacher was 15 but ranged from 6 to 24. Students with intellectual disabilities in kindergarten (4 to 6 years old) and elementary school (7 to 14 years old) predominated (Table 28.4).

Most of the services (63%) were offered at the school where the teachers worked. However, teachers moved to other schools within their regional education coordinator (REC) to provide this specialized care. The frequency of student meetings with the MRR teachers varied from

Table 28.4 Type of disability of students reported by teachers

Type of disability	Number of students (%)
Physical disability	26 (9.92%)
Visual impairment	15 (5.72%)
Intellectual disability	119 (45.41%)
Multiple disability	20 (7.63%)
Hearing disability	24 (9.16%)
Autistic Spectrum Disorder	57 (21.75%)
Others	1 (0.38%)

Source: (Nunes and Schirmer, 2017)

one to four times a week. Activities related to literacy, reading, and writing gained prominence in the agenda of these teachers, as well as teaching the use of hardware such as computers and tablets and software with educational games, adapted materials, and playful activities.

Teaching skills of teachers and their conceptions about AT and AAC resources

After implementation of the in-service training program, we noticed significant changes in the skills reported by teachers. There was an increase in pedagogical skills such as identification of affirmative and negative responses of nonverbal students; identification of the students' specific needs regarding the activities proposed for their reference group; evaluation of the literacy stage at which the students were; and proposition of needed pedagogical adaptations. There has also been an increase in teacher skills regarding resources and materials such as resource production and use, and adaptations for writing, social and academic use of communication boards and other AAC resources. The teachers stated that they began to adapt schoolwork and tests for their non-vocal students. Corroborating the findings of Ascenção (2007) and Zuttin (2008), we found that medium and high technology resources, much needed to assist people with physical and multiple disabilities (such as a voice communicator, adapted mouse, expanded keyboard, special software for writing), were not present in all MRR. This may have been a factor that contributed to the teachers' non-development of these skills. On the other hand, other features – such as a switch activated by pressure, keyboard with acrylic stamping block grid, and Boardmaker with Speaking Dynamically Pro software – that are available in the MEC kit for MRR were being used by more teachers.

At the beginning of the study, teachers associated AT modalities only with resources, disregarding the fact that AT also involves strategies, methodologies, and services. It is important to emphasize that such services were supposed to be provided by these teachers. There was also difficulty in distinguishing the AT modalities. National studies show that teachers are not always prepared to use AT resources at school (Pelosi, 2008; Galvão Filho, 2009; Versussa and Manzini, 2009; Lourenço, 2012). After the training offered, our teachers associated the terms autonomy and independence with AT and stated that they considered the AAC fundamental for the development, communication, and autonomy of speechless students. Prior to the training, teachers recognized the importance of assessing student needs for working with AAC but considered it a "difficult and distressing task". Teachers' feelings of anguish and disability are very common when they face the task of providing instruction to non-vocal students; this is corroborated by national studies conducted by Correia (1999), Beyer (2003), and Rocha et al. (2003). This lack of knowledge about the peculiar aspects of students with severe communication disabilities and their potentialities can drive teachers away from this kind of experience because it may prevent them from developing a pedagogical practice sensitive to the needs of the special needs students included in regular school settings (Pletsch, 2009). In contrast to what they revealed at the beginning of the training program, in 2014, teachers said that AAC needs to be included in teacher planning and the adaptations must be in line with the students' idiosyncratic needs, recognizing that they end up benefiting the whole class.

Continuing education based on the problematization approach and the use of autoscopy

The training program offered provided teachers with a real opportunity to practice their acquired knowledge. Following the precepts of the problematization approach (Colombo and Berbel, 2007), the teachers, gathered in groups of three, conducted case studies of the students who had the most difficulties. Thus, they started with classroom observation, identified pedagogical problems, and chose one as the focus of investigation. Then, they reflected on the possible determinants of the selected problem, defined the key points of the study, and sought and analyzed pieces of information to solve the problem, based on educational theories. Finally, they elaborated theoretical hypotheses of solutions to the problem, applied the procedures indicated by these hypotheses, and then returned to the investigated reality. Throughout this process, teachers were supported by their colleagues, the Experiential Workshop staff, and the researchers. Most groups identified the main problem as communication and interaction difficulties experienced by students and teachers. Thus, they were urged to deepen their knowledge in the areas of AT, especially AAC, to propose solution hypotheses for the cases studied and finally intervene, exercise, and manage situations associated with the problem's solution. For Moraes and Berbel (2006), the problematization approach application allows participants to fix the generated solutions and contemplates their commitment to return to the same reality, transforming it to some degree. It was possible to observe this teacher transformation in relation not only to their posture, both personal and academic, but also with regard to their knowledge and their conceptions.

In a parallel study, two teachers voluntarily submitted to the autoscopy procedure, which offers the teacher the opportunity to film their own teaching performance and later observe themselves on video. By analyzing the recorded material, the teachers observe the environment that surrounds them and, with the researcher's help, can reorganize or reformulate their actions, attitudes, and postures. In fact, after observing their own pedagogical actions provided by autoscopy, both teachers began to better observe their students' needs, introduced AAC resources to stimulate their communication, and provided greater functionality in the proposed school activities. Significant changes in a student were also observed.

What was discussed at the 35 research meetings in 2013–2016

Over the course of four years (2013–2016), the group formed by the MRR teachers, the Experiential Workshop team, and the researchers participated monthly in research meetings lasting approximately three hours. The topics[7] discussed in these 35 meetings were suggested by all participants. Four questions gained prominence in analysis of the statements made by all participants in the research sessions.

MRR working conditions

The Operational Guidelines for Specialized Educational Assistance (ESA) in basic education, in the special education modality for elementary schools, stipulated that:

> the elaboration and execution of the ESA plan are the responsibility of the teachers who work in MRR or ESA centers, in articulation with the other teachers of regular education and with the participation of families.
>
> *(Brasil, 2009, p. 2)*

It is clear from these legal documents that these teachers' duties are numerous and diverse. This professional becomes the main agent of the school inclusion policy, responsible for providing direct attention to the target public of special education and their families, as well as for articulating actions with regular teachers, school staff, and community agencies. One of the most frequent participants complaints referred to the overload of attributions imposed to this position. The MRR teacher is expected to be a super expert, prepared to meet the full range of difficulties of students with different special conditions. In the words of one of the participants in the national studies coordinated by Mendes (2015), "the room is multifunctional but the teacher is not" (Mendes et al., 2015, p. 522). Besides the excessive demand, they resent the low recognition of their work by other school teachers, managers, and even their Regional Education Coordination (REC). The teachers feel the sense of isolation and devaluation. They pointed to obstacles in their own schools and REC for their full participation in this training program. These data are corroborated by the extensive research conducted by Mendes et al. (2015).

Alternative communication resources: pedagogical adaptations × communication

The research sessions emphasized the use of AAC resources in the preparation of adapted material for pedagogical purposes. Since many teachers provide educational care to a variety of students with diverse difficulties, it is justifiable that they had also improved their adapted materials for these pupils by making use of the AAC resources. Nonetheless, it should be emphasized that such resources should prioritize the non-vocal students' social communication. According to the teachers, the conversation between teachers and students and between students is not emphasized in daily school life: "There is no time for conversations, we need to take care of the curriculum". This statement brings us to the third topic, which is the relationship between AAC and language.

AAC and language

The acquisition of communicative competence by non-vocal individuals is related to several aspects. Among them, the linguistic domain stands out, since it is considered critical for such development. People with minimal language competence can express basic needs through non-symbolic actions such as crying, looking, or making facial expressions, but are unable to share more complex ideas, feelings, and thoughts with others (Light, 2003; Deliberato et al., 2014). Just as the capacity of symbolic representation is essential for communication, in its various modalities – oral, gestural, and graphic – interpersonal communication greatly foments the very development of language and cognition. In fact, research has shown that the use of a pictographic system by children with severe communication disorders can stimulate the development of cognitive functions, particularly language (Chun, 2003; Trevizor and Chun, 2004).

Human interaction and alternative and extended communication

The use of new information and communication technologies (ICTs) has spread exponentially in the AAC field, with the development of sophisticated software, adapted mouse, triggering features, boards with digitized or synthesized voice, and more recently mobile technology items (tablets, iPads, and mobile phones) that have touchscreens. In the training offered to the participants of this research, these resources and systems indeed gained prominence, and the teachers devoted themselves to acquiring skills to identify, handle, and master such resources for use with their students. It is important to highlight, however, that the enchantment with these gadgets and consequent focus only on technology can lead professionals to neglect what really matters – the communication with and interaction of the students with their partners (Light and Naughton, 2013). According to Fogel (1993), communication is a continuous process in which partners mutually regulate their behaviors, that is, alter their own actions according to the partner's current and anticipated actions, enabling the joint creation of meaning. We communicate to affect our partner's behavior, thinking, and feeling and negotiate the meaning of our communicative act with them. This emphasis on human interaction must therefore precede any introduction of these technological resources. What is more important is the partner who offers attentive listening to the individual with severe functional speech limitation.

MRR online teacher community

In order to overcome isolation in their teaching activities and promote greater exchange and collaboration with peers, the group of teachers, on their own initiative, created a WhatsApp group named Multifunctional Reference Resource Rooms (MRRR) at the beginning of the training program in 2013. Analysis of the posted messages showed their great commitment to the project and their role as MRR professionals. Chat was used to exchange experiences about the educational space, notably at MRR, and knowledge in special education, AAC, and adapted material. The participants also spoke about the feelings and barriers faced in the school day to day and offered assistance to colleagues and suggestions of solutions to the problems they had to deal with. Information related to everyday life such as politics, culture, leisure, and others was evidenced, but less frequently. The group performance led us to think about the concept of communities of practice, conceived by Wenger (1998) as a group of individuals with distinct knowledge, skills, and experiences, who actively participate in collaborative processes, sharing knowledge, interests, resources, perspectives, activities, and, above all, practices, for producing both personal and collective knowledge, recognizing themselves as competent participants. The concept of communities of practice implies a social perspective of learning, and it should not be disconnected from everyday activities such as reading, shopping, having fun, etc. (Vavoula, 2005). A community of practice can be referred to as an online community when participants, aligned around a common interest, communicate, interact, and build knowledge, synchronously or asynchronously, using digital communication technologies. These practices point to new forms of interaction with knowledge, offering other possibilities of knowledge production that go beyond the conventional perspective of the classroom, MRR, and university and that can make a difference in the continuous in-service teacher training (Lucena, 2016).

Tailored or specially crafted teaching material and AAC resources posted on WhatsApp

The wide range of AT resources that teachers produced and used throughout their training were shown in the Multifunctional Reference Resource Rooms (MRRR) chat. A truly inclusive curriculum for special students is marked by an essential aspect – curriculum adaptation (CA). CAs are the "adjustments" made to the curriculum so that it becomes appropriate to accommodate student diversity. They involve organizational modifications: in the objectives and content, in the methodologies, in the didactic organization, and in the evaluation strategies to meet the educational needs of all pupils in relation to knowledge construction. The special students' needs also create the urge for new and different ways of presenting school content.

An exhausting analysis of the imagery posted from 2013 to 2016 revealed that 148 images in three categories were shared: AAC, Adapted or Specially Developed Material, and Computer Access. The most common types of AAC features developed were cards, followed by AAC boards including photos, pictures, symbols from the PCS and ARASAAC[8] systems, and use of software such as Boardmaker with Speaking Dynamically Pro, Pictovox, Adapt, and TICO. In the category of Adapted or Specially Developed Material, adapted books, pedagogical activities with dynamic boards, school materials, and games were prepared. Among the features of Computer Access, teachers reported using the adapted RCT-Barban mouse, the expanded Intellikeys keyboard, the keyboard with acrylic stamping block grid, and the conventional push-button notebook in various activities.

Indeed, adaptations in activities and materials through AAC devices are important for working on various academic content (Sameshima, 2011; Massaro et al., 2010; Deliberato et al., 2008; Deliberato et al., 2007; Paura and Deliberato, 2007). At school, the educator must provide the acquisition of alternative communication systems, as these resources are not naturally present in the classrooms. AAC is not a natural form of communication, so language development requires a construction and planning process (Von Tetzchner et al., 2005; Von Tetzchner, 2009; Downing, 2009).

Open Rooms: Multifunctional Reference Resource Rooms (MRRR) operating strategies

Open Rooms was the term coined by the participating teachers to refer to their meetings with their MRR colleagues from their Regional Education Coordination (REC). In these meetings, the participant teachers exchanged experiences and reflections and offered pedagogical workshops, especially for beginning MRR teachers and/or those who had students in need of AAC. Such Open Rooms represented, in effect, the operationalization of the movement of extension of the Experiential Workshop's (EW) functions and activities, developed since 1995 to reach an increasing number of teachers in the 11 RECs of the city of Rio de Janeiro. Thus, in 2015, supervised by the EW team and the researchers, the teachers began planning these Open Rooms. Thirty Open Room meetings were held, coordinated by 16 MRR teachers for a total of 333 teachers representing the 11 RECs. In the first Open Room implemented by all participants, the concept of AAC, the resources, and the population that can benefit from this practice were presented. In the following sessions, themes already studied by the teachers during their training were discussed, plus others suggested by the audience itself. The Open Room coordinators conducted activities similar to those employed in their own training. Teachers who attended such meetings generally evaluated Open Rooms as very positive. They highlighted as especially productive aspects: group dynamics, exchange of experiences, case reports, presentation and teaching of the elaboration of adapted materials and communication boards, applicability of the content treated for their classroom work, the psychological support they receive from the group coordinators, and the fact that these coordinators were MMR teachers like themselves. The training was thus a more horizontal one. The audience demanded longer and more frequent meetings to address theoretical aspects of communication, test adaptations, evidence-based literacy procedures, and so on. Workshops were suggested to teach how to make tailored materials and toys and communication boards, design curriculum adaptations, and use AAC software, applications, resources, strategies, and systems. Some Open Rooms coordinators set up WhatsApp groups to keep in touch with the teachers who attended the meetings. Open Rooms seemed to be a true community of practice (Wenger, 1988). In this type of congregation, there are full participants and peripheral ones. The first are those with the most experience, who master the procedures developed by the community; the peripherals are the new members welcomed by the community to initiate their engagement and participation and thus have access to the knowledge produced by the group. The entrance of new participants helps to "oxygenate" the constituted knowledge and promote the search for new solutions for the learning processes, thus favoring the revision of the veterans' practices (Reily, 2015). In this experience, we perceive the MRRR teachers, who coordinated the Open Rooms, as those full participants who welcomed the other teachers, initially considered as peripheral members. These gradually not only came to dominate the knowledge produced by the community but also to favor the rebuilding of new practices, thus imprinting a continuous movement on the community. Thus, if at the beginning of the Open Rooms meetings, the coordinating teachers behaved more like lecturers, over the course of these two years, they gradually established a partnership with the teacher participants, becoming more permeable to their reports of classroom experiences and thus encouraging a collective search for a solution to the difficulties presented. This highlights the extreme importance of the continuity of these Open Rooms with the increasing participation of MRR teachers, especially those with less teaching experience with special students. We believe that the possibility of systematic and more horizontal exchanges between teachers can be configured as a way to make them less isolated and more empowered.

How did SRM teachers evaluate in-service training program?

The training course was a great success and had great social and academic relevance. In the interviews we detected several strengths: participants' maturity; opportunity to attend congresses at Universidade do Estado do Rio de Janeiro (UERJ); practical examples brought by the speakers; sharing experiences with the school community; functional content; case study activities; the use of modern technology; the implementation of Open Rooms; and the links that were created with teachers from other schools. Other aspects, however, were cited as weaknesses in the training program: parallel conversations during the meetings; little time for the development of Open Room activities; the distance between their schools and the Experiential Workshop space; encounters widely spaced from each other; course dates that were scheduled on the same days of class council or students' exams; hard-to-manage software; few theoretical interventions in the appreciation of videos presented in case studies; little time to organize Open Room meetings; and the preference for themes related to children only, not including older students. The training program enabled the teachers to provide better care to the students' parents and to the health professionals who served these pupils. The teachers began to express a different perception of AAC, as well as to the lived and heard experiences and the materials used. This training program gave a voice to teachers who needed training connected to their needs and also to students who lacked pedagogical practices that would help them learn, develop socially and emotionally, and interact with the world. Some suggestions, provided by the participants at the time of the final interview, are worth mentioning: continuity of the training with the same model that has already been done; implementation of Open Rooms throughout Rio de Janeiro's metro school system; review of the excessive attributions of MRR teachers; reassessment of the number of students who are served by the Specialized Educational Assistance (SEA); more time to plan and to make the material needed for the job; the proposal that the MRRR become a space for training and exchange of experiences within each Regional Education Coordination (REC); continuation of the autoscopy process and case studies; expansion of spaces for exchange of experiences; training programs provided by MRR teachers; and prioritization of diverse topics related to students with disabilities. It can be said that the partnership between the Experiential Workshop and the UERJ, in the continuing training program offered to teachers of Multifunctional Resource Rooms, has achieved the proposed objectives, as it has broadened the understanding of political and educational issues aimed at ensuring inclusive education. The work with the MRR teachers has fostered questions and positions regarding teacher education and also the different pedagogical practices and the places where they happen, aiming to ensure the right of all people to qualified school education. Reflections and debates about the social context, the school, and the teacher's performance, in both the regular class and the MRR, will undoubtedly have repercussions on those who desire to build, and dedicate themselves to building, an inclusive society in which human rights are promoted and respected.

Conclusions

The teachers had an active role in all steps of the study. This is suggested by the following aspects: the teachers a) took the initiative of conducting this study, b) helped to choose the methodological procedures, c) brought the cases to be studied by the group, d) recorded their teaching sessions and discussed their content, e) initiated the WhatsApp group to share materials and discuss issues, f) planned, implemented, and evaluated the Open Rooms – and finally g) five teachers authored four chapters of the book entitled *Salas Abertas: formação de professores e práticas pedagógicas em comunicação alternativa e ampliada nas salas de recursos multifuncionais* (*Open Rooms: Teacher Training and Pedagogical Practices in Augmentative and Alternative Communication in Multifunctional Resource Rooms*),[9] published in 2017. This book is a work written by many hands, including teachers, EW staff, researchers, UERJ undergraduates, and graduates in special education. The work was freely distributed to all study participants and offered to schools and to other teachers in the resource classrooms. We also offered to students, teachers, and researchers in special education in Brazil.

Another positive consequence of the training program was the 1st Carioca Alternative Communication Meeting, held in October 2018, in which a workshop was offered by six teachers. We had as audience of approximately 80 MRR teachers and regular class teachers, in addition to UERJ undergraduate and graduate students who made positive comments about the event. The group wants to organize further meetings like this in upcoming years.

The training program had a great impact on participants, other teachers, and education agents in the municipality. This is shown by evidence such as: the evaluation teachers completed at the end of their training, presented in the previous section of this chapter; and the WhatsApp analysis in which information about courses, adapted materials, case reports, etc., continues to be disseminated; the unsystematic observations we make about the program participants' current performance; and testimonials from the Experiential Workshop team.

The facilitating factors of this endeavor were the financial support of two research agencies – FAPERJ and CNPq – which allowed payment of scholarship holders, the purchase of tablets for the teachers, a data show for the Experiential Workshop, and office supplies, plastic for plasticization, and Velcro, among other things, that are scarce in the public school system. In addition, there was the commitment of all the teachers, the EW staff, and the UERJ scholarship holders, and the fact that this formation was institutionalized, that is, it was part of the agenda of EW, besides the duration of the training – four years. The promise of publishing the book with the collaboration of the participants and the planning of the event mentioned above also contributed to the success of this endeavor.

On the other hand, we had some obstacles, such as difficulties in communication between EW, the IHA board, and some school principals, who sometimes did not disclose the group meeting schedule and failed to invite more teachers from the classroom resources to attend Open Rooms.

Future challenges

Several studies point out that one of the major challenges regarding education in the large urban centers of Brazil and especially in Rio de Janeiro is due to a complex context involving aspects such as poverty and violence. The schools attended by the teachers participating in this study were mostly located in underserved communities, and situations involving these aspects were cited as a more complex problem than the needs of the special students included in these schools. Another important factor is the relationship between new technologies and education, which in spite of all discussions in recent decades, remains a major challenge for schools. In a time of intellectual pragmatism, in which the school still assumes the role of transmitting information, and for those special needs students, often excluded from this process, the possibility of communicating, the Alternative Communication and the Assistive Technology might introduce a playful perspective, intended to rescue, in the student, the pleasure and the possibility of social interaction and learning (Schirmer and Nunes, 2009). In order to overcome this, there is a need for investments in both initial and continuing teacher education and in low, medium, or high cost technology. These investments are necessary to ensure not only access to education, but also the effective permanence of these students in school. We also highlight the importance of investments in research in this area, so important to these transformations, that have contributed and may contribute to making the school truly inclusive.

Notes

1 Organ of the Rio de Janeiro Municipal Secretariat of Education responsible for the implementation of public policies aimed at the target population of special education.
2 Service promoted by the Helena Antipoff Institute aimed at the search for strategies and resources of the AT that facilitate the inclusion of special learners in daily school activities.
3 The goal of AT is to promote functionality related to the activity and participation of people with disabilities, disabilities or reduced mobility, aiming at their autonomy, independence, quality of life, and social inclusion (CAT 2007).
4 An area of clinical practice that attempts to compensate, either temporarily or permanently, for impairment and disability patterns of individuals with severe expressive communication disorders (i.e., severely speech-language and writing impaired; ASHA, 1989, p. 107).
5 WhatsApp – a cross-platform instant messaging and voice calling app for smartphones.
6 This is a data collection procedure that records the subject's action through video recording and, subsequently, places him/her as an evaluator of his/her own performance (Nunes et al., 2017).
7 The themes were: description of the cases studied, difficulties, inclusion, AAC resources for the student, suggestions for instructional practices, theoretical–practical questions and conceptions of communication, interaction, language, speech and thought, specialized educational care, family, relationship

between teachers, teacher performance, administrative difficulties, curricular adaptations, individualized educational plan (IEP), problematization approach, reading and writing, naturalistic teaching, open class design, applications, and research data analysis.

8 ARASAAC System is a free license system composed of 15,000 pictograms. Through the ARASAAC Portal, it is possible to have access to symbols and tools such as the Generator of Boards, specifically for the production of printed communication boards. This system was developed by the government of Aragon, Spain. It is available through the website www.catedu.es/arasaac/descargas.php#select (Souza and Pelosi, 2014).

9 www.eduerj.com/eng/?product=salas-abertas-formacao-de-professores-e-praticas-pedagogicas-em-comunicacao-alternativa-e-ampliada-nas-salas-de-recursos-multifuncionais

References

American Speech-Language-Hearing Association Committee on Augmentative Communication (1989). Competencies for speech-language pathologists providing services in augmentative communication. *Asha, 31*(3), 107–110.

Ascenção, M. J. L. (2007). *Ajudas técnicas no atendimento ao aluno com deficiência matriculados na rede regular de ensino de educação infantil* [Technical assistance in the care of students with disabilities enrolled in the regular kindergarten schools]. Unpublished manuscript, Faculdade de Filosofia e Ciências, Universidade Estadual Paulista, Brasil.

Beyer, H. O. (2003). A educação inclusiva: incompletudes escolares e perspectivas de ação. [Inclusive education: school incompleteness and action perspectives]. *Cadernos de Educação Especial, 2*(22), 33–44.

BRASIL. Ministério da Educação. Secretaria da Educação Especial (2009). *Resolução no. 4, de 02 de outubro de 2009* [Resolution no. 4, October 2, 2009]. Brasil, Brasília.

CAT. Ata da Reunião VII, de dezembro de (2007). Comitê de Ajudas Técnicas, Secretaria Especial dos Direitos Humanos da Presidência da República (CORDE/SEDH/PR). [Technical Assistance Committee] Disponível em:http://www.mj.gov.br/sedh/ct/corde/dpdh/corde. Acesso em: 01 jan. 2017.

Chun, R. Y. (2003). Comunicação suplementar e/ou alternativa: favorecimento da linguagem de um sujeito não falante [Augmentative and/or alternative communication: favoring the language of a non-speaking subject]. *Pró-fono, 15*(1), 55–64.

Cochran-Smith, M., & Zeichner, K. (2005). *Studying teacher education: the report of the AERA panel on research and teacher education*. London, Lawrence Erlbaum Associates.

Colombo, A. A., & Berbel, N. A. A. (2007). Metodologia da Problematização com o Arco de Maguerez e sua relação com os saberes de professores [Methodology of Problematization with the Maguerez Arch and its relationship with teachers' knowledge]. *Semina: Ciências Sociais e Humanas, 28*(2), 121–146.

Correia, L. M. (1999). *Alunos com necessidades educativas especiais nas classes regulares* [Students with special educational needs in regular classes]. Porto, Portugal, Porto Edit.

Deliberato, D., Nunes, L. R. P., & Walter, C. C. F. (2014). Linguagem e Comunicação alternativa: caminhos para a interação e comunicação [Language and Alternative Communication: ways for interaction and communication]. In M. A. Almeida & E. G. Mendes (Eds.), *A escola e o público-alvo da educação especial: apontamentos atuais* [The school and the special education target audience: current notes] (pp. 197–210). São Carlos, Marquezine & Manzini; Marília, ABPEE.

Deliberato, D., Paura, A. C., Massaro, M., & Rodrigues, V. (2008). Comunicação suplementar e ou alternativa no contexto da música: recursos e procedimentos para favorecer o processo de inclusão de alunos com deficiência [Augmentative and alternative communication in the context of music: resources and procedures to facilitate the process of inclusion of students with disabilities]. In S. Z. Pinho & J. R. C. Saglietti (Eds.), *Livro eletrônico dos Núcleos de ensino* [Teaching Centers E-Learning Book] (pp. 890–901). São Paulo, Cultura Acadêmica.

Deliberato, D., Paura, A. C., & Neta, D. P. (2007). Comunicação suplementar e alternativa no contexto da música [Augmentive and alternative communication in the context of music]. In L. R. O. P. Nunes, M. B. Pelosi, & M. R. Gomes (Eds.), *Um retrato da comunicação alternativa no Brasil* [A portrait of alternative communication in Brazil] (pp. 77–81). Rio de Janeiro, 4 Pontos /FINEP, v. 1.

Downing, J. E. (2009). Assessment of early communication skills. In G. Soto & C. Zangari (Eds.), *Practically speaking: language, literacy and academic development for students with AAC needs* (pp. 27–46). Baltimore, Paul H. Brookes.

Fogel, A. (1993). *Developing through relationships: origins of communication, self, and culture*. Chicago, University of Chicago Press.

Galvão Filho, T. T. A. (2009). *Tecnologia Assistiva para uma escola inclusiva: apropriação, demandas e perspectivas* [Assistive technology for an inclusive school: ownership, demands, and perspectives]. Unpublished doctoral dissertation, Universidade Federal da Bahia, Brasil.

Light, J. (2003). Shattering the silence: development of communicative competence by individuals who use AAC. In J. C. Light, D. R. Beukelman & J. Reichle (Eds.), *Communicative competence for individuals who use AAC: from research to effective practice* (pp. 3–38). Baltimore, MD, Paul H. Brookes.

Light, J., & Naughton, D. (2013). Putting people first: re-thinking the role of technology in augmentative and alternative communication intervention. *Augmentative and Alternative Communication, 29*(4), 299–309.

Lourenço, G. F. (2012). *Avaliação de um programa de formação sobre recursos de alta tecnologia assistiva e escolarização* [Evaluation of a training program on high technology assistive resources and schooling]. Doctoral dissertation, Universidade Federal de S. Carlos, Brasil. Retrieved from https://repositorio.ufscar.br/bitstream/handle/ufscar/2892/4285.pdf?sequence=1

Lucena, S. (2016). Culturas digitais e tecnologias móveis na educação [Digital cultures and mobile technologies in education]. *Educar em Revista, 59*, 277–290.

Machado, O. V. M. (1999). Novas práxis educativas no ensino de Ciências [New educational practices in Science teaching]. In I.F. Cappelletti, I. F. & L. A. N Lima (Eds.), *Formação de educadores: pesquisas e estudos qualitativos*. [Educational formation: qualitative research studies] (pp. 95–127). São Paulo: Olho D'Água.

Massaro, M., Deliberato, D., & Rodrigues, V. (2010). Augmentative and alternative communication resources in song interpreting and storytelling activities for disabled students. In Proceedings of 14th Biennial Conference of the International Society for Augmentative and Alternative Communication (pp. 1214–1217). Barcelona, ISAAC, v. 1.

Mendes, E. G., Cia, F., & Tannús-Valadão, G. (Eds.). (2015). *Inclusão escolar em foco: organização e funcionamento do Atendimento Educacional Especializado* [School inclusion in focus: organization and operation of Specialized Educational Services] S. Carlos. Marquezine and Manzini, ABPEE.

Moraes, K. C., & Berbel, N. A. (2006). O uso da metodologia da problematização para a investigação sobre avaliação da aprendizagem. O que há de específico para o ensino superior? [The use of the problematization methodology for learning assessment research. What's specific to higher education?]. *Semina: Ciências Sociais e Humanas, 27*(2), 169–186.

Nunes, L. R. O. P., Silva, S. P. N., & Schirmer, C. R. (2017). Salas de Recursos Multifuncionais de Referência no Rio de Janeiro: análise de conteúdo das reuniões de pesquisa – 2013–2016 [Multifunctional Reference Resource Rooms in Rio de Janeiro: Content Analysis of Research Meetings – 2013–2016]. In L. R. O. P. Nunes & C. R. Schirmer (Eds.), *Salas Abertas: formação de professores e práticas pedagógicas em comunicação alternativa e ampliada nas salas de recurso multifuncionais [Open Rooms: Teacher Training and Pedagogical Practices in Augmentative and Alternative Communication in multifunctional resource rooms]* (pp. 29–62). Rio de Janeiro, Eduerj.

Paura, A. C., & Deliberato, D. (2007). Comunicação Alternativa e/ou Suplementar como recurso de apoio no ensino do conteúdo pedagógico de criança deficiente incluída [Alternative and/or Augmentative Communication as a support resource in teaching the pedagogical content of disabled children included] *Proceedings of II Congresso Brasileiro de Comunicação Alternativa* [II Brazilian Congress of Alternative Communication] (pp. 1–8). Campinas, Unicamp.

Pelosi, M. (2008). *Inclusão e Tecnologia Assistiva* [Inclusion and Assistive Technology]. Doctoral dissertation, Universidade do Estado do Rio de Janeiro, Brasil. Retrieved from www.proped.pro.br/teses/teses_pdf/2004_1-72-DO.pdf

Pletsch, M. (2009). *Repensando a Inclusão escolar de pessoas com deficiência mental: diretrizes políticas, currículo e práticas pedagógicas* [Rethinking school inclusion for people with mental deficiency: policy guidelines, curriculum and pedagogical practices]. Doctoral dissertation, Universidade do Estado do Rio de Janeiro, Brasil. Retrieved from www.proped.pro.br/teses/teses_pdf/2006_1-198-DO.pdf

Reily, L. (2015). Comunidades de prática como paisagem da formação em Comunicação Alternativa e Ampliada no Brasil. [Communities of practice as a background for formation in Augmentative and Alternative Communication in Brazil]. In R. Y. Chun et al. (Eds.), *Comunicação Alternativa: ocupando territórios* (pp. 51–67). [Alternative Communication: occupying territories]. São Carlos: Marquezine & Manzini: ABPEE.

Rocha, E. F., Luiz, A., & Zulizan, M. A. R. (2003). Reflexões sobre as possíveis contribuições da terapia ocupacional nos processos de inclusão escolar [Reflections on the possible contributions of occupational therapy to school inclusion processes]. *Revista Terapia Ocupacional[Occupational Therapy Magazine], 14*(2), 72–78.

Sameshima, F. S. (2011). *Capacitação de professores no contexto de sistemas de comunicação suplementar e alternativa* [Teacher training in the context of augmentative and alternative communication systems]. Doctoral dissertation, Universidade Estadual Paulista, Brasil. Retrieved from https://repositorio.unesp.br/bit stream/handle/11449/102185/sameshima_fs_dr_mar.pdf?sequence=1

Schirmer, C. R., & Nunes, L. R. O. P. (2009). *Perfil de alunos de pedagogia que estão frequentando curso de formação inicial de professores para atuação na área de tecnologia assistiva com ênfase em comunicação alternativa/ ampliada* [Profile of pedagogical students attending initial teacher education course for assistive technology with emphasis on alternative/augmentative communication] Paper presented at the V Seminário Nacional de Pesquisa em Educação Especial: Formação de Professores em Foco [V National Research Seminar on Special Education: Teacher Training in Focus]. São Paulo, Brasil.

Schön, D. (2000). *Educando o profissional reflexivo*: um novo design para o ensino e a aprendizagem. [Educating the reflexive professional: A new design to teaching and learning]. Porto Alegre: Artes Médicas.

Souza, V. L. V., & Pelosi, M. B. (2014). Pranchas Estáticas e Dinâmicas Construídas com Símbolos ARASAAC em Softwares de Livre Acesso [Static and Dynamic Boards Built with ARASAAC Symbols on Open Access Software]. *Cadernos de Terapia Ocupacional da UFSCar [Occupational Therapy UFSCar Notebooks], 22,* 301–306.

Trevizor, T. T., & Chun, R. Y. (2004). O desenvolvimento da linguagem por meio do sistema pictográfico de comunicação [Language development through the pictographic communication system]. *Profono, 16*(3), 323–332.

Vavoula, G. N. (2005). D4.4: *A Study of Mobile Learning Practices*: Internal report of MOBI learn Project.

Verussa, E. O., & Manzini, E. J. (2009). Tecnologia Assistiva para o ensino de alunos com deficiência: um estudo com professores do ensino fundamental [Assistive Technology for teaching disabled students: a study with elementary school teachers]. In Paper presented at V *Congresso Brasileiro Multidisciplinar de Educação Especial [V Multidisciplinary Brazilian Congress of Special Education]*, Londrina, Brasil.

Von Teztchner, S. V. (2005). Inclusão de crianças em educação pré-escolar regular utilizando comunicação suplementar e alternativa. [Inclusion of children in regular pre-school education using supplementary and alternative communication]. *Revista Brasileira de Educação Especial [Brazilian Journal of Special Education], 11*(2), 151–184.

Von Tetzchner, S. V. (2009). Suporte ao desenvolvimento da comunicação suplementar e alternativa [Support for the development of supplemental and alternative communication]. In D. Deliberato, M. J. Gonçalves, & E. C. Macedo (Eds.), *Comunicação alternativa: teoria, prática, tecnologias e pesquisa [Alternative communication: theory, practice, technologies and research]* (pp. 14–25). São Paulo, Memnon.

Wenger, E. (1998). *Communities of practice: Learning, meaning and identity.* Cambridge, England: Cambridge University Press.

Zuttin, F. S. (2008). *Tecnologia assistiva na educação: considerações sobre os recursos pedagógicos adaptados* [Assistive technology in education: considerations about adapted pedagogical resources]. Unpublished manuscript, Faculdade de Filosofia e Ciências, Universidade Estadual Paulista, Brasil.

29

DOING MORE THAN TELLING STORIES

Wendy Bryant

Introduction

Being invited into the exclusive world of a university or college can be both an exciting and frightening experience at the same time. The invitation usually rests on an identity of having been disabled or unwell, and probably still being so. Your experiences of professional health and social care are important. There is an opportunity, maybe, to put things right for the future by sharing details of the impact of professional practice. But your story of serious ill health and disability might overshadow that opportunity. Students and lecturers might be worried by what they hear and frightened that it might happen to them (Anderson et al., 2019). They might nurse an even greater fear of failing as they learn professional practices (Smith et al., 2015). That fear will affect their learning.

It is possible to overcome these fears and create learning experiences which enable everyone involved to gain knowledge, skills and understanding. Drawing on work with mental health service users and occupational therapy students Bryant et al. (2012), I share experiences of moving away from storytelling to doing things together. Studying occupation, or doing, is important for pre-registration occupational therapists, as the medium for therapy. However, occupation is relevant to everyone who wants to work together inclusively. It can prevent this:

> The situation was formal, with many people present. The spotlight moved to us, standing in a group. My colleague was mumbling, and looking at his feet. I could not hear the words but the rhythm of the story sounded familiar: his case story. I froze: it was not the story for this event. I hadn't prepared for this.

This happened to me years ago. I was excited by what we had achieved in our collaborative projects but unprepared for events which showcased them. I hadn't explored what my colleagues thought about their presence there, or our occupational identities. My occupational identity was researcher and educator, doing innovative, collaborative research and teaching. The formality of the event heightened anxieties, polarising what we said and thought. Uppermost in my colleague's mind was that he had been invited to join the project because he was a mental health service user. That was his prevalent occupational identity, and so he started to tell the story of his ill health (Cunningham, 2017).

Yet the work we had been doing together extended far beyond mental health services, into the university classrooms and art gallery. To me, he was a colleague. But I hadn't discussed that with him, and so his case story rose up into the conversation. We could have discussed what we were going to say, as our shared story. Focusing on what we were doing together and how it shaped who we were, our occupational identities, could have been a richer conversation. I understand this as an example of an occupational perspective (Njelesani et al., 2012).

In this chapter, after a description of our joint work, an occupational perspective is explained, explored and evaluated. The conventional guest lecture is contrasted with the effects of focusing on the many different things people can do. Examples, drawing on experience, are shared.

You may have observed that I am a solitary author describing collaborative work, which involved mental health service users, occupational therapists, academics and students. However, my involvement has ended now, because of serious ill health, although I am in contact with the others informally, supporting each other with our new, separate projects and challenges. My particular role in creating and leading our work, across research and education, has been most relevant for this chapter. Our work was primarily concerned with research into mental health service user experiences of local services, and living with psychosis (Bryant et al., 2012; Makdisi et al., 2013; Bryant et al., 2019). The local services were closely linked with the university where I worked, because they hosted pre-registration student practice placements and employed many graduates. Local staff and service users gave guest lectures, assessed students, attended special events and advised on programme management and development. The partnership was mutually beneficial and highly valued. Our work was shared as a good example, giving us access to important resources. Initially, we were quite focused on things like libraries and computers. Then we shifted our attention to people (us, other service users, students and staff), finding new ways of doing what we needed to do and thinking about why we needed to do it, another outcome of an occupational perspective.

What is an occupational perspective?

To take a perspective is to see situations in a particular way, bringing some aspects closer and acknowledging others further in the distance. Imagine standing on a hill or at the top of a tall building, and choosing where to look. You will have a keen sense of the place you are in and the places beyond that you cannot see so clearly. To take an occupational perspective is to bring the things people do closer into view (Njelesani et al., 2012). It is based on the belief if we do nothing, we die, and that survival is dependent on occupation (Kosma et al., 2013). Education relies on occupation: students have to do different things to demonstrate their learning, such as examinations. Designing programmes from an occupational perspective involves creating inspiring learning experiences with close attention to the requirements (deadlines, room booking). Learning through doing is a recognized pedagogical approach: from Freire's work, this can be understood as praxis, or learning through activity, interacting with situations (Freire, 1996). Designing research from an occupational perspective similarly involves paying close attention to what people are doing and why they are doing it. This applies equally to the research topic and methods (Bryant et al., 2016a).

There are critical discussions about what an occupational perspective is, because of its infinitely relevant focus (Njelesani et al., 2012). Much of the literature has emerged from occupational science, a body of knowledge about what people do in its broadest sense (Kosma et al., 2013). Three aspects are explored here to help understanding.

Utopias

Many utopias have been described from an occupational perspective (Wilcock, 2001). To describe a perfect world, it is necessary to attend to what people would do in that world (Morris, 2003). Conversely, in a dystopia, everyday lives feature a central and inhuman control over what people do (Zamyatin, 1993). When thinking about how to involve people in education and research, it can be helpful to consider what people would do in an ideal world, to reveal values and hopes of those regulating health and social care professional education programmes (HCPC, 2014; Winn and Lindqvist, 2019). Happell et al. (2015) observed that most accounts of user involvement were based on people being guest lecturers. So, in an ideal world, would the student learning experience consist of a well-structured and engaging talk, by someone who is also able to answer questions at the end? What does this scenario say about the sort of person who is welcomed to share their experience, and the expectations of the students who have come to listen and learn? It could raise questions about inclusion and pedagogic models.

If the focus for involvement were broader, where what people do is a central concern, what happens then? Then lecturers have to consider other activities, such as admissions, research and assessment. For example, Heaslip et al. (2018) described user involvement in recruitment and selection of adult nursing students. There was an important contrast in how candidates were perceived, between professional attributes valued by academic staff and human qualities valued by service users. In an Observed Structured Practical Examination (OSPE), occupational therapy students had to explain the stress response to a service user and an academic. The service user found this an interesting and valuable experience. Although this element caused some students considerable anxiety, they understood the relevance of it to their future professional practice and valued the involvement of a service user. In preparation, they were encouraged to think of their own occupational performance: what could they do to share their knowledge effectively? Would they draw or enact the stress response?

A utopian vision informed our research partnership between service users and occupational therapy staff from local mental health services, and lecturers (Bryant et al., 2019). The vision started with creating a space for user-led research to take place within the university. Teaching emerged from the research, rather than being a goal at the beginning, and so was focused on presenting our collaborative work to students and hosting MSc research projects. Subsequently, some service users became involved in recruitment. Students were appreciated as a continually refreshing resource for our research programme: each year there would be new students keen to learn how to conduct research in partnership with service users (Bryant et al., 2019).

Form, Function and Meaning

William Morris revealed his utopian vision in *News from Nowhere* (2003), based in the Thames Valley (UK) in the late nineteenth century. Industrialisation and poverty were replaced by useful work and shared resources. The Houses of Parliament were repurposed as a compost processing centre, dealing with every sort of organic waste. These changes in form and function were confusing to the narrator, who questioned why people were doing things differently. Similarly, a useful framework for design and process is centred on occupational form, function and meaning (Larson et al., 2003). The idea that form follows function may be familiar from architecture and engineering: the shape of a building or machine is determined by its function, so a house will be different to a warehouse. How were the Houses of Parliament redesigned in Morris's novel to accommodate the new occupations, and how did that affect what people did and the way they did it? Occupational form is the way people do things, and function is why they do it (Bryant, 2016). Rapport (2003) distinguishes between function and meaning, suggesting this:

- Function: *in order to* – I join a research project in order to improve the experience of others.
- Meaning: *because* – I join a research project because I want to share my knowledge and experience.

So, a person may seek to speak to large audiences of students (form), because they are keen to influence as many people as possible (function), but also because they are familiar with public speaking and this is a meaningful way for them to be involved. Another person may be unable to speak formally because of intrusive paranoid thoughts but can work very effectively with one or two students on a project, where relationships can be developed and there is more scope for taking control of the pace of the work (form). Comparing a formal lecture to ongoing project work is to compare occupational forms.

When discussing occupational forms, a hierarchy could be used: occupation, activity, skill and task (Creek, 2003). Imagine service users are working with students to create a visual map to apply theory to practice. The occupation is being a participant in a collaborative learning session; the activity is being involved in a seminar discussion. The skill is concerned with collaboratively producing the visual map. The tasks might be about writing, drawing, listening, holding pens, watching and keeping track of time. Alternatively, consider the different ways of doing in Figure 29.1. Extracting the verbs, or the doing words, from the different tasks takes them out of context for discussion (McKay and Molineux, 2000). One campus building could only be accessed by pressing a green button, which was not immediately visible. Because I worked in the building, it was automatic for me to press the button and open the door. For visitors, it was confusing and off-putting. Bringing students and service users together to explore the campus revealed such barriers. Yet this way of learning might not be obvious as an example

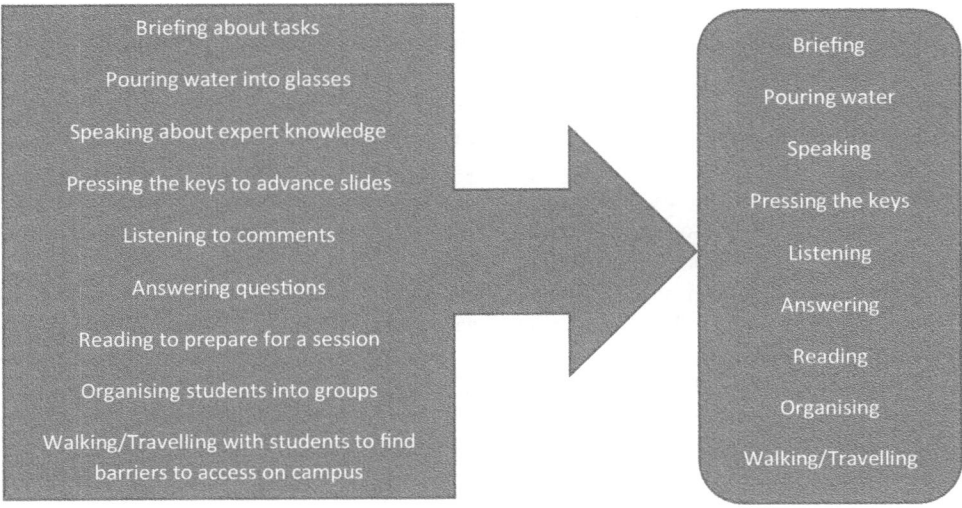

Briefing about tasks	Briefing
Pouring water into glasses	Pouring water
Speaking about expert knowledge	Speaking
Pressing the keys to advance slides	Pressing the keys
Listening to comments	Listening
Answering questions	Answering
Reading to prepare for a session	Reading
Organising students into groups	Organising
Walking/Travelling with students to find barriers to access on campus	Walking/Travelling

Figure 29.1 Creating and negotiating different occupational forms for user involvement means that more people can become involved, enriching the experiences. Looking beyond the good speakers to see who else was interested in being involved is about being inclusive and fair, a justice issue

of user involvement. In preparing the module, talking about walking/travelling (the occupation/task), as well as barriers to access (the goal of the session), opened up new possibilities for involvement.

Occupational justice and injustice

In education, some occupations are valued more highly than others. Listening to an expert is valued so much that a break might be cut short, even though informal discussions in breaks can transform our understanding of complex ideas (Thornburg, 2014). Devaluing occupations such as having a break is an occupational justice issue (Durocher et al., 2014), affecting what people can do. In many situations, we have power to shape how and what we do, but have to negotiate (Freire, 1996). For one presentation, we had to develop a different form, or way of doing it. One co-presenter had an authoritative air and he became an interviewer. The other co-presenter was unable to follow a script, but was very good at making comments. So, I was interviewed about the project we had done together, interrupted with comments in a way that constantly raised the questions: who was in charge? Who had the power?

Denying people the opportunity to shape an occupational form or negotiate its function is an occupational injustice, which can be avoided by careful preparation. Smith et al. (2015) described how a local drama group, Act Too, contributed to pre-registration nursing programmes. The Act Too members, who all had learning disabilities, created and rehearsed their session to lecturers before performing to students. Their shared expertise in drama and performance was significant in the negotiations and preparations. The form the session took belonged to them.

An occupational perspective reveals valued and marginalized occupations (Durocher et al., 2014). Reading is a valued occupation for students, but what about service users? We set up groups to read and discuss articles for student research projects, for collaborative qualitative metasyntheses (Major and Savin-Baden, 2012). The students developed their research question in partnership with a local occupational therapist and former service users. The student would search for relevant literature, provide articles for discussion and lead the discussion, under the supervision of a lecturer. Guidance was provided about where to start. Discussions often developed from the findings before working back to the method and forward to the discussion.

Occupational injustices can take different forms. Consider who is being deprived of the opportunity to be involved, and why that is. Occupational deprivation is a term used to describe how people can be prevented from doing what they need or want to do because of external factors (Durocher et al., 2014). For example, a person may be unable to leave their home. To be involved in student education would depend on lecturers overcoming the barriers between the university and the person's home. A video link could be set up, a pre-recorded film created or an online chat scheduled (Snelgrove et al., 2016).

Occupational alienation is evident when people are doing something, but not in a way that meets their needs (Bryant, 2016). Tokenistic involvement, where the presence of service users is valued above their contribution, is an example of occupational alienation. Students and lecturers can be occupationally alienated, too: showing boredom, frustration and disengagement. This is often because the learning experiences are not meaningful. The lecture, session, project or placement is endured. Active participation overcomes alienation by increasing a sense of ownership over the learning experience, and service users can help with this. Students who did the collaborative qualitative metasyntheses were daunted by the research module. However, service users brought the research articles alive through their comments, observations and critique.

Occupational imbalance is also associated with occupational injustice (Durocher et al., 2014). This is where people do not have control over how much they do, doing too much or too little of the things they value. If a panel of service users were invited to meet students and answer questions, occupational imbalance could be a useful concept to discuss in preparation. Having a panel is to give students access to different perspectives, and so service users can support each other. But, just like the TV panel shows, there are many ways in which people can lose control over how they participate. Attending carefully to how the room is set up, and how people are briefed about the purpose and their respective roles (including the students), can help to demonstrate how involvement is more than getting service users into a classroom. As a guest in the classroom, it is difficult to take control. The lecturer is important to ensure preparations take place.

Occupational deprivation, alienation and imbalance overlap and combine to create other concepts, such as occupational marginalization. In a textbook about occupational therapy and mental health, we (the editors) wanted service user commentaries on the chapters (Bryant et al., 2014). There was a complex process of publicity, recruitment, briefing and support through the writing process. We recognized that people might not get involved because they assumed they were not eligible, not being academic or good at writing. Occupational marginalization, excluding those who could not read and write well, was a risk. It was important to share the function of the commentaries: to provide further insights about the chapter topics, based on direct experience. We encouraged people to use support and to negotiate what they did. The commentaries were diverse, with some academic critiques and others developing the themes of the chapters using personal experiences. They enriched the book as a learning resource (Bryant et al., 2014).

Beyond the guest lecture

Conventionally, users are invited to share their stories of ill-health in pre-registration student education and research (Anderson et al., 2019; Happell et al., 2015). To be empowered to tell their stories, space needs to be created by those in charge of the teaching programme. Driven by the expectation that "users" will be involved in a teaching programme, teaching staff create "slots" in a timetable (Anderson et al., 2019; Happell et al., 2015). In contrast, involvement beyond the guest lecture means the act of storytelling becomes one part of doing things together.

Stories are important to make experiences of ill health coherent and human, engaging the heart as well as the mind (Bocking et al., 2019; Job et al., 2017). Sharing case stories can help people learn about how theory and practice intertwine, but telling a traumatic story repeatedly can be traumatic in itself (Anderson et al., 2019; Sword, 2012). Snelgrove et al. (2016) got around this difficulty by creating "Talking Heads" films as part of teaching psychology to nurses. This was largely successful, but some students and staff questioned the representativeness of the service user. This was partly due to her rare condition, but also because of her apparent lack of distress. Actors were suggested to portray human distress using service user stories (Snelgrove et al., 2016), although the expectation of distress must be challenged. In our collaborative work, we used stories carefully to explore how to share our vulnerabilities safely and for mutual development. Later, I found the work of Thornburg (2014) helpful, distinguishing between the different forms of teaching and introducing the idea of a wise storyteller.

The wise storyteller

Although Thornburg (2014) assumed that the wise storyteller would be a lecturer, there could be the same role for users sharing their story and wisdom, offering personal experiences and observations. Their occupational identities would be important (Cunningham, 2017). If I were to speak about my experiences of health care, I would have two primary occupational identities. As a lecturer, I would want my story to be engaging, informative and thought-provoking. The content would be from my experiences as a service user, but which story do I tell? Having a long-term health problem means repeatedly sharing stories with different people, often on the same day. These stories are tailored to ensure the other person listens. Often health professionals structure the storytelling with a series of questions about my situation. The wisdom is often located in the health professional interpreting my story.

Yet my wisdom is essential, to make the links which the health professionals may not see because of their specialized perspective. A student audience may make unexpected links. I have found some students leap to solutions because of their anxiety about pain. Job et al. (2017) describe how stories can be used to move students from being perplexed, to reflecting deeply about idealized practice and theory to the real world described by a person with direct experience. So, my story needs to provoke deep reflection, not superficial solutions, to capture the significance of my experiences. As a lecturer, I created a seminar structure which involved a short formal presentation by service users. Then students were divided into smaller groups to reflect together on what they had heard and present their reflections back to us. We joined these reflection groups to encourage sharing and help students discuss the importance of their observations.

Bocking et al. (2019) evaluated the COMMUNE project, an international project involving Experts by Experience (users) in pre-registration mental health nursing education. The Experts by Experience co-produced a module as well as delivering it, although details of how this happened are not given. The project was informed by Freire's work (1996), seeing education as a process of dialogue, rather than students being filled with information. Dialogue is important because as it takes place, people can move to indicate their involvement, such as putting a hand up to ask a question. This shifts focus from the primary speakers, offering a chance for an audience to shape the session. They may have stories they want to share.

The story worth telling

Informal and subjective writing is often discouraged, except for specific forms such as reflections and case stories (Sword, 2012). These forms are often limited to a template or appendix, guiding content and structure. It is as if this style of writing distracts from the serious purposes of scholarship, and choices could have been driven by personal preferences, rather than reasoned decisions, based on rigorous study of relevant resources. This belief, especially when applied to module delivery, can restrict user involvement. Yet external non-academic speakers are often highly valued because of their subjectivity, informality and ability to engage students. Students will be exposed to lively and informative stories, which sometimes heighten the contrast between the classroom and the real world. Good speakers and writers can be informal and serious (Sword, 2012). So, what makes a good story? Something can be learned from journalists, who write and present concisely to rapidly engage audiences.

One story I used to share with students as a lecturer involved a policeman, a saucepan and a distressed young man. I shared it very occasionally, not being particularly proud of it but also being acutely aware of its sensationalist properties. As a community occupational therapist concerned for the man's welfare but being unable to access him, I had called the police for help and he had assaulted them. This story had the potential to reduce people to caricatures, distracting from an important message about the difficulties of supporting people with serious illnesses in the community. Caricatures, or stereotypes, are dehumanizing: from an occupational perspective, this can mean unquestioned assumptions about what people do. A story could be constructed from the two people and the saucepan that would resemble a Punch and Judy puppet show. Some journalistic styles engage audiences with sensational stories, and it is important that lecturers do not do the same thing, tempting as it may be to try to sustain weary students.

Managing sensationalism

But sensational stories do take place in health and social care. They could be shared by involving service users in discussions about service developments, ethics and politics. For major adaptations to houses, such as installing a wet room for a wheelchair user, social care occupational therapists usually recommend whether public funding can be provided. There are published stories about disabled people being forced to use unsuitable bathrooms or being trapped at home because public funding is refused or delayed (Preece, 2015, is an example). Discussing these stories in the context of welfare reform and particularly the myth of the "benefit scrounger" is important. Imagine how enriched the discussion could be with the involvement of people who have had their houses adapted and probably also receive welfare benefits in the long term. But this exposes the service user to the unpleasant possibility of being stereotyped and misunderstood (Winn and Lindqvist, 2019).

Shared stories

Bringing people together to create shared stories avoids some of this risk. Our Living with Psychosis research was our shared experience (Researching Psychosis Together, 2012). Individual experiences of psychosis could be presented as part of the bigger story. We agreed to do formal large lectures together, with questions from the students sent to us in advance so we could prepare our responses. Some students had already met us in other places, when on practice placements and attending meetings, which was helpful. Different opportunities need to be created and acknowledged to be inclusive (Bryant et al., 2012). Students, service users, lecturers and others are occupational beings: everyone has different capacities which can be developed in partnership.

Back to the basics

To be more inclusive and imaginative, involvement needs to go back to the basics, such as identifying its purpose and the activities which could be enhanced by service user knowledge and expertise. Bocking et al. (2019) clearly defined the educational goals for the COMMUNE project, aiming to develop specific skills and understanding of complex factors in user experiences, such as stigma. These goals had been identified collaboratively, drawing on focus group findings. Being clear about the pedagogical theory informing curriculum design is important for user involvement. Freire contrasted different pedagogies: depositing knowledge in students, or developing their thinking using dialogue (Job et al., 2017). Students expecting to be given comprehensive information for their future professional practice could be disappointed by user involvement, which is inevitably subjective. This could be the basis for criticisms about representation (Snelgrove et al., 2016). In contrast, active reflection and discussion before, during and after contact with service users is more likely to deepen and enrich understanding (Job et al., 2017).

Heaslip et al. (2018) discussed the challenge of defining who is a service user. They decisively rejected the idea that academic and administrative staff were users of primary care and therefore healthcare service users. Having a significant health condition is very different, giving a person frequent and sometimes distressing contact with health services, rather than occasional consultations with a GP. O'Brien and Dadswell (2017) recognized the difficulties of involving vulnerable people, and the need for pro-active support from academic staff. In a scoping review, they offered insights into different types of educational activities. In the absence of national guidelines, frameworks from different universities were shared. If formal processes are not stated, there is a greater risk of tokenism (Happell et al., 2015). Because of the lack of national guidance, Winn and Lindqvist (2019) drew on experience of involving service users since 2005 to produce guidelines, which were scrutinized by some of those users involved prior to publication. Many practical suggestions were made, with a recurrent theme of remaining mindful of the purpose for involvement. Staff could sustain user involvement with a repeating cycle of briefing, doing and debriefing.

Anderson et al. (2019) evaluated user involvement in interprofessional education, gathering views of service users, students and lecturers. Users could work as co-tutors or mentors. They welcomed the opportunity, feeling less like a "specimen" and more like a colleague, but were wary of the expectations of leadership. Likewise, students were concerned about user capacity for delivering material beyond their direct experience. Recognising that not everyone wants to take a leading role is part of careful preparation, which Anderson et al. (2019) thought was invisible to students but important to users and lecturers. Although practice placements might seem to offer the best form of user involvement, student experience often reflects power differences in the clinical setting, with little opportunity for deep reflection on the implications. The pressure to demonstrate professional competence and work together to provide services can override deep learning about the user experience (Job et al., 2017).

Some examples from experience

Returning to the effects of taking an occupational perspective, Fortune et al. (2016) advise caution with a focus solely on doing. It is equally important to consider how people are with each other, and what they hope to achieve. Working with mutual respect within a collaborative relationship benefits everyone and creates inclusive "spaces for scholarship" (Fortune et al., 2016, p. 313). Employing disabled people and those with direct experience of using services as academics models a broader occupational identity. But employment is scarce because of funding challenges (Happell et al., 2015). Becoming an academic requires a huge shift in identity, engaging with multiple new roles (Ennals et al., 2016). An occasional session is more feasible and appealing for some. Cunningham (2017) described the usefulness of content and process in identity theory. So, an occupational identity might be associated with the content of past occupations, such as being a member of a mental health peer support group. The process of engaging in new occupations such as coming into a university to work with students will add other dimensions to this identity. Understanding this would have been useful for preparation in the example at the beginning of this chapter. Here are some more examples, briefly describing the effects of taking an occupational perspective.

Living with psychosis

This research project was designed by service users, working with occupational therapists. The aim was to explore user experience of psychosis, identifying helpful and unhelpful aspects. After three years of working together, we were ready to recruit an MSc occupational therapy student. The student worked with two service users to publicize, recruit and support other service users to participate in two focus groups. Supervised by another lecturer, she wrote the research up for her dissertation and worked on a journal article, while we shared the findings locally in presentations and a report (Makdisi et al., 2013; Researching Psychosis Together, 2012).

User perspectives on acute mental health

Similarly, for another research thread, two MSc students were recruited to work on a research project with service user advisers and occupational therapists based in the local acute mental health unit. One of the MSc students went on to publish the findings with our support (Bryant et al., 2016b). The project evolved so one of the Living with Psychosis researchers, who was also a peer support worker at the unit, became a co-researcher in a photovoice project (Birken and Bryant, 2019). Meanwhile, the MSc student became a PhD student, taking forward another thread of the research with other service users.

Using action research

One MSc student shared my enthusiasm for action research for her MSc dissertation. She worked jointly with service users in an advisory group for a university research centre, the Centre for Citizen Participation, setting up a working group. She used her experience of project management in a local authority setting, developing it in an academic research context.

Ways of Seeing

I was on the steering group for Ways of Seeing, an innovative project to involve mental health service users as curators at a regional art gallery. We prepared for user involvement by creating a BSc student practice placement to oversee the initial phase. This involved a series of workshops and visits to other galleries. Later, as the project evolved, an MSc student interviewed some of those involved. This project inspired and refreshed our thinking about experiences of mental health, learning and an occupational perspective (Wilson et al., 2015; Lawson et al., 2014).

Conclusion

With an occupational perspective, the gap between practice in theory and practice in the real world can be bridged in an accessible and practical way (Smith et al., 2015). Bridging this gap takes courage and effort but is valued by students, who identify their own learning needs and can embrace sadness, embarrassment and anger, as well as positive feelings associated with greater awareness (Smith et al., 2015). Reflection enables students to critically question their own practice and that of others, understanding how to be more inclusive. Everyone involved is challenged to look beyond professional practice to the person on the receiving end, in a humanizing process (Bocking et al., 2019; Heaslip et al., 2018). Using an occupational perspective can strengthen this humanizing process, as the focus on what people are doing is simultaneously practical and thoughtful, individual and collective, and readily understood by all.

References

Anderson Elizabeth S, Ford Jenny, Thorpe Lucy (2019). Perspectives on patients and carers in leading teaching roles in interprofessional education. *Journal of Interprofessional Care*, 33(2), 216–225. doi:10. 1080/13561820.2018.1531834

Birken M, Bryant W (2019). A photovoice study of user experiences of an occupational therapy department within an acute inpatient mental health setting. *British Journal of Occupational Therapy early online.* doi: 10.1177/0308022619836954

Bocking Julia, Happell B, Scholz B, Horgan A et al. (2019). "It is meant to be heart rather than head"; International perspectives of teaching from lived experience in mental health nursing programs. *International Journal of Mental Health Nursing.* doi:10.1111/inm.12635

Bryant W (2016). The Dr Elizabeth Casson memorial lecture 2016: Occupational alienation – A concept for modelling participation in practice and research. *British Journal of Occupational Therapy*, 79(9), 521–529. doi:10.1177/0308022616662282

Bryant W, Cordingley K, Adomako E, Birken M (2019). Making activism a participatory, inclusive and developmental process: A research programme involving mental health service users. *Disability & Society.* https://doi.org/10.1080/09687599.2019.1613963

Bryant W, Cordingley K, Sims K et al. (2016b). Collaborative research exploring mental health service user perspectives on acute inpatient occupational therapy. *British Journal of Occupational Therapy*, 79(10).

Bryant W, Fieldhouse J, Bannigan K (2014) (Eds.), *Creek's occupational therapy in mental health*, 5th edition. Oxford: Elsevier.

Bryant W, Parsonage J, Tibbs A, Andrews C, Clark J, Franco L (2012). Meeting in the mist: Key considerations in a collaborative research partnership with people with mental health issues. *WORK: A Journal of Prevention, Assessment, and Rehabilitation*, 43(1), 23–31.

Bryant W, Pettican A, Coetzee S (2016a). Designing participatory research to relocate margins, borders and centres. In Pollard N, Sakalleriou D (Eds.), *Occupational therapies without borders*, 2nd edition. Edinburgh: Elsevier.

Creek J (2003). *Occupational therapy defined as a complex intervention.* London: College of Occupational Therapists.

Cunningham Miranda (2017). Broadening understandings of occupational identity. In Sakellariou Dikaios, Pollard Nick (Eds.), *Occupational therapies without borders. Integrating justice with practice*, 2nd edition. Edinburgh: Elsevier.

Department of Health (2010). *Equity and excellence: Liberating the NHS.* The Stationary Office. Retrieved from: www.gov.uk/government/publications/liberating-the-nhs-white-paper

Durocher E, Gibson B, Rappolt S (2014). Occupational justice: A conceptual review. *Journal of Occupational Science*, 21(4), 418–430. doi:10.1080/14427591.2013.775692

Ennals Priscilla, Tracy Fortune, Anne Williams, Kate D'Cruz (2016). Shifting occupational identity: Doing, being, becoming and belonging in the academy. *Higher Education Research & Development*, 35(3), 433–446. doi:10.1080/07294360.2015.1107884

Fortune Tracy, Priscilla Ennals, Anoo Bhopti, Cheryl Neilson, Susan Darzins, Christopher Bruce (2016). Bridging identity "chasms": Occupational therapy academics' reflections on the journey towards scholarship. *Teaching in Higher Education*, 21(3), 313–325. doi:10.1080/13562517.2016.1141289

Freire Paulo (1996). *Pedagogy of the oppressed.* New York: Continuum.

Happell Brenda, Dianne Wynaden, Jenny Tohotoa, Chris Plantania-Phung, Louise Byrne, Graham Martin, Scott Harris (2015). Mental health lived experience academics in tertiary education: The views of nurse academics. *Nurse Education Today*, 35, 113–117.

Health and Care Professions Council (2014). Standards of education and training. Retrieved from: www.hcpc-uk.org/publications/standards/index.asp?id=183

Heaslip Vanessa, Janet Scammell, Anne Mills, Ashley Spriggs, Andrea Addis, Mandy Bond, Carolyn Latchford, Angela Warren, Juliet Borwell, Stephen Tee (2018). Service user engagement in healthcare education as a mechanism for value based recruitment: An evaluation study. *Nurse Education Today*, 60, 107–113.

Job Claire, Ken Yan Wong, Sally Anstey (2017). Patients' stories in healthcare curricula: Creating a reflective environment for the development of practice and professional knowledge. *Journal of Further and Higher Education.* doi:10.1080/0309877X.2017.1404559

Kosma A, Bryant W, Wilson L (2013). Drawing on Wilcock: An investigation of the impact of her published work on occupational therapy practice and research. *British Journal of Occupational Therapy*, 76(4), 179–185.

Larson E, Wood W, Clark F (2003). Occupational science: Building the science and practice of occupation through an academic discipline. In Crepeau E, Cohn E, Schell B (Eds.), *Willard & Spackman's occupational therapy*, 10th edition. Philadelphia: Lippincott, Williams & Wilkins, 15–26.

Lawson, J, Reynolds, F, Bryant, W, Wilson, L (2014). 'It's like having a day of freedom, a day off from being ill': Exploring the experiences of people living with mental health problems who attend a community-based arts project, using interpretative phenomenological analysis. *Journal of Health Psychology*, 19(6), 765–777.

Major Claire Howell, Maggi Savin-Baden (2012). *An introduction to qualitative research synthesis: Managing the information explosion in social science research.* Abingdon: Routledge.

Makdisi Lana, Alison Blank, Wendy Bryant, Christine Andrews, Lucia Franco, Jackie Parsonage (2013). Facilitators and barriers to living with psychosis: An exploratory collaborative study of the perspectives of mental health service users. *British Journal of Occupational Therapy*, 76(9), 418–426.

McKay Elizabeth, Molineux Matthew (2000). Occupation: reaffirming its place in our practice. *British Journal of Occupational Therapy*, 63(5), 241–242

Morris W (2003). *News from nowhere.* Oxford: Oxford University Press.

Njelesani Janet, Tang Anna, Jonsson Hans, Polatajko Helene (2012). Articulating an occupational perspective. *Journal of Occupational Science*, 21(2), 226–235.

O'Brien Niamh, Dadswell Anna (2017). *Developing and showcasing FHSCE Strategy for involving Experts by Experience in Teaching, Learning and Research.* Project Report. Anglia Ruskin University, Chelmsford. Retrieved from: http://arro.anglia.ac.uk/id/eprint/702559

Preece Steven (2015). Councils failing to make homes safe for disabled people, says report. *Welfare Weekly*, April, 29. Retrieved from: https://welfareweekly.com/councils-failing-to-make-homes-safe-for-disabled-people-says-report/ accessed 1/09/2019

Rapport Nigel (2003). *I am dynamite. An alternative anthropology of power.* London: Routledge.

Researching Psychosis Together (2012). *Living with psychosis.* London: Brunel University. Retrieved from: www.brunel.ac.uk/__data/assets/pdf_file/0020/277004/living-with-psychosis-report-FINAL-221012.pdf

Smith P, Ooms A, Marks-Maran D (2015). Active involvement of learning disabilities service users in the development and delivery of a teaching session to pre-registration nurses: Students' perspectives. *Nurse Education in Practice.* doi: 10.1016/j.nepr.2015.09.010

Snelgrove Sherrill, Tait Desiree, Tait Michael (2016). Teaching psychology to student nurses: The use of "Talking Head" videos. *Research in Learning Technology*, 24, 30891. http://dx.doi.org/10.3402/rlt.v24.30891

Sword Helen (2012). *Stylish academic writing.* Cambridge, MA: Harvard University Press.

Thornburg D (2014). *From the campfire to the Holodeck: Creating engaging and powerful 21st century learning environments.* San Francisco: Jossey-Bass.

Wilcock A (2001). Occupational utopias: Back to the future. *Journal of Occupational Science*, 8(1), 5–12.

Wilcock A (2002). *Occupation for health: A journey from prescription to self-health*, Vol. 2. London: College of Occupational Therapists.

Wilson L, Bryant W, Lawson J, Reynolds F (2015). Therapeutic outcomes in a museum? "You don't get them by aiming for them". How a focus on arts participation promotes citizenship and wellbeing. *Arts in Health*, 7(3), 202–215.

Winn Sarah, Lindqvist Susanne (2019). Purposeful involvement of experts by experience. *The Clinical Teacher*, 16, 183–188.

Zamyatin Y (1993). *We.* London: Penguin Books Ltd.

30

INVESTING IN CHILDREN

How a children's human rights organisation contributes to human services research and education

Written by Jordan Dodds and young people from Investing in Children, supported by Dr Felicity Shenton

Introduction

Investing in Children (IiC) is a Community Interest Company (CIC) based in County Durham in the North East of England. It was set up in 1995 by a local authority and the National Health Service (NHS) to promote the human rights of children and young people. This includes their right to express an opinion and to be involved in decision making about their lives. IiC believes in children's agency: i.e. that children know and understand better than anyone what the world looks like to them and can make powerful decisions about their own lives when they are included in decision making processes at both an individual and a community/ collective level.

IiC uses a 'rights-based' approach to create spaces in which children and young people can come together, discuss issues and develop arguments through hands-on research that can support them in entering dialogue with adults who have the power to promote their agenda. Over the 20 or so years of the project's existence, they have been able to demonstrate how this approach can lead to improvements in services as well as have a positive impact on the children and young people themselves.

The main messages from children and young people in the mid-1990s and now are that they feel they are not sufficiently listened to, that adults think they know best and that they are treated differently because of their age.

Investing in Children stands by four main principles:

1   Children are citizens and bear rights, and as such have the right to participate in decisions that affect them.
2   Children and young people know about what is happening around them.
3   Organisations that provide services for children and young people must recognise their right to engage and participate in dialogue aimed at bringing improvements to the service.
4   The means of engaging children and young people must be inclusive and respect the democratic rights of all.

Human rights issues (diversity issues)

Investing in Children describes itself as a children's human rights organisation that exists to promote the human rights of *all* children and young people regardless of age, gender, ethnic origin, sexual orientation, ability or circumstance. These are rights that are enshrined in law in the UK including, for example, in the Children Act 1989 and the Human Rights Act 1998 as well as in the requirements of the United Nations Convention on the Rights of the Child (UNCRC) 1989. Over a period of over 20 years, it has worked alongside children from pre-school age up to care leavers and young adults in their early 20s. It promotes rights-based practice that recognises children and young people as rights bearers and citizens. It has demonstrated that by creating opportunities for children and young people to engage in processes as equal partners with adults, changes can be made to public services designed to meet their needs.

International context

IiC first came to the attention of colleagues in Europe when the project was selected as a model of good practice by the Council of Europe (CoE) Programme for Children at the Cof Europe Conference 'Children at the Dawn of the New Millennium' in Cyprus in 2000. A group of young people from County Durham attended the conference to talk about their efforts to improve the local transport system by making it more responsive to the needs of children and young people (Card et al., 1999; Council of Europe, 2000).

This was followed by the presentation of a paper to the Connections Conference in 2003 on the nature of citizenship in Europe. The paper was based upon a three-year evaluation of Investing in Children conducted by Durham University between 2000 and 2003 (Cairns et al., 2005).

In 2006, IiC entered into a partnership with Alder Hey Children's Hospital in Liverpool to share and develop the IiC approach within a health context. In 2008, this led to IiC contributing to a World Health Organisation (WHO) Task Force on respecting children's rights in hospital (Simonelli and Guerreiro, 2010).

The work in Alder Hey brought IiC to the attention of colleagues in the Republic of Ireland, which eventually led to the following developments:

- In 2014, IiC entered into a partnership with the Youth Advocacy Programme (YAP) in Dublin and Voice of Young People in Care (VOYPIC) in Dublin, which authorised them to promote the Investing in Children approach across Ireland.
- In 2015, IiC was awarded a contract by the Irish government to provide a quality assurance mechanism for TUSLA, the new national Child and Family Agency. TUSLA now has 48 Investing in Children Membership™ sites.

The work in Alder Hey also led to the development of a relationship between IiC and the European Children's Rights Unit (ECRU) at Liverpool University Law School, resulting in numerous collaborations over the years. The most significant of these have been:

- In 2014, IiC and ECRU were commissioned by the Council of Europe to engage children and young people in a review of the Child Friendly Justice Guidelines (Council of Europe, 2010).
- In 2015, IiC and ECRU were the UK representatives in Training Activities for Legal Experts on Children's Rights (TALE), an EEC Horizon 2020 project to develop training for legal professionals working with children and young people (Stalford et al., 2017).

In 2013, IiC was involved in 'Borderless Partnership', an Erasmus + funded project involving Norway, Sweden and the UK, exploring approaches to promoting the effective participation of children and young people in democracy. This resulted in 2017 in the formation of 'Med Ungdom I Fokus', a Norwegian version of Investing in Children.

An introduction to the governance arrangements, including young directors

Young people have an equal role in all aspects of the work carried out within the project. Young people are part of the formal governance structures, and there are Young Directors on the Board of Directors (described below). Young people also help to edit the newsletter and contribute to the website, Twitter, Facebook, Instagram etc. They co-deliver the training and professional development programme and they also carry out peer research. They do not receive formal training to carry out these roles; their contribution is *because* they are young people and their contribution is valued as a young person's perspective.

Investing in Children puts into practice the four principles set out above through the role of Young Director. A Young Director is a position held by a young person involved with IiC; the Young Directors work closely with both service users and the Board of Directors. Young Directors start by chairing or vice chairing a meeting with the Decisions Group of IiC.

The Decisions Group is a collection of the 'service users' of Investing in Children i.e. the children and young people who work alongside the Project Workers. They are all young people who have experience of other aspects of the work carried out by Investing in Children and are, therefore, experienced 'users' and participants in the project. The Young Directors take the feedback collected from the Decisions Group and present to the quarterly meeting of the Board of Directors.

A Young Director of Investing in Children is made fully aware of everything going on with IiC, all topics including project finance, progress and monitoring. All Young Directors are made to feel and are treated like an adult by being given responsibilities to help set up, progress and monitor a project.

Models that Investing in Children use: examples include The Agenda Days™ and the Investing in Children Membership Award™

Throughout all the projects delivered by Investing in Children, Agenda Days™ are used. An Agenda Day™ is an event planned by children and young people, run by children and young people, for children and young people and is an adult-free space.

In all Agenda Day™ events, the format is the floor is open to children and young people with no adults present; this allows for all the information to come from a young person's perspective without interference. At the end of an Agenda Day™, the young person facilitating the event will share the information with IiC Project Workers to help move a project forward.

In one example, an Agenda Day™ was planned around the format of a forum, where all the children and young people sat around a table and discussed the questions presented. Typical questions used in Agenda Day™ events are:

1   Are you happy with this service/project?
2   Do you feel safe at this service/project?
3   Are there improvements you would like to suggest for this service/project?

All events are tailored to the age and ability of the children and young people attending using innovative, creative and interactive tools to engage.

Without adults, the aim of Agenda Day™ events is to help make the children and young people feel more comfortable, as being surrounded by peers can make them feel more open to sharing thoughts and opinions. Agenda Day™ events embody the Investing in Children ethos. Individual issues discussed at an Agenda Day™ are kept completely confidential and not discussed outside of the event, with feedback from the Agenda Day™ event being kept anonymous. Only generic feedback is passed on to adult decision makers.

To help promote the rights of children and young people, Investing in Children have created a quality assurance system, the Investing in Children Membership Award™, which gives organisations national recognition for their good practice and active inclusion of children and young people in *dialogue* resulting in *change*.

The award is broken into two main criteria:

Evidence of dialogue: Dialogue is an interactive and ongoing process and not a 'one off' event. A distinction needs to be made between 'consultation,' where powerful people consult with the powerless, and 'dialogue,' where children and young people are partners with a valid contribution to making, designing, delivering and evaluating services.

Evidence of change: Dialogue should not be the end; dialogue must lead to a change. Having invited children and young people to comment on how a service is provided, we need to make sure young people are then able to influence its development and improvement.

The only evidence that counts is that provided by children and young people themselves. All Membership Award reports are read and approved by the children and young people involved in the process.

The Investing in Children Membership Award™ is the only accreditation where children and young people are at the heart of the award, evidencing how they have a voice and how changes are made based on this.

The Investing in Children Membership Award™ is recognised as good practice and can be used as evidence that certain standards (as defined by young people themselves) are being met. The Investing in Children Membership Award™ has been used as supporting evidence for organisations applying for funding and is recognised by many organisations.

Three examples of projects developed by young people for young people: eXtreme Group, T1KZ and Y-ASC

Through working with children and young people, Investing in Children has helped to develop a spectrum of different groups. The groups are designed to help raise awareness of the needs of children and young people and to design services to meet these needs.

eXtreme Group

The first example is the eXtreme Group, which is a group for children and young people with disabilities, both physical and learning disabilities and those with Special Educational Needs (SEND). The group meets once a month.

The group is an open forum for the members to raise and discuss issues in a judgement-free environment. The agenda of every meeting is driven by the members.

As an example: at one meeting the group was discussing how to make the centre where the group meets more welcoming and inclusive for young people with disabilities.

The group identified one major issue with the centre: the door buzzer button at the centre, is not labelled effectively; the button was too small and there was no signage for the buzzer at all.

The group sat together and brainstormed ideas on how to solve the issue and agreed to suggest the buzzer button be made larger and more visible with both Braille and English signage attached. The group presented the suggestions to the maintenance team of the Centre.

Another point raised by the group members was around planning the next promotional event for the eXtreme Group. Events are run to raise awareness of the group and the work the group is doing. During the discussion, the members suggested two venues: a local college or a local leisure centre.

The group wanted to evaluate both venues to see if they met the needs for disabled people, and they agreed to send two members with one of the project managers to conduct site visits and evaluations on the venues. The venue was chosen based on young people's views.

T1KZ

The work done by this project started in 2001, through Investing in Children working with hospitals in County Durham and Darlington to improve the Paediatric Diabetes Service. This was done by working with the children and young people to make the service better, by listening to children and young people's needs and suggestions. And by engaging with children and young people, the service became popular and led to the creation of the T1KZ groups – a project for children, young people and families living with Type 1 diabetes to come together in a non-clinical environment to get peer support and ultimately improve their health outcomes.

The T1KZ groups started in 2012 and are facilitated by a Project Officer and other support staff from Investing in Children. T1KZ now has three groups based across the North East of England. Two of the groups meet monthly and the other meets on a quarterly basis.

Unlike some IiC groups, T1KZ offers a social space where the children and young people come together to do various activities from sports, arts and crafts, to informal chatting and gaming, even to day trips and activities. These sessions are also a chance for the parents of the children with Type 1 diabetes to come together and share knowledge and get support from one another.

The groups offer an opportunity for professionals such as nurses and sports coaches to come and meet with families in a non-clinical environment and explain how young people can manage their diabetes better. The project is entirely designed and planned by the young people via the Young People's Steering Group.

Families have reported that T1KZ has helped make them feel more confident in managing their condition, feel more positive about the future and have higher self-esteem. The project has helped children and young people feel more confident to say things for themselves in their clinical appointments, championing the Investing in Children mantra of 'Giving children and young people a voice in change.'

One service user described the group as 'a lifeline and an event I look forward to, as the group has helped me come to terms with the condition' and 'it tells me that there is other people out there with the condition.'

The opinion is shared among the parents and other members. Another member described the group, saying, 'I really enjoy the sessions, its [*sic*] great talking to others with diabetes.'

Y-ASC

The third example of a project Investing in Children has helped develop with children and young people is the Young Adults Support Café (Y-ASC), The Y-ASC group was created after a review conducted by Investing in Children into how the Child and Adolescent Mental Health Services (CAMHS) could become younger person-friendly.

The Y-ASC group, run from the Waddington St Centre, a local voluntary sector Mental Health Resource Centre in Durham City, is a safe space for children and young people with Mental Health issues to be honest and open with fellow peers between the ages of 16 to 22.

The group meets every Tuesday evening and is run for the members and by the members. The session is broken into two halves, the first being a café and the second half being an optional art session.

It's by far nothing like after-school clubs; the members are free to participate in anything they wish. From digital artwork to games of cards and even watching films, the session is relaxed for everyone.

Members of the group have described Y-ASC as a 'community of likeminded people,' 'where we can share issues and help one another with issues such as relationships, anxiety and coping strategies.'

The group has been instrumental in improving the transition process from children and young people's services through to adult services, as previous members of the group have successfully managed to transition into the Adult Mental Health Services provided by the Centre.

The Y-ASC group has helped fill a gap in Children and Young People's Mental Health Services by providing a platform for peer support. The group members can feel at ease and not alone in their battles.

> As a young person myself, and having gone through the process of diagnosis of Asperger Syndrome, I see why it is important for children and young people to be given a platform to express their thoughts and raise their voice.
>
> Throughout the process of diagnoses, I was powerless and not listened too. Everything around me was being decided without a single question like 'What do you think?' or 'How would you feel about this?' Having vital decisions that have affected my entire life decided without my input catalysed my lack of confidence.
>
> Being moved schools and having support added and withdrawn without an input from the person needing the support the most, ruined my childhood and has left scars to this day that won't heal.

Seeing how Investing in Children has helped give children and young people a voice is amazing in a world where children and young people are blatantly ignored or their opinions are not considered for services that affect them the most. By giving children and young people the power to decide through Agenda Day™ events, by rewarding those who actively listen and work with children and young people with the Investing in Children Membership Award™ and even supporting vital lifeline groups for children and young people, real changes can be made.

At the end of the day, children and young people are no different from adults. We are all humans and are entitled to our human rights; we all are guaranteed the right of expressing thoughts and opinions, and although our voice isn't normally heard, investing in Children has given children and young people a platform to be heard and to make decisions that will help all children and young people.

Enablers and barriers

The main barrier to ensuring that children and young people have a voice, that they are listened to, and that their views make a difference is almost always that adults think they know best. Making the argument that children and young people should be involved and have a platform to voice their opinions have largely been successful. The Children Act 1989 Section 1, the UNCRC 1989 Article 12 and other mandatory requirements that promoted children's participation in decision-making processes did have an impact. Opportunities have been created for children to voice their opinions. The piece that is often missing is the difference these opportunities have made. Children and young people will often say that they have taken part in school/youth councils, mock elections, shadow cabinets etc. However, the evidence that these processes make a difference is much less convincing, and children are frequently unable to tell us what changes were made to decisions, services or outcomes as a result of young people's involvement. Frequently this is because the adults involved understand that children should be involved but are much less persuaded that children have anything important, valuable or convincing to say. Children and young people's opinions simply do not hold the same weight as adults. Therefore, children have to work twice as hard as adults to be heard, and their views are often considered peripheral.

Enablers, therefore, are people who consider children and young people to have something important to say and who value their contributions. Rights-based practice that creates opportunities for children and young people – 'the powerless' – to participate in processes alongside 'the powerful' enables progress to be made.

Future challenges and learning

The future, as with many things in the current social, political and financial climate, is uncertain. While there have been significant advances made in the field of human rights, particularly in the UK, we are now facing a political regime that appears focused on 'law and order' and on challenging equality, inclusion, openness, transparency and human rights. It is hoped that the significant progress and learning made by such projects as Investing in Children are well enough embedded that this progress will continue.

Bibliography

Cairns, L., Kemp, P., and Williamson, B. (2005). Young People and Civil Society: Lessons from a Case Study of Active Learning and Active Citizenship. In Wildemeersch, D., Stroobant, V., and Bron, M. (Eds.), *Active Citizenship and Multiple Identities in Europe.* Peter Lang: Frankfurt.

Card, E., Douthwaite, S., et al. (1999). *Fares fair: The Investing in Children Transport Group Report.* Investing in Children Archive. Durham County Council.

Council of Europe (2000). *Children at the Dawn of a New Millennium. Consolidated Report.* Council of Europe Programme for Children.

Council of Europe (2010). *Guidelines of the Committee of Ministers of the Council of Europe on Child-friendly Justice.* https://archive.crin.org/. . ./council-europe-guidelines-child-friendly-justice.html

Simonelli, F., and Guerreiro, A. (Eds.). (2010) *Final Report of the Implementation Process of the Self-Evaluation Model and Tool on the Respect of Children's Rights in Hospital.* International Network of Health Promoting Hospitals and Health Services. World Health Organisation.

Stalford, H., Cairns, L., and Marshall, J. (2017). Achieving Child Friendly Justice through Child Friendly Methods: Let's start with the Right to Information. *Social Inclusion,* 5(3), 207–218.

31

DON'T JUDGE A BOOK BY ITS COVER

Lived experiences of the involvement of older people in social work education

*Sarah Lonbay, Shirley Hallam, Patricia Higgins
and Sheila Weatheritt*

Introduction

The involvement of service users and carers in social work education has been strongly encouraged since the 1990s and became mandatory at the turn of the century. It is now considered an essential element of the training for new social workers in the United Kingdom, particularly in enabling them to develop value-driven and competent practice. This involvement allows students to gain the benefit of hearing about not only shared experiences, but also the individual's own unique perspective on that experience. It enables students to learn that, alongside shared experiences, there are individual stories as well. This is the focus of this chapter, which discusses the involvement of older people in social work education and highlights some of the diversity of this "group". The assumption is often made that older people come into contact with services on the basis of needs that arise as a result of "being old". However, being "old" does not qualify one for the receipt of social services, and making assumptions about someone on the basis of their age alone is discriminatory. We should not assume that we know what challenges or experiences an older person brings, just because they are older. In short, we should not judge a book by its cover.

This chapter builds on this starting point to highlight the importance of involving older people in social work education. It does this by drawing on the experience and knowledge of four authors, three of whom are older people themselves with a range of experience of being involved in the education of social work students. The authors share some of their own experiences about social work and their perspectives on being involved in social work programmes. The main aim of the chapter is to challenge assumptions about the homogeneity of this group and to highlight the value of their varied experiences and perspectives as contributions to educating future social workers. Social work students need to be able to understand and respond to the needs of an older population, and for this to occur, as this chapter will demonstrate, they need to learn directly from older people.

Social work involvement as an older person

There are currently over 901 million people in the world who are over the age of 60, and this number is set to increase to 2.1 billion by 2050 (ONS, 2018). This global increase in the older population is reflected within the UK; in 2016 there were close to 12 million older people (over the age of 65) in the UK, an increase of over 2 million since 1991, and the older population is expected to increase a further 8.6 million by 2066 (ONS, 2018). Discourse around the ageing population often focuses on the challenges, rather than the opportunities, that this presents, and older people within this discourse are frequently reduced to a homogenous group. In reality, however, the older population is a very diverse group. There are differences in relation to life stage (whether working or retired), income and wealth, marital status, age (the population age spans from, arguably, 60 through to end of life) and living arrangements, as well as in relation to ethnicity, religion and sexuality, among other things (ONS, 2018). For example, results from the 2011 UK census showed that 8% of people over the age of 65 are BME and 2.1% of people over the age of 50 identify as gay, lesbian or bisexual (AGE UK, 2019). Despite this diversity, services often work from an assumption that the needs of older people are similar and forget to consider the wide range of experience and difference that exists among the older population. Moriarty and Manthorpe (2012, p. 12) found that sexual orientation, religion, belief and gender identity were "almost wholly absent" in research, leading them to conclude that diversity in the older population was being largely ignored. Others have also concluded that sexuality in older age has been "rendered invisible" (Cronin and King, 2010, p. 881). As Milne et al. (2014) have pointed out, the older population, as it grows, will become increasingly diverse, and this needs to be recognised by policy makers, services and social workers. As highlighted within the introduction, older people do not come into contact with services simply by virtue of being an older person. Such experiences arise from a diverse range of reasons, and the route through to involvement in social work education can also vary. Three different experiences are shared below.

Sheila's experience

I have been involved with social services for over 30 years now, which started with the death of my mam. I have also had experiences with social workers due to being a kinship carer. Through this I became involved with Relative Experience, who first introduced me to the university. Relative Experience give support for kinship carers. Kinships carers are grandparents, aunts, uncles and others who are raising a child because the parents are unable to care for them. They deal with drug addiction, alcoholism, parents with a learning disability who can't look after their own children, death in the family and all sorts of other things. They take grandchildren on as adoption or special guardianship, or guardianship. It's not just "looking after the grandchildren"; it's a 24 hour a day job. It is also an unpaid job in most cases. Although we get told in lots of cases, "Well, you are the grandparent so it's part of your life", that is not the case. We take on children who might have been traumatised and don't know how to deal with life. You're giving up the rest of your life as you're starting all over being a parent again. It can also cause you to be cut off from the rest of the family, which is not easy. I don't think when you take a child on like that social services give you enough support, as they don't look at the wider family. They just look at that one person and the child.

Pat's experience

In 2017, I was diagnosed with autism, and since then I have been passionate about raising awareness of the condition, especially in relation to autism and ageing. In 2004 I enrolled on a social work degree; however, due to personal and health issues, I was unable to complete the degree. In 2015 I became a member of a service user reference group which was involved in the recruitment and training of social workers at the same university. Our remit included participating in the selection process, training, design and content of advertising materials, policies and practice documents and their summer school education programme. This included preparing and delivering training, as well as role-play scenarios with students. In every case where there was direct contact with the students, the feedback was always very positive, especially in relation to our sharing personal experiences. Since also becoming involved with the social work department at another university, I have chosen to bring my own experiences of living and ageing with autism, in order to share these experiences and to raise awareness of the complex needs of people with autism. This will hopefully expand the knowledge and skills base of the social work students and future practitioners.

Shirley's experience

Being a carer for my husband has changed my life! My husband was a very complex case of ill health. Following two TIAs (Transient Ischaemic Attacks or "mini strokes"), he suffered a severe stroke when he worked abroad. This left him with lots of side effects, for example short term memory loss, swallowing and choking fits, burst heart with aneurysm, legs at 25 and 35 degrees, as well as a recent cancer scare. Fifteen years ago, he was a very active man, trebling the size of our bungalow in time spent at home when he was not working in the Middle East! He was always outside in the fresh air and a regular walker. He found his lack of mobility very frustrating. He lost 7 stone and said he had become "a crooked man with a crooked stick". I did not know I was a carer until someone made me think that looking after my husband, mother and uncle, I could possibly call myself a carer.

It took me eight years to accept this caring role, and it was only when my mother died and my husband suffered further ill health that I realised I needed help and stepped over the threshold of the local Carer's Centre. Here I was given an instant interview in a caring, quiet environment where I was allowed time to explain my situation. Tears came and went, but when I left the building an hour later, I knew I had found the listening ear I needed. I had found somewhere where staff were empathetic and provided me with the mental support, coping language and signposting to other agencies that I required to be a "carer".

As a carer, it is important to know your rights. I attended one of 16 conferences across the country highlighting human rights. I feel it is vital to have emotional stability and give yourself permission to say "No", or be late, or whatever you need on the day when you feel down. But most of all, don't "judge a book by its cover" and try to retain a sense of humour. It is not easy, but the help of an empathetic social worker can make all the difference to a carer's survival.

The importance of involving older people in social work education

Older people are frequently discussed in often very negative ways, for example, in relation to the "challenges" of an ageing population, or with a focus on ill health or frailty. However, *their* voices are often missing from these discussions. This concurrently excludes them from sharing their own perspectives while allowing assumptions about them, which are often negative and ageist, to flourish. Without direct input from older people within social work education, there is a risk that students risk miss the unique perspectives which can help to challenge a predominantly negative narrative. Duffy (2016, p. 7), for example, stated that the pervasiveness of ageism in society has meant that negative views about older people and ageing are "often accepted as truth and internalised unwittingly". This has been supported by research undertaken by Cherry and Palmore (2008), who reported that ageism was "widespread and frequent" (p. 852) among college students, older adults living in the community and people who were "members of a university community" (p. 851). Allen et al. (2009) also studied the extent to which social work students and practitioners reported engaging in ageist behaviour with similar results. In both studies, participants reported engaging in more "positive ageism" (for example, agreeing with items such as "complement older people on how well they look despite their age", p. 130). However, as the authors pointed out, this could bleed into paternalism, which can undermine and reduce people's choices and independence. Lee et al. (2015, p. 2) also found "generally negative ageist attitudes among social work students". Other research has also provided evidence that ageism is widespread (e.g. AGE UK, 2011; Fealy and McNamara, 2009; Okoye and Obizeke, 2005; Weicht, 2013). Regardless of whether ageism is "positive" ("hold doors open for old people because of their age") or "negative" ("avoid old people because they are cranky"), the impact is predominantly harmful, reflecting as it does an underlying assumption of incapacity (Allen et al., 2009, p. 130). Research by WHO (2002) and O'Brien et al. (2011) also highlighted that older people feel that ageism constitutes, as well as contributes to, abuse.

Given these findings, it is vital for social work students and social workers to reflect carefully on their own perspectives about ageing and for a focus on ageing to be firmly embedded within social work curriculums. Social workers need specialist knowledge in order to work with older people. This includes the need to be aware of theories and models of ageing, to understand the ageing process and to know about health conditions that may be more prevalent in later life, among other things (Milne et al., 2014). Social workers also need to have "knowledge about the local services and the wider community" (p. 17). Through their learning, within which educators by experience play a vital role, social work students are encouraged and supported to reflect on their own misconceptions about ageing. Hearing directly from older people who bring different perspectives and lived experiences into the class room can help them to consider what their prior assumptions have been and how these relate to the experiences that are being shared with them. For example, studies have shown that contact with older people and increased focus on gerontological content in courses can increase students' willingness to work with older people (Curl et al., 2005; Nane, 1999; Ortiz et al., 2012). Ortiz et al. (2012) also found that direct contributions from older people within the curriculum helped students to identify and reflect on ageism, with students making comments such as "I have learned that older adults do not have a lower quality of life simply because they are aging, it is the individual circumstances surrounding the adult" (p. 861). The importance of involving older people in social work education becomes abundantly clear when the impact on the students is considered. The accounts below explore other perspectives about the importance of older people's contributions to social work education.

Pat's perspective

It's important to share personal experiences, so that it can help to inform best practice in social work. I have experienced both negative and positive social work input in the past, and both have had a lasting impact upon my mental health and my life in general. That's why I think it's important to share those experiences, so that in the future more people will have positive experiences instead of negative ones. Perhaps if I had been diagnosed sooner with autism, I might have had more positive experiences and more structured support. I personally feel that sharing my own experiences can contribute to the knowledge base of students, because there are many things which the student cannot learn from books. These include, for example, how someone is feeling and thinking in relation to their life experiences and what impact these experiences can have on a person's ability to cope, or not, as the case may be. They can also learn about exactly what assistance the person requires, instead of making assumptions about their requirements based on reading alone. I know sharing these experiences does make a real difference, because they have told me so. They have completed feedback questionnaires stating how much they enjoyed hearing about my experiences and not only the difference it has made to their understanding of the topic, but also how it will inform their own social work practice and how it broadened their knowledge base.

Shirley's perspective

I hope to support their learning at university in a practical way, to enable them to have a wide range of experiences and to understand the value of their work. By empowering them and working with the university in this way, together we should make a difference and provide the all-round education that will strengthen our social services for the community. We need to encourage the students to use self-help for their physical and mental wellbeing. I want students to be confident and have enough information to be able to make informed decisions and help others do the same. I want them to be aware that "there is more to me than meets the eye".

Sheila's perspective

I think it's a big thing for students to listen to people with the experience because the experience that they get is a wider one; it's not just about my experience as a kinship carer, it's about disability and all sorts of things so they are getting a wide range of what is out there. It has to do some good if everyone is working together to get the same standards in social work. I think over the years that I've been with social services, when we've all worked together as a team (for example, social workers, psychologists – everyone involved with that person), it has worked well, and the students need to know those sorts of things. They need to know what works well and what doesn't work well.

The feedback from students is always really good, and the interest from them is good. They all say they enjoy it, and that is really good to hear. Even if one person comes back and says "I was interested", that's quite good. I have been in lectures with the lecturers where students have fallen asleep – they didn't fall asleep with me! I really think it's a good thing that everyone gets the opportunity to do this. It's certainly done me a lot of good. At the beginning, I was terrified to speak. I'm not really an outgoing person, but I did enjoy talking to the students.

Older people's motivations for engaging with social work education

There is limited research which directly explores the reasons *why* people with lived experience choose to get involved in social work education. Data from my own research (which included older people among other participants involved in this area) suggest that the motivation comes from a desire to give something back and to contribute to bringing about positive change with this profession (Lonbay, in press). Participants in this project also spoke about personal benefits, for example, increased confidence and understanding of social work (Lonbay, in press). These reasons are reflected in research which has explored motivations for becoming involved in other areas. For example, older people involved in a participatory research project spoke about the benefit of the project for others, but also for themselves. Personal benefits included increased knowledge and making new friends (Doyle and Timonen, 2010). Pat and Sheila also speak to this within their accounts below, with a common theme between them also suggesting that a key driver for wanting to be involved in social work education is the aspiration to improve things for others who may find themselves in similar positions.

Pat's motivation

I am motivated to share my experiences because I feel that it is possible to make a real difference to the social work students' experience and that of the social work client. My experiences can help to inform social work practice and in turn help to ensure students have the benefit of life experiences not otherwise available to them. There is no substitute for these experiences, and it is so important for students to have the benefit of hearing those experiences from real people. It also gives students the opportunity to ask questions and receive answers they might not otherwise get. In turn, I have the satisfaction of knowing that I can make a real difference to the experience of students and hopefully clients by helping to inform best practice, especially in the case of autism and ageing, or mental health. I am rewarded through my involvement in social work education, because I am passionate about social work education and the difference it can make to people's lives. I enjoy being part of something that can be such a force for good if it is delivered in the correct way. Since my own chequered experiences of social work, and the impact it has had on me personally, I have been determined to try and improve, or add, to the social work curriculum. That includes sharing my experiences with students, which I hope in turn will in some small way help to prevent other people having negative experiences in the future.

Sheila's motivation

I was introduced by the Relative Experience project to the university because of being involved with them as a kinship carer. I share with the students by speaking to them or teaching a bit about my experiences with social workers. I really just felt like I had a wealth of experience to be able to talk about those experiences. I think it made me feel a lot better because I was telling people all about my situation and letting them hear about it. I've had social work involvement in my life for a long time and the things that I've dealt with over the years have been quite hard, so for someone to be interested in what I had done was really nice as well. It's given me more confidence to be able to speak up. I also think that some of the knowledge that you pick up at the university helps you with the situation that you are in and to feel free to speak up and say how you feel about the situation. For most people, it's a positive experience. They are getting more out of it than they are putting into it. You're talking about personal situations and sometimes it's deep and it hurts, but I feel that people get more out of it than you might realise. I certainly do.

Enablers and barriers to involvement in social work education

Some of the factors which help or hinder involvement with older people have been well documented in various places (see, for example, Lonbay, 2018). For involvement within Higher Education Institutions (HEIs), there is an additional difficulty in relation to how different types of knowledge are valued. For example, there is a drive to produce research-based and "traditional academic knowledge", and this focus does not always leave space for recognising the value of students learning via sources based on more experiential knowledge (Lonbay and Cavener, in press). Both have a role to play in HEIs, particularly when it comes to professional courses such as social work. It is vital that those with lived experience are recognised and valued as a core part of the teaching team, but it is difficult to fully achieve this when they are not formally recognised as employees by HEIs. However, there are steps that can be taken to help move towards that goal. For example, ensuring that fair pay and reimbursement are offered for people's time, offering library or IT access and ensuring that educators by experience are involved, not only in teaching and admission, but in the development of the programme itself. To assist with this, it is also vital that there are clear structures in place for offering support and training (should this be identified as a need by someone). Developing structures and training with experts by experience also helps to ensure that they are useful and actually meeting people's needs (Lonbay and Cavener, in press). For older people, as with others, the important aspect is to ensure that any individual needs or support requirements are met in order that everyone is able to contribute effectively. Clear and effective communication and taking the time to build positive and supportive relationships are therefore both essential components. Pat, Shirley and Sheila share some of the factors which help or hinder their involvement below. Each of them has a slightly different perspective on the most important factors, highlighting again the importance of considering the individual, rather than making assumptions based on age alone.

Shirley's perspective

Every individual has a different "story" to tell. It is not always what you see or hear but what is not said that is important. A calm listening and non-judgemental approach is so important for someone to share "their story", and it takes time to reach the truth by careful questioning, for example asking, "How did you feel when that happened?"

Pat's perspective

Some of the barriers I have experienced have been both physical and psychological. I am physically disabled, and some of the barriers I have faced have included stairs in venues where the education was going to take place. I have hidden disabilities, and it is not always obvious that I am disabled, which is why it is important to ask the person prior to their involvement whether they need any adjustments to the venue. Unfortunately, some of the barriers come from other people's assumptions about my capabilities, especially in relation to my physical and mental health. It has been assumed in the past that autism affects my cognitive abilities and my IQ to the extent that I am unable to contribute or cope within a teaching environment, all of which is untrue. While it is true that I need some adjustments to be made, such as lower lighting and noise levels where possible, or temperature adjustment, I am more than capable in relation to my ability to communicate both verbally and in writing.

Some of the enablers have been in relation to good communication, for example, asking me beforehand if I have any requirements or informing me of the layout of the venue. Having a support worker attend with me and a quiet space where I can unwind if necessary is also helpful. I need to have familiar routines and to feel safe. In physical terms, I only eat and drink certain foods and liquids, so I need to know in advance what will be provided, if anything at all; otherwise I bring my own. Travel can also be difficult for me in terms of accessibility because I am unable to travel using public transport without a support worker. This means using taxis or the car, which can be expensive and prohibitive in terms of cost. Giving some form of reimbursement for travel is a huge help and enables me to participate in social work education. These may seem like simple things, but they make a huge difference to someone with autism and enable me to feel comfortable in the venue and situation, so that I am better able to contribute to the session.

Sheila's perspective

The academic team help a lot; working together at the university is good. The staff have been really helpful and helped us. It's not us and them – "we are the professionals"; we are working together. I get the sense that we are part of the team. When I've been there, the lecturers have helped in a big way. They understand the situations you are in and they will help in any way. People ask after you and want to know how you are. It's also good working with other people who want to do the same thing.

Some key messages for social workers and social work students

A key message within this chapter is that, while we may consider older people as a distinct group, there is in reality a great diversity with the older population, particularly in relation to experiences and individual responses to these. The authors of this chapter also wanted to highlight some key messages for social workers and social work students, which are drawn from their own varied experiences. These are presented below.

Pat's message

Some of the key messages I want social work students to hear from me include the importance of not making assumptions regarding a person's abilities, either mental or physical. If you are in doubt, ask the person, or their support worker, carer or family member. Just because I am someone with high functioning autism, don't assume that I don't have difficulties. For example, I struggle with using public transport, bright lighting, noise, temperature differences, smell and touch; because I am hypersensitive to all of these things, they restrict my socialisation. I can't use public transport and I struggle to read facial expressions; I am vulnerable because I believe what I am told, which can and has led to my being abused in the past. I am also a literal thinker, and this can lead to my interpreting words and meanings wrongly, or literally. It's okay to make mistakes, as long as you are honest about it; explain what has happened and then do something about it. That not only is good practice but also helps to build trust between the social worker and their clients. Even if you can't change the situation, just be honest about it. People really appreciate honesty and clarity, so please don't use jargon either, because it only serves to confuse people and doesn't contribute anything to their experience. It's very important to include clients in the design and implementation of care packages, because it enables them to feel in control and included in the process. It also helps to leave a positive view of social work and social workers.

Sheila's message

The key messages for me that I want social work students to hear are to listen to families and then act on what you've heard, because families know the person better than you do. One of the things I don't like is when they promise to do something for a child or a young adult and then come back and say sorry we can't do it. Never ever promise something to someone unless you can come back and do it.

Social workers also need to empathise – especially with the grandparents, but they also need to think about the wider family. I think as well that they should ask the grandparents, "Can you afford to do what you are doing?", because a lot of financial difficulty comes with this (being a kinship carer) as well and you don't get any support with that. I had my house smashed up on a number of occasions, but no-one asked me "Can you afford to keep doing what you're doing?" I've seen a lot of grandparents like this. As a person looking after someone, I don't like asking for things. I think a lot of people are like that, but we have to ask for it. We don't want to but we have to. People need the help; otherwise they wouldn't be asking for it. It does affect people if you don't want to ask for money or service, but you've got to in some cases. So social workers should ask us what we think we need and show that they can empathise with our situation.

Shirley's message

Nobody tells you how to be a carer, and most people accept it as part of a loving and caring relationship without thought for themselves. Being a carer has to be accepted by "the said person", as well as the "cared for". Pride sometimes gets in the way of acceptance, but if it can be taken on board by both parties, it allows them to gain access to training, "being an expert" during hospital visits and doctor's surgeries, Carer's List and information at a Carer's Centre as well as enabling them to meet other people who have personal knowledge of how it feels. The social worker needs to have lots of helpful hints to encourage this acceptance. Therefore, when social workers are working in this situation, it is very important that the words "You are a carer", if used, are used with sensitivity; it takes a long time for some people to accept this situation, never mind the words themselves. They are reluctant to be "not coping" and therefore shy away from the reality. This can affect their own wellbeing and thus reduce their effectiveness in the Caring role

It is also important for social workers to know what is available for all parties and to give practical advice, because "the carer" does not always know what their rights are and certainly what is available to them to help in their daily lives. For example, check out if they have an Emergency Card from their local NHS or local council.

Conclusion

Each author in this chapter has shared and contributed their ideas about the importance of being involved in social work education. These accounts highlight the differences in people's experiences, which reinforce again the importance of not making assumptions based on someone's membership of a particular "group". However, there are some important similarities as well. All of the authors highlight the importance of involvement being about challenging and changing students' perceptions and ensuring that they think about the individual in front of them, rather than stereotyped ideas about that individual.

This focus was reflected within the "enablers and barriers" section, which also highlighted the importance of tailoring support to be involved in social work education to that individual. As Pat points out, there is a danger in seeing one thing about the person to the exclusion of others. To see someone as only "an older person" means missing other important aspects of that person, which can have negative and exclusionary consequences. To see only the "older person" means to miss so much more. In social work, the consequences of this can be devastating for a person. Involving older people directly in social work should be a core part of increasing gerontological input into social work programmes and is a step towards ensuring that social workers do not "judge a book by its cover".

References

AGE UK (2011). *A Snapshot of Ageism in the UK and Across Europe.* Age UK. Available online at: www.ageuk.org.uk/Documents/EN-GB/ID10180%20Snapshot%20of%20Ageism%20in%20Europe.pdf?dtrk=true (Accessed 10/12/19).

AGE UK (2019). *Later Life in the United Kingdom 2019.* AGE UK. Available online at: www.ageuk.org.uk/globalassets/age-uk/documents/reports-and-publications/later_life_uk_factsheet.pdf (Accessed 10/12/2019).

Allen, P.D., Cherry, K.E. and Palmore, E. (2009). Self-reported ageism in social work practitioners and students. *Journal of Gerontological Social Work, 52*(2), 124–134.

Cherry, K.E. and Palmore, E. (2008). Relating to Older People Evaluation (ROPE): A measure of self-reported ageism. *Educational Gerontology, 34*(10), 849–861.

Cronin, A. and King, A. (2010). Power, inequality and identification: Exploring diversity and intersectionality amongst older LGB adults. *Sociology, 44*(5), 876–982.

Curl, A.L., Simons, K. and Larkin, H. (2005). Factors affecting willingness of social work students to accept jobs in aging. *Journal of Social Work Education, 41*(3), 393–406.

Doyle, M. and Timonen, V. (2010). Lessons from a community-based participatory research project: Older people's and researchers' reflections. *Research on Aging, 32*(2), 244–263.

Duffy, F. (2016). A social work perspective on how ageist language, discourses and understandings negatively frame older people and why taking a critical social work stance is essential. *British Journal of Social Work, 47*(7), 2068–2085.

Fealy, G. and McNamara, M. (2009). Constructing ageing and age identity: A case study of newspaper discourses. *National Centre of the Protection of Older People* Study 1, November 2009.

Lee, H.S., Jung, H.S. and Sumner, A. (2015). A cross-cultural analysis of perception on ageist attitudes between Korean and American social work students. *Korean Social Science Journal, 42*, 25–37.

Lonbay, S.P. (2018). Participatory approaches to social policy in relation to ageing. In Beresford, P. and Carr, S. (Eds.), *Social Policy First Hand*. Bristol: Policy Press.

Lonbay, S.P. (in press). *Developing the Involvement of Educators by Experience in Social Work Education.*

Lonbay, S.P. and Cavener, J. (in press). *Enhancing Experts by Experience Led Education in Social Work: Lessons from a Project to Develop Involvement.*

Milne, A., Sullivan, M.P., Tanner, D., Richards, S., Ray, M., Lloyd, L. and Phillips, J. (2014). Social work with older people: A vision for the future. *The College of Social Work.* Available online at: www.cpa.org.uk/cpa-lga-evidence/College_of_Social_Work/Milneetal(2014)-Socialworkwitholderpeople-avisionforthefuture.pdf (Accessed 10/12/2019).

Moriarty, J. and Manthorpe, J. (2012). *Diversity in Older People and Access to Services – An Evidence Review.* London: Age UK.

Nane, M.N. (1999). Factors affecting social work students' willingness to work with elders with Alzheimer's disease. *Journal of Social Work Education, 35*(1), 71–85.

O'Brien, M., Begley, E., Anand, J.C., Killick, C. and Taylor, B.J. (2011). *A Total Indifference to Our Dignity: Older People's Understandings of Elder Abuse.* Dublin: Centre for Ageing Research and Development.

Okoye, U.O. and Obizeke, D.S. (2005). Stereotypes and perceptions of the elderly by the youth in Nigeria: Implications for social policy. *Journal of Applied Gerontology, 24*(5), 439–452.

ONS (2018). Living Longer: How our population is changing and why it matters. London: Office For National Statistics.

Ortiz, D.V., Cross, S.L. and Day, A. (2012). Insightful learning of life's lessons with older adult guests in the classroom. *Educational Gerontology, 38*(12), 854–866.

Weicht, B. (2013). The making of the "Elderly": Constructing the subject of care. *Journal of Ageing Studies, 27*(2), 188–197.

WHO (2002). *Missing Voices: Views of Elder Persons on Elder Abuse.* Geneva: World Health Organisation.

32

SERVICE USER INVOLVEMENT IN COUNTRIES OF CONFLICT

Joe Duffy

Introduction

This chapter examines service user involvement in the context of countries affected by conflict. The author writes from the perspective of Northern Ireland, a country that has emerged from a protracted period of violent political conflict, but wherein creative opportunities for meaningful service user involvement in social work education have developed in the context of a more peaceful societal milieu following the Peace Agreement of 1998. Northern Ireland will therefore be highlighted as a case study example of service user involvement occurring against a challenging contextual backdrop, one which can point the way forward for other countries experiencing political adversity to consider the development and implementation of similar initiatives.

Background

Service user involvement is very well established in the United Kingdom (U.K.), to such an extent that this is now commonplace and indeed required in key aspects of policy and public services (Duffy et al., 2017; Beresford, 2019). Similar developments have occurred in other international contexts, many reported in this book, but arguably the engrained and mainstreamed presence of service user involvement in the U.K. is unparalleled. The role of the service user movement in the U.K. has been particularly important at a grassroots and political level in terms of championing the need to have the service user voice front and foremost in the delivery of services (Oliver, 1983, 1990; Shaping Our Lives, 2003). Allied to this, service user involvement is also a core feature in the education of many health and social care professionals in the U.K., which, again, has an important impact on reinforcing the importance of lived and experiential knowledge to professional practice in human services work (Beresford, 2019).

This pedagogy of lived experience is, therefore, now a commonplace feature, particularly in social work education, and much has been written and researched on the many ways in which this type of knowledge has impacted on students' competence and practice (Robinson and Webber, 2013). What is less developed, however, is a focus on how service user involvement can find expression in countries and contexts where political upheaval and conflict typify the nature of the wider societal backdrop. This is a new and emerging focus, and this chapter seeks to explore the possibilities and challenges for service user involvement to occur in such situations.

Walter Lorenz recently called for the need to locate social problems within their wider political context when he observed

> the engagement with these wider political issues has always been a contentious issue and it could be said in historical retrospect that the profession overall settled on an attitude of "not rocking the boat" and adjusting both the profession and the users of social services to "given realities", even though in everyday practice the part politics play in the way social problems are generated, or become manifest, is mostly all too obvious.
>
> *(Lorenz, 2019, p. XV)*

Against this backdrop, it is hardly surprising that service user involvement has not taken seed, let alone flourished, in a context where social workers would steer clear of issues deemed political.

However, there is evidence that participatory-based approaches can produce creative and innovative ways to working in otherwise quite dangerous situations imbued with political complexity. Take, for instance, the emphasis reported by social workers in Northern Ireland of working in allied ways with community organizations and community representatives in responding to service users' needs in the context of the Northern Ireland "Troubles" (Duffy et al., 2019). Indeed, some social workers in this research reported risking their own lives in the process of doing so. This type of selfless professional practice could chime with what Lorenz described as "'shared knowledge production' between service users and professionals" (2019, p. xvii). Taking this a step further, in the Northern Ireland context described here, this is also an example of social workers positioning themselves "within and between the state and civil society, a space that is at once risky and dangerous at times of political conflict, but also potentially dynamic and liberating for the social worker and those they seek to help" (Campbell, 2019, p. 10).

Political conflict has a ubiquitous presence for social workers internationally, yet it is difficult to define. Campbell (2019) points out that we are very familiar with some conflicts, such as Northern Ireland, Bosnia and Herzegovina, Israel/Palestine, Cyprus, South Africa and Hong Kong, because quite a lot has been written and described about them. He goes on to argue, however, that by contrast, other very important conflicts in the world, particularly in Africa and Asia, are bereft of such scholarly focus due to an inherent Eurocentric bias in the literature (2019, p. 9). The word "conflict" of itself is also open to interpretation. This could relate to wider discord inherent in society, triggered by the zeitgeist of the political milieu. Consider the issues that, at the time of writing, are prevalent with regard to Brexit and have resulted in political division, upheaval and uncertainty. Issues around immigration and what is referred to as the "refugee crisis", for example, are further manifestations of how "conflict" at a macro (societal) level can emerge at a particular point in time when the impact is acutely witnessed and brought to the fore. The alarming increase in mass shootings in the U.S. is another example of incidents/events occurring at a societal level which can cause disagreement and instability. The adverse impact of climate change has also the potential for upheaval and adverse impact for individuals, groups and communities in parts of the world experiencing the brunt of severe changes to climatic conditions. These eclectic types of examples underscore the need to more broadly envision the meaning of conflict as characterizing instability, displacement, violence and discord. The meaning of conflict is therefore a shifting concept open to varying interpretations and meanings.

This raises the question, core to this chapter, around service user involvement. How can service user involvement fit within the contours of societies affected by conflict and political conflagration, and what are the issues involved? How can a service user perspective find its place in such circumstances? Maglajlic and Basic (2019, p. 69), writing from the experience of the Bosnia and Herzegovina conflict, offer some helpful observations in answering this question when they remark

> that political conflict happens both to service users, practitioners and all other members of a given society alike . . . borders between personal, professional and political in the experiences of social workers become the thinnest and most porous in countries affected by political conflicts.

Service user issues at such times, by implication, are therefore very much to the fore in times of conflict and concomitantly bring a sense of commonality to both service users and social workers. On this point, Maglajlic and Basic remark that "political conflict is the only wider experience where such levelling occurs on a broad scale" (ibid.). Tosone (2019) also concurs about this narrowing of professional boundaries at times of conflict in her reflections of the aftermath of the attacks on the World Trade Center in 2001 in the U.S. and her reference to "shared trauma", a term she uses to describe the similarities in feelings and reactions experienced by clinicians and their clients who were jointly exposed to the same trauma. Tosone observed that "9/11 served as the impetus for enhancing clinical skills and brought about increased compassion and connectivity to clients" (2019, p. 56).

Extending this sense of interconnectivity further, it is conceivable that a background of conflict and instability at a societal level, where there is this proximity and closeness in the relationship between helper and those being helped, can potentially yield opportunities for service user knowledge and experiential lived insights to also have a place alongside more traditional forms of knowledge. Service user involvement can therefore be a natural and progressive manifestation of this type of affinity and levelling out of relationships and distillation of the traditional boundaries between service users and social workers. The next part of this chapter will describe such a pedagogic initiative which has been occurring in Northern Ireland over the past 15 years to address conflict-related issues in the context of social work education where service users with direct lived experience of trauma are involved in teaching.

Northern Ireland – introducing challenging pedagogy to the social work curriculum

Social work education was significantly reformed in 2003 in Northern Ireland, heralding degree-level social work qualifications which would also see service user involvement, like in other parts of the U.K., having a mandatory presence in **all** its core aspects. This was an important milestone to reach with regard to the elevation of service user knowledge and symbolic recognition that this had epistemological gravitas to bring to professional social work training. Northern Ireland, for its part, was at this stage five years into an important peace process, marked by the signing of the Good Friday/Belfast Agreement of 1998; this would mark the end of almost 30 years of violent political conflict, euphemistically referred to as the "Troubles". During the latter period, more than 3,500 people had been killed and significant numbers also injured, bereaved and traumatized as a result of a protracted period of violence (Fay et al., 1999). With a more peaceful and settled societal milieu, the Northern Ireland Social Care Council (NISCC), the regulatory body for social work, creatively responded by also stipulating that social work students in Northern Ireland should be directly taught about the "Northern Ireland Context". This would necessarily entail social work educators openly addressing how this "Context" had adverse impacts at an individual, group and community level in Northern Ireland. This was ground-breaking in many ways, as this is the only part of the world where such a curricular mandatory taught element occurs (Duffy, 2012).

Educators in social work, up until this new initiative, had struggled to openly address these sensitive, difficult and challenging issues in the curriculum (Duffy, 2012; Coulter et al., 2013; Campbell et al., 2013). However, early seeds of innovation were being sown which recognized the potential for victims and survivors of the Northern Ireland "Troubles" to have a direct input in the curriculum (Duffy, 2019). The publication of research by Duffy (2006) provided an additional strategic framework within which these innovative endeavours could reflect the overarching expression of service user and carer involvement in social work teaching in Northern Ireland.

Co-producing a taught curriculum on social work and political conflict

Currently positioned within a 12-week Introduction to Social Work module in the Bachelor of Social Work (BSW) at Queen's University, Belfast, over a two-week period individuals with lived experience of bereavement, injury and trauma, co-produce teaching and tutorials alongside academic colleagues. This co-produced curriculum initiative is facilitated through a long established partnership with the WAVE Trauma Centre, whose members have been actively contributing to social work education at Queen's University.[1] On two full days, morning lectures cover important topics such as: sectarianism and social work; the history of the Troubles in Northern Ireland; understanding trauma; policy perspectives for victims and survivors of the Troubles; the social work role with victims and survivors. The afternoon of each teaching day is then devoted to smaller group tutorials over a two-hour period, where the focus is on bringing the lived experience of victims and survivors to the centre of the students' learning experiences. This is achieved by these *citizen trainers*, the term they prefer to use, openly talking about what happened to them in the Troubles. The tutorials are co-facilitated by the academic team member and citizen trainer, and once the personal narrative of the citizen trainer has been shared, the students then have an opportunity to ask questions and openly talk about the impact of hearing these personally based lived accounts and reflections. After a short break, which is so important given the highly sensitive atmosphere of this teaching, the students then focus on a case study, co-designed by the citizen trainers and academic staff, where the focus is on the application of knowledge, skills and values which the students require to effectively respond in their helping role when working with victims and survivors of the Northern Ireland conflict.

Since beginning this initiative almost 15 years ago, teaching evaluations with the students have raised important findings about the impact of this particular type of pedagogical approach. The following are some of the quotes provided by social work students:

> This learning has enabled me to recognize and understand that many people we will be working with could be affected by the troubles in some way. It's important to have knowledge regarding events and impacts of troubles as it has impacted widely on our society.
>
> It was moving and engaging it made "my history" a reality and more personal rather than "text book".
>
> I felt that bringing people into tutorials who have had traumatic experiences increased learning and brought it home the impact on their lives.
>
> *(cited in Campbell et al., 2013, p. 8)*

It was also important to survey the views of the citizen trainers to reflect on their experiences of this type of service user involvement.

> We are keen take the opportunity to have a constructive input to the system – to change it for the better as we will need social services in the future.
>
> We can't let people forget that although the Troubles are over – they are not over for people struggling with their injuries . . . we have to live with it for the rest of our lives.
>
> *(cited in Duffy, 2012, p. 730)*

Reflections

The latter pedagogic initiative and associated research have been an established feature of the social work curriculum at Queen's University. During this journey, those of us directly involved have learned a lot in regard to: student perspectives, service user/citizen trainer perspectives and impact on ourselves as educators. From a student perspective, our evidence has indicated that their learning has deepened in regard to *threshold concepts* and *troublesome knowledge* (Meyer and Land, 2005; Foote, 2012). Many such students were learning about this topic and experiencing this direct approach through this type of service user involvement for the very first time, and some did question why this was necessary in a society trying to move forward, towards solidified peace and reconciliation. Is it necessary, therefore, to be "going back" when wider society is trying to move forward from conflict? These are important questions that need open engagement (see Duffy, 2012).

In our work, we justified this approach to teaching in the context of the research evidence pointing towards the breadth of legacy issues associated with the Northern Ireland Troubles, such as very high rates of mental illness, addictions, suicide, trauma (PTSD, transgenerational trauma), adverse childhood experiences, etc., which are widely reported (see, for example, O'Neill et al., 2015). When the evidence in this way was further explored and presented, the students were able to clearly see justification of why this approach was so necessary to include in their curriculum. The students then went on to validate the quality of learning through the types of observations cited previously in their evaluations. The literature does also recognize the types of ways in which social work can occupy a middle ground in political conflicts, thereby distancing itself from real and meaningful engagement with more difficult and challenging issues which are inherently political (Smyth and Campbell, 1996; Shamai, 1999; Baum, 2007). Students studying in the midst of on-going political conflict can also experience a sense of isolation (Cunningham (2004; Neumann and Gamble, 1995); however, their openness to active participation in the classroom and directly engaging at an emotional level with these types of lived service user experiences can also result in a deeper and more intense type of learning experience, as noted in the literature (Zembylas, 2007; Maidment and Crisp, 2011; Duffy, 2012).

The service user/citizen trainers in this initiative also valued the experience, as noted from the comments below:

> A great experience – young people coming out as social workers need to be aware of what they will meet as fully qualified – they need all the help they can get.
>
> You want a social worker to come into your home and not judge you – to come in without preconceptions . . . to listen to the hassles I have had with all the agencies, and students to ask themselves how they can simplify the process.
>
> *(cited in Duffy, 2012, p. 731)*

Additionally, when conflict and the potential threat of violence may still be a feature of the background context, even with Northern Ireland as a post-conflict society, it was very important to take account of protections especially in regard to confidentiality, privacy and ground rules:

> The assurance of confidentiality is important for us in telling our stories.
>
> *(cited in Duffy, 2012, p. 730)*

There have also been important messages emerging from this pedagogy about the importance for academic colleagues being openly reflective and reflexive with each other about their own issues, assumptions and potentially inherent biases/prejudices. This type of teaching, therefore, calls for an open and honest dialogue in the triad of relationships that are core to the process: service users with students, students with each other, academics with each other. It is only when this transparency is in place, underpinned by an ethics of care (Hugman, 2005) and attention to detail in preparations (Duffy, 2006), that the involvement of service users in this type of teaching will be able to proceed from a well thought through and solid foundation.

Thinking ahead

In essence, the direct involvement of service users in education in countries affected by conflict will engage what Megan Boler (1999) refers to as a "pedagogy of discomfort". Central to Boler's thinking here is that this area of *discomfort* necessarily involves students and educators stepping outside their "comfort zone" in the classroom context. Outside of this comfort zone is the space where students and educators (and service users in this situation) can collectively self-examine, critique and unpack their established views, opinions, ideas, attitudes, beliefs and values (Boler, 1999; Zembylas and Boler, 2002; Boler and Zembylas, 2003; Coulter et al., 2013). This process of emotional engagement and untangling in learning, argued in the literature, can particularly help students acquire a deepened understanding of social injustices, notably important when the societal backdrop is conflict related (Boler, 1999; Berlak, 2004; Zembylas, 2008; Zembylas and McGlynn, 2012, p. 41). The classroom therefore becomes a site for engaging in alternate ways of thinking, particularly in regard to injustices, but this is dependent on a level of underpinning emotional engagement which potentially will cause discomfort (Ahmed, 2004; Zembylas, 2008; Zembylas and Chubbuck, 2009). This connects in with the reference to "threshold concepts" referred to earlier, citing the work of Foote (2012). Some commentators remark that this type of discomfort is necessary in the complex process of disturbing and questioning established ways of thinking in students. The following quote from Berlak (2004, cited in Zembylas and McGlynn, 2012, p. 43) quite makes this point: "If a major purpose of teaching is to unsettle taken-for-granted views and emotions, then some discomfort is not only unavoidable but may also be necessary".

Conclusion

I have previously noted that this type of teaching approach is not for the *pedagogically faint hearted* (Duffy, 2019). The very notion of causing discomfort in the classroom by exposing students and everyone else involved to these levels of introspection and intrusion is arguably fraught with ethical questions. Having said this, the evidence we have developed in Northern Ireland, reported on earlier in this chapter, would indicate that there is pedagogic value inherent in this approach, as students are learning core aspects of knowledge directly from service users who have lived through the adverse impacts of violent political conflict. This type of knowledge, then, equips students for the types of situations they will encounter when working in the context of human services occurring when conflict is a feature of the wider context.

Achieving a sense of balance of everybody's interests is, however, essential. Attention to detail in regard to care, sensitivity and empathy are the core ingredients to ensuring this type of specialist pedagogy yields positive outcomes for everyone involved. Perhaps it is, therefore, apt to conclude with the following observation by Zembylas and McGlynn (2012, p. 56) that "an ethic of empathy and caring is necessary to provide a safe place for students to examine, challenge, and change their cherished beliefs and assumptions". This type of "safe place" can also encompass the meaningful involvement and active participation of service users in helping students to critically understand the levels of micro (personal) and macro (societal) impact of political conflict.

Note

1 WAVE is a grassroots NGO, established in 1991, which provides support services to people of all ages affected by the Northern Ireland Troubles. See: www.wavetraumacentre.org.uk.

References

Ahmed, S. (2004). *The cultural politics of emotion.* Edinburgh: Edinburgh University Press.

Baum, N. (2007). Social work practice in conflict-ridden areas: Cultural sensitivity is not enough. *British Journal of Social Work*, 37, 873–891.

Beresford, P. (2019). Public participation in health and social care: Exploring the co-production of knowledge. *Frontiers in Sociology*, 3, 41. https://doi.org/10.3389/fsoc.2018.00041

Berlak, A. (2004). Confrontation and pedagogy: Cultural secrets and emotion in antioppressive pedagogies. In *Democratic dialogue in education: Troubling speech, disturbing silence*, edited by Megan Boler, 123–144. New York: Peter Lang.

Boler, M. (1999). *Feeling power: Emotions and education.* New York and London: Routledge.

Boler, M. and Zembylas, M. (2003). Discomforting truths: The emotional terrain of understanding difference. In *Pedagogies of difference: Rethinking education for social change*, edited by P. Trifonas, 110–136. New York: Routledge Falmer.

Campbell, J. (2019). International perspectives on social work and political conflict. In *International perspectives on social work and political conflict*, edited by J. Duffy, J. Campbell and C. Tosone, 8–17. New York. Routledge.

Campbell, J., Duffy, J., Traynor, C., Reilly, I. and Pinkerton, J. (2013). Social work education and political conflict: Preparing students to address the needs of victims and survivors of the Troubles in Northern Ireland. *European Journal of Social Work*, 16(4), 506–520.

Coulter, S., Campbell, J., Duffy, J. and Reilly, I. (2013). Enabling social work students to deal with the consequences of political conflict: Engaging with victim/survivor service users and a pedagogy of discomfort. *Social Work Education – The International Journal*, 32(4), 439–452.

Cunningham, M. (2004). Teaching social workers about Trauma: Reducing the risks of vicarious traumatization in the classroom. *Journal of Social Work Education*, 40, 305–312.

Duffy, J. (2006). *Participating and learning – citizen involvement in social work education in a Northern Ireland context.* London: Social Care Institute for Excellence (SCIE). www.scie.org.uk/publications/misc/citizeninvolvement.pdf

Duffy, J. (2012). Service user involvement in teaching about conflict – an exploration of the issues. *International Social Work* (Special Edition on Social Work and Armed Conflict), 55(5), 720–739.

Duffy, J. (2019). Social work practice and political conflict. In *International perspectives on social work and political conflict*, edited by J. Duffy, J. Campbell and C. Tosone, 17–31. New York. Routledge.

Duffy, J., Campbell, J. and Tosone, C. (eds) (2019). *International perspectives on social work and political conflict.* London: Routledge.

Duffy, J., Gillen, P., Agnew, C., Casson, K., Davidson, G., McGlone, A. and McKeever, B. (2017). *Personal and Public Involvement (PPI) and its impact. Monitoring, measuring and evaluating the impact of PPI in*

Health and Social Care in Northern Ireland. Belfast: Public Health Agency and Patient and Client Council. www.knowledge.hscni.net/Topics/Index/823.

Fay, M.T., Morrissey, M. and Smyth, M. (1999). *Northern Ireland's troubles: The human costs*. London: Pluto.

Foote, W. (2012). Threshold theory and social work education. *Social Work Education: The International Journal*, 32(4), 424–438.

Hugman, R. (2005). *New approaches in ethics for the caring profession*. Basingstoke: Palgrave Macmillan.

Lorenz, W. (2019). Foreword. In *International perspectives on social work and political conflict*, edited by J. Duffy, J. Campbell and C. Tosone, xiv–xviii. New York. Routledge.

Maidment, J. and Crisp, B.R. (2011). The impact of emotions on practicum learning. *Social Work Education*, 30(4), 408–421.

Maglajlic, R.A. and Basic, S. (2019). Critical reflection on the social work experiences in Northern Ireland: Perspectives from Bosnia and Herzegovina. In *International perspectives on social work and political conflict*, edited by J. Duffy, J. Campbell and C. Tosone, 65–79. New York. Routledge.

Meyer, J.H.F. and Land, R. (2005). Threshold concepts and troublesome knowledge (2): epistemological considerations and a conceptual framework for teaching and learning. *Higher Education*, 49(3), 373–388.

Neumann, D.A. and Gamble, S.J. (1995). Issues in the professional development of psychotherapists: Countertransference and vicarious traumatization in the new trauma therapist. *Psychotherapy*, 32, 341–347.

Oliver, M. (1983). *Social work and disabled people*. Basingstoke: Macmillan.

Oliver, M. (1990). *The politics of disablement*. Basingstoke: Macmillan and St Martin's Press.

O'Neill, S., Armour, C., Bolton, D., Bunting, B., Corry, C., Devine, B., Ennis, E., Ferry, F., McKenna, A., McLafferty, M. and Murphy, S. (2015). *Towards a better future: The trans-generational impact of the troubles on mental health*. Belfast: Commission for Victims and Survivors.

Robinson, K. and Webber, M. (2013). Models and effectiveness of service user and carer involvement in social work education: A literature review. *British Journal of Social Work*, 43(5), 925–944.

Shamai, M. (1999). Experiencing and coping with stress of political uncertainty: Gender differences among mental health professionals. *Families in Society*, 1, 41–50.

Shaping Our Lives (2003). *Shaping our lives: From outset to outcome: what people think of the social care services they use*. New York: Joseph Rowntree Foundation.

Smyth, M. and Campbell, J. (1996). Social work, sectarianism and anti-sectarian practice in Northern Ireland. *British Journal of Social Work*, 26(1), 77–92.

Tosone, C. (2019). Shared trauma and social work practice in communal disasters. In *International perspectives on social work and political conflict*, edited by J. Duffy, J. Campbell and C. Tosone, 50–65. New York. Routledge.

Zembylas, M. (2007). Theory and methodology in researching emotions in education. *International Journal of Research & Method in Education*, 30(1), 57–72.

Zembylas, M. (2008). *The politics of trauma in education*. New York: Palgrave Macmillan.

Zembylas, M. and Boler, M. (2002). On the spirit of patriotism: Challenges of a "pedagogy of discomfort". *Teachers College Record Online*. www.tcrecord.org/Content.asp?ContentID=11007

Zembylas, M. and Chubbuck, S. (2009). Emotions and social inequalities: Mobilizing emotions for social justice education. In *Advances in teacher emotion research: The impact on teachers' lives*, edited by P. Schutz and M. Zembylas, 343–363. Dordrecht: Springer.

Zembylas, M. and McGlynn, C. (2012). Discomforting pedagogies: Emotional tensions, ethical dilemmas and transformative possibilities. *British Educational Research Journal*, 38(1), 41–59.

33

NEW ZEALAND'S INDIGENOUS END-OF-LIFE CARE CUSTOMS

A qualitative study on Māori, by Māori, for Māori, with Māori

Tess Moeke-Maxwell, Kathleen Mason and Merryn Gott

Abstract

Background: Pae Herenga is a qualitative study that aims to investigate the traditional end-of-life care customs and protocols employed by indigenous *whānau* (families, including extended family) of Aotearoa, New Zealand, and the facilitators and barriers to their utilisation across different healthcare settings. The *Te Ārai Palliative Care and End of Life Kāhui Kaumātua Rōpū* called for a collaborative study to gather critical information that will strengthen caregiving knowledge of whānau who may be culturally disenfranchised from their caregiving customs through the ethnocentric forces of colonisation, assimilation, and urbanisation. The findings will also support palliative care services which, through New Zealand's founding treatise (1840) and the New Zealand Public Health and Disability Act (2000), are obligated to work in partnership with tangata whenua (people of the land) (Ministry of Health, 2014) to uphold their taonga (treasures). Health is considered a vital taonga by and for Māori (Laing and Pomare, 1994). The findings will help to strengthen the abilities of whānau and the health sector to respond to the projected increase in older Māori deaths over the next 30 years.

Methods: Kaupapa Māori research design, underpinned by indigenous philosophy, values, beliefs, and cultural practices, informs this three-year study. It necessarily places the lived experiences, cultural knowledge, and indigenous caregiving expertise of Māori at the centre of the study. Crucially, it is a project on Māori, by Māori, for Māori, with Māori. Sixty face-to-face interviews and three digital storytelling workshops involving 15 storytellers (whānau, indigenous healers, spiritual healers, Māori health professionals), will be conducted across four geographical sites within Aotearoa, New Zealand. The findings will be disseminated via a public website, peer-reviewed publications, book chapters, conference presentations, and hui (meetings).

Discussion: The Pūrerehua Collaborative Research Framework is introduced to describe the importance of working collaboratively with Māori elders, Community Research Collaborators, and the research participants. For example, the request for this study and the framing question ("What are the traditional customs that whānau use to guide end-of-life care?") was identified by the Te Ārai Kāhui Kaumātua group. A diverse group of researchers, comprised of both Māori and non-Māori researchers, will provide cultural knowledge and academic expertise during the analysis phase. "Community Research Collaborators" will contribute community expertise towards recruiting whānau participants and informing communities about the study, and will participate in disseminating the findings. They will also attend two full research team meetings. Interview participants will collaborate on co-constructing stories based on their personal interview narratives. KMR methods combined with the collaborative efforts of approximately 30 researchers (including seven community researchers and supported by a group of at least ten kaumātua) and over 60 indigenous whānau participants will help to ensure the successful completion and dissemination of the Pae Herenga study.

Background

Palliative care grew out of a desire to champion, and be responsive to, the "voice" of the "voiceless" (Saunders, 2003). However, the extent to which this aspiration has been realised is debatable. While there has been significant support for the principles and aspirations of service user involvement in palliative care at all levels, from individual patient interactions to national policy (Ministry of Health, 2001), the reality is that the voice of the professional continues to dominate. This situation is supported, and exacerbated, by the biomedical research paradigm which determines widely accepted standards regarding what constitutes high quality palliative care research. Adhering to the principles of Evidence Based Medicine, as much palliative care research aspires to, can lead to a side-lining of service user views because, as Greenhalgh et al. (2015) argue, this approach is "biased against patients" (p. 2). This claim relates to the following six features of Evidence Based Medicine that work against the patient agenda: limited patient input to research design; low status given to experience in the hierarchy of evidence; a tendency to conflate patient-centred consulting with use of decision tools; insufficient attention to power imbalances that suppress the patient's voice; over-emphasis on the clinical consultation; and a focus on people who seek and obtain care (rather than the hidden denominator of those that do not seek or cannot access care) (Greenhalgh et al., 2015). Moreover, there is little recognition within palliative care research, practice, and policy of the power differentials that inhibit service user views effecting change, even when "public and patient involvement" is embedded within projects.

In this chapter, we argue that indigenous research methods have much to offer palliative care researchers who are keen to move from the rhetoric of user involvement to effective implementation. Indigenous methodologies provide a framework for building collaborative relationships with research communities to influence positive outcomes for those communities. They recognise and support the self-determination of research participants to express their own priorities for research and service delivery. We use the *pūrerehua* (a Māori musical instrument) metaphor to describe and discuss the importance of collaborative relationships within an indigenous end-of-life study, Pae Herenga. In particular, we describe how the voices of indigenous people have been incorporated into the study to ensure cultural and spiritual integrity of an indigenous end-of-life study.

Pae Herenga study protocol

Health and palliative care services of Aotearoa, New Zealand, are informed by a Western understanding of "a good death" which generally occludes a deeper cultural perspective of indigenous New Zealanders' end-of-life values, beliefs, and customs (Gott et al., 2015). In this section, we introduce a study that has been designed to redress the subjugation of an indigenous perspective of illness, dying, and post-death care through the collection and dissemination of information that is informed by an indigenous end-of-life worldview. We describe the indigenous qualitative research methods used to explore indigenous experiences of using end-of-life care customs.

The Pae Herenga study is reliant on the vital contributions of indigenous peoples. Indigenous people are involved at every level of the study, from conception to recruitment to dissemination, as their knowledge and experiential insights into tribal cultural care customs are critical. The *Te Ārai Kāhui Kaumātua Rōpū* (indigenous elders from the Te Ārai Palliative Care and End of Life Research Group, School of Nursing, University of Auckland[1]) identified the need to conduct this study of Māori end-of-life care *tikanga* (values and principles) and *kawa* (protocols and rules) that Māori individuals, *whānau* (families, including extended family), *iwi* (tribes) and *hapū* (sub-tribes) draw from, and culturally evolve, to inform protective caregiving practices to strengthen whānau at the end of life.

Involvement of Te Ārai Kaumātua

The project will be guided by Te Ārai Kaumātua at every stage of its three-year duration. The importance of *kaumātua* (respected older indigenous people) involvement is evidenced in the contributions they make via their deep cultural and spiritual knowledge (Cram, 2001). To achieve *kotahitanga* (where consensus and unity are achieved through discussion), Te Ārai Kaumātua discussed the need for this project with members of the academic research team. Together, the research objectives were distilled. Kaumātua knowledge was critical in defining the research topic and question, and shaping the project's research design. An example of the influence Te Ārai Kaumātua have in the project concerns the inspiration and direction for the project's title: Pae Herenga.

Te Ārai Kaumātua began the project with a discussion on the meaning of the name they gave to the study. This was an important aspect of the study to get right because our research project's name carries an indigenous holistic view of life and death for Māori people. *Pae Herenga* means the many horizons human encounter from the time of spiritual conception *o te ao wairua* (of the spiritual world) before birth. Spiritual life before birth is the starting point; although formless, the *wairua* (spirit) carries within it the spiritual integrity of *Io-matua-kore* (the Supreme Being). The spirit then progresses through to *te ao kikokiko* (the physical world) where it takes up its physical form before, or during, birth. Now located in the physical realm, the individual experiences being able to action their earthly assignments (given by Io-matua-kore) as they continue to build their characteristics and strengthen the development of their personality through the guidance of *ngā kete o te wānanga* (the three baskets of knowledge). When the person's time on earth expires, they leave their physical form. Upon death, the body dies and the person's spirit returns back to *te ao wairua* (the spiritual world). At death, *ka hoki te wairua ki te ūkaipō* (the spirit returns to their original home), to *te ao wairua te Rangiātea, te Ururangi* (the spiritual world of Rangiātea and Ururangi, in the heavenly realms). Although the pathways are numerous and varied, the cycle of birth, life, death, and birth is something the Te Ārai Kaumātua have expressed that all human beings pass through. After death, the individual benefits from the continuing joint flow of the many parts of the horizon, called *Te Pae Herenga*. According to the Kaumātua, *Tēnei te porohita ō te mana wairua, te mana tāngata, tae noa ki te turanga ō te Puhitau*; this is when the life cycle "promotes maturity of spirit, maturity of humanity in people". When the two parts of metaphysical and physical life experiences are joined together, the standard of *Puhitau* is achieved (the mature, experienced child of Io-matua-kore).

Te Ārai Kaumātua are concerned that the structural and societal changes that have taken place in Aotearoa, New Zealand, since colonisation have influenced Māori peoples' lifestyles, thereby affecting their ability to retain and carry out their traditional end-of-life care customs. The vast and varied cultural changes to Māori society owe their origins to the colonial period, where tribal collectives suffered widespread land loss through land confiscations and the transference of customary tribal land ownership to individual ownership (Kingi, 2008), enabling Māori lands to be more easily procured by the few (Walker, 1990). By the early 1900s, the vast majority of the land in Aotearoa, New Zealand, had been transferred out of Māori customary title (Risenborough and Hutton, 1997). The amalgamation of Māori to the colonial settler society was enabled by the nation's treatise, the Treaty of Waitangi (1840). It is common for contemporary Māori to live away from their tribal lands; this can make it difficult for people to participate regularly in tribal activities where it is likely their unique cultural customs would be role-modelled and handed down through the generations by kaumātua. Assimilationist educational policies of the early twentieth century meant that many Māori became disenfranchised from their language and cultural customs (Jenkins and Morris Matthews, 1998). The urban migration during the 1950s and 1960s saw many Māori move to large cities in search of work (Durie, 1998). With exposure to the white majority cultural norms (of which the health system plays a significant role in Western discourse), the family structures and systems of contemporary Māori whānau often resemble that of the nuclear Pākehā family (white descendants of British settler society).

Pae Herenga aims and objectives

The Pae Herenga study will systematically collect, analyse, and interpret, and disseminate information that describes the traditional customs and protocols that inform and guide the end-of-life care employed by Māori whānau. The objective is to ensure these customs are collected and made available to whānau caregivers who are in need of cultural support. Health and palliative care services are also in need of this information, as it will help to increase their ability to provide culturally safe and congruous end-of-life care. At the conclusion of the study, we will develop an online educational resource to support Māori whānau and their communities (Moeke-Maxwell et al., 2018) and health and palliative care services. This information is urgently needed to support the rapidly growing ageing Māori population and the anticipated increase in Māori palliative care need over the next 30 years (McLeod, 2016). Previous research findings show that Māori cultural customs help to strengthen whānau to carry out end-of-life care activities (Moeke-Maxwell et al., 2014). Hence, the Pae Herenga study has been designed to consult with Māori who have retained their customs, and to share those customs with whānau who have been unable to retain their tribal knowledge due to the impact of colonialism.

A key aim of the study is to describe the end-of-life care customs Māori whānau draw on to strengthen their end-of-life caregiving activities. By extension, we will also explore the observations and experiences of *rongoā* (traditional plant medicine) healers, *tohunga* (spiritual care) practitioners, and Māori health and palliative care providers. Additionally, we will identify the ways in which health and palliative care services help or hinder whānau in using their traditional care customs by identifying any facilitators or barriers that Māori whānau encounter within different care settings (home, hospice, hospital, and aged residential care).

Kaupapa Māori research methods

The Pae Herenga project utilises Kaupapa Māori research (KMR) design; this approach means that the project and its methods are informed by the indigenous philosophy, values, beliefs, and cultural practices of New Zealand Māori (Smith, 1999) and are followed from the beginning to the end of the study (Cram, 2001). The lived experiences, cultural knowledge, and indigenous caregiving expertise of Māori are placed firmly at the centre of the study because "Kaupapa Māori research is philosophy, theory, methodology and practice of research for the benefit of Māori which is also produced by Māori" (Health Research Council of New Zealand, 2010, p. 7).

Research team

The research team recruited for the Pae Herenga study is comprised of kaumātua, academic and community researchers, and Community Research Collaborators from each of the research locations (n=30+). The research team will also be supported by the University of Auckland (UoA) digital storytelling film crew who have been engaged to work collaboratively with selected participants at three digital storytelling workshops, to record and produce stories that talk about an aspect of the participants' end-of-life care journeys.

Research locations

The study will be conducted in four different geographical locations in Aotearoa, New Zealand (Mid-North, Hawkes Bay, Wellington, and Whanganui). These research locations were identified during the pilot study for Pae Herenga (Moeke-Maxwell et al., 2018). There is a high likelihood that many of the Māori people interviewed will be genealogically connected to tribes from those areas.

Key informant groups

Participants for four key informant groups will be recruited to the Pae Herenga study. These groups will be whānau (a person with a life-limiting illness or families caring for a person with a life-limiting illness), rongoā healers (indigenous plant medicine healers), tohunga practitioners (spiritual practitioners), and Māori health professionals (a Māori person(s) working in palliative care or involved with end-of-life care within the broader health sector). Although participants may be recruited to provide information for one research group, we expect that there will be cross-overs between and across the groups. For example, a rongoā healer recruited to participate in the study may also be caring for a family member with a life-limiting illness, or a Māori health professional may also be caring for a family member with a life-limiting illness and be a rongoā practitioner. The key informant group that the participant belongs to will be selected by the participant. Community Research Collaborators (CRCs) in each of the research locations will be engaged to help recruit participants to the study.

Qualitative interviews

The study will include 60 qualitative *kanohi-ki-te-kanohi* (face-to-face) interviews: 15 interviews respectively with each of the four research groups (whānau, rongoā healers, tohunga practitioners, and Māori health professionals) to systematically record the tikanga and kawa used by whānau living in the research locations. The interviews will be digitally recorded and fully transcribed. Using open-ended questions, the researchers will ask participants to describe current or recent activities they have undertaken, or have observed other Māori whānau carrying out, when caring for a family member with a life-limiting illness. We anticipate producing a narrative of lived caregiving experiences containing valuable information on traditional cultural and spiritual practices used by the ill person, or their whānau, that supports the ill and dying person and their family carers across the end-of-life care continuum, and whānau members through the bereavement process. Furthermore, we expect that there will be narratives collected that convey contemporary adaptations of traditional care customs, including those that blend traditional care customs with those from other cultures.

Indigenous hosting methods

Indigenous hosting methods will be called upon to ensure that a high level of cultural safety will be present in the study during all public interactions with Māori communities, with participants during each interview and during the three digital story workshops. For example, establishing *whakawhanaungatanga* (relationship connections), *karakia* (prayer, invocations, and chants), and *waiata* (singing) will help to culturally and spiritually anchor the research environment to provide safety for participants (Gott et al., 2016; Williams et al., 2015, 2018).

Collaborative story production

The Collaborative Story Production (CSP) method is a qualitative member-checking process where participants contribute to the development of a thematically analysed written account of their interview (Moeke-Maxwell et al., 2018). Researchers first identify the interview themes discussed by the interviewee, and present these back to the participant as a summary report for them to provide feedback on. After the digital file has been transcribed, a research assistant cleans the transcript by listening to the recording and amending any typographical errors. A further research team member will craft each story according to the key themes spoken about by the participant(s) and using their words and narrative. In our study, participants will have an opportunity to collaborate with the research team to amend, add, or remove parts of their narrative until it accurately represents their views, from their perspective (Moeke-Maxwell et al., 2018). The lead research writer makes the necessary changes to the summary report, a copy of which will be sent (as either a hard or electronic copy) to the participant.

Coding and analysis

A coding framework will be developed from the 60 summary reports (i.e. not the transcripts) produced via the CSP method. A computer software program (NVivo) will be used to code the data. A thematic analysis will be led by Māori and non-Māori academic team members, with broader involvement from Māori and non-Māori community researchers (includes researchers with clinical skills). CRCs will have an opportunity to review and discuss the developing themes in a further analysis meeting designed for this purpose. There will also be an opportunity for interviewees and digital story participants to provide feedback during site visits that will be held to discuss the study findings.

Digital story workshops

Three digital story workshops will be held in three of the four research sites, producing 15 digital stories. Our previous research has shown digital stories to be a very useful way to capture the lived experiences of indigenous peoples' end-of-life preferences (Moeke-Maxwell et al., 2018; Williams et al., 2015, 2018). They can also help viewers to understand the end-of-life caregiving experiences of indigenous peoples (Williams et al., 2015, 2018). The digital story method has been adapted by Te Ārai members to allow for cultural processes to be woven into the workshops. This will provide a culturally safe introductory method for indigenous participants who will meet the UoA digital story film crew for the first time and share heartfelt stories that could be overwhelming for them in a non-indigenous environmental context. Based on our evaluation of the pilot study, digital stories are helpful for sharing with communities, and are helpful learning resources that represent different aspects of end-of-life caregiving from the perspective of eight Māori whānau (Williams et al., 2015).

Inclusion of spiritual and cultural safety within the study

The inclusion of indigenous peoples' values and customs are critical within end-of-life studies as these provide the cultural safety and spiritual protection for the whānau participants, research data, the CRCs, and broader academic research team. Cultural and spiritual safety must be attended to within the study design if the project is to be successful (Bishop, 1999). This is insured by the ongoing dialogue and cultural advice with Te Ārai Kaumātua and the indigenous communities involved in the study.

Pūrerehua indigenous research framework

New Zealand Māori have always been recognised as an aural society and traditionally have been viewed as masters of *huahuatau* (metaphor). Stories steeped in metaphor are commonly drawn on to communicate important messages, as they are able to convey deep layers of meaning and provide context and deeper understanding to subjects (Hemara, 2000). Customary knowledge has been passed down and across countless generations using this method.

The pūrerehua metaphor is employed to demonstrate that our first priority is to conduct research in a culturally safe and protective way to ensure we produce valuable information and resources to share with whānau and health providers. This information is likely to support equitable health outcomes for Māori because the data gathered will be highly trustworthy and meaningfully relevant to Māori. To provide context for the metaphor, a description of the pūrerehua and its use is provided. We then draw on the pūrerehua metaphor to describe how we incorporate the voices of indigenous people to ensure our research project, Pae Herenga, has the cultural and spiritual integrity required for an indigenous end-of-life study. Finally, we describe and discuss the importance of collaborative relationships for the study.

The pūrerehua

The pūrerehua is an indigenous musical instrument that takes its name from the sound of vibrating, or hovering moths or butterflies. The *Atua* (deity) that governs this instrument is *Tāwhiri-mātea* (Atua of the winds) (Flintoff, 2014). *Kōripo pūrerehua* is the whirling sound that accompanies the twirling pūrerehua. The *pūrerehua* (literal definition: "moth") is a flat oval or diamond-shaped board (paddle) made of stone, bone, or wood (Flintoff, 2004; Melbourne, 2016) and can be made in many of sizes (Flintoff, 2004). Before carving a pūrerehua, the carver has a vision of what the *taonga* (treasured object) will look like and its overarching purpose. The carver may even have an idea about who the pūrerehua will be used by. These details will inform the style, weight, size, and materials used. The pūrerehua paddle can be adorned or carved with indigenous patterns and inset with paua (abalone) shells. The paddle is attached to a *taura* (cord). At the other end of the taura is a *komo* (loop) to slip over the wrist. A *takahuri* (toggle) fastened to the *komo* is grasped in the hand to anchor the chord; the pūrerehua is then twirled through the air in large sweeping circular motions by the *ringapūoro* (musician). As the paddle gains momentum, the *hamumu* (humming sound) emerges as a low whirring vibration that reverberates through the air. In some instances it can be heard at a distance (Melbourne, 2016). The pūrerehua has a number of uses which vary across tribal areas in Aotearoa, New Zealand. In some areas, the pūrerehua is used to summon lizards, and in others to lament the dead (Flintoff, 2004). The pūrerehua, also referred to as a "bullroarer" (Flintoff, 2004; McLean, 1996; Melbourne, 2016; Moyle, 1989), performs its soulful lament as the twirling instrument passes through the domain of *Tāwhiri-mātea* (God of the winds and weather patterns).

The ringapūoro first warms the paddle by gently allowing the paddle to dangle at arms' length before swinging it, secured gently by the taura, back and forth. The paddle is twirled in smallish circles to charge its energy before a full swinging action to launch the paddle high in the air in strong circular sweeping motions above the musician's head. When enlivened, the paddle twirls faster and faster. The vigorous swinging motion permits the deep vibrational hum to fill the air. Different sounds are released depending on the size of the paddle and how fast it is rotated. The humming vibration stirs the soul, connecting the musician and the listeners to *te ao wairua* (spiritual dimension) (Flintoff, 2014). To listen to this ethereal vibration is an emotional experience that uplifts the mind and heart at a time when it is often most vulnerable, during bereavement.

A strong indigenous voice

Inherent within a KMR approach are the voices and perspectives of Māori, and the prospect of creating change based on aspirations, philosophies, and processes that are also Māori (Cram, 2001). The *moemoeā* (vision) for the Pae Herenga study arose out of conversations between kaumātua. They were concerned that many Māori whānau had been affected by the pressures of colonisation and assimilation, and ongoing socio-economic inequities perpetuated by contemporary societal structures, leading to difficulties in retaining their indigenous language and cultural practices. Specifically, they were troubled by the notion that some Māori whānau had been unable to retain their traditional end-of-life care customs. These concerns were brought to the attention of the Te Ārai Palliative Care and End of Life Research Group by the Te Ārai Kaumātua. With the assistance of the core research team, comprised of both Māori and non-Māori academic researchers, the vision and purpose for Pae Herenga were conceptualised. Metaphorically speaking, the hum of the pūrerehua could be compared to the call of the kaumātua, the indigenous voice that informed the vision for the Pae Herenga study.

The indigenous voice is not just limited to the vision or inspiration for the Project, nor is it limited to one source. It is embedded within Pae Herenga and will be heard throughout the duration of the study from multiple indigenous sources. For example, Māori cultural guidance and advice are provided by the Kaumātua, Māori CRCs, and Māori members of the research team. A further example are the indigenous participants from whom qualitative information is collected to inform the findings and online educational resource. It is also intended that the dissemination of the research will be guided by indigenous principles and metaphors, such as the kanohi-ki-te-kanohi dissemination process within the various research locations.

Collaboration

The Pūrerehua indigenous research framework highlights the importance of collaboration. Within a research context, collaboration between the researchers and the researched is vital to the success of an indigenous study. We believe that strong connections are needed to bind everyone involved in the study together. The practice of *whakawhanaungatanga* (establishing relationships) between members of the research team and community is an integral element of KMR (Bishop, 1996), and an essential research priority for the Pae Herenga study. Whakawhanaungatanga embeds the project within te ao wairua, uniting the living with their ancestors to form a unique relationship. By committing to working together, in much the same way that the components of the pūrerehua and ringapūoro synchronise to produce the hamumu, the researchers and the researched can reach the desired outcome. In this instance, achieving the aims and objectives of Pae Herenga relies on each member of the research team (including the Te Ārai Kaumātua), CRCs, UoA digital storytelling film crew, and research participants committing to and carrying out their distinct roles. Collaboration between different roles at different times is required in order to achieve each objective that contributes to the overall aim of the project. Examples of the multiple layers of collaboration required within the Pae Herenga study are further explored below.

Te Ārai Kaumātua and core research team

The ringapūoro is essential to the purpose of the pūrerehua. The musician must be able to swing the parts of the instrument in harmony with the environmental elements to achieve the desired hamumu and rhythm. Timing within the spatial sphere is critical to activate the process that will achieve the desired outcome. The Te Ārai Kaumātua and the core research team (TMM, KM, FS, NS, FT, RW, MG, JW, LN, WT, WH) stand tightly together to action the moemoeā and the call of the kaumātua. As such, we work together to lead the full research team (n=30+) to ensure that the key objectives are met and that the project runs smoothly. Like the grip the ringapūoro keeps on the takahuri of the pūrerehua, a firm grasp is kept on each and every element of the research process in a collaborative effort between the Te Ārai Kaumātua and core research team. Should the grip be too loose, the cord could slip through the fingers, causing the pūrerehua to fly off and smash on the ground and bringing its purpose to an abrupt end.

Community Research Collaborator role

The cord that binds the pūrerehua to its parts is vital to the instrument's purpose. Without the cord connecting its parts, the pūrerehua is lifeless; it would not be able to fly and produce its hum. The cord must be made of strong reliable fibres, and it must be well secured to ensure that the parts do not become separated and cause the pūrerehua's demise. From the conception of Pae Herenga, the research vision included the identification of supportive CRCs and research sites. The CRCs act as a point of contact to support and guide collaboration in each of the research locations. They have been selected for the knowledge they hold of their communities, as well as the high regard in which they are held within those communities. Their role within the project extends to supporting participant recruitment, data collection, analysis, and dissemination of study results. Because they know their communities well, they can provide advice on where, when, and how to engage with the communities and, importantly, who needs to be involved. The CRCs are crucial in the recruitment of participants for each key informant groups (whānau, rongoā, tohunga, and Māori health professionals). Their knowledge of local networks will help to ensure the right balance of participants are recruited to get the information needed to fulfil the aims and objectives of the study. They are an important aspect of gaining the appropriate level of cultural support for participant(s) of the face-to-face interviews and digital storytelling workshops. The CRCs also play a pivotal support role for digital story workshops, connecting the principal investigator (TMM) with local host *marae* (formal gathering place) and other community resources. Furthermore, CRCs will liaise and direct the research team, providing cultural information that will support the reporting of the findings and dissemination of the completed resource through public meetings at each research location.

Research participants and University of Auckland digital storytelling film crew

Digital stories will be produced at the three-day digital storytelling workshops that will be held in three of the four research locations. The production of the digital stories requires collaboration between the research participants and the UoA digital storytelling film crew. Participants will be asked to tell a story about an aspect of their end-of-life care, and to provide photographs, waiata, and other taonga or keepsakes that can augment their narrative. The film crew will work closely with the participants over the workshop to craft the digital story.

Role of the ringawera – core research team and Community Research Collaborators

At different stages of the project, various roles will be required of those involved in Pae Herenga. During the digital storytelling workshops, for example, core research team members and CRCs will work together to take on the role of the *ringawera* (cook). Their main concern will be *manaakitanga* (hospitality, showing care for others) of the research participants, UoA film crew, and other research team members, by preparing and providing *kai* (food) that will help to sustain the workshop participants.

Conclusion

Indigenous kaumātua are greatly concerned that the forces of colonialism have left many whānau culturally disenfranchised and voiceless within the nation, and within the health landscape. Colonialism has created difficulty for some whānau to hold on to their valuable and supportive indigenous end-of-life care customs. This chapter outlined a study on Māori, by Māori, for Māori, with Māori, using a KMR approach to systematically collect information about traditional Māori end-of-life care customs to support whānau to provide end-of-life care. This information will also be useful for health and palliative care services to increase their awareness and understanding. The Pūrerehua Collaborative Research Framework metaphor has been drawn on to show how KMR philosophy relies on research that is led by Māori, to benefit Māori. This type of methodology is more likely to increase Māori engagement before, during, and following the project's life span because it is underpinned by the establishment of whakawhanuangata; this relational approach prioritises the collective relationships of researchers, indigenous stakeholder groups, and participant cohorts.

Conducting research that has a high level of indigenous participation will produce trustworthy data and valuable indigenous knowledge. Furthermore, using participants' kōrero purākau in our dissemination activities (digital stories that use people/families, stories, and photographs/images, for example) means we are more likely to demonstrate tikanga and kawa in ways that contemporary whānau will find interesting, relevant, and sincere. The importance of the Pūrerehua Collaborative Research Framework is that the study will be strengthened by the inclusive and collective unity of indigenous people who will be involved at every level and stage of this end-of-life care study. This will ensure the project's aims, methodological design, fieldwork, analysis, and dissemination will be strengthened by a strong cultural voice that can be heard by those who have been silenced by colonialism.

Funding source

The Pae Herenga study was called for by the Te Ārai Palliative Care and End of Life Research Group, School of Nursing, University of Auckland, with funding from the New Zealand Health Research Council [grant number 17/309].

Authors contributions

TMM and MG contributed to the conception of the idea presented, and TMM developed the proof outline. TMM and KM wrote the manuscript. TMM. MG and KM revised the content and TMM gave final approval for the manuscript.

Author information

We thank the following individuals and groups for their expertise and assistance throughout all aspects of our study and for their help in writing the manuscript.

Associate Professor Janine Wiles
Professor Linda Waimarie Nikora
Mr Rawiri Wharemate
Mrs Whio Wharemate-Hansen
Te Ārai Kāhui Kaumātua

Note

1 The Pae Herenga team includes the Te Ārai Kāhui Kaumātua, research advisors, and community researchers with expertise in palliative care, rongoā (plant medicines), health literacy, and Kaupapa Māori research skills (encompasses Māori research philosophy, values, and ethics).

References

Bishop, R. (1996). Addressing issues of self-determination and legitimation in Kaupapa Māori research. In B. Webber. (Eds), *He paepae korero: Research perspectives in Māori education*. Wellington, NZ: New Zealand Council for Educational Research.

Bishop, R. (1999). Collaborative storytelling: Meeting indigenous peoples' desires for self-determination in research In *Indigenous education around the world: Workshop papers from the World Indigenous People's Conference*. Albuquerque, New Mexico.

Cram, F. (2001). Ranganau Māori: Tona tika, tona pono – the validity and integrity of Māori research. In M. Tolich (Ed.), *Research ethics in Aotearoa New Zealand*. Auckland, NZ: Pearson Education New Zealand Limited.

Durie, M. (1998). *Whaiora: Māori health development* (2nd ed.). Auckland, NZ: Oxford University Press.

Flintoff, B. (2004). *Taonga pūoro: The musical instruments of the Māori*. Nelson, NZ: Craig Cotton Publishing.

Flintoff, B. (2014). Māori musical instruments: Taonga pūoroTe Ara – The encyclopedia of New Zealand. Retrieved from www.teara.govt.nz/en/maori-musical-instruments-taonga-puoro/page-3

Gott, M., Moeke-Maxwell, T., Morgan, T., Black, S., Williams, L., Boyd, M., Waterworth, S., & Hall, D. (2016). Working bi-culturally within a palliative care research context: The development of the Te Ārai Palliative Care and End of Life Research Group. *Mortality*, 1–17. doi:10.1080/13576275.2016.1216955

Gott, M., Moeke-Maxwell, T., Williams, L., Black, S., Trussardi, G., Wiles, J., Mules, R., Rolleston, A., & Kerse, N. (2015). Te Pākeketanga: Living and dying in advanced age – a study protocol. *BMC Palliative Care, 14*(74), 1–8. doi:10.1186/s12904-015-0073-4

Greenhalgh, T., Snow, R., Ryan, S., Rees, S., & Salisbury, H. (2015). Six "biases" against patients and carers in evidenced-based medicine. *BMC Medicine, 13*(200), 1–14. doi:10.1186/s12916-015-0437-x

Health Research Council of New Zealand (2010). *Guidelines for researchers on health research involving Māori.* Auckland, NZ: Author. Retrieved from www.hrc.govt.nz/

Hemara, W. (2000). *Maori pedagogies: a view from the literature.* Wellington, NZ: New Zealand Council for Educational Research.

Jenkins, K., & Morris Matthews, K. (1998). Knowing their place: The political socialisation of Maori women in New Zealand through schooling policy and practice, 1867–1969. *Women's History Review, 7*(1), 85–105.

Kingi, T. (2008). *Maori landownership and land management in New Zealand – making land work: Case studies on customary land and development in the Pacific* (Vol. 2, pp. 129–151). Canberra, Australia: Australian Agency for International Development. Retrieved from www.sprep.org/att/IRC/eCOPIES/Pacific_Region/251.pdf – page=135

Laing, P., & Pomare, E. (1994). Maori health and the health care reforms. *Health Policy, 29,* 143–156. Retrieved from www.sciencedirect.com/science/article/pii/0168851094900124

McLean, M. (1996). *Maori music.* Wellington, NZ: Lilburn Trust and Creative New Zealand.

McLeod, H. (2016). *The need for palliative care in New Zealand.* Technical report prepared for the Ministry of Health.

Melbourne, H. (2016). *Toiapiapi: He huinga o ngā kura puoro a te Māori – A collection of Māori musical instruments.* Hirini Melbourne Whanau Trust 2016.

Ministry of Health (2001). *The New Zealand palliative care strategy.* Wellington, NZ: Author. Retrieved from www.health.govt.nz

Ministry of Health (2014). *The guide to He Korowai Oranga: Māori health strategy 2014.* Wellington, NZ: Author.

Moeke-Maxwell, T., Nikora, L.W., & Te Awekotuku, N. (2014). End-of-life care and Māori Whānau Resilience. *Mai Journal, 3*(2), 140–152.

Moeke-Maxwell, T., Wharemate, R., Black, S., Mason, K., Wiles, J., & Gott, M. (2018). Toku toa, he toa rangatira: A qualitative investigation of New Zealand Māori end-of-life care customs. *IJIH, 13*(2), 30–46. doi:10.18357/ijih.v13i2.29749

Moyle, R. (1989). *The sounds of Oceania.* Auckland, NZ: Auckland Institute and Museum.

New Zealand Public Health and Disability Act, No. 91 (2000). Retrieved from www.legislation.govt.nz

Risenborough, H., & Hutton, J. (1997). *The Crown's engagement with customary tenure in the nineteenth century.* Wellington, NZ: Waitangi Tribunal. Retrieved from www.waitangitribunal.govt.nz

Saunders, C. (2003). A voice for the voiceless. In B. Munroe & Oliviere (Eds.), *Patient participation in palliative care: A voice for the voiceless.* doi:10.1093/acprof:oso/9780198515814.003.0001

Smith, L. (1999). *Decolonizing methodologies.* Dunedin, NZ: University of Otago Press.

Walker, R. (1990). *Ka whawhai tonu matou: Struggle without end.* Auckland, NZ: Penguin.

Williams, L., Gott, M., Moeke-Maxwell, T., Black, S., Kothari, S., Pearson, S., Simpson, P., Morgan, T., Grbin, M., Wharemate, R., & Hansen, W. (2018). Death, dying and digital stories. In P. Beresford & S. Carr (Eds.), *Social policy firsthand.* Bristol: Social Policy Press.

Williams, L., Moeke-Maxwell, T., Kothari, S., Pearson, S., Gott, M., Black, S., & Hansen, W. (2015). Is digital storytelling ka pai for New Zealand Māori? Using digital storytelling as a method to explore whānau end of life caregiving experiences: A pilot study. *BMJ Supportive & Palliative Care, 5,* 23.

34

'MOVING AWAY FROM THE SOUND OF ONE HAND CLAPPING?'

John Stephens, Katherine Baker and Ali Finlayson

Introduction

As a reflection of society in general, contemporary healthcare policy has recognised the growing levels of complexity and uncertainty within professional practice (NHS England, 2017; NHS England, 2014; DH, 2012; DH, 2008; DH, 2006) that have significant implications for pre-registration education and the curricula that support this. The dominance of medicalised research-based standards and specialisation, while advancing diagnosis and treatment, has raised a number of serious challenges. One of the most pervasive of these is a fragmentary approach to 'reality' (Bohm and Peat, 2000); this in turn has impacted on an ever-increasing volume of curriculum content, resulting in an expanding 'null curriculum' (Eisner, 1985), i.e. areas of knowledge, skills, and values for which there isn't space or time to teach. Many of the challenges presented to healthcare and healthcare profession education depend on broad contexts that extend into the whole of society and the life of each individual, reflected in the development of UK Clinical Guidelines and policy over the past five years and perhaps exemplified by *The Five Year Forward View* (NHS England, 2014) and *Next Steps on the Five Year Forward View* (NHS England, 2017). This chapter will discuss co-production of curricular material (primarily with service users, but also includes students) undertaken within pre-registration physiotherapy programmes at Northumbria University, Newcastle upon Tyne.

As identified by Trede (2012), pre-registration education programmes should promote not merely disciplinary knowledge and technical skills but also skills and intelligence related to team working, communication with others, learning ways of working through observation, and how to socialise in different workplace cultures. The largely fragmentary approach to pre-registration education through modularisation within overcrowded, product-driven curricula has arguably been exacerbated by the transformation of how UK higher education is funded. The post-2010 higher education landscape (DH, 2016) has resulted in a shift from publicly funded enterprise towards a regulated market in consumer (student) demand. In meeting the educational needs of contemporary society, Kleiman (2011) argues the necessity for disequilibrium through constant change and evolution where creativity is potent – education on the edge of chaos!

It is against this broad background that we intend to explore possible solutions to these challenges in attempting to move towards a more coherent educational 'whole' through co-production of curricular material with 'service users' and a movement *away from the sound of one hand clapping*. The chapter somewhat naturally falls into three parts. The first section will contextualise contemporary physiotherapy and healthcare profession education within recent developments in higher education and an argument for 'wholeness' via co-production through an emphasis on 'process' within curricula, rather than curricula as 'product'. The second section will explain examples of co-produced curriculum content drawn from our own practice. The third section then seeks to deconstruct and discuss the issues raised within the examples, underpinned by key themes of open dialogue, space for reflection, creativity, and order, framed by theoretical frameworks designed to provide insight to the processes of our approach. Some broad guidance for those keen to undertake a similar approach is articulated for those who wish to generate not merely a *sound* but a discernible *tune* in their approach to co-production within professional education.

Broad picture

Contemporary higher education, healthcare, and healthcare professional education in the UK is changing continuously and quickly. Change is changing (Bevan, 2017). As of September 2017, undergraduate pre-registration healthcare programmes in England moved away from public funding to student self-funding (UK Government, 2016), although the two-year accelerated pre-registration MSc programmes were assured public funding for 2017–18. In addition, there are a plethora of pre-registration routes proposed by the UK Government, including apprenticeships, two year BSc (Hons), integrated master's, and doctoral-level education (UK Government, 2016, Council of Deans, 2017). This at a time when the role of physiotherapists, nurses, and allied health professionals is rapidly changing with demand growing.

The UK Government has argued the NHS, independent care and social care sector, students, universities, and wider public sector will all benefit from introducing the same reforms in health professional education that have taken place across the rest of higher education (UK Government, 2016). This is predicted to provide a greater number of healthcare professionals, reduce costs and reliance on agency staff, and enable a greater number of students to realise an ambition to enter the profession of their choice. A broader range of pathways to gain professional registration claims to provide benefits to students, healthcare organisations, and HEIs, e.g. programmes of shorter duration, it being quicker to gain employment, or being in employment for the duration of study (apprenticeships). All of this arrives at a time when consumer demand (student choice) is predominant in what is offered by service providers, universities, and other education providers.

Within the contemporary landscape of healthcare and healthcare professional education, there is an interesting relationship with Foucault's analysis of knowledge-power and surveillance (Foucault, 2005) and a perceived dominance of competency-based, product-driven education. For Foucault, power and knowledge are inseparable; knowledge doesn't represent the truth of what is, but promotes what is taken to be true. Power is exercised through 'knowledgeable' practices and dialogue that observe, measure, categorise, and regulate. Pre-registration healthcare professional education in the UK is required not only to shape learning to meet academic requirements of the awarded degree, but also to 'direct' enculturation of learners to meet the requirements of Professional Statutory Regulatory Bodies (PSRBs). This shaping of subjectivity is achieved through the curriculum and the pedagogy that supports this (Osberg and Biesta, 2008).

Our approach at Northumbria in the co-production of learning with service users – People With Experience (PWE; Jones et al., 2009) being our preferred term – has been based around an emphasis on process-driven rather than product-driven education (O'Neil, 2015), and what

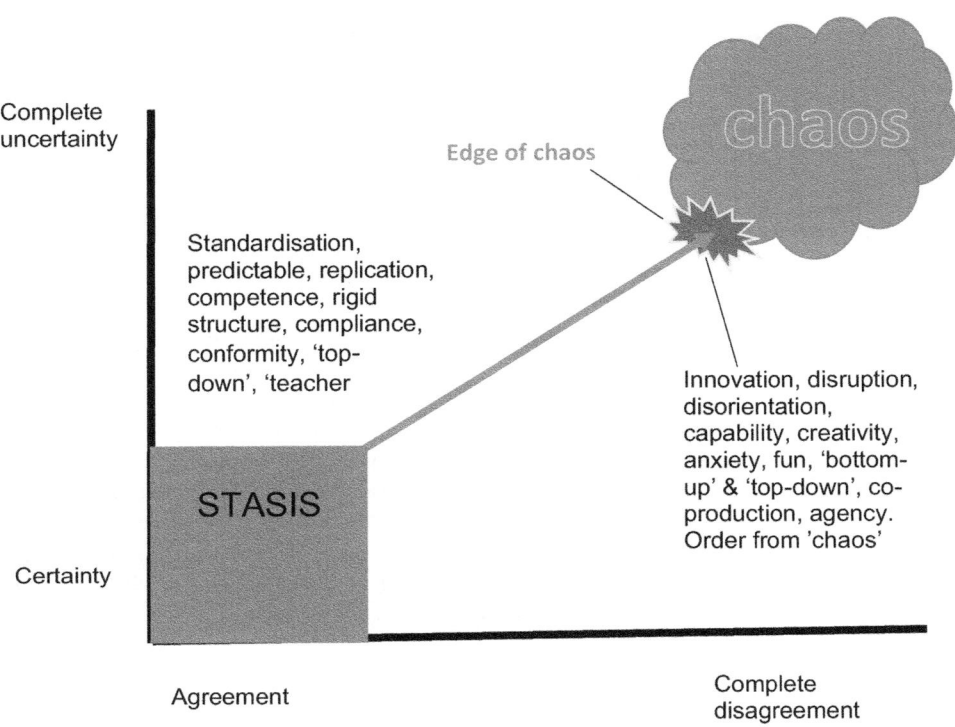

Figure 34.1   Education on the edge of chaos
Source: Adapted from Kleiman, 2011

Kleiman (2011) terms education 'at the edge of chaos' (Figure 34.1). In meeting the educational needs to shape proficient contemporary healthcare professionals, we would argue the necessity for disequilibrium through constant change where creativity is potent, driven by a process of open dialogue (Bohm, 2004). This has been a feature of our approach in pursuing a coherent whole in curriculum design and learning.

The title of this chapter is adapted from a Zen Buddhist koan – *Two hands clap and there is a sound. What is the sound of one hand?* The definition of the term 'koan' is 'a paradoxical anecdote or riddle without a solution to demonstrate the inadequacy of logical reasoning' (Oxford Dictionaries, 2018). Within the context of our work, the term is used as a metaphor to highlight the inadequacy of linear, 'top-down', product-driven education (one hand clapping). Our stance seeks to embrace education at the edge of chaos (Kleiman, 2011), as an interdependent process for which participation (Stephens, 2015; Stephens et al., 2011) is essential. With reference to 'patient' involvement in education, Tew et al. (2004) described five levels of involvement with curriculum design. At Level 1, the curriculum is planned, delivered, and managed with no consultation or involvement of service users, while Level 5 sees all pertinent parties involved, working together in a systematic, interdependent manner underpinned by clear values – moving away from the sound of one hand clapping.

The following section provides an outline description and explanation to four examples of our approach. This will be followed by a deconstruction of our process, framed within a participatory learning model (Stephens, 2015; Jones et al., 2009).

Examples of our practice: description and explanation

The drive by government policies over the past decade or so to involve patients, service users, carers, and the public (cf. People With Experience) in service development and education has been largely targeted at the provision of individualised care (Gov UK, 2013; Gov UK, 2012). The values underpinning our approach within the pre-registration physiotherapy programmes at Northumbria University include those of open dialogue (Bohm, 2004) and participation (Stephens et al., 2011, p. 678) – 'the willingness to be involved with confidence and without fear of not being accepted. Being aware of both professional and social role within the context'.

Our understanding and application of the term *dialogue* is as derived from the Greek *dia* (through) and *logos* (the word), as a free-flow of meaning between people in communication (Bohm, 2000). This is not merely in terms of the spoken word but open exchange of ideas through symbols, gesture, sound, and so forth (Blumer, 1969) in an attempt to promote movement towards shared meaning that reflects contemporary life and healthcare as continuously changing. A common feature of our approach is the creation of disequilibrium through the use of 'creative' approaches to co-produced workshops in the facilitation of dialogue and learning. Four examples from our programmes will be briefly described and explained below, with key emergent themes framed within a participatory learning model (Stephens, 2015; Jones et al., 2009) discussed in the final section of the chapter.

Example 1: Prose and poetry

Within a Year 1 module providing students with an introduction to neurology, there is a danger of an over-emphasis on a biomedical approach, and thereby loss of focus on the 'person' due to having to cover foundation-level anatomy and pathology. To maintain the focus on the individual, a bank of poems, prose, and pictures created by a woman who lived with Parkinson's is used to provide a personal context for students' developing knowledge and skills. The creative material describes the experience of living with Parkinson's, highlighting the difficulties, coping strategies, impact on relationships, and so forth (Powell et al., 2013; Jones et al., 2011). The students draw on the material and interpret through mapping this personal narrative against the framework of the International Classification of Functioning (WHO, 2001) to inform open dialogue of the group's understanding of Parkinson's – linking the applied anatomy and physiology, and pathophysiology to interpretation of the creative writing material.

Students are uncertain but curious about the work and the process of learning at first, initially at least, as it is a very different approach to engaging with learning from their previous experience. The session evaluates very positively, with many students and graduates citing the workshop as one of the sessions that really 'sticks'.

Example 2: Working with actors

The Lawnmowers are an independent theatre company run by and for people with learning difficulties. Within Year 2 of our undergraduate programmes, a series of interprofessional workshops are held as part of a Creative Health Awareness Training (CHAT) project (Lawnmowers, 2018). Students interact with the actors via a scripted scene and discussion to raise awareness of 'best practice' in healthcare. Students also have the opportunity to take part in a freeform case scenario, where two students will work with an actor to undertake a simulated clinical assessment for a given injury or health problem.

Thus, students have a valuable opportunity to 'practice' in a safe but authentic scenario, considering their communication skills and reflecting on how certain scenarios may be perceived by people with learning difficulties. The workshop is concluded with an open dialogue session involving all participants, with constructive feedback for future development provided from the actors and workshop facilitators. The students evaluate their level of confidence in working with people with learning difficulties at the beginning and end of the workshop, which has always resulted in a positive impact for learning and development.

Example 3: What is life? Physiotherapy perspectives of health and healthy living

Two workshops within a final year module based on physiotherapy for 'early life and later life' enable students to create space to reflect on their role working with families and also with people living with a mental health diagnosis. The first workshop involves a young adult and his parents discussing their experience of him growing up with cerebral palsy, reflecting on what has made experiences within healthcare (specifically physiotherapy) positive or negative. Using the life course narrative from the perspective of different members of the family helps the students to appreciate the complexity of working with young people within a family context.

The second workshop involves open dialogue with four people living with mental health diagnosis. The broader context for dialogue is that of related mental health policy, and concepts of mental and physical health, which highlights the relevance of the relationship between mental and physical health for physiotherapy practice and how, why, and when we should approach this with people. An outcome of the session is co-production of 'good practice pointers' between students, service users, and academics.

Example 4: Baddiel and Skinner Unplanned

This workshop has been used to facilitate open dialogue between PWE, students, and an academic facilitator, based on the popular television programme *Baddiel and Skinner Unplanned* (Wikipedia, 2018). The format and content of the session is designed and delivered by the invited PWE and a member of academic staff, and is based on individual experience of physiotherapy with a focus on decision-making.

Freeform discussion is usually based around two themes, the first relating to PWE life with an introduction to their health 'problem'. Students then lead discussion on what they feel the main issues relating to physiotherapy intervention may be. Two volunteer 'secretaries' from the student group record what they perceive to be key points as notes, diagrams, or sketches on flipchart paper or whiteboard. The PWE is invited to bring along an artefact that represents part of their life to further facilitate discussion. Examples of artefacts have been photographs of family members, a photograph of the PWE's Harley Davidson motorcycle, exercise equipment, a young baby, and self-penned creative writing or poetry. Ali Finlayson, who has Parkinson's, has contributed to a number of the workshops through his creative writing, as well as contributing to this chapter.

The second phase then focuses on dialogue of the actual experience of the PWE and results in a powerful learning experience for all involved (Stephens, 2015). One of Ali's shorter compositions, 'The Deal' (Box 1), based on the experience of living with Parkinson's and the role that a healthcare professional or any individual can offer as a person, is a powerful piece of writing that has stimulated a great deal of valuable learning. The raw emotion of the piece facilitates a safe environment for disruption and disequilibrium to promote learning that is enhanced by the process of participation and the provision of space for reflection and open dialogue.

Box 1   The Deal by Ali Finlayson

Give me the scolding fury of your tears
Let it soak into my listening shoulder.
Give me the waiting 'horror' of your alone-ness
Let its ambush vanish with the arrival of my understanding.
Give me the mad conversation of your stuttering footsteps
Let me sooth their stammering with the balm of my words.
Give me the moment of your falling
Let my arms catch you before the hard slap of the welcoming ground.
Give me the rigid prison of your locked limbs
Let its doors be flung wide by the medicine of my wishes.
May you dance through those doors.
All I ask in return is some of your courage.
And the sound of the sun
On your dancing floors

A framework of knowledge, skills, values, and behaviours for physiotherapists has been articulated by the Chartered Society of Physiotherapy (CSP, 2013), the professional body for physiotherapy in the UK. Within the examples provided, reflective of our general position regarding professional education, is a view of knowledge as part of the total flux of process in learning that seeks to provide a more orderly, individualised approach to physiotherapy and healthcare rather than static, fragmentary products. The recognition of knowledge (thinking, and therefore skills, values, and behaviours) as a process that is for people by people and therefore interdependent, necessitates the promotion of co-production in seeking to guard against falling into the trap of treating learning content tacitly as a final and essentially static reality, independent of thought. Common themes across the examples provided thus include participation, the value of space for reflection, and open dialogue in an attempt to create a co-produced, coherent whole in learning that is driven by process rather than product. The final section of the chapter provides a theoretical exploration of our work and some recommendations for practice – 'top tips' for those wishing to engage in a similar approach.

Authenticity, creativity, and order . . . and having fun!

The term 'curriculum' holds a wide variation of definition beyond broad statements relating to a careful, systemic use of a well-defined set of ideas (Fraser and Bosanquet, 2006). Pertinent to healthcare professional education, Fotheringham et al. (2012) expand on this position in the identification of a discipline-focused approach that is dominated by professional regulatory requirements and employability (i.e. a product). This, when the nature of contemporary society is characterised by rapid change, would suggest a need to provide a more holistic approach to education that relates not just to what is taught but also the experiences of PWE, students, clinicians, and academics, supported by the appropriate pedagogical approaches, i.e. an emphasis on process-driven curricula and co-production.

The dangers of a fragmented approach to education, raised at the introduction to this chapter, can often be exacerbated by scientific research, in taking the content of our thought 'as is', i.e. an objectively true description of the world (Bohm, 2007; Bohm and Peat, 2000). As human thought tends to discriminate and classify (through distinction and difference), there is a tendency to look at these as real divisions and the world as broken into fragments rather than a coherent whole. A motivation towards co-production is therefore to pursue a process of learning that recognises a coherent whole that is constantly changing, and that within this chaos/complexity (Kleiman, 2011) order (learning) will emerge.

The following discussion is framed within the participatory learning model (Stephens, 2015; Jones et al., 2009). Clearly articulating the underpinning concepts and theories of our work is useful in providing valuable insight of our approach for those wishing to adopt a similar approach. The participatory learning model (Figure 34.2) originated from an adaptation of participatory research methodology (Reason and Rowan, 1981) developed to support the series of workshops delivered across Years 1 to 3 of undergraduate physiotherapy education and also within a master's pre-registration programme. An appreciation of the underpinning concepts of the model, which include appreciative inquiry (Hammond, 1998) and communicative ethics (Scambler, 2001), will help to provide added perspective to a methodology of symbolic interactionism (Blumer, 1969) and key themes of space for reflection, and open dialogue that informs our approach. At this point, it is well worth highlighting a key principle for success in the development and delivery of co-produced learning, that of 'letting go' and encouraging creative, authentic activity that is fun and meaningful. In accepting what is perhaps a different

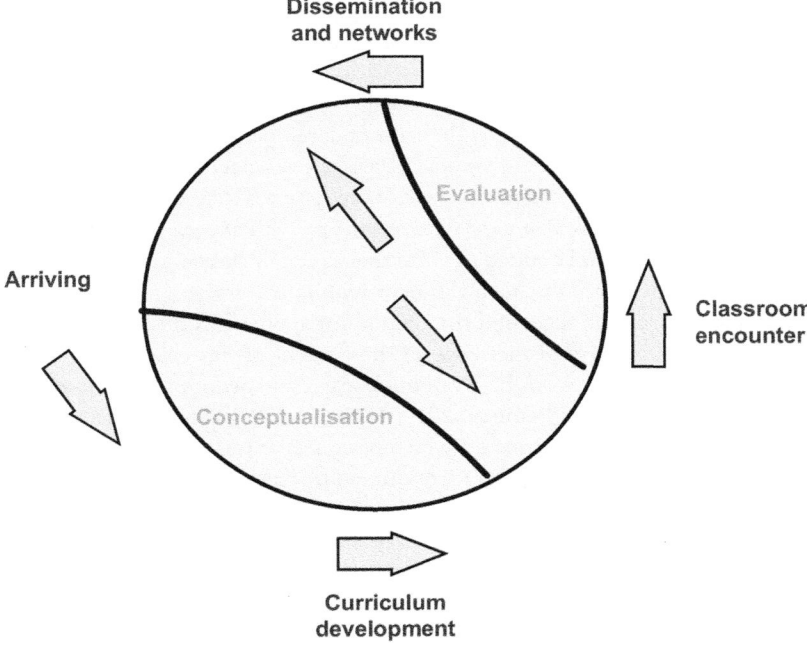

Figure 34.2   The participatory learning model

Source: Adapted from Stephens, 2015; Jones et al., 2009

kind of power-knowledge (Foucault, 2005), and in keeping with the inclusion of an adapted Zen koan as a metaphor to illustrate our approach, the following quote will prove informative and also, hopefully, entertaining:

> Even though you try to put people under control, it is impossible. You cannot do it. The best way to control people is to encourage them to be mischievous. Then they will be in control in a wider sense. To give your sheep or cow a large spacious meadow is the way to control him. So it is with people: first let them do what they want, and watch them. This is the best policy. To ignore them is not good. That is the worst policy. The second worst is trying to control them. The best one is to watch them, just to watch them, without trying to control them.
>
> *(Shunryu Suzuki, 2011, p. 15)*

Our personal motivations for authentic co-production, in an attempt to address the socially constructed reality of individualised physiotherapy practice in education, has resulted in 'arriving' at a participatory approach, as articulated at Figure 34.2. The creation and development of networks and partnerships have been critical across all four of the examples provided earlier in moving away from a unilateral, product-driven approach to curriculum design – to move away from the sound of one hand clapping. This involves contact with PWE, often established through networks with clinical colleagues.

An inward movement to 'Conceptualisation' is in sharing and agreeing core values related to open dialogue based on suspension of personal bias or discrimination (Bohm, 2004). This embraces 'communicative ethics' (Scambler, 2001), whereby participants are free to articulate opinions (or not) and have their views listened to and respected. Open dialogue accepts the importance of individuals' experience of the world and the opportunities presented of offering a different or new view in learning. The broad focus of the workshops is to focus on 'when things go well' – appreciative inquiry (Hammond, 1998) – and solution-oriented dialogue. This being the case, any individual, whether at the stage of developing or delivering material, has full 'permission' to participate in expression of values, wishes, and needs; introduce a topic into the discourse or question any area; or remain silent at any point if they wish. At this point, it is a pertinent reminder to recognise that everyone is someone with experience of healthcare and so quite legitimately are PWE and entitled to voice their opinion and contribute to production of curriculum content whether at the design stage or within delivery.

An important factor in the successful running of our approach is that of time and therefore space to reflect. Although beyond the scope of the content of this chapter, it is important to appreciate the relationship that exists between time, space, and being and therefore the relationship with learning and identity (Bauman, 2010; Katagiri, 2007). Each of the provided examples captures a focused area of practice on which to concentrate, but an area of practice that is always based on a whole. For example, in working with actors, the conversations are based on the preceding acted scenes, and within the *Baddiel and Skinner Unplanned* workshops, conversation is based on the broad background of the PWE and students' perceptions of what they may experience and expect to happen if they were in that position. The attraction of co-produced development and delivery is in the focus on the 'whole' to produce action based on the 'whole', rather than a one hand clapping, taught ('teacher knows best') approach often reflective of product/competency-driven approaches to education (Figure 34.3).

The process of open dialogue and learning, based on the 'whole' illustrated in Figure 34.3, underpins 'curriculum development' (design of workshops) and 'classroom encounter' (delivery). At the development stage, discussion is based around identification of an agreed focus for

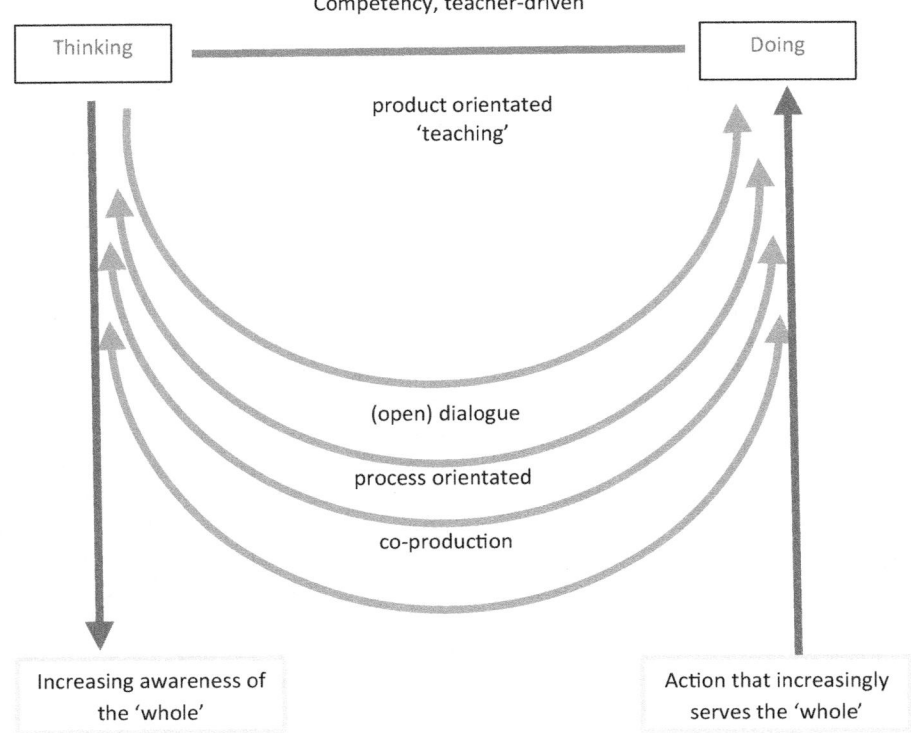

Competency, teacher-driven

Thinking

Doing

product orientated
'teaching'

(open) dialogue

process orientated

co-production

Increasing awareness of
the 'whole'

Action that increasingly
serves the 'whole'

Figure 34.3 Co-production; the 'whole' picture

Source: Adapted from Stephens and Rickard 2016; Senge et al., 2010

workshops, for example, providing insight of the relevance of applied anatomy and physiology to the lived experience of Parkinson's (Example 1), or people's lives in the context of their families (Examples 3, 4), or communication in healthcare (Example 2). Pragmatic environmental and economic factors also require consideration, such as appropriate room booking for workshop delivery, travel and access to buildings, and expenses/payment, and address any possible impact this may have for anyone in receipt of benefit payments. Workshops are generally delivered across two to three hours to provide opportunity for adequate breaks for participants, and also to ensure adequate space for reflection.

The 'classroom encounter', the delivery of the agreed session in each case, does require responsibility to be taken by the staff facilitator in the running of a successful collaborative learning opportunity. However, this role may not necessarily be filled by an academic member of staff, for instance Example 2, working with actors, where the acting group facilitator takes a lead role, and on occasion within Example 4, *Baddiel and Skinner Unplanned*, where the PWE and academic facilitator may run the workshop as a team. Co-production involving students, and therefore involving all participants, can also be integrated into workshops, for example at *Baddiel and Skinner Unplanned*, students are provided with an opportunity (and time) to write their own individual outcomes for the workshop once the background to the workshop has been introduced. As part of the introduction to all workshops, it is appropriate to discuss any ground rules based on the concepts articulated earlier within

'Conceptualisation', in essence, reassurance of the processes of communicative ethics, appreciative inquiry, and 'participation'.

Within the premise of communicative ethics, it is important to explain the process of open dialogue (Bohm, 2004) in terms of participants taking time to suspend any personal beliefs in accepting any expressed opinions at face value and as a basis for further dialogue. This is consistent with our view of knowledge and learning expressed earlier. A useful way of understanding this further is through the methodology of symbolic interactionism (Blumer, 1969), which is worthy of consideration as a broader 'methodological' framework to encompass co-production activity.

Symbolic interactionism is a methodological framework derived primarily from the work of Mead and articulated by Herbert Blumer, a student of Mead's. The underlying principle of symbolic interactionism is that of individual selves as social products that are purposive and creative. Symbolic interactionism presents an illustration of life in action through social interaction (Blumer, 1969). The common process across co-production, as illustrated through the examples drawn from our practice, can be based on the premises of symbolic interactionism: a) humans act towards 'things' based on the meanings 'things' have for them, b) meanings arise from social interaction, and c) meanings are handled and modified through an interpretive process by the person(s) interacting with 'things'. In the case of our approach, the symbols are largely the spoken word (open dialogue), but are also based on gesture, posture, and the written word in establishing a shared understanding of 'things'. Learning is thus shaped through a dynamic process of individuals' social definitions. People respond not merely to a physical reality but also to the social understanding of reality based on interdependence rather than through hierarchy and surveillance (Foucault, 2005). A useful analogy of learning and co-production is expressed through Bauman's (Bauman, 2010) metaphor of a jigsaw in relation to human identity. In building a jigsaw, one starts from a position of the final image being known beforehand, with all pieces being present i.e. learning and identity as a 'set' product. Within co-produced learning, each participant starts from a number of pieces that seem worthy of having. Through a process of open dialogue, pieces are ordered, added to, re-ordered to get some pleasing pictures – or perhaps within the metaphor of moving away from one hand clapping – some pleasing sounds, i.e. meaningful learning.

As happens at the end of the workshop examples, it is important to obtain feedback from all participants as part of the inward movement to 'Evaluation'. This may be written feedback via a pre-prepared form, but should also include feedback within open dialogue and a broader understanding of feedback as something more than discriminatory like, dislike, or indifference. Within dialogue, there are opportunities to capture feedback from a social perspective (*is everyone okay?*, thanking each other for contributions and so forth) and a developmental perspective (what will individuals do next, how could future workshops be developed and so forth) as well as discriminatory (did it generally go well, not well, not bothered!).

Finally, 'Dissemination and Networks' is an outward movement to provide feedback into a wider circle that includes publication through local discussion, conference outputs, written articles, and continuing to a new point of 'arrival'.

Conclusions

The frameworks offered by the participatory learning model, open dialogue, and symbolic interactionism hold real potential to develop and deliver co-produced learning opportunities that are based on process rather than product. The opportunities offered by this approach to curriculum development can be established through an authentic attempt to create order from an understanding of complexities in the pursuit of contemporary person-centred physiotherapy/healthcare: in the realisation of 'education on the edge of chaos'.

There is a focus on the 'whole' rather than 'fragments', which has the potential to impact on learning and development for all participants in understanding the importance of relationships, the value (and limitations) of physiotherapy/healthcare, and the interdependent nature of individuals, groups, and organisations. We would argue that the design and delivery of education that is relevant not just to contemporary society but also to the future requires a movement towards educational disequilibrium. This position is supported by an appreciation of successful education being for people by people, context relevant, authentic (evidenced-based and creative), and morally sound. Collaboration in accessing and identifying partners, developing materials/learning sessions, activities, evaluation, and dissemination is key to success and (predictably) iterative in nature. Open dialogue, the ability to suspend personal prejudicial thought, and participation require more than a degree of honesty and bravery, the main message here being one of patience and effort. A little resilience and 'graft' may be required – but is well worth it.

References

Bauman Z. (2010) *Identity*. Chichester: Wiley.

Bevan H. (2017) Leading Change into the Future HEA Annual Conference. University of Manchester, July 4, 2017.

Blumer H. (1969) *Symbolic Interactionism. Perspective and Method*. Los Angeles: University of California Press.

Bohm D. (2004) *On Dialogue*. London: Routledge.

Bohm D. (2007) *Wholeness and the Implicate Order*. London: Routledge.

Bohm D., and Peat D. (2000) *Science, Order, and Creativity*. London: Routledge.

Chartered Society of Physiotherapy (CSP) (2013) CSP Physiotherapy Framework. Available at https://v3.pebblepad.co.uk/v3portfolio/csp/Asset/View/6jqbh3GzhGWrrcGqpknwmZzh8Z

Council of Deans (2017) *Apprenticeships in Nursing and the Allied Health Professions*. London: Council of Deans. Available at https://councilofdeans.org.uk/wp-content/uploads/2017/07/071117-Apprenticeships-paper-version-7.pdf

Department of Health (DH) (2006) *Our Health, Our Care, Our Say: A New Direction for Community Services*. Available at www.dh.gov.uk/en/Publicationsandstatistics/Publications/PublicationsPolicyAndGuidance/DH_4127602 accessed 04.03.2015.

Department of Health (DH) (2008) *Real Involvement: Working with People to Improve Health Services*. Available at www.dh.gov.uk/en/Publicationsandstatistics/Publications/PublicationsPolicyAndGuidance/DH_089787 accessed 04.03.2015.

Department of Health (DH) (2012) *The Health and Social Care Act*. Available at www.dh.gov.uk/health/2012/06/act-explained/

Department of Health (DH) (2016) *Reforming Healthcare Education Funding: Creating a Sustainable Workforce*. Government Response to Public Consultation. Available at https://assets.publishing.service.gov.uk/government/uploads/system/uploads/attachment_data/file/539774/health-education-funding-response.pdf

Eisner E. (1985) *The Educational Imagination*. New York: Macmillan.

Fotheringham J., Strickland K., & Aitchison K. (2012) *Curriculum: Directions, Decisions and Debate*. Glasgow: QAA. Available at www.enhancementthemes.ac.uk/docs/publications/curriculum-directions-decisions-and-debate.pdf

Foucault M. (2005) *The Order of Things*. Abingdon: Routledge Classics.

Fraser S.P., & Bosanquet A.M. (2006) The curriculum? That's just a unit outline isn't it? *Studies in Higher Education*, 31(3), 269–284.

Gov. UK (2012) *The Health and Social Care Act*. Available at www.gov.uk/government/publications/health-and-social-care-act-2012-fact-sheets

Gov. UK (2013) *Report of the Mid Staffordshire NHS Foundation Trust Public Inquiry*. Available at www.gov.uk/government/publications/report-of-the-mid-staffordshire-nhs-foundation-trust-public-inquiry

Hammond S.A. (1998) *The Thin Book of Appreciative Inquiry*. Bend: Thin Book Publishing Co.

Jones D., Stephens J., Innes W., Rashburn A., & Stack E. (2009) Service user and carer involvement in physiotherapy practice, education and research: getting involved for a change. *NZ Journal of Physiotherapy*, 37(1), 29–35.

Jones D., Taylor T., Powell S., Scott J., & Scott L. (2011) Parkinson's Disease in Prose and Pictures: Neurological Narratives in Physiotherapy Education. Prize Winning Poster – Outstanding Abstract and Presentation Award in the Special Interest Poster Display Category, World Physical Therapy, 16th International WCPT Congress, June 2011, Amsterdam, Holland.

Katagiri D. (2000) *You have to say something: Manifesting Zen Insight.* Boston: Shambhala Books.

Katagiri D. (2007) *Each Moment is the Universe.* Boston: Shambhala Books.

Kleiman P. (2011) Learning at the edge of Chaos. *All Ireland Journal of Teaching and Learning in Higher Education (AISHE-J)*, 3(2), 62.1–62.11.

Lawnmowers (2018) *Creative Health Awareness Training.* Available at www.thelawnmowers.co.uk/content/creative-health-awareness-training-0

Mead, G.H (1934:2015) *Mind, Self and Society.* Chicago: University of Chicago Press.

NHS England (2014) *The Five Year Forward View.* Available at www.england.nhs.uk/wp-content/uploads/2014/10/5yfv-web.pdf

NHS England (2017) *Next Steps on the Five Year Forward View.* Available at www.england.nhs.uk/wp-content/uploads/2017/03/NEXT-STEPS-ON-THE-NHS-FIVE-YEAR-FORWARD-VIEW.pdf

O'Neil G. (2015) *Curriculum Design in Higher Education: Theory to Practice.* E-book. Available at www.ucd.ie/t4cms/UCDTLP0068.pdf

Osberg D., & Biesta G. (2008) The emergent curriculum: Navigating a complex course between unguided learning and planned enculturation. *Journal of Curriculum Studies*, 40(3), 313–328.

Oxford Dictionaries (2018) *Koan.* Available at https://en.oxforddictionaries.com/definition/koan

Powell S., Scott J., Jones D., & Scott L. (2013) An online narrative archive of service user experiences to support the education of undergraduate physiotherapy and social work students in North East England: An evaluation study. *Education for Health*, 26(1), 25–31.

Reason P., & Rowan J. (1981) *Human Inquiry. A Sourcebook of New Paradigm Research.* Chichester: Wiley.

Scambler G. (2001) *Habermas, Critical Theory and Health.* London: Routledge.

Senge P.M., Scharmer C.O., Jaworski J., & Flowers B.S. (2010) *Presence: Exploring Profound Change in People, Organizations and Society.* London: Nicholas Brealey Publishing.

Stephens J. (2015) A participatory learning model and person-centred healthcare: Moving away from 'one hand clapping'. *European Journal for Person Centred Healthcare*, 3(3), 279–287.

Stephens J., Abbott-Brailey H., & Platt A. (2011) Appearing the team; from practice to simulation. *The International Journal of Therapy and Rehabilitation*, 18(12), 672–682.

Stephens J., & Rickard N. (2016) 'We rather than me'. Involvement and its measurement in pulmonary rehabilitation. Poster presentation, *4th European Congress of the European Region of the World Confederation of Physical Therapy.* Liverpool, UK, 11–12 November 2016.

Suzuki S. (2011) *Zen Mind, Beginner's Mind.* Boulder: Shambhala.

Tew J., Gell C., & Foster S. (2004) *Learning from Experience. Involving Service Users from and Carers in Mental Health Education and Training.* Nottingham: Higher Education Academy/National Institute for Mental Health in England/Trent Workforce Development Confederation.

Trede F. (2012) Role of work-integrated learning in developing professionalism and professional identity. *Asia-Pacific Journal of Cooperative Education*, 13(3), 159–167.

UK Government (2016) *The Case for Health Education Funding Reform.* Available at www.gov.uk/government/consultations/changing-how-healthcare-education-is-funded/the-case-for-health-education-funding-reform

WHO (2001) *International Classification of Functioning, Disability and Health.* Available at www.who.int/classifications/icf/en/

Wikipedia (2018) *Baddiel and Skinner Unplanned.* Available at https://en.wikipedia.org/wiki/Baddiel_and_Skinner_Unplanned

35

SOCIAL PEDAGOGY, COLLABORATIVE LEARNING AND OUTCOMES IN SERVICE USER AND CARER INVOLVEMENT IN SOCIAL WORK EDUCATION

Susan Levy, Claire Ferrier, Elinor Dowson and Jordan Risbridger

Introduction

Social work is a profession that engages with social justice and social change to enhance the life chances of people. The International Federation of Social Workers (IFSW) defines the profession as promoting 'social change and development, social cohesion, and the empowerment and liberation of people' (IFSW, 2014). It is a profession, along with the other caring/people professions, characterised by complexity (Bondi et al., 2011), which is addressed through prioritising the human and ethical dimensions of practice. That is the art of being, and connecting, with people to co-produce authentic relationships (Eichsteller and Holthoff, 2012); and it is the 'art' of social work that can serve as the catalyst for social change (England, 1986; Levy, 2018; Rapoport, 1968). Embedding meaningful service user and carer involvement (SUCI) into social work education can centre student learning on the art of social work, on developing relationship-based practice, grounded in active citizenship for social change.

This chapter extends previous work on service user and carer involvement (SUCI) and an outcomes-based model of SUCI in social work education at the University of Dundee, Scotland (Levy et al., 2016), to offer new thinking on the topic. Social pedagogy's *Head, Heart and Hands* is used to frame discussion of the model to demonstrate how collaborative learning between service users, carers and social work students is preparing students for future person-centred and relationship-based practice (Cabiati, 2017). The chapter has uniquely been co-authored by a social work lecturer, MSc Social Work student, recent graduate/newly qualified social work practitioner and a carer, and is in three main sections. First, the literature on SUCI in social work education provides a context for the chapter, with a focus on SUCI leading to social change framed by social pedagogy. Second, the *Caring within Integrated Services* module (*Caring* module) is introduced. This is a core module on the MSc Social Work, a qualifying social work programme at the University of Dundee. The module integrates SUCI into a collaborative learning/outcomes model. Third, three of the co-authors – Risbridger (MSc student), Dowson (carer) and Ferrier (newly qualified social worker) – offer a reflection on their individual perspectives and experiences of the *Caring* module, using the *Head* (knowledge/learning), *Heart* (relationships/feeling) and *Hands* (practice/doing) of social pedagogy.

Situating user and carer involvement in social work education

Service user and carer involvement (SUCI) within social work education has been mandatory for over 15 years in Scotland (Scottish Executive, 2003) and the rest of the UK (Department of Health, 2002). The detail of the 'What?' and 'How?' of SUCI was left open for interpretation by the individual universities, leading to wide variation in practice. Both within the UK and elsewhere, achieving clarity over a form of meaningful SUCI which is consistent with social work values continues to be elusive and contested. An expanding area of SUCI literature contributing to clarifying this debate is focusing on models of involvement that are framed around social change, empowerment (Askheim et al., 2017; Hatton, 2017; Heule et al., 2017), impact and outcomes (Hughes, 2017; Levy et al., 2016; Tanner et al., 2015). These approaches can be understood through the lens of social pedagogy (Hatton, 2017) and point to the social aspect of education (Hamalainen, 2012).

Empowerment through service user and carer involvement in social work education

The professionalisation of social work poses several challenges for meaningful SUCI; for a profession to exist, it must have its own distinct disciplinary knowledge. This disciplinary, expert knowledge informs and shapes professional practice. Despite indigenous knowledge being integral to the international definition of social work (IFSW, 2014), there are challenges integrating 'other'/indigenous forms of knowledge, local and experiential, into social work education and practice. This bifurcation has led to dualistic outcomes (the privileging of one form of knowledge over the 'other') and is a barrier to collaborative, democratic practice. A hierarchical lens has the power to create stigma and prejudice which social work students, despite their choosing to align themselves with social work, can, and do, hold and share with the wider public (Askheim et al., 2017). The alternative, developing authentic and reciprocal relationships built on valuing different forms of knowledge, involves the unsettling deconstruction of prevailing power relations and appropriation of knowledge. Cabiati and Raineri (2016), in their study of Italian SUCI social work education, note that being involved in the process of critiquing oppressive structures has liberating and emancipating potential.

A hybrid approach to knowledge creation allows for a re-alignment away from hierarchical and unnecessary divisions, to the blending of expert and experiential knowledges, and opens a dialogical space for social work students/social workers and service users/carers to work in collaboration. A *Gap-mending* pedagogy (Askheim et al., 2017; Heule et al., 2017) aims to bridge the 'gaps' that emerge through binary thinking and practice, the gaps that can engender prejudice and stigma. The *Gap-mending* pedagogy emerged out of work at the University of Lund, Sweden, and the development of the *Mobilisation* module (Askheim et al., 2017; Heule et al., 2017). The module involves service users/carers and social work students studying and working together on a group project and aims to advance democracy and citizenship through challenging embedded prejudices within social work practice. Conceptually, *Gap-mending* is premised on acknowledging and valuing intersectionality and multi-layered identities. Each and every one of us is a complex human individual, with strengths and weaknesses, none of which are fixed and unchanging; labels, identities and boundaries are all fluid. Social work practitioners, students and service users/carers can all hold expert social work knowledge alongside experiential knowledge gleaned from being carers and/or service users as well as experience of oppression (Beresford and Croft, 2004). As a pedagogy, *Gap-mending* is framing SUCI in social work education in European countries (Driessens et al., 2016; Grodofsky and Gutman, 2017).

> As different parties engage in a common cause, new important social bonds develop, and can contribute to fewer gaps and an increased sense of mutual recognition.
>
> *(Heule et al., 2017, p. 398)*

Social work moves beyond narrow definitions and judgements of service users/carers and is responsive to the rich diversity of individual lives. Valuing differences and other knowledges is at the core of relationship-based practice and a 'caring' profession based on trust, 'empathic understanding' (Bondi, 2008), active listening and acknowledgement of the inter-dependency of relationships. This requires a commitment to demonstrate care through action, through an ethical conscience that is not undermined by task-oriented dependency. Such an approach supports an ethics of care perspective, that as humans we are inherently relational, responsive beings and the human condition is one of connectedness or inter-dependence (Gilligan, 1982). An ethics of care serves as a useful starting point for developing SUCI in social work education, particularly Tronto's (1993) five elements for effective caring relationships:

1   Attentiveness: recognising the needs of others.
2   Responsibility: doing the 'right thing'.
3   Competence: meeting the needs of others.
4   Responsiveness: ensuring the needs of others have been met.
5   Integrity: all of the above combined.

Gap-mending and an ethics of care have informed recent enhancements to the *Caring* module at the University of Dundee, as has a social pedagogical approach.

Social pedagogy and service user involvement in social work education

The *Gap-mending* pedagogy aligns with approaches that advocate for the role of education in achieving social change. This includes Freire's work on 'conscientisation' and education as a conduit to enable people to become 'more fully human in the world in which they exist' (Freire, 1972, p. 94); and on social pedagogy, seeking educational solutions to social problems (Hamalainen, 2003; Smith and Whyte, 2008). It is a social pedagogy approach that is explored here and the role of collaborative learning to realise

> people's *political imagination* so that they can envision an alternative experience, a different way of experiencing and delivering welfare and social work services . . . [and] changing the way issues are framed so that service users are not seen as 'problems' . . . but as active partners.
>
> *(Hatton, 2017, p. 160, italics in the original)*

Forming meaningful and trusting relationships, improving social inclusion and contributing to active citizenship are all central to social pedagogy and are achieved through transformative and collaborative learning (Hamalainen, 2012). This is a process that requires time. Social pedagogy, Eichsteller and Holtoff (2012, p. 33) argue, is all about '*being* . . . about being with others and forming relationships . . . about being there in a supportive, empowering manner'. 'It is the "art" of working with and being with service users and carers, engaging as equals, learning with and from each other' (Levy and Young, 2020, pp. 68–79).

The three key tenets of social pedagogy are *Haltung, Common Third* and using the *Head, Heart and Hands. Haltung* has German roots and refers to mindset, to empathy and the personal values professionals bring to their practice. The *Common Third* is a Danish concept and refers to the practice of joint, collaborative working to achieve outcomes, in particular the use of creative methods and finding a joint purpose through working on a joint project. The collaborative learning that is integral to and embedded in the *Caring* module at the University of Dundee is an example of the *Common Third* in practice. The use of the *Head, Heart and Hands* stems from the work of Pestalozzi, a Swiss pedagogue writing in the late 18th/early 19th century with a focus on social justice and education (see Brühlmeier, 2010, for an overview of Pestalozzi's work in English). The *Head* (learning/knowledge), *Heart* (relationships/feeling) and *Hands* (doing/practice) can be contextualised within SUCI in social work education as:

Head: service users/carers and social work students learning and developing as equals;
Heart: service users/carers and social work students developing meaningful relationships based on trust and understanding;
Hands: service users/carers and social work students developing creative approaches to enhance social inclusion and active citizenship.

The use of the *Head, Heart and Hands* are of equal importance in professional relationships (Ruch et al., 2017) and require practitioners to have a strong sense of self, self-awareness and self-reflection.

Caring within Integrated Services *module, University of Dundee*

The Framework for Social Work Education in Scotland (Scottish Executive, 2003) led to the mandatory requirement to include SUCI in all social work qualifying programmes in Scotland. This was the driver for the development of a Carer and Users (CU) group in the School of Education and Social Work at the University of Dundee. Over the past 15 years, the CU group has been actively involved in the social work undergraduate and postgraduate qualifying programmes, in particular, the *Caring within Integrated Services* module (*Caring* module), a core module on the MSc Social Work. The *Caring* module (originally entitled: *Making Sense of the Caring Experience*) was introduced in 2008. The module offered students experiential learning through spending up to 24 hours over a period of weeks with a carer, in the carer's home. The experience enabled students to develop meaningful and trusting relationships in a safe space, to observe and to learn from their carer (Gee et al., 2009). Over the last decade, the module has evolved, leading to some key changes: students spending time with a carer and/or service user, and the original 24 hours was changed to a minimum of 15 hours (Levy et al., 2016). Students and service users/carers now meet as a group instead of one-to-one, and meetings take place on the university campus instead of at the service users/carers' home. Each evolving iteration of the module has retained and strengthened its essence; of social work students learning from and with service users/carers, of valuing different knowledges, and developing meaningful relationships as core to effective and affective person-centred practice. The module requires everyone involved to bring honesty and a sense of 'self' to the relationship as the basis for collaborative learning. Each new enhancement of the module has emerged through feedback from students and CU group members and is evidence of meaningful partnership working between the module leader and the CU group. The *Caring* module can usefully be understood through the *Head, Heart and Hands* lens of social pedagogy (Table 35.1).

The introduction of groupwork into the *Caring* module has shifted the focus from service users sharing their experiences with students, to students and service users/carers drawing on the range of the group's experiences to collectively work to address an identified challenge through a group project, culminating in a joint presentation. The module articulates the interdependency between students and service users/carers to co-produce an outcome (group presentation). All group members contribute to identifying the social care challenge to be addressed in their presentation, as well being integral to the development and delivery of the presentation. Through involvement in the module, service users/carers understand that they can be part of the change they want to see in their lives. Bringing service users/carers into the university to work collaboratively on a group project has brought to the fore the *Caring* module's contribution and scope for the empowerment of group members. Feedback from service users/carers involved in the *Caring* module point to the experience being empowering and that these outcomes have emerged through the development of meaningful relationships between service users/carers and social work students.

Service User and Carer feedback on their involvement in the *Caring within Integrated Services* module (2018)

'Made me feel good because the group didn't see my disability, they saw me as a person'.

'They worked well with me, very collaboratively, very pleased to have been included with them'.

'The strengths of this group were their collaborative approach, we (service users) were always a central and important part of this piece of work'.

'Made me feel proud'.

Table 35.1 Social pedagogy framing the *Caring within Integrated Services* module

	Head	Heart	Hands
Concept	Service users/carers and social work students learning and developing as equals.	Service users/carers and social work students developing meaningful relationships based on trust and understanding.	Service users/carers and social work students developing creative approaches to enhance social inclusion and active citizenship.
Caring module	Social work students and members of the Carers and Users group form working groups comprising approximately 8 students and 1–2 service users/carers. Groups meet weekly for 2 hours over 6 weeks.	Group members contribute as equals, each bringing unique knowledge and strengths. Meaningful and trusting relationships emerge from collaborative working and a shared project.	Each group works towards a group presentation. Creative approaches are used for group presentations, ensuring everyone is included and is able to contribute.

Through working democratically, valuing the strengths, knowledge and experience that each brings, group members are surpassing narrowly defined identities associated with being a service user/carer and/or student. These are the elements of the module that can facilitate for social change, and are markers of meaningful involvement (Beresford, 2005).

Robinson and Webber (2013), in their review of the SUCI in social work education literature, observed that impact on practice was an area of weakness. This lacuna is being addressed by the *Caring* module and the development of the Outcomes Focused SUCI model (Levy et al., 2016). The model creates a bridge between SUCI in social work education and social work practice.

> The outcomes-based model of SUCI used . . . is premised on social justice and operates at the intersection where the voices of service users and carers, student learning and social work practice interconnect to develop meaningful, sustainable and outcomes focused SUCI in social work education.
>
> *(Levy et al., 2016, p. 876)*

The Outcomes Focused SUCI model (Levy et al., 2016) has been revised in response to the introduction of groupwork and group presentations into the *Caring* module (Figure 35.1). The initial Stage 2, *Knowledge Creation*, has been renamed *Collaborative Learning* to recognise the process leading to knowledge creation. Stage 3, initially *Applying Knowledge to Practice*, has also been renamed *Empowerment for Social Change*, to provide greater insight into the process behind the development of new knowledge and the impact of collaborative learning. Stage 4, *Knowledge Exchange*, remains unchanged and is supported through the sharing of module learning with practitioners and relevant stakeholders at knowledge exchange events to impact organisational culture and practice (Eichsteller and Holthoff, 2012).

The Collaborative Learning and Outcomes Focused SUCI model provides a practical and sustainable framework for SUCI in social work education. It mirrors good practice that strengthens the ethical orientation of working with service users and carers. The dynamic of

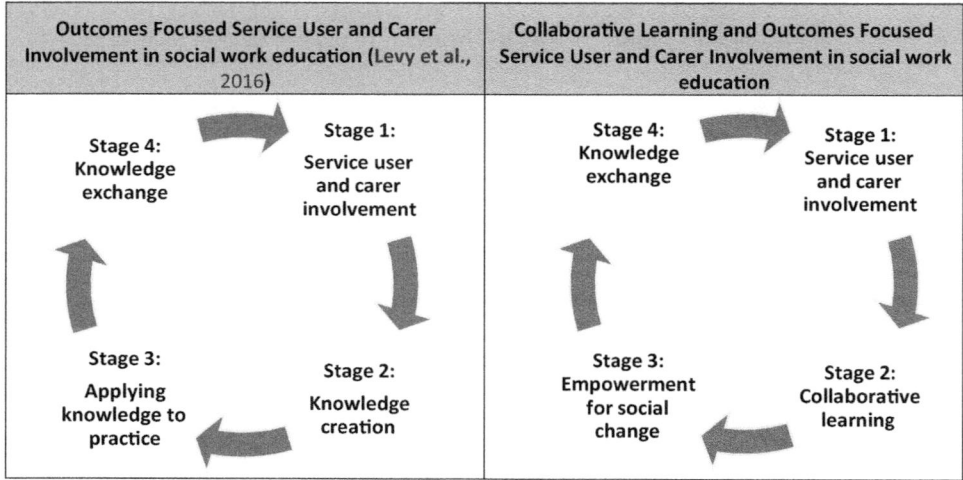

Figure 35.1 Outcomes Focused Service User and Carer Involvement in social work education models (2016 and 2018)

collaborative learning, and the establishment of reciprocal, inter-dependent and caring relationships is not unproblematic, however. It adds a layer of complexity, of precariousness, that may be unsettling for both students and service users/carers. This complexity may be manifest in a sense of 'strangeness', in feelings of vulnerability and uncertainty. 'Strangeness' and complexity are inherent within the spaces of the people professions (Bondi et al., 2011); but we should be nurturing capacities to enable people to flourish amid 'strangeness' (Kreber, 2014). Working with complexity and being open to other knowledges, to (re)aligning moral boundaries, should be welcomed as a necessary skill for future social work practice, rather than an unwelcome nemesis. The *Caring* module is creating opportunities for students to immerse themselves in 'strangeness', in the complexity of people's lives, within a safe and collaborative space, as a conduit for learning, empowerment and social change.

The following section offers three reflections on the *Caring* module: from Risbridger, a current MSc Social Work student on his experience of studying the module (*Head*); from Dowson, a carer who has been involved with the module from its inception, who offers her thoughts on the module and how it has changed over time (*Heart*); and Ferrier, a recent graduate/newly qualified practitioner, reflects on her experience of applying the learning from the *Caring* module to social work practice (*Hands*). Each author has identified a key challenge for the future development of SUCI; the future challenges are introduced in the final section of the chapter.

Meaningful engagement? perspectives from a social work student, newly qualified social worker and carer

Head (knowledge/learning together)

One of the central strengths of the module was the opportunity it afforded students to visualise the boundaries between abstracted theoretical approaches to care and the lived experiential knowledge of service users and carers. Throughout our academic careers, we are encouraged to engage critically with learning materials and adapt and shape our knowledge base accordingly. The *Caring* module promotes student critical consciousness, and effective co-production enables a more open and dynamic alternative to established epistemological hierarchies.

Working alongside service users within a group helped to challenge the preconceptions of the value and efficacy of a professional knowledge base. Weekly meetings with the service users in our group helped to promote a wider understanding of the nuance of the theories, policy and legislation that we were being introduced to. The lived reality of trying to negotiate the planning and organisation of care and the continuing stress about costs was made readily apparent and provoked a need to engage fully with the idea of people's lives being central to interventions. As aspirational and as liberating as the changes in health and social care policy have been in Scotland, we discovered that there are significant systemic problems that are evidenced every day by service users/carers (and their families) who require support from services.

Considering the communication between professionals and people who require services was a fertile area for our group presentation. Following introductions, both service users in my group explained that they identified themselves as 'service specialists'. The adoption of the term helps them to feel empowered in a system that privileges professional knowledge and reduces levels of inclusivity. The 'specialists' shared a number of anecdotes about how they had, at times, felt marginalised within their own care plans due to an unwillingness to simply listen to their concerns. The dependence on highly codified and prescriptive practice had led to feelings of mistrust and ostracisation. Meaningful co-production has at its core a mutual understanding of each person's perspective and the ability to cede ground if you uncover inequality. The knowledge that each service user/carer has of their own need is something that any skilled practitioner should be willing to uncover and engage with. There was a tacit understanding that the success of the groupwork would rely on trusting each other; to respect differing views and work co-operatively when we encountered differing viewpoints.

Subsequently, subjectivity was very often a central theme of our group discussions; and the understanding that the objective focus of care also requires significant room for the voices experiencing this care to be heard. Learning that different methods of support can be experienced in manifestly different ways is a key way of reminding practitioners to think creatively and responsively to the individual needs of those families they work with. With the *Caring* module group project, discussion that included the service specialists offered insights into the direction we were headed or suggestions as to how we might improve a point. The dynamic of the group allowed for the service specialists to be equal arbiters in what was seen to be relevant for the presentation.

Heart (relationships)

Reflecting back, as a family carer, the *Caring* module began as a response to a heartfelt plea from a family carer, that if only students could spend 24 hours 'in her shoes' they would be better able to understand the needs of her 'cared for' person and her own needs. Students initially spent 24 hours as guests of carers (and then carers and services users), who shared their life/ lives. It was a 'safe and intimate' space for students to learn from the carer/service user. Students witnessed first-hand what had helped and what had hindered establishing good communication and building meaningful relationships with social workers on their journey of care, and how they had developed strengths which helped them cope on that journey.

Students learnt that social work performed a dual role in the lives of their carers/service users: as solution providers, but also at times, and often as a result of poor communication, social work could be part of the problem. Students witnessed first-hand how this dual role could build tension and conflict and lead to emotional turmoil. I recall students, on hearing these harrowing stories, would want to share their concerns about how they should act in these circumstances, and to use self-reflection to examine their own emotional response.

I remember how each year students wondered in advance how they would get on in this new and 'strange' experience. Likewise, carers/service users hoped that the student would want to learn and would 'fit' into their household. There were only a few students over the years who failed to treat their hosts with respect and saw them only as a resource. Most students grew in confidence and developed the skills of self-reflection and self-awareness. These were positive outcomes for both students and carers/service users, with the latter perceiving their involvement in the *Caring* module as contributing towards better social work practice.

On reflection, the *Caring* module has evolved alongside broader developments in social work practice around co-production and collaborative working that is (re)placing relationships at the heart of social work practice. The new phase of the *Caring* module, framed by social pedagogy and with a focus on groupwork, sits ideally with the skills practised already in earlier phases of the module. In addition, it builds on them and connects with my involvement with the recovery agenda in Scotland, which shifts practice from 'doing to' to 'doing with' and 'being alongside' service users/carers.

This approach has been encapsulated in the groupwork for the *Caring* module. On the first day I was faced with six students, all looking expectantly at me, and, feeling a little anxious myself as I did not know anyone, I asked them if they would mind sharing something about themselves. Laughter followed and we started to build up a group jigsaw, unknowingly, at first, but each time we met we tried to remember with warmth what had been shared before. Through these small beginnings, we wove a tapestry effortlessly of our strengths, fears, seeming prejudices, differing beliefs and varying cultures. Over the coming weeks, we learnt a lot from each other, why we believed in a certain way of acting or had certain attitudes, and the seeming gulf between us grew less. As these conversations unfolded, it became apparent who had certain strengths or fears regarding the forthcoming presentation, and we offered group support to anyone who wanted to move beyond where they felt comfortable in order to take part.

I felt respected and supported by the group and felt 'safe' in this collaborative space. Through collaborative learning we formed relationships, made friendships and benefitted far beyond our expectations from the original remit of working on a group presentation. For me, and from the reactions of the other group members, this way of forming relationships between service users/carers and students, learning with each other and facing fears in a warm supportive environment, is a worthy and timely next step forward in the life of the *Caring* module.

Hands (practice/doing together)

The *Caring* module is a tangible and symbolic example of what social work practice can be; practice is learning about each other, exploring outcomes through relationships. There are challenges in practice; often the managerial nature of social work can devalue the unquantifiable: the subjective care enabled by the relationships we build with service users/carers. The pressure of practice manifests in issues of absenteeism and retention (Ravavlier, 2018), and the impact on individual workers, teams and the profession itself cannot be underestimated. This reflection of practice does not seek to minimise this reality, but instead to illuminate the opportunities for value-based, social change-orientated practice through the integration of *Head, Heart and Hands*.

In the first year of my MSc, I spoke with a social work writer and practitioner about how he managed to do 'radical' practice in a local authority. He said to me, 'you have to really know your stuff'. He meant that a case for practice that was relationship and citizenship focused could be made, not despite policy, procedure or legislation, but because of it, if one was sufficiently cogent in their assessment and proposal for an intervention or no intervention at all. The interplay and distinction between agency and structure (Bourdieu, 1977) is a useful framework for social work practice. It enables a worker to be realistic about the limitations while maintaining a professional and moral responsibility, or *agency*, to practice social work with passion, creativity and a commitment to professional development, person-centred care and social change. Should we absolve responsibility to neoliberalism, managerialism or austerity, our silence will only strengthen that which limits achieving the aims of social work.

Time is often a scarce resource in practice and the perennial concern of too little time with people and too much desk time persists. Relationships are good in themselves; when people encounter social work, it is as a result of oppression and vulnerability, usually involuntary. Communicating your values with openness, care and preparedness to share some of your world acts in a reciprocal way, to both support and encourage service users/carers and to reinforce and continually reproduce a social work identity which is morally and critically motivated. Thus, relationships are the 'cornerstone' for change (Dewane, 2006). When trust is built and a vision for change is shared and owned between the practitioner and the service users/carers, achieving outcomes becomes more likely.

From my experience from working with carers with significant anxiety about their caring role, it is talking through their concerns, to some extent rationalising them, which enables carers to be more embracing of positive risks. This can be liberating for cared-for people. It is also important to recognise the technical-rational quality of relationships; it is the deeper understanding of service users/carers which results through spending time together that increases the quality of information of need, risk and identifying informal networks that can reduce the burden on public services. When I am working with people to identify their outcomes and manage risk, it is often not from direct questioning, but from a personal narrative. The *Caring* module lays down the foundations of relationship and citizenship-based practice by providing opportunities for students to build relationships: to feel equal to, and an ally of, service users/carers.

Future challenges

The emergence of models of SUCI that are achieving social change and empowerment and are outcomes focused are addressing the need to 'develop a more holistic and complex way of understanding how service users/carers can contribute to social work education; . . . as co-producers and partners in the educational experience' (Hatton, 2017, p. 155). The *Caring* module at the University of Dundee uses an innovative model, framed within social pedagogy, to integrate collaborative learning, with a focus on the collective and reciprocal relationships as agents for social change. This work exposes the social dynamic within social work education to prepare students to be 'caring' and ethical practitioners of the future who understand and work with service users/carers from a citizenship and social justice perspective.

Looking to the future, the authors have identified three key challenges for SUCI in social work education:

1 **Ensuring that there are opportunities for service users/carers and social work students to engage in collaborative learning.**

From a social work student perspective, I feel that one of the primary challenges is the continuity of this form of knowledge creation. With practice placement opportunities forming such a central part of our learning it is incumbent on students to engage critically with the ways in which knowledge of practice, as it is formed through professional institutions, can negate meaningful involvement with service users and carers.

2 **Ensuring SUCI in social work education is sustainable.**

From a carer perspective, my identified challenge for the future is to ensure universities have enough funding for SUCI to enable innovative work which empowers service users/carers and students to work creatively and to ensure a foundation for future ethical and relationship-based social work.

3 **Ensuring service users/carers are valued as citizens with agency in their lives and society.**

From a newly qualified practitioner perspective, I would suggest that the notion of a modern professional social worker be broadened to (re)incorporate political and democratic literacy and for citizenship to be recognised in its broadest sense. Service user/carer participation is more than voice being captured in an assessment; it means empowerment and having a stake in society. Some people require (social work) support to achieve this level of agency. The *Caring* Module has the potential to instil this through *learning, creating relationships and doing* together.

The *Caring* module, framed by a collaborative learning/outcomes-focused SUCI model, is supporting the development of thoughtful future social workers – practitioners who understand the 'art' of social work – and developing moral practice based on reciprocal and trusting relationships. A focus on groupwork in the module has created a space for students and service users/carers to collectively address challenges and social problems. In doing so, the *Caring* module is mirroring the ambitions of co-production and outcomes-based practice, and demonstrating that the module is a tangible and symbolic example of what social work practice can and should be.

References

Askheim, O.P., Beresford, P. and Heule, C. (2017) 'Mend the gap – strategies for user involvement in social work education', *Social Work Education: An International Journal*, 36(2), 128–140.

Beresford, P. (2005) 'Theory and practice of user involvement in research: making the connection with public policy and practice', In L. Lowes and A. Hulatt (eds.), *Involving Service Users in Health and Social Care Research* (pp. 6–17). London, Routledge.

Beresford, P. and Croft, S. (2004) 'Service users and practitioners reunited: the key component for social work reform', *British Journal of Social Work*, 34(1), 53–68.

Bondi, L. (2008) 'On the relational dynamics of caring: a psychotherapeutic approach to emotional and power dimensions of women's care work', *Gender, Place and Culture*, 15(3), 227–243.

Bondi, L., Carr, D., Clark, C. and Clegg, C. (2011) *Towards Professional Wisdom: Practical Deliberation in the People Professions*. Farnham, Ashgate.

Bourdieu, P. (1977) *Outline of a Theory of Practice*. Cambridge, Cambridge University Press.

Brühlmeier, A. (2010) *Head, Heart and Hand: Education in the Spirit of Pestalozzi*. Cambridge, Sophia Books.

Cabiati, E. (2017) 'Social work education: the relational way', *Relational Social Work*, 1(1), 61–79.

Cabiati, E. and Raineri, M.L. (2016) 'Learning from service users' involvement: a research about changing stigmatizing attitudes in social work students', *Social Work Education: An International Journal*, 35(8), 982–966.

Department of Health (2002) *Requirements for Social Work Training*. London, Department of Health.

Dewane, C.J. (2006) 'Use of self: a primer revisited', *Clinical Social Work Journal*, 34(4), 543–558.

Driessens, K., McLaughlin, H. and van Doorn, L. (2016) 'The meaningful involvement of service users in social work education: examples from Belgium and the Netherlands', *Social Work Education: An International Journal*, 35(7), 739–751.

Eichsteller, G. and Holthoff, S. (2012) 'The art of being a social pedagogue: developing cultural change in children's homes in Essex', *The International Journal of Social Pedagogy*, 1(1), 30–46.

England, H. (1986) *Social Work as Art: Making Sense for Good Practice*. London, Allen and Unwin.

Freire, P. (1972) *Pedagogy of the Oppressed*. Penguin, Harmondsworth.

Gee, M., Ager, W. and Haddow, A. (2009) 'The caring experience: learning about community care through spending 24 hours with people who use services and family carers', *Social Work Education*, 28(7), 691–706.

Gilligan, C. (1982) *In a Different Voice: Psychological Theory and Women's Development*. Cambridge, MA, Harvard University Press.

Grodofsky, M.M. and Gutman, C. (2017) 'Social work undergraduates and service users as co-learners and researchers', *Social Work Education: An International Journal*, 36(2), 141–153.

Hamalainen, J. (2003) 'The concept of social pedagogy in the field of social work', *Journal of Social Work*, 3(1), 69–80.

Hamalainen, J. (2012) 'Social pedagogical eyes in the midst of diverse understandings, conceptualisations and activities', *International Journal of Social Pedagogy*, 1(1), 3–16.

Hatton, K. (2017) 'A critical examination of the knowledge contribution service user and carer involvement brings to social work education', *Social Work Education: An International Journal*, 36(2), 154–171.

Heule, C., Knutagard, M. and Kristiansen, A. (2017) 'Mending the gaps in social work education and research: two examples from a Swedish context', *European Journal of Social Work*, 20(3), 396–408.

Hughes, M. (2017) 'What difference does it make? Findings of an impact study of service user and carer involvement on social work students' subsequent practice', *Social Work Education: The International Journal*, 36(2), 203–216.

IFSW (2014) *International Federation of Social Workers, Global Definition of Social Work*. www.ifsw.org/what-is-social-work/global-definition-of-social-work/

Kreber, C. (2014) 'Rationalising the nature of "graduateness" through philosophical accounts of authenticity', *Teaching in Higher Education*, 19(1), 90–100.

Levy, S. (2018) 'Re-creating the social work imagination: embedding the arts in social work discourse in Scotland', In E. Huss and E. Bos (eds.), *Art in Social Work Practice: Theory and Practice: International Perspectives* (pp. 44–56). London, Routledge.

Levy, S., Aiton, R., Doig, J., Dow, J., McNeil, R., Brown, S. and Hunter, L. (2016) 'Outcomes focused user involvement in social work education: applying knowledge to practice', *Social Work Education: The International Journal*, 35(8), 866–877.

Levy, S. and Young, H. (2020) 'Arts, disability and crip theory: temporal re-imagining in social care for people with profound and multiple learning disabilities', *Scandinavian Journal of Disability Research*, 22(1), 68–79. doi:http://doi.org/10.16993/sjdr.620

Rapoport, L. (1968) 'Creativity in Social Work', *Smith College Studies in Social Work*, 18(3), 139–161.

Ravavlier, J. (2018) 'UK social workers: working conditions and wellbeing', *British Association of Social Workers*. www.basw.co.uk/resources/uk-social-workers-working-conditions-and-wellbeing-0

Robinson, K. and Webber, M. (2013) 'Models and effectiveness of service user and carer involvement in social work education: a literature review', *British Journal of Social Work*, 43(5), 925–944.

Ruch, G., Winter, K., Cree, V., Hallets, S., Morrison, F. and Hadfield, M. (2017) 'Making meaningful connections: using insights from social pedagogy in statutory child and family social work practice', *Child and Family Social Work*, 22(2), 1015–1023.

Scottish Executive (2003) *The Framework for Social Work Education in Scotland*. Edinburgh, The Stationary Office.

Smith, M. and Whyte, B. (2008) 'Social education and social pedagogy: reclaiming a Scottish tradition in social work', *European Journal of Social Work*, 11(1), 15–28.

Tanner, D., Littlechild, R., Duffy, J. and Hayes, D. (2015) 'Making it real: evaluating the impact of service user and carer involvement in social work education', *British Journal of Social Work*, 47(2), 467–486.

Tronto, J. (1993) *Moral Boundaries: A Political Argument for an Ethic of Care*. London, Routledge.

SECTION 4

Service user involvement in research in the human services

36

LESSONS OF INCLUSIVE LEARNING

The value of experiential knowledge of persons with a learning disability in social work education

Jean Pierre Wilken, Jeroen Knevel and Sascha van Gijzel
in collaboration with Ellis Jongerius, Caron Landzaat,
Idman Nur-Voskens, experts by experience in our team

Introduction

Unlike England, where it is mandatory to include service users in all different aspects of social work education, in the Netherlands, like many other countries, service user involvement is still in many ways in the early stages of development (Driessens et al., 2018). But interest is growing; all over the country new initiatives are being taken, aimed at bridging the gap between experiential, academic, and practitioner knowledge.

Over the past ten years, experiential knowledge has become an important thread in our work at Utrecht University of Applied Sciences in the Netherlands. We acknowledge that for healthy social work, practitioners, academics, and students should be in a continuous dialogue with service users and carers, learning with and from each other (McLaughlin et al., 2018, p. 2). We deem experiential knowledge a primary source of knowledge, equal value to academic and practitioner knowledge. Experiential knowledge can be defined in different ways, for instance as 'truth based on personal experience with a phenomenon' (Borkman, 1976) or 'the often implicit, lived experiences of individuals with their bodies and their illnesses as well as with care and cure' (Caron-Flinterman et al., 2005). When individuals share experiential knowledge, the communal body of knowledge exceeds the boundaries of individual experiences. This body of knowledge has been as collective experiential expertise. This expertise is mostly developed in peer communities. Individuals can also become 'experts by experience' through training. Experts by experience are capable of expressing their personal experiences, reflecting on them, and transforming them into collective knowledge. Furthermore, experts by experience actively convey this collective knowledge to a wide audience of peers, social workers, support workers, policy makers, management, educators, researchers, and students.

In this chapter, we describe our experiences with fostering the inclusion of persons with a mild learning disability and their experiences in our research and education programmes. We present some of our projects in which we have piloted different roles of experts by experience, like (co)lecturer, trainer, instructor, researcher, and team member. First, we introduce the context of our work and the theoretical notions we use. Then, we describe three examples of pilot projects: Inclusive Project-Based Learning, Tandem Cooperation, and Gap Mending. We conclude with some general learnings and directions for the future.

Context

Our research group is called 'Participation, Care and Support'. It is part of the Research Centre for Social Innovation at Utrecht University of Applied Sciences. Studying the value and application of experiential knowledge is one of our research programmes. This theme is closely connected to one of our other programmes: social inclusion of people with a disability. We study these themes from the perspective of persons with a learning disability, a mental disability, acquired brain damage, and physical disability. In this chapter, we focus on people with a learning disability.

Our vision is 'practice what you preach'. This means that our R&D methodology should be inclusive as well. We use methods of participatory action research, focusing on the improvement of practices, especially of social support services and disability care.

Walmsley (2001) coined the term 'inclusive research' to denote research involving people with a learning disability as 'more than just subjects or respondents'. The inclusion in research of people with disability, their families, and representative organizations is now more and more embedded in the strategies of national funding agencies in the Netherlands. But in reality, we are just at the beginning of integrating this into our practices. The same goes for 'inclusive education'. Dutch policy promotes the inclusion of children with a disability in primary schools and other levels of education, and there is wide public acknowledgement that this is the way to go. Yet we are facing obstacles caused by a shortage of teachers and insufficient knowledge to provide children who require special attention with the pedagogical climate and safety which they need. In secondary and higher education, inclusiveness receives massive attention, but it is clear that there is a lot to do in order to make curricula and knowledge of lecturers more inclusive. Our research group seeks to find answers and to provide knowledge and good examples, in order to make education and research more inclusive. Our focus is higher education: we use our own university and the campus as a field lab. In our research, we often opt for a design approach. In communities of practice (we call these 'communities of development'), we bring all the stakeholders together to design and test more inclusive practices. In these communities, we involve people with a disability, students, professionals, and family members (Wilken et al., 2020). Experiential learning is the preferred mode of working.

Our research group is working closely together with the Institute for Social Work, which has bachelor's and master's programmes in social work. We provide knowledge for the social work curriculum. One of the current spear points of the bachelor's is the acknowledgement, utilization, and facilitation of experience-based knowledge. The institute endorses this by explicitly describing in its qualifications that students must use experience-based knowledge for the benefit of service users.

For a number of years, we have commenced a partnership with the LFB, which is a national advocacy organization of people with learning disabilities in the Netherlands. Part of their mission is to offer training and education to people with a learning disability who wish to develop experience-based knowledge and learn skills for the benefit of themselves and others. The objective is to empower the person by articulating his or her experience-based knowledge. Increasingly, care organizations want to work with experts by experience, and the LFB is asked to provide the training programme in-company, using an action learning approach. Persons with a learning disability and their coach, usually a support worker, both participate in the training so as to encourage learning together. Subjects being addressed comprise sharing your story, strengthening your social network and that of peers, political participation, advocacy, and so on. Besides delivering support services, they deploy peer experts in various professional activities such as teaching and co-teaching, research and co-research, co-design, presentations, and workshops. Over recent years, three trainers with experiential knowledge have been seconded to our university, recognized as our colleagues in teaching and research.

Theoretical frame

We employ three primary perspectives: social inclusion, human rights, and experiential knowledge.

Social inclusion can be defined in many ways. It is often described as the opposite effect to 'social exclusion'. It is about enabling people or communities to fully participate in society. The key elements of promoting social inclusion appear to be:

- Supporting socially excluded people and communities to overcome inequality and disadvantage, arising as a result of the circumstances an individual is born into, or as a result of his or her particular circumstances; and
- Promoting equality of opportunities, which is related to eliminating discrimination and the promotion of diversity (Charity Commission, 2001).

Schuurman and Nass (2015, p. 245) define inclusion from the perspective of the person:

> The situation in which a person experiences no obstacles preventing him or her from participating in society and specific measures for people with disabilities are virtually unnecessary. It means that anyone, irrespective of background or current situation, is self-evidently part of society, feels welcome and can engage with those around them.

Succinctly, definitions of social inclusion contain notions of participation and belonging. Social inclusion indicates an amalgamation of elements of being engaged in meaningful social roles and activities in networks and communities, and feeling valued by other members of these communities.

For the human rights perspective, we reference the United Nations Convention on the Rights of Persons with Disabilities (UN CRPD), which aims for the 'full and effective participation and inclusion in society' of people with disabilities (United Nations, 2006, art. 1).

These frames are interlinked. The UN CRPD emphasizes the same rights people with a disability have as other citizens, for example regarding education, housing, and labour. Although the notion of social inclusion is not well defined, throughout the CRPD the spirit of inclusion is there. Adopted in 2006, the United Nations Convention on the Rights of Persons with Disabilities (CRPD) represents a modern human rights treaty with innovative components (Bielefeldt, 2009; Stein, 2010; Anderson and Philips, 2012; Sabatello and Schulze, 2014; Degener, 2016). Among the innovative potentials of the Convention, it provides for a new understanding of equality i.e. transformative equality (Biholar, 2014; Fredman, 2016), and an extended notion of discrimination (Graumann, 2012; Goldschmidt, 2012), and it pursues a further conceptualization of disability i.e. a human rights model deeming disabled persons as rights holders and human rights subjects (Van Weele, 2012; Degener, 2016). Anderson and Philips (2012) add to it that the CRPD constitutes a paramount milestone that has brought about a paradigm shift in conceptions of disability and human rights, not by introducing 'new rights' but by expanding and 'deepening our understanding of the universal scope of human rights' (see also Degener and Koster-Dreese, 1995; Harnacke and Graumann, 2012; Sabatello and Schulze, 2014). The CRPD represents a vision and ambition of 'wide inclusion' containing civil, political, social, economic, and cultural rights.

Experiential knowledge can be defined as knowledge based upon personal experience. The specific experiential knowledge of people with a learning disability emerges when they acquire knowledge through becoming familiar with their disability, with the personal and social consequences of the impairment, and with the support services they receive. Collective experiential knowledge is developed by compiling the personal experiences of individuals in the same area, for example, experiences with special education or with labour participation. Verbrugge and Embregts (2013) distinguish four stages in the development of experimental knowledge: 1. naming one's own experience; 2. insight into one's own experience; 3. insight into collective experiences; 4. applying experiential knowledge to others. Research (Verbrugge and Embregts, 2013; Groutars et al., 2015; Gijzel, 2017) on development and the implementation of experiential knowledge of people with learning disabilities shows that partnership with a coach is needed to gain insight into collective experiences and conveying this knowledge to others.

We consider experiential knowledge a pivotal asset to advance social inclusion, and as a touchstone for the implementation of the CRPD. The proof of the pudding is in the eating. The personal and collective experiences pertaining to social inclusion or exclusion, and with rights ensured or denied, are crucial sources to assess where we are on the road, and what should be praised or changed.

Below, we present three projects: Inclusive Project-Based Learning, Tandem Cooperation, and Gap Mending. For each project we highlight context, objectives, content, outcomes, and experiences.

Inclusive Project-Based Learning

Context

The adoption of the UN CRPD prompted our School of Social Work to pay much more attention to the concepts and dynamics that underlie the UN CRPD, to wit social inclusion, anti-discrimination, equality, equal dignity, disability oppression, empowerment, the concept of disability, and so on. With the ratification of the convention in 2016 by the Dutch government, the importance of these concepts was again stressed. Professionals in the social work field also bear responsibility for the application of the Convention. However, research carried out has shown that professionals are not yet focused or equipped to work on social inclusion (Knevel and Wilken, 2015, 2016; Wilken and Knevel, 2016). The UN Convention and its implications are still barely known in the professional field. This also applies to vocational education and training. Furthermore, we noted very little involvement of people with a mild learning disability themselves in our School of Social Work, which is pivotal in case of the pursuit of wanting to be an inclusive school. This sparked us to devise methods of co-creation requiring inclusive collaboration between university students and persons with a mild learning disability. This amounted to an inclusive approach of project-based learning.

Objectives

At our School of Social Work, we offer a degree minor focusing on learning disability. The degree minor envisages an inclusive society; hence, the learning objectives are geared towards this:

1) The student supports persons with learning disabilities to actively engage themselves in society
2) The student is able to work via an inclusive process with persons with learning disabilities
3) The student is able to collaborate on an equal basis with persons with learning disabilities
4) The student promotes equality of persons with mild learning disabilities
5) The student reflects on the notions of inclusion, equality and equal dignity, power and power relations, empowerment, and emancipation.

Project-based learning (PBL) is a model that organizes learning around projects. According to the definitions found in PBL handbooks for lecturers, projects are complex tasks, based on challenging questions or problems, that involve students in design, problem-solving, decision making, or investigative activities; give students the opportunity to work relatively autonomously over a certain period of time; and culminate in realistic products or presentations (Jones et al., 1997; Thomas et al., 1999). In our minor, persons with a learning disability are included in different roles in the projects the students work on. Ideally, the persons and the students work together on an equal basis, in a process of co-creation, using an action learning approach. We have called this 'inclusive cooperation'.

Content

We offer the course entitled Inclusive Projects once a year to our fourth-year undergraduate social work students, starting in September and ending in January. It encompasses theory, which is, however, made subordinate to practice; the project is conducted following the model of project-based learning (PBL).

The degree minor addresses various interlinked topics such as power, power structures, power (im)balances between service users (i.e. persons with mild learning disabilities), and support workers, enabling and impeding conditions of and pathways to and from inclusion, inclusive approaches, (in)equality, (un)equal dignity, empowerment, and emancipation.

In essence, the lecturer's task is limited to supporting the process and at times offering more in-depth content to encourage students to delve deeply into the notions mentioned above.

One of the instruments used to support the reflections of students and the persons with mild learning disabilities is shown in Figure 36.1 (Van Hove, 2015). The model depicts the dynamics of shifting power balance between the persons with mild learning disabilities and the student at our University of Applied Sciences. The model serves as an aid to reflect on the balance of power. However, students employing this model have criticized the terminology and power relationship depicted. Students are given the freedom to deviate from this model by devising their own modified form.

In the practice part, students can choose from three options, varying in the degree they are structured, from more formal to more informal:

1) Conducting an inclusive research project
2) Designing an innovative product
3) Conducting a social inclusion project.

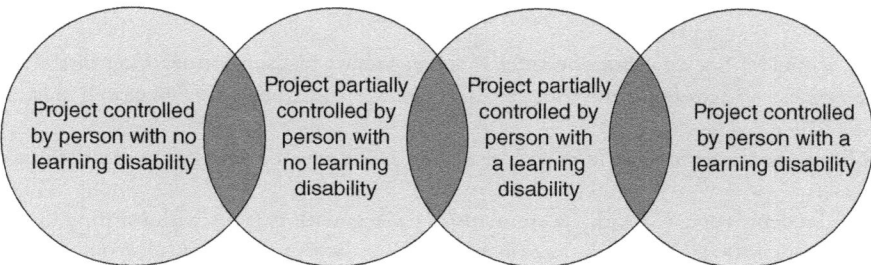

Figure 36.1 Balance of power

Source: Adapted from Hove, G. van (2015). Gewoon Bijzonder: Nationaal Programma Gehandicapten. The Hague: ZonMW/VUmc/LFB

The learning objectives are identical (see section above), cooperation between university students and persons with a mild learning disability is required, and the range of challenges for the student is similar.

Inclusive research expects the student to form a research team with one or more persons with a learning disability. The entire research process is completed as one team. The research team is completely free to determine the subject to be investigated, the research question, and research methods. Reporting and presentation of the process and results is allowed in any fashion, provided that it meets the requirements of accessible communication.

Product innovation is about designing and producing a tangible product aimed at improving the quality of life of persons with a learning disability. The product has to be an innovation for the field of learning disability care or support, either for people with a learning disability or support workers. The product innovation assignment expects students to assemble a team with one or more persons with a learning disability. The entire process of innovation is completed as one team. Reporting and presentation of the process and product is allowed in any fashion, provided that it meets the requirements of accessible communication.

Conducting a social inclusion project means that the student works on improving the accessibility of a certain environment for people with a learning disability. These social contexts may include a neighbourhood, a workplace, or a setting where leisure activities are being organized (sports club, music club, and the like). This project has the character of 'social pioneering', accomplishing meaningful social encounters between people with and without disabilities, people with different backgrounds, thus creating connections and adding social value. Students are expected to assemble a team with one or more persons with a learning disability. The assignment is undertaken as one 'inclusive team'. This team organizes for example an event in the community. In this project, the principles of 'bridge-building' are applied (Kal et al., 2012). One of these principles is 'creating a welcoming space'.

The project may also be aimed at combating stigmatization and self-stigmatization of persons with learning disabilities, exclusion, and discrimination. Realization of welcoming spaces in society is achieved in many different ways e.g. through sports events, art events, music and dance, culinary events, nature activities and so on.

In all three projects, it is crucial that the team reflects on notions such as power, power relations, (in)equality, equal dignity, empowerment, and inclusion. Reflections on these notions derive from experiences students have had in their collaboration.

Outcomes and experiences

We have been running this IBPL course for four years. To date, 60 students and approximately 60 persons with mild learning disabilities have participated. Third-year bachelor's university students and students in their graduation year (fourth): 54 female students, 6 male students aged between 20–45 years of age. Eighty percent students from Utrecht University of Applied Sciences, 20% students from other Universities of Applied Sciences around the country. Persons with mild learning disabilities: a mix of male and female service users aged 10–60 years. Persons with mild learning disabilities have different backgrounds: mostly Dutch, Caucasian, sheltered living in residential groups or supported living independently in the community. Some of them have additional psychiatric disorders, most of them not. Most importantly, they have the curiosity, the wish to develop competencies, to explore new opportunities, to learn new things, to have influence on issues (policies, decisions) regarding their lives etc.

Students were very enthusiastic about this way of learning and the learning outcomes. Most students had experiences in working with service users during their internship or (for part-time students) their professional work, but working together as a learning experience is quite new.

At the beginning, this gives quite some confusion, because traditional frameworks are turned upside down. Students learn for instance to adapt communication and pace, and to negotiate about goals and activities in order to reach consensus what to achieve and what to do.

> At first, I thought equality was a certain attitude that you had to have towards your client. But the fact that you have the power to use a certain attitude already makes the relationship unequal.
>
> *(social work student)*

Subjects that students come up with in their projects vary significantly, for instance accessibility of music festivals, becoming an assistant lecturer at primary school, intimacy and friendships, doing household chores (bathroom, kitchen, toilet cleaning) with the prospect of living independently, preparing healthy meals, sign language to support people with complex disabilities to communicate, taking care of your pets, awareness raising of substance use among youths with a learning disability. Events realized for bridge building comprised sports events (volleyball, tennis, football), bingo, community dinners, creative arts at secondary school, and photography exhibitions.

Gap Mending

Context

In September 2018, we developed a more formally structured, project-based learning method called the Gap Mending course. The main difference with the previous approaches is that people with learning disabilities participate in the role of students and attend classes together with the social work students. The inclusive projects discussed in the previous section require students to assemble a team themselves with one or more persons with a learning disability. In the Gap Mending course, people with lived experiences are participating from the start onwards and form a couple with a student in order to work on a common project.

'Mend the gap' means that two different groups of people are learning together. In this way, despite the differences between the persons, they come closer to each other, inviting each other to better understand one another's world. It is about sharing experiences and views on topics such as dependency, disability, ability, quality of services, discrimination, independent living, work, friendships and relations, politics etc.

In a 'Gap Mending course', the idea is that when you both participate in the social valued role of student and engage in a learning process together, the gap between the social work students and services users is reduced or 'mended'. In such a learning situation, the participants often experience a certain degree of shared inconvenience. This shared uncertainty ensures that the gap between social work students and service users is narrowed and that they have a more equal starting position as course participants. Both the students and service need to let go of a role they are familiar with. The Gap Mending course is inspired by the Mobility course of the Lund University from Sweden University (Heule et al., 2017; and the Gap Mending principles of the PowerUs network (Askheim et al., 2018; powerus.org).

> I gave a lot of explanations to my co-student, although I wanted to avoid this. On the other hand, it isn't possible to cooperate if she doesn't understand what the project is about. She won't be able to participate in the research in an equal way. This is something I struggled with during the project.
>
> *(social work student)*

Besides incorporating elements of the course 'Inclusive Learning', this course was devised in collaboration with our partners LFB, Amerpoort, and De Wilg (organizations providing support services to people with learning disabilities). This partnership is crucial for the development and execution of a Gap Mending course. Trainers with experiential knowledge from LFB were involved in the development of the course. One of the experts by experience was co-lecturer during the course we taught in tandem.

Objectives

In addition to the learning objectives of the course 'Inclusive Learning', described earlier, we formulated the following objectives.

Students attending the Gap Mending course will learn to:

1) Collaborate with social work students and students with learning disabilities
2) Collectively learn with social work students and students with learning disabilities.

Similar to the inclusive projects, the collaboration and learning process revolves around inclusion, equality, power and powerlessness, and empowerment.

Content

In this course, students experience what social inclusion means, what social exclusion may look like, and what discrimination encompasses. Students reflect on the conceptualization of social inclusion, and what inclusive cooperation requires. Similarly, students will experience what inequality and equality mean and reflect on the concept of equality – in terms of equal opportunity, equal worth of persons, and dignity. Attached to these concepts are power, powerlessness, and empowerment. Again, students experience what these concepts look like, how they feel, and how power operates in social relations.

Outcomes and experiences

The course has been piloted twice so far. The first experiment was done with six persons with a learning disability (one quit after the first lesson) and six social work students in the fourth year of the bachelor's programme. The second time the course was offered for second year students. Nine persons with a learning disability from different organizations and six social work students participated in this course.

We evaluated the experiences both groupwise and individually, using interviews. The overall experiences were very positive. All students of the course felt it was meaningful for them to participate, and some of them have become real ambassadors of the course. For the students with lived experience, the value was in the chance to be on a university campus, have contact with new young people, learn new skills, and work on a problem or issue they think is urgent. Social work students appreciate that they became aware of, even though confronting, the misbalance of power between themselves and the people they support in their practice. They better understand big abstract concepts like inclusion and equality. Examples of issues that were addressed were loneliness among people with a learning disability and the lack of possibilities for further education for people with learning disabilities.

> I would rather have that they hurt us a little and be honest instead of being correct and nice all the time.
>
> *(expert student)*

Next to this, some of the students with user expertise became aware of that they tend to lean back, 'be the client', and let social work students take the lead. They had to get used to the fact that they had another role, not as a service user but as a student and a peer expert.

Social work students and expert students had a different interest and motivation to participate in the course. Although expert students received a certificate and supplements which they appreciated and valued, social work students received 5 European credits as part of their bachelor. This created a power unbalance in some situations, where expert students thought 'Ah well, let them decide, their diploma depends on it!' It is recommended this aspect be taken into account and solutions for future courses looked for to mend this gap.

> I have learned about doing research and what it means. I've learned a lot from the accessible summaries social work students made.
>
> *(expert student)*

Assessment of the process and the student's reflection on it are most important in order to earn credits. The project results (research report, newly developed product) merely serve as a vehicle to get the process going. Unsurprisingly, students were inclined to focus on the results i.e. the product instead of the process. This is partly due to the logic of the current education system within our School of Social Work. Hence, more time and effort are required to encourage students to reflect on inclusive collaboration and related topics.

A social work student shares:

> I was angry to the fact that I was serving my own interests for a good grade, but my power has unconsciously been employed in a way that made A. and R. feel behind. I also felt that I had gone too far in creating a safe environment in which they could develop. There is little room for development if you can only watch.

However, stimulating students to evaluate and reflect on the collaboration together eventually helped for example an expert student to better stand up for himself: 'After evaluating and saying what we wanted different in our team we had a better collaboration and it felt more equal'.

The course was given by a university lecturer and a lecturer with expertise by experience. Despite having already worked in tandem before, this course was quite a challenge for them. The focus on the process and moving with the group was difficult. It resulted in a power imbalance where the university lecturer often took the lead and the role of the co-lecturer was less clear. It was essential to reflect on this but also to share this with the group. So, we could make our own troubles in our collaboration useful by sharing them and discussing them in the group.

The focus on the process during the course needs a lecturer and co-lecturer who are able to move with the group. It requires coaching skills and the ability to react to what is happening in the group. This takes time and reflection. The university lecturer needs to create space for the co-lecturer by letting go of his agenda, and the co-lecturer must be able to tell what he or she needs, to have a meaningful role during the course. A skill that can be helpful is to ask critical questions and not be scared to issue what is socially or politically correct.

Inclusive projects contain elements of action learning and reflective learning. Action learning is a good way of learning about inclusion, equality, power, empowerment, and social entrepreneurship. We learn that inclusive projects take time. It is not always guaranteed that the assignment can be finished in time (within the period of the course), and success is not always guaranteed. But part of the learning experience is that tuning to the pace and possibilities of the person you work with is more important than getting results within a set time frame.

Inclusive projects and Gap Mending: commonalities and distinctions

The above account of the inclusive project (informal) and the Gap Mending (formal) methods harbour obvious commonalities and distinctions. In short, both methods have in common that, first, the learning objectives are identical; second, cooperation between university students and people with mild mental disabilities is required and is paramount; and third, the challenges are equal.

Distinctions between the two methods are listed below. Features of the inclusive projects (IP) encompass:

1) Encounters between university students and experts by experience primarily occur outside the classroom and off campus
2) There is no tandem collaboration between university lecturer and expert by experience; there is no co-lecturer involved
3) Does not offer a pre-structured programme: we offer a structure, although it merely serves as a tool, not as a rule
4) Experts by experience are not recruited by the university lecturers, but by the students themselves
5) Persons with a learning disability are not required to be trained experts by experience
6) Students do not receive a certificate; only students enrolled at the university can obtain credits.

Features of the Gap Mending course encompass:

1) The encounters between university students and students who are trained to be experts by experience mainly happen in the classroom on campus
2) There is tandem collaboration between the university lecturer and the expert by experience i.e. co-lecturer

3) Experts by experience are recruited by university lecturers and support workers of the service providers we work with
4) All students attending the Gap Mending course obtain a certificate. This certificate does not accord with the European Credit Transfer and Accumulation System (ECTS). In addition to that certificate, students enrolled at the university obtain credits.

The tandem cooperation constitutes an indispensable property of the gap mending course. The next session provides a further elaboration of how we have shaped this concept at our School of Social Work.

Tandem cooperation

Context

Tandem collaboration is our third example of experiential knowledge being implemented in higher education and university research. The tandem concept was developed in Flanders by Driessens and others (Driessens and Van Regenmortel, 2006; Vansevenant et al., 2008). In this concept, an expert by experience and a professional, often a social worker, work side by side. Coalescing experience-based and professional knowledge amounts to knowledge in which the 'good' of both sources is harnessed as soon as inclusion and empowerment of people with learning disabilities are taken as starting point. The partnership typical to this relationship is based on principles of empowerment and complements both sources of knowledge (Groutars et al., 2015; Gijzel, 2017). We have translated the tandem collaboration concept to a classroom environment. This implies that a university lecturer, together with the expert by experience, prepares and executes classroom activities. It is a side-by-side collaboration.

Objective

Within the curriculum of our School of Social Work and our research activities at the Research Centre, we are searching for ways to expand the use of experience-based knowledge. By working in tandem, we interlink experiential, theoretical, and practitioner knowledge.

Acknowledging experience-based knowledge by means of tandem collaboration, reciprocity between students and service users is fostered and critical thinking encouraged.

Content

The core of tandem collaboration is that a lecturer and a person with lived experience are both working together as lecturers. The peer expert gets the support of the lecturer to remove obstacles and create a discretionary and welcoming space to use and share his knowledge during preparations of the lessons as well as in the classroom. We teach our students about social inclusion, social (in)justice, power and powerlessness, empowerment, and social role valorization. We wish for students to recognize the expertise of service users and to integrate it with their professional body of knowledge. Through the tandem collaboration, we demonstrate how students can perform similar collaborations in their social work practice.

Outcomes and experiences

Between 2016 and 2018, more than 200 future social workers from the first, second, third, and fourth year have been reached. Based on evaluations among students, lecturers, and experts by

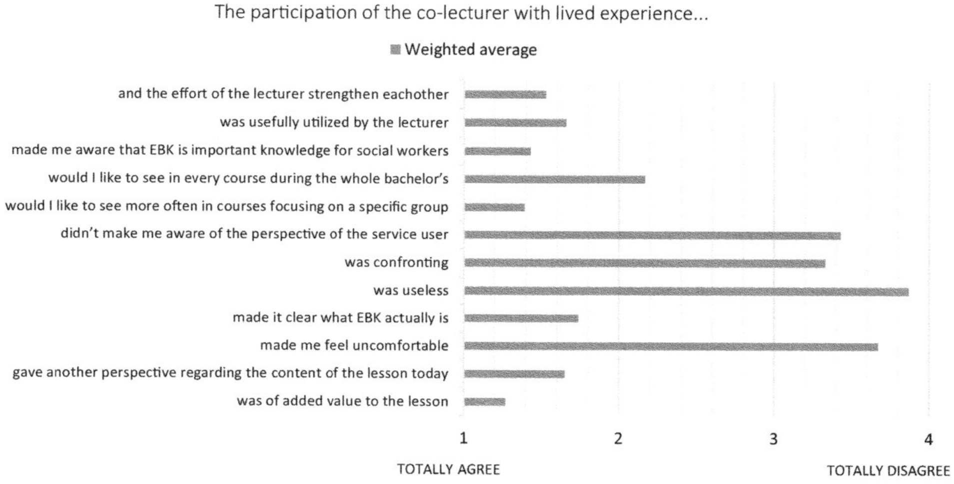

The participation of the co-lecturer with lived experience...

■ Weighted average

Figure 36.2   The participation of the co-lecturer with lived experience

experience, we can conclude that tandem collaboration is appreciated (Figure 36.2). Students appreciated the involvement of the co-lecturer with an average of 8.8 (N123) on a scale of 1 to 10.

Students find the course very innovative, in terms of the tandem lecturing and the content. The added value is huge given the evaluation results and what students learn and the raise of their level of awareness.

First-year students usually have stereotypical images of persons with learning disabilities. Once they meet genuine examples of how people with learning disabilities manifest themselves, these images alter. Hence, co-lecturers have a crucial influence on positive imaging amongst students about people with learning disabilities. This good practice inspired other lecturers to work together with experts by experiences and new initiatives are worked on for the second year of the new programme.

> I personally found this a very informative lesson. I feel that I really want to work with people with learning disabilities.
>
> *(first-year social work student)*

Students value the expert by experience because she has a different credibility than the university lecturer. For example, in our classes we promote a strength-based approach, and our colleagues with lived experiences are living examples of how this approach has contributed to their quality of life. Experiences shared by our colleagues on what works in supporting them or what they find valuable skills of a 'good' social worker really grab the attention of our students. A co-lecturer's participation and presence challenges superficial ideas and persistent views of what we consider to be 'normal', thereby encouraging critical thinking.

> First year social work student: Through these lessons you will look at things from a different perspective, this will allow you to see things that you would otherwise not be aware of.
>
> *(first-year social work student)*

The partnership between the university lecturer and co-lecturer can be seen as an example of what the collaboration and use of experience knowledge can look like in the social practice where students work or will work. It is key that lecturer and co-lecturer be able to reflect on the spot about dynamics in the classroom which are not always purely positive. The university lecturer more or less needs to guide the process in the group and has to make sure that not only students but also the expert by experience interact productively. This is in line with the findings of Driessens and De Clerck (2014), who state that lecturers play a facilitating role: providing a safe space, encouraging open dialogue, and connecting the stories of service users to theory, frameworks and vision.

> A good example was with the lesson Ellis. We were given assessment tools that we could test. Ellis could tell how it worked for her. This made it very clear.
>
> *(fourth-year social work student)*

> You learn a lot more with an expert by experience present. The lecturer cooperates well together with the expert by experience.
>
> *(third-year social work student)*

Bringing experts by experience into a group of students sometimes introduces uncomfortable situations or a kind of awkwardness among students. One of the experts experiences a certain reluctance with students towards her because they don't want to hurt her feelings. She suspects students wouldn't hold back when they only had to deal with the university lecturer. This kind of situation is meaningful to discuss with students on the spot. This, of course, requires a safe atmosphere in the group and good communication between lecturer and co-lecturer.

In the light of the principle of equal cooperation, our own struggles and achievements in the classroom are exemplary for students. Willingness to show vulnerability, and the lecturer being transparent about what enables and what impedes the cooperation, is significant to reflect on the power imbalances between the lecturer and co-lecturer. This was particularly valuable with regards to the further development of the Gap Mending course.

We learned that a number of conditions are needed to make this concept successful. For example, it is necessary to have a coordinating lecturer within the University with whom experts are familiar. The coordinator receives and processes requests of university colleagues and carefully introduces the experts by experience to lecturers who start working in a tandem cooperation.

For meaningful participation, the expert must have lived experience related to the subject addressed in class and/or be involved in the design of the classroom activities. So, it is important to make a good match. For this, the coordinating lecturer must know the experts by experience well.

Conclusion and reflection

Although our experiences with new ways of bringing persons with a disability and their perspectives into research and education are still quite new, we can assert the great added value. Students at our School of Social Work strongly appreciate learning about complex concepts and theories through inclusive projects (appreciation scores 8 to 9.5 on a scale of 0–10). It helps them to understand comprehensive concepts and theories such as social inclusion, empowerment, equality, equal dignity, emancipatory practice, power, and powerlessness. Inclusive projects set up by students are suitable methods for promoting social inclusion of persons with a mild learning disability. It empowers persons with a learning disability.

Evaluations among the students show a high appreciation of learning in an inclusive way, and learning from experts by experience. Students discovered that service users have more competencies than students were aware of, more than they believed that persons with learning disability would have. Students also became aware of the power and control social workers have, leading to a power imbalance. In terms of competencies, students increased their communication and collaboration skills.

The experts by experience value their collaboration and participation a lot. They feel they have an important and valued role. They are being heard and appreciated by the students and are happy that they can contribute to their development. In addition, they learn from the lecturer and students; they meet new people and visit new places. Our evaluations show that people feel empowered. They mention that they feel their experiences have been acknowledged. They feel proud stepping into a new role, which opens new perspectives in their lives. They indicate that their competences have been increased.

As lecturers and researchers, we have developed together with our lived experience colleagues and their coaches several didactical forms, which are structured in different ways. It is good to have this variety, since this offers different options for inclusive learning.

Further exploration of collaborative reflection by student and life-expert on the project, its objectives, and the cooperation between the researcher and co-researcher is needed. Helpful tools to achieve equal input in collaborative reflection specifically for students and life-experts with a mild learning disability are needed and have to be developed. For example: methods to stimulate, structure, and deepen reflection.

We have learned that certain conditions are indispensable. First, a group of dedicated lecturers is important, people who believe in the value of bringing lived experiences into the classroom. People who want to spend time and energy in connecting to people with a learning disability and supporting them in taking their role. Second, to develop courses, workshops, or lectures in co-creation requires time, commitment, and thus enough financial means. In the Gap Mending course, we were able to develop the whole course together with experts by experience and teach the whole course in tandem. Power and equality are also important themes in the tandem collaboration. There is a power imbalance in this collaboration because the expert by experience is quite dependent on the lecturer to provide her the space and time she needs to participate meaningfully. To guarantee this, it is important to determine roles and divide tasks in advance and always create time to evaluate. Our findings confirm the experiences of Ward et al. (2016), that inclusive involvement requires positive guidance and continuous support.

Working inclusively with persons with lived experiences brings about a paradigm shift. It results in a better understanding of their perspective, needs, and preferences. It creates a common ground for partnership and person-centred care. In Table 36.1, we summarize a number of challenges social workers and social work students are facing, and the benefits resulting from introducing peer expertise directly in the social work curriculum.

Our studies confirm the findings of other researchers, like Ward et al. (2016), who state that an important value of direct teaching by people with a disability is that negative stereotyping is challenged, including the belief that people with a learning disability are childlike and not able to speak for themselves. This is a significant barrier to inclusive involvement and to the way professional social workers are approaching service users.

The principle of the service user movement, 'nothing about us without us', is not obvious in social work practice, research, and education. Inclusive projects and tandem cooperation can help to change this. The next step is to extend and integrate the principles and methods from the

Table 36.1 Challenges and benefits

Challenges		Benefits	
For the person with lived experience	*For the student*	*For the person with lived experience*	*For the student*
Emotional wellbeing Student is over-demanding, expecting too much, which may cause distress.	**Control** Balancing between taking and giving control.	**Feeling acknowledged** The person with learning disabilities expressed thoughts and feelings of feeling acknowledged. The acknowledgement is harboured in the fact that they are asked for their experiences, their knowledge, their perspective, and the influence they have on the project, have a recognized role as team member, and feel welcomed at the university – a place they often regard as 'outer world', a bastion of learning life.	**Awareness of power relationship with service users** First, students began to understand the concept of power, the inevitable presence of power between support workers, persons with a learning disability. Furthermore, students learned to accept the reality of power, the dynamics of power, and the fruitful and ugly face of power.
Protection Protectiveness of social worker or coach may hinder allowing involvement of persons with a learning disability to join an inclusive project.	**Accessible language** University students find it hard to switch to accessible language.	**Feeling competent** Active participation in the inclusive projects offers opportunities to reveal competences which often remain undisclosed in a dependent relationship between service user and practitioner. Persons with disabilities felt valued due to genuine commitment of the university students to cooperate and the influence they had in decisions to be taken. Feeling acknowledged and feeling competent are interwoven experiences.	**Capabilities** Students came to realize that persons with a learning disability are often underestimated by the students themselves, the support workers, and outsiders regarding competencies they have and their undiscovered potentials.
Commitment Team member stops halfway through the process. In Gap Mending course, wasn't available for working outside the planned sessions.	**Time consuming** Process of cooperation in inclusive projects is time consuming. It is time consuming to undertake an inclusive project, so much more that students misjudge time needed to complete it.	**Being proud; feeling empowered**	

(Continued)

Table 36.1 (Continued)

Challenges		Benefits	
For the person with lived experience	*For the student*	*For the person with lived experience*	*For the student*
Lack of knowledge Persons with learning disabilities lack knowledge and experience in conducting research, which may hinder the fulfilment of the project.	**Convincing practitioners** Students must assemble their own inclusive team. In doing so, they face support workers who are not convinced that such a project (i.e. inclusive research) can be interesting and informative for co-researcher, service users, and social work professionals.	**Experiencing new social valued roles**	**Parallel insights** Through inclusive projects students gained insights into their own attitude and behaviour as a support worker in training. The inclusive projects thus acted as a mirror.
	Dealing with hurtful situations Students share knowledge from scientific sources with the team members with learning disabilities. What the books say about people with learning disabilities is not always flattering or may even be insulting for the persons with learning disabilities. Still, the university student needs to address this knowledge, too. This evokes hurtful situations. Assembling an inclusive team. Finding persons with learning disabilities who are interested and willing to invest time and effort. Equal input in collaborative reflection student and life-expert.	**Opening new perspectives** Expanding lifeworld	**Understanding comprehensive concepts** Better understanding of comprehensive concepts such as inclusion, equality, empowerment, emancipatory practice.

400

degree minor to the major curriculum to guarantee a sustainable incorporation of experience-based knowledge of persons with learning disabilities throughout the whole curriculum.

Literature

Anderson, J.H. and Philips, J.P.M. (eds.) (2012). *Disability and Universal Human Rights: Legal, Ethical, and Conceptual Implications of the Convention on the Rights of Persons with Disabilities*. SIM Special Issue 35. Utrecht.

Askheim, O.P., Beresford, P. and Heule, C. (2018). Mend the gap – strategies for user involvement in social work education. In McLaughlin, H., Duffy, J., McKeever, B. and Sadd, J. (eds.), *Service User Involvement in Social Work Education*, 151–163. London: Routledge.

Bielefeldt, H. (2009). *Zum Innovationspotenzial der UN-Behindertenrechts-konvention*. Berlin: Deutsches Institut für Menschenrechte.

Biholar, R. (2014). *Moving from Formal to Substantive Equality. Challenging the Barriers to Real Equality: Transformative Equality. Annual Gathering of the Group of Women Parliamentarians*. Mexico City, June 24–25. www.parlamericas.org/uploads/documents/article-ramona-biholar-en.pdf

Borkman, T. (1976). Experiential knowledge: A new concept for the analysis of self-help groups. *Social Service Review*, 50(3), 445–456.

Caron-Flinterman, F., Broerse, J.E.W. and Bunders, J.F.G. (2005). The experiential knowledge of patients: A new resource for biomedical research? *Social Science & Medicine*, 60(11), 2575–2584.

Charity Commission (2001). *The Promotion of Social Inclusion*. London: Charity Commission.

Degener, T. (2016). Disability in a human rights context. *Laws*, 5(3), 35.

Degener, T. and Koster-Dreese, Y. (eds.) (1995). *Human Rights and Disabled Persons: Essays and Relevant Human Rights Instruments*. Dordrecht: Nijhoff.

Driessens, K. and De Clerck, W. (2014). Ervaringsdeskundigen als tandempartners in hogeschoolopleidingen (experts by experience as tandem partners in professional bachelor programmes in University Colleges). *Welwijs*, 25, 30–33.

Driessens, K., McLaughlin, H. and Van Doorn, L. (2018). The meaningful involvement of service users in social work education: Examples from Belgium and the Netherlands. In McLaughlin, H., Duffy, J., McKeever, B. and Sadd J. (eds.), *Service User Involvement in Social Work Education*, 138–150. Abingdon: Routledge.

Driessens, K. and Van Regenmortel, T. (2006). *Bind-Kracht in Armoede. Leefwereld en Hulpverlening*. Leuven: LannooCampus.

Fredman, S., Campbell, M., Atrey, S., Brickhill, J., Ramalekana, N. and Samtani, S. (2016). *Achieving Transformative Equality for Persons with Disabilities: Submission to the CRPD Committee for General Comment No. 6 on Article 5 of the UN Convention on the Rights of Persons with Disabilities*. Oxford Human Rights Hub. University of Oxford.

Gijzel, S. van (2017). *Met veilig vallen en samen opstaan; masterthesis*. Amsterdam: HvA.

Goldschmidt (2012). Shifting the Burden of proof: How the CRPD is transforming our understanding of discrimination, intersectionality, and priorities. In Anderson, J. and Philips, J. (eds.), *Disability and Universal Human Rights: Legal, Ethical, and Conceptual Implications of the Convention on the Rights of Persons with Disabilities*. SIM Special Issue 35. Utrecht.

Graumann (2012). Resolving the Tension between Equality and Difference: Towards a New Understanding of Discrimination. In Anderson, J. and Philips, J. (eds.), *Disability and Universal Human Rights: Legal, Ethical, and Conceptual Implications of the Convention on the Rights of Persons with Disabilities*. SIM Special Issue 35. Utrecht.

Groutars, G., Schipper, N. and Tilburg, H.v. (2015). *Ervaringswerk; handreiking ervaringswerk in revalidatiecentra en bij organisaties voor mensen met een verstandelijke beperking*. Amsterdam: VakVereniging voor Ervaringswerkers.

Harnacke and Graumann (2012). Core principles of the UN convention on the rights of persons with disabilities: An overview. In Anderson, J. and Philips, J. (eds.), *Disability and Universal Human Rights: Legal, Ethical, and Conceptual Implications of the Convention on the Rights of Persons with Disabilities*. SIM Special Issue 35. Utrecht.

Heule, C., Knutagård, M. and Kristiansen, A. (2017). Mending the gaps in social work education and research: Two examples from a Swedish context. *European Journal of Social Work*. 396–408.

Hove, G. van (2015). *Gewoon Bijzonder: Nationaal Programma Gehandicapten. Bijlage 5: Inclusief/Participatief onderzoek (werkpakket C)*. ZonMW/VUmc/LFB.

Jones, B.F., Rasmussen, C.M. and Moffitt, M.C. (1997). *Real-life Problem Solving: A Collaborative Approach to Interdisciplinary Learning*. Washington, DC: American Psychological Association.

Kal, D., Post, R. and Scholtens, G. (2012). *Meedoen gaat niet vanzelf: kwartiermaken in theorie en praktijk*. Amsterdam: Tobi Vroegh.

Knevel, J. and Wilken, J.P. (2015). *Inclusie, (on)gewoon doen!* Utrecht/Amersfoort: Kenniscentrum Sociale Innovatie.

Knevel, J. and Wilken, J.P. (2016). Zo werk je Inclusiegericht: Het recht op meedoen en meetellen. *In Sozio*, (2).

McLaughlin, H., Duffy, J., McKeever, B. and Sadd, J. (2018). *Service User Involvement in Social Work Education*, 1st ed. Abingdon: Routledge.

National Institute for Learning Disabilities (2009). *All We Want to Say: Life in Ireland for People with Learning Disabilities Report*. Dublin: Trinity University.

Nicki Ward, Christian Raphael, Matthew Clark & Vicki Raphael (2016) Involving people with profound and multiple learning disabilities in social work education: Building inclusive practice. *Social Work Education*, 35(8), 918–932.

Sabatello, M. and Schulze, M. (eds.) (2014). *Human Rights and Disability Advocacy*. Philadelphia: University of Pennsylvania Press.

Schuurman, M. and Nass, G. (2015). Mensen met verstandelijke beperkingen in de Wmo: verheldering van concepten en handelingsmogelijkheden. *NTZ*, 3, 244–251.

Stein, M.A (2010). Monitoring the convention on the rights of persons with disabilities: Innovations, lost opportunities, and future potential. *Human Rights Quarterly*, 31. https://ssrn.com/abstract=1533482

Thomas, J.W., Mergendoller, J.R. and Michaelson, A. (1999). *Project-based Learning: A Handbook for Middle and High School Teachers*. Novato, CA: The Buck Institute for Education.

United Nations (2006). *United Nations Convention on the Rights of Persons with Disabilities (UN CRPD)*. New York: United Nations.

Vansevenant, K., Driessens, K. and Van Regenmortel, T. (2008). *Bind-Kracht in Armoede. Krachtgerichte hulpverlening in dialoog*. Leuven: LannooCampus.

Verbrugge, C.J.J.M. and Embregts, P.J.C.M. (2013). *Een opleiding ervaringsdeskundigheid voor mensen met een verstandelijke beperking*. Tilburg: Prismaprint.

Walmsley, J. (2001). Normalisation, emancipatory research and inclusive research in learning disability. *Disability & Society*, 16(2), 187–205.

Walmsley, J. and Johnson, K. (2003). *Inclusive Research with People with Learning Disabilities: Past, Present and Futures*. London: Jessica Kingsley.

Ward, N., Raphael, C., Clark, M. & Raphael, V. (2016). Involving people with profound and multiple learning disabilities in social work education: Building inclusive practice. *Social Work Education*, 35(8), 918–932.

Weele, E. van (2012). The UN convention on the rights of persons with disabilities in the context of human rights law. In Anderson, J. and Philips, J. (eds.), *Disability and Universal Human Rights: Legal, Ethical, and Conceptual Implications of the Convention on the Rights of Persons with Disabilities*. SIM Special Issue 35. Utrecht.

Wilken, J.P. and Knevel, J. (2016). Werken aan inclusie. Lessen uit zeven proeftuinen. *Nederlands Tijdschrift voor de Zorg aan mensen met een verstandelijke beperking*, 42(3), 182–195.

Wilken, J.P. et al. (2020). *The Community of Development. A Model for Learning, Research and Innovation*. Submitted for publication.

37

HOW CAN WE SURVIVE
AND THRIVE AS SURVIVOR[1]
RESEARCHERS?

Jacqui Lovell-Norton, Konstantina (Dina) Poursanidou,
Karen Machin, Stephen Jeffreys and Holly Dale

(ALL AUTHORS ARE MEMBERS OF THE SURVIVOR RESEARCHER NETWORK
[SRN] WORKING GROUP IN THE UK)

Introduction

This chapter documents the impact of undertaking research-related activities asking the over-arching question, 'How can we survive and thrive as survivor researchers?' A brief summary of the Survivor Researcher Network (SRN) is given and the impact of the current context of *austerity* in the *United Kingdom* (UK) outlined. Following this, the 4Pi National Involvement Standards (4Pi-NIS) developed by the National Survivor User Network (NSUN) (2015) act as the starting point in this critical reflection. The addition of further P's to the 4Pi-NIS relating to issues of privilege, power, parity and progression in survivor-led research processes are discussed. In addition, a number of autoethnographic[2] poems, collectively known as *Expanded I poems* (Lovell, 2017), are interspersed throughout the body of the text to support the issues raised, placing lived experience firmly at the top of the hierarchy of evidence presented. Building on Gilligan et al.'s (2003) voice-centred relational data analysis process, the poems are constructed from our spoken words to foster critical reflection across personal (I), interpersonal (you), objectified (it), group (we) and community (they) levels of experience. These *Expanded I poems* function as an 'alternative performance' (Madison, 2006, p. 322) to both explore and illustrate issues raised in aiming to 'resist the repetitive and hegemonic[3] power to reinscribe identity and value'. Our hope in doing so is to heighten readers' awareness of the systemic and other changes needed for us to both survive and thrive as survivor researchers. This is of critical importance when working with and indeed in the current hierarchical neoliberal societies in which we reside and over which we have little or, more often than not, no control. Four projects are described that reflect resistance in action, including: MaDCaff and their peer-led performance cafes in community spaces across Wales; the democratisation of knowledge in commissioning services; decolonising history through play production; and crit-walking with White privilege and supremacy in youth education. Lastly, we outline our intention to remain 'in difficulty' (Maileo, 2017, n.p.) with ourselves in relation to our 'Whiteliness'[4] (Tate and Page, 2018, p. 141) and other areas of intersectional inequity as SRN members. We commence with a discussion of equality as it relates to SRN and the impact a sustained period of austerity has had upon diverse disabled people residing in the UK.

The Survivor Researcher Network (SRN)

SRN aims to support researchers of varying genders (including people who identify as non-binary); ethnicities; sexualities; ages; disabilities; classes; cultures; and beliefs. SRN does so to challenge the marginalisation of individuals and communities in mental *health*[5] research in relation to access to resources, participation and leadership. SRN does this through promoting evidence based on lived experience as fundamental not only to the knowledge base of mental *health* but also to human rights and social justice. SRN challenges the current hierarchy of knowledge that exists in mental *health* research, and promotes alternatives to dominant models drawing on the social model of disability (Oliver, 2013), madness and distress (Beresford et al., 2016) in doing so. As Cohen (2016, p. 210) critically stated 'as neoliberalism has infected higher education, research on "mental *health* issues" in the academy has become increasingly conservative' (italics added). SRN are aware of the need to

> think critically about the mental health system, to be able to challenge the work of the psy-professions, to interrogate meaningfully the production of knowledge claims on 'mental disease,' and to adequately contextualise the expansion of the psychiatric discourse with reference to theoretical sets of ideas which refer to labelling, power, and social control.
>
> *(Cohen, 2016, p. 210)*

A number of National Survivor User Network (NSUN) and Survivor Research Network (SRN) members past and present have been prolific in these areas, including Beresford (2003, 2007, 2019), Carr (2005, 2014, 2016), Faulkner (2004), Kalathil (2008, 2009, 2011), Lovell (2017), Lovell and Akhurst (2015, 2018) and Rose and Kalathil (2019). In 2013, SRN conducted a survey[6] of 46 NSUN members, who expressed an interest in research to aid in the development of its aims, objectives and planned work. These include providing people who have used mental health services and survivors of mental distress interested in or undertaking research with a forum for networking and information sharing and a space within which to enact our shared values through mutual support, of especial importance in the current climate of economic austerity.

Neoliberalism and austerity

Recovery in the Bin (RITB) (2019, n.p.) describe neoliberalism as 'the dominant ideology of many major governments around the world. Its "holy trinity" is deregulation, privatisation and the cutting of social provision'. According to the World Social Forum (WSF) (2015, n.p.), the current '*crisis* in health and social *care* and *protection*[7] is a direct consequence of global neoliberal politics' (italics added). With the (WSF, 2015, n.p.) 'major burden of the current crisis being faced by those people already marginalised namely women, children, migrants, the poor, people living with disabilities, workers and peasants'. WSF position health as a fundamental human right that is effectively denied to growing numbers of people worldwide. More recently, Philip Alston, the United Nations Human Rights Council Special Rapporteur, undertook a mission to the UK to review the situation in relation to both extreme poverty and human rights. Alston[8] (2019) reported that despite being the world's fifth largest economy, of the approximately 66 million people who live in the UK, almost one-fifth (approx. 14 million people) live in poverty, roughly one-tenth of whom (1.5 million people) experienced destitution in 2017. This includes people across all age groups. Alston (2019, p. 4) noted that 'Government reforms have often denied benefits to people with severe disabilities and pushed them into unsuitable work', while mental health *care* has 'deteriorated dramatically' as

> austerity policies have deliberately gutted local authorities and thereby effectively eliminated many social services . . . closed libraries in record numbers, shrunk community and youth centres, and sold off public spaces and buildings including parks and recreation centres. It is hardly surprising that civil society has reported unheard-of levels of loneliness and isolation . . . [t]he bottom line is that much of the glue that has held British society together since the Second World War has been deliberately removed and replaced with a harsh and uncaring ethos.

Indeed, disabled people (Ryan, 2019) under the current *austerity regime* are economically impacted at a proportion that is between 9 and 19[9] times greater than average. Suicide rates (ONS,[10] 2019) have risen accordingly. A current campaign led by NSUN[11] (2019) highlights the value of user-led groups, recognising how many groups have already closed. This further increases the social isolation of disabled people. As Cummins (2018, n.p.) concluded, the politics of *austerity* has increased 'the overall burden of mental distress and marginalisation within the UK'. This is the context within which NSUN and the Survivor Researcher Network (SRN) are located.

NSUN's 4Pi principles of involvement

SRN draws on the 4Pi National Involvement Standards (4Pi-NIS) (NSUN, 2015, p. 1) to support 'meaningful involvement' in survivor research. Organisations utilising these standards commit to 'valuing the contribution of service users and carers equally to those of professionals'. SRN does so to support survivor research with 'a diversity of service users and carers . . . involved at all levels and all stages of an organisation or project'. NSUN (2015, p. 1) proposed that collectively working to enact the 4Pi-NIS has the potential to 'improve outcomes for all'. There are, however, some concerns (Thompson and Machin, forthcoming) that survivor research can be co-opted

> into 'public and patient involvement' by the NHS, academia and large corporate mental health charities. User involvement and 'co-production' initiatives are conceptually very different to survivor research where people with lived experience are creating their own knowledge and theories, . . . People with lived experience are now more likely to be included in research studies through 'co-production' initiatives and can make a valuable contribution, but often the research that is produced continues to reflect one narrow perspective.

Thompson and Machin (forthcoming) suggest it is time to explore how 4Pi-NIS are used in co-productive and co-creative purposes. As Brosnan (2012, p. 45) observes, 'power is all pervasive within mental health services yet often overlooked in official discourse on user-involvement'. Therefore, it would be useful to know (Thompson and Machin, forthcoming) if organisations signed up to 4Pi-NIS have merely undertaken the minimum or threshold standard of involvement,

> with few [organisations] having moved beyond minimum recommended payments and no differentiation between the different levels of expertise brought to the role,

either from lived experience of distress, previous experiences of involvement, or the relevant expertise and skills of the person or group.

SRN further suggest it may be useful to reflect on the P's of privilege, power, parity and progression to reflect the complexity of survivor research involvement. We do so, asking the following questions:

1   What actions can we take (from our location in the Northern hemisphere) within our praxis[12] to reflect lived experience of mental distress as survivor researchers? [Privilege]
2   What power within the research process, including the allocation of resources, do survivor researchers have? [Power]
3   What are the support needs of survivor researchers? [Parity]
4   What actions can we take to challenge inequity in mental *health* research? [Parity]
5   What are the opportunities for survivor researchers? [Progression]
6   What opportunities should and could there be? [Progression]

It is necessary, however, to take a broader view than that offered within the (Grande, 2004; Rose and Kalathil, 2019) Westernised medical model with its Cartesian duality of mind and body. This approach led to a hierarchical distinction with 'thoughts' (as opposed to feelings, spirituality and other embodied experiences) and cognition dominating fields of enquiry including mental *health*. Focusing on White Western privilege and this epistemic injustice, we ask:

1   What actions can we take (from our location in the Northern hemisphere) within our praxis to reflect lived experience of mental distress as survivor researchers?

Privilege

Strega (2005, p. 214), an Indigenous researcher, reminds us that as White Western people (albeit people who have experienced oppression), the differential benefits of privilege within the current system confer power over the process, asking 'what epistemology, what methodology, will allow us to speak truth to the power of White men's dominance?' Strega (2005, p. 199) concludes that

> for researchers concerned with social justice, the answers represent not just methodological choices, but choices about resistance and allegiance to the hegemony[13] of Eurocentric thought and research traditions – the master's tools.

DiAngelo (2011) suggests that 'if whites cannot engage with an exploration of alternate racial perspectives, they can only reinscribe white perspectives as universal'. We agree with Grande (2004) and Cohen (2016) that Indigenous and critical research can form a resistance to hegemony. Freire and Macedo (1995, p. 381) raised the need for a 'unity' between theory and practice, coupled with 'epistemological curiosity' about what can be known. Freire (1970, p. 126) further contends 'a theory of transforming action . . . cannot fail to assign the people a fundamental role in the transformation process'. Although Cornish (2004, p. 30) cautions:

> when there are few, if any, avenues through which to take action on those structures, to recognise the powerful societal sources of one's disadvantage may be experienced as profoundly disempowering rather than as empowering. That is, reflection is not always liberation.

hooks (1990, p. 147) observed in critical theory that 'there is an effort to remember that is expressive of the need to create spaces where one is able to redeem and reclaim the past legacies of pain, suffering and triumph in ways that transform present reality'. Indeed, the realities that exist for Black, disabled, Mad, crip and spoonie[14] people and people of differing sexualities, ethnicities and genders, including people who identify as non-binary, certainly need transforming. It is easy to see how the tasks we need to *perform* grow daily in the face of kyriarchy and the White privileged, neoliberal, capitalist, ableist, racist, sexist, anti-feminist, heterosexist, classist, ageist, supremacist people, spaces and places that proliferate in our world (Lovell, 2015). It is in the *performance* of survivor research that we explore 'what is possible', understanding that

> our research practices are *performative*, pedagogical, and political. Through our writing and our talk, we enact the worlds we study. These *performances* are messy and pedagogical. They instruct our readers about this world and how we see it. The pedagogical is always moral and political; by enacting a way of seeing and being, it challenges, contests, or endorses the official, hegemonic ways of seeing and representing the *other*.
>
> *(Denzin, 2006, p. 422; italics added)*

Including our voices in the form of *Expanded I poems* that re-present our lived experience challenges hegemonic ways of seeing and representing people who experience mental distress as *other*.

Extract from I poem 1

I wasn't doing
my job properly
I felt like
I was honour bound to resign erm
as a result of where
I was at the time, I mean
my mental distress was on the ceiling
I was all over the place
I lost the capacity to read and to
process information and then
I really struggled with that

Extract from I poem 5

my, my attitude towards
my mental distress and my
my mental health service use and also
my being a service user researcher has

got a lot of ambivalence in
me that can see how
my experiential knowledge and
me that wishes that
I never had anything to do with all
I've lost because of all the trauma and so . . .
What was the question again?

Extract from We poem 1

for service user researchers in particular
because of our gaps in
our CV's because of for example
not having the publications
we could have had if
we didn't have all these breaks in
our employment trajectory
we don't start in the same sort of place
our mental health fluctuates
we can't be as productive

As survivor researchers, we struggle to sustain ourselves not only in our roles but also with the trauma and loss that result from lived experience of mental distress. Madison (2006), however, contests that when the focus is the self, as is often the case, we individualise and do nothing to incentivise calls for the 'dialogical performative . . . to widen the door of our caravan and to clear more space for Others to enter and ride' (p. 321). As Madison (2006, p. 322) stated, doing so requires 'a reinvigoration of our thinking about the Other that takes shape through a multiplicity of what is possible'. Indeed, Madison (2006, p. 322; italics added), referring to Bhabha (1994) and Dolan (1993), links

> the *performative* to the punctum, a break in the flow of expectation that resists the repetitive and hegemonic power to reinscribe identity and value. The performative is a *subversive performativity* that opens up the possibility for *alternative performances* and alternative citations.

This *alternative performance* reflects our voices and the centrality of our individual and collective lived experience and *acts* as a means to challenge the production of knowledge within mainstream mental *health* research. Our second question therefore asks:

2 What *power* within the research process, including the allocation of resources, do survivor researchers have?

Power

Table 37.1 outlines the experiences and skills of the 46 people who responded[15] to a survey of SRN members' involvement in and experience of the research process (SRN, 2013). Showing the diversity of experience and skills of people, it also indicates an inequity in respondents' experience of peer review and research ethics committees; teaching of research methodology; training researchers; and project management.

This was despite over 50% of respondents documenting they have the skills to involve people from under-represented groups and communities; design research; advise research teams; write research reports; and analyse quantitative and qualitative data. No questions relating to survivor researcher involvement in decisions on the allocation of mental *health* research funding were included. The questions we don't ask are often as important as those we do. Does this absence of questions signify a resignation on the part of survivor researchers of ever being involved; or

Table 37.1 Information taken from SRN's Members' Survey Summary (2013, p.2)

Experiences and skills of respondents	
Serving on peer review and research ethics committees	9%
Teaching research methodology	17%
Training researchers	28%
Project managing research	33%
Conducting literature reviews	48%
Involving marginalised groups in research (reaching out to people normally overlooked by mainstream research)	52%
Designing research (e.g., writing proposals, preparing research tools)	52%
Advising research teams	54%
Writing research reports	57%
Analysing data (quantitative or qualitative)	57%
Participating in research as research subjects (participants)	65%
Conducting research (e.g., interviewing, doing surveys)	74%

does it reflect existing exclusion from this aspect of research *involvement* process? Or both? Or are other factors involved?

Most recently, the National Institute for Health Research (NIHR) and INVOLVE[16] (2019, p. 1) produced a list of prompts for researchers planning public *involvement* in health research that includes:

> checking your power; valuing the people you work with; using language carefully; considering inclusive locations; listening and seeking agreement; getting from A to B perhaps via Z; collaboration; investment in the workforce; commitment to a relationship; evidencing, evaluating, sharing and reflecting on the research involvement process; while acting small and thinking big

and lastly, 'being values based and socially innovative supporting the ideas of the diverse and the many, not the few'.

It is noted, however, that survivor researchers operating outside of the academy are currently excluded from leading research funding applications to NIHR. It appears diversity doesn't extend to *all* of 'the many', just the chosen and academically approved 'few'. Perhaps NIHR need to reflect on and take account of their own 'prompts' when working to *involve* survivor researchers. While funders like NIHR fail to adequately recognise and share resources, survivor-led researchers are denied equitable parity of opportunity to participate. In addition, NIHR exclude survivor researchers holding doctorates from involvement as peer reviewers in a 'lay person' capacity, even if your doctorate was undertaken as a survivor researcher. One assumes having a doctorate makes the person just too much of an 'expert by experience'. This is despite principles of involvement being enshrined within the Department of Health's (2005a) Research Governance Framework. There exists a lack of reciprocity in the involvement process that is reflected in the disparity of inclusion of survivor researchers. According to Cook et al. (2011, p. 25) 'relationships need to be reciprocal for change to happen'. We therefore ask the question,

3   What are the support needs of survivor researchers?

Parity

Extract from I poem 6

I don't think
I will ever do anything more difficult than
I couldn't believe the kinds of
childhood some of
I was like being exposed to
I mean, I remember going home and
feeling knackered because absorbing all
I mean very, very severely
I mean attempting suicide

Extract from It poem 6

it's the secondary trauma isn't
it like being er because

in all the pieces of work
that in particular and all this
it was part of a programme
very intensive ethnography
that was very difficult, very challenging
that, that was,
that was secondary trauma
that was well
that was very traumatic to be part of . . .

Extract from I poem 9

I think what
I would have wanted was perhaps some
*   mentoring for*

me to be able to erm progress with	I would be doing the project,
publications and	my research idea
also with getting funding research funding so	I wrote the proposal
I can do my own project	I worked for the whole summer to get,
I can do my own research.	some erm, because
I had a research idea that	I needed to have
I worked on but in order to apply for money	I did a lot of work trying to get
I could apply for money to do and	I did not submit it

Potts and Brown (2005) describe power and knowledge as intrinsically relational and political, enacted in relationships between people with the potential to be both oppressive or resistant and note 'often it is a complex combination of both'. Further, they observe that

> knowledge does not exist in and of itself, isolated from people. Rather, it is produced through the interactions of people, and as all people are socially located in race, gender, ability, class identities, and so on with biases, privileges, and differing power relations, so too is the creation of knowledge socially located, socially constructed. Recognizing that knowledge is socially constructed means understanding that knowledge doesn't exist 'out there' but is embedded in people and the power relations between us.
>
> *(p. 261)*

Disparity

The disparity of experience in survivor research in relation to people from a range of ethnicities, sexualities, ages, disabilities and genders (or none) has a long his-story in the National Health Service (National Institute for Mental Health in England [NIMHE], 2003), despite calls for reform in mental *health* care *for* people from diverse ethnic backgrounds. Indeed, 'integration' of 'knowledge of BME community service providers' was supposed to support development both 'inside the mental health system and outside' (DoH, 2005b, p. 59) and led to the development of a Delivering Race Equality (DRE) Action Plan (DoH, 2005b). This ill-fated *plan* blamed the communities it aimed to serve, suggesting they needed to be more *engaged* while not recognising how engaged they already were. Evidence, however, suggested *institutional racism* within services would likely impact upon DRE (Hackett, 2008). Rather than focus inwardly on institutional racism, the DoH cites a 'lack of good evidence of effective services and strategies as a barrier to improving the mental *health* of BME groups' (Department of Health [DoH], 2005b, p. 65; emphasis added). Despite DoH rhetoric, there was an unwillingness to undertake research or evaluation of services from the diverse perspectives of people using them (Sainsbury Centre for Mental Health [SCMH], 2005). In addition, 2005 heralded changes through the formation of a National Mental Health Research Network. This research network in mental *health* supports large randomised controlled trials as the 'gold standard' (DoH, 2005a). It seems, far from loosening its grip on research, the establishment further entrenched mental *health* research within it. Kalathil (2008, p. 1) noted that 'Black and *Minority*[17] Ethnic (BME) service user research is stuck between a rock and a hard place', with 'very little opportunity to explore issues that we want to explore'. Kalathil (2009, p. 12) added, 'consultation is not involvement', suggesting that

> if there has to be meaningful involvement of service users/survivors from black and minority ethnic communities in mainstream initiatives, there has to be structural changes in hierarchies, ways of working, assumptions, power structures within

institutions, resource allocation, the location of decision making, and the way people are treated within mental health services and outside them.

As previously, we draw on the summary of SRN's survey of members (Table 37.2) to assist in answering our question, rightly recognising its limitations (Kalathil, 2009).

Table 37.2 documents the percentage of respondents (SRN, 2013, p. 3) who want support from SRN in relation to different aspects of involvement in the research process. Demonstrating the *give and take* of reciprocity, some respondents anticipated contributing and participating in the network, strengthening survivor research through a range of activities, including 'bringing the experience of survivors from marginalised communities into mainstream survivor research'. Surprisingly, this vital aspect of involvement was under-represented, with only two respondents saying there was a need for survivor researchers' specific contribution and they were interested in contributing to developing knowledge, experience and interest in this area. This was despite over half of respondents recognising that 'involving marginalised groups in research' was one of their areas of expertise. There are other aspects to this process, however, including the impact of undertaking survivor research on us as individuals and the lack of mentorship available illustrated by extracts from 'They poems' presented below.

Extract from They poem 1

they designed this post erm
as part of the application
they hadn't thought about support
they thought that
they would just throw somebody in there and
the person would cope
they bullied people, they bullied me,
they have bullied others

Extract from They poem 2

all researchers are faced with,
as others because of
they would want to keep
they didn't find the funds but
they wanted to find funds as
they did with other people that
they would have found the funds

In acknowledging all of the above, we ask further questions, including:

4   What actions can we take to challenge and reduce inequity in survivor research?
5   What are the opportunities for survivor researchers?

Table 37.2 Information taken from SRN's Members' Survey Summary (2013, p. 3)

Support and opportunities expected	
Networking with other researchers	83%
Opportunities for collaboration	83%
A forum for discussion	78%
Opportunities for research work	78%
Finding funding for research	74%
Help with specific research projects	72%
Skills development opportunities	70%
Training in research methodologies	67%
Presentations of research work	52%
Delivering training on research	50%

Extract from I poem 10

I think
I'm struggling with some of the issues,
where do
I go and who am
I gonna ally myself to?
I've been looking around
I could slide into
feeling like well
I was, when
I was saying well look
I've got my PhD but what use is it,
what use if I'm not actually putting
I got it, I mean just the fact that

for me, me as an individual getting that PhD
I mean it took
researcher roles are all doing things that
I really don't have an investment in doing
     because
I no longer believe in

Extract from We poem 2

where do we go
for us to be on an equal par
with each other when
we're doing the work and trying to find
someone who will go along with
our bottom up style of working

Progression

Galeano (1977, p. 19; italics authors) reminds us

> *we are what we do, and above all what we do to change what we are*: our identity lies in action and struggle. That is why the revelation of what we are implies denunciation of what prevents us being what we can be.

While Moiloa (2017, n.p.), drawing on Galeano, suggests that through our writing and literature we 'attempt disruption, to find a place of unease' that (Galeano, 1977, p. 20) 'does not set out to bury its own dead, but to perpetuate them; which refuses to clear up the ashes and tries on the contrary to light the fire'. For as hooks (1990, p. 146) stated, 'language is also a place of struggle. The oppressed struggle in language to renew ourselves, to reconcile, to reunite, to renew. Our words are not without meaning, they are an action, a resistance'. What follows are some practical examples of resistance in action across a range of fields; all, however, share a broad focus on the recognition of lived experience and aim to support people who have experienced mental distress using a range of mediums and media.

Example 1: Mad people, spaces, places and performances

MaDCaff[18] provides a place for all people with lived experience of mental distress who share an interest in music, dance, poetry and prose to perform through community-based, 'pressure-free' performance cafes for musicians, dancers, groups and anyone affected by mental illness[19] to have a friendly place to meet interesting people in order to 'end unnecessary stigmas'. Originally funded by Time to Change Wales and Disability Arts Cymru, following their winning of an Epic Award (2015) and further funding from Voluntary Arts Week, they hosted events during Mental Health Arts Festivals in Wales throughout 2016 and 2017. In 2019, MaDCaff gained funding from Wales Community Voluntary Agency (WCVA) via a Volunteering in Wales grant. This supported them to establish a further seven groups. MaDCaff is evaluating their *performance* using mixed methods based on participatory evaluation approaches with a view to sustaining the work that they do into the future.

Example 2: knowledge democratisation in service provision

Walker et al. (2018, p. 759) undertook 'research straddling the boundary between academic inquiry and political activism [that] speaks to the many issues that are prevalent in the changing HE sector as well as NHS privatisation, health commissioning and public sector cuts'. Walker et al. (2018, pp. 763–764) recognise that 'margins and opportunities exist that allow room for manoeuvre toward the construction and implementation of alternative engagement practices'. In these spaces, communities can 'play a key role in balancing the rational pragmatics of cost control with forms of protest informed by the lived experiences of health outcomes'.

> Having developed the Brighton Citizen's Health Services Survey (BCHSS) this was utilised to 'explore and potentially challenge how knowledge is used and by whom in the production of local health commissioning institutions and relations'. The survey contained an 'animating set of questions' in order 'to open up spaces through which to make visible some of the ways of knowing and valuing the NHS and health services that had been minimised through the commensuration practices of post-2012 public engagement'. This democratisation of knowledge and the space that it opened were used to present varying 'health publics' facilitating further exploration to ultimately 'broaden participative engagement opportunities'.

Example 3: decolonising history

Journalist and playwright Satinder Chohan (2019) was one of five playwrights who took up residence in the History Department of the School of Oriental and African Studies (SOAS) in London. From an earlier reading of Urvashi Butalia's *The Other Side of Silence*, documenting oral histories and untold stories of partition survivors, Chohan (2019, n.p.) learned 'about the subcontinental holocaust of partition in more detail, through both its big and small players'. She reported being 'both fascinated and alarmed by Britain's collective historical amnesia'. As a result of her learning and experiences, Chohan developed an audio drama, entitled *Scar Tissue*, inspired by what she had found relaying the history of partition through the eyes of an elderly grandmother. Chohan suggests we recognise that 'crimes and wrongdoings have happened within families and nations and while we can't change them, we don't have to turn away from ugly, violent history out of ignorance, shame, guilt or denial'. Chohan views the *Decolonising History* project she was involved with as part of 'an attempt at a more honest, grown-up debate, so that we can learn more about who we all are and how we relate to one another, to our past and our future in 21st century Britain', adding, 'this is especially so in a Brexit Britain, overshadowed by Britain's "glorious" past in an amnesiac nation that has never dealt with its loss of empire – raising pressing questions for us all about how history should live today'.

Example 4: critwalking colonialism, imperialism and White privilege

Locke and Getachew (2019), through a process of 'critwalking', have utilised a 400-year historical timeline of slavery and White privilege as a form of critical pedagogy to pictorially document and share the history of White supremacy enacted across the United States of America (USA). This intervention effectively holds up pictures of the past through a range of media to White, predominantly middle-class educators. In addition, they share the history of legislation that was designed to protect the rights of people. In doing so, Locke and Getachew (2019, pp. 144–145) provide a

> 'bird's eye' view of the history of U.S. policies and practices that harm and marginalize individuals and groups, which exposes systemic, legal, and political systems that support White supremacy (rather than a focus on individual acts of racism), [that] illustrates the rootedness and intergenerationality of White supremacy and how it evolves and resurfaces.

When speaking of the education system in the United States, Locke and Getachew (2019, p. 144) are clear that those who need fixing are those with power in the schools – the teachers and leaders whose charge is the education of *all* students. What needs to be fixed is our view of lives and communities as ahistorical and unrelated to the racist and white supremacist history.

In light of all the above, we ask:

6   What opportunities for survivor research could there be?

The Reclaiming, Challenging and Reviving Survivor Research' Event (SRN, 2016, n.p.) created a space for researchers whose 'voices have not historically been present or included' to consider issues around survivor research, whiteness and heteronormativity',[20] with conversations led by people from BME and LGBT groups to ensure 'the inclusion of black and minority ethnic survivors' as participants and to invite people who were less familiar with SRN.[21] Recommendations and conclusions of relevance to this discussion include (SRN, 2016, n.p.):

• There is a real need to break patterns of oppression within and outside of survivor research. 'Whiteness' and 'straightness' continue to be constructed as universal and invisible. We need to acknowledge and openly address the racism and homophobia in our society.
• We all need to reflect on our own privilege, recognise our own racialisation and understand how we all contribute to oppressive systems in society. This might be difficult to do when we have been oppressed ourselves. But if real, lasting change is to take place, it cannot be the responsibility of people from racialised and LGB and T communities alone.

DiAngelo (2011, p. 55) recognised that 'white racial insulation is somewhat mediated by social class (with poor and working class urban whites being generally less racially insulated than suburban or rural whites)'. King et al. (2009, p. 40) remind us that

> despite extensive research into this [racism] and other aspects of potential discrimination in the assessment of mental health issues, little progress has been made . . . [o]ur experience suggests that this may well be because the critical issues are and remain, as one of us (CK) has graphically put it, masked by 'the theatre of theoretical indulgence'.

King (2016, p. 224) asks the question, 'How do we expose and challenge whiteness that has become the ghost of past theories that continues to fill the context of mental health settings?' This is one of the opportunities that SRN has to engage with the task of revealing its 'Whiteliness' (Tate & Page, 2018) within survivor histories. This process of learning about racism and the intersection with ableism, heteronormativity, sexism, classism and ageism is much needed if we are to reframe and decentre all forms of privilege. It is the application of this learning within our local contexts that would make the greatest difference to people who experience intersectional discrimination and the social isolation that mental distress and *austerity* bring. Recognising we need to be cautious of 'White fragility' (DiAngelo, 2011) and 'applause' Moiloa (2017) suggests we 'resolve to remain in difficulty with ourselves, to challenge our relevance head-on in the midst of those who question us and to deny again and again the right to feel comfortable – particularly in the imagining of easier, better worlds'. Our hope as SRN members is to do so in connection with people who have experienced mental distress, in the UK, Europe, Northern and Southern hemispheres, firm in our 'resolve to remain in difficulty with ourselves' in order to (SRN, 2016, n.p.) 'develop new, creative methodologies in this area that foreground user-generated experiential knowledge and address diversity and complexity as standard'.

Notes

1 Authors are aware of other terms such as service user, patient or client and adopt the term 'survivor' to position SRN politically as an organisation led and run by people who have attempted (and for some of us still are) to 'survive' mental distress and/or psychiatric services.

2 Ethnography (Merriam-Webster [online] 2019, n.p.) is defined as 'the study and systematic recording of human cultures and also a descriptive work produced from such research' (www.merriam-webster. com/dictionary/ethnography). Autoethnography is the application of this research process in relation to the self as a means of critically reflecting upon I/my/your/our lived experience.

3 Hegemony (Merriam-Webster [online], 2019, n.p.) as a concept is defined as 'the social, cultural, ideological, or economic influence exerted by a dominant group' (www.merriam-webster.com/dictionary/ hegemony#other-words).

4 'Whiteliness' is the term used by Tate and Page (2018) when discussing manifestations of 'hidden' institutional racism in White people.

5 Italics are used here to demonstrate the incompatibility of this statement given that SRN's perspective is far broader than the purely 'health' aspects of mental distress as per the social model of disability (Oliver, 2013).

6 SRN's Survey Report can be found at www.nsun.org.uk/FAQs/survivor-researcher-network-srn.

7 We use these words advisedly given their appropriation in the neoliberal agenda of domination and control.

8 The full UNHCR report can be found at http://ap.ohchr.org/documents/dpage_e.aspx?si=A/HRC/ 41/39/Add.1.

9 This figure is dependent upon the person and the degree to which the environment is disabling of them.

10 The Office of National Statistics (2019) in the UK found that 'in 2018 there were 6,507 suicides registered with an age-standardised rate of 11.2 deaths per 100,000 population; the latest rate is significantly higher than 2017 and represents the first increase since 2013. The UK male suicide rate of 17.2 deaths per 100,000 represents a significant increase from 2017. Three-quarters of registered deaths in 2018 were among men (4,903 deaths)'. Further info at www.ons.gov.uk/peoplepopulationandcommunity/ birthsdeathsandmarriages/deaths/bulletins/suicidesintheunitedkingdom/2018registrations.

11 For more information on NSUN's Importance of User Led Group Campaign, see here www.nsun.org. uk/faqs/the-value-of-user-led-groups-2019-campaign.

12 Praxis according to Merriam-Webster Dictionary [online] is defined as the 'exercise or practice of an art, science, or skill; customary practice or conduct; or practical application of a theory'. In this instance it refers to the practical application of theory in practice (www.merriam-webster.com/dictionary/praxis).

13 According to the Collins English Dictionary [online], hegemony 'is a situation in which one country, organisation, or group has more power, control, or importance than others' (www.collinsdictionary. com/dictionary/english/hegemony).

14 Spoonie is a term used by people who live with chronic conditions and relates to Miserandino's spoon theory, available at the following link: https://butyoudontlooksick.com/articles/written-by-christine/ the-spoon-theory/.

15 Initially 198 people were contacted, therefore the response rate was 23%. This is a ratio of approximately one person for every four people who were asked to complete the survey.

16 This guidance document was compiled by INVOLVE's Diversity and Inclusion Group and the National Institute for Health Research (NIHR). NIHR direct and inform the work of the Department of Health (DoH) in the UK, and INVOLVE are an organisation that support the involvement of *patients* across all areas of health.

17 Although Black people and people from many ethnic backgrounds account for the global majority, White Europeans continue to use this 'label' which, when shortened, erases the words Black and Ethnic. A similar process happens when we use labels such as LGBTQIi to represent people who identify as Lesbian, Gay, Bisexual, Trans, Queer, Intersex and interested. What this makes 'invisible' are those of us who may not 'fit' neatly into these 'labels'.

18 More information on MaDCaff is available at http://madcaff.rocks/.

19 The term illness is the term used by members of MaDCaff and as such it has not been altered.

20 Heteronormativity is a world view that promotes heterosexuality as the *normal* or preferred sexual orientation.

21 For further information about the planning of the event, please see the working group statement: www.nsun.org.uk/assets/downloadableFiles/SRN-July2016-STATEMENTSRNFINALVERSION22.pdf.

References

Alston, P. (2019) *Report of the Special Rapporteur on Extreme Poverty and Human Rights on His Visit to the United Kingdom of Great Britain and Northern Ireland.* Geneva: UN Human Rights Council. Retrieved from http://ap.ohchr.org/documents/dpage_e.aspx?si=A/HRC/41/39/Add.1

Beresford, P. (2003) *It's Our Lives: A Short Theory of Knowledge, Distance and Experience.* London: Citizens Press in Association with Shaping Our Lives.

Beresford, P. (2007) User involvement, research and health inequalities: Developing new directions. *Health and Social Care in the Community*, 15, 306–312.

Beresford, P. (2019) Including our self in struggle: Challenging the neo-liberal psycho-system's subversion of us, our ideas and action. *Canadian Journal of Disability Studies Special Issue Survivals, Ruptures, Resiliences: Perspectives from Disability Scholarship, Art and Activism*, 8, 31–59.

Beresford, P., Perring, R., Nettle, M. & Wallcraft, J. (2016) *From Mental Illness to a Social Model of Madness and Distress.* London: Citizens Press in Association with Shaping Our Lives.

Beresford, P. & Russo, J. (2016) Supporting the sustainability of mad studies and preventing its co-option. *Disability and Society*, 31, 270–274. Retrieved from http://dx.doi.org/10.1080/09687599.2016.1145380

Bhabha, H. K. (1994) *The Location of Culture.* New York: Routledge.

Brosnan, L. (2012) Power and participation: An examination of the dynamics of mental health service-user involvement in Ireland. *Studies in Social Justice*, 6, 45–66.

Carr, S. (2005) 'The sickness label infected everything we said': Lesbian and gay perspectives on mental distress. In J. Tew (Ed.), *Social Perspectives in Mental Health* (168–183). London: Jessica Kingsley Press.

Carr, S. (2014) Individual narrative and collective knowledge: Capturing lesbian, gay and bisexual service user experiences. In P. Staddon (Ed.), *Mental Health Service Users in Research: Critical Sociological Perspectives* (135–152). Bristol: Policy Press.

Carr, S. (2016) Narrative research and service user/survivor stories: A new frontier for research ethics? *Philosophy, Psychiatry and Psychology*, 23, 233–236.

Chohan, S. (2019, 11th Sept.) *Both Fascinated and Alarmed by Britain's Collective Historical Amnesia, I Had to Be Involved in a Project That Sought to Decolonise History.* [Online blog]. Tamasha Digital. Retrieved from https://tamashablog.wordpress.com/2019/09/11/both-fascinated-and-alarmed-by-britains-collective-historical-amnesia-i-had-to-be-involved-in-a-project-that-sought-to-decolonise-history/

Cooke, A., Friedli, L., Coggins, T., Edmonds, N., Michaelson, J., O'Hara, K., Snowden, L., Stansfield, J., Steuer, N. & Scott-Samuel, A. (2011) *The Mental Wellbeing Impact Assessment (MWIA)* (3rd ed.). London: National MWIA Collaborative.

Cohen, B. M. Z. (2016) *Psychiatric Hegemony: A Marxist Theory of Mental Illness.* London: Palgrave Macmillan.

Cornish, F. (2004) Making 'context' concrete: A dialogical approach to the society-health relation. *Journal of Health Psychology*, 9, 281–294. Retrieved from http://eprints.lse.ac.uk/47790/

Cummins, I. (2018) The impact of austerity on mental health service provision: A UK perspective. *International Journal of Environmental Research and Public Health*, 15, 1–11.

Denzin, N. (2006) Analytic autoethnography, or Déjà Vu all over again. *Journal of Contemporary Ethnography*, 35, 419–428.

Department of Health. (2005a) *Research Governance Framework for Health and Social Care* (2nd ed.). London: The Stationery Office.

Department of Health. (2005b) *Delivering Race Equality In Mental Health Care, an Action Plan for Reform Inside and Outside Services; and the Government's Response to the Independent Inquiry into the Death of David Bennett.* London: The Stationery Office.

DiAngelo, R. (2011) White fragility. *International Journal of Critical Pedagogy,* 3, 54–70. Retrieved from https://libjournal.uncg.edu/ijcp/article/viewFile/249/116

Dolan, J. (1993) Geographies of learning: Theatre studies, performance, and the performative. *Theatre Journal,* 45, 417–41.

Faulkner, A. (2004) *The Ethics of Survivor Research; Guidelines for the Ethical Conduct of Research Carried Out by Mental Health Service Users and Survivors.* Bristol: The Policy Press.

Freire, P. (1970) *Pedagogy of the Oppressed.* Harmondsworth: Penguin.

Freire, P. & Macedo, D.P. (1995) A dialogue: Culture, language and race. *Harvard Educational Review.* 65(3), 377–402.

Galeano, E. (1977) In defence of the word. *Index on Censorship* [Trans. Rowe, W.], 6, 15–20. Retrieved from https://journals.sagepub.com/doi/abs/10.1080/03064227708532670

Gilligan, C., Spencer, R., Weinberg, M. K. & Bertsch, T. (2003) On the listening guide a voice centered relational method. In P. M. Camic, J. E. Rhodes & L. Yardley (Eds.), *Qualitative Research in Psychology: Expanding Perspectives in Methodology and Design* (pp. 157–172). Washington, DC: American Psychological Association.

Grande, S. (2004) *Red Pedagogy: Native American Social and Political Thought.* New York: Rowman & Littlefield.

Hackett, R. (2008) Improving quality of mental health care for BME clients. *Nursing Times,* 104, 35–36.

hooks, b. (1990) *Yearning: Race, Gender, and Cultural Politics.* Boston, MA: South End Press.

Kalathil, J. (2008) *Mapping User-Controlled Research in BME Mental Health Observations for the INVOLVE Project.* [Online]. Retrieved from www.survivor-research.com/images/documents/observations%20 for%20involve%20project.pdf

Kalathil, J. (2009) *Dancing to Our Own Tunes: Reassessing Black and Minority Ethnic Mental Health Service User Involvement.* London: National Service User Network (NSUN), The Afiya Trust.

Kalathil, J. (2011) *Dancing to Our Own Tunes: Reassessing Black and Minority Ethnic Mental Health Service User Involvement: Reprint of the 2008 Report with a Review of Work Undertaken to Take the Recommendations Forward.* London: NSUN.

King, C. (2016) Whiteness in psychiatry: The madness of European misdiagnoses. In J. Russo & A. Sweeney (Eds.), *Searching for a Rose Garden* (69–76). Monmouth: PCCS Books.

King, C., Fulford, B., Williamson, T., Dhillon, K. & Vasiliou-Theodore, C. (2009) *Model Values? Race, Values and Models in Mental Health.* London: Mental Health Foundation.

Locke, L. A. & Getachew, E. (2019) Understanding stubborn inequities: A critical lesson in history. *International Journal of Critical Pedagogy,* 10, 127–153.

Lovell, J. (2015) *To PhD or not to PhD That Is the Question, the Process and the Answer?* [Online]. Retrieved from http://jacquiluvslife.blogspot.co.uk/2015/08/to-phd-or-not-to-phd-that-is-question_42.html

Lovell, J. (2017) *So What's Changed? Participatory Action Research Through Which Diverse Members Co-Evaluate Their Community Organisation to Creatively Document Their Experiences and Outcomes.* PhD Thesis. Retrieved from http://etheses.whiterose.ac.uk/18274/1/So%20Whats%20Changed%20Jacqui%20 Lovell%201.08.2017.pdf

Lovell, J. & Akhurst, J. (2015) Financial capability considered from a community psychology-informed process in the North East of England. In S. M. Değirmencioğlu & C. Walker (Eds.), *Social and Psychological Dimensions of Personal Debt and the Debt Industry.* (180–202). London: Palgrave Macmillan.

Lovell, J. & Akhurst, J. (2018) The dilemmas of a participatory action research process evaluating a community cooperative: Whose party was this? In C. Macleod, J. Marx, P. Mnyaka & G. Treharne (Eds.), *Handbook of Ethics in Critical Research: Stories from the Field.* Basingstoke: Palgrave Macmillan.

Madison, S. (2006) The dialogic performative in critical ethnography. *Text and Performance Quarterly,* 26, 320–324.

Moiloa, M. (2017) Remaining in difficulty with ourselves. In T. Kurgan & T. Murinik (Eds.), *Wide Angle.* [Online]. Johannesburg, South Africa: Goethe-Institute, Wits School of Arts and the Market Photo Workshop. Retrieved from http://fourthwallbooks.com/wp-content/uploads/2015/08/Wide-Angle_Final.pdf

National Institute for Health Research [NIHR]/INVOLVE. (2019) *Being Inclusive in Public Involvement (PI) in Health Research: Things to Think About for Researchers and Practitioners.* London: NIHR/INVOLVE, Manchester University NHS Foundation Trust.

National Institute for Mental Health in England [NIMHE]. (2003) *Inside Outside: Improving Mental Health Services for Black and Minority Ethnic Communities in England.* Leeds: National Institute for Mental Health in England.

National Survivor User Network. (2015) *4Pi National Involvement Standards: Involvement for Influence.* London: National Involvement Partnership. Retrieved from www.nsun.org.uk/Handlers/Download. ashx?IDMF=995617f8-1cd7-40af-8128-5eaaf2953b8e

Office of National Statistics (2019) Statistical bulletin. Suicides in the UK: 2018 registrations. Newport: Office for National Statistics. Retrieved from https://www.ons.gov.uk/peoplepopulationandcommunity/ birthsdeathsandmarriages/deaths/bulletins/suicidesintheunitedkingdom/latest

Oliver, M. (2013) The social model of disability: Thirty years on. *Disability & Society*, 28, 1024–1026.

Potts, K. & Brown, L. (2005) Becoming an anti-oppressive researcher. In L. Brown & S. Strega (Eds.), *Research as Resistance: Critical, Indigenous, and Anti-Oppressive Approaches.* (255–286). Toronto: Canadian Scholar's Press.

Recovery in the Bin [RITB], Edwards, B. M., Burgess, R., & Thomas, E. (2019) *Neorecovery: A Survivor Led Conceptualisation and Critique.* [Online Transcript]. Keynote presented at the 25th International Mental Health Nursing Research Conference, The Royal College of Nursing, London. Retrieved from https://recoveryinthebin.org/2019/09/16/__trashed-2/

Rose, D. & Kalathil, J. (2019) Power, privilege and knowledge: The untenable promise of co-production in mental 'health'. *Frontiers in Sociology*, 4:57, 1–11.

Ryan, F. (2019) *Crippled: Austerity and the Demonization of Disabled People.* London: Verso Books.

Sainsbury Centre for Mental Health. (2005) *Briefing Paper 31: Choice in Mental Health Care.* [Online]. London: Sainsbury Centre for Mental Health. Retrieved from www.centreformentalhealth.org.uk/pdfs/ briefing31_choice_in_mental_health_care.pdf

Strega, S. (2005) The view from the poststructural margins: Epistemology and methodology resistance. In L. Brown & S. Strega (Eds.), *Research as Resistance: Critical, Indigenous, and Anti-Oppressive Approaches* (199–236). Toronto: Canadian Scholar's Press.

Survivor Research Network. (2013) *Summary of Findings from the National Survivor User Network Members' Survey.* London: National Survivor User Network. Retrieved from www.nsun.org.uk/FAQs/ survivor-researcher-network-srn

Survivor Research Network. (2016) *Statement from the Event Organisers 'The Reclaiming, Challenging and Reviving Survivor Research' Event Report.* London: NSUN. Retrieved from www.nsun.org.uk/FAQs/ survivor-researcher-network-srn

Thomson, S. & Machin, K. (forthcoming) *4Pi and Survivor Research – A Thought paper*

Tate, S. A. & Page, D. (2018) Whiteliness and institutional racism: Hiding behind (un)conscious bias. *Ethics and Education*, 13, 141–155.

Walker, C., Artaraza, K., Darkinga, M., Davies C., Fleischer S., Grabera, R., Mwalea, S., Speed, E., Terrya, J. & Zoli, A. (2018) Building spaces for controversial public engagement – exploring and challenging democratic deficits in NHS marketization [Special Issue]. *Journal of Social and Political Psychology*, 6, 759–775.

World Social Forum. (2015) *World Social Forum/Forum Social Mondial – Final Declaration.* [Online]. Retrieved from https://fsm2015.org/en

38

THE TROUBLE WITH COPRODUCTION

Nick Watson

Introduction

The concept of coproduction and the social model of disability, emancipatory research and the Independent Living Movement are all concepts strongly associated with both disability studies and the disabled people's movement. Together they form the bedrock of what defines our discipline and our movement, neatly encapsulated by the overarching principle of "Nothing About Us Without Us". The call for greater involvement in the design and delivery of services and in research by the disabled people's movement challenged and changed both the way that disabled people were treated by society and the very definition of disability itself. It provided a radical alternative to the disablism that was restricting and reducing disabled people's inclusion and opportunities. Through these approaches, the disabled people's movement sought to change policies by governments and others who tried to define what disability was and what disabled people could and could not do, and where they could and could not live.

Dissatisfied with their prolonged and continued exclusion from the benefits of growth that marked the post-war years, both here in Europe and in the US, disabled people demanded change. The growing inequality of disabled people's experience compared to their nondisabled peers drove disabled people to call for a more equitable and just solution. Not only did it expand the sense of injustice that surrounded disability, it also sought to recreate disability as a social problem and as a problem of social justice (Oliver, 1990). It located that problem within state-led capitalism, which was seen as the source of much of the problem. State-led capitalism was responsible for the delivery of care and support that were part of the oppressive regimes that served to exclude disabled people. These organisations and structures worked to legitimate disabled people's exclusion on the grounds that they were not able to live on their own, to form relationships or to work as fast or produce the equivalent of their nondisabled peers.

Importantly, for the disabled people's movement, coproduction also meant greater involvement in the design and production of research and is strongly linked to the emancipatory research paradigm, as outlined by Oliver (1992). The disabled people's movement and their allies, working within a broadly emancipatory paradigm and with disabled people as equal partners, provided a critique of these services and made the case of distinct dimensions of injustice experienced by disabled people across economic, political and cultural domains, both historically and contemporarily (Barnes, 1991). They demonstrated how services such as special schools, care homes, rehabilitation units, segregated workshops, segregated housing and other services aimed at disabled people disadvantaged and excluded disabled people from the mainstream, denying them the opportunities afforded to their nondisabled peers.

Coproduction has become a key methodological approach in disability research, particularly in research with people with a learning disability (Strnadová and Walmsley, 2018). It is important, however, to remember that it is not confined to the research process; it is "a rather heterogeneous umbrella concept" (Verschuere et al., 2012, p. 1094) and plays a key role in the design and delivery of our public services. Neither is it confined to a single activity; it covers a range of different processes and may occur at different phases in either the research process in the design and delivery of public services. Nabatchi et al. (2017) identify four phases where coproduction may occur. First is the actual commissioning process, where ideas for identifying and prioritising research topics or public services occurs. Here researchers work together with commissioners of research or public services to jointly develop activities for later action. Second is the actual design of the projects. Here service users/research participants and their communities work together with commissioners or researchers to try and create a service or a research project that is of greatest benefit to all those involved and that takes account of their needs or interests. Third is the co-delivery of a project. This is where people work together to carry out the activity. Fourth is the monitoring and evaluation stage, where people work together to access the actual quality of an intervention or the success of a research project.

There is no doubting that coproduction has led to some significant successes and that it has changed the mode of both research production and the design and delivery of our public services (Armstrong et al., 2019). It is not, however, a trouble-free area, and there are some concerns about the approach that are worthy of consideration. Further, the impact of the financial crises and the resulting austerity have seen the possibility for retrenchment in this area. There is a danger that some of the ideals and demands of the disabled people's movement are now being employed by those who seek to reduce the role of the state in the delivery of care and support, cut costs and withdraw benefits to legitimate their actions. Direct payments and the personalisation of social care, ideals strongly associated with coproduction, for example, have unwittingly acted as a key driver for the end of socialised social care and the dominance of the private sector in the delivery of care and support (Pearson and Ridley, 2017).

This chapter will seek to address some of these concerns. The aim of this chapter is not to debunk coproduction or to argue that it is an inappropriate methodology; rather, I want to point out some of the concerns and weaknesses of the approach. If people are aware of these, then action can be taken to modify them. It opens with a brief overview, mapping out the emergence of coproduction and how it has become one of the driving ideas for the emancipation of disabled people. It reconstructs the concepts that have underpinned this approach and in doing so seeks to shed light on some of the challenges faced today. In constructing its critique, the chapter draws heavily on the work of Nancy Fraser, Simon Winlow and Steve Hall and argues that the changing world economy and responses to the economic collapse present new challenges to coproduction and its role in tackling disablement and promoting social justice. It starts with a brief overview of the concept of coproduction and then moves on to locate that practice within disability research and the development of public services for disabled people.

The development of coproduction in the design and delivery of public service

Coproduction as a concept emerged in the 1970s, and its origin is closely associated with the work of Nobel Prize-winning economist, Elinor Ostrom (1972, 2012). She was trying to understand why crime rates rose when police moved off the beat and into patrol cars. She concluded that if the police were to be successful in their tasks, they required the cooperation and involvement of the public. In creating a distance between themselves and the public, the police lost access to important information about the community, information that was crucial to preventing and solving crime. Effective services, Ostrom argued, required the active participation of those who received them (1996). The principles of coproduction marked a direct challenge to the then-prevailing orthodoxy that services should be hierarchical, with government directly providing services to the public based on rules and formal procedures (Sorrentino et al., 2018, p. 279). Coproduction moves citizens from being passive recipients of services to active agents:

> Coproduction implies that citizens can play an active role in producing public goods and services of consequence to them.
>
> *(Ostrom, 1996, p. 1073)*

Coproduction fell out of fashion through the late 1980s and 1990s as the trend moved more towards the idea that the market was the best means through which improvements in public services could be delivered. This era, loosely defined as New Public Management (NPM), saw the ideas of coproduction being challenged with a focus on service users as consumers rather than producers. Consumer choice was the dominant discourse and coproduction was no longer inherent to the process; rather, it was "something that can be added to the repertoire of service delivery arrangements available to public managers in the attempt to increase efficiency and do more with less" (Sorrentino et al., 2018, p. 279). Key services, such as those providing health and social care, became perceived as goods or services that could be bought or sold and were treated in the same way as other commodities. The original formulation of the Independent Living Movement is very much centred on this consumerist model, as de Jong made clear with his assertion that

> because disabled persons are the best judges of their own interests, they should have the larger voice in determining what services are provided in the disability services market.
>
> *(1979, p. 439)*

Through the 1990s, coproduction moved to the mainstream and has now become central to the reform of public services (Sorrentino et al., 2018). For example, in Scotland the Christie Commission on the Future Delivery of Public Services (2011), which has set the agenda for public service reform in Scotland, states that "effective services must be designed with and for people and communities – not delivered 'top down' for administrative convenience" (2011, p. ix). Public services, it argues, have to be "built around people and communities, their needs, aspirations, capacities and skills, and work to build up their autonomy and resilience" (2011, p. 23).

In this next section, I want to focus on a critique of coproduction. Following Fraser (2013), I will argue that its ideas have been conscripted as part of a project that can run counter to its original intentions and that, far from promoting a more just society, coproduction may have been co-opted to lay the path towards a new, neoliberal, transnational form of capitalism based on consumerism. Fraser makes the point that second wave feminism emerged at the same time as neoliberalism, arguing that there existed some "perverse subterranean affinity between them" (p. 218), and while this may be a heretical claim, it is nonetheless one that is important to bear in mind and one that I think that we should consider in relation to disability.

Some problems with coproduction

Coproduction and the delivery of coproduced services can point to an impressive bank of evidence to support its claims that lives have been transformed. So successful has this been that it has now been adopted and rolled out as the model for a wide range of public service delivery, and it is a well-established research approach. There are, however, costs attached to this model.

There is a danger that coproduction can have difficulties examining and unpacking the way that the exclusion of disabled people is fundamentally underpinned by the structures, processes and values of a liberalist–capitalist political economy and the social and cultural consequences this has for disabled people (Winlow and Hall, 2013). We have moved from a mainly macro-approach to a mainly micro-analysis of exclusion. So, for example, we hear a great deal about the ways that particular disabled people create fear in nondisabled people, or the ways that "othering" results in social policy initiatives that exclude disabled people, all of which help in our understanding of the disability experience. However, what this analysis fails to do is to address the fact that simply removing these labels will not remove or even ameliorate what Winlow and Hall (2013, p. 31) term the "multidimensional structural pressures – whose nexus is located deeply in the logic of the financialised global economy". It is this that puts disabled people where they are and continues to reproduce their socio-economic and cultural exclusion.

Daniel Wight, in an ethnographic study of a Scottish village that he called Cauldmoss, puts a very good case for our need to understand that lay perceptions of inequality are experienced in immediate ways:

> It is striking that the things which most concern people in Cauldmoss on a daily basis were, in terms of mainstream sociological theory, generally considered trivia . . . for instance the cleanliness of children's clothes, the relative expense of wedding presents or personal reputation in the village. This was the stuff of status distinctions. Factors deemed to be of sociological importance . . . occupation, class, voting behaviour, were usually experienced by villagers as the inevitable parameters of their condition, and therefore rather futile to dwell on. Within these bounds they led their lives, exercised by issues that were subject to their influence.
>
> *(Wight, 1993, p. 7)*

These are, of course, important issues, but they do not get to the root structural issues that construct disablism and other macro concerns such as class, gender and ethnicity. Coproduction does not challenge these structural inequities which can shape people's lives.

In a recently published article, Oliver and her colleagues point to a number of other concerns around coproduction (2019). It is expensive, they argue, time consuming, resource demanding, and it requires a high degree of skill, particularly if we are to include those with the greatest need. For example, poor health can affect an individual's ability to participate, and some people with mental health problems or other conditions may find participation itself an issue

(Vennik et al., 2015). Gender and ethnicity can also impact on people's willingness to engage. Power to the people can become power to the already powerful people.

It is well documented that large numbers of disabled people do not identify themselves as disabled. For example, large numbers of disabled people either do not identify as disabled people or do not identify with the disabled people's movement, as Ligget argues:

> In order to participate in their own management disabled people have had to participate as disabled. Even among the politically active, the price of being heard is understanding that it is the disabled who are speaking.
>
> *(1988, p. 271ff)*

Research by the Equality and Human Rights Commission suggests that nearly half of those who are covered by the disability element of the Single Equality Act in the UK do not see themselves as disabled. Many disabled people do not want to see themselves as disabled; there is a cost to identity politics (Shakespeare and Watson, 2001).

There are problems around representation and who is entitled to speak for a community (Warren, 2008). Who has the authority to speak on behalf of a group and how is accountability ensured? The most normal route into coproduction is through self-selection, and this can lead to domination by organised interests (Fishken, 2009, p. 98).

There are also issues around the status of those who take part in the process, and it can, albeit inadvertently, reinforce the researcher or official/disabled divide (Watson, 2019). In research, for example, it is common to see disabled people who are acting as researchers referred to as co-researchers (Liddiard et al., 2018). This marks them out as different and separate from the researchers or officials.

Oliver et al. also point to the personal demands coproduction makes on researchers and others involved in the process. It can create interpersonal conflict, and managing disagreements can be demanding. Coproduction works well until people disagree. There are also reputational risks for all those involved. Participants run the risk of having to produce and agree to outcomes that they may not fully agree with, and this might harm them, either politically or personally. All those involved may be seen as being partisan; the outcomes may be employed to add legitimacy to political positions that they neither endorse nor accept. Criticism of the outcomes negotiated can become difficult. For example, many organisations of disabled people are now inextricably involved in the delivery of personalisation and have lost their ability to act as an independent voice and to speak up for service users. The Centres for Inclusive Living are now so closely aligned with the delivery of personalised support and social care that there is no space for critical engagement with the personalisation agenda.

In Glasgow, for example, the delivery of Self-Directed Support, a service coproduced with disabled people and their organisations, coincided with an 11 per cent cut from the £89 million social care budget during 2012/13 (Main, 2013 in Pearson and Ridley, 2017). In explaining the cuts, the local authority claimed that they could be justified because of efficiencies resulting from coproduced services and personalisation. How coproduction can result in these efficiencies was not made clear (Pearson and Ridley, 2017; Pearson et al., 2018). What we do know is that there has been a significant worsening in the working conditions of care workers with a growth in zero-hour contracts, loss of holiday and sick pay and pension entitlement. The private sector has moved in and a perspective aimed originally at transforming state power into a vehicle to empower disabled people and promote social justice has been used to legitimate both marketisation and state retrenchment. The disabled people's movement has to take some of the blame here, for we originally sold the concept on its ability to not only improve the delivery of care but also to cut costs (Zarb and Nadish, 1994).

Coproduction also requires sharing of what might be sensitive information; people may have to expose vulnerabilities or uncertainties, and even when these are shared, they may still not make a difference (Maybin, 2016). It has potential to open up those who are researched to even greater surveillance (Baistow, 1994). Further, as Oliver et al. argue, the omission of people's views or perspectives from a final report or outcome may make people feel they have been ignored.

Many of these problems are of course not insurmountable, but they have to be considered and have to form part of any planned initiative involving coproduction.

Conclusion

There is no doubting the potential coproduction offers in terms of improving outcomes, in both the design and delivery of public services and research, as many of the other chapters in this collection demonstrate. However, this is not a cost-free approach, and there are many risks associated. The links between consumerism and coproduction have created problems and the accompanying neoliberal onslaught has instrumentalised some of our best ideas. For coproduction to work, we need to reclaim them, and we need to develop a way of critiquing neoliberalism while at the same time critiquing traditional authority, which is where many of our ideas have come from. We don't want a return to paternalistic welfarism, where decisions are made for disabled people. We must reactivate the promise of coproduction, but do so in a way that allows for a fully formed and three-dimensional account of what it is like to be disabled: that unpacks, explores and examines what we mean by terms such as independence, inclusion and rights for all disabled people in a way that takes account of the axis of experience, including gender, class, ethnicity, geography and impairment effects. An approach that will allow us to work at the micro, meso and macro levels and analyse both the social and structural investment required for social change to ensure social justice for disabled people.

There is a danger that the valorising of coproduction in current policy discourse is still closely associated with the consumerist approach of NPM. In his Reith Lectures for the BBC in 2013, the artist Greyson Perry employed the term "subversive compliance" to describe the relationship between modern art and capitalism. On the one hand, he argued, artists feign to oppose capitalism, while capitalism itself loves modern art: it gives them new ways of spending money. Capitalism, as Marx pointed out, is constantly seeking new ways to re-invent itself and to generate new markets. I want to argue that a similar relationship may have emerged through coproduction between disability activists, disabled people's organisations and capitalism. Disability activists have, it could be argued unwittingly, helped what Boltanski and Chiapello have termed "the new spirit of capitalism", which has emerged to replace the state-led capitalism that existed in the 1960s, 1970s and 1980s and that these new forms of capitalism that have emerged are producing new forms of oppression.

Drawing on Nancy Fraser's analysis of the discourses of feminism and its links with calls for greater participation, we can see that coproduction with disabled people pointed towards two different outcomes (2013). In a first scenario, there is the potential for an outcome in which emancipation for disabled people goes hand in hand with increased participation and through that greater social solidarity. In a second, it opens up the possibility of a new form of liberalism, one that through increased participation would afford disabled people equal access to the goods of individual autonomy, increased choice and meritocratic advancement. Perhaps a case could be made that the latter has become more dominant at the expense of the former. We have challenged the welfarist, authoritarian services that have traditionally constructed the lives of disabled people. In doing so we have perhaps, as Fraser argues with respect to feminism, created an affinity with neoliberalism. In trying to challenge the subjection that accompanied the way disabled people were treated and excluded and the traditional forms of care and support, and to emancipate disabled people from oppressive care regimes or to challenge their oppressive representation, we have inadvertently opened the door to capitalism. Previous state-controlled regimes, such as those that provided social care and support, and the authority associated with them obstructed or prevented capitalism from entering this market. Welfarist authorities, through their paternalism, protected disabled people and their supporters from capitalism. This is a critique that capitalism itself employed in its assaults on traditional forms of power and traditional authority. These two critiques, one driven by the emancipatory movement of disabled people, the other by capitalism, appear to converge, and we have, to cite Grayson Perry's term, been subversively compliant in the rolling out of capitalism in the lives of disabled people. Coproduction, and the discourse of consumerism that has accompanied this approach, has played a part in this action.

References

Armstrong, A., Cansdale, M., Collis, A., Collis, B., Rice, S. and Walmsley, J. (2019). What makes a good self-advocacy project? The added value of co-production. *Disability & Society*, 34(7–8), 1289–1311.

Baistow, K. (1994). Liberation and regulation: Some paradoxes of empowerment. *Critical Social Policy*, 42, 34–46.

Barnes, C. (1991). *Disabled people in Britain and discrimination: A case for anti-discrimination legislation*. London: C. Hurst & Co. Publishers.

Dejong, G. (1979). Independent living: From social movement to analytic paradigm. *Archives of Physical Medicine and Rehabilitation*, 60, 435–446.

Fishkin, J.S. (2009). *When the people speak, deliberative democracy and public consultation*. Oxford: Oxford University Press.

Fraser, N. (2013). *Fortunes of feminism: From state-managed capitalism to neoliberal crisis*. Brooklyn, NY: Verso Books.

Liddiard, K., Runswick-Cole, K., Goodley, D., Whitney, S., Vogelmann, E. and Watts, M.B.E.L. (2018). "I was excited by the idea of a project that focuses on those unasked questions" co-producing disability research with disabled young people. *Children & Society*, 33(2), 154–167.

Liggett, H. (1988). Stars are not born: An interpretive approach to the politics of disability. *Disability, Handicap & Society*, 3(3), 263–275.

Main, J. (2013). Personalisation – Plus ça change? In: Beresford, P. ed. *Personalisation*. Bristol: Policy Press.

Maybin, J. (2016). *Producing health policy: Knowledge and knowing in government policy work*. New York: Springer.

Nabatchi, T., Sancino, A. and Sicilia, M. (2017). Varieties of participation in public services: The who, when, and what of coproduction. *Public Administration Review*. doi:10.1111/puar.12765

Oliver, M. (1990). *Politics of disablement*. Basingstoke: Palgrave Macmillan.

Oliver, M. (1992). Changing the social relations of research production? *Disability, Handicap & Society*, 7(2), 101–114.

Ostrom, E. (1972). Metropolitan reform: Propositions derived from two traditions. *Social Science Quarterly*, 53(3), 474–493.

Ostrom, E. (1996). Crossing the great divide: Coproduction, synergy, and development. *World Development*, 24(6), 1073–1087.

Ostrom, E. (2012). Foreword. In: Pestoff, V., Brandsen, T. and Verschuere, B. eds. *New public governance, the third sector and co-production*. London: Routledge, xii–vii.

Pearson, C. and Ridley, J. (2017). Is personalization the right plan at the wrong time? Re-thinking cash-for-care in an age of austerity. *Social Policy & Administration*, 51(7), 1042–1059.

Pearson, C., Watson, N. and Manji, K. (2018). Changing the culture of social care in Scotland: Has a shift to personalization brought about transformative change? *Social Policy & Administration*, 52(3), 662–676.

Perry, G. (2013). *Democracy has a bad taste BBC Reith lectures*. www.bbc.co.uk/programmes/b03969vt (accessed December 12 2019).

Shakespeare, T., and Watson, N. (2001). The social model of disability: An outdated ideology. *Research in Social Science and Disability*, 2(1), 9–28.

Sorrentino, M., Sicilia, M. and Howlett, M. (2018). Understanding co-production as a new public governance tool. *Policy and Society*, 37(3), 277–293. doi:10.1080/14494035.2018.1521676

Strnadová, I., & Walmsley, J. (2018). Peer-reviewed articles on inclusive research: Do co-researchers with intellectual disabilities have a voice? *Journal of Applied Research in Intellectual Disabilities*, 31(1), 132–141.

Vennik, F.D., van de Bovenkamp, H.M., Putters, K., et al. (2015). Co-production in healthcare: rhetoric and practice. *International Review of Administrative Sciences*, 82(1), 150–168.

Verschuere, B., Brandsen, T. and Pestoff, V. (2012). Co-production: The state of the art in research and the future agenda. *Voluntas*, 23(4), 1083–1101.

Warren, M.E. (2008). Citizen representatives. In: Warren, M.E. and Pearse, H. eds. *Designing deliberative democracy: The British Columbia citizens' assembly*. Cambridge: Cambridge University Press.

Watson, N. (2019). Agency, structure and emancipatory research. In: Watson, N. and Vehmas, S. eds. *The Routledge handbook of disability studies* London: Routledge.

Wight, D. (1993). *Workers or wasters: Masculine responsibility, consumption and employment in Central Scotland*. Edinburgh: Edinburgh University Press.

Winlow, S. and Hall, S. (2013). *Rethinking social exclusion: The end of the social?* London: Sage.

Zarb, G. and Nadash, P. (1994). *Cashing in on independence*. Derby: British Council of Organisations of Disabled People.

39

AUGMENTED COMMUNICATION

Patient and public involvement in research: rhetoric and reality

Liz Moulam, Stuart Meredith, Helen Whittle,
Yvonne Lynch and Janice Murray

Introduction

We recently completed a three-year research project funded by the UK's National Institute of Health Research (NIHR). The NIHR is fully funded by the UK government's Department of Health and Social Care, which oversees the National Health Service (NHS) in England. Health services are devolved in Scotland, Wales and Northern Ireland.

The project, identifying appropriate symbol communication aids for children (I-ASC), was a research collaboration that included six service users within the research team. The main aim of the project had been to explore ways to improve the health and wellbeing outcomes for children and young people who have little or no intelligible speech and need to use communication aids to communicate.

The NIHR encourage public involvement (PI) in the research they fund. Their gold standard is for the active involvement of service users in every aspect of co-producing research, but as a minimum, they state service users should be involved in funding bids, advising on processes and supporting dissemination. When the I-ASC research project began, the team was clear that service users, and their families, would be essential partners in delivering the best possible results for the project, and with roles throughout the life of the project rather than being involved in a limited capacity, for example, as project advisors.

This chapter outlines what we discovered from the literature about how others were approaching PI research, the latest UK guidance on what good PI research should look like and how the I-ASC team co-created their project. This was not always straightforward, but the hope is that readers will see the challenges and benefits and be able to apply the learnings in their own PI research projects.

What the literature tells us

There are many different ways to describe patient and service user involvement in research. The terms the I-ASC team chose to use are defined in the relevant sections.

The acronym PI means involving service users in research to ensure it reflects the views of all stakeholder groups. This is not a new concept; for 20 years, the UK Health Service (NHS) has stated they wanted patient and public involvement in all research and that their involvement is essential to good research. Our funders (NIHR) intend that by 2025, patient and public involvement will be an integral part of every bid. More recently, PI has been redefined to make it clear who should be involved in research: 'patients, service users, survivors, carers and family members' (National Standards, 2018, p. 4).

Existing literature suggests the best type of research takes account of everyone involved in a particular field or area. According to Sackett et al. (1997), and later Dolloghan (2007), evidence-based practice is when researchers seek evidence from stakeholders or patients, search out internal clinical evidence and draw on scientific research evidence. Despite these good intentions, Snow (2016) found most published research has few participants and often only looks at the variables, options or interventions important to the clinician. Frankena et al. (2016) go as far as to raise three concerns regarding PI research: the lack of clarity around the best methodologies to choose for successful inclusion of co-researchers, little or no evaluation or assessment of how those involved in PI research benefitted and if the robustness and credibility of the research improved with co-researcher input.

Policy interpretation and governance variations

The literature revealed key themes for consideration. It became apparent other fields of research were not involving service users in the same way as planned by the I-ASC collaboration. The reality has been that the UK Department of Health (Health Education England, 2018) and the NIHR (Denegri, 2015) have published explicit guidance on patient and public involvement, but thus far this has resulted in variable implementation. This might be explained by the way the NHS operates in England: with national policy, regional operations and local agendas. What happens within one clinical specialism appears to be very different from another; for instance, there are large national clinical trials for some conditions like lung cancer, where other conditions may be more locally focused with pockets of good practice. This means that there appears to be uncertainty about what good (PI) practice looks like across different types of health research. It appears much of the current PI research is tokenistic, often undertaken in the easiest way possible, and is a box that managers can tick (Boaz, 2014; Green, 2016; Ocloo and Matthews, 2016). This has been evidenced by the frequent use of the same small pools of participants, those vocal few who want to make a difference, or by filling out of questionnaires and surveys rather than in depth participation, e.g., general practitioner's surgeries handing out satisfaction questionnaires.

Power imbalances

One positive outcome of the advent of PI is that it has drawn attention to power imbalances that have traditionally existed between health professionals and their patients (Shen et al., 2016). In most areas of health, it seems the service user or patient's voice is often viewed from an intervention perspective, rather than taking account of the patient's experiences, feelings and emotions prior to and during interventions that may be on offer (Snow, 2016). In some clinical research, while there is an acknowledgement the public can support some activities, there was a reluctance to share control or power with lay persons (Boza, 2014). Researchers may appear threatened by patient challenge (Shen et al., 2016), and with increased access to the internet, if anyone is worried about a symptom or diagnosed with a new condition, the first thing they probably do is find out as much as they can about their own situation. Researchers, and research practitioners, may not have the time, funding, training or resources to engage meaningfully with service users who have low incidence conditions and in-depth lived experience which makes them experts in their own lives. One result is that the richness of service user experiences and input can be lost in a typical consultation and implementation plan (Snow, 2016).

Empowering service users

The literature suggests that there has been concern around empowering service users in research, with a degree of opposition from some researchers that PI contributors would not understand or have the knowledge to share co-production or co-creation of a study (Boaz, 2014). With regard to severe communication impairment, there appears to be a view that these groups are too hard to involve; they are difficult to reach, making meaningful contact both costly and time consuming (Ocloo and Matthews, 2016). What also comes across from the literature is that these groups are often perceived as having nothing to add to the research evidence and speaking to a proxy is good enough (Ocloo and Matthews, 2016). This cannot be acceptable; parents, for instance, may be a constant in a child's life, but their perspective is different to their child's, young adult's or adult's perspective, suggesting the views of everyone must be essential to the research process (Shen et al., 2016), albeit through alternative means, e.g., communication aid technologies.

Effective guidance

The process of meaningful involvement of service users with complex communication impairments in research is reflected in the literature, suggesting existing guidance is lacking in reach by being unable to suggest reasonable adjustments for participants with additional needs (Frankena et al., 2016). Firstly, most guidance on public participation has been produced with adult patients in mind, and at best the mainstream population who are cognitively able, or those with acquired conditions where their cognition is not impacted. Secondly, where guidance exists for children and young people, there appears to be little of relevance to children with lifelong conditions. Children are different from adults; they are both currently being and yet growing and developing. They are individuals who live in families, suggesting that one approach to research involvement does not fit all (Denegri, 2015). Where PI guidance for research involvement does exist, to date it fails to support best practice for PI delivery in research with those who are potentially more difficult to reach or engage. In particular there is an absence of guidance to navigate ethical issues, environmental challenges, institutional and/or cultural practices and procedures, personal circumstances and individual needs related to specific conditions.

Strategies for success

Consideration of the literature suggests there are four key strategies for successful patient and public involvement. This includes greater clarity on who can be involved in research roles; the new UK National Standards for Public Involvement in Research (2018) were welcomed. The clearer guidance paves the way for improved research recruitment processes by defining participation: those who might want to take part in a research study, and co-researcher roles; those actively working as part of a research team. Researchers have a responsibility to ensure methodologies are accessible, relevant and meaningful to the participant groups; the PI co-researcher(s) helps ensure the participant is central to all planning, delivery, dissemination and evaluation of a project by bringing lived experience to every stage of the research process. All research meetings that engage with co-researchers may need to be adapted to be jargon free and allow PI input meaningfully, for instance help with pre-meeting planning, scaffolding input or allowing extra time. Finally, researchers must balance the time needed for effective co-researcher involvement with ensuring research progress is made and funder outcomes and key milestones are met, even if the work takes longer. These strategies dovetail with the National Standards for Public Involvement in Research (2018) to ensure diverse viewpoints are considered throughout the research cycle.

The UK National Standards for Public Involvement (NSPIR) (2018)

The 2018 launch of the new NSPIR is timely. Along with the new definitions of public involvement roles, there are six core features to guide improvements in collaborative working. These are statements of guidance on what to do, which are then broken down into key indicators of best practice for researchers to demonstrate or measure their success in the co-production of research. The standards suggest the essential factors for any collaborative research project with public contributors should include inclusive opportunities, working together, support and learning, communications, impact and governance. This guidance makes it clear that PI contributors to research may come into and out of a project as it progresses, often inputting in their area of interest only.

Inclusive opportunities refer to reaching out to those people who would benefit from the research by including them on the research team. Best practice would be to involve people from the planning stages through to developing outcome measures in ways that are suited to individual interests and skill sets. In order to make this happen, any barriers to participation need addressing, including payment of expenses and having meetings in convenient locations, and at a time that is best for the PI contributors. The project team is expected to be open and transparent in the way they recruit to the research team, avoiding overuse of the same few known people.

The importance of working together focuses on valuing all research contributors, from whatever background, with the aim of building strong and mutually supportive research relationships. It is suggested that this can be achieved through a top-down, bottom-up approach, from an organisational culture perspective and from a service user lived experience. Collaborative working can result in co-creating research plans, delivery of involvement plans and sharing roles, responsibilities and expectations through the life of a study. Ultimately, a measure of success is PI researchers being actively engaged in meetings and decision making.

Support and learning should be offered in an appropriate way to PI contributors in research. This might be evidenced by ensuring budgets reflect accurately the cost of public involvement, for instance pay for the work undertaken, support for access needs such as a personal assistant and travel. Other specific considerations might be the need for mentoring and emotional support or counselling. Good practice includes having a PI section on the research organisation's website and having a designated PI lead for all research contributors to contact if needed; each participant in the research cycle should have access to appropriate learning and support activities, including training. The research team are responsible for regularly evaluating their activities and sharing their findings with others through PI activities, such as workshops, presentations and forum.

Communication should be central to every research project, with the focus of the PI on improving research and outcomes; this might be delivered through providing updates in plain language and a regularly updated communications plan. Where needed, the research team should provide different formats of information, for instance easy read documents or a face-to-face meeting instead of emails, with regular updates.

There is an imperative to learn from PI research, from what works well and what might be improved. The impact of research is critical for future funding and can be achieved by understanding and sharing the difference public involvement makes during the research cycle. The key indicators of impact success would be to involve service users in assessing the PI roles in research, for the research team with PI contributors to record what they expect to gain from PI input and agree together projected study outcomes before the research commences, then record actual achievements through the life of the award. Best practice might then be not just to publish the research findings, but to reflect and publish what has been learned from a PI perspective during the research, and the impact of this.

Finally, the National Standards for PI in research recommend involving the public, or service users, in governance and leadership of research by actively engaging them in decision making around research focus, how PI might contribute to research agendas and developing, delivering and monitoring their involvement in research. Organisations demonstrating best practice will have a public involvement in research plan with a designated senior manager responsible for implementation, with funds allocated for effective PI research.

What has become clear is that, in summarising the literature review and the best practice guidance from the NSPIR, it is not a simple matter to categorise challenges and opportunities for working with service users into neat boxes. Each area of concern or development interacts; governance affects ways of working in the field as well as the strategic vision and operationalisation of an organisation. Empowering service users is not just a goal but a cultural shift which pervades every aspect of opportunity, working together, support and learning as well as how we all communicate to deliver impactful research with meaningful outcomes.

The I-ASC reality of 'service user' involvement in the co-creation and co-production of research

The I-ASC research project (identifying appropriate symbol communication aids for children who are non-speaking: enhancing clinical decision making [HS&DR number: 14/70/153]) began with two key questions to underpin the effective delivery of PI research.

1   How do we apply the previously published quality indicators from a PI perspective to ensure our research approach and outputs meet with best practice standards?
2   How do we minimise any risk of tokenism while at the same time delivering effective, externally funded research with critical deadlines?

Within the I-ASC project team of ten, there were two PI co-researchers: an adult with a severe speech impairment who used augmentative and alternative communication (AAC) and a parent of a young adult who also used AAC. The project also appointed an NIHR Advisory Board with four members, which included a parent of a young adult who uses AAC, and a Critical Friends Group of eight members, including one adult who uses AAC and one parent of a young adult using AAC.

I-ASC and defining terminology

The lack of clarity around roles, and the diversity of descriptions within the field of public involvement, led to the I-ASC team defining team roles to support the project objectives:

Co-researcher: a service user actively engaged in the day-to-day activities of the I-ASC project from concept through to evaluation.

Researcher: a paid academic researcher or research practitioner who was engaged in the day-to-day activities and/or in specific tasks during the project from concept through to evaluation.

Research advisor: a service user, practitioner or professional actively engaged in specific activities relating to the project, e.g., NIHR Advisory Board, Critical Friends Group.

This lack of clarity also extended to the way in which different people interfaced with the project. These interactions were defined by the I-ASC team as:

Co-creation: the activities where the members of the research team who worked together to create the project from concept, writing the funding bid, the full research cycle and then through to evaluation, or tasks where team members were heavily involved in developing and delivering the systematic reviews, and the qualitative and quantitative elements of the study. This included researchers and co-researchers.

Co-production: the ad hoc or specific activities where those who joined the team post-award took on paid and voluntary roles to review resources, attend advisory and evaluation meetings, transcribe data. This included researchers and research advisors.

While not the subject of this chapter, the research participants who were interviewed were co-producers of the findings; they were the service users, families and professionals we collaborated with to understand their ways of working, expectations and experiences. Some service users, who were already 'experienced' participants in other AAC research, were invited to be research advisors to ensure 'fresh' views were gained from new participants.

The I-ASC methodology

The I-ASC project adopted an evidence-based approach to the investigation, within a participatory action research (PAR) paradigm. PAR methodologies aim to empower those involved in a particular section of the population to take action and actively create the way knowledge is produced (Nieuwenhuys, 2004), especially in relation to what is normally considered professional knowledge as specialists working within their field. In the case of the I-ASC project, this meant empowering those who use AAC and their family members. This approach is not without challenge, as communication through AAC is slower; it can be time consuming and add cost to the research budget. By involving those who are central to the research though every stage of the process, the theory is the power balance moves from the professional 'expert' perspective to those who will benefit most from the project outputs (Nieuwenuys, 2004).

Balancing power and inclusive opportunities with the I-ASC project

From the beginning, the research team leads were determined that service users – people with severe speech impairment and who use AAC, and/or their family members – would be involved in every aspect and stage of the research. This began with co-creating the project, conceptualising the study and working collaboratively to put together the funding application to the NIHR. The team was delighted when the funders highly commended them for their public involvement approach. Within the field of AAC research, it is not unusual to actively engage with service users and their families, and the research team gave the public involvement co-researchers a key role in leading on dissemination, as well as working alongside them designing and testing the methodological tools, collecting and analysing the data and developing resources for the website.

Out of pocket expenses were available for all PI contributors; meetings were timed to allow those who needed to travel, or accommodate the needs of their personal assistants, to take part. The co-researchers were invited to all full team meetings, where they contributed equally to all discussions, entered into the debate in hand and ensured the project remained focused on the research population needs (children and young people using AAC). The AAC population is a small cohort; however, every effort was made to widen the net and engage with new PI contributors rather than relying on those people who were well known within the field for 'having a say'. From the research perspective, there were three types of opportunity for the co-researchers (n=2) who were actively involved in developing the funding application and stayed as part of the project team through to evaluation. Then the NIHR Advisory Board member (n=1) who represented the funder at annual review meetings, and the Critical Friends Group (n=2) who met twice a year to provide feedback on progress, share experiences and help develop project resources and tools.

It was essential to overcome any barriers to inclusion. The Occupational Health team undertook assessments for all project team members and recommended that there should be a break-out area for the co-researcher using AAC, in case of fatigue. The university operates an open plan working environment, but accommodated this by agreeing a designated project room which could be used for relaxation when attending research team meetings. The co-researcher who uses AAC has said 'I have enjoyed and [I am] still enjoying being a co-researcher on this project even so sometimes I feel like going into a darkened room'. The added benefit for the whole project team was that the co-researcher and advisory group members using AAC could have private conversations if needed without synthesised voices carrying across the office.

Ethics and governance at a regional level proved challenging. In this context, this refers to meeting the guidelines and standards for university and NHS ethics and governance. At an early stage, the co-researcher who used AAC was unable to get an NHS research passport for clearance through health service governance to collect data on health service premises or with health service patients and/or staff. It was agreed unanimously by the whole team that neither co-researcher would undertake this portion of data collection. Ensuring accessibility is a key consideration for the project team. The University building is new and accessible, although there were some unexpected challenges, such as the co-researcher who uses a wheelchair and who has limited dexterity not being able to access a room alone due to the weight of the doors and the swipe card locking system. In addition, the project team, including the co-researchers, had not considered that visiting a special school educating physically disabled children and young people might be a challenge for an adult wheelchair user; however, in hindsight, either asking access questions before the visit or carrying out a risk assessment might have been prudent, as on one occasion the facilities were less accessible than anticipated.

Balancing power and working together on the I-ASC project

Every effort was made to ensure that the co-researchers had parity within the research team. This was not just listening to their views, giving them time to contribute and asking them to be party to decision making. Throughout the project, they undertook tasks that played to their strengths, undertaking tasks where they had experience, e.g., one co-researcher had considerable experience as an advocate, training mentor and public speaker; the other had bid writing, project management and marketing experience. Together, they took on the role as dissemination leads for the project. The co-researchers received training alongside other members of the project team, for instance, in research skills, where the team then developed the semi-structured interviews for children and young people who used AAC and the teams around them (parents, school staff, allied health professionals and others). As part of this, the whole team undertook mock interviews with members of the wider I-ASC research advisory team, giving and receiving 360-degree feedback on the activity before going out and collect data.

With hindsight, one of the reasons the I-ASC project perhaps did not neatly fit within the NIHR and National Standards for Public Involvement in Research (2018) guidance was the continuous in-depth nature of co-creating the project, with the co-researchers being integral to the research team throughout the life of the project. It was impossible to note separately each time the co-researchers participated in a meeting or decision; their central and essential role within the team was viewed from the beginning as the norm. In the same way that an employed researcher can take holiday and sick leave, the co-researchers were absent for holidays, bereavements and recovery from major surgery. In this time, where appropriate, they were kept informed by email, phone and other online media of the project's progress. During the project, other team members had extended periods of leave and sickness; early on, some of the research team were replaced due to availability, and this impacted some project activities more than the PI absences.

As knowledge of the I-ASC research grew, so did interest in the roles of the co-researchers. From the very early stages this led to the opportunity for them to present both internally within the university, to the NIHR Advisory Board and the Critical Friends Group, and externally at conferences, about the 'rhetoric and reality of PI research'. This became an unexpected offshoot from the main project.

Support and learning, within and outside of the I-ASC research team

Co-researchers had been costed into the budget from the go live date. Unfortunately, pre-award bids do not normally allow for fees/reward for involvement to be claimed; the university team was fortunate in the co-creating phase of the project that both people were willing to give their time and expertise for free, although they were reimbursed for travel costs. There was a variance in terms of how PI contributors were paid or rewarded; this depended on their personal financial situation with relation to claiming benefits or being able to be employed, but reward was in line with UK national guidance for public involvement in research (NIHR INVOLVE, 2016). Monetary or in kind reward is not just the motivator for involvement; both co-researchers reported learning new skills, growing in confidence in the work place and feeling valued for their input. This level of reciprocity benefits both the project and the individual. The parent co-researcher said: 'after several years out of the paid workplace this opportunity made me realise I still have skills, experience and knowledge to offer'.

One co-researcher needed a personal assistant (PA) at all times, initially often bringing a different member of their own team to meetings. After discussion between them and the chief investigator, it was felt a consistent assistant would support their input to the project. This resulted in the project team assisting the co-researcher in recruiting support workers though the university student workforce. Unfortunately, as student cohorts change, it became clear there was a need for a longer-term commitment for continuity for the co-researcher and to the project. Fortunately, a part-time member of the existing project team was able to step in to provide this assistance role. This solution proved vital in terms of knowledge, skill, reliability, expectations and understanding, enabling even greater levels of input to meetings and output outside of the team meeting and planning days.

The NSPIR (2018) recommend emotional support for co-researchers. Each member of the team was offered the opportunity to undertake counselling at any stage of the project through the university, if they felt it warranted after any research related activity, e.g., conducting individual interviews and coping with any revelations that arose. In addition, during data collection, the team who interviewed participants were encouraged to write field notes and discuss their experiences with another team member or the lead investigator. It was felt the interviews might create emotional challenges for those who used AAC and their families; to address this, each interviewee, including professionals, were provided with contact details of the co-researchers so they could follow up on their experiences – another reason why the support for co-researchers was seen as important.

Learning and support have been part of the overall plan for all team members. PI co-researchers attended team training sessions alongside the research team, and when needed had their own training sessions with the chief investigator. All team members were offered mentoring via their own line manager and when needed the chief investigator. Mentoring is a role which for the future might be more clearly defined.

Communication and empowerment

Communication has been a key theme running throughout the project. The team took the decision not to produce lay summaries of materials for the research team; it was viewed as important that everyone was treated alike. The team culture allowed everyone to participate equally, and so if a PI co-researcher, or any other team member, wanted to ask for clarification or discuss a point raised, this was seen as completely acceptable. In contrast, the team were aware that research participants who use AAC and their families might not have the same access to information and support as co-researchers; the team produced alternative accessible formats of materials for research participants with additional needs. This work was co-created and produced with the PI co-researchers and included plain language documents and a video to explain informed consent, story books to explain the assessment process for a communication aid and symbol boards with appropriate graphic representations for each individual to facilitate their decision making.

It might have been challenging for the co-researchers using AAC to participate in meetings, or the other team members to be patient and wait for them to contribute. However, whether this was the result of the I-ASC project being within the field of speech and language therapy and everyone being aware of the need to provide a supportive communication environment, or just the project culture of inclusion, each member of the team was given time and space to share their views, be heard and take part in decision making. Ground rules were established in the initial meeting and honoured throughout the project. One co-researcher noted ways his assistant helped to give him the opportunity to read materials distributed in meetings, and that having papers sent ahead of meetings meant he could think about his responses.

The project culture was established from when the I-ASC bid was first conceived, that of parity within the team. This may have led initially to some uncomfortable moments for the academic and practitioner researchers who were less used to being challenged by a group they normally saw as service users. By empowering the PI co-researchers, the door was opened for unexpected challenge and questions; when new people joined the team, this open and frank discussion was sometimes a surprise.

The NIHR Advisory Board and the Critical Friends Group provided valuable feedback throughout the life of the project; the Critical Friends Group was a project choice and not required by the funders. Both groups were supportive yet willing to give frank evaluations on progress and outputs, both as groups and as individuals in the areas of interest to them. For instance, a video produced to explain informed consent was modified following their feedback, and role playing of interviews was tested to the limit when a critical friend who used AAC had a technology failure and couldn't *speak* through his preferred medium, something that can easily happen in real life.

Having a co-researcher with the same range of communication impairments as the child and young people participants led to some interesting interactions during interview data collection, including surprise by parents that someone using AAC could be a researcher. The co-researcher's role in interviewing demonstrated to all participants what can be achieved by a person who uses a communication aid, once leaving education.

Both co-researchers presented as part of the team at the dissemination events in Manchester, at the Scottish Parliament and the House of Commons in London, sharing key findings, policy implications and the resources they had co-created with the wider team. This created a strong impact with panellists and workshop participants, who explicitly welcomed the inclusion of people who use AAC and family members within the research team, as well as the findings from PI participants.

Impact of the I-ASC project

The co-researchers have together been co-authors on the outputs from the project as essential team members every step of the way during the study; their input, as mentioned earlier, was not recorded separately, as they were integral to all activities. Within the field of AAC, the team had gone out in the first year to engage with as wide an audience as possible. Communication Matters (the UK branch of the International Society of Augmentative and Alternative Communication (ISAAC)) hold an annual, well-attended conference. This provided a platform to gain feedback from those who use AAC, family members and professionals throughout the course of the project, and then share as the keynote speakers the findings from the project. The later full dissemination of findings have built on this, spreading the word widely with those who use AAC, families/carers, national and local policy makers, commissioners of services, funders, practitioners and technology manufacturers that public involvement delivers good research.

In terms of demonstrating PI impact on the research output, this chapter is one attempt to share widely the initial learnings from the I-ASC project approach to PI co-construction of research. Achieving good impact is essential for all funders and research establishments. The NIHR want by 2025 for every research project to be inclusive of PI contributors. The I-ASC approach appears to be ahead of the curve; what we thought was common place in our field, and within research generally, now appears ground-breaking.

Governance and leadership

In this context, the NSPIR (2018) refer to organisational and institutional governance and its leadership. Each research establishment in the UK is encouraged to have a PI engagement plan, enabling public contributors to be part of senior-level decision making on research strategy, then monitoring, reviewing and reporting on plans. This is less about research project delivery and more about public accountability and visibility. The Faculty of Health, Psychology and Social Care within Manchester Metropolitan University have a clear focus on this, and within the I-ASC project the research team have gone above and beyond the minimum standards laid out for best practice. Saying this, it is also clear there is still much to be learned in effective PI research, and the I-ASC team see this project as one they too can learn from for the future.

Returning to the key I-ASC research questions for PI

1   How do we apply the previously published quality indicators from a PI perspective to ensure our research approach and outputs meet with best practice standards?

The most recent quality indicators are those from the NSPIR (2018) and are further along than anything published when the project was conceived. The team have measured progress in PI research against these latest standards and feel the culture and approach of the project has gone above and beyond the indicators published for good practice.

2   How do we minimise any risk of tokenism while at the same time delivering effective, externally funded research with critical deadlines?

There was some slippage within the project; however, it cannot be said to be wholly or in part due to the PI co-researchers. Some tasks have just taken longer than planned, but sickness and absences within the rest of the project team also resulted in setbacks. On the other hand, the parent co-researcher stepping in to help out with additional tasks when deadlines needed to be met is not the norm for a PI co-researcher and should not be viewed as good practice. At the time, this was right for the project, but in reality this has blurred the lines between the PI co-researcher role and their undertaking project management activities. In hindsight, it might have been preferable to have replaced them with a new PI co-researcher or employed another researcher part time.

In summary, the new National Standards for PI re-frame good practice; however, even now it seems the I-ASC project has been innovative in ambition for PI co-produced research. The next step is to thoroughly evaluate the process and PI contributions during the I-ASC project in order to produce a toolkit and online resources that support other researchers and those who wish to participate in the co-production of PI research. One aim of this evaluation is to show the ways in which PI co-created and co-produced research delivers benefits for both a research study in the short term and the wider population in the longer term.

Recommendations

Naively, the I-ASC project team thought at the outset that this approach to PI research was the norm. Based on the setbacks, pitfalls and unexpected bonuses along the way, we would recommend:

*   Understand time constraints, payment and the personal circumstances of PI co-researchers to agree appropriate rewards as part of the bid process.
*   Have clearly defined roles for all team members, including the PI contributors.
*   Discuss and agree the ways PI contributors with communication impairments prefer to be supported and ensure all team members understand the strategies to be used so everyone will be heard, valued and empowered.
*   Where possible, find funding for PI co-researchers to be involved in the co-creation of research, allowing for pre-award payment.
*   Explore what the co-researcher can bring to the project besides their lived experiences.

- Obtain, with their permission, the support of family and support network of co-researchers who need assistance to participate, to establish the best support mechanisms.
- Understand the potential timelines, constraints and challenges that may occur through national and local policy, institutional and organisational procedures, for instance in relation to taking up references (in the UK, everyone working with children and vulnerable adults needs clearance from the Disclosure Barring Service). Occupational Health, ethics etc.
- Ensure the project team understands the potential constraints for data collection and site visits e.g. co-researchers who need specific access requirements or personal assistance, carrying out site visits/risk assessments beforehand where necessary.
- Ensure all partners and team members understand every team role, expectations of all roles and the parity of input by everyone, agreeing at the first opportunity ground rules for joint collaborative working.

In summary, the new National Standards for PI re-frame good practice; however, even now it seems the I-ASC project has been ahead of the curve in ambition for PI co-produced research. The next step is to thoroughly evaluate the process and PI contributions during the I-ASC project in order to produce a toolkit and online resources that support other researchers and those who wish to participate in the co-production of PI research and, in addition, to demonstrate that with a cohort renowned for being difficult to reach, and time and resource heavy to engage with. Use the main I-ASC project methodologies and approaches to demonstrate how to make research accessible, relevant and meaningful to those with communication impairments, including day-to-day adjustments. Finally, showing PI co-created and co-produced research delivers benefits for both a research study in the short term and the wider population in the longer term.

References

Boaz, A., Biri, B., and McKeitt, C. (2014). Rethinking the relationship between science and society: Has there been a shift in attitudes to patient and public involvement and public engagement in science in the United Kingdom. *Health Expectations*, 19, pp592–601.

Denegri, S. (2015). *Going the extra mile: Improving the nation's health and wellbeing through public involvement in research.* www.nihr.ac.uk.

Dollaghan, C. A. (2007). *The handbook for evidence-based practice in communication disorders.* Baltimore, MD: Paul H. Brookes Publishing.

Frankena, T. K., Naaldenberg, J., Cardol, M., et al. (2016). Exploring academics' views on designs, methods, characteristics and outcomes of inclusive health research with people with intellectual disabilities: A modified Delphi study. *BMJ Open*, 6:e011861. doi:10.1136/bmjopen-2016-011861

Green, G. (2016). Power to the people: To what extent has public involvement in applied health research achieved this? *Research Involvement and Engagement*, 2:28, pp1–13.

National Standards for Public Involvement in Research. (2018). https://sites.google.com/nihr.ac.uk/pi-standards/home.

Nieuwenhuys, O. (2004). Participatory action research in the majority world. In S. Fraser, V. Lewis, S. Ding, M. Kellett and C. Robinson (Eds.), *Doing research with children and young people.* London: Sage Publications.

Ocloo, J., and Matthews, R. (2016). From tokenism to empowerment: Progressing patient and public involvement in healthcare improvement. *BMJ Quality & Safety*, pp1–7, Online First.

Sackett, D., Straus, S., Richardson, W., Rosenberg, W., and Haynes, R. (1997). *Evidence based medicine: How to practice and teach EBM.* New York: Churchill Livingstone.

Shen, S., Doyle-Thomas, K., Beesley, L., Karmali, A., Williams, L., Tanel, N., and McPherson, A. (2017). How and why should we engage parents as co-researchers in health research? A scoping review of current practices. *Health Expectations*, pp1–12. doi:10.1111/hex.12490.

Snow, R. (2016). *What makes a real patient?* BMJ Blogs. https://blogs.bmj.com/bmj/2016/07/19/rosamund-snow-what-makes-a-real-patient/.

Online resources

NHS Health Education England. (2018). *Patient advisory forum annual review: Involving patients and the public in the decisions of health education England.* www.hee.nhs.uk/sites/default/files/documents/PAF%20 Annual%20Review%20v7%20low%20res.pdf [accessed 19 September 2019].

NIHR INVOLVE. (2016). Guidance for Researchers: PPI Feedback. https://www.clahrc-eoe.nihr.ac.uk/ wp-content/uploads/2016/05/Guidance-for-Researchers-PPI-Feedback_2018.pdf

40

FROM TOKENISM TO FULL PARTICIPATION

Autistic involvement in research and the delivery of services

Damian Milton

Introduction

Historically, autistic people have often been framed out of contributing towards the decisions that directly affect their own lives. This is despite a background of changing national and international policy and legislation regarding obtaining the views of disabled people in the delivery of services and within research practices (Pellicano et al., 2013). This is possibly most highlighted by the lack of autistic involvement and representation in many of the organisations that have been set up to advocate for the needs of autistic people. As this chapter indicates, however, this is perhaps slowly beginning to change in some contexts, although many barriers still exist in regard to participation in wider social life, with many autistic-led advocacy groups rallying behind the call for 'nothing about us, without us' (e.g. *ASAN*, 2011; *Autistic-UK*, 2019). As autistic self-advocacy and rights groups have grown over the last two or three decades, there has also been a growing conflict between the autistic community 'voice' often championing the concept of neurodiversity and a social model of disability (or some variant thereof) and a discourse based in an individualised medical model of dysfunction, deficiency and dependency. In this chapter, an overview will be given to numerous participatory projects based primarily in the context of work happening in the United Kingdom. This is due to how the UK could be said to be further along this path than most. Reference will also be made to efforts outside the UK.

Neurodiversity and the challenge to traditional autism research

Originating as a term in the late 1990s and coined by the Australian sociologist Judy Singer (2017), herself an autistic person, 'neurodiversity' was proposed at its base as a 'brute fact', in the sense that all brains and their development are in some ways unique (using an analogy with the term 'biodiversity'). Walker (2014), in their overview of the main concepts related to neurodiversity, also distinguishes between the 'neurodiversity movement' (relating to the championing of human rights for all 'neurodivergent' people) and the 'neurodiversity paradigm' that saw such diversity as part of natural diversity, rather than something to be pathologised using a purely individualised and medical model of disability. From this, one can see that these ideas are often rooted in the social model of disability (or variations thereof). Such conceptualisations of autism and neurodiversity are at odds, though, with the dominant views within autism research and education (Pellicano et al., 2013), which primarily frames autism as a set of impairments to be alleviated or remedied through medical intervention, rarely employing a sociological imagination (Mills, 2000) to such experiences. While within sociological contexts issues regarding insider and outsider knowledge have long been debated (Merton, 1972) or championed (Harraway, 2003), it has been more recent that such calls have been made regarding autism research and practice (Milton and Bracher, 2013; Pellicano et al., 2013).

> Right from the start, from the time someone came up with the word 'autism', the condition has been judged from the outside, by its appearances, and not from the inside according to how it is experienced.
>
> *(Williams, 1996, p. 14)*

Until recently, autistic people have rarely been seen in the role of the producer or interpreter of research, cut off behind what Mike Bracher (in Milton and Bracher, 2013) described as the 'glass sub-heading' – always written about and for rather than leading on the interpretation of findings. As Pellicano et al. (2013) showed in their report, *A Future Made Together*, less than 1% of autism research could have been described as 'social research', with the vast majority also looking at autistic children rather than through the whole lifespan. In recent times, however, this lack of full participation in research and the design and delivery of support services has been challenged by autistic-led writers and groups such as the Participatory Autism Research Collective (*PARC*, 2019). As autistic people have moved into the field of autism research, standard ideas of the goals of research and intervention have been highly criticised, particularly those reliant on an idealised notion of normalcy and in deep contrast to goals defined by behavioural outcomes and 'social skills' (as defined by non-autistic onlookers).

Participatory Autism Research

In the view being expressed here, participatory research should not be seen as a strict set of practices to follow but more of an ethos to work towards, often encompassing a wide range of theoretical and methodological approaches, the primary aim of which is to cede power from the researcher to the subjects of such research, who are often community members of community-based organisations. In participatory research, it is the participants themselves who should have control over the research agenda, processes and actions taken. Most importantly, it is the participants who should have the power to analyse and reflect upon the information generated. This is not to say that there is not value in traditional research methods or sometimes the purposes they are set to (although one can often be critical of these, too); the randomised controlled trial of an intervention and whether it actually does what it says it will, for example. Or, alongside this, the building of collaborative communities of practice (Wenger, 1998) and the value of theories and methods aimed at capturing the lived experiences of those being researched.

Autistic participation in research is not without pragmatic difficulties, however, particularly in the intersection between autism and significant learning/intellectual disability. The cognitive and linguistic demands of research may limit the full involvement of participants with such experiences (Lewis and Porter, 2004). Alongside this, the representativeness of proxy informants have also been questioned (Lewis and Porter, 2004), as well as the accuracy of utilising views as reported through means such as visual pictures and schedules and whether such activities can fully grasp the views of participants (Preece and Jordan, 2009). Informed consent is therefore also at issue. Having said this, however, just because participation can be difficult does not mean we should not at least try the best one can to increase participation of autistic people with learning/intellectual disability. As a recent study by Russell et al. (2019) suggested, the vast majority of autism research is carried out with those without significant learning/intellectual disability. There has also been innovative work using a number of mediums to increase participation, such as through artwork, collage, photography, modelling, concrete manipulation (such as sorting into piles of like and dislike) and the use of 'aide-memoirs' (Greenstein, 2014; Milton, 2018; Ridout, 2017; Williams and Hanke, 2007).

> Traditional methods of consulting and working in partnership may not always be effective, and new avenues for connection may need to be sought, however when collaborative ventures are pursued, and when people on the autism spectrum feel included and empowered, the ability to live as one chooses greatly increases.
>
> *(Milton, 2014)*

Examples of autistic participation in research

Through my own work, I have been fortunate enough to be part of a growing push for greater participation in research, and this has included numerous projects. In 2012, I was enlisted to work on projects for the Autism Education Trust (*AET*, 2019) as an autistic consultant, which also led on to work on the Transform Autism Education project (*TAE*, 2019). This latter project involved working with teams in Italy and Greece in reworking the materials that had been produced by the AET in those contexts. All these projects involved the design and delivery of training and resources for educational practitioners. In the TAE project, it also involved work increasing the level of participation of autistic people more generally into this production. I was also employed by London South Bank University as a researcher for a project regarding mentoring for autistic adults. This project involved the autistic mentees along with a mixture of autistic and non-autistic mentors, and an advisory group mostly made up of autistic people. The goals of the mentoring process were led by the autistic mentees. Although only a small pilot project, this process showed significant benefits for many involved (Martin et al. 2017). I was also a co-investigator in the 'Shaping Autism Research UK' seminar series project that grew out of the report by Pellicano et al. (2013). This seminar series involved six events across the UK and brought together autistic people with researchers and other stakeholders in order to address a range of topics. A key theme that was prevalent in this series was the issue of participation, with one of the seminar events dedicated to the issue, and it was a key focus in subsequent articles about the project (Fletcher-Watson et al., 2019). This seminar series also produced a 'participation toolkit' for researchers that is freely available (*Shaping Autism Research*, 2019).

Recent years have also seen the establishment of autistic-led open access journals such as *Autonomy: The Critical Interdisciplinary Journal of Autism Studies* (*Autonomy*, 2012) and *Autism, Policy and Practice* (*APP*, 2019), as well as the Autism Arts Festival, hosted annually at the University of Kent (*Autism Arts Festival*, 2019).

The Participatory Autism Research Collective (PARC)

The Participatory Autism Research Collective (PARC) was set up to bring autistic people, including scholars and activists, together with early career researchers and practitioners who work with autistic people. Its first meeting was held in April 2015. The aim of this collective was to build a community network where those who wish to see more significant involvement of autistic people in autism research could share their knowledge and expertise (and not just those already involved in research). The initial objectives of PARC were set out to:

- Address the isolation felt by many autistic researchers
- Ensure that research carried out by autistic people can be found and used
- Raise the reputation of participatory research methods in the field
- Critically comment on autism research which does not empower autistic people.

In order to achieve these objectives, it was suggested that PARC would:

- Encourage autistic people starting out in research
- Provide peer feedback on research and support with accessing funding
- Hold meetings and events.

In the near five years since its inception, the PARC network has been successful in some of these objectives, although attracting funding has remained a problematic issue, both for the network itself and for participatory projects. Despite this, the PARC network has been able to attract good interest in both its website (*PARC*, 2019) and in numerous events that it has hosted, such as regular seminar events, a yearly 'critical autism studies' conference held at London South Bank University, partnerships with events such as the Lancaster University Disability Studies conference (holding a specialist stream on neurodiversity), the Learning Disability Today conference and a fringe event to the 50th anniversary conference for Scottish Autism, as well as seminar events and meetings held in Birmingham, Sheffield, Nottingham and Canterbury. The PARC network has also been involved in publishing special editions of journals such as *Advances in Autism*, and book publications through a partnership with Pavilion Press (e.g. Milton, 2017; Ridout, 2018).

The National Autistic Taskforce

Not all efforts have been in the area of autism research, though. Following on from the National Autism Project (*NAP*, 2019), where the involvement of an autistic advisory panel was highly impactful, the Shirley Foundation commissioned and funded the setting up of an independent National Autistic Taskforce (*NAT*, 2019):

> The National Autistic Taskforce was established to give autistic adults a stronger voice in the decisions and directions of our own lives – especially those with highest support needs and, often, least autonomy. We draw on deep knowledge of rights and obligations, already enshrined in law but rarely respected in practice, to increase autonomy in Autistic lives. We seek to ensure autistic voices are included alongside those of families, policy makers and professionals.
>
> *(National Autistic Taskforce, 2019)*

The NAT project has contributed to a variety of government consultations and working groups, but most importantly (thus far) has also produced an independent guide to quality care for autistic people. This document aimed at the implementing of policy initiatives and improvements in practice, re-framing issues around behaviour (addressed as linked to distress) and communication, as well as highlighting issues such as personal autonomy, fighting stigma and discrimination and encouraging positive autistic identity.

Remaining issues and challenges

While the above initiatives and projects have been a large step forward in the participation of autistic people in research, the education of professionals working with autistic people and the design and delivery of services, these efforts remain somewhat on the periphery of autism discourse and practice. There is also still a very long way to go to address wider issues in respect of autistic participation. As already mentioned, there is a need to do further work on the inclusion of autistic people with significant learning/intellectual disability (Russell et al., 2019), although the same can often be said regarding learning disability research, which often does not fully account for sub-groups within and often only is acknowledged as a 'co-morbidity'. This siloed nature of the respective fields is a block to progress in both and the intersection between.

There are also the intersections of autism with gender and sexuality. While there is increasing recognition of the underdiagnosis of autistic women (*SWAN*, 2019) and the higher proportions of autistic people with non-binary gender and sexual identities, there is still much work to be done to address these intersections in terms of autistic advocacy and participation more generally. Such under-representation can also be seen regarding ethnicity and culture, with the vast proportion of efforts being in the Global North. Autism associated events and discourse are thus often dominated by white, middle-class males. Although PARC has partnered with groups such as *Autism Voice UK* (2019) to hold events and training sessions, such efforts are even further on the margins and need to be held centre-stage in future.

References

Autism Arts Festival. (2019). Accessed online at: https://autismartsfestival.org/, 29/11/19.
Autism Education Trust (AET). (2019). Accessed online at: www.autismeducationtrust.org.uk/, 29/11/19.
Autism, Policy and Practice. (2019). Accessed online at: www.openaccessautism.org/index.php/app, 29/11/19.
Autism Voice UK. (2019). Accessed online at: www.autismvoice.org.uk/, 29/11/19.
Autistic Self-Advocacy Network (ASAN). (2011). *Our Motto: What Is 'Nothing About Us Without Us'?* Accessed online at: https://autisticadvocacy.org/about-asan/position-statements/, 29/11/19.
Autistic-UK. (2019). Accessed online at: https://autisticuk.org/, 29/11/19.
Autonomy, the Critical Journal of Interdisciplinary Autism Studies. (2012). Accessed at: www.larry-arnold.net/Autonomy/index.php/autonomy/index, 29/11/19.
Fletcher-Watson, S., Adams, J., Brook, K., Charman, T., Crane, L., Cusack, J., Leekham, S., Milton, D., Parr, J. and Pellicano, E. (2019). Making the future together: Shaping autism research through meaningful participation. *Autism*, 23(4), 943–953.
Greenstein, A. (2014). Today's learning objective is to have a party: Playing research with students in a secondary school special needs unit. *Journal of Research in Special Educational Needs*, 14(2), 71–81.
Haraway, D. (2003). Situated knowledges: The science question in feminism and the privilege of partial perspective. *Turning Points in Qualitative Research: Tying Knots in a Handkerchief, 2003*, 21–46.
Lewis, A. and Porter, J. (2004). Interviewing children and young people with learning disabilities: guidelines for researchers and multi-professional practice. *British Journal of Learning Disabilities*, 32, 191–197.
Martin, N., Milton, D. E. M., Sims, T., Dawkins, G., Baron-Cohen, S. and Mills, R. (2017). Does 'mentoring' offer effective support to autistic adults? A mixed-methods pilot study. *Advances in Autism*, 3(4), 229–239.
Merton, R. K. (1972). Insiders and outsiders: A chapter in the sociology of knowledge. *American Journal of Sociology*, 78(1), 9–47.
Mills, C. W. (2000). *The sociological imagination*. Oxford: Oxford University Press.
Milton, D. (2014). *What is meant by participation and inclusion, and why it can be difficult to achieve*. NAS Ask autism conference, Participation and inclusion from the inside-out: Autism from an autistic perspective, London.
Milton, D. (2017). *A mismatch of salience: Explorations of the nature of autism from theory to practice*. Hove: Pavilion Press.
Milton, D. (2018). Autistic development, trauma and personhood: Beyond the frame of the neoliberal individual. In *The Palgrave handbook of disabled children's childhood studies* (pp. 461–476). London: Palgrave Macmillan.

Milton, D., and Bracher, M. (2013) Autistics speak but are they heard? *Medical Sociology Online,* 7(2), 61–69.

National Autism Project (NAP). (2019). Accessed online at: http://nationalautismproject.org.uk/, 29/11/19.

National Autistic Taskforce (NAT). (2019). Accessed online at: https://nationalautistictaskforce.org.uk/, 29/11/19.

The Participatory Autism Research Collective (PARC). (2019). Accessed online at: https://PARCautism.co.uk, 29/11/19.

Pellicano, L., Dinsmore, A., and Charman, T. (2013). *A future shaped together: Shaping autism research in the UK.* London: Institute of Education.

Preece, D., and Jordan, R. (2009). Obtaining the views of children and young people with autism spectrum disorders about their experience of daily life and social care support. *British Journal of Learning Disabilities, 38,* 10–20.

Ridout, S. (2017). The autistic voice and creative methodologies. *Qualitative Research Journal, 17*(1), 52–64.

Ridout, S. (2018). *Autism and mental well-being in higher education: A practical resource for students, mentors and study skills support workers.* Hove: Pavilion Press.

Russell, G., Mandy, W., Elliott, D., White, R., Pittwood, T., and Ford, T. (2019). Selection bias on intellectual ability in autism research: A cross-sectional review and meta-analysis. *Molecular Autism, 10*(1), 9.

Scottish Women's Autism Network (SWAN). (2019). Accessed online at: http://swanscotland.org/, 29/11/19.

Shaping Autism Research UK. (2019). Accessed online at: www.shapingautismresearch.co.uk/, 29/11/19.

Singer, J. (2017). *Neurodiversity: The birth of an idea.* Lexington, KY: n.p.

Transform Autism Education (TAE). (2019). Accessed online at: www.transformautismeducation.org/, 29/11/19.

Walker, N. (2014). *Neurodiversity: Some basic terms and definitions.* Accessed online at: https://neurocosmopolitanism.com/neurodiversity-some-basic-terms-definitions/, 29/11/19.

Wenger, E. (1998). *Communities of practice: Learning, meaning and identity.* Cambridge: Cambridge University Press.

Williams, D. (1996). *Autism: An inside-out approach.* London: Jessica Kingsley.

Williams, J., and Hanke, D. (2007). 'Do you know what sort of school I want?': Optimum features of school provision for pupils with autistic spectrum disorder. *Good Autism Practice (GAP), 8*(2), 51–63.

41

THE POSSIBILITIES AND CONSTRAINTS OF SERVICE USER RESEARCH COLLABORATIONS

The Peer Qualitative Research Group

Jijian Voronka, Jill Grant, Deb Wise Harris,
Arianna Kennedy and Janina Komaroff

Collaborations in context

In recent decades, Western countries (especially Canada, the US, the UK, Australia, and New Zealand) have prioritized and mandated inclusionary practices in mental health and social care policy. This turn was conceived as a response to the advocacy demands of service user/consumer/survivor activists that there be "nothing about us without us." However, it is also part of a broader trend in which the ethos of *inclusion* is deployed in mainstream organizations as a strategy to purportedly tackle social injustice. Philosophies of normalization and independent living, the emergence of specific support services for women, racialized and LGBTQ2S+ communities, and progressive professionals working within the system to change organizational process all contributed to the mainstreaming of participatory practices (Beresford, 2012, p. 25). In Canada, inclusion of mental health service users in the systems that affect us has been taking place since the 1980s (Church and Reville, 1990; Grant, 2007). As service user participation has evolved, these roles have formalized and in some cases been professionalized into more official categories of "peer work." To be a peer worker, you must have lived experience that is conceived as similar to those experienced by people that a system serves. As a result, usually denigrated experiences (distress, incarceration, drug use, sex work, migration, homelessness) have become qualifications.

Peer workers are employed to support clients directly, to represent and advocate for service user communities within social service organizations, and sometimes as members of the research teams investigating those communities. Peer workers are found in locations as diverse as homeless shelters, drop-in services, outreach efforts, clinical hospital wards, veteran and workplace mental health supports, and forensic units. They have increasingly become key paraprofessional figures, whose labour is harnessed in the governance of others like themselves.

As this ethos of inclusion becomes normalized, people have begun to map how such inclusion measures are organized in situ, highlighting critiques of these governing practices. Critiques of inclusion and diversity efforts in the fields of Critical Race (Ahmed, 2012; Joseph,

446

2015), Indigenous (Coulthard, 2014; Million, 2013), Queer (Puar, 2007; Spade, 2015) Disability (Mitchell and Snyder, 2015), and Mad Studies (Brosnan, 2019; Voronka and Costa, 2019) have pointed to the ways in which inclusion methods simply incorporate marginalized subjects into pre-existing systems of power without significantly recalibrating such systems. In the field of mental health research, service users and their allies have been producing knowledge on how to do inclusion as ethically as possible (Barber et al., 2011; Desai et al., 2019; Wallcraft et al., 2009), as well as documenting the conditions and limits of such participatory practices (Daya et al., 2019; Rose and Kalathil, 2019; Rose, 2019). With this chapter, we document the effort, process, and results of developing the Peer Qualitative Research Group (PQRG), a research group entirely made up of people with lived experiences of mental health issues and/or homelessness. Yet we do so with a critical eye to the conditions and limits of how this group was able to work within dominant mental health epistemes. Specifically, we show that the PQRG was still constrained by the expectations of conventional research funding timelines, practices, and disciplinary standards.

A decade ago, the At Home/Chez Soi project, a large national research demonstration project, set out to study the most effective ways to house and support homeless people with mental health issues. The study sought to implement and evaluate the Housing First program model, which offers housing and support choice to service users, and compare the outcomes of this model to whatever pre-existing services were available in five cities across Canada. A randomized controlled trial, the research project nevertheless invested in considerable and sustained community outreach in order to achieve enough "buy-in" from provincial and municipal governments, local health and social service providers, researchers and service users. One of the many ways in which this was done was to invest in the involvement of "people with lived experience" of homelessness and/or mental health issues in project peer work positions. By merging common community-based research practices of including those communities in which you seek to research within this larger RCT, the project positioned itself as invested in inclusion practices, and thus community. Sites were encouraged to develop local PWLE groups to consult on local research, service, and housing activities; local research teams were encouraged to hire peer researchers; service providers hired peer support workers on their mental health service teams. Nationally, the project incorporated PWLE into their governance structures and supported the development of a peer-only advisory board.

This inclusion did several things. It positioned a core project principle as valuing lived experience as expertise and thus invested in community. This principle worked to secure others working in community who are invested in inclusion practices to invest to the project. It also added peer workers into diverse workplace settings, some of which were used and equipped to work alongside community members, other workplaces less so. In local research teams, some sites were led by researchers experienced in community-based research (CBR) practices and thus enthusiastic in working with peer researchers. In other sites, researcher teams were less familiar with CBR and less clear on how to make use of peer researchers. In sum, the ways in which peer researchers were hired, the work that they did, and the environments that they worked within varied drastically across this national project.

The development of the Peer Qualitative Research Group (PQRG) emerged from the context of this wider research project. Part of the lead author's role was to ensure meaningful engagement of peer researchers, yet in practice there was little way of ensuring this and was beyond her purview to enforce. Most local research teams hired two peer researchers onto their teams: most of them were hired as part-time contractual labour, and most of them were involved in conducting qualitative interviews with project participants. Yet whether and how peer researchers would inform analytic approaches to the data, whether they would be involved in data analysis, and whether they would be involved in writing and co-authorship activities remained to be seen. After raising these questions with the national qualitative research team, rooting these queries as concerns that are often cited in CBR more broadly (Janes, 2015; Kirkwood, 2012; Roche, 2011), discussion about the possibilities of creating a peer-only qualitative research subgroup ensued.

Logics for developing a peer-only research group within this wider project included that it would ensure that peer researchers would have paid time to contribute to analysis and write-up. Often, members of a research team who are on contract only get paid for data collection, coding, and perhaps analysis stages of research, as oftentimes grant funding ends before writing begins. This means that usually principal and co-investigators, members who are in academic positions and are salaried to do writing as part of their work, dominate the writing stages, and thus the final products of the research. In practice, this translates into knowledge outputs that are produced by people who are living and working in protected, financially stable worlds with research agendas and careers that they are invested in. This in turn influences their priorities of what constitutes valuable "research output." This matters because a) in the academic knowledge economy, what constitutes valuable knowledge, findings, and outputs is influenced by dominant pre-existing frameworks, which are influenced by bureaucratic and professional values that may not align with community needs, knowledges, and values. And b) due to these pressures, those left in charge of writing up the research may prioritize the demands of their jobs and their disciplines and overlook alternative ways that this data could be used and written up for publication. This can lead to c) similar knowledge, findings, and outputs dominating and replicating, leaving little room for alternative perspectives and knowledges to be valorised as knowledge proper.

The PQRG could help counter this by working in a setting that wasn't *as* influenced by such academic pressures, which might open the possibility for findings otherwise not of interest to traditional research teams. We also hoped that there might be a level of community-building and comfort in working in a peer-only research group setting. Up until this point, all peer researchers were working in mixed-research teams, and it was a goal to bring us together across disparate work environments to pool our resources and prioritize our own analysis.

Building the Peer Qualitative Research Group

However, first we had to make it happen. This meant developing a proposal that would make sense to the broader research project leads by using the language of "capacity-building" and working within what have come to be liberal frameworks of inclusion. Often, when the language of capacity-building is used within mental health contexts, emphasis is on the need for marginalized individuals to develop a set of skills or knowledge that they are assumed to be lacking. Knowing this, the proposal used the language of capacity-building strategically to point to the ways in which the development of this group would also "capacity build" at organizational and structural levels. That is, build on the capacity and the quality of mental health research and contribute to social justice work that is committed to understanding how best to improve service systems from those who use them. We also hoped that the paper produced from our work would demonstrate to research teams that peer researchers have the capacity to be involved in all stages of the research project, including data analysis and writing. This will position peer researchers as having demonstrated capacity of doing such work, and further encourage local research teams to better incorporate peers meaningfully within their own research endeavours.

The proposal for the development of the PQRG articulated that the development of this research group would ensure that peer research involvement would be more than consultation and incorporation, and allow for peer-only research collaboration. To allow PWLE to establish their claim as knowledge producers within scholarly activities, and to offer PWLE the opportunity to develop process, analytic, and writing skills among peers in a self-determining manner. We also noted some conditions to the development of the PQRG to be clear about our process and autonomy: that the research topic/questions will be identified by peers within the group; the data will be analysed and interpreted by peers within the group; the group will have editorial and write-up control; the group will be responsible for dissemination of the final product (an academic, publisher-ready article – as well as the possibility for write-up for other audiences).

After some discussion and an outline of process and budget, the national qualitative research team initially granted $40,500 of funding for the development of the PQRG, which was later cut to $32,000. The majority of this funding was towards bringing the research group together for in-person meetings, and to hire a research assistant. In mid-2011, Voronka invited Grant in as co-lead for this project, and by summer we secured Wise Harris as the PQRG research assistant. These three members held employment positions/contracts that effectively compensated them for the labour involved in organizing, analysing, and writing up the research. All other group members were compensated in a more precarious way: local research teams were informed of this project and asked that they consider this opportunity for their peer RAs as part of their job responsibilities, and financially compensate them for the hours that they put in working with the PQRG. While all local research teams enthusiastically supported this, in practice it meant that all members were paid for work that was within a set start and end period of eight months (Fall 2011–Spring 2012). We secured a peer researcher from Moncton, New Brunswick, who initially participated in the group but with whom we lost contact with about half-way through our collaboration. Other PQRG members included Janina Kamaroff (Montreal), Arianna Kennedy (Vancouver), Dawn Boyle (Winnipeg), and Deb Wise Harris (Toronto, and also the PQRG research assistant).

The PQRG undertook secondary data analysis of 30 baseline qualitative interviews that were purposively sampled to reflect the demographics of the overall At Home/Chez Soi study. Thus, on the inclusion continuum, this project was a collaborative effort that involved peer researchers conducting a user-led component within a larger research project (Rose, 2009, p. 171). For those eight months, we set up a pretty traditional working order, with bi-monthly teleconferences and an in-person meeting in November 2011 that brought us all together. We collectively pulled themes that emerged from the transcripts and the research assistant carried the heavy weight of developing a master code list. We decided (after some discussion) to focus on how participants were talking about help – the kind of help they wanted, the kind of help that they received, and the disconnect between the services they wanted and what was available to them. In these eight months, we chose themes that emerged from the data, collectively coded the data, and by the time that our funding was up, we had all contributed some analysis and writing of a draft paper, but were nowhere near finished. When our formal funding period ended, Voronka, Wise Harris, and Grant took the lead in finishing the paper, while in periodic contact with the rest of the members for reviews, edits, and finishing touches. In essence, the group ran into the same pitfalls that often befall CBR-informed research teams: those with more secure work positions ended up heavily shaping the article end product.

Making it work

The two-day in-person meeting held early on in our collaboration was crucial for team building and helped orient ourselves to the work and each other. At the time, having the budget to do this felt extravagant, yet in retrospect it's standard research practice. Perhaps it felt extravagant because we were replicating standard research travel practices that the larger project research teams relied on, and those felt extravagant. Regardless, it's difficult to work remotely from one another, and this team meeting helped build rapport and team spirit. We spent the first day working through the transcripts, discussing themes, and deciding on the theme of un/helpful help, and particularly how participants emphasised the need for social supports (financial, housing, employment) but instead received middle-class textbook responses that were disconnected from their expressed needs. Notes from the lead author's in-person meeting include "Help! I need somebody. Help! Not just anybody." Day two's theme was "How we are going to write it," and the day's agenda started with a planned discussion on theoretical frameworks and conceptual ways to approach the themes, followed by how to write an academic paper and assigning work and roles.

When we started on the agenda item of "theoretical frameworks," the lead author had mapped out and was prepared to guide a group discussion summarizing critical approaches to knowledge production that was very much working within the confines of scholarly ways of learning. Foucault was on the agenda, and armed with flip board and felt pen, the lead author was ready to reproduce ways of knowing that centred disembodied canonical theoretical knowledge. This quickly unravelled, as research team members took the lead in articulating the constraints of working within dominant mental health epistemes and the ways in which their own experiences were interpreted in limiting ways in their work and everyday lives. We discussed the ramifications of this for us as peers, and for the research participants when they present their knowledge in narratives that are then analysed by those that are working within "textbook" ways of thinking about mental health and homelessness. This marked a moment of unlearning for the lead author: of loosening up traditional ways of "training" by allowing collective knowledge to not only emerge but take over.

The first in-person meeting was a success, which allowed for concentrated immersion in the transcripts, thematic consensus, and determining work tasks, but most importantly that we could work together. One thing that we didn't do was designate time to discuss our own histories of lived experience and how we came to occupy peer work positions. Some of us would have appreciated time to discuss and reflect on this collectively as a working group, while others of us felt relief in not having to share what makes us a peer. The change of the original plan of having us come together again in-person towards the end of our analysis no doubt hindered our collective, but we managed to work through this limitation through consistent teleconferencing.

We argued for the development of the PQRG by contending that peer research could produce knowledge that might not be generated otherwise. Here's one way in which we made use of the qualitative data differently. We analysed baseline qualitative interviews only, while the larger research study largely used both baseline and 18-month follow-up interviews to compare participant changes (in social integration, housing stability, mental health etc.). This was largely a structural issue. Had we wanted to do a comparative study to explore participants' transcripts pre- and post-intervention, the project itself would have been close to ending, and funding and payment for research team members would have been compromised. In practice, only analysing the baseline interviews meant that we were "restricted" to analysing and honouring the knowledge that participants came into the study already holding. By engaging only with the baseline qualitative interviews, our purpose was to learn what service users had to say about their encounters with mental health and social service systems prior to study intervention. In essence, we were working with what they already know, and making system change recommendations based on lived experiences of moving through these systems, without the requirement of a mental health intervention to make these changes.

We also made ample room for interview data that heavily critiqued common health and social services practices. We made sure to include lots of full quotes that articulated these critiques in participants' own words. These included distain for mental health and social service practitioners, services offered, experiences of forced drugging, lack of informed consent, and confinement. We worried that this knowledge would be overlooked by conventional researchers. Or, even worse, that it might not be considered knowledge at all, but rather that narrations of such experiences could be interpreted as signs/symptoms of mental illness. By contextualizing and collating individual participants' interviews collectively, we were able to build an analysis of their experiences that pointed to structural issues and systems failures, rather than reducing their critiques to individual deficits/mental illness.

Negotiating disciplinary constraints

Early on in our meetings, we had discussions about what this was all for: the point of undertaking this work, why we were doing it, and who we wanted to engage as our audience. One of the ways that we organized our thoughts about this was by talking through where we wanted to publish. Did we want to try to publish in a traditional mental health medical journal in an effort to gain exposure from a "hard to reach" audience? Did we aim for a liberal helping professions journal working within community mental health frameworks? Or did we preach to the choir and aim for a critical studies publication? We ultimately decided to aim for what we called a "middle of the road" social work and mental health journal. We wanted to reach an audience that would be open to the notions of peer research and knowledge – exposed but not over-exposed.

We settled on submitting our paper to the journal *Social Work & Mental Health*, which meant that we would be reaching an audience of largely social work and allied scholars/professionals. We crafted a paper that at once honoured the experiential knowledge that service users hold by moving through service systems, as well as content that directly pointed to failures in service systems and service provider practice (see Voronka et al., 2014). This exercise demonstrated that even when working within a peer-only research setting, you are still working within the confines of larger disciplinary fields and the expectations of what constitutes a "research paper" proper in that field. We were reminded of this when we received our peer review comments. While positive, the main work that we were advised to do to make the paper publication-ready was to reorganize the paper so that it fit within "standard research paper format." This meant organizing and creating content under thematic heads that traditionally organize social work research articles, such as research methods, analysis, findings, summary, and implications. In essence, we are still expected to meet the writing traditions of social work disciplinary standards if we want publication.

This restricts the work that peer researchers can produce. The goal of peer researchers cannot be to reproduce the standards of what counts as knowledge and research in dominant disciplines. This replicates a similar tension that has been found when implementing peer support services in clinical settings. While the need to develop alternative, peer -led initiatives is recognized, in practice these initiatives "become more medicalized over time, and for long-term sustainability a program often thus depends on its ability to align with the established medical system's characteristics" (Mathers et al., 2014, p. 726). By choosing to publish in a mainstream journal, we were required to fold our writing in ways that were recognizable to conventional knowledges. One reviewer's comments noted how they were familiar with the larger research project and understood it as rigorous, and thus understood our data to be sound. Which invites the question of whether our paper would have been considered equally valid had the research project been designed and conducted by peers. Lastly, we learned that peer-only research collaborations are still hard to comprehend, as one reviewer still required clarification as to whether all of the authors of the paper were people with lived experience, despite our elaborate explanation of the development of the PQRG within the larger context of peer research.

Despite these constraints, the article itself has been useful in education settings. Grant has used the article for several years when teaching an advanced direct practice course in a Master of Social Work program in Canada. Used to both question "expert knowledge" and to support the need to focus on the perspectives of service users when planning services, the paper has stimulated classroom discussion about the most helpful approaches to service provision as well as challenging notions of expertise. Some social work students struggle with the question of their role when we privilege the knowledge and decisions of service users, sometimes becoming protective of their own expertise ("I've spent a lot of money on my education, becoming an expert . . ."). The article has also been taught for several years in "A History of Madness," an upper-year undergraduate Disability Studies course taught at Ryerson University, Toronto, Canada. Students from across disciplines take this class as a liberal arts elective "crash-course" in mad history, politics, and resistance. By the end of the course, students are often left with the question "what do we do with all of this," which instructors interpret as a desire for applied examples of what all of this unlearning is good for (Snyder et al., 2019). We have used this article as a way to answer some of their expressed ambiguity about how the knowledge that they have been exposed to can translate in praxis. The article works as a practical example of how a) people with lived experience already know the problems and resources needed to fix health and social service systems; b) people with lived experience can also be researchers and c) the "theoretical frameworks" that they have been learning in class can have practical applications in "real world" environments.

Challenging the future

The Peer Qualitative Research Group helped us to challenge notions of expertise, highlight the knowledges of people with lived experience, and show that we can learn from those knowledges. We began the project with a strong commitment to challenging the dominant academic conceptualization of expertise by publishing in an academic journal. It was important for us to publish in an academic journal so that the level of prestige assigned to papers *about* people with lived experience of mental illness and/or homelessness might be assigned to a paper *by* people with lived experience. The publication, in and of itself, questions whose voices ought to inform practice; our process does the same in many ways.

Our experience with this collaborative writing project leaves us committed to the need for people with lived experience to do more than "consult"; in order to have an impact, we need to find ways to be in control of the outputs of research. Yet, the reality that we found ourselves restricted in format reflected our desire to claim a presence in the dominant academic venue. At the same time, it meant that our desire to unsettle the process of publishing was hindered by the very structure we were attempting to influence.

The PQRG experienced process constraints that are already well detailed in service user and community-based research. Despite being familiar with these "best practice" methods, we still wrestled with, tried to resist, but also ended up reproducing some of these constraints. These include replicating unrealistic research timelines that might work in labs but not in community-engaged research development; team hierarchies in paid time and pay-scale; enduring cuts to the research budget while expected outputs remain the same; and contending with disciplinary expectations that restrict the ways that knowledge can be presented. Despite these constraints, we are still committed to the possibilities of service user research and working these structural tensions through until they bend, if not break.

References

Ahmed, S. (2012). *On being included: Racism and diversity in institutional life*. London: Duke University Press.

Barber, R., Beresford, P., Boote, J. Cooper, C., & Faulkner, A. (2011). Evaluating the impact of service user involvement on research: A prospective case study. *International Journal of Consumer Studies*, Vol. 35, 609–615.

Beresford, P. (2012). The theory and philosophy behind user involvement. In P. Beresford & S. Carr (Eds.), *Social care, service users and user involvement* (pp. 21–36). Philadelphia: Jessica Kingsley Publishers.

Brosnan, L. (2019). "The lion's den": The epistemic dimensions of invisible emotional labour in service-user involvement spaces. *Journal of Ethics in Mental Health*, Vol. 10, 1–16.

Church, K., & Reville, D. (1990). Do the right thing* right. *Canadian Review of Social Policy*, Vol. 26, 77–81.

Coulthard, G. S. (2014). *Red skin, white masks: Rejecting the colonial politics of recognition*. Minneapolis: University of Minnesota Press.

Daya, I., Hamilton, B., & Roper, C. (2019). Authentic engagement: A conceptual model for welcoming diverse and challenging consumer and survivor views in mental health research, policy, and practice. *International Journal of Mental Health Nursing*, https://doi.org/10.1111/inm.12653.

Desai, M. U., Bellamy, C., Guy, K., Costa, M., O'Connell, M. J., & Davidson, L. (2019). "If you want to know about the book, ask the author": Enhancing community engagement through participatory research in clinical mental health settings. *Behavioural Medicine*, Vol. 45(2), 177–187.

Grant, J. (2007). The participation of mental health service users in Ontario, Canada: A Canadian application of the consumer participation questionnaire. *International Journal of Social Psychiatry*, Vol. 53(2), 148–158.

Janes, J. (2015). Democratic encounters? Epistemic privilege, power, and community-based participatory action research. *Action Research*, Vol. 14(1), 72–87.

Joseph, A. (2015). The necessity of an attention to eurocentrism and colonial technologies: An addition to critical mental health literature. *Disability & Society*, Vol. 30(7), 1021–1041.

Kirkwood, R. (2012). Projects through partnership: Promoting participatory values throughout the research process. In M. Barnes & P. Cotterell (Eds.), *Critical perspectives on user involvement* (pp. 169–180). Bristol: The Policy Press.

Mathers, J., Taylor, R., & Parry, J. (2014). The challenge of implementing peer-led initiatives in a professionalized service: A case study of the national health trainers service in England. *The Millbank Quarterly*, Vol. 92(4), 725–753.

Million, D. (2013). *Therapeutic nations: Healing in an age of indigenous human rights*. Tucson: University of Arizona Press.

Mitchell, D. T., & Snyder, S. L. (2015). *The biopolitics of disability: Neoliberalism, ablenationalism, and peripheral embodiment*. Ann Arbor: University of Michigan Press.

Puar, J. (2007). *Terrorist assemblages: Homonationalism in queer times*. Durham: Duke University Press.

Roche, B. (2011). *New directions in community-based research*. Toronto: Wellesley Institute.

Rose, D. (2009). Is collaborative research possible? In J. Wallcraft, B. Schrank & M. Amering (Eds.), *Handbook of Service User Involvement in Mental Health Research* (pp.169–180). Chichester: Wiley-Blackwell.

Rose, D. (2019). Navigating an insider/outsider identity in exclusive academic spaces: How far can boundaries be pushed? *Journal of Ethics in Mental Health*, Vol. 10, 1–18.

Rose, D., & Kalathil, J. (2019). Power, privilege and knowledge: The untenable promise of co-production in mental "health." *Frontiers in Sociology*, Vol. 4, article 57, doi.org/10.3389/fsoc.2019.00057.

Snyder, S., Pitt, K., Shanouda, F., Voronka, J., Reid, J., & Landry, D. (2019). Unlearning through mad studies: Disruptive pedagogical praxis. *Curriculum Inquiry*, Vol. 49(4), 485–502.

Spade, D. (2015). *Normal life: Administrative violence, critical trans politics, and the limits of the law*. Durham and London: Duke University Press.

Voronka, J., & Costa, L. (2019). Disordering social inclusion: Ethics, critiques, collaborations, futurities. *Journal of Ethics in Mental Health*, Vol. 10, 1–9.

Voronka, J., Wise Harris, D., Grant, J., Komaroff, J., Boyle, D., & Kennedy, A. (2014). Un/helpful help and its discontents: Peer researchers paying attention to street life narratives to inform social work policy and practice. *Social Work in Mental Health*, Vol. 12(3), 249–279.

Wallcraft, J., Schrank, B., & Amering, M. (Eds.). (2009). *Handbook of service user involvement in mental health research*. West Sussex: Wiley-Blackwell.

42

RHETORIC TO REALITY

Challenges and opportunities for embedding young people's involvement in health research

Louca-Mai Brady

Introduction

While there is growing awareness of the case for children and young people's involvement across the public sector, there is limited evidence on how this apparent commitment to involvement and children's rights translates into professional practice and young people's experience of involvement in health research. There are also disparities in the characteristics of young people likely to be involved, the types of decisions they are involved in making, and the extent to which this involvement is meaningful and effective.

Involvement should lead to research, and ultimately services, that better reflect young people's priorities and concerns. This is especially important for young people deemed to be more 'vulnerable', whose voices are often absent from the literature. This chapter draws on learning from a research study which involved young people with experience of drug and alcohol services to explore the potential for new approaches which would do more to transfer power to young people and presents a rights-based framework for embedding young people's involvement in research in ways that are meaningful, effective, and sustainable.

The rhetoric: the case for children and young people's involvement in research

Public involvement in research refers to research carried out 'with' or 'by' members of the public rather than 'to', 'about', or 'for' them' (INVOLVE, 2012). In other words, working with people with relevant lived experience in the design, delivery, and dissemination of research, as opposed to their being involved as research participants, i.e. sources of data. All publicly funded health research in the UK is now expected to have some element of public involvement (Evans et al., 2014). There are two principle arguments for involving children and young people in health research: a rights-based moral argument that it is the 'right' thing to do; and an impact, or evidence, based argument that involvement has benefits for the children and young people participating, for research and for the services and policies which draw on this research evidence (Brady and Graham, 2018).

Public involvement is seen as a right when a group of people might be affected by the research topic, or 'as part of good governance in ensuring transparency of decisions and accountability in the use of public funds' (Oliver et al., 2015, p. 206). The rights-based argument centres on the United Nations Convention on the Rights of the Child (UN, 1989), which established international recognition that all children have a right to have a say in decisions that affect them. The CRC is the most widely ratified human rights treaty in the world, accepted by all UN member states except the United States of America. It sets out children's rights in terms of both their protection and their participation in society and 'asserts children's right to have a voice in decision-making, as well as rights to freedom of thought and expression' (Percy-Smith and Thomas, 2010, p. 1). The key article relating to participation, Article 12, states that:

> States Parties shall assure to the child who is capable of forming his or her own views the right to express those views freely in all matters affecting the child.
>
> *(UN, 1989)*

The CRC-informed understanding that children and young people should be involved in decisions which affect them is increasingly reflected in law, regulation, policy, and research guidance. Further, Article 13 states that children have the right to seek, receive, and impart information and ideas of all kinds. The realisation of children's participation rights requires their translation into policy and practice, as well as children and young people's participation in conceptualising and realising these rights (Spronk, 2014). Children's rights have been reflected in increasing interest in children and young people's involvement in research (e.g. Kellet, 2005; INVOLVE, 2016; Powell and Smith, 2009; Brady and Graham, 2018) both as sources of data and, the focus of this chapter, through their active involvement in the research process.

The evidence-based argument is that involving those who are the focus of health research has been found to have a positive impact on what is researched, how research is conducted, and the impact of research findings on services and in the lives of those involved (Brett et al., 2014; Staley, 2009). Involvement should lead to research, and ultimately services, that better reflect young people's priorities and concerns (Brady et al., 2018; Fleming and Boeck, 2012). By making use of people's knowledge, lived experience, and networks, researchers can provide more relevant, higher quality research that is more widely communicated (Barber et al., 2011; Stewart and Liabo, 2012). But while the evidence base for public involvement has expanded over the past decade, the quality of reporting is often inconsistent, which limits understanding of how it works, for whom, and why (Staniszewska et al., 2017). Research which actively involves young people, if used to inform decision-making or policy formulation, should lead to policies and services that reflect children's priorities and concerns and help to promote a more participative culture (Brady et al., 2012; Fleming and Boeck, 2012).

The reality: children and young people's involvement in health services and research

The global evidence for children's participation in health services is growing rapidly, and international examples of children's voices informing healthcare decision-making and services include the Youth Friendly Hospital Programme in Australia, Give Youth a Voice in Canada (Weil et al., 2015), and the World Health Organisation's *Adolescent Friendly Health Services: an Agenda for Change* (WHO, 2002). Council of Europe Guidelines for Child Friendly Healthcare set out three levels at which children should be provided with opportunities for participation: individual decision-making, providing feedback on their experience of services, and in the policy-making and planning processes of the health services they use (CoE, 2011). But public involvement in health policy tends to focus on adult input, and services for children are seen as the 'poor relation' to adult services within the NHS (Evans, 2016). Children and young people's involvement in healthcare focuses on consultation with children about their individual health needs rather than collaboration in the commissioning, design, delivery, or evaluation of health services or the research which informs this (Brady et al., 2018; Ocloo and Matthews, 2016): In the UK examples of children and young people's involvement in health research include the GenerationR alliance of young people's advisory groups (YPAGs) which support the design and delivery of paediatric health research in the UK[1] and ALPHA DECIPHer, a group of young people aged 14–25 who advise researchers on public health research.[2] Internationally the European Young Person's Advocacy Group (eYPAGnet[3]) is a virtual consortium of YPAGs which aims to support the development of new YPAGs within Europe, and to provide the necessary infrastructure to support meaningful and valued involvement of children and young people (CYP) in clinical trial design and health research. The International Children's Advisory Network (iCAN[4]) is a worldwide consortium of children's advisory groups which works to promote and develop greater global understanding about the importance of the paediatric patient and caregiver voice in healthcare, clinical trials, and research.

However, despite these projects and networks, there is a still a lack of robust evidence on children and young people's participation in health research (Brady, 2017; Wilson et al., 2015). Less attention has been paid to the experiences and impact of involving children and young people than to the involvement of adults in research (Bird et al., 2013), and the evidence base in this area is still developing (Parsons et al., 2017).

Whose voices?

'Children and young people' are far from a homogenous group; age and other aspects of social background such as race and ethnicity, disability, social class, family background, and use of services

> intersect as aspects of who [young people] are, their social position, and what researchers need to consider' in designing research approaches appropriate to the young people they wish to involve.
>
> *(Clavering and McLaughlin, 2010, p. 604)*

There are disparities in the characteristics of children and young people likely to participate, the types of decisions they are involved in making, and the extent to which this involvement is meaningful and effective (Cockburn, 2005; Percy-Smith, 2010). The mechanisms of formal involvement may also privilege the already privileged (Crowley, 2015). Young children (presecondary school age), disabled children and young people, and children and young people in care, among other 'less frequently heard' groups, were still not routinely or systematically involved in individual or strategic decision-making in health services (CRAE, 2015a, 2015b). The voices of children and young people deemed to be more 'vulnerable' are also often absent from the literature on children and young people's participation in research (Powell and Smith, 2009; Mawn et al., 2015; Richards et al., 2015).

The Y-SBNT study

Note: This section draws on a recent paper by the author and colleagues (Brady et al., 2018) and an associated doctoral thesis (Brady, 2017).

The Youth Social Behaviour and Network Therapy (Y-SBNT) study (Watson et al., 2015, 2017) was a randomised controlled trial which aimed to demonstrate the feasibility of recruiting young people to a specifically developed family and wider social network-based intervention by adapting and then testing a version of adult social behaviour and network therapy (SBNT) (Copello et al., 2009).

Evolving plans for involvement

The initial plan for young people's involvement in the Y-SBNT study was to form a young people's advisory group (YPAG) of 10–12 young people with previous experience of drug and alcohol treatment services. The original aim was for the young advisors to work alongside the research team, supported by the study's public involvement leads, through a series of group meetings. But recruitment proved slower than anticipated, and initial meetings were poorly attended. We therefore worked with young advisors to develop a more flexible model that focused on what worked for the young people, recruiting through services known to the study team and in our localities. In total, 17 young people from across England were involved as young advisors in some capacity during the project. The young advisors included 12 females and 5 males ranging in age from 16 to 21 years. Ten young people were involved in the study once, five twice, and two on five or more occasions. We met young people face-to-face on 20 occasions, both one-to-one at locations convenient for them and in group meetings in academic or professional settings. This was supplemented with e-mails, text messages, telephone conversations and postal correspondence depending on the preferences of the young people involved. Young people were given the option of ongoing involvement as a young advisor, without obligation to do so. Regular newsletters, with contributions from young advisors where possible, were sent to all the involved young people, with the aim of keeping them informed even if they were unable to attend meetings or be involved in other ways (Brady et al., 2018).

The young advisors contributed to all three phases of the study. During phase one (intervention development), they contributed to the design of the intervention, ensuring it was acceptable and relevant to the Y-SBNT study's target groups. During phase two (the randomised controlled feasibility trial) and phase three (analysis and reporting of data from the feasibility trial), young people's involvement included input into the design of recruitment and training materials, data collection tools, data analysis and interpretation, reporting, and dissemination (Brady et al., 2018).

'Why we got involved': young advisor's perspectives

I think it's important to involve young people in the Y-SBNT project because we have sort of walked the walk, so we know that stuff that other young people using services have to go through on a daily basis. I wanted to get involved with this project because I've always wanted to do something like this to show others that it is possible and there is light at the end of the tunnel – and that no matter what circumstances they're in they've always got a voice. I want to make things better.

(Young advisor A)

I got involved in the project because I think that it's important that young people can get the help that they need in the most helpful and supportive way so it doesn't damage them. I think I've gained an insight into research with young people and the opinions of young people held by social agencies and professional networks. A project for young people should definitely consult young people and should be based around their views. Young people who have used drug and alcohol services will be able to reflect on their past use of services and give relevant feedback. . . . I'm very much used to discussing my substance use history in a very negative light with no real benefit at the end, but this project has helped me realise that a negative experience has made me wiser.

(Young advisor B)

Louca-Mai Brady

The need for flexibility

We found that facilitating the input from young people needed to be dynamic and flexible in relation to the rhythms, preferences, and commitments in their own lives:

> My mental health has sometimes made it difficult for me to be involved [in the project]. . . . But I like how, if I can't come to a meeting, we can have a phone call instead or you're just a text [message] away, or we can do stuff by post. I've not always been well enough to come and see people face-to-face but that doesn't mean I couldn't be involved in things, whereas some organisations I've been involved with would have said 'you're ill or you couldn't come to a meeting so you can't be involved.'
>
> *(Young advisor A)*

> What I've liked is the flexibility. I've never had to make my own way to one of these meetings . . . of course it is a research project so there is a certain amount of formality about it but [individual involvement] keeps it relevant and convenient for to the young person.
>
> *(Young advisor B)*

But while adults think it is useful for young people to participate, and indeed young people may perceive benefits to involvement, we found that the young advisors often had other priorities:

> Young people in my age group are in a very transitional stage of life, it's hard to commit long term. Some young people relapse, or simply don't like discussing their problem in depth.
>
> *(Young advisor B)*

Keeping in touch was also sometimes problematic; many of the young people we worked with were in hostel or other temporary accommodation, moving several times during the course of the project, as well as changing mobile phones. Lack of internet access and other personal reasons also meant that many did not have regular access to a computer or the internet or chose not to use e-mail or social media.

The need for sensitivity

Involvement in the study required young advisors to draw on their own experiences as users of drug and alcohol services, as well as considering the ways in which their family and wider networks had helped or hindered their recovery. Young advisors pointed out that, in this context, individual involvement may sometimes be more appropriate than group meetings:

> This project talks about really personal stuff and the only way I can talk openly and honestly is because I've had a chance to get to know you [public involvement lead] face-to-face and because I trust you. It wouldn't work otherwise.
>
> *(Young advisor A)*

The skills and experience young people can gain is often cited as a benefit of involvement, but we found that in a study such as this, crediting young people's involvement can be problematic:

> As much as I would love to put on my CV that I've been involved . . . people might wonder why I've been an advisor to a drug project . . . it just raises a few question

marks. . . . I do always have that worry that they're going to think 'Oh she was a drug-gie' and yes it's the truth but I don't want every employer knowing that stuff.

(Young advisor B)

Young people with complex needs may feel powerless about decisions affecting their life and find it difficult to actively say 'no' to involvement, instead opting out by remaining silent or not responding to contact (Waldman, 2005). This was certainly our experience, as all the young people who opted out of further involvement did so by not responding to contact rather than actively opting out. However, both of the two long-standing young advisors quoted in this chapter had periods when they were unable to be involved in the project but subsequently re-engaged when circumstances changed. It was important to maintain a balance between keeping in contact and leaving the door open for future re-engagement, and not making young people feel 'hassled'.

The need for sensitivity also came up in another piece of work in which I was involved: supporting the involvement of young people in a systematic review on what helps improve the lives of people with experience of adverse childhood experiences (ACEs). In this case, we held a one-off workshop during the early stages of the review process to help verify whether the evidence found was relevant to YP's lived experience. The learning from this workshop is discussed further in an associated blog (Lester and Brady, 2018), but a key learning point was the need to manage disclosure. We explained to the young people early in the process that, although they were at the workshop because of their lived experience of ACEs, they did not need to share any personal details. However, several chose to do so, and this needed to be managed carefully to create a safe and comfortable space for everyone involved. Some of the young people who attended were also still going through difficult experiences, and supporting their involvement required both flexibility and sensitivity to individual circumstances.

The role of services

The involvement of children and young people in research also often includes adults, either parents and carers or professionals, who may as act as 'gatekeepers' and both enable and potentially constrain children and young people's involvement (Cree et al., 2002; Moules, 2005). Children and young people can be reliant on significant adults to decide what information they should be given and whether they can be involved (Powell and Smith, 2009). Gatekeepers play a significant role in whether and how children and young people's efforts to be involved are facilitated and supported (Brady and Graham, 2018). Although gatekeepers often play an important role in safeguarding the interests of children and young people, 'they can also act to exert power over young people to prevent their voices being heard' (Moules, 2005, p. 142). Professionals and parents play a significant role in whether and how children and young people's efforts to participate are facilitated and supported in clinical settings, and many have reservations or concerns about children and young people's active involvement (Coyne, 2008).

It was sometimes difficult to engage the interest of services in the potential opportunities that involvement could provide for young people:

Some professionals don't see the value of these projects and don't commit to recruiting young people. Without this you just can't engage young people and do projects like this.

(Young advisor B)

Some services were reluctant to pass information on to young people because they were concerned about young people being too vulnerable or, conversely, because they thought that young people might not be 'academic' or reliable enough. But when we were able to successfully involve young people in the project, the role of services was crucial both in recruitment and in supporting their ongoing engagement. The young people who become engaged almost all did so because someone in a service understood what we were doing and actively promoted the opportunity to young people and supported their engagement.

Developing a different approach to involving young people

Despite the challenges we faced in identifying and recruiting young people with experience of alcohol and/or drug problems for ongoing involvement in the study, young people were actively involved through all stages of the research. Towards the end of the study, we worked with the young advisors to reflect on what we had learnt and how we might best involve young people in future studies. Both researchers and young advisors felt that, ultimately, some form of ongoing group was the best way to involve young people; but one that was more flexible and young people-centred than a fixed-location YPAG with a largely static membership. Instead, what emerged was the need for a more fluid 'community of practice' (Wenger, 1998) in which young people can gradually develop capacity for engagement on their own terms, in what Lave and Wenger (1991) refer to as 'legitimate peripheral participation'. The new approach was a 'hub and spoke' model with a core ongoing group of young advisors, who might change over time, alongside one-to-one and small group work and one-off consultations for those young people who were unable to attend group meetings or commit to ongoing involvement (Brady et al., 2018).

A framework for involvement

In considering the issues outlined above, the following rights-based framework (Figure 42.1) pulls together many of the ideas discussed in this chapter, drawing on our experience of what is needed for children and young people's involvement to be embedded in research and evaluation in ways that are meaningful, effective, and sustainable:

Children and young people are at the centre of the framework because of the centrality of children's rights to this approach, as well as the importance of developing involvement in child and young person-centred ways and in collaboration with children and young people in ways that work for them.

Scope: What might enable or limit children and young people's involvement in the project or programme? E.g. policies and processes of the organisation and systems in which involvement will takes place, requirements of commissioning and regulatory bodies, gatekeepers etc.

Within 'scope' there are a series of interconnected dimensions, set out in Table 42.1, all of which play a part in determining both what children and young people will be involved in and how they will be involved.

Different levels and types of involvement will be appropriate and valid for different children and young people, the nature of the specific research project or programme, and the available resources. No level of involvement is intended to be 'better' than another.

Discussion

Embedding children and young people's involvement in health research requires an understanding of how people conceptualise participation and children's rights and how these understandings

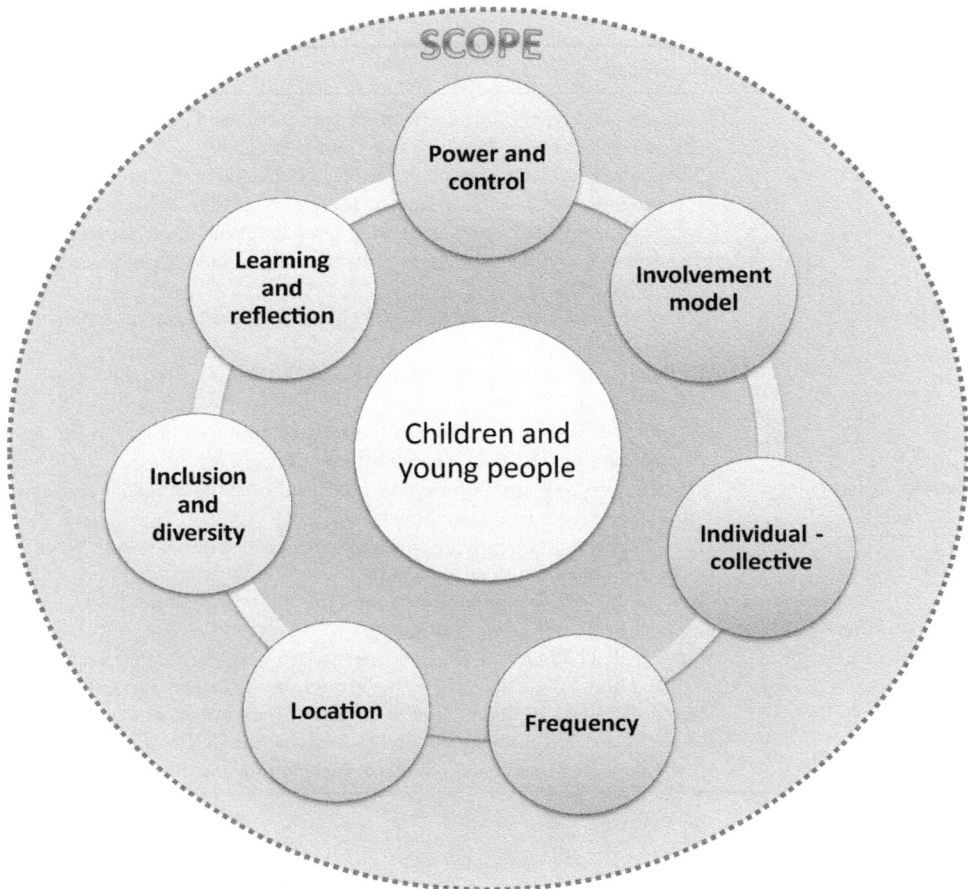

Figure 42.1 A framework for embedding children and young people's involvement in research

Source: Brady (2017)

inform culture and practice, as well as how the cultures and ways of working inform how participation is understood. Participation needs to be embedded in everyday practices, systems, and cultures, but at the same time young people and those facilitating their participation need to be able to be 'critical friends' and to have the independence and resources to be able to drive a more ambitious vision of participatory, inclusive, and socially just participation (Todd, 2012). Without this, participation can too easily revert to be a top-down, 'tick box' exercise which does not stimulate meaningful change in practice and in the relationships between young people and professionals.

How and when children and young people are involved in research is still largely determined and controlled by adults (Brady, 2017; Boyden and Ennew, 1997). It is adult researchers who generally do the asking and the listening and who have the power to put into practice (or not) decisions which children and young people are involved in making. It is important to consider whether children and young people are contributing 'on their own terms and of their own volition . . . [rather than being] expected to fit into adult ways of participating' (Cockburn, 2005, p. 116). The Y-SBNT study, as with many studies involving young people in health research, began with an adult-led set up in which plans for involvement were established before young

Table 42.1 Framework dimensions

Dimension	Key questions to consider
Model of involvement	What level and types of involvement are appropriate and possible for the project/programme? At which stages of the research?
Individual–collective	Will children and young people be involved individually, in a group, or both?
Frequency	How often does involvement happen? Is it a one-off, does it happen at key points/intermittently, or is it ongoing throughout the research process?
	How will this work best for the project/programme and for children and young people?
Location	Where does involvement take place? In fixed or varied-locations, online or in a physical location?
	Do children and young people come into adult settings or do adults go to young people?
	Does involvement involve going to pre-existing groups or other forums or establishing new ones, or a combination of both?
Inclusion and diversity	Who needs to be included for the involvement to be meaningful and relevant to the service, organisation, or project?
	Who is and is not currently or potentially included in involvement? What would enable them to be included?
	What might limit their involvement, and can this be addressed?
Power and control	Consider in relation to all of the above:
	What say do children and young people have in what they are participating in, and how, when, and where they participate (structures and systems)?
	Who decides what is done with the outputs of the involvement?
	Who evaluates involvement and decides on what the success measures are?
Learning and reflection	How will you evaluate impact and learning from the involvement process?

people became involved, rather than collaboratively exploring with young people what would work best for them. In this case, the time taken to establish a group of young advisors and the lack of established YPAG members with relevant experience meant it was difficult to involve young people in the initial stages of the project. If the primary purpose of young people's involvement in research is for them to comment on how to make research materials more 'young people-friendly', this is nearer to consultation than authentic participation (Cockburn, 2005), co-production, or emancipatory models of involvement (Beresford, 2013; Gibson et al., 2012). The dominant discourses and cultures of health services and research, for example the YPAG model, does not necessarily sit easily with co-production or partnership initiatives with young people (Todd, 2012). The framework above provides a means to consider how participation in health services and research could be driven by discourses on children's rights and participatory practice as well as agendas of public involvement, engagement, 'patient experience', and 'voice'.

There are legal and ethical implications to consider when involving children and young people in research (INVOLVE, 2016). The young people involved in the Y-SBNT study and the ACEs systematic review (Lester and Brady, 2018) spoke about the benefits of involvement for their wider peer group as well as personal benefits, including being able to use difficult personal experiences to create positive change. But doing so safely required building trust and being sensitive to individual circumstances. When working with young people on sensitive topics, the emotional health and wellbeing of the young people involved needs to be a priority for everyone involved, particularly when the topics being discussed may act as triggers (Dunn et al., 2018). Young people have a right to be involved in matters that affect them, but in exercising that right, they should be able to influence how they participate as well as exercise the right not to be involved. Individuals who may be under significant stress might see limited personal benefit in being involved as a research collaborator (Beresford, 2000). It can be particularly difficult to involve young people in research on sensitive topics, such as those that are private, stressful, or 'potentially expose stigmatising, or incriminating information' (Lee, 1993). Supporting such involvement requires the adults involved to be 'vigilant, sensitive and supportive'(Dunn et al., 2018). Inclusive involvement should seek to provide opportunities for any young people who want to be involved to do so in ways that work for them, but acknowledge that if, when, and how they can be involved is ultimately a matter of individual choice.

Returning to the distinction at the start of this chapter between rights and evidence-based arguments for children and young people's involvement in research, these arguments are not in opposition but rather can support and reinforce each other. While the evidence base for public involvement has expanded over the past decade, the quality of reporting is often inconsistent, which limits understanding of how it works, for whom, and why (Staniszewska et al., 2017). There is a need to collate, understand, and disseminate more evidence on the nature, extent, and impact of young people's involvement in research (Brady and Preston, 2017). The current climate of austerity and increasing privatisation has implications for children and young people's involvement research, both for the continuation of YPAGs and other projects and in ensuring that learning is captured or shared. Embedding participation requires critical reflection and shared learning as well as an understanding of the wider systems and structures which can facilitate or present barriers to participative practice.

Acknowledgements

Grateful thanks to all the young people who have been involved in the Y-SBNT study, and to the members of the study team, including Alex Copello, Lorna Templeton, Paul Toner, and Judith Watson, co-authors of the Brady et al. (2018) paper on which this article draws.

The Y-SBNT study was funded by the NIHR Health Technology Assessment Programme (project number 11/60/01). The views and opinions expressed in this chapter are those of the author and do not necessarily reflect those of the Health Technology Assessment Programme, NIHR, NHS, or the Department of Health. The study was coordinated by the University of Birmingham and sponsored by Birmingham and Solihull Mental Health Foundation Trust.

The associated PhD (Brady, 2017) was supported by a bursary from the University of the West of England, supervised by Barry Percy-Smith and David Evans.

Notes

1 https://generationr.org.uk/
2 http://decipher.uk.net/public-involvement/young-people/
3 www.eypagnet.eu/
4 www.icanresearch.org/

References

Barber, R., Beresford, P., Boote, J., Cooper, C., and Faulkner, A. (2011). Evaluating the impact of service user involvement on research: a prospective case study. *International Journal of Consumer Studies* 35 (6), pp. 609–615.
Beresford, P. (2000). Service users' knowledges and social work theory: conflict or collaboration? *British Journal of Social Work* 30 (4), pp. 489–503.

Beresford, P. (2013). From 'other' to involved: user involvement in research: an emerging paradigm. *Nordic Social Work Research* 3 (2), pp. 139–148.

Bird, D., Culley, L., and Lakhanpaul, M. (2013). Why collaborate with children in health research?: an analysis of the risks and benefits of collaboration with children. *Archives of Disease in Childhood: Education and Practice Edition* 98 (2), pp. 42–48.

Boyden, J., and Ennew, J. (1997). *Children in focus: a manual for participatory research with children.* Stockholm: Radda Barnen.

Brady, L. M. (2017). *Rhetoric to reality: an inquiry into embedding young people's participation in health services and research.* PhD, University of the West of England. Available from: http://eprints.uwe. ac.uk/29885

Brady, L. M., Davey, C., Shaw, C., and Blades, R. (2012). Involving children and young people in research – principles into practice. In Beresford, P. and Carr, S. (eds), *Social care, service users and user involvement: building on research.* London: Jessica Kingsley, pp. 226–242, 2018.

Brady, L. M., and Graham, B. (2018). *Social research with children and young people: a practical guide.* Bristol: The Policy Press.

Brady, L. M., Hathway, F., and Roberts, R. (2018). A case study of children's participation in health policy and practice. In Beresford, P. and Carr, S. (eds), *Social policy first hand.* Bristol: The Policy Press, pp. 62–73, 2018.

Brady, L. M., and Preston, J. (2017). *Evaluating the extent and impact of young people's involvement in national institute for health research (NIHR) studies: an assessment of feasibility.* Report of a project commissioned by the James Lind Initiative. Available from: http://generationr.org.uk/?p=1375

Brady, L. M., Templeton, L., Toner, P., Watson, J., Evans, D., Percy-Smith, B., and Copello, A. (2018). Involving young people in drug and alcohol research. *Drugs and Alcohol Today* 18 (1), pp. 28–38. Available from: https://doi.org/10.1108/DAT-08-2017-0039

Brett, J., Staniszewska, S., Mockford, C., Herron-Marx, S., Hughes, J., Tysall, C., & Suleman, R. (2014). Mapping the impact of patient and public involvement on health and social care research: a systematic review. *Health Expectations* 17 (5), pp. 637–650.

Children's Rights Alliance for England. (2015a). *UK implementation of the UN convention on the rights of the child: civil society alternative report 2015 to the UN committee – England.* London: CRAE [online]. Available from: www.crae.org.uk/news/crae-submits-two-child-rights-reports-to-un/

Children's Rights Alliance for England. (2015b). *See it, say it, change it: submission to the UN committee on the rights of the child.* London: CRAE [online]. Available from: www.crae.org.uk/news/crae-submits-two-child-rights-reports-to-un/

Clavering, E. K., and McLaughlin, J. (2010). Children's participation in health research: from objects to agents? *Child: Care, Health and Development* 36(5), pp. 603–611.

Cockburn, T. (2005). Children's participation in social policy: inclusion, chimera or authenticity? *Social Policy and Society* 4 (2), pp. 109–119.

Copello, A., Orford, J., Hodgson, R., and Tober, G. (2009). *Social behaviour and network therapy for alcohol problems.* London: Routledge.

Council of Europe Committee of Ministers. (2011). *Council of Europe guidelines on child-friendly health care* [online]. Available from: www.coe.int/en/web/children/child-friendly-healthcare

Coyne, I. (2008). Children's participation in consultations and decision-making at health service level: a review of the literature. *International Journal of Nursing Studies* 45, pp. 1682–1689.

Cree, V. E., Kay, H., and Tisdall, K. (2002). Research with children: sharing the dilemmas. *Child and Family Social Work* 7 (1), pp. 47–56.

Crowley, A. (2015). Is anyone listening?: the impact of children's participation on public policy. *International Journal of Children's Rights* 23 (3), pp. 602–621.

Dunn, V., O'Keefe, S., Stapley, E., and Midgley, N. (2018). Facing shadows: working with young people to coproduce a short film about depression. *Research Involvement and Engagement* 4 (46). Available from: https://doi.org/10.1186/s40900-018-0126-y

Evans, D., Coad, J., Cottrell, K., Dalrymple, J., Davies, R., Donald, C., Laterza, V., Long, A., Longley, A., Moule, P., Pollard, K., Powell, J., Puddicombe, A. R., Rice, C., and Sayers, R. (2014). Public involvement in research: assessing impact through a realist evaluation. *Health Services and Delivery Research* 2 (36), pp. 1–128.

Evans, K. (2016). Listen and learn. *Journal of Family Health* 26 (3), pp. 44–46.

Fleming, J., and Boeke, T., eds. (2012). *Involving children and young people in health and social care research.* London: Routledge.

Gibson, A., Britten, N., and Lynch, J. (2012). Theoretical directions for an emancipatory concept of patient and public involvement. *Health* 16 (5), pp. 531–547.

INVOLVE. (2012). *Briefing notes for researchers: public involvement in NHS, public health and social care research.* Southampton: NIHR INVOLVE [online]. Available from: www.invo.org.uk/resource-centre/resource-for-researchers/

INVOLVE. (2016). *Involving children and young people in research: top tips for researchers.* Southampton: NIHR INVOLVE [online]. Available from: www.invo.org.uk/posttypenews/involving-children-and-young-people-in-research-top-tips-and-key-issues/

Kellet, M. (2005). *How to develop children as researchers: a step by step guide to teaching the research process.* London: Sage Publications.

Lave, J., and Wenger, E. (1991). *Situated learning: legitimate peripheral participation.* Cambridge: Cambridge University Press.

Lee, R. M. (1993). *Doing research on sensitive topics.* London: Sage Publications.

Lester, S., and Brady, L. M. (2018). *Blog: involving young people with lived experience of adverse childhood experience (ACEs) in a systematic review.* EPPI Centre Blog, UCL. Available from: https://eppi.ioe.ac.uk/cms/Default.aspx?tabid=3681&articleType=ArticleView&articleId=175

Mawn, L., Welsh, P., Stain, H. J., and Windebank, P. (2015). Youth speak: increasing engagement of young people in mental health research. *Journal of Mental Health* 24 (5), pp. 271–275.

Moules, T. (2005). Research with children who use NHS services: sharing the experience. In Lowes, L. and Hulatt, I., eds. *Involving service users in health and social care research.* London: Routledge, pp. 140–151.

Ocloo, J., and Matthews, R. (2016). From tokenism to empowerment: progressing patient and public involvement in healthcare improvement. *BMJ Quality and Safety* (March), pp. 1–7. Available from: http://qualitysafety.bmj.com/content/early/2016/03/18/bmjqs-2015-004839.abstract

Oliver, K., Rees, R., Brady, L. M., Kavanagh, J., Oliver, S., and Thomas, J. (2015). Broadening public participation in systematic reviews: a case example involving young people in two configurative reviews. *Research Synthesis Methods* 6 (2), pp. 206–217. Available from: http://onlinelibrary.wiley.com/doi/10.1002/jrsm.1145/full

Parsons, S., Thomson, W., Cresswell, K., Starling, B., McDonagh, J. E., and On Behalf of the Barbara Ansell National Network for Adolescent Rheumatology. (2017). What do young people with rheumatic disease believe to be important to research about their condition?: a UK-wide study. *Pediatric Rheumatology Online Journal* 15 (53). http://doi.org/10.1186/s12969-017-0181-1

Percy-Smith, B. (2010). Councils, consultation and community: rethinking the spaces for children and young people's participation. *Children's Geographies* 8 (2), pp. 107–122.

Percy-Smith, B., and Thomas, N., eds. (2010). *A handbook of children's participation: perspectives from theory and practice.* London: Routledge.

Powell, M. A., and Smith, A. B. (2009). Children's participation rights in research. *Childhood* 16, pp. 124–142.

Richards, S., Clark, J., and Boggis, A. (2015). *Ethical research with children: untold narratives and taboos.* Basingstoke: Palgrave Macmillan.

Spronk, S. (2014). Realizing children's right to health. *International Journal of Children's Rights* 22, pp. 189–204.

Staley, K. (2009). *Exploring impact: public involvement in NHS, public health and social care research.* Southampton: INVOLVE [online]. Available from: www.invo.org.uk/posttypepublication/exploring-impact-public-involvement-in-nhs-public-health-and-social-care-research/

Staniszewska, S., Brett, J., Simera, I., Seers, K., Mockford, C., Goodlad, S., Altman, D.G., Moher, D., Barber, R., Denegri, S., Entwistle, A., Littlejohns, P., Morris, C., Suleman, R., Thomas, V., and Tysall, C. (2017). GRIPP2 reporting checklists: tools to improve reporting of patient and public involvement in research. *Research Involvement and Engagement* 3 (13). Available from: https://researchinvolvement.biomedcentral.com/articles/10.1186/s40900-017-0062-2

Stewart, R., and Liabo, K. (2012). Involvement in research without compromising research quality. *Journal of Health Services Research and Policy* 17 (4), pp. 248–251. Available from: http://hsr.sagepub.com/content/17/4/248.abstract

Todd, L. (2012). Critical dialogue, critical methodology: bridging the research gap to young people's participation in evaluating children's services. *Children's Geographies* 10 (2), pp. 187–200.

United Nations. (1989). *Convention on the rights of the child.* Available from: www.ohchr.org/EN/ProfessionalInterest/Pages/CRC.aspx

Waldman, J. (2005). From rhetoric to reality: the involvement of children and young people with mental ill health in research. In Lowes, L. and Hulatt, I., eds. *Involving service users in health and social care research.* London: Routledge, pp. 152–162.

Watson, J., Back, D., Toner, P., Lloyd, C., Day, E., Brady, L. M., Templeton, L., Ambegaokar, S., Parrott, S., Torgerson. D., Cocks, K., Gilvarry, E., McArdle, P., and Copello, A. (2015). A randomised controlled feasibility trial of family and social network intervention for young people who misuse alcohol and drugs: study protocol (Y-SBNT). *Pilot and Feasibility Studies* 1 (8). Available from: https:// pilotfeasibilitystudies.biomedcentral.com/articles/10.1186/s40814-015-0004-4

Watson, J., Toner, P., Day, E., Back, D., Brady, L. M., Fairhurst, C., Renwick, C., Templeton, L., Akhtar, S., Lloyd, C., Li, J., Cocks, K., Ambegaokar, S., Parrott, S., McArdle, P., Gilvarry, E., and Copello, A. (2017). Youth social behaviour and network therapy (Y-SBNT): adaptation of a family and social network intervention for young people who misuse alcohol and drugs a randomised controlled feasibility trial. *Health Technology Assessment* 21 (15). Available from: www.journalslibrary.nihr.ac.uk/hta/ hta21150/#/abstract

Weil, L. G., Lemer, C., Webb, E., and Hargreaves, D. S. (2015). The voices of children and young people in health: where are we now? *Archives of Disease in Childhood* 100 (10), pp. 915–919.

Wenger, E. (1998). *Communities of practice: learning, meaning and identity.* Cambridge: Cambridge University Press.

WHO. (2002). *Adolescent friendly health services: an agenda for change.* Geneva: World Health Organisation.

Wilson, P., Mathie, E., Keenan, J., McNeilly, E., Goodman, C., Howe, A., Poland, F., Staniszewska, S., Kendall, S., Munday, D., Cowe, M., and Peckham, S. (2015). Research with patient and public involvement: a realist evaluation – the RAPPORT study. *Health Services and Delivery Research* 3 (38). [online]. Available from: www.ncbi.nlm.nih.gov/pubmed/26378332

43

"RECENTLY, I HAVE FELT LIKE A SERVICE USER AGAIN"

Conflicts in collaborative research, a case from Norway

Sidsel Natland

Introduction

In Norway, as in other Western countries, the welfare service delivery system has become increasingly entangled with political pressures to reform the system and increase the quality of public social services. The government has initiated several programs to meet these aims. The program in focus in this article was named HUSK.[1] It was linked to the National Strategy for Quality Improvement in Health and Social Services policy and launched by the Directorate of Health and Social Care. The Directorate claimed there was too big a gap between research, education, and practice, and with the HUSK program they called for research and development projects aiming at reaching three strategic goals:

1   Promote structures and arenas for equal collaboration between municipal social service providers, social service users, social researchers, and social work/welfare educators
2   Reinforce practice-based social research
3   Reinforce the knowledge designed to inform practice

The program was established and funded to 8.97 million euro for six years (2006–2011). Four universities in different regions of Norway were selected to provide regional leadership for local projects, connected to municipal social services and social work educational programs. Each region carried out 10–15 local projects. They were free to develop their own organizational structure and processes. Unique to the HUSK program was the requirement of *active involvement of service users* in addition to the ideal of "equal collaboration". The term *partnership* emerged later, promoted by the service user representatives to underscore their demand to be recognized as equal partners (Austin and Johannessen, 2015; Johannessen et al., 2011). Outcomes of the program were externally evaluated and concluded that HUSK reinforced the value of service users' experiences, but concrete outcomes, such as new models that can be applied in practice, were not implemented (Gjernes and Bliksvaer, 2011).

This chapter is based on a case study of one local project that performed promisingly with regard to achieving concrete outcomes, but at the same time faced conflicts that affected the group's ability to fulfil its tasks. The case is suited for providing an analysis of the occurrence and meaning of *conflicts* in collaborative research (Natland and Hansen, 2016).[2]

Partnership

The terms "partnership" and "collaboration" are often used interchangeably. However, partnership describes different constructs, ranging from loose networks to institutionalized joint ventures, whereas collaboration can refer to people agreeing to work jointly in a more informal way (Caplan and Stott 2008). Svensson and Nilsson (2008) approach partnership as:

> a form of work used in social planning and development in which actors with complementary and sometimes overlapping interests and areas of responsibility are involved in a common planning decision-making and implementation process.
>
> *(2008, 10)*

Partnership projects between service providers, academics, and users are increasingly promoted as means to improve research and health and human services, and there exists an extensive body of empirical research on partnerships (Beresford, 2005; Boydell, 2007; Fleming et al., 2013; Lasker et al., 2001). Partnership implies a process through which parties, encountering problems from different angles, can explore differences and search for solutions that go beyond their own limited vision of what is possible. *Advantages* include the potential of addressing complex social challenges by bringing in a team with diverse experience and knowledge; creating appropriate research questions; addressing problems within a societal context; reducing power differentials; creating empowering and learning processes. However, there are also *disadvantages*, in particular related to conflicts about status, leadership, and communication. Partnerships require considerable amounts of time and resources and may generate frustrations, tensions, and conflicts, even the potential of being destructive, particularly for the "weaker" partnership members. Efforts to establish a partnership can absorb energy that should be devoted to improvement of services (Arieli et al., 2009; Lasker et al., 2001; Smith et al., 2010).

Partnership should be a means to improve something, which preferably implies the involvement of those affected by the outcomes (Fleming et al., 2013; Fletcher, 2006). One significant part is the employment of a *double strategy* for the outcome, involving both working on a concrete project and emphasizing personal outcomes of participation (Svensson and Nilsson, 2008). To achieve this, the partnership depends on a good *process*, which calls for studies that capture *participants' own sense-making* of the development of collaborative projects (Perrault et al., 2011). Further, there is a need for more analysis of collaborations that were *not* successful.

Partnership and empowerment

Empowerment refers to the process of attaining influence on events and outcomes of importance, and may unfold at individual, group, and organizational level (Fawcett et al., 1995). Empowerment may also be related to *recognition*. Recognition in both private and public spheres is required for individuals to achieve a positive sense of self, and empowerment cannot take place before this has been constructed. Going through such a process may release energy and strength, but not power. Individual development needs to be combined with *collective* action. Partnership may offer such an arena. Larsson (2008, pp. 109–113) identifies three steps in an empowering process that service users in a partnership may experience: the *retaining of control* over one's life (increasing resources on both an individual and collective level); the *capacity to act* (the ability to define and achieve goals as well as degrees of motivation, feeling of meaningfulness, and the purpose of action); and the possibility for *active participation and self-determination* (opportunities for developing competence and self-efficacy).

Empowerment is regarded a desirable partnership requirement as it promotes the voice and presence of those who otherwise may be marginalized or excluded. However, partnership and empowerment are not the same, and partnership is not necessarily based on equal power relationships. This raises issues around power, mutual need, relationships, and the value of the variation of the partners' resources and contributions (Caplan and Stott, 2008, pp. 24–31).

Partnership and conflict

Conflict is a predictable element in partnership projects, and it is important to understand and resolve them as they occur. Conflicts can be related to both tasks and relationships and may also be approached as a *process* in which one part finds that its interests are opposed or negatively affected by another party (Dechurch and Marks, 2001, p. 5). Conflicts can also be

> an expressed struggle between at least two interdependent parties who perceive incompatible goals, scarce rewards and potential interference from the other part in achieving their goals.
>
> *(Putnam, 1994, p. 284)*

Conflicts should also be approached as both *productive*, as they may balance power relationships, promote flexibility, and prevent stagnation of work units, and as *destructive force*, which can lead to unification of coalitions or interest groups under a set of issues, beliefs, or values, and exaggeration of differences and power relations between partners. To handle conflicts, *negotiation* can help, as it symbolizes willingness to cope with problems, listen, and pay attention to the complaints, a way of minimizing status differences and emphasizing equality. However, negotiation rarely deals with the underlying conflicts of interest that formed the basis of the conflict or helps to reach the best solution. Negotiation may be a means of coping rather than sharing power (Putnam, 1994, pp. 294–296).

The case

The particular HUSK project was an interesting case. It performed promisingly; the local municipality supported it and approved what they conducted (see below). However, at the same time, the project group faced conflicts to such an extent that it terminated and faded away before HUSK was finished. In retrospect, the educator's representative in the project and I decided to study the incidents, aiming at turning them into learning experiences for future partnership projects. We met and discussed this with the rest of the group, and all agreed that we should do this, even if it meant that conflicts would be written about and published in an article, and how this required careful ethical reflections.

We interviewed the participants and got access to meeting records. The data is anonymized. The Norwegian Social Science Data Services (NSD) approved the project (Natland and Hansen, 2016).[3]

The focus on conflicts does not contradict the existence of positive experiences, which underscores partnerships' complexity, but our aim was to understand why conflicts occurred. Analytically, we approach the partnership process with a division into three phases: the initial, operational, and terminational phases (Andersson et al., 2005, p. 9–10).

The initial phase – organization and a contested excursion

The project started in 2007. Representatives from the regional steering group and the university met with representatives from the social services in a local municipality to discuss participation in the HUSK program. The municipality wanted a project based on challenges in the practice field. The local social services agency had already developed project applications, hoping that HUSK funding would help realize them. The conclusion of the meeting was to proceed with one of these projects. It was also decided to assign leadership to the local manager at the social services, who also had developed the agency's original applications. After this, representatives from social services recruited local service users. This may affect the selection of user representatives, that persons are selected who already have a good relationship with the case workers or users that they regard competent to take part. At this point, half of the group members were represented by long-term service users. The group had 16 participants and met and interacted on a regular basis throughout the project period. Usually six to eight participants attended.

A major challenge at the start was to understand the implications of a HUSK project. The wide framework given to the local project leaders was unique and formed the basis for creativity and innovative thinking, but also undefined expectations regarding activities and outcomes. The partners had little experience from such collaboration.[4]

The service users reported that in this phase they were encouraged to "tell our stories", but for what purpose? One practitioner said:

> The project leader had an agenda for the meetings, but my experience was that all after a while found it to be very theoretical and that it was difficult to proceed on how to actually carry it out, as well as too much focus were put on the social services. So it was a challenge to acknowledge that users should be involved in actually carrying out of the project.

The early anchoring in the practice field may have contributed to regarding practitioners as the main actors. The decision on projects without involving all stakeholders also generated different opinions regarding the status of various activities in the group's later work. Should those first topics be regarded as a starting point, open for negotiations, or were they fixed for the whole period?

The first year the group planned an excursion to visit a successful program for long-term social service users in another city to learn and share experiences. However, one and a half months before the excursion, the local project leader informed the group that it was cancelled. Twenty employees from the municipal social services were to go instead. The reason given was that the excursion was important for the practitioners' development of competencies in follow-up work and to increase their interest in HUSK projects.[5] This decision triggered strong emotions in the group. The regional leadership made it clear that an excursion where only one of the partners was invited would not be supported. The result was that the employees from social services went alone, financed by their employer. In retrospect, the local project leader explains that she found her position challenging, experiencing competing demands, and not having sufficient support from her own agency:

> I felt like a lonely locomotive that tried to produce its own fuel, and that is difficult. I was alone. I tried my best. And I do not think it made me a nice colleague, and it affected the project group.

She tried to compensate by inviting her colleagues to the excursion. The result was diminishing trust from the rest of the project group.

The operational phase – negotiations and empowering processes

One part of the original application was to conduct an evaluation of a project started by the municipality's social services, offering psychological assessment for long-term service users. The group had ongoing discussions about its relevance within the HUSK context. It involved only one of the partners and took a considerable part of the budget. However, it appeared impossible to leave out; it was already included in that year's budget.

This made the rest of the group aware of the importance of taking part in *all* discussions concerning applications and budgets. The following year all participants were involved, the majority still wanting to leave this project out. However, it appeared to be of significant importance to the project leader. Disagreements continued till the local municipality agreed to transfer the whole project to their ordinary services. The following year, the municipality reduced their financial contribution to the HUSK project. The consequences were diminished space for the group's activities since the project leader's salary took a large share of the funds.

During 2008, something took place that affected the group's process. The service user organization involved in HUSK developed and carried out "Courses for Changing Attitudes", focusing on empowerment, involvement, and recognition of experiential knowledge. Service users were the target group, but all partners were invited, so there were often a mix of participants.[6] All the users in the project group except one participated, and this impacted their empowering process (Natland and Dalen, 2015). One practitioner commented: "It was fun to see. It gave them confidence and they seemed to develop a sense of 'we'". Another noted how they "dared to raise their voice" and "developed into stronger persons".

Within the project group, the users now asked for clearer focus for activities and goals, and to be recognized as equal partners in planning and decision making. In a meeting with the regional leadership in October 2008, they underscored the importance of *partnership* as the requisite for succeeding. They emphasized their role as "new and in the making" and that they would "bring their experiences, personal competence and other resources into the HUSK partnership". The meeting concluded with following agreements in regard to the group's goals: *Explore and develop new methods for long-term changes in the social service system*; all partners willing to *surrender power* and *consistent user influence* all the way.

One concrete task raised by the practice field was to evaluate their social service provisions. The users agreed to prioritize this on one condition: if they could influence *how* to conduct the evaluation. They presented a need for an alternative to the annual questionnaire used by social services. The project leader suggested *dialogue seminars*. This is a method of creating an equal dialogue between different parties to interact with the current situation, challenges, and future solutions. It is also a method that facilitates user participation and developing conditions for collaboration between, for example, users and employees (Natland et al., 2019). The group decided to employ this method as they found it well suited to assess securing the service users' point of views of the services they received and having a great potential regarding their aim of developing a new practice: bottom-up evaluations of the local services. However, disagreement arose concerning what kind of information the evaluation should focus on. The users wanted a totally new approach, with open-ended questions with a future focus. The practitioners expressed doubt if this would provide valuable information to improve services. The group negotiated this topic for three months, in weekly or fortnightly meetings and e-mail correspondence. One of the practitioners recalls this phase as "exhausting". Negotiations constructed "we-them-positions". He felt positioned as negative, not acknowledging the service users: "[It] did not feel good. Often I felt I had to agree and sympathize with the users' perspectives".

The service users' ideas were finally accepted. The group arranged three dialogue seminars, the first with 31 local users, the second with 28 practitioners, and then a joint seminar (11 users, 14 practitioners). The user representatives moderated and took the lead of the last seminar. Users and practitioners came up with several ideas that they agreed might improve social services. The dialogue seminars aroused interest from the county municipality, who now wanted to try dialogue seminars when evaluating other services. The service users recall this process as "liberating".

The terminational phase – change of leadership

Despite the positive development with dialogue seminars, frustrations had accumulated within the group. The users still felt less involved and recognized. Of importance for the group's interaction was that some of them now had organized themselves in the users' organization, which led to a division between organized/non-organized users. The organized ones now informed their organization and the regional HUSK leadership of their frustrations. A meeting was scheduled (March 2009). The regional leadership, the users' organization, and the project group attended. The group members said that the project leader still made decisions they did not support, and if shared decision making was conducted, they were likely to be overruled. The users said that being a partner was challenging. One expressed how his personal process, succeeding in becoming an active participant, now reversed: "Recently I have felt like a user again". The local project leader claimed that she "felt responsible for the quality of the project, and that you could not change the conditions every year, but stick to them for the whole project period".

The meeting concluded that each group member should decide whether they wanted to proceed and inform the regional leader within an agreed time limit. However, after this meeting, the organized users had a separate meeting with the regional leadership. They demanded a shift to a new leadership appointed by their user organization. If not, they would withdraw from the project.

The rest of the group were unfamiliar with this and had in the meantime decided to use their next meeting to work on topics like group dynamics and leadership. The initiative came from the educator's representative. The intention was to reflect and turn their challenges into a learning situation. The group decided to continue this work, except from the organized users, who did not see the point in continuing until the regional leadership had come to a decision. It was not until now that the other partners were informed of the organized users' demand and the separate meeting with the regional leadership. They reacted strongly and asked the regional leadership to postpone appointing a new leadership until all participants had been heard. Nevertheless, the regional leadership decided that the user organization was to be delegated the responsibility appointing a new leadership. The user organization recruited two new project members for this task. This had a negative effect on the rest of the group, who now felt abandoned by both the organized users and the regional leadership. The local users said that the situation made them feel less recognized: "Why were not we as local users heard, only the organized ones?"

The third joint meeting of the dialogue seminars was arranged in this phase. The new project leaders were only observing as they were unfamiliar with the project. The seminars were followed up by written reports, including discussions of requirements for succeeding in implementing dialogue seminars as permanent evaluation of services. However, conflicts affected the group's ability to follow up with proposals and delivery. Many now found the process towards partnership so filled with strains that they decided to withdraw, and the project group fell apart.

The new leadership faced challenges trying to re-establish credibility, having little legitimacy to influence the local social services.

Conflicts and empowering processes in the phases

The involvement of users in the HUSK program illustrates how interaction with institutions and professionals may increase attributions of personal responsibility, at the same time negotiating individual and structural inequalities. In some phases of the collaboration, identities such as being an "incapable user" was reinforced, individualizing the users' structural disempowerment and oppression. When it comes to the goals of the HUSK program, the group did not succeed in implementing concrete outcomes. The dialogue seminars and bottom-up evaluations of services attracted interest in municipality, promising for implementing a new practice of benefit for the users. But handling the unfolding process took attention and energy away.

The processual analysis enables an understanding on how participation and leadership is carried out in the phases: how users in the project were involved, and how leadership supported group interaction. In the partnership's *initial phase*, conditions set by funding authorities limited the service users' involvement and influence on the planning of the project. The *operational phase* was characterized by the users' *empowering process*. It was marked by changes, in particular by the agreement on "partnership" which marked a development towards more democratic collaboration: agreements on sharing power and decision making. The service users reached the step that Larsson (2008) identifies as *capacity to act*. During dialogue seminars, the third step was achieved, actively *participating*, involved in a way that was an opportunity to learn, develop competences, and self-efficacy.

Conflicts had already started in the initial phase and increased in the operational phase. The leader still overruled partnership agreements, followed by increased displeasure with the leadership. However, *conflicts also facilitated breakthroughs* since they next resulted in progress regarding involvement in organizational matters and budget planning. The users' empowering process took place as a way towards recognition. Different aspects of conflict and reconciliation relieved each other. The fact that they kept going and faced conflicts in the operational phase indicates confidence and self-awareness.

The termination phase was characterized by the strongly contested decision to change to user leadership without involving all partners. The incident was a key marker of the users' empowering process that started in the initial and early operational phase where the users felt excluded, to a return with knowledge and skills to take part in negotiations. But it is complex, as it also signifies the *collective* as part of an empowering process. It was the organized users who had the power needed to demand this change. Did they now run counter to partnership' ideals that the users themselves had promoted? The organization of users led to a division between organized/not-organized users, which adds important complexity to understanding issues in collaborative research projects: power issues may occur also *among* one of the partners. The incident created new conflicts, and this time also of a destructive character.

By focusing on how conflicts emerged in different phases of the partnership, this case illustrates that conflicts in collaborative research might be interpreted within the context of empowerment and management. The case indicates how partnership working may benefit users as they often find themselves in the position of being powerless. It is then highly important that the leader secures each member's participation and acknowledgement on the basis of their particular experiences and competences, and that all are allowed to influence the decision making. Especially important is the *conflict perspective*, which should be acknowledged in initial phases as this may secure confidence in the operational phases.

Lessons learned

The case offers many learning experiences for future collaborative research. It demonstrates 1) how such research should be approached processual to identify how its *phases* are signified by different conditions regarding the involvement of service users, and 2) how conflict must be acknowledged as part of the process. Learning to handle conflicts in an open way might produce better outcomes, and this is why a deeper understanding of conflicts in such research is of importance for future research and practice. Then we must understand when conflicts arise, what triggers them, how they should be handled and how one can avoid destructive conflicts.

This case showed conflicts that fall into the categories of conflicts *within* the partnership: the contested leadership, disagreements between the individual partners in regard to roles, power, and expectations. It also shows that if conflicts in an earlier phase of a project are not acknowledged or solved, they tend to come to the surface again at later stages of the project. Most remarkable, however, is that the case represents an important reminder when it comes to interpreting *conflicts as indicating increased empowerment* on behalf of the usual weakest part: the service users.

The case taught us the importance of identifying *conflict triggers* to avoid conflicts of a destructive kind. Conflict triggers are conditions and/or behaviours that lead to tensions and disagreements. The unclear expectations about the aim and how to conduct collaborative research triggered conflicts as this resulted in the social services taking both about *priorities, budgets, decision making and leadership.* Along the way, *cultural and epistemic clashes* between the practitioners' and users' views occurred, on topics like how to carry out research, how to develop evaluation forms, how to acknowledge experiential knowledge. This resulted in mistrust and a *lack of shared vision.* Also, a conflict trigger was lack of reflection and dialogue as the case showed how conflicts arose because the service users felt that they were not "seen and heard".

Further, the case reminds us that *partnership projects need strategies for handling conflicts. Dialogue* and *listening* to each other is a crucial element. The dialogue should be carried out by *validating* the participants' concerns and *responding* as this might secure a feeling of being involved and not a dismissal or denial of their view of reality.

Related to this is also that such partnership projects should be marked by focusing on assets: what kind of knowledge, experiences, and resources do the participants bring into the project? This would especially benefit the service user representatives, as it may result in them not being positioned as "clients in need" but rather as subjects with agency, as citizens with skills and talents useful for the project.

Of particular significance is the contested concept of *leadership* and how well it supported partners' interaction. Mary (2005) draws a distinction between "management" and "leadership"; managing means to accomplish activities and manage routines, whereas leadership involves the influence of others and the creation of visions for change or empowerment. Skills like clarifying purpose and role, search for feedback, respond to feelings and indirect communication, and refinement of activities versus shared goals and tasks are crucial for successful processes. Research indicates that if professionals take the lead in a partnership, other partners tend to be treated as objects of concern or sources of data rather than peers in problem solving, running counter to the objectives of empowerment. Partners working together in all phases of the partnership are more appropriate for an empowering process since it facilitates the practice of power *with* rather than over (Lasker and Weiss, 2003). *User leadership* is increasingly promoted, but also faces barriers due to both negative attitudes and funding difficulties (Callard and Rose, 2012). Roussos and Fawcett (2000) argue that partnerships may benefit from a *diverse* leadership team including various people with various experiences and skills. In this HUSK project, a shared leadership between users and practitioners may have been a better alternative.

It is of importance that the leader has a clear idea of how the interaction within the group is taking place and how this interaction is linked to important aspects of the partnership process. Should it be about liberation or power play? Johnsen and Normann (2004) argue that there are two modes of relationships between attitudes, processes, and results, one leading to collaboration, the other conflict. To secure collaboration, the group's interaction should be based on understanding and disagreements handled through *reflectivity and adjustment of values*. This *communicative attitude* leads to deliberation. The opposite is a *strategic attitude* where interaction is based in interest and disagreements handled through negotiations and power play. This may lead the partners into a circle of power, where no trust is gained and the result is increased probability of conflicts (2004, p. 230).

Conflicts can be transformed into productive action if they are dealt with in a proper way. An important lesson learnt with implications for future research is that all such projects should start with bringing in all participants, and time should be devoted to information and knowledge about what such research is, what is expected from the partners, and what the outcome should be. Attention must be paid not only to *who* is involved in the partnership and *how*: the case strongly demonstrates that such preparation also must include *why*.

Notes

1 HUSK is the Norwegian abbreviation for "The University Research Program to Support Selected Municipal Social Service Offices".
2 Please see this for detailed information about methods, data collection, and analysis.
3 Please see this for detailed information about methods, data collection, and analysis.
4 It should, however, be commented that this kind of collaboration was new for all parts, even the project leaders in each region. The regional project leadership in this region was also very much preoccupied with the idea that all research projects and activities should be allowed to develop from "below". Openness and local autonomy in each sub-group can of course be a premise for making new and useful experiences.
5 The educators' representative refused an invitation to take part in the excursion.
6 The courses were partly funded by HUSK.

References

Andersson, M., L. Svensson, S. Wistus & C. Aaberg (2005). *On the Art of Developing Partnerships*. Stockholm: Arbetslivsinstitutet [Institute of Work Research].

Arieli, D., V. J. Friedman & K. Agbaria (2009). The Paradox of Participation in Action Research. *Action Research*, 7(3), 263–290.

Austin, M. & A. Johannessen (eds.) (2015). Enhancing the Quality of Public Social Services Through the Involvement of Users: The Norwegian HUSK Projects. Special Issue. *Journal of Evidence-Informed Social Work*, 12(1).

Beresford, P. (2005). Theory and Practice of User Involvement in Research: Making the Connection with Public Policy and Practice In: Lowes, L. & I. Hulatt (eds.) *Involving Service Users in Health and Social Care Research* (pp. 6–18). Oxford and New York: Routledge.

Boydell, L. (2007). *Partnerships: A Literary Review*. Dublin: Institute of Public Health in Ireland.

Callard, F. & D. Rose (2012). The Mental Health Strategy for Europe: Why Service User Leadership in Research Is Indispensable. *Journal of Mental Health*, 21(3), 219–226.

Caplan, K. & L. Stott (2008). Defining Our Terms and Clarifying Our Language. In: Svensson, L. & B. Nilsson (eds.) *Partnership – As a Strategy for Social Innovation and Sustainable Change* (pp. 23–35). Stockholm: Santèrus Academic Press.

DeChurch, L. A. & M. A. Marks (2001). Maximizing the Benefits of Task Conflict: The Role of Conflict Management. *The International Journal of Conflict Management*, 12(1), 4–22.

Fawcett, S. B., A. Paine-Andrews, V. T. Fransisco, J. A. Schultz, K. P. Richter, R. K. Lewis, E. L. Williams, K. J. Harris, J. Y. Berkley, J. L. Fisher & C. M. Lopez (1995). Using Empowerment Theory in

Collaborative Partnerships for Community Health and Development. *American Journal of Community Psychology*, 23(5), 677–697.

Fleming, J., P. Beresford, C. Bewley, S. Croft, F. Branfield, K. Postle & M. Turner (2013). Working Together – Innovative Collaboration in Social Care Research. *Qualitative Social Work*, 13(5), 706–722.

Fletcher, K. (2006). *Partnerships in Social Care: A Handbook for Developing Effective Service*. London and Philadelphia: Jessica Kingsley Publishers.

Gjernes, T. & T. Bliksvaer (2011). *Nye samarbeidsformer – nye læringsformer. Sluttrapport fra evalueringen av forsøket Høgskole-og universitetssosialkontor (HUSK).* [*New Collaborations – New Learning: Evaluation of the HUSK Program*]. NF-report7/2011. Bodø: Nordland Research Institute.

Johannessen, A., S. Natland & A. M. Støkken (eds.) (2011). *Samarbeidsforskning i praksis. Erfaringer fra HUSK-prosjektet.* [*Collaborative Research in Practice – Experiences from HUSK*]. Oslo: Universitetsforlaget.

Johnsen, H. C. & R. Normann (2004). When Research and Practice Collide: The Role of Action Research When There Is a Conflict of Interest with Stakeholders. *Systemic Practice and Action Research*, 17(3), 207–235.

Larsson, A. C. (2008). You're Welcome to Participate – but on Whose Terms? – On Empowerment and Structural Impact. In: Svensson, L. & B. Nilsson (eds.) *Partnership – as a Strategy for Social Innovation and Sustainable Change* (pp. 101–120). Stockholm: Santèrus Academic Press.

Lasker, R. D. & E. S. Weiss (2003). Creating Partnership Synergy: The Critical Role of Community Stakeholders. *Journal of Health & Humans Services Administration*, 26(1), 119–139.

Lasker, R. D., E. S. Weiss & R. Miller (2001). Partnership Synergy: A Practical Framework for Studying and Strengthening the Collaborative Advantage. *The Milbank Quarterly*, 79(2), 179–205.

Mary, N. L. (2005). Transformational Leadership in Human Service Organizations. *Administration in Social Work*, 29(2), 105–118.

Natland, S., E. Bjerke & T. B. Torstensen (2019). Opplevelser av god hjelp i møter med Nav. Fontene forskning [Service Users' Experiences and Perceptions of Helpful Relationships with the Welfare Services]. *Fontene Research*, 12(1), 17–29.

Natland, S. & H. Dalen (2015). Service Users' Self-Narratives on Their Journey from Shame to Pride: Tales of Transition. *Journal of Evidence-Informed Social Work*, 12(1), 50–63.

Natland, S. & R. Hansen (2016). Conflicts and Empowerment – a Processual Perspective on the Development of a Partnership. *European Journal of Social Work*, 20(4), 497–508.

Perrault, E., R. McClelland, C. Austin & J. Siepert (2011). Working Together in Collaborations: Successful Process Factors for Community Collaboration. *Administration in Social Work*, 35(3), 282–298.

Putnam, L. (1994). Productive Conflict: Negotiation as Implicit Coordination. *International Journal of Conflict Management*, 5(3), 84–298.

Roussos, S. T. & S. B. Fawcett (2000). A Review of Collaborative Partnerships as a Strategy for Improving Community Health. *Annual Reviews Public Health*, 21, 369–402.

Smith, L., L. Bratini, D. Chambers, R. V. Jensen & L. Romero (2010). Between Idealism and Reality: Meeting the Challenges of Participatory Action Research. *Action Research*, 8(4), 407–425.

Svensson, L. & B. Nilsson (eds.) (2008). *Partnership – As a Strategy for Social Innovation and Sustainable Change*. Stockholm: Santèrus Academic Press.

44

WHAT DIFFERENCE DOES IT MAKE? THE SERVICE USER CONTRIBUTION TO EVALUATION

Claire Russell and Roger Smith

The context: setting the scene

This chapter is based on our experience of evaluating one of the recently implemented 'fast track' social work qualifying programmes in England. The lead body (Think Ahead) had itself established a service user consultative group, and it was committed to ensuring that teaching and learning on the programme incorporated a range of perspectives from people who were 'experts by experience' by virtue of their involvement with mental health services. As part of the programme's own commitment to improvement and future development, it sought to commission an external evaluation of its organisation, delivery and outcomes. Our proposal followed a fairly conventional structure, but we did seek to ensure that the service user perspective was acknowledged and the evaluation team therefore included an expert by experience who was familiar with the service area to which the project related, that is, mental health social work. Our submission was worded as follows:

> For this particular project, we have . . . included Claire Russell in the team, who will bring her extensive experience as an educator in mental health services; and as someone who has used services previously. She has specific experience of assessing practice-based exercises undertaken by social work students which we believe will be of particular value in this evaluation.

Despite our 'good intentions', even at this point, the tensions and challenges facing us were fairly clear. Ambiguity seems to be an inevitable feature of this kind of project. Despite what are by now well-established principles and values, and recognition of the inherent worth of the service user/expert by experience perspective, negotiating uncertainty is almost certain to follow.

CR: My experiences, not just as a service user/expert by experience, but also an educator has helped my understanding from multiple viewpoints.

[But I was] unsure before the project started how we would work together and what my role would look like.

RS: Likewise, although I had been involved in joint working with people who use services before, every project is different, and there's always an element of learning as you go along, I think. On the other hand, being too prescriptive about involving experts by experience doesn't feel right either.

The organisational base for the evaluation was a university, so clearly not a service user-led body, but also one with its own formal systems and representations of what counts as knowledge and who is deemed to be an 'expert', and awarded recognition as such. As many readers will no doubt be aware, even before we get into the substance of carrying out the evaluation in a way which recognises the importance of incorporating service user expertise, the operational context almost inevitably embeds a number of difficulties in the process. We faced questions of how the expert by experience is going to be recognised as a legitimate member of the team; how they are going to be paid, and on what basis; how they will be accorded access to institutional resources and facilities; and (as it happened, one of our most frustrating and annoying obstacles), how their insurance status is going to be established!

This sort of challenge is all too familiar to those who seek to establish effective partnerships between service users and large organisations, whether the academy or elsewhere in the public sector. It probably does not come as a surprise in the present context, and we will not dwell on the matter, except to observe that it acts as a constant reminder of the impermanence of the recognition of expertise based on experience, and the continual effort involved in fighting and (sometimes) winning the same battles repeatedly.

Other perspectives

Of course, we are not alone in encountering and addressing the challenges of effective and productive service user involvement in research and evaluation, and some of the key issues are helpfully summarised elsewhere (Barber et al., 2011, notably). Advantages of direct involvement of service users as co-researchers can be expected in terms of better data quality (more open responses), more insightful analysis, shaping the reporting of evidence, and more authoritative dissemination. On the other hand, disadvantages may be observed in terms of practical challenges (costs, time, and administration), lack of experience and preparation for the research field, and lack of understanding between researchers/evaluators from different backgrounds (Barber et al., 2011, p. 610).

It is also well-established by now that the 'range and extent' of involvement of experts by experience in evaluation and research are very wide (Beresford, 2013, p. 142), extending from direct involvement in specifying the initial framing of the study, through planning and organising, undertaking fieldwork and analysis, writing and disseminating, to the end point of deciding what to do next with the evidence and its implications. Peter Beresford (2013, p. 142) offers a helpful typology of service user involvement in research, differentiating between those projects where service user 'input' is used to supplement 'existing arrangements'; where service users and researchers develop and carry out 'collaborative' research activities; and where the research is initiated and led by service users or their organisations. Our evaluation would fit most closely with the first of these, since the specifications and structure of the evaluation were already in place before CR became involved as a member of the research team. This does raise important considerations, of course, as to whether this particular exercise could expect to involve the service user perspective effectively, and what specific steps would need to be taken to ensure that this was the case. Beresford (2013, p. 145) goes on to warn of the risk of treating user involvement as a 'box ticking' exercise, where there may be material and symbolic gains for academic researchers but little benefit to service users and little recognition of their expertise.

Where we came from

For both authors, this was a different, if not entirely new, experience. Our task was to undertake a complex programme evaluation, and to ensure that the service user perspective was both present (methodologically) in the structure and delivery of the evaluation project, on the one hand; and captured (empirically) through the representation of service user involvement and experiences of the programme itself, on the other. Either element could have been incorporated independently, but the particular challenge here was to bring them together and ensure that there was some sense of alignment between them.

The involvement of 'experts by experience' in social work education, and other forms of programme delivery, including research, was familiar to both of us from our separate and shared prior experience; but this was new territory nonetheless. Perhaps it is the case that each project or programme that seeks to involve service users effectively is unique, but there was perhaps an expectation on our part that we could bring previous learning and 'best practice' to this particular project fairly easily, and this was certainly not always the case. Almost certainly, in some respects, previous mistakes were repeated, and existing structural constraints proved as problematic as they always seem to be in such cases – such as the status of the expert by experience in the evaluation team (alongside established academics); or the frustrations of service user programme participants at being listened to but not always heard.

Aims and rationale

Decisions about involving service users in evaluation should be discussed at an early stage in the project. . . . Be prepared to do things differently from standard evaluation processes.

(Evaluation Support Scotland, 2015, p. 39)

At the outset, our aim was relatively straightforward, and this was to ensure that the service user perspective was represented in the evaluation, not simply through listening to experts by experience but also by drawing on this expertise to help shape our approach and improve our capacity to obtain and incorporate the service user perspective:

the closer the link between direct experience and knowledge, the more reliable that knowledge is likely to be.

(Beresford, 2003, p. 22)

CR was already associated with the social work programme on which RS taught, and thus became the obvious candidate to take on this role, with expertise drawn both from experience of using services and from being a social work educator. This offered us a 'win–win' opportunity because CR was able to incorporate a number of different perspectives from her own knowledge and prior involvement.

CR: [As the] SU/EBE research team member [I] was able to give views on: education delivery/content, participants and utilising user groups from an 'end user' point of view.

The emphasis on the service user perspective was apparent in the provider agency's documentation, and we think that this meant that our attempt to 'mirror' this in the construction of our proposal was recognised favourably. It certainly meant that the provider was willing to enable us to have access to the various service user groups associated with the programme in some way. This was an important starting point for us, and for CR, whose prior experience did not include a great deal of involvement in research or evaluation. In this sense, having a clear and identifiable role and rationale for involvement may have been helpful, but there was still a considerable amount of learning through being part of the process. This was sometimes uncomfortable because some aspects of the work did take longer simply because of lack of familiarity. Although reassurance may be offered, it is perhaps understandable that someone taking on a new role might feel somewhat deskilled, despite efforts to ensure that their contribution is validated and valued.

As at all points, there are practical consequences which it is difficult to resolve – taking longer to do things might mean using your own (unpaid) time to keep up. Although efforts may be made to cost in the extra time and resources required to support user involvement (recognised as good practice in research design), this is not an exact science. Once budgets are set, it may prove difficult to recognise in a practical sense the extra time and effort put in. This aspect of involving experts by experience in all aspects of learning and research is unfortunately all too familiar, and others have similarly observed similar barriers to involvement, including devising appropriate means of payment and negotiating criminal records checks (Grayson et al., 2013, p. 35).

Enabling effective service user involvement

We did anticipate some, but not all, of the problems we might encounter. We knew that it was important, for example, to build in regular 'catch up meetings', especially in the early stages, to foster the working relationship and to enable CR 'to slowly grasp and carve out for myself' a role within the team.

> **CR**: Time is a crucial factor to build a working relationship and understanding of role/project. To be guided in my role was of paramount importance to me and impossible to do via email/phone.
> **RS**: Having worked on research projects with service users previously, I thought I knew this, but arguably we still did not build enough time/money into the project proposal to enable us to spend enough time at the beginning learning how to work together effectively.

At the same time, we tried to maintain a balance between the specialist areas of activity, for which CR was best placed – engaging with other experts by experience directly – and involvement in the wider evaluation activities – such as observing student learning on their recall days from practice. This we found to be another aspect of the project where tensions could have arisen. We did not want CR's contribution solely to be based around service users and their perspectives on the programme, since this might have been experienced as exclusive; but it would also have denied us access to her insights and expertise relating to the project as a whole. As the work progressed, CR certainly became an active and insightful contributor to other aspects of the evaluation, such as the complex exercises which comprised 'analysis days', and which in the end gave us the overarching framework to make sense of our findings. As the evaluation progressed, CR naturally acquired a fuller grasp of the overall project, and as a result became more confident in sharing her own views and expertise; and as a result, certain insights were undoubtedly sharpened, such as our collective understanding of the pressures and stress experienced by participants/learners on the fast track programme.

In addition, though, it is undoubtedly the case that the service user groups involved with the qualifying programme valued the opportunity to share their thoughts and concerns with someone who did share their perspective and some of their own understandings of being marginalised and problematised. 'Credibility' is an important word here, but it was clearly evident from the level of openness with which service users linked with the programme shared their views, even where these were critical. Others on the team might have been able to achieve this level of mutual confidence, but it would undoubtedly have taken longer and would have afforded less rich material in evidence.

CR: My own service user/expert by experience background came out naturally during meetings with SU/EBEs.

This asset was further enhanced to the extent that CR was able both to elicit service user views but also to show sensitivity to their concerns and recognise the adverse impact of some aspects of their involvement – sometimes apparently small omissions such as failure to recognise the practical and emotional 'work' involved in undertaking some tasks, and the tendency to take contributions for granted when they have been the result of considerable effort.

As the evaluation progressed, we had to develop an effective way of working which reflected the ethos and values of the project, but without much of a blueprint. Although, on both sides, we had fairly substantial prior experience of service user/practitioner, service user/educator, or service user/researcher collaborations, significant aspects of this particular exercise were unknown territory for all of us. There were a number of 'givens' which presented problems we needed to address.

Firstly, of course, it is in the nature of evaluations that they are commissioned according to external specifications, in this case the host organisation of the programme which was the subject of inquiry. So, the extent to which experts by experience were involved in developing those specifications was a matter for them. Fortunately, they were very positive about our proposal to include a significant service user element in the evaluation, and have continued to facilitate that throughout the process.

In addition, though, the precise nature of the task itself required careful planning to ensure that the expertise and insights of the team's expert by experience was fully integrated into the overall programme. The questions we were asked to address related largely to the quality and outcomes of the qualifying programme. Although ultimately this is about preparing effective and committed practitioners able to work in the best interests of service users, the evaluation itself was largely concerned with what might be called 'proxy indicators', in terms of the acquisition and demonstration of professional skills, knowledge, and values; and other important outcomes, such as successful programme completion and transition to the social work workforce.

In order to address these questions, much of our investigative activity focused on two key aspects of the programme; namely, the teaching and learning activities, and the experiences of programme participants, that is, qualifying mental health social workers. Arising from this, legitimate substantive questions would be the extent to which experts by experience are involved, and involved effectively, in the delivery of teaching and learning; and, in turn, the extent and manner in which that involvement had impacted on the programme participants (learners). In light of this, the methodological questions for us included identifying the best ways to address these questions. The argument for involving people who have direct experience of using services at this point is not simply a matter of principle, vitally important though that is; it is our contention that this is also about enhancing the quality of the research itself.

In this particular instance, we sought evidence representing the service user perspective in a number of ways:

- Individual and group interviews with service user interests involved with the programme, in delivery or at a strategic level;
- Observations of service user involvement in teaching and learning activities in the classroom;
- Interviews with programme participants/observations of structured case 'consultations' with practice supervisors.

Here, then, different types of evidence were gathered and incorporated into our overall analytical framework. Importantly, while a number of methods were utilised in the conduct of the study, each source of evidence had to be accorded similar weight and value:

> Experiential knowledge needs to be viewed as complementary to rather than competing with empirical knowledge.
>
> *(Millar et al., 2015, p. 214)*

This is effectively to give substance to the expectation applied in service settings that we should not allow an implicit hierarchy of knowledge to develop where information gathered from any one source might be viewed as having greater purity or reliability. This is, of course, a temptation where paid professional researchers might be inclined to trust their own methods and findings more readily than those obtained from other sources, such as experts by experience.

Implementation

In working out CR's role and potential contribution, we were aware that some aspects of the overall project clearly necessitated that she take the lead, specifically in working with the various service user groups associated with the programme in both strategic planning and delivery roles. It was important, though, that this did not become a sort of 'side project', and so we had to ensure that clear links were maintained between this element and other aspects of the evaluation. Similarly, as far as CR was concerned, it was crucial that she did not become detached from the remainder of the research team's activities; this proved a somewhat challenging balancing act, as we tried to manage time and resources.

Our partial solution to this was to ensure that she played a part in all aspects of the evaluation, attending teaching observations, taking part in site visits, engaging in interviews with participants, playing a full part in our analysis days, and contributing to our strategic discussions.

It did seem that the strategy we adopted had some distinct advantages. Access to the various service user groups was reasonably straightforward, and their comments and feedback suggested that they did value the opportunity to engage with an evaluator who shared their perspective and had a degree of empathy and 'insider' knowledge. It was not an experiment, of course, so we cannot tell whether the same quality of response would have been obtained by a non-service user researcher, but it is undoubtedly the case that CR's involvement was viewed positively by other experts by experience involved in various aspects of the fast track programme.

Notwithstanding these advantages, we also had to recognise that CR was not a particularly experienced researcher, and here there was undoubtedly a degree of 'learning on the job', where the input of RS and other members of the team was important. So, in terms of practical tasks, such as designing interview schedules and carrying out observations, perhaps more conventionally understood researcher 'expertise' came into play. This is a line to tread carefully, since there is a risk here of re-establishing hierarchical relationships, or devaluing the very service user expertise we claim to rely on.

> **CR**: Over time, I've felt my understanding of the project has deepened and so my confidence has grown as a result.
>
> **RS**: I think this reflects a wider team philosophy which values different expertise and experience as carrying equal weight, and it is reassuring, as well as providing another indicator of 'credibility'.

A different feel?

Given that the research activities undertaken appeared very similar to those featuring in any conventional mixed methods evaluation, in what ways can we be sure that our inquiry was enhanced by way of the service user contribution? Perhaps we cannot be sure, but there are several possibilities which certainly justify the effort.

Firstly, this very approach acts as an important reminder to consider the user perspective and to ensure that the overall evaluation actually does maintain this as its central focus and justification.

Secondly, the direct engagement of someone with expert insights based on direct experience appears to have been reassuring to others who had used mental health services. This was certainly expressed as such in the form of direct feedback.

Thirdly, there were cues and messages which might not have been clear to the research team without input from the perspective of an expert by experience – particularly in terms of the intensity of impact of some of the 'little things' which indicate to service users that their views and experiences are not being acknowledged properly. In this context, complaints about the structure of teaching sessions, and feeling unprepared and rushed, were picked up and had a direct impact in terms of future planning and adaptation.

> **CR**: Dissatisfaction from people was expressed to me – and I was able to facilitate open discussions around issues and understand peoples' experiences.

As a result of these observable gains, the evaluation's findings will clearly have been enriched. There will be a sharper focus on the key questions of the extent of service user involvement in programme design and delivery, the nature and experience of that involvement, its impact on programme participants, and the overall quality and achievements of the fast track programme itself.

What could have been better?

We should not idealise our own achievements, however, and it is important to acknowledge some of the mistakes and limitations of the evaluation project. Undoubtedly, the initial plans did not provide sufficiently for the level of involvement required of the expert by experience team member. This was partly an oversight at the outset, and partly a consequence of the level of complexity of the role, as it became clear that sustained engagement with several different service user groups would be required. It is well established by now that there are specific costs associated with research which involves people who use services, but it is an inexact science trying to predict exactly what these might be.

As already acknowledged, there were several very frustrating practical difficulties, including the treatment of our colleague for insurance purposes, which was not well handled by the university and indicated a very limited awareness of the particular nature of this kind of research activity. Institutional barriers of all kinds are only too familiar to service users, so in a sense this was just one more confirmation of their inferior status.

Lessons learned: partial achievements and perennial pitfalls

Reflections

CR: I guess one question would be not necessarily how to make people the same – I believe in teams that have a diversity of people with differing skills and abilities – and wouldn't want everyone to be the same, because then (a bit like the Facebook or Twitter algorithm) you get reinforced what you already think anyway.

A team with a diversity of people naturally lends itself to a hierarchy. The question is how to make sure the hierarchy is based on competence, not power. And how the different competences are valued. The relationships within the team, I feel, are important for this and that everyone supports the inclusion of those with a different perspective than in usual research teams (i.e. service users).

Also, I do think we could recommend considering support for an individual – someone unrelated to the project. Me having a) supervision sessions with my counsellor and b) having my friend coming to sit with me and sort through my thinking has helped me to better understand the project. This has been done by talking about and explaining things – and in doing so has helped me to talk through my ideas and thoughts associated with my tasks, which in turn has helped me be more involved and feel more confident within the team.

I know you have mentioned the extra time needed to resource service users; however, this independent support has been of specific benefit to me.

RS: It has felt like a positive experience, although quite challenging. I was clearly invested with the authority of being 'principal investigator' for the evaluation, so would be faced with the normal expectations of managing a leadership role in an enabling and respectful manner, quite apart from considerations of working with someone whose own experience, expertise, and 'authority' stemmed from quite a different source.

I like Claire's idea of a 'hierarchy of competence' and I think I'll use it again, with her permission! Certainly that is the approach I've tried to take to the different team roles occupied by Claire and other team members in this process. At the same time, I cling to the assumption that I am involved in a particular capacity because of my own experience and expertise, which need to be deployed in order to achieve a successful outcome, where one of the success criteria is, of course, that the service user voice and experience are properly reported and influence our conclusions and recommendations.

It is very much an exercise in blending talents and perspectives, and I'm wary of prescribing a 'right way' to do things, although a strong value base is always important, as are principles of inclusion and 'equal value', given to all and any contribution made to the team effort.

Did we/I get it right? I don't know, but the experience has confirmed for me that it is undoubtedly worth making the effort.

For any such project, where the aim is to establish full and productive involvement of service users, there are essentially two main tests. Firstly, the extent and manner of user involvement has to be determined; and, secondly, as our chapter title suggests, we need to get some idea of what difference this actually makes.

In our example, the first question itself is two-sided, in that we were seeking to utilise the insights of one 'expert by experience' to gain access to the thoughts and experiences of others. However, we cannot just assume that this will achieve positive results simply by putting people next to each other. Effective communication and knowledge sharing are not guaranteed simply because those involved have had similar experiences. This is where role expectations were effectively matched to competence. CR brought a range of personal qualities and skills to the exercise which enabled her to build on pre-existing common ground.

> **CR**: This is true and was one of my personal highlights: having expertise in group facilitation together with active listening skills meant the honesty and quality of the responses received was high and the SU group members felt heard by me.

In this context, planning and preparation are as important as in any other aspect of the research task. Professional and practical support for the evaluation team's service user researcher were key elements of the process, and as already indicated we achieved some aspects of that requirement better than others. It did, though, provide validation for RS and other colleagues to the extent that our own research skills and experience could be drawn upon as positive resources rather than being divisive. Becoming part of the team was important for CR (and for the team), but we also recognised that we had to ensure that she retain her independence and distinctive perspective, especially where the technical aspects or constraints of the overall task threatened to impede a fuller understanding of the service user perspective. Mundane and self-evident as it may seem to the reader, the importance of making every effort to sustain full and equal involvement in all aspects of the evaluation (such as team meetings, skype calls, analysis days, and, of course, fieldwork) became increasingly clear to us as the project progressed.

Mirroring this aspect of the evaluation, though, was the requirement to ensure that service user participants could recognise and respond to our expert by experience evaluator. There would be little point beyond asserting a matter of principle if service user involvement in the process did not have some concrete impact on the outcome, in terms of the nature and quality of our findings and the perspectives articulated. Here, then, the construction of service user engagement as a discrete aspect of the study, where CR exercised a considerable degree of autonomy, seemed very important. At the same time, it was equally important to ensure that participants recognised and responded to this as a form of encounter between peers. For verification of this, we have relied partly on the quality of findings obtained, where views were clearly expressed forcefully and openly in ways which might not have happened otherwise. And as well, for our own reassurance, we did seek the views of service users as to whether they felt CR's involvement had helped them to express themselves effectively, on completion. For some, this was undoubtedly the case, and there were explicit examples of the value they placed on this – one, for instance, commented specifically on CR's valuable 'de-briefing' role. While this certainly validated the methodological approach on the one hand, it was also indicative of a possible negative finding on the other, in that it suggested that the level of engagement and support offered by the lead body was not always as helpful to service users as it could have been. In other respects, though, both service users and programme participants spoke very highly of the educational value of the contribution of experts by experience; and this finding, too, gained more emphasis as a consequence of the evaluation strategy adopted.

This was not an experiment, so we are not able to say whether the evaluation was enhanced as a result of the initial decision to involve an expert by experience in carrying out the exercise.

We have some indication that CR's role and activities were valued by participants, and we do know that she played a full and distinctive part in contributing to the conduct of the study and the analysis and reporting of findings.

> **CR**: It has been worth it to me. My involvement, I feel, has got better and better and I'm sad that it is coming to an end when I just feel like I am learning how to work in a research team.

We believe that the contributions made by a service user evaluator are demonstrably distinctive, and we have tried to point to some evidence of the added value that this offers. For us, it has certainly felt like a positive experience, and the 'right thing to do'. We believe that it also offers grounds for the inclusion of experts by experience/service users in service and service-related evaluation exercises as a 'good practice' standard.

References

Barber, R., Beresford, P., Boote, J., Cooper, C. and Faulkner, A. (2011) 'Evaluating the impact of service user involvement on research: a prospective case study', *International Journal of Consumer Studies*, 35, 6, pp. 609–615

Beresford, P. (2003) *It's our lives*, London, Citizen Press, Shaping Our Lives

Beresford, P. (2013) 'From "other" to involved: user involvement in research: an emerging paradigm', *Nordic Social Work Research*, 3, 2, pp. 139–148

Evaluation Support Scotland (2015) *Why bother involving people in evaluation?*, Edinburgh, Evaluation Support Scotland

Grayson, T., Tsang, Y., Jolly, D., Karban, K., Lomax, P., Midgley, C., O'Rourke, I., Paley, C., Sinson, J., Willcock, K. and Williams, P. (2013) 'Include me in: user involvement in research and evaluation', *Mental Health and Social Inclusion*, 17, 1, pp. 35–42

Millar, S., Chambers, M. and Giles, M. (2015) 'Service user involvement in mental health care: an evolutionary concept analysis', *Health Expectations*, 19, pp. 209–221

45

TALKING HEADS

Reflections of a researcher with multiple impairments: Raising the voices of young disabled people preparing for life beyond segregated school

Paul Doyle

This chapter is based on my experience of carrying out research for my doctoral thesis. The fieldwork for the research took place in a special school where I did advocacy work with young disabled people who had a range of impairments. I am myself someone who has multiple impairments. In this chapter, I will reflect upon some of the insights I gained during this process. I will also discuss some of the struggles – as well as some positive outcomes – I experienced as a disabled researcher working alongside teachers and teaching assistants.

By 2002, I already had a BSc and an MSc in psychology, graduating in 1997 and 2002. In between these, I had been looking unsuccessfully for employment. I had only been interviewed once during this time. Then I received an email from one of the tutors from where I obtained my psychology degrees, informing me that Sheffield University was offering bursaries to people who wanted to take up doctoral studies. I applied for one of these and was delighted that I was successful. I started my PhD in July 2003.

I knew that I wanted my PhD thesis to be based around inclusive education, but at first I did not know what angle I should take. I was introduced to a special school in the North of England by my PhD supervisor at Sheffield University. I spent the first few months at the school talking to and observing people, coming to a decision that my research should focus on self-advocacy for young people preparing to leave school. After this, one of the teachers told me that some of the young people at the school wanted to talk to me.

My very first day at the school where I carried out the fieldwork for my PhD was a Wednesday. I remember it was a Wednesday because that was when the school café was open. The young people ran the café with the staff. The purpose of the café was to give the young people independence training.

There were three young people in the initial group, all due to leave school in the next academic year. They wanted to speak with me about leaving school. I have been to two special schools myself and so I was able to tell the young people of my own transition from special school into mainstream college and mainstream society.

In this, the original advocacy group, there were three young people. Being at a special school, all had impairments with various levels of speech impairments as well. I also have a speech impairment myself. This was the scenario, then. I always have a personal assistant with me, who also acts as an interpreter for when people do not understand what I am saying. Most of the time, as well, the young people had teaching assistants with them, also acting as interpreters.

Prior to my PhD, I carried out several pieces of research at college and university. All the research pieces involved disabled people with a range of impairments. Before my PhD, I had not really thought about the actual research process and how to ensure that people were able to fully participate in research procedures. For my other pieces of research, I had followed the rules of mainstream methods and mainstream methodology. I will give you an example. Whenever I was interviewing someone who had a speech impairment and they had a personal assistant with them, an interpreter, and I had the same, I had never acknowledged the personal assistants when I was writing up. Thinking about it now, this was wrong of me. It was like I was hiding the fact of my co-researchers' and my own impairments.

For this particular piece of research, I took a qualitative approach. Qualitative research helps to understand people and groups of people's underlying reasons, opinions and motivations. The methods to gather qualitative research data include interviews (structured and semi-structured), observation and group discussion.

The methodology that I chose to collect the data for my doctoral research was ethnography. The reason that I elected ethnography was that I could see people in their natural setting. The texts on ethnography say that with this particular type of methodology, the researcher *immerses themselves in* with the participants. With having gone to special schools myself, I was always comparing my schools to the special school where I was working.

On one of my very first visits to the school, I held a group interview. This took place in the café. As always, the café was extremely noisy while I was trying to conduct this group interview. There were five or six young people, three members of staff and my personal assistant and I sitting around a large table in the café. It was so loud in the room nobody could concentrate or hear what anyone was saying. I recall as well that the teaching assistants were talking amongst themselves and literally telling the young people what to say. The teachers were having a laugh. I do not know whether this was to put the young people at ease, or something like that, but I thought that it was very unprofessional. With all this confusion, I never did this type of interview again.

A part of ethnography is autoethnography. Autoethnography is to systematically analyse personal experience in order to understand cultural experience. While I was carrying out the fieldwork at the school, I was constantly thinking about my own special educational experience and comparing the two. Talking to the young people, I told them about my own educational experience, and this encouraged the conversations to expand.

A little more theory. There are two types of interview, structured and unstructured. The structured interview has a certain number of questions; these would be closed questions, which have to be answered in the exact order as they are asked. Structured interviews are quick. The limitations of structured interviews are they are not flexible and they lack detail.

With an unstructured interview, an interview schedule does not necessarily have to be used, and if a schedule is used, the questions would be open-ended. The questions can be asked in any order, and some of the questions might be missed out and some other questions can be added. Unstructured interviews can be adapted and changed depending on the respondents' answers.

When I talk about interviews here, I include the advocacy sessions which I have already mentioned, conversations with the staff at the school and some talks with some of the parents of the young people at the school.

Realistically, it is almost impossible to follow the mainstream research process when researching alongside people with complex impairments. I have already explained the situation involving young people with speech impairments. I also worked with young people with learning disabilities, something I will talk about again later in the chapter. One of the symptoms of a learning disability is short attention span and poor memory.

This chapter will discuss two topics. Firstly, the way young people with different types of impairments and/or more than one impairment interact with the research process. Secondly, my own experiences of carrying out postgraduate research as a person with an impairment. I will give you an example of the second. I had just got in the school entrance and we, my personal assistant and I, were signing in at reception. Someone came over to us and looked at my personal assistant and said, "I bet he's going swimming, isn't he?" It was obvious they were talking about me. I tried to tell them that I was at the school to work, but they just looked at my personal assistant again and said, "I bet he is, isn't he?" Things like this are so frustrating.

I was in the school café one day, having a break between advocacy sessions, and members of staff would come up to me and say things like "You only come here on a Wednesday because the café's open, don't you?" Again, so frustrating. I just could not get it into anybody's head that I was at the school to work with the young people. I do not think that I even tried to tell them that I was studying for a PhD. I think that would have been too much for them to take in.

On my first few visits to the school I was not entirely sure what my PhD was going to be about. At one point, someone suggested that I do some work on communication aids for those young people who could not speak, non-verbal. On a previous week, one of the teachers told me that there was a young person who relied upon her communication aid quite heavily but it was broken. This must have been exasperating for the student.

The next week when I was at the school, I was sat in the café at the school and the student had her communication aid back. The student was moving her head around and seemed to be looking at me. I was just going to send my personal assistant over to see what she wanted but someone was already helping her. This is another example of where an observation can be misinterpreted. The moving of the student's head must have been a muscle spasm and I misinterpreted it.

For me, one of the main outcomes of my PhD research is that people have to be patient with people with impairments. I was talking to the same student with the communication aid. She indicated to the teaching assistant, I think it was her own personal assistant actually, that she wanted to sit up in her wheelchair. It took at least five minutes to make her comfortable. I can relate to this because sometimes I need re-positioning in my wheelchair and it can take time. I wonder whether a non-disabled researcher would understand and have patience in this kind of situation. A non-disabled researcher may be more concerned about getting the interview done and moving on to the next. If this were the case, many disabled people may miss out on taking part in research. Not only would this be an injustice to the disabled person themselves, but the world of research would miss out on this particular population.

Whilst I was carrying out the fieldwork at the special school, I could not help comparing the school with the two special schools where I spent my own school days. The main differences between these schools, on which this chapter is based, is that there are lots more support staff here. This means that all the young people are able to join in everything. Everyone is able to get on with their schoolwork. When I was at school, I was lucky if I got 20 minutes of help per day. I cannot write using my hands and this was before I got a typewriter. Many of my schooldays were very frustrating as I wanted to get on with my academic work but I could not.

All the way through my school years, I was taken out of my classes and sent to physiotherapy. This was annoying as I really enjoyed my learning. What was very strange was the fact that the teachers did not have a say on whether I should go to physiotherapy or not. Someone would come into the classroom and say, "Could Paul Doyle come to physio?" and before the teacher could say anything I was being "frogmarched" up the corridor and into physiotherapy. I never understood this. It was as though physiotherapy was more important than my academic lessons.

I have co-ordinated advocacy sessions where one of the teachers would come into the room and go up to one of young people, say something quietly to them and just wheel them out, without paying any attention to me whatsoever. This scenario has two points. One, again it takes away the young person from airing their views and, two, it is disrespectful to me. I know that I was there carrying out postgraduate research, and not a member of staff, but I thought I would have deserved a little more courtesy. I wonder whether it would have been different if I was not disabled.

This brings me nicely on to an observation that I carried out at the special school. This was the Foundation Class. As I got into the room, the children were having their break. In here there was an occupational therapist and a speech therapist, as well as the teacher and teaching assistants. There was a girl sitting at a table pointing to cards to indicate what she wanted to eat or drink next. This demonstrates that the school carries out most of the young peoples' therapy in the classroom. This means that the young people do not have to leave their lessons, and they are not alienated from their classmates the way I was at my school.

In the first proper advocacy session at the school, there were three young people. Not long after this meeting, I referred to these young people as the "original group", we all got on so well. There were also four teaching assistants in the room. I started off the session by telling the young people about my own education, and more importantly, my transition from special school to mainstream college. This, I feel, formed the basis of future sessions.

The three young people in the first advocacy session were due to leave school the following year, and they had all applied to go to a special boarding college. In my opinion, this is not the way forward. I have visited several special boarding colleges and from what I have observed, they are similar to special schools, but I did not say this to the group.

One of the young people in the group asked whether they had telephones at college. Reading between the lines, the young person must have been concerned about keeping contact with his family while he was away. The advocacy sessions aimed to prepare the young people at the school for life outside the special education needs system. Having telephones around may seem trivial to some people, but after being "hidden away" from society, locked in a special school, this is how I was at boarding school, and this would be a worry. Again, on the subject of boarding college, one of the young people said, "I can't wait, I can't wait". She was really looking forward to moving on.

I have two regular personal assistants, and they do change from time to time for whatever reason. Just so that you know, my personal assistants assist me with all my personal care such as taking me to the toilet, feeding me and making sure that I am comfortable in my wheelchair. When I was working at the school, my personal assistant took me to where I needed to go within the school. They took notes for me in the advocacy sessions and, as the reader already knows, they act as interpreters for me. Each time I had a new personal assistant with me at the school, I had to explain what I wanted and needed them to do for me. My father and one of my nephews came to the school with me when my personal assistants were off.

The post-16 part of the school mainly offered vocational courses, such as office work, gardening, car maintenance and working in the school café. As well as talking about what the young people wanted to do when they leave school in the advocacy sessions, the young people also spoke about how they felt regarding their current school. A few weeks before the conversation which I am going briefly explain, I was listening to two teachers talking about whether students who cannot use their hands actually enjoy subjects such as gardening. One of the teachers said that they were given a choice and the other said that they did not think that they did.

There was an advocacy session where only one young person turned up, from the original group. The student had similar impairments to me. I took this opportunity to ask him whether he enjoyed vocational subjects such as gardening. The student said that he did not like gardening as he could not take part himself. I told him that was exactly my experience when I was at school. I thought about alternative classes that people like the student in question could do. An idea that I had was to have workshops about independent living and giving people advice on how to express their wishes and needs to other people. The young person said that this sounded a good idea. I was going to suggest this to the school but, unfortunately, I did not get the chance. I wish that I had done as I think it is very important.

Sometimes when I had been expecting to see five or six students in an advocacy session, only two or three turned up. I had the impression that one teacher in particular did not like me working with the young people. I say this because whenever I had finished a session such as this and was going around the school, to get my lunch for example, I would see one of the young people who I thought would have been in the advocacy session. They would say that they had wanted to see me but they had to do something else. It turned out that the "something else" was nothing other than another lesson. It does not seem fair if someone wants to be somewhere, the advocacy session in this instance, that another person can prevent you. This is taking away freedom of choice.

One of the topics that the young people wanted to talk about in the advocacy sessions was independent living. As far as I am aware, this was not discussed in the school. As a disabled person who lives independently and who employs two full-time personal assistants, I felt qualified enough to talk to the young person about independent living. I always think that information and advice is better coming from someone who has experience of the topic in question.

Attitudes was another subject that came up in the advocacy sessions. I think that this is a big issue for people who have been in special schools all their lives. Being at special schools not only affects children and young people with impairments, it also has an impact on non-impaired and/or non-disabled people. Special schools, and special education as a whole, split up the two groups of people, and the majority may never meet until they are 25 years of age. The age of 25 is when the transition period ends

Even after three or four years of co-ordinating the advocacy sessions at the school and talking with the same young people over this period, I still had to explain the meaning of certain words, such as advocacy. This is part of having a learning disability. This is why I say that patience was one of the key elements of my research. If researchers did not have any patience with a respondent with a learning disability, they would probably obtain very little data.

Whenever I spoke to young people who were in the school proper, and not in the post-16 section of the school, I was concerned whether these were ready to talk about leaving the school. I found that some were ready and some were not. For those who did not want to talk about life beyond school, I turned these conversations round and gave the young people the opportunity to talk about their current school and their current situation.

When the young people were not talking about leaving school, they began to tell me about what they were doing in their lessons. One of the young people said that they were writing about a "Flying Cow" and another was writing about two cats. Sometimes I thought that the young people and I ought to be talking about leaving school. Then I considered the fact that the advocacy sessions are all about the young people talking about whatever they want to talk about, and so I just let these kinds of conversations flow.

An interesting situation that I faced considered confidentiality. Before one of the advocacy sessions, a young person came over to me and asked whether he could speak to me on his own after the session. This particular group was talking about bullying. When the group had finished, the young person had stayed behind. He told me that he was being bullied and said who it was that was tormenting him. I felt a little awkward during this conversation because my personal assistant was sat with me and this should have been a one-to-one discussion between the young person and I. Prior to this, I did have a talk with my personal assistants about these kinds of situations and we agreed that they would be kept confidential.

At times, when there have been teachers and/or teaching assistants in the advocacy sessions, it has not worked the way that I had intended. Ideally, the advocacy sessions should be attended by the young people alone so that they are able to speak up for themselves where there are no staff around. This gives the young people the freedom to say what they like and not feel afraid of saying the wrong thing in front of their teachers

Particularly when I first started the advocacy sessions at the school and the staff sat in with the young people, sometimes the staff members would start to talk amongst themselves; this was really annoying, especially when they talking about something that was nothing to do with the session. I do not know what the young people thought about it; I wish that I had asked. If this would have happened to me when I was a young person, this would have frustrated me so much, especially if it prevented me from saying what I wanted to say.

At other times, it was difficult to decide whether having members of staff in the sessions was useful or not. Sometimes it was quite a strain for me to get the young people to talk. In these situations, the staff did encourage the young people to speak up for themselves, for which I was really grateful. This can go another way as well, where if the young people were not talking and teachers and/or teaching assistants were trying to encourage them to talk, there is the danger that the staff may put words into the young people's mouths.

Most of the time, however, having teaching assistants in the advocacy sessions was really helpful. As well as acting as interpreters for those young people with speech impairments, they were there if any of the young people needed anything. For example, one of the young people used a deaf aid and it was not working properly and a teaching assistant put it right.

One of the young people in one of the advocacy groups had epilepsy and he could have a seizure at any time. This meant that there always had to be a teaching assistant in the room. There were also times when the assistants put what a young person said into context for me. For example, one of the young people was talking about "the Keresforth Centre"; I knew where this was, but I did not know *what* it was, and one of the teaching assistants told me that the centre is where the young people go in order to give their parents respite breaks.

In another advocacy session, school was being discussed. I asked the young people what they liked about school and some of them said that the staff and the meals are nice. I wondered whether the young people would have said this about the staff if there had been none in the room. I have always hoped that having staff members in advocacy sessions has never influenced what a young person had said.

As the advocacy groups were based around leaving school, the sessions were technically centred on the transition period. The transition period for young disabled people is from the ages of 14–25. Fourteen years of age is when young people start to plan for their future. Basically, the transition discussions are around the topics that we, the young people and I, talk about in the advocacy sessions that are held in the school: leaving school, and going to college or looking for a job. In the advocacy sessions, nearly all the young people said that they had not heard anyone actually say the word *transition* to them before.

As I cannot use a pen or pencil to write with and I cannot use a standardised laptop, my personal assistants took notes for me in the advocacy sessions. It was almost impossible for me to tell them what to write without disturbing the advocacy sessions. What I actually did was, when I got home from the school that evening, I typed up the notes that my personal assistant had taken and used their notes and my memory to type up the full field notes.

I felt extremely lucky concerning the placement, the special school, for the fieldwork for my research. It was my supervisor who introduced me. I have tried to get in special schools before to carry out some work on behalf of several disability organisations, but I have not been able to establish myself anywhere. It seems that because I have impairments myself, people think that I am unable to work with young people who also have impairments. Another way of looking at this is that a special school is a "closed community". Once people step inside these buildings, it is like they are locked away from the world and the staff are over-protective towards the children and young people. Finding a placement for this particular PhD may well have been more difficult if it was not for my supervisor.

Of course, when working with children, young persons and vulnerable adults, you have to have a police check. As I have a personal assistant with me all the time, including when I was working with the young people, they also had to have a police check. I really felt very awkward asking my personal assistants about this, but I needed to do this in order for me to continue with the fieldwork.

One of the most difficult encounters I experienced whilst I was studying for my PhD was the literature research. Using libraries when you use a wheelchair is quite difficult. Technically, speaking from personal experience, you can only see two bookshelves, as they are at my own eye level; the other shelves are either too high up or too low down. I have to tell my personal assistants which books I want to look at and they would get the book for me and hold it and turn the pages.

Another problem with the library at the University of Sheffield was that the books for my particular studies were on the mezzanine, where there was no lift access. On my second visit to the library, the librarian who assisted students with additional needs brought down two trolley loads of books. I felt really awkward about this and I remember thinking "She can't be doing this every time I come into the library". As my time at university went on, more and more materials became available online in the form of ebooks and journals, and these made a massive difference as I could access these from home.

As well as my research saying that young disabled people can, indeed, speak up for themselves and make their own choices and important decisions that will affect the rest of their lives, there is another major aspect to this thesis. As the reader knows, I consider myself as having multiple impairments. I use a wheelchair full-time; I have very little use of my hands and I have a speech impairment. As is well known in the world of disability, there are conflicting models of disability, the social model of disability and the medical model of disability being the two most frequently referred to. The medical model is based on the premise that disability is a problem of the individual person directly caused by disease, trauma or other health condition. The social model sees the issue of "disability" as a socially created problem and a matter of the full inclusion of individuals in society.

Years ago, when the medical model was dominant, I, as a person with multiple impairments, would have probably not have had the opportunity to do doctoral studies. People would just see me in my wheelchair and look at my involuntary movements, and they would think that I was incapable of gaining an English or Maths GCSE, let alone a PhD. This demonstrates that certain barriers have come down regarding disabled people within society, but there is still a long, long way to go.

It was important that the advocacy sessions at the special school were based upon the social model of disability. If these sessions were being carried out with the medical model in mind, there would be no positive outcomes. Before the social model was developed by the Union of the Physically Impaired Against Segregation in the early 1970s, people with impairments did not have a say on how they wanted to live their lives, and research like mine would have been unthinkable.

I hope that my PhD research thesis will encourage more disabled people to do more research. In conjunction to this, researchers must encourage people, and young people in particular, to take part in research in order to create a platform where they can have a better say on how they want to lead their lives.

There is lots of really good research carried out by disabled people and concerning this group of the general population. In my work, I have discussed my own experience of the mechanics and the techniques of carrying out disability research. It is really important that *everybody*, regardless of severity of impairment, has an opportunity to fully take part in the research process.

As in my PhD research, where the participants and the researchers all have multiple impairments, there is much to think about. To begin, you have to make sure that the space where the research is being conducted is big enough, thinking about how many researchers and co-researchers will be using wheelchairs, how many personal assistants there will be. It is important that everyone is able to see each other in case people have to lip read. And, of course, research with people with multiple impairments takes a longer period of time.

I feel that my methodological ideas and practices could be used in general situations. For example, particularly when I was younger, I remember teachers at school talking about what, in their opinion, was best for me, and I could understand everything that they were saying. I think this about social workers as well. If the so-called professionals had more time and patience to listen to disabled people, we would have a better chance of leading our lives the way we want.

For further reading

Doyle, P. (2014) "A study to raise the voices of young disabled people preparing for life beyond segregated school: the power of disability research in promoting advocacy". University of Sheffield. [Online]. http://etheses.whiterose.ac.uk/7064/

46

TALKING HEADS

Reflections on learning from gap mending participants: Experiences matter

Compiled by Helen Casey, Cecilia Heule and Arne Kristiansen

(INTERNATIONAL CO-ORDINATORS, POWERUS)

Introduction

The gap mending approach originated at Lund University in Sweden in 2005; it was then taken up by Lillehammer University Norway 2009, and in 2012 a partnership with Shaping Our Lives (UK) was established as a new international network called PowerUs. PowerUs has a growing membership currently consisting of 19 countries (2019). The concept and practice of gap mending is written about elsewhere in this book. This chapter is based upon key gaps which have initiated so much interest in this approach, that is, recognition that the experiences of people as an important source of knowledge have largely been neglected in professional education, practice and research.

This chapter aims to show that experiences matter by sharing reflections from participants of gap mending programmes in the North East of England and Lund, Sweden. A range of voices are heard to convey the benefits of substantive mutual learning outside of the traditional classroom environment.

> I was very excited to be part of the first mend the gap project however, very apprehensive on how the students were going to react on hearing my thoughts, feelings and experience. I really appreciated how from the start it was service user led and then constructed in to a programme. It was pleasing to know that the social service students are just as "normal" as me. An example of this being the students explained they have dishes and piles of washing, however, a service user cannot due to neglectful home condition. When talking about this, there became an understanding regarding the difference between them getting done that day, to the situation escalating to neglectful home conditions. This conversation inspired me to write a poem (see below).
>
> I appreciated the input of how the system works and being able to understand the process in which they must follow. This gave me some closure to my own experiences that I never had before.
>
> During the programme I was able to voice my concerns regarding contact, black marks (no show social workers compared to no show service users) and regards to feelings from children been taking away. I felt this section of the programme resulted in

a lot of shock factor moments, and the inability to make suggested changes to senior social workers – who had not trained with service user involvement. My hope was to shape the next generation and how they practice, that they would think out the box, not be quick to judge and that "life is not a text book nor is it a ticky box."

My time on this programme was a rollercoaster of emotions however I feel it was met with total respect, empathy and admiration. I would do it all again.

(Louise, parent)

Keyhole

Look through the key hole what do you see?
Do you see the not so quite clean kitchen floor?
  Or the brand-new mop propped up by the door.
Do you see a person sat down?
  Or a person having a rest while the kids run around.
Do you see a baby unattended in a play pen?
  Or a person keeping them out of harm's way.
Do you see that person down?
  Or that tiredness as come around.
Do you see that washing pile?
  Or that she's a mum of five.
Do you see the past?
  Or the potential in me.

Just think for a moment . . .

If we looked through your keyhole what would we see?

(Louise)

Mend the Gap was an excellent way to voice my opinions and have my views heard after so long. I had believed that such a lot of my living years and experiences did not matter – to me or anyone else. I have learned that they do matter and I have been able to relate to others who have been on a similar journey to myself. I have also been able to relate this to students training to be social workers. I have even attended social work conferences in different locations in the UK. I used to go to conferences blind-folded thinking that everything that I thought was wrong. Through finding my voice and confidence in Mend the Gap I re-discovered my self-belief that I knew many things that were right. Things about how parents should be treated by professionals, no matter how difficult the circumstances are. I remember being told I should ask for help and when I did I did not get any. That's how professionals make you feel you are wrong. As my confidence and self-belief started to grow I started to mend gaps with my family. I felt I had the tools and resources I needed to do this. I learned that I can be creative when putting pen to paper and listening to others; this inspired me to write a poem which won an award in a local addiction support service.

This is my main message to all;
"Never give up on your dreams and let yourself be an inspiration to others."

(Jackie, parent)

Lady Heroin

I am ashamed to say that I had a sad torrid affair with you so many years ago.
I sold practically every piece of clothing and jewelry so, I could support my craving for you.
I robbed people of their money and burgled people's homes just so I could that hit
    I needed to feel again what I thought was normal.
I was often called derogatory names, kicked and punched because of my appearance and
    for the drug that I was on.
Time after time I tried to give up.
This medication, that medication but, it felt like nothing was working.
I was given a lifeline and second chance so, I took it by the horns because I thought it
    was what I needed right there right then.
Nowadays I can hold my head up high with dignity and say "Yes, I've done it and at last
    I'm finally free of you Lady Heroin."
I've given myself a pat on my back for every year that I've remained abstinent from you.
Bridges have been built and crossed over the years and I've been forgiven from everybody
    I ever hurt.
Got money in my pocket and in the bank, nice clothes on me back and nice perfumes to
    make me smell nice.
Two lovely boys to name and a very loving partner whose been the most supportive
    throughout my ups and downs.
If you get a second chance like I did then take heed and listen to what's on offer.
It may just be the thing that you need most to, sort your life out and get yourself back on
    track.

(Jackie)

I had had a notion that the meeting with the student from service user organizations would be complicated. This because I assumed that a "we" and "them" would be created. The first day I had come early to university. In the classroom, a service user student sat at a table. I asked if I could sit down. I got a grave serious "No" in response. Nervously laughing at this harsh jargon, I nevertheless sat down and the silence occurred. During the smoke break, I heard another service student say, "Well, that's the way it is. . . . They don't know anything about reality, that's the difference between us and them" and pointed to the classroom. I interpreted this as a contempt for social students: "I don't understand what I came here to do. After all, no one listens to what I have to say. Social workers are just a bunch of assholes." . . . the smoke breaks came to serve as a forum where our cemented roles began to be loosened up through constant meetings. The person who brazenly rejected me on the first day wanted day two lunch with me. He continued: "I thought I'd be at a cruel disadvantage. But I feel like I'm king of the world. I feel like I own the university!" After this conclusion, the person opened up.

(Magnus, social work student)

When I got to Lund and university on day one, I am of course nervous but full of expectancy. After stepping into the classroom and sitting among a lot of social students, it didn't get any easier. But to my delight there were also a few from different user associations so I became a bit calmer.

(David, student from service user organization)

I remember a coffee break during the future workshop when I and a couple of fellow students spoke us warmly in the face of some common passions. Where one got us into more increasingly subspecialized interests that we were a part of with subspecialized vocabulary (which most people would probably have a hard time relating to). What is so sad is that because of our various group affiliations in society, we would not normally have received this amazing exchange of funny anecdotes, the comparison of techniques and crazy ingenious ideas. But what was so amazing now, was that no one thought about the things that might have separated us and that would unfortunately have made our meeting in this country quite unthinkable in other contexts. There we would be seen on as a 22-year-old, sweet and a little protected but idealistic and very talented student who had it safe financially all my life and not had to forgive anything, A much older woman who has not attended high school but for decades been completely depleted, often not had food for the day or any steady accommodation, and lived in an environment where she constantly has to be on her guard so as not to get blown and cheated in ways that may prove to be deadly, exploited in various more or less degrading or violent ways. A woman who is also very idealistic, filled with passionate commitment and creativity, which had come back after having been close to dying with her. As now grew as her self-image and self-worth increased, the longer she kept herself completely away from the drugs, and thanks to her strength and stubbornness. And then there was also a middle-aged, of illness ravaged man, a reduced rubble of his former self who believed in all those who told him it was too late to get up again and when both doctors and the social authorities gave up on him. But he didn't think about it now (and even if he did, he would no longer have believed in them, because he started to see that he didn't share their picture of what he had to be and achieve to be successful, because he had others, his own way he could feel proud and significant in), but now he was just there, laughed and listened to some who didn't expect him to be anything special, but just that he was a human being who shared something with them.

(Johan, student from service user organization)

So including students from service user organizations or experts by experience, is both innovative, new and ground-breaking. . . . it's a new level where we people with our multifaceted experiences look at problems and together try to find new ways. It's not a situation where people are taken advantage of and where the quick solutions are the answer or the right thing. It's taking collective responsibility and taking the time to look at new solutions where we see each other not as problems but resources.

(Mikaela, student from service user organization)

In the end, I can't help but thinking back to how this conversation about belonging in academia started with the student from a service user organization. Through the presentations we found out that we both created poetry as a way of expressing our thoughts and I am sure I had not been able to understand how she thought from her horizon if I had not read a poem that she had written about it. People that come together in a creative melting dough and makes innovative projects, it is almost that the Mobilization course itself is a kind of poetry that breaks through old walls and systems between a rusty we and them.

(Adrian, social work student)

The mobilisation course has provided me with several important insights. One is that much of what we read about social studies and theories only makes sense when it is combined with practical examples and in the meeting with people, which is why the mobilization course is and has been an incredibly important and important element of education.

(Adam, social work)

What the Mobilisation course strives for, and in all likelihood also succeeds, is to give people with experience of being service users, an insight that their own experiences are highly valued and that they have the power to define their own problems. As social work students, we are forced to develop the concrete knowledge and tools we have that we can use to create change for the individual. When these two entrances to social work occur in reality, the results will be sustainable in the long term.

(Betty, social work student)

Unlike all previous courses I have attended, a dynamic and trust was created in the group which is difficult to describe but has been valuable on so many levels. By acting with recognition of each other, I also noticed that we started to form good relationships early. It is mainly what I bring from this moment, how valuable it has been to build relationships with the people you work with.

(Marta, social work student)

To use the power as a social worker to also resist, seems reasonable and important. It feels incredibly important in professional life to be a brave social worker who dares to stand up to social injustices and work so that those we meet have the opportunity to make their voices heard and influence the work with the knowledge and experience they have.

(Susanne, social work student)

Through this course I have come closer to who I am as a social worker. Through my experience of social work in general and life in particular, I have been able to blur the boundaries between ourselves and those we learn to see as service users. In this course we are all equal.

(Kathrine, social work student)

This course has taught me a lot, in a way that previous courses could not do. I appreciate how the Mobilisation course goes from the traditional way of learning that we have learned earlier in the education and how the course challenges and activates us. It has given me an even greater commitment to working forward and I now hopefully look at the opportunity to create social change, although there may only be small changes that I can contribute, there is something to do. I also got a clear and convincing picture of how important it is with service user influence and to listen to the knowledge that is gained through experience.

(Theresia, social work student)

We cannot change social work ourselves as social workers, but we need to bring with us the people we work with to gain knowledge and experience. The mobilization course is really mobilizing and I think also it is the beginning of a change in society.

(Evelyn, social work student)

We have learned a lot during the course, not least that people who come from different backgrounds and have different experiences can sit and do something good together. We have taken advantage of each other's strengths and seen it to the capacity and potential each individual has to offer. We are different and do not always think the same, but at the same time we have shown how equal we are. We have gone from a we and them to a we, shared memories and stories we may not have even talked about in the past.

(Roberto, social work student)

Something I take with me from the course is that nothing is impossible and that we should be persistent in the goals we set to change social work and society. We are not the first to change and not the last. Many before us have succeeded with the impossible and many after us will succeed with the impossible. What we need is to value our goals and democracy enough to be on the train of change!

(Hannah, social work student)

I was offered the opportunity to take part in a "mend the gap" programme which I was not quite sure what this involved but I was struck by the fact that the participants were not only single mothers to young children but they had fled violent home countries to seek refuge in Britain. The weekly sessions offered a window into the daily trials and tribulations of what it is like to be an "asylum seeker" and all the uncertainty that comes with that title. It was made abundantly clear that not only did they have to deal with the discourse around the label of "asylum seeker" but also with culturally insensitive and housing not fit for purpose, severely restricted budgets, the legacies of escaping their homelands (with the trauma of conflict as well as leaving families behind) as well as having issues around communication as some struggled with their English. While I am ardent pupil of current affairs and geopolitics, especially in Africa as that is my heritage, I found myself learning lots of new facts about the issues that had led them to come to Britain. I learned about political strife in Eritrea, the legacy and practice of Female Genital Mutilation in Sierra Leone as well as Gender Based Violence in Algeria and Zimbabwe. I strongly believe that Mend the Gap is a good foundation for social workers to learn alongside people with such experiences.

(Rob, social work student)

I was able to be part of the first "Gap Mending" programme. The powerful stories and experiences parents shared came to life within a space that allowed me to critically analyse and reflect on my practice and experiences to aid my learning. I was able to look at my role both through the lens of a social worker and also as a parent experiencing a social worker within their lives.

What resonated with me was the power bestowed upon the social worker, particularly in the position of safeguarding children. As a child's safeguarding social worker your main focus is always the safety and welfare of the child which will at times be disempowering for the parents you are working with, as there are times when decisions need to be made which parents do not agree with. However, what became apparent from this Gap Mending programme was that this was accepted by the parents in terms of social workers acting out their statutory duties under the law. Parents highlighted through their experiences how they struggled with the way in which social workers used their power and implemented their duties within their practice. What was highlighted to me was the importance of building effective relationships with the parents through adapting an open and transparent approach with coordinated communication.

As I have moved in to a more senior role as a Consultant Social Worker, I have been able to place a strong focus on relationship based practice which has given me the chance to shape and support a number of social work students as part of their journey in to the social work profession. The social work programme, in which I am involved, recognises the positive impact "Experts by Experience" have on the learning and development of social work students and also the importance of relationship based practice. This aligns with my approach to practice which has been embedded throughout my learning journey. Within the units I have managed we have a strong focus on relationship based practice and how service users are at the center of how we approach our practice and deliver support to them. I feel that my involvement with the Gap Mending approach has shaped my practice and continues to influence future practitioners.

(Neil, social worker)

I really enjoyed the mend the gap program because of the continuity which helped build trust throughout the weeks. I found the group to be positive and constructive unlike some other groups I have previously been involved in. Social interaction was a very important part of this, I was upset when the group came to an end.

(Allan, service user, participant)

I was invited to attend an 8 week program called Mend the Gap which was run by the Open University in conjunction with partners such as the Department for Work and Pensions (DWP). I was supported by "Empowerment" (service user led support service) beforehand as I knew that I had issues with this Government Department. I felt safe and valued throughout these meetings and it was quite a turning point for my social anxieties. For the first time in 10 years I felt included and encouraged to participate. This ultimately led to a trip to London to participate in a huge convention of very academic people, social workers, asylum seekers, support workers and service users. It was an outstanding experience and one that I am keen to enjoy again.

(Mike, service user participant)

I found Mend the Gap extremely positive. It was a chance to look at what needs to be done in order for people to have a better understanding of Social Work, and for Social Workers to understand how clients feel when they believe that their needs are not being met and how this makes people feel "ignored." It gave clients a chance to say what was wrong about services as well as what works for them, as well as giving Social Workers the chance to respond and share how they feel, especially when they cannot do what they want to do for their clients. I had more empathy with the Social Workers after hearing their frustrations. Overall the program gave us an opportunity to try and change the way both Social Workers and clients feel about each other and help improve working practices.

(Louise, service user participant)

My experience of Mend the Gap has been invaluable as a student Social Worker. It has broadened my understanding of the profession and gave me a unique insight into the lives of many different people. I was given the opportunity to work alongside genuine, honest people, who were willing to share experiences good and bad in order to see future services improved. I believe I will be a better Social Worker because of my involvement with this program.

(Maria, social work student)

It was a good idea to get people together with different disabilities in one program. Listening to what they had to say. It was well attended and well facilitated. It was a shame that the group could not have more funding to continue beyond the program. It was so good for people to be able to get out and have a purpose to meet together. People can become isolated very easily.

(John, service user participant)

I had worked towards developing a Mend the Gap program for disabled people with other participants for some time. However, I could not visualize how successful it would be until we actually put it together. It worked because of the commitment of the group members. It was truly User led. The topics discussed were raised by disabled people, so it was issues which impacted them directly. The other important point was the trust developed between the disabled people, the students and professional partners involved, which led to real openness. This also led to a feeling of progression, and many of the service users who were involved have expressed interest in being involved in a future program. As "Empowerment" was a newly formed business at the time that we developed the program, Mend the Gap has become very much a model which we use in other areas of our work. We have since used the model around Hate Crime Awareness Raising and we are planning a future program to highlight Employment Barriers facing disabled people.

(Ian, service user co-facilitator)

I have been involved in social work education attending University courses which has helped me with my road to recovery. I have gained so much confidence getting involved with things I never would have thought about doing. This provided me with opportunities to put my bad experiences into positive use. Working alongside social work lecturers I was treated as though I was another colleague and not a service user. By taking part in a mend the gap programme there was much more opportunity to share my experiences with students and professionals and also to learn from them. It was more of a two way exchange than going into a classroom.

(Julie, service user participant)

Whilst I thought that my own lived experiences brought a level of "realness" to my understanding of hardship and challenges, I had never really experienced listening to the stories of others as they progressed from strangers to co-participants over the weeks and how having social services intervene in their lives; whether wanted or not, actually impacted on them. Work based placements were not the same, everyone involved in the Gap Mending project were starting from the same point. Parents set the agenda by identifying the gaps which most affected them although we all identified with these gaps from our roles and shared fully the dialogue.

During one session, I recall it brought home to me how a parent might be anxiously anticipating being judged poorly over an ordinary every-day occurrence. A participant's baby daughter had been crawling around on the floor in the crèche resulting in her tights becoming dirty. Her father felt he needed to explain this to us and whilst doing so appeared to genuinely be concerned of our reaction: that somehow the dirt on her tights stemmed from his poor parenting. I remember feeling shocked and worried that I had subconsciously reacted in a way which might have triggered this behaviour. It seems we were trying to evaluate the boundaries of our relationship and that despite the work we were doing, these "relationships" remained somewhat precarious. During my studies we were taught about power imbalances and I recalled thinking I would never abuse that power. It hadn't occurred to me that I would have to actively "work" at showing families I was not going to abuse that power, and that in itself highlighted the power imbalance. I have found the gap mending experience immersive and motivating and I know that the experience has had an intensively positive impact as it has reinforced the development of my practice along my social work journey.

(Gaynor, social worker)

Thank you to all contributors. There are many more gap mending participants who have contributed their reflective feedback from courses, which has not been included in this collection but has been significant to developing experiential knowledge. PowerUs, as a network of 19 countries and growing, is committed to finding channels for promoting voices as widely as possible. Some service user students, for example at Utrecht University in the Netherlands, do not have speech and their University lecturers have found creative ways to gather their feedback and emotions. Everyone has experiences to share and learn from. When we come together as people first, it is possible to recognize each person's unique experiential knowledge as a service user, student, practitioner or other role. When we start with the recognition that every person's view point is equally valid, we can find solutions together to create new knowledge and insight and where possible improve policy and practice. PowerUs is committed to supporting new groups who wish to take forward a gap mending approach. Feel free to contact us via our website. We are an informal network promoting people's rights to be included in professional education and practice contexts.

www.powerus.se

SECTION 5

Future challenges and opportunities

47

PROFESSIONAL EDUCATION

Does service user involvement make a difference?

Colin Cameron, Helen Casey and Joe Duffy

In this chapter, we approach the question 'Does service user involvement make a difference to professional education?' with caution. At the outset, when we started planning this book, we would have had no hesitation in answering the question positively and straightforwardly. Yes, of course it makes a difference, we would have said. Yes, of course, it is a very important thing. And yes, of course, it is necessary.

But to say that service user involvement is a very important thing, and that it is necessary, is not the same as saying that it makes a difference. Having been involved in both editing and writing for this book, we would now qualify our answer by saying that it *can* and *should* make a difference when it is carried out meaningfully and when it is allowed to have an impact. But it seems that this is not always the case. In this chapter, we will comment upon and make observations about this notion of impact through reflecting back both on the chapters we have been involved in editing and in the wider context of attendant issues on the topic.

The lead author writes from a background as a disabled activist with considerable experience and specialism in Disability Studies. Most of the contributing authors he has worked with have, therefore, been involved with disability, either through personal experience or in terms of professional practice. What is interesting to note is that of the chapters he has been involved with, those written by non-disabled academics in partnership with service users – with disabled people and older people – have tended to be more positive than the others. Sarah Lonbay, Shirley Hallam, Patricia Higgins and Sheila Weatheritt, for example, have talked about the value of bringing and sharing their own experiences in order 'to expand the knowledge and skills base of the social work students and future practitioners'. They highlight the importance of involvement being about challenging and changing students' perceptions, about the importance of user involvement in helping students move beyond regarding people they work with in terms of stereotyped ideas. And this is excellent. Undoubtedly, students who have been taught by Hallam, Higgins and Weatheritt will have been positively changed by the experience and learned about the importance of anti-oppressive practice.

John Stephens, Katherine Baker and Ali Finlayson have suggested the possibility of open dialogue and acceptance between educators, students and service users. But their optimism is tempered. They recognise the requirement for moving towards educational disequilibrium – an unsettling and disturbance of existing ways of looking, thinking and talking – and point out that

> open dialogue, the ability to suspend personal prejudicial thought and participation requires more than a degree of honesty and bravery, the main message here being one of patience and effort.

It is far from our intention to dampen anybody's enthusiasm for and commitment to service user involvement. But it is important, in trying to answer the question 'Does service user involvement make a difference?', to reflect on what has been written by the authors we have worked with. It is striking to note the greater reservations expressed about this in the chapters that have been written singly or collaboratively by disabled people as service users, whether in academic roles or otherwise.

Peter Kearns and Susan Carton, disabled and non-disabled academics at St Angela's College in Sligo, Ireland, talk about McDonnell's (2003) discussion of the two different structural levels at which educational systems work. McDonnell, they note, suggests that while at the surface level the day-to-day practices in the organisation of educational institutions are often attended to, the deeper structures of underlying theories, concepts, assumptions and beliefs are rarely challenged or changed. Kearns and Carton highlight that educational institutions need to address these deeper structures and discuss how the establishment of Disability Studies at St Angela's, involving and grounded in perspectives developed by disabled people, represents an attempt to do this. In doing so, they reveal the deep structural nature of disabling professional practices and the difficulty of bringing about real change.

Paul Doyle emphasises the importance of disability research in educational settings. That is, research designed and led by disabled people and grounded in the social model. Again, this requires moving away from thinking of disability as something people 'have' and recognising disability as a structural issue, something requiring social structural change rather than just a shift of people's attitudes.

These perspectives are not new, as Colin Cameron, Maggie Cameron and Colin Hambrook point out. In what is now approaching five decades since the development of the social model as an analytical tool, disabled people have been demanding change in terms of the removal of physical and social barriers to education, employment, housing, public transport, information, leisure activities. These barriers, disabled people have argued, are the real causes of disablement, the exclusion of people with impairments from the social mainstream – the perspective explained and outlined in Disability Equality Training. Yet universities largely continue to maintain narratives and practices which reinforce ways of looking that continue to regard disability as an individual characteristic, an embodied condition that is understood primarily in terms of loss and abnormality. For all the talk of listening to service users within professional education – and for all the excellent examples of where this has happened – the persistent attachment to individual model thinking implies either an unwillingness to *really* act on service users' views or an outright rejection of these. This has a real impact both on service users' everyday experiences of education, as Joanne Molloy-Graham's and Maggie Cameron's accounts of their experiences illustrate, and on their perceptions of the value of involvement activities.

The Shaping Our Lives guide by Becki Meakin and Joanna Matthews emerged as an outcome of research in which service users had identified a number of recurrent unsatisfying experiences as service user representatives. Central to these was an imbalance of power manifested, for example, in situations when there was no meaningful outcome from the involvement; in involvement processes which were inflexible, too long or tokenistic; and at times where they felt their views had neither been listened to nor acted upon by the professionals involved. Power is exercised through the control of discourse and, until the disabling impact of medical model judgements is acknowledged and addressed, relations between professionals and service users will remain skewed, however well intended people are.

Nick Watson echoes this point, identifying social and structural investment at micro, meso and macro levels as necessary to ensure social justice for disabled people. While he acknowledges the potential co-production has in terms of improving outcomes in both the design and delivery of services, he is concerned about the links between consumerism and co-production. In other words, while co-production has been presented as an uncontroversial and benign idea, a strategy for promoting the empowerment and inclusion of service users, it has been used to co-opt disabled people and to involve them in the compromise and watering-down of their ideas. In this sense, user involvement has not, in fact, signified a straightforward advance in terms of improvement of opportunities but is rather part of a new way of exercising disciplinary control. Watson calls for a reactivation of the promise of co-production, but for this to involve the unpacking, exploration and examination of what it is like to be disabled: to involve a critical gaze at the deeper structures of underlying theories, concepts, assumptions and beliefs held about disability.

Damian Milton has identified the conflict between the ideas of the 'neurodiversity movement' which identifies autism and neurodiversity as part of natural human diversity, and dominant views within autism research, framing autism 'as a set of impairments to be alleviated or remedied through medical intervention'. While he discusses a number of initiatives and projects signifying a large step forward in the participation of autistic people in research, the education of professionals working with autistic people and the design and delivery of services, he observes that these efforts remain somewhat on the periphery of autism discourse and practice. His reference to C. Wright Mills' (2000) *The Sociological Imagination* expresses a desire to have the disability experienced by autistic people regarded as a social issue rather than as a personal trouble. Like the other disabled writers discussed here, Milton is suggesting that real change will only be achieved with recognition of the structural nature of disability.

Therefore, a fair way of summarising the different views discussed here in response to the question 'Does service user involvement make a difference?' would be to say that most authors believe that it can but are not necessarily convinced that it will. There are, of course, different ways of looking at it, and we suppose a fuller answer to the question would require a discussion of what we mean by *change*. Undoubtedly, small-scale changes in terms of individual professionals' outlooks and practice will result from closer and more equal involvement with service users, but structures of education are about more than just individuals' thoughts and behaviours. There is an incessant interplay between these and organisational cultures, between these and broader, established ways of understanding. Individual professionals may be the loveliest of people, but if their working culture is characterised by an unacknowledged institutional disablism, participation within that culture may easily lead to unintentionally oppressive practice. Every time the expression 'people with disabilities' is used, for example, the medical model is strengthened. If there is a certain scepticism among the disabled authors considered here about the likelihood of user involvement to bring about real change, this is perhaps because they are more attuned to this reality.

Of course, user involvement makes a difference. Charden Pouo's accounts of his community activism and community education activities in Congo Brazzaville represent a context very different to the others, in the UK and Ireland, so far discussed. Pouo describes a situation where meaningful service user involvement is far from a reality: a situation where the ideas of rights and entitlements to services at all, let alone rights and entitlements to have a say in how those services are planned and delivered, are alien to many people. Couleurs Congolaises was established in order to develop a critical consciousness among some of the most disenfranchised people in the world. Its activities involved education to awaken people to their rights. It is no secret that the original leaders of Couleurs Congolaises experienced government harassment and intimidation as a result of their activities. They had to scatter, flee and disappear because of government response to their activities. This would not have happened if user involvement did not have the power to make a difference.

As a concept, looking at impact and outcomes in the context of service user involvement in human services education has far-reaching implications. This is tied in with the need for such involvement to be both non-tokenistic (Campbell, 1996) and honest (McLaughlin, 2009) so that service users who have been involved will be left feeling that their participation not only has been valued, but also has resulted in some sort of change and narrowing of distance (Duffy, 2008). As a result, the likelihood of growing and increasing service user involvement going forward is improved. Research tells us that if service users are not in receipt of feedback in regard to the impact and outcomes from their involvement activities, they are more likely to be left feeling not only empty, but also sceptical about engaging in similar involvement activities in the future (Levin, 2004; Duffy, 2006, 2008; Duffy et al., 2017). They need to know that their involvement is making a difference.

Reflecting back on the earlier chapter in this collection written by Gillian Buck, Paula Harriott, Kemi Ryan, Natasha Ryan and Philippa Tomczak, this sense of scepticism towards involvement is powerfully expressed: 'Many prisoners reject involvement advances, sensing them as tokenistic and offering false hope'. These authors also make an additionally important point in their chapter about the need to express value in the form of payment to people who have given of their time to be involved; again, the following quote from their paper starkly underscores this:

> Another barrier to meaningful participation is the exploitation of people with criminal records for organisational ends. We have been brought in to 'educate' others and told what to say and no one is paid. When a person is trying to rebuild their life they should be paid, there should be real opportunities and buy in to rehabilitation.

The related challenge here is that there are not large numbers of people with lived experience who want to be involved, particularly in education, so it is, therefore, vital that the service users who are involved are made fully aware and informed of the impact of their involvement (Levin, 2004). Of equal importance is the need to pay attention to detail in regard to supporting and attending to the more practical aspects of involvement as this will yield future positive benefits (Levin, 2004; Duffy, 2008; Duffy et al., 2017).

This book contains many examples of how service user involvement works to make a difference. Building in *evaluation* and *feedback* to service user involvement is a very important practical way of ensuring that evidence of difference can be shown. This in turn can then be reported back to everybody involved and fits within the realms of pedagogic research. The chapter by Raes Begum Baig, Kar-Choi Chan and Jim Campbell is one such example of a 'measurement' approach to evidencing impact of the use of e-learning videos on students' understanding, knowledge and skills in working with ethnic minority service users in the context of social work education in Hong Kong. This is an important methodological approach in regard to evidencing impact, and this chapter effectively expresses confident findings as a result. Actively promoting service user involvement in this project was also regarded by these authors as having added significance to the outcomes and impact, as can be seen from the following excerpt:

It is argued that the breadth of this multidisciplinary partnership would contribute the necessary, diverse knowledge and expertise to enable the construction of suitable e-learning materials. A significant innovation was the production of e-learning videos involving a process of user participation.

This measurement type approach has also been very effective in evidencing the impact of service user involvement in Northern Ireland, particularly in evaluating the impact of the involvement of victims and survivors of the 'Troubles' on the knowledge and skills development of social work students (see Duffy, 2012; Campbell et al., 2013; Coulter et al., 2013).

Confident expression of impact and outcomes from service user initiatives in education is increasingly important, particularly given that the literature currently points to a lack of evidence around the reporting of such evaluations (Robinson and Webber, 2013). Until now, therefore, empirical evidence in this area is underdeveloped. Nonetheless, there are important examples of recent pedagogic research which have provided degrees of measurement to provide quantitative expressions evidencing the impact of service user involvement. Tanner et al. (2017), for example, followed a cohort of newly qualified social workers into their first year in practice across two sites: Birmingham and Belfast. This study provided evidence that service user involvement in social work education 'produces changes in attitudes, knowledge and skills; prompts changes in students' own practice and, through this, some change in organisational practice; and leads to beneficial outcomes for service users' (2017, p. 483). While it is encouraging to note such impact, the effects of the overly procedural, target driven and regulated nature of practice was also found to have a detrimental impact on these newly qualified social workers being able to stay true to the powerful messages they had received from service users during the course of their social work studies. This finding is also noted in other parts of the literature (Scheyett and Diehl, 2004; Skilton, 2011). Recent work by Susan Levy and colleagues in Scotland has also innovatively introduced a new model of outcomes-focused service user involvement in social work education, so it is encouraging to see that this is now becoming a more prevalent direction of travel with regard to elevating the focus on impact (Levy et al., 2018).

Brendan McKeever's chapter earlier in this collection offers a refreshing and powerful example of the power of parents of disabled children to bring about monumental change in housing policy, firstly in Northern Ireland and then in other parts of the UK, really showing *making a difference* in action. Brendan's chapter is littered with poignant examples of how impact can be achieved, and the reader at once is left with the sense that this should not be over complicated: 'We had won, the voices of those most marginalised in our society had been listened to and acted upon' is one such example of lived/experiential knowledge of parents being given deserved recognition with the announcement of an abolished means test in Northern Ireland for parents of disabled children seeking to make adaptations to their homes. Brendan portrays the 'housing campaign' as a powerful example of service users campaigning to make a real difference and, within this, shares what he argues were the essential ingredients for achieving this:

> Trust, openness, respect, commitment and acknowledging human values were not just topics for discussion they were thrashed out on the anvil of the campaign, they were real and evident throughout. Partnership and empowerment again were demonstrated day and daily as supporters struggled to get the message across, change was necessary.

Joanne Sansome's earlier chapter, focusing on the extent to which people with impairments in Northern Ireland are involved in public life as the topic of her master's research, again brings us back to the importance of not over-complicating things when it comes to service user involvement: 'The concept of building capacity could work in reality, if people could "just ask" everyone involved what do you need support with to enable achievement'. This chimes with what Brendan McKeever referred to as the core ingredient that worked in the housing campaign when he refers to the importance of trust and openness. Without such core practices, it is hard to envisage how honest, non-tokenistic and impactful involvement can occur. Joanne goes on to remind us, making a similar point to Gillian Buck et al.'s chapter, previously mentioned, that for people with impairments: 'experiences of discrimination and not being treated fairly are major obstacles (barriers) towards meaningful participation'. She goes on to make the point 'that there is no recognition that society is at fault or needs to change (Drake, 1999). Within society, there is a notion that disabled people need to build their capacity or create ideas to fit the existing social norms'.

On reflection, it is notable that there are a number of contributions to this book which demonstrate the impact of mutual learning in social work education, which is first and foremost what sets this book apart from being a book 'about' service user and carer involvement to being a book 'with' service user and carer involvement. This book, therefore, provides a context for new ideas to be presented, and a strong theme presented throughout the chapters is an identified need for more comprehensive co-produced learning. The voices of participants from Mend the Gap programmes in the UK, Europe and Canada demonstrate the capacity and potential for co-produced learning in social work to provide a broader range of professional insights, develop appreciative critical learning skills and co-create new knowledge through experiential learning. As was explained in one chapter proposing a model for radical co-production (Helen Casey, Dan Vale, Maryam Zonouzi), there is an appetite for co-production and opportunity to take co-production further than it has been taken in social work by promoting a radical co-production alternative to the existing consensual model. The mantra to stop people being seen as 'passive recipients of services' has been around too long. We need to change this mantra. A key message which stands out from this chapter that achieves this is 'in radical co-production; equality is not the destination, it is the starting point'.

It should also be acknowledged that there are many groups promoting collective action and initiatives beyond the contributions in this book. For example, there is a well-established co-production group co-facilitated by Sarah Jane Waters and Abyd Quinn Aziz at Cardiff University who ensure individuals and organisations like Cardiff People First make a difference to social work education. Similarly, the Unity group at Stirling University convened by Sandra Engstrom, some of whose members have contributed to chapter 23, who positively impact on student's learning, despite government funding being removed from supporting this activity in Scotland a decade ago.

Co-production is a key concept in public services, yet social work students are not being prepared for taking this forward in their education. What is most striking from the Talking Heads Mend the Gap reflections is how much more insight can be gained for us all when we commit to working together in partnership to overcome differences and gain a better understanding of ourselves and our roles. In the UK context, when the formal commitment to service user involvement was introduced with the introduction of the social work degree in 2003, there were many attempts to establish reference groups and involve people with lived experiences in teaching and learning contexts. This, however, led to an absence of the involvement of people who were 'seldom heard', which subsequently led to the identification of four main seldom heard groups: homeless people with addiction problems, people from black and ethnic minorities, people with communication impairments and people with dementia (Dime et al., SCIE, 2008).

SCIE identified that the most effective approach was an 'integrated approach' based on a value base which placed people at the centre of services, with staff supporting them by developing trust, mutual understanding and respect (Dime et al., ibid.). An interesting conclusion to attribute to people who are defined as 'hard to reach' almost by implication suggests that the 'seldom heard' person is in some way difficult to engage with. Larry Sylvester, as a social worker from Nigeria, has explained very straightforwardly that without creating the right environment, Black Minority Ethnic (BME) communities would never share their problems as culturally this would bring too much stigma and shame. Mend the Gap approaches clearly build on some of the ideas from SCIE's research a decade ago and provide us with a model for promoting methods of mutual learning to be more culturally effective and supporting the empowerment of marginalised and discriminated groups in society. Chapters in this book also show that there is a rich and growing amount of data to evidence the effectiveness of this approach, which has challenged existing classroom-based structures and established a model of good practice internationally. The example shared by parents whose voices ultimately influenced Home Office decision making around accommodation is an extremely important example of what is possible to achieve through co-learning, similar in many ways to what Brendan McKeever writes about in his chapter. Still, however, there are huge gaps between policy, research and practice that need to be mended. Gap Mending participants have expressed the benefits of co-creating a learning space where people who feel most marginalised and stigmatised initiate the agenda. This is similar to the model proposed by Ginger Giraffe for conceptualising co-production which requires structures to change.

On reflection, it is our contention in this discussion that existing social work education structures have not been reviewed since the social work degree was established in 2003 in the UK; this book provides a timely opportunity to reflect upon what has worked well over a substantive period of time. For example, Elizabeth Anderson, Jenny Ford and Emma Smith share the findings of an 'inter-professional education' model which has been established for over 20 years, yet still this is not widely incorporated in health and social care educational contexts. By now this model could surely be implemented across all health and social care curricula to ensure that patients and students everywhere can access these valuable learning opportunities. That said, innovative models which can make a difference to service users, students and practitioners raise the precarious issue of funding which is necessary to value and sustain meaningful involvement. Government funding for service user involvement in social work education is unique to some parts of the UK. Our worry is if this funding does not continue and expand, the future of meaningful involvement is under serious threat, which could have adverse consequences for people whose voices could never, not just seldom, be heard. As Beverley Burke and Andrea Newman point out in their chapter on the ethics of involvement, it is important to highlight how much power practitioners within their role and institutional structures have with the potential to discriminate and oppress. We need to continue to redress the balance of power by valuing how everyone's experiential knowledge can challenge discrimination and oppression; otherwise we risk having unequal relationships and poor practice.

Writing at a time in the UK when a newly established right-wing Government is determined on continuing to implement cuts and damaging policies which impact most harshly on vulnerable people, the case for making a difference in professional education, to ensure that those in professional support roles can help people, has never been stronger or more necessary than now.

References

Campbell, J., Duffy, J., Traynor, C., Reilly, I., & Pinkerton, J. (2013). Social work education and political conflict: Preparing students to address the needs of victims and survivors of the Troubles in Northern Ireland. *European Journal of Social Work*, 16(4), 506–520.

Campbell, P. (1996). The history of the user movement in the United Kingdom. In T. Heller, J. Reynolds, R. Gomm, R. Muston & S. Pattison (eds.), *Mental Health Matters*. Basingstoke: Macmillan, pp: 218–225.

Coulter, S., Campbell, J., Duffy, J., & Reilly, I. (2013). Enabling social work students to deal with the consequences of political conflict: Engaging with victim/survivor service users and a pedagogy of discomfort. *Social Work Education – The International Journal*, 32(4), 439–452.

Dime, N., Hernandez, L., Litherland, R., Sampson, A. and Robson, P. in Social Care Institute for Excellence (SCIE) Position paper 10: seldom heard-Developing inclusive participation in social care, 2008. https://www.scie.org.uk/publications/positionpapers/pp10.asp accessed 28/04/2020.

Drake, R. F. (1999). *Understanding Disability Policies*. London: Palgrave Macmillan.

Duffy, J. (2006). *Participating and Learning: Citizen Involvement in Social Work Education in a Northern Ireland Context*. London: Social Care Institute for Excellence.

Duffy, J. (2008). *Looking Out from the Middle: User Involvement in Health and Social Care in Northern Ireland*. London: Social Care Institute for Excellence (SCIE). www.scie.org.uk/publications/reports/report18.asp

Duffy, J. (2012). Service user involvement in teaching about conflict – an exploration of the issues. *International Social Work (Special Edition on Social Work and Armed Conflict)*, 55(5), 720–739.

Duffy, J., Gillen, P., Agnew, C., Casson, K., Davidson, G., McGlone, A., & McKeever, B. (2017). *Personal and Public Involvement (PPI) and Its Impact: Monitoring, Measuring and Evaluating the Impact of PPI in Health and Social Care in Northern Ireland*. Belfast: Public Health Agency and Patient and Client Council. www.knowledge.hscni.net/Topics/Index/823.

Levin, E. (2004). *Involving Service Users and Carers in Social Work Education*. London: Social Care Institute for Excellence.

Levy, S., Aiton, R., Doig, J., Dow, J. P. L., Brown, S., Hunter, L., & McNeil, R. (2018). Outcomes focused user involvement in social work education: Applying knowledge to practice. In H. McLaughlin, J. Duffy, B. McKeever & J. Sadd (eds.), *Service User Involvement in Social Work Education*. London and New York: Routledge.

McDonnell, P. (2003). Chapter 2: Education policy. In S. Quin & B. Redmond (eds.), *Disability and Social Policy in Ireland*. Dublin: UCD Press.

McLaughlin, H. (2009). Keeping service user involvement in research honest. *British Journal of Social Work*, 1–18. Doi:10.1093/bjsw/bcp064.

Mills, C. W. (2000). *The Sociological Imagination*. Oxford: Oxford University Press.

Robinson, K., & Webber, M. (2013). Models and effectiveness of service user and carer involvement in social work education: A literature review. *British Journal of Social Work*, 43(5), 925–944.

Scheyett, A., & Diehl, M. J. (2004). Walking our talk in social work education: Partnership with consumers of mental health services. *Social Work Education – The International Journal*, 23(4), 435–450.

Skilton, C. J. (2011). Involving experts by experience in assessing students' readiness to practise. *Social Work Education*, 30(3), 299–311. www.scie.org.uk/search?sq=seldom+heard accessed 18 December, 2019.

Tanner, D., Littlechild, R., Duffy, J., & Hayes, D. (2017). 'Making it real': evaluating the impact of service user and carer involvement in social work education. *British Journal of Social Work*, 47(2), 467–486.

48

SERVICE USER INVOLVEMENT IN RESEARCH

What difference does it make?

Peter Beresford and Hugh McLaughlin

Introduction

From very humble beginnings, user involvement in research and user-led research have increasingly impacted on political, policy, professional and public understandings about the nature, methods and purpose of research. This development has been international in its influence and spread. However, as this book shows, its growth is neither assured nor universal, as Alam (2020) documents about the US, Cirano (2020) about Spain and Pouo about Congo Brazzaville.

In this chapter, we will try to look particularly at what difference these developments have made. But, in doing so, we must not only avoid any desire to over-claim for them – this is work still very much in progress – but also equally avoid glossing over the complexity and uncertainty of progress in this field. It is important to remember that the pressure for greater user involvement in, and indeed leadership of, research can now be traced back to the 1970s – nearly half a century. This is no new discovery. But it is also one that arguably is transformative in its implications and effects and one which opens the door to new paradigms in many domains, from knowledge formation through professional development to transforming social and public policy.

There have been distinct phases in the development of user involvement in research, just as there have been more broadly in the development of participatory initiatives in states and societies. We will begin with the first of these, the emergence of emancipatory disability research and its implications, emphasising their incapacity and reinforcing their marginalisation.

What research is for

Through the first half of the twentieth century, prevailing understandings of disability were predominantly individualised and medicalised – it was seen as an isolated personal tragedy, and the response was primarily one of segregating disabled people and lumping them together as defective (Oliver, 1983; Hunt, 2019). In the UK, a group of institutionalised disabled people sought to challenge this, believing that with the right kind of support, they could lead independent lives in mainstream society. They approached a group of social researchers to evidence their ability to live independently but were then shocked when these researchers wrote them off as 'social parasites' who would inevitably be dependent on society (Beresford, 2016, pp. 218–219; Hunt, 2019). This was a turning point in disability research. It led disabled activists to feel that if they wanted research which truly reflected their experience, situation and interests, then they must carry it out and control it *themselves*. Such research became an important part of the emerging international disabled people's movement and was seen as a form of collective self-advocacy. Key characteristics of such research were that it would:

- equalise relationships between researcher and researcher;
- be empowering for research participants;
- lead to political and social change in line with the interests of disabled people;

and was

- not only participatory, but emancipatory in purpose.

As Mike Oliver, the disabled academic and activist, wrote, this was a different kind of research to that of the mainstream:

> the research is not an attempt to change the world through the process of investigation but an attempt to change the world by producing ourselves and others in differing ways from those we have produced before.
>
> *(Oliver, 2009, p. 116)*

This is a fundamental distinction to draw. Such a philosophy, with its purpose of democratising research and directing it to the empowerment and liberation of oppressed people, has developed more broadly into user-controlled and 'survivor' research as more groups have taken it forward, particularly in the twenty-first century.

However, the pressure for change in research also prompted a response from research itself. This has been reflected in a growing range of formal requirements for participation, or what has become known as 'public, patient involvement' (PPI) in:

- accessing different sources of funding, both statutory and non-statutory;
- planning and undertaking research projects;
- disseminating their findings and acting on them.

Perhaps most important was the establishment of what became known as the National Institute for Health Research (NIHR) INVOLVE (www.invo.org.uk/resource-centre/) in 1996 to support and encourage involvement in health, public health and social care research. Over this period, we have seen such participation extend to processes of research governance, research organisations, peer-reviewed journals and other research publications, as well as to research conferences.

While Director General of Research at the Department of Health, Dame Sally Davies stated:

> I have always taken the view that public involvement in research should be the rule not the exception. It is fundamental to ensure high quality research that brings real benefits for patients, the public and the NHS.
>
> *(Staley, 2009, p. 14)*

Increasingly, service users have been able to gain research qualifications (pioneered by the Centre for Disability Studies at the University of Leeds, initially established in association with the UK disabled people's movement), with growing numbers gaining PhDs and entering academia and research organisations as researchers. This reminds us that being a service user, or a researcher, is not a mutually exclusive identity; it is possible to be both.

The increasing numbers of service user PhDs entering academia and research organisations are significant developments. However, they should not be exaggerated, and there is no doubt that progress has been patchy and inconsistent, with the achievement in some areas, organisations and academic and research institutions much more substantial than in others.

Of course, the key question, and the one which this chapter asks, is: what difference does involvement in research make? We know from service users that whenever they are asked why they get involved – whether we are talking about research, policy or practice – they say it is to make a positive difference and bring about real improvements in people's lives, in line with their rights and needs.

We also know that the major complaint from disabled people and service users is that invitations to get involved are often no more than tokenistic, and seem to be for a researcher to tick a box in a research proposal. There are widespread feelings that decisions have often already been made when they are asked and that frequently little notice is taken of what they say they want (Beresford and Croft, 1993). It is important to recognise that service users usually have no say in prioritising what the research question is and are often recruited after this has been decided. But there is more to this issue than a reluctance on the part of some services and policymakers to take user involvement seriously or variations in enthusiasm and commitment, although it is often explained in such terms.

At a more profound level, what we are also seeing is the working out of different, competing ideologies in relation to participation and user involvement which can be explained by the conflicting origins of pressure for this development over the period in question.

As we have seen, this originated with people on the receiving end of public policy, particularly marginalised groups like disabled people and mental health service users/survivors, seeking to redress what they experienced as an imbalance of power by working for more say and control in policies and services which affected them and their lives. They can be seen as in the same tradition and reflecting the goals of other new social movements like the women's, Black civil rights and LGBTQ movements. Their aim has been to democratise public policy and services, redistribute power downwards and remake provision in to serve a liberatory and supportive role.

At roughly the same time, government and service systems and associated research institutions have been developing their provisions for participation, usually in the form of consultative market research and related provisions. But here there has generally not been any suggestion of redistributing power. Instead, developments have more clearly come within a consumerist framework tied to a market-based model. Thus, the involvement, views and contribution of service users are sought, just as they are with conventional commercial goods and products to maximise their knowledge-base, marketability and profitability through inputting the views, intelligence and preferences of service users. This is essentially a process of extraction rather than empowerment. Control remains where it has always been: with those making the decisions about what notice to take of service user input. To put it in conventional market terms, being asked your views is far from the same as being offered a place on the board.

In our view, here lies the origin of the major misunderstanding in conventional provider-led approaches to involvement. It is a misunderstanding that has played a major part in stymying user involvement. Being asked to give your views is not the same as having a direct say in decision-making, and it is the confusion between these two different approaches and offers that has led to much user frustration and accusations of tokenism and 'rubber stamping' in participatory arrangements. What is needed, therefore, is greater clarity in what kind of involvement is being offered, so that service users and their organisations can decide if it is an offer they want to accept, ignore or challenge. The fact that consumerist and democratic approaches to involvement – in research as elsewhere – are couched in very much the same language has of course increased the confusion and misunderstanding. It is therefore important to attempt to be clear about differences in values, aims and objectives when it comes to user involvement. Failure to do that is only likely to result in misunderstanding and distrust.

This situation is made all the more difficult as we have come to accept an increasingly neo-liberalist hegemony and continued government chosen austerity (Jones, 2018). This has led to increasing individualism and reduction in the welfare state and state benefits coupled with rising eligibility thresholds. In the UK, this has led to the UN Special Rapporteur on Extreme Poverty and Human Rights to claim that 'British compassion for those who are suffering has been replaced by a punitive, mean spirited, and often callous approach' (Alston, 2018, p. 3). This makes it all the more important that service users contribute to prioritising research questions and act as researchers and co-researchers in addressing key questions of design, delivery and effectiveness of human services provision.

Research is about finding things out, whether it's focus is on us or our wider world, and trying to do so in the most reliable, consistent and accurate way possible. However, what we have been learning throughout this book, and during the course of this particular chapter, is that we can come at this from many different vantage points, with diverse, sometimes competing concerns. So, we need to be clear in advance not only what kind of involvement in research is under consideration but also, *whose* knowledge is research primarily concerned with revealing, making available and to whom? Historically, research was primarily intended to prioritise the expert knowledge of policymakers, professionals and politicians. Since the advent of user involvement, a new concern has arisen: to identify, make available and act on the knowledge of people traditionally on the receiving end of public policies, services and professionals, that is to say, their experiential knowledge – the knowledge emerging from their lived experience (Sweeney et al., 2009). This knowledge is essential to understand and respond effectively to the issues and challenges of those in receipt of services, as it is only they who experience both the intended and unintended consequences of public policies, services and professionals (Beresford, 2000). To ignore this perspective is to negate any identified recommendations for change as at best partial and at worst mis-informed.

Thus, we really need to be clear whose knowledge we want to bring to the fore, recognising that if there's one thing user involvement has taught us, it is that the search for knowledge can be a battleground. Put simply, the big pharma want to mine user knowledge about their mental health drugs for very different reasons to many service users themselves. And as a result, findings and conclusions can be very different. This was the clear finding when, for the first time, a systematic review with user involvement was carried out on Electro Convulsive Therapy (ECT), a very contentious 'treatment' long used on some mental health patients. Instead of the unproblematic findings of much traditional research, serious problems were identified in this study in the administration by professionals of this procedure (Rose et al., 2003). Once we recognise that the great opportunity offered by user involvement in research is to include the experiential knowledge of service users, then we have the chance of maximising its potential as an agent of change.

Importance of including all perspectives

A major reason for making additional specific provision for eliciting the views of people as health, care and other professional service users is because of the increasing view that their views have not emerged from the conventional processes of representative politics and thus additional efforts were needed to elicit them. Pressure for involvement in public services and professions arises from the sense of a gap or shortcoming in mainstream democratic arrangements. But as we have developed our skills and understanding about such user involvement, so we have also come to appreciate that it can have its own limitations. The 'Beyond the Usual Suspects' project carried out by Shaping Our Lives with funding support from the UK Department of Health highlighted that many people continued to be marginalised in such participatory initiatives. These included:

- Equality issues: in relation to gender, sexuality, race, class, culture, belief, age, impairment and more;
- where people live: if they are homeless, in prison, in welfare institutions, refugees and so on;
- communicating differently: if they do not speak the prevailing language, it is not their first language, they are deaf and used sign language etc.;
- the nature of their impairments: which are seen as too complex or severe to mean they could or would want to contribute;
- where they are seen as unwanted voices: they did not necessarily say what authorities want to hear, are seen as a problem, disruptive etc. (Beresford, 2013)

Only when serious efforts are made to include these neglected, often devalued, perspectives can user involvement in research make its potential difference for everyone, rather than just those whose experience and identity match groups valued more in society. This demands that for service user involvement to be taken seriously, researchers need to be believe in the added value of such an approach, be committed to a process of learning that will require time, effort and funding for service user's time, which is not always going to proceed smoothly and is likely to challenge hierarchies and power dynamics (see Natland, 2020, in this volume). However, for us, the potential for better, greater quality research and its meaningfulness for those on the receiving end of services more than makes up for the effort required.

Conclusions

As the many chapters in this book ably illustrate, there is a wealth of knowledge and skill in working participatively with different client groups in a range of different settings in different countries. By bringing together this collection of experiences, we hope we will inspire others to join us: service user, researcher, service user researcher or whichever identity you wish to claim. If we accept that differing knowledges and experiences contribute to a fuller understanding of human services issues and challenges it then becomes essential that we embrace the experiential knowledge of service users otherwise any claims to a full understanding of a research problem will be inherently untruthful. Service user involvement in research can and will make a difference; however, it is precarious in many countries, while in others it is yet to be viewed as a legitimate form of research. On top of this, we have already noted that it can be tokenistic, and we need to continue to strive to ensure that it is meaningful, and that we collect examples, like we have in this book, where it has made a positive difference and brought about real improvements in people's lives – that is the challenge!

References

Alston, P. (2018), *Statement on the Visit to the United Kingdom, by Professor Phillip Alston, United Nations Special Rapporteur on Extreme Poverty and Human Rights.* www.ohchr.org/Documents/Issues/Poverty/EOM_GB_16Nov2018.pdf

Beresford, P. (2000), 'Users' knowledges and social work theory: Conflict or collaboration', *British Journal of Social Work*, 30 (4), 495–503.

Beresford, P. (2013), *Beyond the Usual Suspects: Towards Inclusive User Involvement – Research Report*, London, Shaping Our Lives.

Beresford, P. (2016), *All Our Welfare: Towards Participatory Social Policy*, Bristol, Policy Press.

Beresford, P., Croft, S. (1993), *Citizen Involvement: A Practical Guide for Change*, Basingstoke: Palgrave Macmillan.

Hunt, J. (2019), *No Limits: The Disabled People's Movement – a Radical History*, Manchester, TBR Imprint.

Jones, R. (2018), *In Whose Interest? The Privatisation of Child Protection and Social Work,* Bristol, Policy Press.

Natland, S. (2020) "Recently, I have felt like a service user again": Conflicts in collaborative research, a case from Norway, in McLaughlin, H., Beresford, P., Casey, H., Cameron, C. and Duffy, J. (eds.), *Routledge International Handbook of Service User Involvement in Education and Research*. Abingdon, Routledge.

Oliver, M. (1983), *Social Work and Disabled People*, Basingstoke, Palgrave Macmillan.

Oliver, M. (2009), *Understanding Disability: from Theory to Practice*, Basingstoke, Palgrave Macmillan

Rose, D., Wykes, T., Leese, M., Bindman, J., Fleischmann, P. (2003), 'Patients' perspectives on electro convulsive therapy: Systematic review', *British Medical Journal*, 326, 1363–1366.

Staley, K. (2009), *Exploring Impact: Public Involvement in the NHS, Public Health and Social Care Research*, Eastleigh, INVOLVE.

Sweeney, A., Beresford, P., Faulkner, A., Nettle, M., Rose, D. (editors), (2009), *This Is Survivor Research*, Ross-on-Wye, PCSS Books.

INDEX

Dorling, D. 30–31
Dorozenko, K.P. 117, 183
Dowson, Elinor 371
Doyle, Paul 4, 487, 508
Drake, R.F. 168
Driessens, K. 397
Duffy, Joe 2–4, 339, 342, 507

Earle, Rod 286
economic and social inequality 10
economic austerity 404
economic crisis 30–31
Edith Cowan University, Social Work programme 113–121
education 311, 316
educational curriculum on racial equality and anti-racism 157–158
educational disequilibrium 368, 507–508
educational infrastructure 277
educational institutions 132
educational processes 206
educational services in Rio De Janeiro 296–297; AAC and language 301–302; AAC resources 303; alternative communication resources 301; human interaction and alternative 302; MRR online teacher community 302; MRR working conditions 301; multifunctional reference resource rooms (MRRR) operating strategies 303–304; participating teachers and students 297–299; problematization approach 300; purpose and study steps 297; research meetings in 2013–2016 300; teaching skills of teachers 299–300
educational teacher training in Brazil 3
education and safeguarding 95
educators 251, 342
EEC Horizon 2020 project 323
elasticity 209
e-learning project on anti-racial discrimination 154–155; coverage and usage 158–159; e-learning videos 156–159; evaluation 157–158; and racial equality 155–159
e-learning videos 151, 156–159, 510
Electro Convulsive Therapy (ECT) 107, 518
emancipation 389, 397
embedding participation 463
Embregts, P.J.C.M. 388
emotional arousal 155
emotional distress 115
emotional engagement 344
emotional subjectivity 75–77
emotion management 65, 75–77
empathic understanding 373
employment/employment opportunities 165
empowering and learning processes 468
empowerment 65, 236, 389–390, 397, 502; and augmented communication 435–436; and

partnership 219, 468–469; for social change 376
end-of-life care customs 350
epistemic injustice 406
epistemic violence 47–48
equal dignity 390, 397
equality 19–20, 32, 387, 397
Equality and Human Rights Commission 423
Equal Opportunities Commission (EOC) 153
equal participation 24
equal partnership 207
EQUAL program 143–144
equity pedagogy 154
Ericson, R.V. 33
ethical conscience 373
ethical involvement of service users 54–57; learning point 58–61; practice examples 57–58
ethical misalignment in culture of educational institutions 215
ethical theories 56
ethics and governance 433
ethics of care 373
ethnic-Chinese social workers 158
ethnicities 404, 407
ethnic minority: actors 156; populations 151–152
ethnography 415n2, 488
European Children's Rights Unit (ECRU) 323
European Credit Transfer and Accumulation System (ECTS) 395
European Young Person's Advocacy Group (eYPAGnet) 456
evidence-based argument 455
evidence-based medicine 45
exclusion 390
Expanded I poems 403
experience-based co-design (EBCD) 208
experience-based knowledge 144, 386, 395, 479
experiences and individual responses 336
experiential knowledge 334, 385, 388, 451, 482
experiential knowledge in mental health services: context 41; co-production and community participation 50–51; culture and exclusion 44–45; defined 42; emancipatory discourse 43; implications for research 46; knowledge authentication and epistemic violence 47–48; liberal, radical and critical perspectives 49–50; medical hegemony 43–44; mental health education 45–46; research, race and epistemic exclusion 48–49; survivor research 46–47
experiential learning 386
experiential workshop (EW) 296, 306
experimental knowledge 388
experts by experience 36–38, 181–182, 316, 485
exploitation 182, 510
eXtreme Group 325–326